The Economics of Women, Men, and Work

The Economics of Women, Men, and Work

Eighth Edition

FRANCINE D. BLAU
Cornell University

ANNE E. WINKLER
University of Missouri—St. Louis

New York   Oxford
OXFORD UNIVERSITY PRESS

About the Authors

Francine D. Blau is Frances Perkins Professor of Industrial and Labor Relations and professor of economics at Cornell University. She is also a research associate of the National Bureau of Economic Research (NBER) and a research fellow of the Institute for the Study of Labor (IZA). She received her Ph.D. in economics from Harvard University and her B.S. from the School of Industrial and Labor Relations at Cornell University. Before returning to Cornell in 1994, she was for many years on the faculty of the University of Illinois, Urbana-Champaign. Professor Blau has served as president of the Society of Labor Economists (SOLE) and of the Labor and Employment Relations Association (LERA), vice president of the American Economic Association (AEA), president of the Midwest Economics Association (MEA), and chair of the AEA's Committee on the Status of Women in the Economics Profession (CSWEP). She is a fellow of the Society of Labor Economists, the American Academy of Political and Social Science, and the Labor and Employment Relations Association. In 2010, she received the IZA Prize for outstanding achievement in labor economics (the first female recipient) and, in 2017, the Jacob Mincer Award for lifetime contributions to the field of labor economics from SOLE. She was also the 2001 recipient of the Carolyn Shaw Bell Award from CSWEP for furthering the status of women in the economics profession. She is an associate editor of *Labour Economics* and was formerly an editor of the *Journal of Labor Economics* and an associate editor of the *Journal of Economic Perspectives*. She serves or has served on numerous editorial boards, including of the *American Economic Review*, the *Journal of Labor Economics*, the *Journal of Economic Perspectives*, the *ILR Review, Feminist Economics, Signs,* and *The Annals,* among others. Professor Blau has written extensively on gender issues, wage inequality, immigration, and international comparisons of labor market outcomes. She has published widely in refereed journals and is the author of *Equal Pay in the Office* and of *Gender, Inequality, and Wages* and, with Lawrence Kahn, of *At Home and Abroad: U.S. Labor Market Performance in International Perspective.* She is also coeditor of *The Economic and Fiscal Consequences of Immigration, The Declining Significance of Gender?,* and *Gender and Family Issues in the Workplace.*

Anne E. Winkler is professor of economics and public policy administration at the University of Missouri–St. Louis (UMSL). She is also a research fellow at IZA (the Institute for the Study of Labor). She received her Ph.D. in economics from the University of Illinois at Urbana-Champaign and her undergraduate degree in economics from Wesleyan University. She has been a faculty member at UMSL since 1989. She serves on the editorial boards of *Social Science Quarterly* and *Journal of Labor Research*. She previously served as second vice president of the Midwest Economics Association and as president of the St. Louis Chapter of the National Association for Business Economics (NABE). She also served as board member of the American Economic Association's Committee on the Status of Women in the Economics Profession (CSWEP). Her main areas of research interest are in the economics of gender, the economics of the family, and welfare and poverty. Her work has appeared in economics and broader social science journals including *Journal of Human Resources, Research in Labor Economics, Monthly Labor Review, Demography, Journal of Policy Analysis and Management, Journal of Urban Economics, Management Science,* and *IZA World of Labor.*

A Note from the Authors

In publishing this eighth edition with Oxford University Press, we honor the memory and warmly acknowledge the enduring influence of our longtime coauthor and dear friend, Marianne A. Ferber. Marianne Ferber and Francine Blau collaborated on *The Economics of Women, Men, and Work,* the first-ever textbook on this topic, in the early 1980s. Anne Winkler joined with the third edition, and the book was coauthored by all three through the seventh edition, all of which were published by Prentice-Hall/Pearson. This is the first edition that does not bear Marianne Ferber's name. We encourage readers to learn more about her remarkable life and professional contributions.*

It is our hope that Marianne Ferber's legacy—her professional achievements, personal story, and long-lasting influence on this text—will inspire young women to pursue in life what is most meaningful to them and, for those pursuing a profession, to have the opportunity to rise to the highest echelons of their field.

FDB and AEW
June 2017

---

*Committee on the Status of Women in Economics, "An Interview with the 2001 Carolyn Shaw Bell Award Co-recipients Marianne A. Ferber and Francine D. Blau," *CSWEP Newsletter* (Fall 2002); and Francine D. Blau and Anne E. Winkler, "Remembering Marianne A. Ferber," *CSWEP Newsletter* (Winter 2014), https://www.aeaweb.org/about-aea/committees/cswep

Brief Contents

Contents

PART II   THE ALLOCATION OF TIME BETWEEN THE HOUSEHOLD AND THE LABOR MARKET   39

3   The Family as an Economic Unit: Theoretical Perspectives   41

PART III   LABOR MARKET OUTCOMES: THEORY, EVIDENCE, AND POLICY   155

 ## 7   Evidence on Gender Differences in Labor Market Outcomes   157

8   Gender Differences in Educational Attainment: Theory and Evidence   191

11 | Labor Market Discrimination: Theory   301

12 Government Policies to Combat Employment Discrimination   323

PART IV   THE ECONOMICS OF THE FAMILY: THEORY, EVIDENCE, AND POLICY   347

13 Changing Work Roles and Family Formation   349

14   The Changing American Family and Implications for Family Well-Being   381

15   Government Policies Affecting Family Well-Being   399

16   Balancing the Competing Demands of Work and Family   425

PART V   THE ECONOMIC STATUS OF THE WORLD'S WOMEN   457

Preface

We wrote *The Economics of Women, Men, and Work* because we saw a need for a text that would acquaint students with the findings of research on women, men, and work in the labor market and the household. We are extremely gratified on the publication of the eighth edition to reflect that this belief was justified and hope that this fully revised and updated edition will serve as effectively as the earlier ones.

Overview of the Text

The book is written at a level that should both utilize and enhance students' knowledge of economic concepts and analysis and do so in terms intelligible to those not versed in advanced theory. Even though we assume a knowledge of introductory economics on the part of the reader, an interested and determined individual wanting to learn more about the economic status of women compared to men could benefit considerably from the material offered here. The book also draws upon research in the other social sciences. The text, used in its entirety, is primarily intended for courses on gender from an economics perspective. Such a course may have a variety of names—*Women in the Economy*, *Women in the Labor Market*, *Economics of Gender*, and *Work, Family, and Public Policy*, to name a few. However, this book could be used to good advantage in interdisciplinary women's studies courses as well as introductory-level courses in economic problems. Selected readings would also make a useful supplement to round out a general labor economics course or a course in the economics of the family. In addition, this book would serve as a useful reference work for those not familiar with the rapidly growing body of literature on women, men, and work as well as for practicing economists looking for a single volume on this topic.

We have prepared some materials for instructors to help you teach with the Eighth Edition, including answers to the end-of-chapter questions and a set of Power-Point slides containing the figures from the book for use in lectures and assignments. You'll find these materials and some additional teaching tips, such as how to teach more difficult concepts and ideas for supplementary assignments, on the Ancillary Resource Center found at www.oup-arc.com/blau. In addition, we offer a discussion of how the gender economics this course can enhance student learning in a chapter

---

[1]Francine D. Blau and Anne E. Winkler, "Women, Men, and the Economy," in *International Handbook on Teaching and Learning Economics*, ed. Gail M. Hoyt and KimMarie McGoldrick (Cheltenham, UK: Edward Elgar, 2012), 693–702.

entitled "Women, Men, and the Economy" published in the *International Handbook on Teaching and Learning Economics*.[1] Courses like this offer an opportunity for students to apply their microeconomic knowledge to gender-related policy issues and can be used to motivate useful discussions about data, research methods, and interpreting mixed research findings. Our handbook chapter also points to ways to fully engage students in the course material and offers suggestions about how to teach more difficult concepts as well as provides ideas for supplementary assignments, in addition to the end-of-chapter questions and Internet-based data exercises in the textbook.

Significant Features of the Eighth Edition

The eighth edition reflects the numerous changes in the labor market and in the family that have occurred in recent years. All data and tables have been updated, and discussions and references take into account the most recent research on each subject covered. As in the recent prior editions, questions are provided at the end of each chapter to review major concepts and to stimulate further discussion among students and instructors. In the seventh edition, we introduced Internet-based data exercises, and in this eighth edition, we have expanded that content.

Key updates in the eighth edition include the following:

- We highlight recent developments in the labor market and their consequences for women and men. These developments include the increasingly divergent outcomes for individuals and families by level of educational attainment, as well as the lasting impacts of the Great Recession, which began in December 2007 and lasted until June 2009, for both individuals and families. In Chapter 10, we provide new evidence on the sources of the existing gender wage gap as well as the reasons for its decline compared to previous years. In this discussion, we also present new research that looks at the size of and changes in the gender wage gap for those at the top, middle, and bottom of the wage distribution.

- We updated and expanded the content on differences in labor market outcomes by race and ethnicity (Chapters 5–8). In this regard, for example, in Chapter 6, which looks at employment difficulties for black men, we discuss the disproportionate impact of the criminal justice system on black men and their employment prospects. In chapters on the family (Chapters 13 and 14), we emphasize situations in which race differences are widening (the share currently married) as well as situations where they are narrowing (rates of unmarried births).

- In keeping with changing demographics, in Chapter 13, the book incorporates an expanded discussion of same-sex marriage including its legalization throughout the United States. Chapter 13 also discusses the rising age at first marriage for all women and the rise in gray divorce (divorce among older women). Further, it examines changing dimensions of fertility, including the rise in serial cohabitation and multipartner fertility, the considerable recent decline in teen birth rates, as well as the leveling off in the proportion of births to unmarried women.

- New sections discuss "hot topics" in the news. In this eighth edition, we discuss the fall of all gender barriers in the military (women can now serve in combat on the front lines), the minimum wage campaigns sweeping the nation, the impact of Title IX on sexual harassment and sexual violence in schools, recent efforts to combat employment discrimination based on sexual orientation and gender identity, and action at the state level to extend paid leave to workers to help them balance work and family.

- The material in the international chapters has been reorganized so that Chapter 17 focuses on the world's women, while Chapter 18 compares women's economic status in the United States to that in other economically advanced countries. Chapter 17 emphasizes the dramatic changes occurring across the globe, including rapid declines in fertility in nearly all regions, as well as dramatic increases in women's education in developing countries. We also discuss a major policy change in China: the official end of the one-child policy. Chapter 18 emphasizes key policy differences among economically advanced countries, such as the extent and generosity of paid family leave and childcare subsidies. International differences in policies and institutions help us to better understand the variation we see in women's labor force participation, the gender pay gap, and the fertility rate.

Acknowledgments

We have both taught a course on women in the labor market for some time, and we wish to acknowledge that this book has benefited from the experience and the insights we have gained from our students. Over the years, a large and diverse group of colleagues, from a number of disciplines, have contributed material and provided valuable comments on the various editions. We warmly acknowledge their contributions, including a few who have since passed away, including our dear coauthor Marianne A. Ferber.

Deborah Anderson

Orley C. Ashenfelter, Princeton University

Nancy S. Barrett, Western Michigan University, Kalamazoo

Andrea H. Beller, University of Illinois, Urbana–Champaign

Lourdes Beneria, Cornell University

Barbara R. Bergmann, American University

Gunseli Berik, University of Utah

Sherrilyn Billger, Illinois State University

Judy Bowman, Baylor University

Charles Brown, University of Michigan

Clair Brown, University of California, Berkeley

Michael Brun, University of Illinois, Urbana–Champaign and Illinois State University

Cheryl Carleton, Villanova University

Mary Corcoran, University of Michigan

Ann Davis, Marist College

Greg J. Duncan, University of California, Irvine

Margaret C. Dunkle, American Association of University Women, Educational Foundation

Cristina Echevarria, University of Saskatchewan

Paula England, New York University

Robert Fairlie, University of California, Santa Cruz

Belton M. Fleisher, Ohio State University

David Gillette, Truman State University

Claudia D. Goldin, Harvard University

Janet Gornick, Baruch College, City University of New York

Ulla Grapard, Colgate University

Shoshana Grossbard, San Diego State University

Sara Gundersen, Valparaiso University

Daniel S. Hamermesh, University of Texas, Austin

Francis Horvath, Bureau of Labor Statistics

Joan A. Huber, Ohio State University

Randy Ilg, Bureau of Labor Statistics

Thomas R. Ireland, University of Missouri–St. Louis

Debra Israel, Indiana State University

John Johnson IV, University of Illinois, Urbana–Champaign

Heather Joshi, City University, London

Joan R. Kahn, University of Maryland

Lawrence M. Kahn, Cornell University

Lisa Blau Kahn, Yale University

Charlene Kalenkoski, Texas Tech University

Kristen Keith, University of Toledo

Mahruq Khan, University of Wisconsin–La Crosse

Mark R. Killingsworth, Rutgers University

Andrew Kohen, James Madison University

Marcia Brumit Kropf, Girls Incorporated

Edith Kuiper, State University of New York at New Paltz

Fidan Kurtulus, University of Massachusetts, Amherst

Pareena Lawrence, University of Minnesota

Phillip Levine, Wellesley College

Hilarie Lieb, Northwestern University

Susan J. Linz, Michigan State University

Shelly J. Lundberg, University of California, Santa Barbara

Elaine McCrate, University of Vermont

Kristin Mammen, Columbia University

Julie A. Matthaei, Wellesley College

Nara Mijid, Central Connecticut State University

Joan Moriarty, UNITE HERE

Catherine P. Mulder, John Jay College of Criminal Justice–CUNY

Kathryn Nantz, Fairfield University

Janet Norwood, Urban Institute

Elizabeth Peters, Urban Institute

Leila Pratt, University of Tennessee at Chattanooga

Harriet B. Presser, University of Maryland

Smita Ramnarain, Siena College

Barbara B. Reagan, Southern Methodist University

Barbara F. Reskin, University of Washington, Seattle

Patricia A. Roos, State University of New York, Stony Brook

Elaina Rose, University of Washington, Seattle

Steven H. Sandell, US Department of Health and Human Services

Lisa Saunders, University of Massachusetts, Amherst

Richard Stratton, University of Akron

Myra H. Strober, Stanford University

Louise A. Tilly, New School University

Donald J. Treiman, University of California, Los Angeles

Jane Waldfogel, Columbia University

Jennifer Ward-Batts, Wayne State University

Alison Wellington, The College of Wooster

H. F. (Bill) Williamson, University of Illinois, Urbana–Champaign

Frances Woolley, Carleton University, Ottawa

Brenda A. Wyss, Wheaton College

Without their help, this book would have had many more deficiencies. For those that remain, as well as for all opinions expressed, we, of course, take complete responsibility. This list of acknowledgments would be incomplete if we did not also thank Amanda Eng, Chao Huang, and Christopher Cunningham, the research assistants who helped us track down sources and references and prepare tables and graphs for this edition. We also thank Donna Battista, Vice President, Business Publishing, at Pearson Education, for her strong support over the years.

Finally, we are immensely grateful to our editor, Ann West, Senior Editor, Business, Economics, and Finance, Oxford University Press, for her sage advice and help throughout this process. We would also like to thank Elizabeth Kelly, Project Manager, SPi Global; and the rest of the team who helped bring forth this new edition.

FDB
AEW

PART I

Introduction and Historical Perspectives

Introduction

1

CHAPTER HIGHLIGHTS

- ■ What Economics Is About
- ■ Uses of Economic Theory
- ■ The Scope of Economics
- ■ Individuals, Families, and Households
- ■ A Further Note on Terminology
- ■ Outline of the Book
- ■ Appendix 1A: A Review of Supply and Demand in the Labor Market

Courses in economics abound at universities and colleges, along with an ample supply of texts focusing on the many facets of this discipline. These courses and books increasingly recognize that women play an important role in the economy as workers and consumers and that in many ways their behavior and their problems differ from those of men. However, male patterns often receive the major emphasis, just as patterns of the majority racial and ethnic groups do, while gender differences are, at best, just one of many topics covered. For example, workers are often assumed to enter the labor market after completing their education and to remain until their retirement. Although women in growing numbers are spending an increasing proportion of their time working for pay, their lives and their world continue to be significantly different from those of men, and more of their time continues to be spent in nonmarket activities.

Considerable attention has been focused on the increase in women's labor force participation rates and particularly on the changing economic roles of married women. Much has been made, especially in the popular media, of the growing representation of women in nontraditional occupations, not to mention the publicity received by "the first woman" in a given field, whether it be the first woman to win a major car race or to become the presidential nominee of a major political party. All this focus tends to obscure both the continued responsibility of most women for the bulk of nonmarket work and the large occupational and wage differences between men and women that remain, despite considerable progress. As long as this situation persists, there is a need to address these issues in depth, as is done in this book.

Although economic behavior is clearly not isolated from the remainder of human existence, the primary focus of this book is on the economic behavior of women and men, on economic institutions, and on economic outcomes. To refresh the memory of students who have some acquaintance with economics and to provide a minimal background for those who do not, we begin with a brief introduction to the tools of economics. Neoclassical or mainstream economic theory provides the major emphasis of this book. However, students need to be aware that we endeavor to constantly stretch and challenge the existing theories to shed light on issues related to gender and work. So, in addition to presenting conventional analyses, we sometimes offer critiques of existing approaches. We discuss the importance and implications of gender inequities in the labor market and in the household, to the extent they exist, and we make every effort to take note of diversity by race and ethnicity where space permits. In addition, we point to the increasingly divergent outcomes for individuals and families by level of educational attainment. Finally, we take account of alternative perspectives and the insights of other disciplines where relevant.[1]

Throughout this book, but especially in those segments where we deal with policy, we are confronted by a dilemma common to the social sciences. On the one hand, much of what we present is positive, rather than normative, in the sense that we present facts and research results as we find them. Furthermore, we try to avoid value judgments and prescriptive attitudes; personal values should not be permitted to intrude upon objective analysis. On the other hand, it is unrealistic to claim that the choice of topics, the emphasis in discussions, and the references provided are, or even can be, entirely value-free. A reasonable solution is to present various sides of controversial questions, while making clear that different premises will lead to different conclusions and that the policies one should adopt depend on the goals one wants to reach. We follow this approach.

At the same time, the tenor of this book is undoubtedly colored to some extent by our feminist perspective. Thus, we recognize, for instance, the extent to which persons of the same sex may differ and persons of the opposite sex may be similar. And, like other feminists, in considering gender differences, we are increasingly aware of how these differences vary by race and ethnicity.[2] Our feminist perspective also means we believe that, as much as possible, individuals should have the opportunity to live up to their potential, rather than be forced to conform to stereotypical roles. Most of all, it means that, while recognizing differences between women and men, some possibly caused by biological factors and others by the way girls and boys are reared in our society, we are less inclined to emphasize the differences between them than the common humanity that unites them.

---

[1]We point interested readers to Marianne A. Ferber and Julie A. Nelson, eds., *Beyond Economic Man* (Chicago: University of Chicago Press, 1993). This is the first book that examined economics from a feminist perspective.

[2]Scholars refer to the study of the overlap or intersection of the social constructs of gender, race, ethnicity, and class as "intersectionality." For the application of this concept to analysis of the labor market, see Irene Browne and Joya Misra, "The Intersection of Gender and Race in the Labor Market," *Annual Review of Sociology* 29 (2003): 487–513.

What Economics Is About

Neoclassical or mainstream economics is concerned with decision-making under conditions of **scarcity**, which means that not enough resources are available to satisfy everyone's wants and choices have to be made about how these resources are used. Given this constraint, it is crucial to recognize that using labor, capital, and land to produce one good means that fewer of these inputs will be available for producing other goods. Hence, in the most basic sense, the cost of having more of one good is forgoing the opportunity of having more of another. This idea of cost is captured by the notion of **opportunity cost**, which is the value of the best alternative foregone.

The concept of opportunity cost is fundamental to an understanding of the central economic problem—how to allocate scarce resources so as to maximize well-being. In order to make a rational decision whether to spend money to buy a new coat or whether to spend time going for a hike, knowing how much **utility** (or satisfaction) will be derived from each is not sufficient. Because the amount of money and time is limited and we cannot buy and do everything, it is also crucial to be aware of how much satisfaction is lost by giving up desirable alternatives—that is, we must know the opportunity cost of our choice. **Rationality**, as economists use the term, involves some knowledge of available opportunities and the terms on which they are available. Only on the basis of such information is it possible to weigh the alternatives and choose those that provide more utility than any others.

One of the most fundamental assumptions in traditional economics is that people may be expected to behave rationally in this sense. It does not mean, as critics have occasionally suggested, that only monetary costs and benefits are considered. It is entirely rational to take into account nonpecuniary (nonmonetary) factors because it is *utility*, not, say, money income, that is to be maximized. This definition is so broad that almost everyone might be expected to behave this way. Nonetheless, rationality cannot be taken for granted. It is not satisfactory simply to argue that whatever a person does must provide more utility than any alternative course of action because he or she would otherwise have made a different choice. Such an argument amounts to a mere tautology. An individual who blindly follows the traditional course of action without considering costs and benefits or who fails to consider long-run implications or indirect effects is not necessarily rational. Nor is it uncommon to find persons who, with surprising regularity, make choices that they later appear to regret. Most of us have probably known someone whose behavior fits one or more of these patterns.

These qualifications should be kept in mind, lest we accept too readily that whatever people do must be for the best. Nonetheless, as a first approximation, it is probably more realistic to assume that people tend to try to maximize their well-being rather than that they are indifferent to it. We shall, for the most part, accept this as a reasonable generalization, while recognizing that it is not necessarily appropriate in every instance. Specifically, one must keep in mind that the knowledge needed to make optimal decisions is often difficult and costly to obtain. When this cost is likely to exceed the gain derived, it is rational to *satisfice* (select an option that meets a minimum standard of acceptability) rather than to insist on maximization.[3] By the same token, however, when additional information can be provided relatively cheaply and easily, it is likely to be useful in improving decision-making.

---

[3]This concept was first proposed by Nobel laureate Herbert Simon in *Models of Man* (New York: Wiley, 1957). He argued that when the knowledge needed to make optimal decisions is difficult and costly to obtain, an individual may be content with selecting a "satisfactory" alternative.

Uses of Economic Theory

That individuals are rational is only one of the many simplifying assumptions economists tend to make in formulating **theories** (explanations for why an event might have occurred) and building **economic models** (frameworks that explain human behavior). The justification for making such assumptions is that, much like laboratory experiments in the biological and physical sciences, these abstractions help to focus economists' attention on the particular issue they are attempting to clarify and on the main relationships they want to understand.

In many instances, the approach is to examine the effects of changes in a single variable, such as price or income, while assuming that all else remains the same. This approach does not suggest that economists believe the real world actually works in such a simple way. An aerospace engineer finds it useful to test a plane in a tunnel where everything except wind speed is artificially stabilized, even though the vehicle will later have to fly in an environment where temperature, atmospheric pressure, and humidity vary. Similarly, the social scientist finds it helpful to begin by abstracting from numerous complications.

A theory is not intended to be a full description of the underlying reality. A description is like a photograph, which shows reality in all its details. A theory may be likened to a modern painting, which at most shows the broad outlines of its subject but may provide deeper insight than a more realistic picture would. Hence, a theory or model should not be judged primarily by its detailed resemblance to reality but rather by the extent to which it enables us to grasp the salient features of that reality. Thus, economic theory, at its best, can help us understand the present and correctly predict the future.

Economists should not, therefore, be faulted for making simplifying assumptions or using abstractions, as long as economic models yield useful insights and their predictions are tested against empirical evidence, which is drawn from the real world with all its complexities. Unfortunately, such testing is not always easy to do. Computers enable us to process vast amounts of information, and econometricians have made substantial progress in developing better methods for doing so. However, the availability, timeliness, and quality of the data often still leave much to be desired.

Collecting data is a slow, expensive, and generally unglamorous undertaking. The US government does more and better work in this respect than governments of many other countries. Even so, collecting, compiling, and making the information available may take quite some time. Some data are, in any case, collected only intermittently and other data, not at all. For a variety of reasons, including the government's appropriate reluctance to invade certain areas as well as cost constraints that preclude government data collection on all topics that might potentially be of interest, some substantial gaps occur in official data collection. Private research organizations endeavor to fill these gaps to a degree, but they are even more likely to be constrained by lack of necessary funds. Moreover, the data from such special surveys are particularly likely to be collected sporadically or at lengthy intervals. Despite these difficulties, the possibilities for empirical work have improved beyond the wildest dreams of economists of even one or two generations ago.

When suitable data are available, evidence for some relationships can be obtained using such simple devices as averages and cross-tabulations. In other instances, however, sophisticated statistical methods are required to analyze the data. Such studies are time-consuming, and rarely are conclusions from any one study regarded as final. At times ambiguities occur, with different sets of data or various approaches producing inconsistent results. Even so, such studies enhance the progress of science and help us to identify important areas for future research.

Because of these difficulties of data collection and analysis, timely and definitive answers are simply not available for every question. We have, however, done our best to summarize existing knowledge on each topic considered in this book.

The Scope of Economics

Traditionally, and for the most part even today, economics has focused on the market and on the government. In the market, goods and services are sold. Government is itself a major buyer and seller of goods and services as well as an agent that regulates and otherwise influences the economy. As we shall see, an important change is that many mainstream economists now devote significant attention to the allocation of time within the household itself, but such material is still typically not included in general economics courses. Also, for the most part, the value of nonmarket household production is ignored when aggregate indicators of economic welfare, such as gross domestic product (GDP), are computed. This exclusion is a matter of concern in part because women play the dominant role in the nonmarket sector. One way this book is different is that we focus on the allocation of time within the household, providing both theory and evidence about this decision as well as presenting estimates of the value of nonmarket production.

In its microeconomics section, the typical introductory economics course puts primary emphasis on the analysis of product market transactions, with the firm as seller, concerned with maximizing profits, and the household as buyer, concerned with maximizing satisfaction or utility. Later it introduces markets for factors of production, specifically labor, in which the household is generally the supplier and the firm the purchaser. As a rule, however, this discussion is a brief portion in the section on factors of production, and most students may well come away with a view of the market as chiefly an institution where goods and services are supplied by businesses and the demand for them comes from the household.

In this book, our interest is most specifically in women and men, their work in the labor market and in the household, and the interdependence among individuals within the household. Therefore, we briefly review supply and demand in the labor market in Appendix 1A at the end of this chapter.

In a market economy, the forces of **supply and demand for labor** determine both the jobs that will be available and how much workers will be paid for doing them. Much of our analysis throughout this book is concerned with the determinants of the supply of labor. We shall examine how individuals and their families decide to allocate their time between housework and market work and how women's changing roles in this regard are affecting their own well-being and that of their families. Also on the supply side, workers may influence their productivity by attending school or getting training on the job. We shall consider the determinants of such human capital investment decisions and their role in producing gender differences in labor market outcomes.

Demand is essentially determined by the behavior of employers, who are in turn influenced by the business climate in which they operate. In the simplest case, their goal is to maximize profits, and their demand for labor is related to its productivity in making the goods or producing the services sold by the firm. Thus, the firm's demand for labor is *derived* from the demand of consumers for its final product. It is, however, possible that employers depart from the dictates of profit maximization and consider aspects of workers that are not directly related to their productivity. Discrimination is one such aspect. In this book, discrimination against women in the labor market and its role in producing wage and occupational differences between women and men is another topic that we shall explore in some depth.

A major focus of our analysis of the sources of gender differences in labor market outcomes is to better understand the role played by supply-side versus demand-side explanations in producing gender differentials. Supply-side explanations emphasize the role of gender differences in preferences and human capital investments, while demand-side explanations focus chiefly on labor market discrimination. We also point out that labor market discrimination can *indirectly* lower women's earnings and occupational attainment by reducing their incentives and opportunities to acquire education and training. Supply- and demand-side explanations are not mutually exclusive, however, and it is our view that both play a role in producing the gender differences in outcomes that we observe in the labor market.

Individuals, Families, and Households

Throughout this book, we shall at times focus on the behavior of families and at other times on that of individuals. A **family** is officially defined in US government statistics as consisting of two or more persons, related by blood, marriage, or adoption, living in the same household. This definition includes what might be regarded as a traditional nuclear family—a married-couple family where both parents are the biological or adoptive parents of the children—but it also includes other types of families, including a growing number of single-parent families, blended families (families where one parent is a step-parent), and multigenerational families (e.g., those that include grandparents). Cohabiting couples, who are also growing more prevalent, are not counted as a family in the government's definition. An important recent change is that with the 2015 Supreme Court decision legalizing same-sex marriage, same-sex couples are now permitted to marry in all US states (and the District of Columbia) and, when married, are now counted as a family in government statistics.

While it is, of course, the individual who, in the last analysis, consumes commodities and supplies labor, it is often appropriate to treat the family as the relevant economic unit because decisions of various members within a family are interdependent, much of their consumption is joint, and it is common for them to pool income. At the same time, it is important not to lose sight of the fact that the composition of families may change as individuals move in and out (e.g., a child may grow up and live on his or her own or a single mother may remarry) and that the interests of family members may diverge to a greater or lesser extent (e.g., a married couple may disagree as to how to allocate their income). We shall return to these issues throughout this book as we discuss the status of women and men within the family and in the labor market.

The broader concept of the **household** is also relevant to economic decision-making and is becoming increasingly more so. A household consists of one or more persons living in one dwelling unit and sharing living expenses. Thus, all families are households, but one-person households or those composed of unrelated individuals are not families. The term *household* is more general than *family* and does greater justice to the increasing prevalence of alternative living arrangements; however, because families still constitute a substantial majority of households that include more than one person and because the term *family* is more familiar and connotes a more uniform set of relationships, in this book we choose to use it primarily.

A Further Note on Terminology

Traditionally the terms *sex* and *gender* were used interchangeably to refer to the biological and social differences between women and men. Now, the term *sex* is generally used to refer to the biological differences between males and females and the term *gender* is used to encompass the distinctions society has erected on this biological base.[4] Thus, *gender* connotes a cultural or social construct, including distinctions in roles and behaviors as well as mental and emotional characteristics.[5] We have generally observed the distinction between *sex* and *gender* in this book. In recent years, there has been growing attention to the distinction between biological sex at birth and an individual's **gender identity**, that is, how a person self-identifies, as policies are formulated to address the rights of transgender individuals in schools and in the workplace.[6] The topic of discrimination based on gender identity is often discussed in conjunction with sexual orientation discrimination. **Sexual orientation** refers to the gender one is sexually or romantically attracted to.[7]

Another area in which the question of appropriate terminology arises is with respect to racial and ethnic groups. Historically, people of African origin in the United States were generally called *Negroes*. Several decades ago the term *black* came into use, followed more recently by *African American*. In this book, we use both terms but generally use *black*, mainly because *black* is the term that continues to be used in the official government statistics on which we frequently rely. For the same reason, that is, its use in government statistics, we use the term *Hispanic* rather than alternatives such as *Latino*.

In government statistics, race (e.g., white, black, Asian) and ethnicity (e.g., Hispanic, non-Hispanic) are identified as separate categories.[8] In recent years, the US Census Bureau and the Department of Labor have, in some cases, made available data for the category "white, non-Hispanic." Where feasible, we provide statistics on this group rather than all whites. The reason is that many persons of Hispanic ethnicity self-identify as white and they comprise a large and growing disadvantaged group among whites. Thus, to most clearly gauge the progress of minority groups (including

---

[4]Francine D. Blau, "Gender," in *The New Palgrave: A Dictionary of Economic Theory and Doctrine*, ed. John Eatwell, Murray Milgate, and Peter Newman, vol. 2 (London: MacMillan Press, 1987), 492.
[5]Helen Tierney, ed., *Women's Studies Encyclopedia* (New York: Greenwood Press, 1989), 153.
[6]Growing attention to the concept of gender identity has also raised new discussions about the language that we use in referring to individuals, including our choice of pronouns (he/she/they); see Amanda Hess, "Who's They," *New York Times*, March 29, 2016.
[7]While there is no single definition of gender identity and sexual orientation, see for instance, Anti-Defamation League, "Definitions Related to Sexual Orientation and Gender Identity," accessed November 2, 2016, www.adl.org; and Human Rights Campaign, accessed November 2, 2016, www.hrc.org.
[8]Researchers are actively debating the US Census Bureau's use of these classifications and the meaningfulness of them. See, for instance, Kenneth Prewitt, *What Is Your Race? The Census and Our Flawed Efforts to Classify Americans* (Princeton, NJ: Princeton University Press, 2013).

Hispanics) we compare them to their white, non-Hispanic counterparts. Also, starting with the 2000 census, individuals are permitted to select more than one race group to describe themselves. Due to space considerations, however, it is not possible to fully reflect the rich variation in the racial background of the US population. Thus, the figures on specific race groups presented in the book continue to report data for the major race categories of white, black, and Asian (the vast majority of the population) and do not report data for those of two or more races as a separate category.

There is also the issue of terminology to describe male–female and same-sex couples. It remains the terminology of the US Census Bureau, and we maintain it here, that male–female couples are described as *opposite sex*. However, we acknowledge that there is rising usage of the phrase *different-sex* couples. In referring to marriage between persons of the same sex, we largely use the term *same-sex marriage*, as does the Census Bureau, though it is often also referred to as *gay marriage*.

Outline of the Book

This book is divided into five parts, with each part further subdivided into a number of related chapters. Part I provides an introduction and offers historical perspectives, including a consideration of the sources of gender differences between women and men (nature versus nurture) and an examination of the changing roles of men and women over the course of economic development, with particular focus on the United States. Part II considers the allocation of time between the household and the labor market. First we consider the gender division of labor within the family, providing both theory and evidence regarding the allocation of housework and market work between husbands and wives. Next we focus on the labor supply decision itself and analyze an individual's decision about how to allocate his or her time between the household and the labor market, with emphasis placed on explaining the factors behind trends in women's and men's labor force participation.

Part III deals specifically with women's position in the labor market compared to that of men, beginning with an overview of gender differences in occupations, earnings, and types of employment, followed by an in-depth examination of the various explanations of the existing situation. We first review the human capital explanation for gender differences in education and on-the-job training and examine other supply-side sources of gender differences in outcomes. The next several chapters concentrate on discrimination as a possible cause of women's less favorable labor market outcomes. We first examine empirical evidence on the importance of supply-side factors and the possible role of unexplained differences that could be due to discrimination. We then examine theoretical explanations for discrimination and consider government policies to address this issue.

In Part IV we return to the economics of the family. We examine economic explanations for family formation, including the effect of women's rising labor force participation, and look at the impact of recent changes in family structure on the well-being of family members, as measured by the incidence of poverty and children's outcomes. The subsequent two chapters focus on policies affecting family well-being, including policies designed to alleviate poverty, government tax policies, and the growing number of "family-friendly" policies designed to assist individuals in balancing paid work and family responsibilities.

Finally, in Part V we compare the economic status of women relative to that of men throughout the world. In the first of two chapters, we begin with an overview of the status of the "world's women." Topics covered include the societal benefits of educating women, skewed sex ratios at birth, and the relationship between women's status, economic development, and globalization. The next and final chapter analyzes the similarities of and differences in labor market and family outcomes between the United States and other economically advanced nations.

Questions for Review and Discussion

1. Define *scarcity*, and explain why the concept is so central to neoclassical economics.

2. In everyday language *cost* generally means the amount of money it takes to purchase a commodity. Can this meaning be tied to the concept of opportunity cost and, if so, how?

3. Discuss the uses and abuses of simplifying assumptions in economic models.

4. This question draws on the supply and demand analysis presented in Appendix 1A. Using a graph, show how each of the following labor markets (assumed to be competitive and initially in equilibrium) is affected by the following changes. Explain your reasoning fully.

   a. Labor market for math and science teachers.

      Wages available in private industries utilizing these skills rise.

   b. Labor market for university professors.

      College enrollments expand.

   c. Labor market for low-skilled workers.

      The 1996 federal welfare reform legislation requires that a much larger fraction of welfare recipients work than in the past.

   d. Labor market for workers who completed high school only.

      The workplace becomes more computerized and technically sophisticated.

   e. Labor market for workers who completed college or more.

      The workplace becomes more computerized and technically sophisticated.

Key Terms

scarcity (5)

opportunity cost (5)

utility (5)

rationality (5)

theories (6)

economic models (6)

supply and demand for labor (7)

family (8)

household (8)

gender identity (9)

sexual orientation (9)

demand curve (12)

diminishing marginal productivity (12)

substitution effect (12)

scale effect (13)

supply curve (13)

equilibrium (13)

APPENDIX 1A

A Review of Supply and Demand in the Labor Market

As we explained earlier, supply and demand provide economists with a framework for analyzing labor markets. We briefly review these concepts here in the context of a particular type of labor, clerical workers.

Curve *DD* in Figure 1-1 shows the typical downward-sloping **demand curve**. Wage rate (price) is on the vertical axis, and quantity (number of workers) is on the horizontal axis. The demand curve represents the various amounts of labor that would be hired at various wages by firms in this labor market over a given period of time. If all else remains the same, including methods of production and prices of other inputs, changes in the wage rate cause movements along this curve. In this case, a change occurs in the *quantity demanded*, but demand (i.e., the demand curve) remains the same. If, on the other hand, other factors do not remain the same, the entire demand curve may shift.

Demand curves are normally expected to slope downward to the right, which means that the firm will hire more workers at a lower wage rate and fewer at a higher wage rate. There are several reasons for this. The first is that in the short run there is **diminishing marginal productivity** of labor, meaning that additional units of labor provide progressively less additional output when combined with fixed amounts of capital (plant and equipment). Capital can only be expanded or contracted over a longer period of time, which means that the only way to immediately increase output is to hire additional workers or to have workers put in longer hours. The second is the **substitution effect**. When the price of a particular input changes, while prices of potential substitutes remain the same, the tendency is for profit-maximizing employers

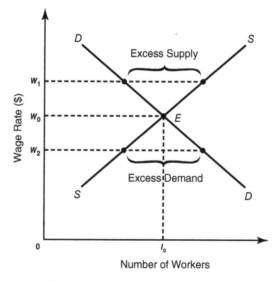

FIGURE 1-1 The Market for Clerical Workers

to use more of the input that is now relatively cheaper and less of the input that is now relatively more expensive. In the short run, for example, less-skilled labor may be substituted for more-skilled workers. In the long run, it may be possible to substitute capital for labor. Last, the **scale effect** can operate in both the short run and the long run. As wages increase, the price of the product will go up, less of it will be purchased, and fewer workers will be employed. The scale effect is likely to be especially large when wages constitute a substantial part of the costs of production, as is usually the case for services. These factors cause the quantity of labor hired to decrease as the wage rate increases, but the movements are along a given demand curve and do not involve a shift of the demand curve.

The **supply curve**, shown by *SS* in Figure 1-1, slopes upward and to the right. It shows the number of workers who would be willing to do clerical work at all possible wages. The supply curve is upward sloping because, if rewards for one type of job increase while those for all others remain the same, additional workers will be attracted from related occupations. So, for example, an increase in the wages of clerical workers may induce individuals who are currently employed in other jobs to improve their clerical skills and compete for clerical positions. Similarly, if pay for clerical work declines relative to others, the quantity of labor supplied to clerical jobs is expected to decline as workers move to other sectors.

It is important to emphasize that the supply curve depicted in Figure 1-1 represents the number of individuals available for a particular line of work. As we shall see in greater detail in Chapter 6, the number of hours supplied to the market by any particular individual may not increase when wages rise. This situation may happen because, at a higher wage rate, an individual who participates in the labor market may choose to allocate more of his or her time to nonmarket activities and the satisfactions they bring.

The intersection of the supply and demand curves shown in Figure 1-1 represents a stable **equilibrium**. An equilibrium exists when all persons willing to work at the going wage rate are able to find employment and all employers willing to hire someone at the going wage rate are able to find workers. In other words, the quantity of labor demanded and the quantity of labor supplied are equal at *E*, and there are no forces causing the wage to move from its present level as long as no external shocks take place. In this case, the equilibrium wage is w_0 and the equilibrium quantity of labor employed is l_0. To illustrate why point *E* represents a *stable* equilibrium, let us assume that, for whatever reason, the wage rate is initially set higher than w_0, say at w_1. At this point, the quantity of labor supplied would exceed the quantity of labor demanded and push wages down toward *E*. Conversely, if wages were initially set at w_2, the opposite would occur. In short, we have a stable equilibrium when there is no tendency to move away from *E*. If an external shock were to cause a deviation, the tendency would be to return to *E*.

Of course, external shocks may occur. If external shocks do occur, they may cause *shifts* in demand, supply, or both, leading to a new equilibrium. Such shocks may come from changes in markets for goods, for nonlabor inputs, or for other types of labor; and they are extremely common. Therefore, a stable equilibrium is not necessarily one that remains fixed for any length of time. It merely means that at any given time the tendency is toward convergence at the point where the quantity of labor supplied equals the quantity of labor demanded, until conditions cause this point to shift.

It may be instructive to consider a couple of examples of shifts in the supply or demand curves. These sample situations can help clarify the difference between factors that cause a movement along an existing supply or demand curve and those that cause a shift in the entire curve. We shall also be able to see how the new equilibrium position is established.

Suppose that the government issues a report on the dangers of credit spending and that, as a result, there is a reduction in the demand for such services provided by the banking industry. That is, at any given price of these services, consumers demand less of them. Because this industry employs a substantial number of clerical workers, such a change would cause an inward shift in the market-wide demand curve for clerical workers, from DD to $D'D'$ in Figure 1-2a. At any given wage rate, then, firms are willing to hire fewer clerical workers. This example illustrates that

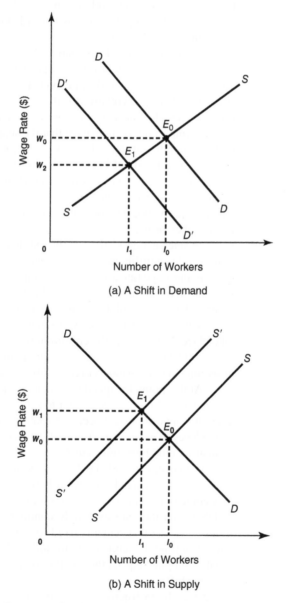

(a) A Shift in Demand

(b) A Shift in Supply

FIGURE 1-2 An Illustration of Shifts in the Supply and Demand Curves

the demand for labor is a *derived* demand: it is derived from consumer demand for the goods and services that the workers produce. A new equilibrium will occur at E_1, where the quantity of labor supplied again equals the (new) quantity of labor demanded. At E_1, fewer individuals are employed as clerical workers and a lower wage rate is determined for that occupation.

Shifts in supply curves can also alter the market equilibrium, as shown in Figure 1-2b. For instance, suppose that the government's antidiscrimination policies increase opportunities for women in managerial jobs, raising their wages in these jobs and making it easier for them to obtain such employment. This change will result in a reduction in the supply (inward shift in the supply curve) of clerical workers, an occupation staffed primarily by women, from SS to $S'S'$. At any given wage, fewer women would be available to work in clerical jobs than previously. At the new equilibrium (E_1), the wages are higher and the number of workers employed is lower than in the initial situation (E_0). This example illustrates that improved opportunities for women in traditionally male jobs can potentially improve the economic welfare even of those women who remain in traditionally female pursuits.

2

Women and Men: Historical Perspectives

CHAPTER HIGHLIGHTS

- ■ The Source of Gender Differences: Nature versus Nurture—The Ongoing Debate
- ■ Factors Influencing Women's Relative Status
- ■ Women's Roles and Economic Development
- ■ The US Experience

We are constantly told today that we live in an era of rapid change—change in economic conditions and technology, in economic and social institutions, in mores and beliefs. And so we do. Changes in the roles of women and men, their relations to each other, and the nature of the families in which most of them continue to live take place at an unprecedented speed. This situation inevitably creates stresses and strains. Not surprisingly, people who feel insecure in a world of shifting boundaries and values are prone to look back with nostalgia to the "good old days" when women were women and men were men and both "knew their proper place."

How realistic is this picture some hold of traditional gender roles, unchanging for all time and pervasive for all places, which is supposed to have existed before the recent era of turmoil and upheaval? The answer has substantial practical implications. If the same roles of women and men have existed always and everywhere, some may conclude that these roles are biologically determined and that they probably cannot, and perhaps should not, be changed. If, on the other hand, the roles of men and women have varied a good deal over time and space, it is likely that there is also room for flexibility now and in the future.

For this reason, gaining insight into the nature of gender roles and how they have changed over time is valuable. We begin by considering the sources of gender differences between women and men, with specific attention to what has been termed the *nature versus nurture debate*. Next we consider the changing roles of men and women in the household and in the economy and the evolution of the family over the course of economic development, with particular focus on the United States. Although other factors are not ignored, economic causation is the primary focus of our investigation of the forces shaping these changes.

The Source of Gender Differences: Nature Versus Nurture— The Ongoing Debate

In understanding gender differences between women and men, whether in regard to their selection of mates or math test scores, the question is often raised as to whether "**nature**" (biology, genes) or "**nurture**" (social environment, culture) is responsible for the observed differences.

Some have emphasized biology and particularly the biological origins of differences between men and women.[1] The emphasis on biology gained particular traction following the publication of Edward O. Wilson's *Sociobiology: The New Synthesis* in 1975. Advocates of **sociobiology** and those in the related field of **evolutionary psychology** appeal to Darwin's theory of natural selection to argue that genes determine behavioral traits for humans as well as other animals.[2]

Other scholars, such as Alice Eagly and Wendy Wood, take a **social structural approach**, emphasizing the role of the social environment and **culture** in determining gender roles and behavior. *Culture* refers to "knowledge, beliefs, and evaluations shared among members of a society." In this view, biology constrains, but does not determine, human behavior. The roles of men and women depend on many factors, including not only men's greater size and physical strength and women's reproductive activities but also the society's economy and social organization, which is in turn influenced by its technology.[3] Biological nature is seen as a broad base upon which a variety of structures, with respect to socially determined gender differences, can be built.

This view leaves greater room for adaptation in behavior to changing circumstances. For example, women's lives were severely constrained by biology during earlier historical periods when women were pregnant or nursing virtually all their adult lives and infants were entirely dependent on mother's milk for their survival. This situation changed considerably with reductions in family size and the arrival of bottle-feeding.[4] Moreover, it has been increasingly recognized that the environment may influence and condition biological structures and responses. For example, research evidence on the adult brain indicates that it is "remarkably responsive, even

---

[1]Influential early exponents include Robert Ardrey, *The Territorial Imperative* (New York: Atheneum Press, 1966), and Desmond Morris, *The Naked Ape: A Zoologist's Study of the Human Animal* (New York: McGraw-Hill, 1967).

[2]See, Edward O. Wilson, *Sociobiology: The New Synthesis* (Cambridge, MA: Belknap Press of Harvard University Press, 1975), and Linnda R. Caporael, "Evolutionary Psychology: Towards a Unifying Theory and a Hybrid Science," *Annual Review of Psychology* 52 (February 2001): 607–28. Efforts to integrate a biological perspective also underlie the development of evolutionary anthropology and bioeconomics.

[3]Alice H. Eagly and Wendy Wood, "The Origins of Sex Differences in Human Behavior: Evolved Dispositions versus Social Roles," *American Psychologist* 54, no. 6 (June 1999): 408–23; quotation is from p. 414. See also, Shoshana Grossbard-Schechtman, "Biology versus Economics and Culture in Research on the Family," *Journal of Bioeconomics* 4 (2002): 191–94.

[4]Joan Huber, *On the Origins of Gender Inequality* (Boulder, CO, and London: Paradigm Publishers, 2007). See also Stefania Albanesi and Claudia Olivetti, "Gender Roles and Medical Progress," *Journal of Political Economy* 124, no. 3 (June 2016): 650–95.

in terms of its structure, to experience, as well as to hormones."[5] And scientists are increasingly recognizing that gene expression or suppression may to some extent be influenced by environmental factors.[6]

Evidence on what women and men look for in their mates provides a useful example of the possible role of biology compared to environment and culture in explaining human behavior, as well as of the difficulty in discriminating between these two sets of explanations.[7] Much research has found that men tend to place a higher value on physical appearance in selecting mates, while women tend to focus on intelligence and other qualities plausibly associated with being a good provider. For example, in an experiment, researchers arranged for study participants to meet a number of potential mates in a speed-dating setting and gave them the opportunity to accept or reject each partner. Subjects also rated each potential partner on a number attributes. It was found that, in making their selections, women put greater emphasis on the intelligence of the partner, while men put greater emphasis on physical attractiveness.[8] Another study that reached a similar conclusion used information on the mate search behavior of users of an online dating service in two US metropolitan areas. Users of the service could view photos and information on a variety of attributes of potential partners. Utilizing data on users' browsing behavior and decisions to initiate a first contact with a potential mate, researchers were able to analyze male and female preferences for potential partners. This study also found that women have a stronger preference than men for income compared to physical attributes.[9]

A proponent of evolutionary psychology might view this behavior as, to some extent, the result of different selection pressures experienced by ancestral humans. In that period, women's preferences reflected their need for mates who were able to provide the resources to support them and their children, while men's preferences were for partners who would bear and nurture their children and for attributes that signaled that capability. Physical attractiveness is one such attribute, it is argued, because women's reproductive capacity is time-limited,[10] and presumably attractiveness is correlated with youth and robust health. Those with such preferences experienced greater reproductive success than those who did not and passed their genes on to their offspring. Thus, in this view, these "evolved psychological dispositions are built into the human psyche"[11] and maintained, to a greater or lesser extent, throughout the world to this day. While this does not rule out a role for

[5]Melissa Hines, *Brain Gender* (New York: Oxford University Press, 2004), 228; see also Deborah Blum, *Sex on the Brain: The Biological Differences between Men and Women* (New York: Viking Penguin, 1997), 41.

[6]Judith Shulevitz, "Why Fathers Really Matter," *New York Times*, September 8, 2012.

[7]Donald Cox cautions that "to cast culture and biology as *presumed* alternatives (thereby ruling out that they might work together) risks an incomplete and perhaps over-simplified approach to sex based differences in mating preferences"; see "Biological Basics and the Economics of the Family," *Journal of Economic Perspectives* 21, no. 2 (Spring 2007): 91–108; quotation is from p. 101.

[8]Raymond Fisman, Sheena S. Iyengar, Emir Kamenica, and Itamar Simonson, "Gender Differences in Mate Selection: Evidence from a Speed Dating Experiment," *Quarterly Journal of Economics* 121, no. 2 (May 2006): 673–97.

[9]Gunter J. Hitsch, Ali Hortagsu, and Dan Ariely, "What Makes You Click? Mate Preferences in Online Dating," *Quantitative Marketing and Economics* 8, no. 4 (December 2010): 393–427.

[10]David M. Buss, "Toward an Evolutionary Psychology of Human Mating," *Behavioral and Brain Sciences* 12 (1989): 1–14. Our discussion in this section draws on the review and comparison of evolutionary psychology and social structural theory in Eagly and Wood, "Origins of Sex Differences."

[11]Eagly and Wood, "The Origins of Sex Differences," 412. See also Buss, "Toward an Evolutionary Psychology."

environmental factors,[12] one might be tempted to conclude that such genetically encoded dispositions will not change much even as circumstances are altered.

Although the observed gender differences in mating preferences are consistent with evolutionary theory, social structural theory can provide an alternative explanation based on the contemporary environment and the impact of culture. Proponents of this view would point out that the preference patterns found in the speed-dating experiment and the analysis of online dating correspond to what would be expected based on traditional gender roles. Under a traditional division of labor, men are the breadwinners; thus, their earning capabilities are important to potential mates. Women are valued for their prowess at household production and may exchange that and other attributes, like beauty, to obtain a high-earning partner. Observed gender preferences for mates may thus reflect the realities of men's and women's circumstances in earlier times.

But why should preferences grounded in traditional gender roles persist into the present? There are at least two reasons, both of which may be operative. First, even today, many significant differences between men and women remain that could plausibly reinforce these preferences. Despite important changes, women continue to have lower labor force participation rates than men; to be clustered in lower-paying female occupations; and, in most couples, to earn less than their partners. Therefore, while men are no longer the only breadwinners in most families, they are generally the higher-earning spouse, which provides an incentive for women to value earning capability in a potential partner more than men do. Moreover, as we shall see in Chapter 4, in most families women continue to do the majority of housework, making it reasonable for men to put greater emphasis on a potential partner's abilities in this area than women do. Second, to the extent that gender roles are changing, the preferences of men and women may continue to reflect the gender roles of an earlier period if preferences and attitudes are handed down to later generations through cultural transmission. In Chapter 6, we review some evidence that is consistent with a role of culture in influencing women's labor supply decisions.

Due to the impact of culture, even a social structural analysis suggests considerable staying power for gender differences in roles and preferences over time. However, an important difference from evolutionary psychology is that an analysis based on social structure does lead us to expect that, as women continue to enter traditionally male occupations and increase their earning power and as men engage in more caregiving responsibilities, the desired traits in a mate will also eventually change. Indeed, as we discuss in subsequent chapters, with the increase in two-earner couples, partners' skills and interests are likely becoming more similar. One consequence is that marriage may increasingly occur as a result of gains from shared consumption between the members of the couple rather than on the basis of gains from specialization in household production and market work. Some empirical evidence supports the expectation that the desired traits in a mate will change as gender roles change. A study that examined gender differences in preferences for mates in 37 cultures around the globe did find that, in all cultures, men placed greater emphasis on domestic skill in a mate and women placed greater emphasis on earning potential. Very importantly, however, the gender differences lessened with increasing gender equality in the society—as indexed by the United Nations' Gender Empowerment

---

[12]Cox, "Biological Basics and the Economics of the Family," 94, explains that "biological causality ranges from distal to proximate, a parade of forces increasingly interactive with, and contingent upon, environmental conditions."

Measure.[13] This variation in preferences suggests that more than genetics explains mate selection and other gender differences in preferences and that preferences may be influenced by contemporary environmental factors.

It has also been argued that placing too much emphasis on a biological explanation is problematic, resulting in a tendency to overemphasize the *differences* between men and women rather than recognizing their many similarities, as well as the great diversities *within* each group.[14] For example, it is common to stress the differences between men and women in the averages of height, strength, math SAT scores, and so forth, rather than the fact that the range for each group substantially overlaps. Indeed, as we shall see in Chapter 9, the gender difference in math SAT scores in the United States has decreased over time. In fact, there is no gender difference in demonstrated math abilities in some countries; and in Iceland, girls' average math scores are higher than boys'.[15]

To sum up, just as biology may play some role in explaining gender differences, so too do the environment and the opportunities society provides for overcoming biological limitations. Therefore, in thinking about the role of biology compared to environment and culture, it may be more useful to think about each as emphasizing one dimension (nature) relative to the other (nurture), rather than as posing a stark dichotomy between the two (nature vs. nurture). This perspective ascribes an important role to history in influencing where we are now and to progress in determining where we will be in the future.

Factors Influencing Women's Relative Status

There is general agreement that the relative status of women has varied over time and across societies, but there is less agreement regarding the factors determining their relative position. Here we point to two likely factors. First, women's relative status is positively influenced by the importance of their *role in production*, which is in turn shaped by the technology employed by the society in producing the necessities of life.[16] For example, as pointed out by Esther Boserup, two technologies practiced in traditional agriculture—shifting cultivation and plow cultivation—had very different impacts on women's role in production. Under shifting cultivation, handheld tools that do not require a great deal of physical strength like the hoe and digging stick are used. In contrast, under plow cultivation, more upper body strength is required and activities are less compatible with caring for children at the same time. These technologies, which varied in their rates of adoption depending on geographical and climatic conditions and the crop being cultivated, significantly affected the roles of women in these societies. Women actively participated in farmwork under shifting

---

[13]Eagly and Wood, "The Origins of Sex Differences." For further evidence, see Marcel Zentner and Klaudia Mitura, "Stepping Out of the Caveman's Shadow: Nations' Gender Gap Predicts Degree of Sex Differentiation in Mate Preferences," *Pyschological Science* 25, no. 10 (2012): 1176–85.
[14]Ruth Hubbard, "Race and Sex as Biological Categories," in *Challenging Racism and Sexism: Alternatives to Genetic Explanations*, ed. Ethel Tobach and Betty Rosoff (New York: Feminist Press of the City University of New York, 1994), 11–21; and Blum, *Sex on the Brain*.
[15]Luigi Guiso, Ferdinando Monte, Paola Sapienza, and Luigi Zingales, "Culture, Gender, and Math," *Science* 320 (May 30, 2008): 1164–65.
[16]See, for example, Ernestine Friedl, *Women and Men: An Anthropologist's View* (New York: Holt, Rinehart & Winston, 1975); Esther Boserup, *Women's Role in Economic Development* (London: George Allen & Unwin, 1970); and Alberto F. Alesina, Paola Giuliano, and Nathan Nunn, "On the Origins of Gender Roles: Women and the Plough," *Quarterly Journal of Economics*, 128, no. 2 (2013): 469–530.

cultivation. However, plow agriculture tended to result in a gender division of labor where men worked outside the home in the fields using the plow and women worked in or near the home.[17] Such societies developed the belief that "women's place" is in the home. In fact, recent evidence suggests such beliefs tend to persist even to the present day, as reflected by the lower rates of female labor force participation in areas where the plow took hold in earlier times.[18]

Second, while engaging in productive work plays an important role in determining the economic status of women, as the foregoing discussion suggests, another factor influencing women's relative status is the extent of their *participation in productive activities outside the home and family*, what has been termed the *public sphere*. As Claudia Goldin notes, "there is considerable evidence that as women's work moves out from the home and family, even if such work was previously market oriented, women gain freedoms in the polity, in the society, and in their own households."[19] Part of the explanation for women's relatively lower status in earlier times is that their activities were confined to the home, while the public sphere was monopolized by men.

As we shall see in the next section, the productive role of women has tended to vary over the course of economic development. This helps us to understand not only differences in the roles of women across countries at different stages of economic development today but also how gender roles changed in the course of economic development in the United States.

Women's Roles and Economic Development

Using data from countries around the globe and insights from economic theory, Claudia Goldin and other researchers have traced out a **U-shaped relationship** between women's labor force participation and economic development.[20] Figure 2-1 provides a useful graphic of this relationship. **Gross domestic product (GDP) per capita**, which measures the total value of goods and services produced within a nation divided by the population, is shown along the horizontal axis and serves as a proxy for economic development. The indicator of **labor force participation** on the vertical axis is the share of the female population that is economically active, where economic activity includes not only conventional employment for pay in the labor market but also the work of unpaid family members on family farms and in family businesses, individuals working for pay *within* the home, and the self-employed. While the curve in Figure 2-1 is hypothetical, it aligns well with empirical data

---

[17]Boserup, *Women's Role in Economic Development*, based on the summary of Boserup and additional information provided in Alesina, Giuliano, and Nunn, "On the Origins of Gender Roles." Similarly, Eliana Carranza observes that in rural areas of India with loamy soil that requires male strength to work it, women are less economically valued, as reflected by sex ratios of children that favor boys. The converse is also true: in areas where female labor is more highly valued, sex ratios are less skewed toward boys. See "Soil Endowments, Female Labor Force Participation, and the Demographic Deficit of Women in India," *American Economic Journal: Applied Economics* 6, no. 4 (2014): 197–225.

[18]Alesina, Giuliano, and Nunn, "On the Origins of Gender Roles."

[19]Claudia Goldin, "The U-Shaped Female Labor Force Function in Economic Development and Economic History," in *Investment in Women's Human Capital*, ed. T. Paul Schultz (Chicago: University of Chicago Press, 1995), 61–90; quotation is from p. 63. See also Michelle Z. Rosaldo, "Women, Culture, and Society: A Theoretical Overview," in *Women, Culture, and Society*, ed. Michelle Z. Rosaldo and Louise Lamphere (Stanford, CA: Stanford University Press, 1974).

[20]Goldin, "The U-Shaped Female Labor Force Function."

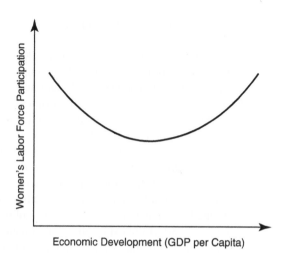

FIGURE 2-1 The U-Shaped Relationship between Women's Labor Force Participation and Economic Development

showing the current-day relationship between female labor force participation and economic development among a cross section of countries.[21]

Looking to the far left of the U, female labor force participation is found to be high at earlier stages of economic development, when women tend to be heavily involved as family workers on the farm or in family businesses or otherwise working for pay or producing for the market within the household. As shown by the declining portion of the U, women's labor force participation initially falls in the course of economic development as the locus of production moves out of the household and family enterprises and into factories and offices and as the nature of agricultural work changes and becomes wage-based.[22]

To understand the decline in female labor force participation at this stage and its subsequent increase with further economic development along the U-shaped curve in Figure 2-1, it is useful to apply two economic concepts that we consider in greater detail in Chapter 6: the income effect and the substitution effect. The **income effect** is the change in a wife's labor supply associated with a change in family income, all else equal. The income effect is expected to be negative because an increase in family income, all else remaining the same, will increase the family's demand for all goods from which it derives satisfaction, including the wife's contributions within the home and, as a result, she is less likely to participate in the labor force. The

[21]See Goldin, "The U-Shaped Female Labor Force Function;" Kristen Mammen and Christina Paxson, "Women's Work and Economic Development," *Journal of Economic Perspectives* 14, no. 4 (Fall 2000): 141–64; Shelly Lundberg, "The Sexual Division of Labour" in *The Shape of the Division of Labour: Nations, Industries and Households*, ed. Robert M. Solow and Jean-Philippe Touffut (Cheltenham, UK, and Northampton, MA: Edward Elgar, 2010); and Claudia Olivetti, "The Female Labor Force and Long-Run Development: The American Experience in Comparative Perspective," in *Human Capital in History: The American Record*, ed. L. Platt Boustan, C. Frydman, and R.A. Margo (Chicago: University of Chicago Press, 2014).

[22]Looking at the set of Organisation for Economic Co-operation and Development (OECD) countries, Olivetti, "The Female Labor Force," finds weaker evidence of the declining part of the U for those that joined the OECD later (after the mid-1970s), perhaps because manufacturing required less brawn or was associated with better working conditions than in earlier periods. Recent work by Isis Gaddis and Stephan Klasen similarly finds weak evidence for the declining part of the U for those countries currently defined as "developing"; see "Economic Development, Structural Change, and Women's Labor Force Participation: A Reexamination of the Feminization U Hypothesis," *Journal of Population Economics* 27 (2014): 639–81.

substitution effect is the change in a wife's labor supply associated with a change in the wage that she can earn in the labor market, all else equal. The substitution effect is expected to be positive because an increase in the wife's potential market wage, all else remaining the same (including family income), will increase her opportunity cost of time spent in the home and, as a result, she is more likely to participate in the labor force.

One reason for the decrease in women's participation along the declining portion of the U is that the higher family income associated with economic development causes an income effect that reduces female labor force participation. Further, Goldin has argued, societal norms often work against married women performing manual wage labor in agriculture or manufacturing. This work was regarded as unattractive or inappropriate for married women; therefore, if a married woman undertook it, her husband was stigmatized as a poor provider.

As economic development progresses, however, women's education and consequent opportunities for white-collar employment rise. Women's labor force participation once again increases both because the higher wages available to women lead to a substitution effect, increasing their labor force participation, and because white-collar employment does not share the same stigma as factory work and wage labor on farms. This corresponds to the rising portion of the U.[23]

While the broad sweep of economic development thus appears to foster gender equality by drawing women into the labor force,[24] the U-shaped relationship between women's labor force participation and economic development means that the initial phases of development may be associated with declining female labor force participation and, to the extent that women's relative status depends on their productive roles, declining relative status of women. However, two qualifications are warranted. First, it has been noted that the rising incomes associated with economic development benefit society as a whole, including women. These benefits can be substantial, leading, as development economist Esther Duflo has observed, to a "relaxing [of] the constraints poor households face, thus reducing the frequency at which they are placed in the position to make life or death choices."[25] Thus, for women who are members of these households, the overall effect of development on their *well-being*, even at the bottom of the U, is not entirely negative. Second, it is not just women's productive role but also where this activity takes place that is important. For this reason, even though women's participation rates are high at lower levels of economic development (the far left of the U), to the extent that this activity takes place within the confines of the home or a family enterprise, women's status is probably not as high as it will be later, in the rising portion of the U, when women are drawn out of the home and into the labor market.

Thus, in the last phase (the rising portion of the U), women's status is arguably highest because they are increasingly engaged in the paid labor market and in employment outside of the confines of the home. However, it is important to note that economic development does not lead to improvements in women's status

---

[23]Interestingly, for the current period, Robert Jensen points to the dramatic growth of IT "call centers" in India as having a similar impact on women's labor force participation there; see "Do Labor Market Opportunities Affect Young Women's Work and Family Decisions? Experimental Evidence from India," *Quarterly Journal of Economics* 127 (2012): 753–92.

[24]Goldin, "The U-Shaped Female Labor Force Function."

[25]Esther Duflo, "Women Empowerment and Economic Development," *Journal of Economic Literature* 50, no. 4 (December 2012): 1051–79.

in every respect. One need only look at the situation for girls in China and India, both countries where boys are generally preferred. As income has increased, so has sex-selective abortion. Finally, in thinking about the relationship between economic development and women's status, it is important to realize that the relationship goes *both ways*: Policies that promote gender equality, in particular those that open up opportunities for women in the paid labor market, have the potential to advance economic development from which all members of society benefit and, in particular, to improve the well-being of children.[26] These topics are discussed at length in Chapter 17.

The US Experience

The history of the United States provides a useful illustrative example of how women's roles in the labor market and household, and accordingly their relative status, have changed over time. As we shall see, over the course of US economic development, women's labor force participation exhibited the expected U-shaped pattern. The case of the United States is in some respects unique, even in comparison to other economically advanced countries. In particular, the frontier experience was shared by only a few of these countries, such as Canada and Australia. Nonetheless, the broad contours of the shifts outlined here are to some extent applicable to many economically advanced nations. Indeed, the alteration of men's and women's work roles that we have observed in the United States may be seen as part of a transformation taking place in much of the industrialized world. (Recent developments in other countries are discussed in Chapters 17 and 18.)

Colonial America: The Preindustrial Period

The start of **colonial America** is often dated to 1607, when the first English settlement in the New World was established in Jamestown, Virginia. In colonial America, as in other preindustrial economies, the family enterprise was the dominant economic unit and production was the major function of the family.[27] The family was largely self-sufficient, with the household producing most of the necessities itself. Although some exchange of goods and services, chiefly barter, took place, it was not until well into the nineteenth century that production outside the home for sale came to dominate the economy.

Both women and men held the same *economic role*—producer—but their *tasks* differed. Women did household work, such as cooking, cleaning, and care of children, but also what might today be called "light manufacturing," such as spinning, weaving, sewing, and soap and candle making. They also tended a garden, cared for farm animals, and provided seasonal help with the crops. Men were responsible for the majority of the more physically demanding agricultural work, including plowing. Most of the food and other raw materials consumed were grown or produced on the farm.

---

[26]World Bank, *World Development Report 2012: Gender Equality and Development* (Washington, DC: World Bank).

[27]A more detailed account of the position of women during the colonial era and the early years of the Republic may be found in Alice Kessler-Harris, *Out to Work: A History of America's Wage Earning Women* (New York: Oxford University Press, 1982), 3–45.

All members of the family capable of making any contribution participated in production, including young children, from the time they were able. Indeed, the important economic role of children, as well as the plentiful availability of land, encouraged large families. Birth rates in the colonies were high compared to Europe, as observed by Benjamin Franklin, among others, at the time. While fertility data are not available for the colonial period, data for 1800 indicate that the typical American woman averaged about seven children.[28]

Of course, there were exceptions to the general patterns discussed here. Widows sometimes took over the family enterprise when the need arose, and wealthy women were primarily managers, not workers, within the household. The poorest women were often indentured servants and were not permitted to marry during their years of servitude. The most important exception to keep in mind is that this was a time when the vast majority of African American women and men were slaves. They had to work very hard with no claim on the fruits of their labor, or indeed any other legal rights, and could have their family entirely disrupted by their owners' choice to sell a family member.

Period of Industrialization

The late eighteenth and early nineteenth centuries mark the establishment of **industrialization** in the United States, which began with the development of the textile industry. Samuel Slater opened the first textile mill in 1789 in Rhode Island. Young single women and children left their family farms to work in the new factories. The employment of these young women in the early textile factories may have appeared quite natural to observers at the time. They were doing much the same type of work they had done in the home, only in a new location and under the supervision of a foreman rather than the head of the household.[29] The young women worked long hours, nearly 13 hours per day, 6 days per week, and lived in corporate boarding houses. Conditions in the mills were difficult, including loud noise from the machinery and little ventilation. Still, these jobs enabled these young women to supplement family income, and they were able to retain some of their earnings to accumulate a "dowry" that would make them more desirable marriage partners. Once married, women generally left their jobs to look after their own households. Notably, many children worked alongside the young women in the mills; such work was regarded as a valuable activity for both groups given the Puritan view of the "virtue of industry."[30]

By the 1840s, immigrant women had largely replaced the New England farm girls in the factories. While it was not uncommon for immigrant wives to work outside the home, such employment remained rare for white, native-born married women and for married women overall. Moreover, although early industries did employ women, mainly young single ones, the more technologically advanced

---

[28]Michael Haines, "Fertility and Mortality in the United States," *EH.Net Encyclopedia*, ed. Robert Whaples, March 19, 2008, accessed July 31, 2012, https://eh.net/encyclopedia. Data are for whites; data on blacks, which are available starting in 1850, indicate that they had higher fertility and higher mortality than whites.

[29]This similarity was pointed out by Edith Abbott, *Women in Industry* (New York: Appleton & Company, 1910). For a more recent discussion of the evolution of women's paid work, see Dora L. Costa, "From Mill Town to Board Room: The Rise of Women's Paid Labor," *Journal of Economic Perspectives* 14, no. 4 (Fall 2000): 101–22.

[30]Abbott, *Women in Industry*.

industries that subsequently developed relied almost entirely on male workers. The earliest available data from the 1890 US census indicate that the labor force participation rate for men was 84 percent but only 18 percent of all women were in the paid labor force. The percentage of married women who worked outside the home was even smaller—only 5 percent overall and less than 3 percent for white women.[31]

Married women's employment differed substantially by race and ethnicity. As we have seen, married immigrant women were more likely to work outside the home than the native-born. Participation rates were also considerably higher for African American women than for native-born whites. About 23 percent of black wives were employed; most worked either as domestics or in agriculture in the rural South, the same jobs they had held under slavery.[32] The higher participation rates for these married women were likely due in large part to the low earnings of their spouses. As our earlier discussion suggested, married women's employment was associated with economic need, and it was uncommon for wives to remain in the labor force once their husbands earned enough to support their family.

Returning to our discussion of the overall pattern of married women's labor force participation over the course of economic development in the United States, the evidence suggests that it corresponds to the U-shaped relationship shown in Figure 2-1. From the colonial period through early industrialization, married women's labor force participation appears to have decreased, consistent with the left-hand portion of the U. Married women were quite active in family farms and enterprises during the colonial period but were not employed extensively outside the home as industrialization became established. Their participation declined subsequently with industrialization but then began to increase as economic development proceeded further.

Unfortunately, official government data, like those cited earlier, do not provide a complete picture of the relationship between women's labor force participation and economic development that would demonstrate the U-shaped pattern. For one thing, meaningful statistics date back only to 1890 and thus do not capture the early period of high participation in family farms and businesses. In addition, as found by economic historian Claudia Goldin, even in 1890, quite a bit of married women's work was not fully counted. Undercounted activities include work performed for income in the home (e.g., taking in boarders or doing piecework), unpaid work in family farms and businesses, and even wage work in manufacturing. When the data are adjusted to account for the omission of these activities, Goldin estimates that participation rates for all women and married women in 1890 were about the same as their participation rates in 1940.[33] And, as we have noted, married women's participation

---

[31]The labor force participation figures cited here and later in this chapter are from Claudia Goldin, *Understanding the Gender Gap: An Economic History of American Women* (New York: Oxford University Press, 1990), with the exception of the overall male and female participation rates, which are from US Census Bureau, *Historical Statistics of the United States: Colonial Times to 1970*, part 1 (1975), 131–32.
[32]For further discussion of differences by race and ethnicity, see Teresa L. Amott and Julie A. Matthaei, *Race, Gender, and Work: A Multicultural Economic History of Women in the United States* (Boston: South End Press, 1996); and Leah Platt Boustan and William J. Collins, "The Origin and Persistence of Black–White Differences in Women's Labor Force Participation," in *Human Capital in History: The American Record*, ed. Leah Platt Bouston, Carola Fryman, and Robert A. Margo (Chicago: University of Chicago Press, 2014).
[33]The adjustments made by Goldin are detailed in Table 2.9 of *Understanding the Gender Gap*. See also Goldin, "The U-Shaped Female Labor Force Function." Unfortunately, these data are provided only for whites. As we have seen, official statistics indicate that married black women had higher participation rates than married white women.

was likely even higher prior to 1890, given their active role in family farms and businesses.

Thus, in accordance with the U-shaped relationship, married women's participation in the United States at first fell with industrialization, reaching the bottom of the U probably around the 1920s. It then rose dramatically, particularly in the post-1940 period, tracing out the rising portion of the U.[34] The growth in female labor force participation in the post-1940 period will be examined in detail in Chapters 5 and 6.

The Evolution of the Family and Women's Labor Force Participation

As industrialization and urbanization progressed over the course of the nineteenth century, many husbands followed the shifting locus of production into factories and offices and, with their earnings, were able to purchase newly available factory-produced goods for their family. At the same time, wives' opportunities to help out on a family farm or with a family business diminished. As a consequence of these changes, the family shifted from a production unit, as was the case in the preindustrial period, to a consumption unit. Redistribution became an important function for the family as the wife and children became the economic dependents of the market-productive husband. Now, not only did specific *tasks* differ between men and women, as they always had, but men and women had different *economic roles* as well. Husbands took on the role of breadwinner, and wives assumed the role of homemaker; and what has come to be known as the **traditional family** was established.[35]

Husbands had the primary (and often sole) responsibility for earning a living. As household head, they also made decisions about how income was to be spent, thereby occupying dominant roles in both the public (market) and private spheres.[36] Married women's role was limited to the domestic (private) sphere: taking care of their children, nurturing their husbands, and maintaining the home. Indeed, exclusive dedication to the role of mother and wife was widely accepted as the only proper and fulfilling life for a woman. Nonetheless, market work was still quite common among single women. In addition, as we have seen, among the poor, particularly blacks and immigrants, it was often economically necessary for wives to enter the labor market. There were even a relatively small number of women, particularly college graduates, who chose careers over marriage as a lifelong vocation.

---

[34]See Goldin, *Understanding the Gender Gap* and "The U-Shaped Female Labor Force Function." See also Costa, "From Mill Town to Board Room."

[35]Historian Carl N. Degler termed this shift the *first transformation*. In his view, the second transformation came in the 1940s, when married women began to enter the labor market in large numbers; see *At Odds: Women and the Family in America from the Revolution to the Present* (New York: Oxford University Press, 1980). For an excellent recent discussion of the evolution of women's and men's roles, see Andrea Rees Davies and Brenda D. Frink, "The Origins of the Ideal Worker: The Separation of Work and Home in the United States from the Market Revolution to 1950," *Work and Occupations* 41, no. 1 (February 2014): 18–39. The ideal paradigm of the breadwinner-husband and homemaker-wife family was also fostered by male workers and their trade unions, who wanted to protect their jobs; see Alice Kessler-Harris, "Organizing the Unorganizable: Three Jewish Women and Their Union," in *Class, Sex and the Woman Worker*, ed. Milton Cantor and Bruce Laurie (Westport, CT: Greenwood Press, 1977).

[36]See, for instance, Janet R. Wilkie, "Marriage, Family Life, and Women's Employment," in *Women Working*, ed. Ann H. Stromberg and Shirley Harkess (Mountain View, CA: Mayfield Publishing, 1988), 149–66.

As a consequence of industrialization and urbanization, housework itself was altered. More goods and services used by households began to be produced outside the home, and advances in household technology (like indoor plumbing and electrification) and household appliances made housework less burdensome. While it might have been expected that these developments would have reduced the time spent on housework, norms changed as well. Groceries purchased at the market and a gas or electric oven made cooking easier, but elaborate multicourse meals replaced a pot of stew. As washing machines and vacuum cleaners made cleaning easier, new standards of cleanliness developed that housewives were expected to meet.[37] The net result was that the number of hours that full-time homemakers devoted to housework, more than 50 per week, did not change from the early 1900s to the 1960s.[38] However, while the hours of work of the housewife remained long, the emphasis on her productive role diminished. Whereas the colonial wife was valued for her industriousness, industrialization brought with it the **cult of true womanhood**, which equated piety, purity, domesticity, and submissiveness with the femininity to which all women were expected to aspire.[39] As Nancy Folbre observes, "ironically the moral elevation of the home was accompanied by the economic devaluation of the work performed there."[40]

Another important development in the evolution of the family during this period was the steady decline in fertility that began at least by 1800. The decrease in fertility that accompanied industrialization, which occurred at various times in all of the economically developed nations, is termed the **fertility transition**. As we shall see in greater detail in Chapter 14, drawing on the work of Nobel laureate Gary Becker, economists analyze fertility in a demand framework: children are regarded as a "commodity" from which individuals derive utility or satisfaction, and the demand for children depends on prices (i.e., the costs of having and rearing children) and the level of family income.[41] This framework is useful in understanding the decline in the number of children that women had during the period of industrialization.[42] As we have seen, in earlier times children made substantial economic contributions to the family; these contributions helped to offset the costs of children. However, with industrialization and urbanization, children had fewer opportunities to make an

---

[37]Research by Joel Mokyr points to the importance of cleanliness to raising a healthy family, see, "Why 'More Work for Mother'? Knowledge and Household Behavior, 1870–1945," *Journal of Economic History* 60, no. 1 (March 2000): 1–41.

[38]See Joann Vanek, "Time Spent in Housework," *Scientific American* 231, no. 5 (November 1974): 116–20; and Ruth Schwartz Cowan, *More Work for Mother: The Ironies of Household Technology from the Open Hearth to the Microwave* (New York: Basic Books, 1983). It was not until the 1970s that this situation changed; see our discussion in Chapter 4.

[39]Barbara Easton, "Industrialization and Femininity: A Case Study of Nineteenth Century New England," *Social Problems* 23, no. 4 (April 1976): 389–401; and Barbara Welter, "The Cult of True Womanhood, 1820–1860," in *The American Family in Social–Historical Perspective*, ed. Michael Gordon (New York: St. Martin's Press, 1978), 313–33.

[40]Nancy Folbre, "The Unproductive Housewife: The Evolution in Nineteenth Century Economic Thought," *Signs: Journal of Women in Culture and Society* 16, no. 31 (1991): 463–83; quotation is from p. 465.

[41]Gary S. Becker, *A Treatise on the Family* (Cambridge, MA: Harvard University Press, 1991).

[42]Our discussion of the explanation of declining fertility draws heavily on Timothy W. Guinnane, "The Historical Fertility Transition: A Guide for Economists," *Journal of Economic Literature* 49, no. 3 (September 2011): 587–614. See also Martha J. Bailey and Brad J. Hershbein "U.S. Fertility Rates and Childbearing 1800 to 2010," *Oxford Handbook of American Economic History* (Oxford and New York: Oxford University Press, forthcoming); and Larry E. Jones and Michele Tertilt, "An Economic History of Fertility in the U.S.: 1826–1960" in *Frontiers of Family Economics*, ed. Peter Rupert (Bingley, UK: Emerald Group, 2008).

economic contribution to the family than they had on the farm or in the early manu-facturing establishments. This increased the costs of children and contributed to a reduction in fertility, as did the high housing costs in cities, which further reduced incentives to have large families.[43] At the same time, family incomes rose. Rising family income might be expected to increase the demand for children and thus in-crease fertility. However, following Becker, economists believe that higher incomes increase the demand of parents for **child quality** (investments in children), leading them to invest more in the education and health of each of their children rather than to have a larger number of children.[44] Beginning in the mid-nineteenth century, this preference was reinforced by the spread of free public education, which lowered the costs of investing in child quality. Thus, while women had an average of 7 children in 1800, this figure fell to 5.5 births per woman for the cohort born in the early nine-teenth century and about 3 births for those born toward the end of the nineteenth century.[45] (A **cohort** is a group of individuals who all experienced a particular event during the same time span. In this case, the term refers to individuals who were born in the same period.)

By the dawn of the twentieth century, important changes occurred both within and outside of the household. Within the household, as we have seen, the household sphere was shrinking as family size declined and as market substitutes, technologi-cal advancements, and household appliances made housework easier and *potentially* less time-consuming. Beyond the household, several important changes occurred. First, as we previously mentioned, the growing availability of public schooling led to a dramatic increase in elementary as well as secondary schooling for both boys and girls. In fact, around 1900, girls outnumbered boys among high school graduates. Second, expansions in white-collar (office) work transformed work roles for women and men. For white middle-class men, the norm of the **ideal worker** emerged. The ideal worker was "a man completely devoted to his employer, his faithfulness re-warded by promotions." Basically, career success meant focusing on the job and leaving all household responsibilities, including care of children, to their wives.[46] At the same time, increased demand for clerical workers in offices created new labor market opportunities for the growing number of (single) female high school gradu-ates. This employment paid higher wages and did not carry the stigma of manufac-turing employment.

Thus, important changes both within and outside the household set the stage for an influx of married women into the labor market. An important puzzle is the question of why married women's labor force participation rates remained quite

---

[43]Guinnane, "The Historical Fertility Transition," also points out that, starting in the mid-nineteenth century, states began passing child labor laws that restricted the employment of minors. Notably, he discounts the importance of two often-cited factors: declining child mortality and the wider availability of contraception (condoms). He observes that the fertility decline in the United States began prior to the decline in child mortality, and condoms, which became available in the mid-1850s, were expensive, limiting their use.

[44]This is sometimes referred to as the quantity–quality trade-off. See Becker, *A Treatise on the Family*; and Gary S. Becker and Nigel Tomes, "Child Endowments and the Quantity and Quality of Children," *Journal of Political Economy* 84, no. 4, part 2 (August 1976): S143–62.

[45]Karl E. Taeuber and James A. Sweet, "Family and Work: The Social Life Cycle of Women," in *Women and the American Economy: A Look to the 1980s*, ed. Juanita M. Kreps (Englewood Cliffs, NJ: Prentice Hall, 1976), 31–60; and Jones and Tertilt, "An Economic History of Fertility."

[46]The quote and description are from Davies and Frink, "Origins of the Ideal Worker," 26. As discussed in Chapter 16, this norm continues to prevail in many workplaces, though it is being challenged as both women and men seek to balance jobs and family.

low until 1940, when the stage was set for a rise by 1920, in terms of both women's qualifications (the large number of female high school graduates) and their opportunities for employment (increased demand for clerical work), as well as changes in the household sphere that potentially reduced their workload (reduced fertility rates, technological advances, and more market substitutes and household appliances). Claudia Goldin, who raised this issue, has offered two explanations: first, the presence of marriage bars in teaching and clerical work and, second, the lack of part-time opportunities.[47] **Marriage bars**, which prohibited the employment of married women, were first instituted in the late 1800s and were particularly prevalent in teaching and clerical work. They thus constituted a significant barrier to employment in the two occupations that were to become among the most common for married women in later years. Marriage bars were expanded during the Great Depression of the 1930s and not fully abandoned until 1950. Another obstacle to married women's employment outside the home was the lack of availability of part-time work at a time when women's household responsibilities were still quite demanding.

Why did marriage bars begin to fall by the wayside in the 1940s? At that time, employers began to face a shortage of the young single women they had traditionally employed in clerical and teaching jobs, thereby providing an incentive to permit married women into these occupations. That shortage was due to three developments. First, birth rates were low in the 1920s and 1930s, resulting in small cohorts of women in the younger age group traditionally favored for these jobs in the 1940s and 1950s. Second, rising educational attainment for women meant that an increasing share of the young women who would otherwise have been available for employment were pursuing their schooling. And, finally, as a result of the post–World War II baby boom, women were marrying younger and having larger families, further diminishing the availability of single women in this age group. Employers responded by discarding the marriage bars and offering more options for part-time employment.

After 1940, women's labor force participation did begin to increase dramatically; these overall increases were driven by a sharp increase in the participation of married women. From 1940 through the mid-1990s, women's participation rate rose from 28 to nearly 60 percent, and rates have remained at roughly that level since then.[48] The causes of this increase are examined in greater detail in Chapter 6; however, the shrinkage of the household sphere combined with the increase in women's education and the growth in the demand for clerical workers undoubtedly played important roles. The box on "Economic Incentives" provides an interesting discussion of how the economic changes we have reviewed created incentives for extending property rights to women.

Historical Evidence on Occupations and Earnings

Not only were relatively few women employed during the early years of the twentieth century, but they also tended to work in different occupations from men and were

---

[47]Goldin, *Understanding the Gender Gap*, 159–84. For further discussion of obstacles faced by women, see Rosalind Chait Barnett, "Preface: Women and Work: Where Are We, Where Did We Come from and Where Are We Going?" *Journal of Social Issues* 60, no. 4 (December 2004): 667–74.

[48]For more detailed historical data, including differences by race and marital status, see Goldin, *Understanding the Gender Gap*, chap. 2.

Economic Incentives: An Engine of Change for Women's Property Rights

In 1848, in the Declaration of Sentiments and Resolutions issued at the Seneca Falls Convention, Elizabeth Cady Stanton and other prominent women's rights activists set forth a list of demands.* One of the best known was a demand for the right to vote, which women ultimately gained in 1920 when the Nineteenth Amendment to the US Constitution was passed. Another demand was for the right for women to own their own wages and property. As of 1840, in most of the then 27 US states, wives were not permitted to buy, sell, or own property, nor did they have ownership of their own labor market earnings. Once women were married, their husbands had legal claim to their earnings and property, under a system known as "patriarchal property rights." Only starting in the middle of the 1890s did states begin to extend to married women property rights to their earnings and property holdings. By 1920, married women in all but three states had such rights. What precipitated these changes in state laws governing married women's property rights? Research points to the pivotal role of economic incentives as the catalyst for change.

Rich Geddes and Dean Lueck argue that, prior to industrialization, economic incentives to change existing property laws for women were minimal because women had few opportunities to buy or sell goods or to get paid jobs. However, by the latter part of the nineteenth century, industrialization was in full swing, cities were growing, wealth was increasing, and a larger proportion of women had some education. As opportunities for women in the market economy expanded, the existing set of patriarchal property rights became, in the authors' words, a "relatively costly institution." That is, without legal ownership of their own earnings, married women had little economic incentive to participate in the growing economy, which in turn constrained families' potential income. Hence, Geddes and Lueck argue, it was in the interests of both women and men to extend property rights to married women. Further, once married women were given the legal ownership of their wages, their incentives to get an education, invest in market skills, and participate in the market economy were further increased.**

Matthias Doepke and Michelle Tertilt provide an interesting alternative explanation for this change in women's property rights. They argue that men might have been willing to vote for these expansions not because of increased labor market opportunities for their wives but rather to improve the well-being and economic prospects of their daughters and granddaughters.*** In both cases, we are reminded that economic incentives can be an important force for changing long-standing, seemingly immutable institutional arrangements. Moreover, these examples illustrate that improvements in women's rights and opportunities can benefit society at large.

*Elizabeth Cady Stanton, "Declaration of Sentiments and Resolutions," Seneca Falls Convention, 1848.
**Rick Geddes and Dean Lueck, "The Gains from Self-Ownership and the Expansion of Women's Rights," American Economic Review 92, no. 4 (September 2002): 1079–92. This discussion also draws on Elissa Braunstein and Nancy Folbre,

"To Honor and Obey: Efficiency, Inequality, and Patriarchal Property Rights," Feminist Economics 7, no. 1 (March 2001): 25–44.
***Matthias Doepke and Michelle Tertilt, "Women's Liberation: What's in It for Men?" Quarterly Journal of Economics 124, no. 4 (2009): 1541–91.

concentrated in relatively few jobs. This may be seen in Table 2-1, which gives the occupational distribution of men and women workers around the turn of the century. At that time, a very large share of men—42 percent—still worked in agricultural jobs; women's concentration in this sector was substantially less at only 19 percent. Manufacturing accounted for a sizable share of both men and women workers, although here again the percentage of women in such jobs (28 percent) was

TABLE 2-1 DISTRIBUTION OF WORKERS BY OCCUPATION, RACE AND GENDER, 1890/1900

	MEN	WOMEN		
	Total (%)	Total (%)	White (%)	Nonwhite (%)
Professional	10.2	9.6	12.5	0.9
Clerical	2.8	4.0	5.2	0.4
Sales	4.6	4.3	5.7	0.1
Service[a]	3.1	35.5	31.3	48.2
Manufacturing	37.6	27.7	34.7	6.4
Agricultural	41.7	19.0	10.8	44.0
Total Employed	100.0	100.0	100.0	100.0

Note: [a]For women, service primarily refers to domestic service.
Sources: From *Understanding the Gender Gap: An Economic History of American Women*, by Claudia Dale Goldin, Tables 3.2 and 3.3. Copyright (c) 1990 by Claudia Dale Goldin. Used by permission of Oxford Unversity Press, Inc.

considerably less than that of men (38 percent), and virtually all the women in manufacturing were in just three industries—textiles, clothing, and tobacco. Perhaps the sharpest contrast was for service jobs. Relatively few men, 3 percent, were in service jobs (e.g., waiter or barber), while nearly 36 percent of women were in the service sector, with the majority employed in domestic service. Table 2-1 further shows that more than 90 percent of black women worked either as domestic servants or as farm laborers compared with only 42 percent of white women. It was also the case that foreign-born white women were overrepresented in manufacturing and domestic service compared with native-born white women, though these figures are not shown separately here.

A similar share of men and women, 18 percent, held white-collar jobs (professional, clerical, and sales combined). Just over one-half of white-collar workers of both sexes were in the professional category, but the jobs held by these men and women differed considerably. Almost all the women were schoolteachers or nurses, whereas men were more likely to be managers and proprietors. While the "female" professions of schoolteacher and nurse, like domestic service, might be regarded as extensions of women's domestic role, interestingly, initially almost all schoolteachers were men.[49] The remainder of men and women white-collar workers were in clerical and sales occupations.

Like teaching, clerical work was originally a primarily male occupation. Although Table 2-1 indicates that a somewhat higher share of female than male workers held clerical jobs, the number of men in clerical positions greatly exceeded that of

---

[49]Teaching became feminized in the latter half of the nineteenth century; see Myra H. Strober and Audri Gordon Lanford, "The Feminization of Public School Teaching: Cross-Sectional Analysis, 1850–1880," *Signs* 11, no. 2 (Winter 1986): 212–73.

women because women were such a small share of the labor force at that time. Thus, as late as the turn of the twentieth century, 85 percent of all clerical workers were men. It was not until after 1900 that women's employment in this sector began to increase markedly, eventually absorbing a substantial proportion of employed women. By the early 1970s, when the share of employed women in clerical jobs peaked, nearly one-third of all women workers were in such occupations.

A wide variety of factors contributed to the rapid growth of female clerical employment. Among these was the growth of large corporations, which greatly increased the volume of paperwork and thus the demand for clerical workers. The large proportion of women with a high school education who needed little or no on-the-job training to perform such work provided an inexpensive labor pool to satisfy this expanding demand. Employers were willing to hire these women, even when they were not expected to stay on the job for a long time; this practice became all the more common after these positions came to serve a purely clerical function rather than as a training ground for advancement. Women, in turn, were likely to find these jobs attractive because relevant skills did not tend to depreciate much during periods out of the labor force, and therefore reentry was relatively easy. It is also possible that, as we have seen, many preferred clean white-collar jobs to dirtier, noisier, and at times more physically demanding blue-collar jobs. In any case, they generally had few alternatives.[50]

Available data from the nineteenth century also point to substantial differences between women's and men's earnings. In the early years, we have information only for the manufacturing and agricultural sectors, rather than for the economy as a whole. Around 1815, the **gender pay ratio** (women's pay divided by men's pay) in agricultural and domestic activities was as low as 29 percent (i.e., women earned 29 percent of what men earned). They did better in the early manufacturing establishments where the gender pay ratio was in the range of 30 to 37 percent in 1820. The gender gap in both sectors narrowed from this time, around the start of early industrialization, through the turn of the twentieth century. Later data, which are available for the economy as a whole, indicate that the gender pay ratio increased from 46 percent in 1890 to 56 percent by 1930. The rise over these 40 years was largely due to an increase in the relative wages of women within broad occupations, though it also reflects some movement of women into higher-paying sectors.[51] Subsequently, little change took place until about 1980, but since then the ratio has risen considerably, reaching 79 percent. We present recent trends in the gender pay ratio in greater detail in Chapter 7.

As labor market opportunities expanded for women and they increasingly joined the workforce, they faced the challenge of shaping the roles that work and family would play in their lives. This is an issue that has considerable resonance

[50]For analyses of women's occupational choices and of their entry into clerical work, see Mary C. Brinton, "Gendered Offices: A Comparative-Historical Examination of Clerical Work in Japan and the United States," in *The Political Economy of Japan's Low Fertility*, ed. Frances McCall Rosenbluth (Stanford, CA: Stanford University Press, 2007), 87–111; Claudia Goldin, "Historical Evolution of Female Earnings Functions and Occupations," *Explorations in Economic History* 21, no. 1 (January 1984): 1–27; and Margery Davies, "Woman's Place Is at the Typewriter: The Feminization of the Clerical Labor Force," in *Labor Market Segmentation*, ed. Richard C. Edwards, Michael Reich, and David M. Gordon (Lexington, MA: D.C. Health, 1975), 279–96.
[51]Goldin, *Understanding the Gender Gap*, 58–63.

College-Educated Women Over the Last 100 Years: Work, Family, or Both?

Research by economic historian Claudia Goldin points to dramatic changes over the twentieth century in the ability of women who are relatively career-oriented—those who are college-educated—to combine paid work and family.* Her work provides a useful historical context for understanding the challenges faced by career-oriented women today.

Goldin begins with a cohort of women who graduated from college about 1910. She finds that they experienced a "stark choice" between a career (most often teaching) and having a family. Indeed, fully 50 percent did not marry or, if married, did not have children compared to only 22 percent of their contemporaries who did not attend college. Their experience suggests that prevailing social norms strongly discouraged married women from working outside the home.

The cohort of women who graduated from college about 1955 was more demographically similar to other women in the general population. During a time when Americans were generally marrying younger and having more children, college women were part of the trend, with only 18 percent not married or, if married, childless. Moreover, in contrast to their predecessors, many were able to have both a family and a job, though for the most part they did these activities in stages. Like many other women at that time, they first had a family and took a job later. For this group, college provided an economic reward, not only because it increased their potential earnings but also because college women were more likely to marry college men (who outnumbered them 2 to 1). Thus, they reaped the added benefit of a higher-earning husband. Even though the experience of this cohort suggests that it was becoming more acceptable for married women to work for pay, even the college-educated generally had "jobs" rather than "careers," which require substantial human capital investment and more continuous labor force participation.

Among the cohort of women graduating college about 1972, a larger share sought to have careers,

rather than simply jobs. Because of the investment required to do this, many women in this cohort delayed childbearing and pursued the route of career first, family later. Still, Goldin's data suggest that the proportion of those who were able to "have it all," that is, family and career, was surprisingly small. Only 13 to 18 percent of women in this cohort achieved both goals by about age 40, when *family* is defined as having given birth to at least one child and *career* as having earnings over a certain amount during the 2 to 3 preceding years.** The most recent cohort she examined are women who graduated college in the early 1980s and were followed to about age 40. Using the same definitions, Goldin finds that 21 to 27 percent of these women attained family and career, still low but certainly an improvement over the early 1970s cohort.

Of course, career is a difficult concept to define, and the proportion of women found to have careers varies with the definition. Moreover, the estimates of career may be low among the age group surveyed because of the presence of young children among a substantial proportion of the women who had families. Yet even this qualification suggests that women face the need to make decisions and trade-offs seldom confronted by their male counterparts. Goldin's findings regarding the difficulty of combining family and career are reinforced by considerable evidence suggesting that, among women as a group, children have a negative effect on earnings and employment.

Nonetheless, there may be reason to be optimistic about prospects for future cohorts. Access to family leave, for example, has been found to substantially mitigate the negative effect of children on women's wages. While access to such leave likely remains inadequate, it has increased with the passage of the federal Family and Medical Leave Act in 1993, which mandated that firms provide 12 weeks of *unpaid* leave, and as firms increasingly choose to provide leave beyond that required by the law. This development and other emerging leave policies are discussed at length in Chapter 16. Moreover,

continues

as discrimination in the labor market continues to decline, marriages gradually become more egalitarian, and various other family-friendly policies are offered on a more widespread basis in the workplace, more women who want to "have it all" should be able to do so.

*Claudia Goldin, "Career and Family: College Women Look to the Past," in Gender and Family Issues in the Workplace, ed. Francine D. Blau and Ronald G. Ehrenberg (New York: Russell Sage Foundation, 1997), 20–59; and Claudia Goldin, "The Long Road to the Fast Track: Career and Family," Annals of the American Academy of Political and Social Science 596, no. 1 (2004): 20–35. Evidence on the impact of children and the availability of maternity leave on women's earnings is from Jane Waldfogel, "Understanding the 'Family Gap' in Pay for Women with Children," Journal of Economic Perspectives 12, no. 1 (Winter 1998): 157–70.

**Specifically, having income or average hourly earnings at least as high as a man's at the 25th percentile of the college-educated male earnings distribution. When Goldin, instead, defines career as working full time during the preceding 3 years, she obtains a somewhat higher estimate of 22 percent. In related work, Marianne A. Ferber and Carole Green examined a sample of women predominantly in their 50s and found a larger share who meet the definition of career and family; see "Career or Family: What Choices Do College Women Have?" Journal of Labor Research 24, no. 1 (Winter 2003): 143–51.

even today. In the "College-Educated Women" box, we summarize research by Claudia Goldin on how work and family roles evolved for one relatively career-oriented group, college-educated women.

Conclusion

The overview provided here suggests that the roles of men and women and the social norms that prescribe appropriate behavior for each are not shaped by biology alone. Rather, while biology may play a part, gender roles and women's status are also determined by the interaction of technology, the role of women in production, and a variety of social and political factors. It is also likely that, due to the lingering impact of culture, the roles of men and women, which developed initially as a rational response to conditions that existed at an earlier time in the course of economic development, continued their hold even after they ceased to be functional.

We also pointed out the important relationship between women's participation in productive work, particularly in the public (market) sphere, and their relative status. In the case of US economic development, married women's labor force participation and likely their relative status declined during the period of early industrialization as the locus of production shifted from the home to the market. However, as women's educational attainment increased and opportunities in the clerical sector became available, their participation rose with a corresponding increase in their relative status. As we shall see in upcoming chapters, women have made considerable advances in the labor market since the 1940s, where this chapter leaves off. Nonetheless, although considerable progress has been made, substantial differences between women and men in family roles and labor market outcomes remain. Fully understanding the reasons for these differences and the appropriate policy responses to them will constitute much of the focus of the remaining chapters.

Questions for Review and Discussion

1. What is the relationship between economic development and women's labor force participation?

2. Explain how women's and men's roles in the United States changed between the colonial period and early industrialization.

3. From a historical perspective, how has the labor market experience of black and white women differed?

4. In view of our discussion of evolutionary psychology and the social structural approach, to what extent can traditional roles of men and women be expected to change with changing economic conditions?

5. Explain how the relationship between economic development and the expansion of women's rights may operate in both directions.

6. What factors account for the decline in fertility that occurred in the course of industrialization?

Suggested Readings

Amott, Teresa L., and Julie A. Matthaei. *Race, Gender, and Work: A Multicultural Economic History of Women in the United States*. Boston: South End Press, 1996.

Bouston, Leah Platt, Carola Frydman, and Robert A. Margo, eds. *Human Capital in History: The American Record*. Chicago: University of Chicago Press, 2014.

Costa, Dora L. "From Mill Town to Board Room: The Rise of Women's Paid Labor." *Journal of Economic Perspectives* 14, no. 4 (Fall 2000): 101–22.

Davies, Andrea Rees, and Brenda D. Frink. "The Origins of the Ideal Worker: The Separation of Work and Home in the United States from the Market Revolution to 1950." *Work and Occupations* 41, no. 1 (February 2014): 18–39.

Eagly, Alice H., and Wendy Wood. "The Origins of Sex Differences in Human Behavior: Evolved Dispositions versus Social Roles." *American Psychologist* 54, no. 6 (June 1999): 408–23.

Goldin, Claudia. "The Quiet Revolution That Transformed Women's Employment, Education and Family." *American Economic Review* 96, no. 2 (May 2006): 1–15.

Goldin, Claudia. "The U-Shaped Female Labor Force Function in Economic Development and Economic History." In *Investments in Women's Human Capital*, edited by T. Paul Schultz, 61–90. Chicago: University of Chicago Press, 1995.

Goldin, Claudia. *Understanding the Gender Gap: An Economic History of American Women*. New York: Oxford University Press, 1990.

Hines, Melissa. *Brain Gender*. New York: Oxford University Press, 2004.

Huber, Joan. *On the Origins of Gender Inequality*. Boulder, CO, and London: Paradigm Publishers, 2007.

Lundberg, Shelly. "The Sexual Division of Labour." In *The Shape of the Division of Labour: Nations, Industries and Households*, edited by Robert M. Solow and Jean-Philippe Touffut, 122–48. Cheltenham, UK: Edward Elgar, 2010.

Mammen, Kristin, and Christina Paxson. "Women's Work and Economic Development." *Journal of Economic Perspectives* 14, no. 4 (Fall 2000): 141–64.

Ruggles, Steven. "Marriage, Family Systems, and Economic Opportunity in the United States Since 1850." In *Gender and Couple Relationships*, edited by Susan M. McHale, Valarie King, Jennifer J. Van Hook, and Alan A. Booth, 3–41. Heidelberg, Germany: Springer, 2016.

Wilson, Edward O. "What Is Sociobiology?" *Society* 15, no. 6 (1978): 10–14.

Key Terms

nature (17)

nurture (17)

sociobiology (17)

evolutionary psychology (17)

social structural approach (17)

culture (17)

U-shaped relationship (21)

gross domestic product (GDP) per capita (21)

labor force participation (21)

income effect (22)

substitution effect (23)

colonial America (24)

industrialization (25)

traditional family (27)

cult of true womanhood (28)

fertility transition (28)

child quality (29)

cohort (29)

ideal worker (29)

marriage bars (30)

gender pay ratio (33)

PART II

The Allocation of Time between the Household and the Labor Market

The Family as an Economic Unit: Theoretical Perspectives

3

CHAPTER HIGHLIGHTS

- ■ The Simple Neoclassical Model: Specialization and Exchange
- ■ Disadvantages of Specialization
- ■ Advantages of Families beyond Specialization
- ■ Transaction Cost and Bargaining Approaches
- ■ Appendix 3A: Specialization and Exchange: A Graphical Analysis

For a long time, neoclassical economics, the dominant school of economics in the United States and most of the rest of the world today and the approach we primarily draw on in this text, concerned itself largely with the behavior of "economic man." It was, of course, acknowledged that this man interacted with others, in competition or in cooperation, but it was his individual well-being that he would attempt to maximize. Consumer economics had long recognized the existence of the family and its importance as a unit of consumption. However, it was not until the 1960s, with the pathbreaking work of Gary Becker and Jacob Mincer, that mainstream economists began to concern themselves with the issues confronted by men and women in allocating their time and income so as to maximize family well-being.[1] Since then, using sophisticated theory

---

[1]Their foundational articles are Gary S. Becker, "A Theory of the Allocation of Time," *Economic Journal* 75, no. 299 (September 1965): 493–517; and Jacob Mincer, "Labor Force Participation of Married Women," in *Aspects of Labor Economics*, ed. H. Gregg Lewis, Universities National Bureau of Economic Research Conference Series 14 (Princeton, NJ: Princeton University Press, 1962), 63–97. An early pioneer was Margaret G. Reid, *Economics of Household Production* (New York: Wiley, 1934), but her ideas received relatively little attention by economists at the time. For a full development of the "new home economics," see Gary S. Becker, *A Treatise on the Family* (Cambridge, MA: Harvard University Press, 1981, enlarged ed., 1991). For theoretical critiques and extensions of Becker's work, see, for instance, Robert A. Pollak, "Gary Becker's Contributions to Family and Household Economics," *Review of Economics of the Household* 1, no. 1–2 (January/April 2002): 111–41; and Paula England, "Separate and Soluble Selves: Dichotomous Thinking in Economics," in *Feminist Economics Today*, ed. Marianne A. Ferber and Julie A. Nelson (Chicago: University of Chicago, 2003), 61–80.

and advanced econometric methods, economists have developed and tested models that have produced important insights in this area. Yet, many of these models are not altogether satisfactory because the tendency is still to treat even this multiperson family as a single-minded, indivisible, utility-maximizing unit.

In this chapter, we draw heavily upon neoclassical economic analysis, with appropriate simplifying assumptions, to better understand the determinants of the division of labor in the family. Because a substantial majority of people continue to live in married-couple families, we focus largely on the division of labor between husbands and wives. At the same time, it would be a mistake to overlook the considerable increase in the number of cohabiting opposite-sex couples or the presence of gay and lesbian couples, both unmarried and married.[2] We shall examine both types of couples in Chapter 13.

Our focus on economic analysis does not mean that we believe families are established or dissolved entirely, or even primarily, for economic reasons. On the contrary, human need for companionship, sexual attraction, affection, and the desire to have children all play a substantial part in family formation. Human need for independence and privacy as well as incompatibilities and preference for a variety of partners all play a large part in family breakups. Nonetheless, it is our belief that economic factors are important and that focusing upon them considerably enhances our understanding of the determinants of the division of labor in the family.

After presenting the neoclassical model of the family, we provide an evaluation and critique of this approach and introduce a more complex reality. In particular, the simple neoclassical model points to important efficiency gains arising from the traditional division of labor in which the husband specializes in market work and the wife specializes in home work. Nevertheless, such an arrangement is less and less prevalent. Moreover, individuals continue to form families despite this decrease in specialization. We shed light on the reasons for these developments by extending the simple model in two ways.[3]

- We examine the disadvantages of the traditional division of labor, particularly for women, which are not considered in the simple neoclassical model. These disadvantages help explain the decline of the traditional division of labor.

- We point out other types of economic benefits of forming families besides specialization. Thus, couples may discard specialization and still reap economic gains from living in families. These economic benefits help explain the persistence of the married-couple family, even as specialization diminishes.

We then briefly discuss the alternative neoclassical approaches of transaction costs and bargaining models. These models provide additional insights into family decision-making.

---

[2]In 2014, Massachusetts became the first US state to legalize same-sex marriage. In 2015, following the Supreme Court decision of United States v. Windsor, same-sex marriage became legal throughout the United States. The Netherlands was the first country to legalize same-sex marriage in 2001, and as of 2016, 20 countries had followed suit.

[3]Much of this material was first developed in Marianne A. Ferber and Bonnie G. Birnbaum, "The New Home Economics: Retrospect and Prospects," *Journal of Consumer Research* 4, no. 4 (June 1977): 19–28. For an updated discussion, see Marianne A. Ferber, "A Feminist Critique of the Neoclassical Theory of the Family," in *Women, Family, and Work: Writings on the Economics of Gender*, ed. Karine S. Moe (Oxford: Blackwell, 2003), chap. 1.

The Simple Neoclassical Model: Specialization and Exchange

The neoclassical analysis of the family relies on the following basic underlying assumption: the family is a unit whose adult members make informed and rational decisions that result in maximizing the utility or well-being of the unit. Beginning with this premise, economic analysis has been applied to understanding the division of labor within the family. Such economic models have also been used to explain women's rising labor force participation rates, trends in divorce rates and fertility, the greater emphasis on children's education, and a number of other aspects of people's behavior as members of families.

The simplest model assumes that the family's goal is to maximize its utility or satisfaction by selecting the combination of **commodities** from which its members derive the greatest possible amount of utility. Commodities are produced by combining the home time of family members with goods and services purchased in the market using labor market earnings.

Virtually all purchased goods and services require an infusion of home time to transform them into the commodities that provide utility—from food that needs to be bought and prepared and furniture that needs to be purchased, arranged in the home, and maintained to childcare centers, which must be carefully chosen and where children must be dropped off and picked up. Similarly, even time spent in leisure generally requires the input of market goods and services to be enjoyable—from flat-screen televisions and Blu-ray players to rock concerts and baseball games. Thus, time spent on paid work produces the income necessary to purchase market goods, which in turn are needed together with home time to produce commodities. A crucial question for the family is how the time of each individual should be allocated between home and market most efficiently in order to maximize satisfaction.

Comparative Advantage

Under certain conditions, commodity production is carried out most efficiently if one member of the family specializes, at least to some extent, in market production while the other specializes, at least to some extent, in home production. They may then exchange their output or pool the fruits of their labor to achieve their utility-maximizing combination of commodities. For there to be gains from this arrangement, it is necessary for the **comparative advantage** in home and market production of the two individuals to differ. That is to say, one partner must be *relatively* better in household production compared to market work than is the other partner, while the other partner must be *relatively* better in market work compared to household production.[4] The key concept that underlies comparative advantage is **opportunity cost**. Recall from Chapter 1 that opportunity cost refers to the value of the best alternative foregone when you make a decision. As we shall see in greater detail later, the partner who is relatively better in household production compared to market work has the lower opportunity cost of spending an hour in household production and

---

[4]The case for specialization as a way to maximize the well-being of the family is similar to that for international trade, where each country specializes in production for which it has a relative advantage. Among the important differences between the two situations, however, is that countries generally need not rely on a single trading partner, allowing somewhat less opportunity for the stronger partner to take advantage of the weaker one. Another difference is that couples, unlike countries, must also share a good deal of consumption.

thus has a comparative advantage in that activity. And the partner who is relatively better in market work compared to household production has the lower opportunity cost of spending an hour in market work and thus has a comparative advantage in that activity.

Is it generally the case that women are relatively more productive in the home and men are relatively more productive in the market? Whether or not one assumes, as some have, that women are biologically better suited for housework because they bear children, it is frequently the case that women have a comparative advantage in household production and men have a comparative advantage in market work. The reason is that men and women are traditionally raised with different expectations and receive different education and training. It may also be the case that women have been discriminated against in the labor market, lowering their market earnings. Moreover, the traditional division of labor itself is likely to magnify differences in the household and market skills of men and women because both types of skills tend to increase with experience "on the job." Thus, even a small initial gender difference in comparative advantage is likely to increase considerably over time.

Although each of the preceding factors tends to produce gender differences in comparative advantage for homemaking compared to market work, it is not necessarily the case that the traditional division of labor is the optimal arrangement. Treating children according to gender rather than individual talents and discriminating against women workers in the labor market clearly introduce distortions. Even more obvious is the fact that circular reasoning is involved when women supposedly specialize in housework because they do it better, but, in fact, they do it better because they specialize in it. To the extent that women's relative advantage for housework is socially determined and reflects unequal access to market opportunities, the traditional division of labor is not always efficient, let alone desirable, particularly when, as we shall see, it entails many disadvantages for women.

In the following discussion we assume that women have a comparative advantage in housework relative to men because the reality that we seek to explain is one in which women generally assume primary responsibility for homemaking. We do not mean to imply, however, that the traditional division of labor is inevitable or that it will persist indefinitely into the future. Indeed, we are also concerned with better understanding the reasons why traditional patterns are changing.

Specialization and Exchange: Numerical Examples

Two simple examples will help clarify the notion of comparative advantage and illustrate the efficiency of specialization and exchange. The analysis is analogous to the standard proof of gains from international trade and is illustrated in Table 3-1.

CASE 1: EACH INDIVIDUAL HAS AN ABSOLUTE ADVANTAGE IN ONE ACTIVITY   Consider first the case where one individual (John) has an absolute advantage in market work, while the other individual (Jane) has an absolute advantage in household production (e.g., producing home-cooked meals). **Absolute advantage** means that the individual can produce more total output of a good in a given period. Specifically, suppose in 1 hour John can earn $10 by working in the labor market, thereby allowing him to purchase $10 worth of market goods (M), or he can produce $5 worth of home goods ($H$). On the other hand, in 1 hour, Jane can earn $5 in the labor market, thereby allowing her to purchase $5 worth of market goods, or she can produce $10 worth of home goods. We can see that John has an absolute advantage in market goods because the value of his market time is higher, while Jane has an absolute advantage in home production because the value of home goods she can produce in 1 hour is higher. In this case, it makes intuitive sense that John and Jane's combined level of economic well-being will be greater if they each specialize, at least to some extent. For example, John, who has an absolute advantage in market work, can spend all his time in the labor market earning money, while Jane, who has an absolute advantage in home production, can do the grocery shopping, cooking, cleaning, and so forth, although she may also allocate some time to market work.

The answer to the question of how the couple should divide their time between household production and market work may seem fairly obvious for this couple, but reasoning out comparative advantage for them will be helpful for us in better understanding comparative advantage and the benefits of specialization. For John, the opportunity cost of $1 worth of market goods in terms of home production foregone is $.5H$ (since the two goods exchange at a rate of $10 of M for $5 of H). For Jane, the opportunity cost of $1 worth of M is $2H$. Since John's opportunity cost of $1M$ is lower ($.5H < $2H), he has the comparative advantage in market production. Jane has the comparative advantage in home production because her opportunity cost of home production is lower than his: the opportunity cost of $1H$ is $.5M$ for Jane but $2M$ for John.

To further illustrate that John and Jane can benefit by specialization, let us consider their combined level of economic well-being when each produces for himself

TABLE 3-1 AN ILLUSTRATION OF THE GAINS FROM SPECIALIZATION AND EXCHANGE

(a) Case 1: EACH INDIVIDUAL HAS AN ABSOLUTE ADVANTAGE IN ONE ACTIVITY

SEPARATE PRODUCTION			
	Value of Market Goods (M)	Value of Home Goods (H)	Total Income
John	(6 hrs. × $10)	(2 hrs. × $5)	
	$60 +	$10 =	$ 70
Jane	(7 hrs. × $5)	(1 hr. × $10)	
	$35 +	$10 =	$ 45
Total (John and Jane)	$95	$20	$115

SPECIALIZATION AND EXCHANGE			
	Value of Market Goods (M)	Value of Home Goods (H)	Total Income
John	(8 hrs. × $10)	(0 hrs. × $5)	
	$80 +	$0 =	$ 80
Jane	(5 hrs. × $5)	(3 hrs. × $10)	
	$25 +	$30 =	$ 55
Total (John and Jane)	$105	$30	$135

(b) Case 2: ONE INDIVIDUAL HAS AN ABSOLUTE ADVANTAGE IN BOTH ACTIVITIES

SEPARATE PRODUCTION			
	Value of Market Goods (M)	Value of Home Goods (H)	Total Income
Dave	(6 hrs. × $10)	(2 hrs. × $5)	
	$60 +	$10 =	$ 70
Diane	(7 hrs. × $15)	(1 hr. × $15)	
	$105 +	$15 =	$120
Total (Dave and Diane)	$165	$25	$190

SPECIALIZATION AND EXCHANGE			
	Value of Market Goods (M)	Value of Home Goods (H)	Total Income
Dave	(8 hrs. × $10)	(0 hrs. × $5)	
	$80 +	$0 =	$ 80
Diane	(6 hrs. × $15)	(2 hrs. × $15)	
	$90 +	$30 =	$120
Total (Dave and Diane)	$170	$30	$200

or herself alone (without collaboration) and then when they specialize according to comparative advantage and pool their incomes. As we shall see, John and Jane's income and potential well-being are higher when they collaborate. The two scenarios are illustrated in panel a of Table 3-1. Initially, as shown in the top section of panel a, John and Jane are each self-sufficient, and both allocate some time in their 8-hour day to market work and some time to home production. John devotes 6 hours to earning income and 2 hours to home production. His total income (including the value of home production) is $70. Jane spends 7 hours in the market and 1 hour on home production. Her total income is $45. The sum of their two incomes (although they are not necessarily sharing at this point) is $115.

If they collaborate, each spouse has the option of specializing to a greater extent in the activity at which he or she is relatively better and then exchanging (or pooling) their output, as shown in the bottom section of panel a. Suppose John decides to devote all his time to the market (for which he has a comparative advantage), and Jane transfers 2 additional hours from market work to home production (for which she has a comparative advantage). By reallocating their time, the couple is able to raise their total income from $115 to $135.

CASE 2: ONE INDIVIDUAL HAS AN ABSOLUTE ADVANTAGE IN BOTH ACTIVITIES   Less obvious is the fact that specialization can also raise the income of a couple when one individual has an absolute advantage both in the labor market and in home production. Consider the case of Dave and Diane. Suppose for each hour, Dave could earn $10, thereby allowing him to purchase $10 worth of market goods, or he can produce $5 worth of home goods. In the same period of time, Diane could earn $15, thereby allowing her to purchase $15 worth of market goods, or she can produce $15 worth of home goods. In this case, Diane has an absolute advantage in both activities, but the important point is that she has a comparative advantage in home production; that is, she is relatively much better at home production than Dave. Returning to the concept of opportunity cost, for Diane, 1M$ = 1H$ (since the two goods exchange at a rate of $15 of M for $15 of H), while for Dave, 1M$ = $.5$H$. Since Dave's opportunity cost in market work is lower (for 1M$, he gives up only $.5$H$ instead of 1H$ for Diane), he has a comparative advantage in market work. Diane has a comparative advantage in home production because her opportunity cost in that activity is lower: the opportunity cost of 1H$ is 1M$ for Diane but 2M$ for Dave. Panel b of Table 3-1 shows that through specialization according to comparative advantage and exchange, the couple can increase their total output of both market goods and home goods and raise their total income from $190 to $200.

Decreasing Gains to Specialization and Exchange and the Shift Away from the Traditional Family

These examples illustrate the potential gain in the output of specialization and exchange. They do not, however, tell us how much time John and Jane will actually spend on each type of work; the hours indicated in Table 3-1 are just illustrative. The goal of the family is to maximize utility or satisfaction. Thus, the value attached to various commodities and the time allocation actually chosen by each couple will depend on their preferences for market- versus home-produced goods. Many outcomes are possible. For example, perhaps Jane and John have such a strong preference for market goods that their well-being would be maximized by both of them working only for pay and purchasing all the goods and services they consume rather than producing any at home. Or Diane and Dave might have such a strong preference for home production that Diane would entirely specialize in housework and Dave would divide his time between market and home production. In Appendix 3A, we present a more comprehensive treatment of the decision-making process that explicitly takes into account both the production possibilities available to the couple and their preferences for each type of good.

In any case, however, each couple will seek to produce their desired combination of market and home goods in the most efficient way. Thus, the analysis suggests that as long as they produce some of each type of good, if the wife has a comparative advantage in housework (relative to the husband) and the husband has a comparative advantage in market work (relative to the wife), they will choose to specialize, at least to some extent.

It would appear, then, that this analysis provides an explanation for the traditional family with a male breadwinner and a female homemaker. Each may help the other if demand is high for the production he or she is not particularly qualified for, but each has a clearly defined sphere of primary responsibility. Assuming that the partners have different comparative advantages, whenever such specialization does not take place, the couple will fail to maximize their output and, potentially, their well-being.

Yet, as we know, the traditional family has become much less common in recent years, as families in which both husband and wife work in the labor market have become the norm. Within the context of the model, this shift may be traced in part to trends that narrow differences in women's and men's comparative advantage. As discussed in greater detail in Chapters 8 and 9, women's educational attainment and labor market experience have substantially increased, and it is likely that the extent of labor market discrimination against women has declined. As a result, women's wages have increased.[5] At the same time, the relative value of nonmarket time has fallen, with the rapid adoption of appliances, such as the microwave oven, and the increased consumption of market substitutes for home-produced goods, like fast food and purchased meals from grocery stores in place of home-cooked meals. In addition, more out-of-home childcare is available than in the past, though issues of access, affordability, and quality remain, as discussed further in Chapter 16.

The direction of causality for such changes is difficult to establish, and the effects are likely to be mutually reinforcing. For example, rising educational attainment of women may reduce their comparative advantage in household work, but, at the same time, women's reduced desire to adhere to the traditional division of labor in the family is likely a factor explaining their rising educational attainment. As another example, greater availability of fast food is expected to reduce women's comparative advantage in household work but is no doubt also a response to the growing demand for purchased meals due to women's rising labor force participation. However, the important point from the perspective of the issues we are considering here is that such shifts in comparative advantage of women and men substantially reduce the gains to marriage. Thus, it is not surprising that the share of currently married adults has fallen, as discussed in Chapter 13. Nevertheless, a substantial majority of people continue to marry.

Part of the reason for the continued prevalence of marriage is that gender differences in comparative advantages have not completely disappeared. Women continue

---

[5]If women's wages rise relative to men's (and nothing else changes), less specialization is expected.

to earn less than men in the labor market, and the data presented in the next chapter show that they continue to do the bulk of the housework, even when they are employed outside the home. Moreover, as we shall see in a later section, there are important economic gains to marriage beyond specialization. These other economic benefits to marriage, which are not considered in the simple model, mean that even as the differences in comparative advantage between wives and husbands diminish, indeed even if they disappear entirely, there will still be economic incentives to marry. And, of course, as we acknowledged in the beginning of this chapter, there are important noneconomic advantages.

Disadvantages of Specialization

As we have seen, the simple model suggests that specialization and exchange is the economic foundation of marriage. Here we consider reasons why specialization and a gender-based division of labor may not always be desirable, particularly for women, even when specialization and exchange does yield some economic gains to the family. These potential disadvantages of specialization, which are generally not discussed in standard models, are nonetheless important and, as our previous discussion suggests, may provide insights into why the traditional division of labor is breaking down.

Lack of Sharing of Housework

Even if a wife has a comparative advantage in doing housework compared to her husband, a thorough consideration of the issues suggests a number of reasons why a couple might often find it desirable to share the housework rather than for each spouse to specialize completely. First, the simple model assumes only one type of home good (or, in our example, a generic catch-all category of "home goods") and a value associated with production of this activity. In fact, the tasks typically performed within the household are quite varied, including not only childcare, house cleaning, cooking, and shopping but also gardening, home repairs, car maintenance, and taking care of the family finances. Contrary to the assumption in the simple model, it is unlikely that the wife will have a comparative advantage in performing all of these tasks compared to the husband; rather, it is likely that he will have a comparative advantage in at least some of them, even taking his often larger market earnings into account. Of course, once the wife is at home because she is better at some, or many, of the household tasks, it may be more efficient for her to do other related work as well. But the sweeping assumption that women have a comparative advantage in all household tasks and thus should do all the housework seems unrealistic.

Second, it is worthwhile to consider the utility or disutility that people derive from work itself. The simple model considers only the utility derived from the consumption of market-produced and home-produced goods. Yet most people spend much of their time working, and their well-being is influenced by the satisfaction or dissatisfaction directly associated with their work. If everyone always enjoyed more (or disliked less) the kind of work they do more efficiently, the gains from specialization would be even greater than those indicated by the simple model; and that may be the case to some degree. However, this line of reasoning ignores the possibility that how we feel about doing particular tasks depends on how much time we have to spend on them. Persons who dislike a particular type of work to begin with are likely to increasingly hate this activity as they do more of it. Even those individuals who like what they do are, nonetheless, likely to become less enthusiastic.[6] The stronger this effect, the less likely are the gains in utility from complete specialization suggested by the simple model.

Life Cycle Changes

A serious shortcoming of the simple model is that comparative advantage likely varies over the life cycle. One would expect women's comparative advantage in home production to be larger when young children are present than when they have grown up and left home. At the same time, labor market earnings and career opportunities tend to increase with work experience and decline during years out of the labor force. If a woman withdraws from the labor force for a considerable period of time for child-rearing, she is likely to pay a high price in terms of career advancement and earnings when she reenters the labor market. Hence, while wives' specialization in home production may maximize family well-being in the short run, this allocation of time may not be advantageous to the wife or to her family in the long run. This is particularly the case as women have come to increasingly value career success in the labor market. It might be argued that offsetting these disadvantages for the wife's career, and the lifetime income of the family, is the opportunity for a stay-at-home mother to spend more time with her children. However, as discussed in the next chapter, differences in the amount of time that employed and nonemployed mothers spend with children appear to be quite modest. Also, maternal care is only one factor, of many, that affects children's well-being and achievement, as discussed further in Chapter 14.

Costs of Interdependence

While, as we have seen, specialization may improve the well-being of the couple under certain circumstances, this arrangement may leave them less prepared to deal with some unforeseen developments than if they had each spent time in both the market and household production. For instance, suppose the husband is laid off or does not get a promotion or the wife becomes ill and needs care instead of providing it for the rest of the family. In situations like these, each partner will be better equipped to keep the household and family afloat if he or she is already participating in both home and market activities. Each partner will also be better able to manage alone in the event of divorce, separation, or death. A related critique is that complete specialization poses a particular risk for full-time homemakers, most notably in the event the relationship ends. In such a case, a homemaker may have market skills that have substantially depreciated or become obsolete. The challenges faced by female-headed families are discussed more fully in Chapter 14.

Tastes and Bargaining Power

In our development of the simple model, we did not consider how the couple determines the allocation of income and of time to the various commodities the family would enjoy. The decision will be relatively simple if they both have the same tastes

---

[6]The reasoning is analogous to diminishing marginal utility as additional units of the same good are consumed.

and preferences and opt for the same combination of goods and services to be shared. If, however, their tastes differ significantly, the question arises as to how they will decide on the combination of commodities to be produced and consumed. One can easily imagine cases in which spouses have differing tastes and preferences, whether in regard to purchasing a car, giving to charitable organizations, or spending money on children. If so, whose preferences (husband's or wife's) will receive greater weight? The answer largely rests with who has greater bargaining power. In the traditional breadwinner-husband, homemaker-wife family, the husband may be viewed as having the "power of the purse" and, therefore, be accorded a greater say in spending decisions and quite possibly in other respects. Further, contributing to the husband's bargaining power is the wife's economic dependence. If the marriage were to break up, she would not have her own resources to support herself (and children), weakening her own bargaining position in the marriage. Women's earning power changes this dynamic. As women's relative earnings increase, so does their relative position in the marriage and control over household decisions. Economists have developed models that specifically address the role of bargaining in family decision-making. Later in the chapter, we examine these models and provide evidence on the impact of bargaining on family outcomes.

Domestic Violence

An additional disadvantage of specialization is that it will tend to limit opportunities for women to get out of an abusive, harmful situation.[7] That is, women who are not employed outside the home are less likely to have the financial means to leave an abusive relationship or to effectively persuade their husband that they will leave the marriage if the abuse does not stop. Therefore, it is not surprising that research identifies a link between improvements in women's economic status and reduced domestic violence. For example, one study found that the increase in the female–male wage ratio over the 1990–2003 period led to a 9 percent decline in domestic violence against women.[8] Similarly, changes in factors external to the family, such as the easing of divorce laws (e.g., the adoption of unilateral divorce), have been found to reduce abuse against women, arguably because such changes improve their bargaining power in the family.[9] The availability of services for victims of domestic violence, such as shelters, counseling, and legal advice, would be expected to have a similar effect.

---

[7]Recent statistics on domestic violence are cited in Shannon Catalano, "Intimate Partner Violence: Attributes of Victimization, 1993–2011," Special Report (Washington, DC: US Department of Justice, November 21, 2013), and can be found at the US Department of Justice website, www.bjs.gov. Robert Pollak formalizes the notion of a cycle of domestic violence in "An Intergenerational Model of Domestic Violence," *Journal of Population Economics* 17, no. 2 (June 2004): 311–29.

[8]Anna Aizer, "The Gender Wage Gap and Domestic Violence," *American Economic Review* 100, no. 4 (September 2010): 1847–59. See also Derek A. Kreager, Richard B. Felson, Cody Warner, and Marin R. Wenger, "Women's Education, Marital Violence, and Divorce: A Social Exchange Perspective," *Journal of Marriage and the Family* 75, no. 3 (June 2013): 565–81.

[9]In the language of formal bargaining models discussed in a subsequent section, an easing of divorce laws (or, similarly, an increase in a person's own economic resources) raises the "threat point" of divorce and, in turn, bargaining power. For evidence on the impact of changes in divorce laws, see Pablo Brassiolo, "Domestic Violence and Divorce Law: When Divorce Threats Become Credible," *Journal of Labor Economics* 34, no. 2, pt. 1 (2016): 443–77; and Betsey Stevenson and Justin Wolfers, "Bargaining in the Shadow of the Law: Divorce Laws and Family Distress," *Quarterly Journal of Economics* 12, no. 121 (February 2006): 267–88.

Dealing with spousal abuse, whether the aggressor be a husband or occasionally a wife, is often made more difficult by the ambivalent attitudes of society. Many believe that such battering is a family matter and that the legal system should not intrude or may even suggest that the victim might have "asked for it." Another complication is that children in the household may further add to the emotional as well as the financial difficulty of leaving.

The consequences of domestic violence likely vary, depending on the length and severity of the abuse, and may include both psychological difficulties and physical injuries. Domestic violence may also affect employment and earnings. Interestingly, studies find that the labor force participation rates of women who are victims of domestic violence are the same as or even higher than those of otherwise similar women who are not victims. This finding could be because battered women seek employment outside the home as a refuge or as a means of achieving economic independence (in preparation for leaving). On the other hand, some evidence indicates that abuse negatively affects women's job performance and consequently may lower their wages.[10]

Advantages of Families beyond Specialization

There are a number of economic advantages to forming families apart from specialization, although these benefits are not considered in the simple model. This means that when husbands and wives have very similar, or even precisely the same, relative abilities in the market and in home production, there will still be economic advantages to marriage, thus shedding light on the persistence of marriage in the face of the declining difference in the comparative advantage of wives and husbands. Arguably, most of these benefits do not necessarily require a married husband–wife family, but they are likely to be enhanced when individuals expect to have a long-term relationship with a strong degree of commitment.

Economies of Scale

Economies of scale exist when an increase in the scale of operation of a productive unit can result in increased output at decreasing per unit cost. To the extent that a couple is able to benefit from such economies of scale, both in the production of some home goods and in purchasing market goods and services, economic gains result from living together. For example, housing for two usually costs less than the combined amount each would pay for his or her housing separately. Meals for two generally take less than twice as much time to prepare as meals for one, and so forth.[11]

Public Goods

A **public good** has the unique characteristic that the consumption or enjoyment of the item by one person does not diminish the consumption or enjoyment of the same

---

[10]Amy Farmer and Jill Tiefenthaler, "Family Dysfunction," in *The Economics of the Family: How the Household Affects Markets and Economic Growth*, ed. Esther Redmount (Santa Barbara, CA: ABC-CLIO, 2015), 179–208.

[11]Economies of scale also explain the advantages of larger groups living together. The fact that such arrangements are not common in affluent societies suggests that most people value additional privacy highly once they can afford it.

item by others.[12] Within the family, many goods are likely to have this characteristic. For example, one partner's enjoyment of a television program is unlikely to be reduced by the fact that the other partner is also watching. Similarly, the delight of a parent in his or her child's adorable antics is not apt to be diminished by the other parent's pleasure.[13] Many aspects of housing—the views from the windows and the decoration of the rooms—also have public goods aspects. In fact, as we discuss shortly, the enjoyment of these goods by one partner may even enhance that of the other. To the extent that public goods are important, the gains from joint consumption are increased because two individuals derive more total satisfaction from sharing a given stock of public goods and services by living together than they would by living separately.

Externalities in Consumption

Externalities in consumption occur when the consumption of a good or service by one of the partners affects the well-being of the other who does not consume it. When these externalities are positive—one person derives enjoyment from the other's consumption—gains will be greater than those indicated by the simple model. For example, a husband's purchase of a new suit may increase his wife's utility as well as his own. Of course, these externalities may be negative as well, for example, when one partner's cigarette smoking reduces the other partner's well-being. But, in general, we would expect there to be considerable positive externalities and for these to constitute an important gain to marriage. Indeed, when two people care for one another, one partner may even derive satisfaction simply from the enjoyment and happiness of the other.

Gains from Shared Consumption

Individuals tend to derive greater utility from doing activities (whether making a gourmet meal or international travel) with others who have a shared interest, rather than doing these activities alone or with someone who has less interest. While gains from shared consumption are possible for all couples, they are likely greater for dual-earner couples who tend to pair up on the basis of more similar interests, rather than for single-earner couples who pair up on the basis of the gains to specialization and exchange.[14] Consistent with this thinking, a recent study shows that married couples who have more similar hours in paid work also spend more leisure time together, as would be expected if marriage is based on gains from shared consumption.[15]

---

[12]A *pure* public good also has the characteristic that others cannot be excluded from using or enjoying it or that it is, at any rate, too difficult or costly to exclude them. For further discussion of public goods and the concept that follows, externalities, see Jonathan Gruber, *Public Finance and Public Policy*, 4th ed. (New York: Worth Publishers, 2013).

[13]As Nancy Folbre points out, children not only provide benefits to their parents—in earlier days for their economic contribution to the family and today largely in the form of enjoyment—but they also provide benefits to the larger society; children are the innovators and taxpayers of tomorrow. See "Children as Public Goods," *American Economic Review* 84, no. 2 (May 1994): 86–90.

[14]This rationale is emphasized by Betsey Stevenson and Justin Wolfers, "Marriage and Divorce: Changes and Their Driving Forces," *Journal of Economic Perspectives* 21, no. 2 (Spring 2007): 27–52.

[15]Hani Mansour and Terra McKinnish, "Couples' Time Together: Complementarities in Production Versus Consumption," *Journal of Population Economics* 27, no. 4 (2014): 1127–44. The authors, however, do not find this relationship for parents with very young children; one explanation offered is that parents also derive shared benefits from children, even if the adults themselves are not spending time together.

Marriage-Specific Investments

Marriage-specific investments refer to skills and knowledge developed in marriage and other investments made during a marriage that are worth more within the marriage than they would be if the marriage were terminated.[16] Examples of such investments include learning to cook each other's favorite meals or learning to do the same recreational activities, such as skiing or rock climbing. Marriage, since it is a legal arrangement and one that is generally costly to exit, fosters long-term commitments and hence these types of investments. Perhaps the prime example of a marriage-specific investment is the rearing of children. Parents devote considerable time and energy to nurturing their children and fostering the values that they share.[17] While children provide considerable satisfaction to parents within the marriage, they may not provide such satisfaction to a different partner, and their presence may even be an obstacle to forming and maintaining a new relationship.[18]

Risk Pooling

Married-couple families have the advantage that if one of the spouses becomes unemployed, he or she may be able to rely on the earning power of the other partner to cover at least part of their family's expenses. In bad economic times, if the husband loses his job or his earnings decline, even a traditional homemaker may enter the labor market to maintain family income. This "added worker" effect is discussed in Chapter 6. However, the advantage of risk pooling is likely to be larger for two-earner couples. This is, in a sense, the opposite of the interdependency disadvantage of specialization that we discussed previously. Similarly, couples, again particularly two-earner couples, have much greater flexibility to switch jobs, change careers, or pursue additional education or job training because they can rely on the other spouse's earning power.

Institutional Advantages

Married couples also frequently enjoy institutional advantages. In the United States, these include coverage by a spouse's health insurance, pension rights, and Social Security benefits. Some employers extend benefits such as health insurance to the unmarried partners of opposite-sex and same-sex couples, but to date this practice is far from universal. As discussed in the box "The State of Unions in the United States" in Chapter 4, following the landmark Supreme Court decision of United States v. Windsor in 2015, same-sex couples can now legally marry throughout the United States and are entitled to the same federal and state benefits and rights granted to opposite-sex married couples.

---

[16]See Becker, *A Treatise on the Family*; and Robert A. Pollak, "A Transaction Cost Approach to Families and Households," *Journal of Economic Literature* 23, no. 2 (June 1985): 581–608.

[17]Robert Pollak and Shelly Lundberg suggest that a key reason why college graduates are marrying at relatively higher rates these days is that they are best positioned to reap the benefits of marriage-specific investments in children; these parents have the greatest amount of financial resources to do so; see "The Evolving Role of Marriage, 1956–2010," *The Future of Children* 25, no. 2 (Fall 2015): 29–50.

[18]See, for instance, Carmel U. Chiswick and Evelyn Lehrer, "On Marriage-Specific Human Capital: Its Role as a Determinant of Remarriage," *Journal of Population Economics* 3, no. 3 (October 1990): 193–213.

Transaction Cost and Bargaining Approaches

One of the shortcomings of the neoclassical model of the family highlighted by the preceding discussion of the disadvantages of specialization is that it ignores the internal decision-making structure of the family. The model simply assumes that the family operates efficiently and without friction either because of a consensus on preferences within the family or because decisions are made by an altruistic family head and accepted by all other members.[19] In this model of the family, power is irrelevant; earnings and resources from household members are "pooled together," so it is only total income (not who brings the income into the family) that affects household decisions regarding spending and other outcomes.

Not surprisingly, this simple model has been challenged. Alternative approaches that emphasize transaction costs and bargaining have sought to unlock the "black box" of the family and more accurately characterize family decision-making.[20] The **transaction cost approach**, for instance, focuses on the role of institutions in structuring complex, long-term relationships so as to minimize transaction costs. That is, just as a merger between firms eliminates the costs of negotiating repeated contracts and ensures that the initially separate firms will do business together for years to come, a marriage fosters a long-term relationship between partners. Marriage incorporates rules both about the nature of the ongoing relationship and about the rights of each individual should the union break up. Hence, marriage might be seen as a contractual affiliation that is "flexible enough to allow adaptive sequential decision making in the face of unfolding events."[21]

Because marriage is intended to be a long-term relationship, spouses must make numerous decisions over the course of their life together. While they might discuss some issues in advance, they cannot realistically anticipate and plan for all possible situations that may arise.[22] It is also quite unlikely that husbands and wives share the same preferences regarding all consumption and production decisions. Thus, bargaining between the partners is likely to be very important. A class of **bargaining models** has been developed that allows for husbands and wives to have different preferences, with outcomes determined through a process of bargaining.[23]

---

[19]The consensus model was proposed by Paul Samuelson, "Social Indifference Curves," *Quarterly Journal of Economics* 70, no. 1 (February 1956): 1–22. The altruist model was introduced by Gary S. Becker, "A Theory of Marriage: Part II," *Journal of Political Economy* 82, no. 2 (March/April 1974): 11–26.

[20]Even though this section focuses on decision-making among spouses, bargaining models are applicable to unmarried couples and have also been applied to decisions made by a parent and an adult child. See, for instance, Lilliana E. Pezzin, Robert A. Pollak, and Barbara S. Schone, "Efficiency in Family Bargaining: Living Arrangements and Caregiving Decisions of Adult Children and Disabled Elderly Parents," *Review of Economic Studies* 53, no. 1 (March 2007): 69–96.

[21]See Pollak, "A Transaction Cost Approach;" quotation is from p. 595.

[22]For a discussion, see Paula England and George Farkas, *Households, Employment and Gender: A Social, Economic, and Demographic View* (New York: Aldine Publishing, 1986).

[23]For reviews of the literature, see Susan Himmelweit, Cristina Santos, Almudena Sevilla, and Catherine Sofer, "Sharing of Resources within the Family and the Economics of Household Decision Making," *Journal of Family and Marriage* 75, no. 3 (June 2013): 625–39; Shelly J. Lundberg and Robert A. Pollak, "Family Decision Making," *New Palgrave Dictionary of Economics*, 2nd ed., ed. Steven N. Durlauf and Lawrence E. Blume (New York: Palgrave Macmillan, 2008), 254–60; and Bina Agarwal, "'Bargaining' and Gender Relations: Within and Beyond the Household," *Feminist Economics* 3, no. 1 (March 1997): 1–51. For early work in this area, see Mary Jean Horney and Marjorie B. McElroy, "Nash-Bargained Household Decisions: Toward a Generalization of the Theory of Demand," *International Economic Review* 22, no. 2 (June 1981): 333–49; and Marilyn Manser and Murray Brown, "Marriage and Household Decision Making," *International Economic Review* 21, no. 1 (February 1980): 31–44.

In these models, the bargaining power of each spouse is determined by his or her *threat point*—the level of well-being that each would attain if the couple cannot reach agreement within the marriage. In the most common type of family bargaining model, termed **divorce-threat** **bargaining models**, the threat point depends on the well-being of each individual if the marriage were to end.[24] As in the case of negotiations between a vendor and a customer, decisions reached by the two parties are likely to more closely reflect the preferences of the party with the stronger threat effect, the one who is better able to "walk away" from the deal. In the case of a divorce-threat model, the two parties are the married spouses and "the deal" is the marriage.

What factors might affect each partner's threat point? One key factor is each partner's own labor market earnings (or potential earnings, if not already in the labor market, given their human capital). Greater earnings confer increased bargaining power. In addition, factors external to the family may affect one or both of the partners' threat points. These might include laws defining the division of marital property if divorce were to occur, laws governing divorce itself, and each individual's probability of remarriage as well as available government support in the event of a breakup.[25]

To better understand the differences between the neoclassical model and the divorce-threat bargaining model and their implications, let's reconsider the example of John and Jane, one of the married couples discussed earlier. They maximized total family income by specializing: Jane split her time between home production and market work, while John did only market work, with no time spent in home production. Once total income is maximized, the next issue to decide is how to allocate this joint income among the different commodities the family might want. The neoclassical model assumes that John and Jane have common preferences or that John is an altruistic head who considers Jane's and other family members' preferences. Bargaining models explicitly allow for the possibility that John's and Jane's preferences might differ and that there is no family head who would determine decisions in that case. For instance, while the spouses may agree on the amount they want to spend on their children (thus, they have a common preference in this regard), they may differ on whether they should spend some of it on music lessons or karate classes. As another example, one spouse may prefer to spend discretionary income on a ski trip, while the other may prefer a beach vacation.

In a divorce-threat bargaining model, it is John's and Jane's threat points that affect their relative bargaining power and thus determine what consumption decisions will be made. Given the traditional division of labor in their marriage, Jane is expected to have less bargaining power because she has a weaker threat point. If they were to divorce, she would likely have more difficulty supporting herself (and their children) because she has mainly invested in marriage-specific rather than market skills. Even if she has a college degree, she has lost out on valuable labor

---

[24]Shelly J. Lundberg and Robert A. Pollak suggest an alternative threat point within the marriage itself, in which the partners fully specialize in the provision of public goods according to traditional gender roles; for example, the wife provides all the childcare, while the husband does all the outdoor work. In this "separate spheres" model, family behavior depends not on the incomes each spouse would receive after divorce but on the resources each spouse controls within marriage; see "Separate Spheres Bargaining and the Marriage Market," *Journal of Political Economy* 101, no. 6 (December 1993): 988–1010.

[25]Marjorie B. McElroy, "The Empirical Content of Nash-Bargained Household Behavior," *Journal of Human Resources* 25, no. 4 (Fall 1990): 559–83. For an excellent graphical exposition of bargaining models, see Susan Himmelweit, Roberto Simonetti, and Andrew Trigg, *Microeconomics: Neoclassical and Institutionalist Perspectives on Economic Behavior* (Boston: Cengage Learning, 2001), 143–78.

market experience. Her bargaining power is also affected by rules and laws in place, including the amount of child support she will receive (assuming she has at least partial physical custody of the children), government support (e.g., welfare benefits or the Earned Income Credit), and her chances for remarriage. John, on the other hand, is likely to be in a much stronger bargaining position because, during the marriage, he remained fully attached to the labor market. However, once divorced, John may need to pay alimony and child support, and he may also have less contact with his children, depending on the provisions of the child custody agreement. In addition, he may have to purchase some household services formerly produced by his wife.

One way that researchers empirically investigate whether husbands' and wives' preferences are the same or different is to see if the husband and wife would spend their personal income in the same way (consistent with the neoclassical model) or if they would spend their income differently (consistent with a bargaining model because control over resources matters). To investigate this point, two studies examined the effect of a policy change in the United Kingdom in the 1970s that transferred receipt of income, in the form of a child benefit, from the father to the mother. Both found that this change led to an *increase* in expenditures on children's consumption (as measured in one study by expenditures on children's clothing and, in the other, by expenditures on children's clothing, toys, and "pocket" money).[26] These studies, among others, suggest that the "common preference" assumption of the simple model does not hold up; in other words, who controls the income matters. Indeed, mounting evidence shows that, consistent with bargaining models, who controls family resources affects a wide array of outcomes beyond consumption expenditures, including how each spouse allocates his or her time as well as decisions regarding charitable giving.[27] In addition, as discussed earlier, women who have greater economic resources are less likely to experience domestic violence.

In our preceding discussion, we focused on expenditures on children's clothing as an illustrative example of a case in which husbands and wives differ in their spending patterns. In fact, a growing body of research suggests that mothers generally allocate more resources and place greater emphasis on their children's well-being than do fathers. Notably, in developing countries where resources are scarce, children's health and survival probabilities have been found to improve when mothers have greater control over family resources.[28]

One implication of this research is that the government has the potential to promote certain outcomes, to the extent that its policies and laws affect the distribution of

---

[26]Shelly J. Lundberg, Robert. A. Pollak, and Terence J. Wales, "Do Husbands and Wives Pool Their Resources? Evidence from the U.K. Child Benefit," *Journal of Human Resources* 32, no. 3 (Summer 1997): 463–80; and Jennifer Ward-Batts, "Out of the Wallet and into the Purse: Using Micro Data to Test Income Pooling," *Journal of Human Resources* 43, no. 2 (Spring 2008): 325–51.

[27]Regarding the labor supply of married couples, see Paul Schultz, "Testing the Neoclassical Model of Family Labor Supply and Fertility," *Journal of Human Resources* 25, no. 4 (Fall 1990): 599–634; and for cohabitors, see Anne E. Winkler, "Economic Decision Making among Cohabitors: Findings Regarding Income Pooling," *Applied Economics* 29, no. 8 (August 1997): 1079–90. Regarding charitable contributions, see James Andreoni, Eleanor Brown, and Isaac Rischall, "Charitable Giving by Married Couples: Who Decides and Why Does It Matter?" *Journal of Human Resources* 38, no. 1 (Winter 2003): 111–33.

[28]For reviews of the evidence, see Esther Duflo, "Women Empowerment and Economic Development," *Journal of Economic Literature* 50, no. 4 (December 2012): 1051–79; and Cheryl Doss, "Intrahousehold Bargaining and Resource Allocation in Developing Countries," *The World Bank Research Observer* 28, no. 1 (2013): 52–78. For an influential early study, see Duncan Thomas, "Intra-Household Resource Allocation: An Inferential Approach," *Journal of Human Resources* 25, no. 4 (Fall 1990): 635–64.

resources between men and women, both inside and outside marriage.[29] As we have seen, in the United Kingdom, when the government paid the child benefit to mothers rather than fathers, expenditures on children increased. Another way that government may affect families is through laws that govern the distribution of marital assets in the case of divorce. For example, adopting a community property law (which mandates equal division of property upon divorce) would generally give the wife a larger share of marital assets and hence increase her bargaining power within marriage compared to following common law. Interestingly, one study found that marital property laws that favor women are associated with wives' increased labor supply and reduced time in housework.[30] Similarly, as discussed earlier, the adoption of unilateral divorce laws has been found to reduce domestic violence, again most likely by increasing women's bargaining power. It has been further suggested that changes in men's and women's relative bargaining power may affect not only decisions *within* existing marriages but even the decisions of unmarried individuals, such as whether to get married.[31]

Conclusion

We saw in Chapter 2 how what has come to be known as the traditional married-couple family—the breadwinner-husband and homemaker-wife—evolved over time. The simple neoclassical model explains how such a division of labor may be advantageous under appropriate conditions. However, it cannot be taken for granted that these conditions are satisfied at any given point in time, let alone that they will be for the rest of each person's life.

The traditional division of labor became established during a time when family size was large and life was short, a considerable amount of time was spent in household production, and market wages in jobs available to women were low so that women's relative advantage for home work was great. With many children and a shorter life expectancy, the problem of the decline in the value of housework after the children grew up was far less serious. Also, with severe social and religious sanctions against divorce, women were less likely to find themselves and their children on their own, without financial support from their husbands. However, as these conditions changed, the advantages of the traditional division of labor decreased and the costs associated with it, particularly for women, increased.

Growing recognition of the drawbacks of the traditional division of responsibilities between husband and wife is likely an important factor that contributed to the increase in women's labor force participation and the decline of the traditional married-couple family. Furthermore, these changes together with improvements in women's labor market opportunities are also likely related to the decline in marriage, the increase in divorce, and the rise in cohabitation that have occurred since the 1960s. Nonetheless, as we will see in Chapter 13, marriage rates remain high in the United States compared with other nations around the world.

---

[29]Agarwal, "'Bargaining' and Gender Relations."
[30]Jeffrey S. Gray, "Divorce-Law Changes and Married Women's Labor Supply," *American Economic Review* 88, no. 3 (June 1998): 628–51; and Kristie M. Engemann and Michael T. Owyang, "Splitsville, The Economics of Unilateral Divorce," *The Regional Economist* (January 2008): 12–16.
[31]Lundberg and Pollak, "Family Decision Making." For instance, the UK child benefit discussed in the text, which transferred income from husbands to wives, effectively made marriage more attractive to potential wives and less attractive to potential husbands.

Questions for Review and Discussion

1. Explain why husbands and wives benefit from specialization and exchange. Under what conditions are these benefits likely to be large?

2. Jason and Jennifer are married. If Jason works in the labor market, he can earn a wage of $20 per hour, while Jennifer can earn a wage of $10 per hour.

   a. Who has an absolute advantage in the labor market? How do you know?

   b. Suppose we want to know who has a comparative advantage in the labor market. What specific information do we need to know? Discuss.

3. In view of the advantages of specialization and exchange pointed out by Becker, explain why families are increasingly moving away from the traditional division of labor.

4. To what extent is the presumption that women have a comparative advantage in housework justified?

5. Explain under what conditions it would be rational for a woman who could earn more than her husband in the labor market to specialize (to some extent) in housework.

6. What is a "bargaining approach" to decision making? Why is this approach more realistic than the standard neoclassical model?

7. Suggest some factors that would improve the bargaining power of married women.

Suggested Readings

Becker, Gary S. *A Treatise on the Family*. Cambridge, MA: Harvard University Press, 1981, enlarged ed., 1991.

Bergmann, Barbara. *The Economic Emergence of Women*, 2nd ed. New York: Palgrave Macmillan, 2005.

Ferber, Marianne A. "A Feminist Critique of the Neoclassical Theory of the Family." In *Women, Family, and Work: Writings on the Economics of Gender*, edited by Karine S. Moe. Oxford: Blackwell, 2003, chap. 1.

Ferber, Marianne A., and Julie A. Nelson, eds. *Beyond Economic Man*. Chicago: University of Chicago Press, 1993.

Ferber, Marianne A., and Julie A. Nelson, eds. *Feminist Economics Today*. Chicago: University of Chicago, 2003.

Lundberg, Shelly. "The Sexual Division of Labour." In *The Shape of the Division of Labour: Nations, Industries and Households*, edited by Robert M. Solow and Jean-Philippe Touffut, 122–48. Cheltenham, UK: Edward Elgar, 2010.

Lundberg, Shelly, and Robert A. Pollak. "The American Family and Family Economics." *Journal of Economic Perspectives* 21, no. 2 (Spring 2007): 3–26.

Key Terms

commodities (43)

comparative advantage (43)

opportunity cost (43)

absolute advantage (44)

economies of scale (51)

public good (51)

externalities in consumption (52)

marriage-specific investments (53)

transaction cost approach (54)

bargaining models (54)

divorce-threat bargaining models (55)

APPENDIX 3A

Specialization and Exchange: A Graphical Analysis

As discussed in this chapter, a complete analysis of the division of labor between the individuals who make up a couple takes into account both their production possibilities and their preferences for different goods. This appendix provides a more comprehensive examination of the simple neoclassical model in the context of a graphical analysis and reaches the same conclusions as to the value of specialization and exchange as those based on the examples presented in Table 3-1.

For simplicity, we assume that individuals derive utility from only two types of goods—home goods, produced with inputs of home time, and market goods, purchased with market income. In Figure 3-1, H and M measure the dollar value of household output and market goods, respectively. Two persons, Kathy and Jim, each allocate their time between market work (M production) and housework (H production).[32]

If Kathy and Jim are each dependent on their own output, their consumption opportunities are limited to their individual *production possibility frontiers*. The production possibility frontier shows the largest feasible combinations of the two outputs that can be produced with given resources (in this case, time inputs) and know-how. M_1H_1 indicates the combinations of household and market outputs available to Jim, while M_2H_2 shows the options from which Kathy can choose. For example, if Jim devotes full time to market work (M production), he can produce a maximum of $80 worth of market goods. If he spends all his time on household activities, he can produce $30 worth of home goods.

The slope of the line M_1H_1 tells us the money value of the market goods Jim must give up to get an additional dollar of home goods. The fact that M_1H_1 is more steeply sloped than M_2H_2 means that Jim must give up more market goods to get an additional dollar of home goods than Kathy. Specifically, Jim must give up $2.67 of

---

[32]We also assume fixed proportions production functions for H and M for each individual. For example, an additional hour spent on the production of H by Kathy increases output by the same amount, regardless of how much H she already produced. This simplifying assumption results in the straight-line production possibility frontiers shown in Figure 3-1. For a discussion of this point, along with a consideration of other ways the standard theoretical model might be made more realistic, see Pollak, "Gary Becker's Contributions."

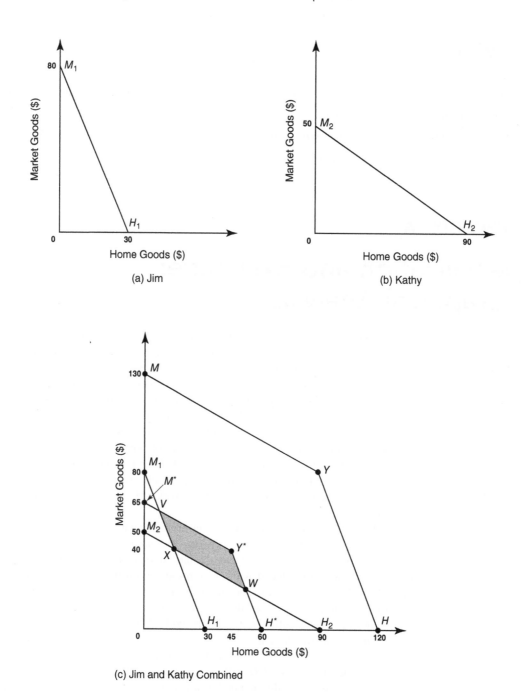

FIGURE 3-1 Separate and Combined Production Possibility Frontiers

market goods to get an additional dollar of home goods ($80/$30), whereas Kathy needs to give up only $.56 of market goods to get an additional dollar of home goods ($50/$90). Viewing the matter somewhat differently, Kathy must forgo more home goods to get an additional dollar of market goods than Jim. Kathy would have to give up $1.80 worth of home goods to get an additional dollar of market goods ($90/$50), while Jim needs to give up only $.38 worth of home goods to get an additional dollar of market goods ($30/$80). Thus, Jim has a comparative advantage in market work and Kathy has a comparative advantage in home production.

If Jim and Kathy decide to collaborate, their combined production possibility curve will be MYH, as shown in panel c. At point M both Jim and Kathy specialize entirely in market work, producing $130 ($80 + 50) of market goods. If they prefer to have some home goods, it will pay for only Kathy to do housework, up to the point where she does no market work at all (point Y), because she adds more to home production ($1.80) for every dollar of market goods given up than Jim would add ($.38). Therefore, the segment MY has the same slope as M_2H_2, showing that as long as only Kathy is dividing her time between market and home, it is Kathy's slope that is relevant. Jim will do some housework only if a mix of more household production and fewer market goods are desired than segment MY represents. Beyond that point, the slope of M_1H_1 becomes relevant as it is only Jim who is dividing his time between home and market. At the extreme, at point H, both Jim and Kathy work only in the home, producing $120 ($30 + $90) of home goods.

The combined production possibility frontier (MYH) makes feasible some combinations of M and H that would not be attainable by Kathy and Jim on their separate production possibility frontiers. These gains from specialization and exchange may be illustrated by putting the output combinations represented by production possibility frontier MYH on a per capita or per person basis. This is shown by production possibility frontier $M*Y*H$ that is obtained by dividing MYH by 2. (For instance, point Y reflects $90 worth of home goods and $80 worth of market goods, while point $Y*$ reflects $45 worth of home goods and $40 worth of market goods.) $M*Y*H$ may be compared to the options represented by Jim and Kathy's individual production possibility frontiers, M_1H_1 and M_2H_2 (panel c). The shaded area $WXVY*$ represents the increased per capita output that is now available. This gain in output may potentially be distributed between Jim and Kathy so as to make them both better off than they would have been separately. To obtain the gains represented by $WXVY*$, the couple must produce a nontrivial amount of both market and home goods, for it is the production of both commodities that gives each of them the opportunity to specialize in the area of their comparative advantage.

This analysis also illustrates that the gains from specialization will be larger the more the two individuals differ in their comparative advantages. To see this relationship, imagine the extreme case in which Kathy and Jim both have the same production possibility frontier, say M_1H_1. The combined production possibility frontier would then be $2 \times M_1H_1$. On a per capita basis (dividing the combined production possibility frontier in half), we would simply be left with M_1H_1. Kathy and Jim would do no better combining forces than they would each do separately. Based on this simple analysis alone, it is not clear what the economic gains of collaborating are for such a couple. However, as we saw in this chapter, economic gains are likely even in this case because two people can use many goods and services more efficiently than a single person can. Here, however, we focus on a couple who can potentially increase their income through joint production.

To provide a link between the potential increase in output due to collaboration and the goal of maximizing satisfaction, we need to introduce an additional tool of economic analysis and pursue our inquiry one step further. So far we established the various combinations of the two types of outputs that Kathy and Jim could produce. Which of these they would choose depends on their tastes, that is to say, on their preferences for market goods compared to home goods. To considerably simplify the analysis, we will assume that they have identical tastes. If home goods are valued more highly than market goods, the couple will be willing to give up a considerable amount of market goods in order to get an additional dollar of home goods, and vice versa if market goods are valued more highly. This relationship can be illustrated using indifference curves, as seen in Figure 3-2.

Let us assume that Kathy and Jim have been told that they could have the combination of market and home goods represented by point A in panel a. They are then asked to find various other combinations of H and M from which they would derive exactly the same amount of satisfaction or utility. These other points can all be connected into one indifference curve, U_2, so named because the couple is indifferent about being at various points on the curve. The U_2 curve is *negatively sloped*; the reason for the negative slope is that if the amount of market or home goods is decreased, the amount of the other good must be increased for the couple to remain equally well off.

Notice too that indifference curve U_2 is convex to the origin. That is, it gets steeper as we move to the left and flatter as we move to the right. What this means is that at a point like C, where M goods are relatively plentiful and H goods are relatively scarce, it takes a fairly large amount of M ($15 worth) to induce the couple to give up a fairly small amount of H ($5 worth) and remain equally well off. On the other hand, at a point like E, where M goods are relatively scarce and H goods are relatively plentiful, the couple is willing to give up a fairly large amount of H ($20 worth) to get even a small additional amount of scarce M ($2 worth). The convex shape depicted here is generally realistic to the extent that relatively scarce goods are valued more highly.

However, Kathy and Jim have not just one indifference curve but rather a whole family of higher and lower indifference curves. For example, it is possible to choose a point like G on curve U_3 that offers more of both M and H and is therefore clearly preferable to point A on curve U_2. Hence, all points on curve U_3 will, by extension, be preferable to (give more satisfaction than) all points on curve U_2. Similarly, it is possible to choose a point like J on curve U_1 that offers less of both M and H than at point A. Point J is clearly less desirable than point A, and, by extension, all points

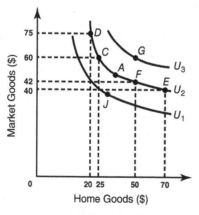

(a) Relatively Strong Preferences
for Market Goods

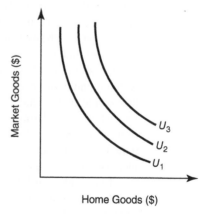

(b) Relatively Strong Preferences
for Home Goods

FIGURE 3-2 Indifference Curves

on curve U_1 are less desirable (give less satisfaction) than all points on curve U_2. It should be clear that indifference curves can never intersect. All points on any one curve represent an equal amount of utility, while any point above (below) represents a larger (smaller) amount of utility. At the point where two curves intersect, they clearly represent the same amount of utility, yet at all other points they do not. This is a logical impossibility.

On the other hand, another couple's preferences might look like those depicted in panel b of Figure 3-2. These indifference curves are steeper and show that this couple places a relatively higher value on home goods compared with market goods than Kathy and Jim do. In general, it would take a larger amount of market goods to induce them to give up a dollar's worth of home goods while remaining equally well off.

To determine the division of labor (or time allocation) a couple will actually choose, we must consider both their production possibilities and their tastes or preferences. In Figure 3-3, we superimpose the couple's hypothetical indifference map on the production possibility frontier shown in Figure 3-1, panel c. It is then readily

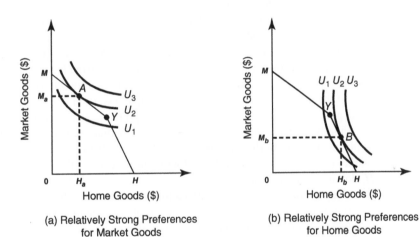

(a) Relatively Strong Preferences for Market Goods

(b) Relatively Strong Preferences for Home Goods

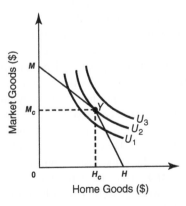

(c) Intermediate Preferences

FIGURE 3-3 The Role of Tastes in Determining the Household Division of Labor

possible to determine the combination of home-produced and market-produced goods that a rational couple with those tastes (indifference curves) will choose. It will always be the point where the production possibility curve just touches the highest indifference curve it reaches. The reason is simple—the couple always prefers to be on a higher indifference curve (by definition, as we have seen), but because they are constrained to the possible combinations of output represented by the production possibility frontier, they cannot realistically reach an indifference curve that at all points lies above the frontier.

In Figure 3-3, we illustrate the impact of the couple's preferences on their time allocation. The combined production possibility curve for the couple, *MYH*, shows the various combinations of *H* and *M* the couple can produce while taking full advantage of their combined resources and the comparative advantage each has in producing one of the goods. Let us continue to assume that the wife has a comparative advantage in home production and that the husband has a comparative advantage in market work.

As may be seen in panel a, a couple with relatively strong preferences for market goods will maximize satisfaction at point *A* along segment *MY*. The husband will specialize entirely in market production, and the wife will do all the housework and supply some time to the market. They will consume M_a dollars of market goods and H_a dollars of home goods.

Panel b shows a couple with stronger preferences for home-produced goods. They will maximize utility at point *B*. The wife will devote herself entirely to household production, while the husband will do some housework as well as supplying time to the market. Such a couple will consume fewer market goods (M_b) and more home goods (H_b) than a couple with stronger preferences for market goods.

Finally, panel c shows a couple with intermediate tastes. They will maximize utility at point *Y*. Both wife and husband will each fully specialize in home and market production, respectively, and will consume M_c dollars of market goods and H_c dollars of home goods.

Couples may differ in their allocation of tasks within the family, not solely due to differences in tastes. The relative productivity of each member of the family in the production of market and home goods will also be an important factor. We already noted that if both husband and wife are equally productive in each endeavor, they will not realize any gains from specialization or division of labor within the family. However, even if we assume that the wife has a comparative advantage in household production and that the husband has a comparative advantage in market work, the relative productivities of each individual in home and market production are still relevant, which are illustrated in Figure 3-4.

Panel a shows two hypothetical production possibility frontiers. In *MYH*, the segment corresponding to the wife's frontier (*MY*) is relatively flat, indicating that she is considerably more productive in the home than in the market. For given tastes (represented by indifference curve *U*), the couple maximizes utility at point *Y*, where the wife specializes entirely in home production and the husband specializes completely in market work. However, if the couple's production possibility frontier were *MY'H'*, even with the same tastes (indifference curve), they would choose point *A* along segment *M'Y'*. Here the wife will continue to do all the housework but will do some market work as well. This is because *MY'* is steeper than *MY*, indicating a higher ratio of the wife's market productivity relative to her home productivity. The opportunity cost of home goods in terms of market goods forgone has increased, and as a result the family consumes less home goods.

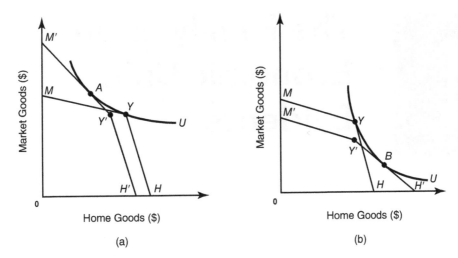

FIGURE 3-4 The Role of the Production Possibility Frontier in Determining the Household Division of Labor

Similarly, as shown in panel b, the couple's time allocation may also depend on the husband's relative productivity in the home and the market. For given tastes (represented by indifference curve U), the couple will choose point Y when the husband's productivity in the home is extremely low relative to his market productivity. (This is indicated by the relatively steep slope of segment YH on frontier MYH.) They are more likely to choose a point like B along the flatter segment $Y'H'$ on frontier $M'Y'H$ where the husband does some housework as well as market work, when his market productivity is lower relative to his home productivity. At B, the couple consumes more of the now relatively cheaper home-produced goods than at Y.

Figure 3-4 shows how the relative productivity of the husband and the wife in the home and the market influences the division of labor in the family and the combination of home- and market-produced goods that they choose to consume. Nonetheless, as long as the comparative advantages of husband and wife differ in this simple model, some degree of specialization will be efficient. As we have seen, the greater the difference between the two in their comparative advantage, the greater the gains to specialization and exchange.

Thus, the more comprehensive analysis presented here supports the conclusions reached on the basis of the numerical example provided in this chapter. In this case too, however, the same qualifications hold: first, the traditional division of labor is not without its disadvantages, particularly for women, and, second, potential economic benefits to marriage include more than just specialization and exchange.

The Family as an Economic Unit: Evidence

CHAPTER HIGHLIGHTS

- ■ Time Spent in Nonmarket Work
- ■ Estimating the Value of Nonmarket Production
- ■ The American Family in the Twenty-First Century

Economists have traditionally focused their attention on market work, although much work is performed outside the market, both in the household and in the voluntary sector. Such unpaid work substantially contributes to the well-being of individuals, their families, and society at large. First we examine available evidence on the allocation of time to market work, housework, childcare, and volunteer work by men and women, as well as changes in this allocation during recent decades. Next we look at how the value of nonmarket production might be estimated and recent efforts to do so. We conclude by looking at the American family in the twenty-first century. As we shall see, married couples, the focus of this chapter, have been declining as a share of all households. We briefly summarize the changes that have occurred and point to the increasing complexity of families in the United States. Chapters 13 and 14 provide more detailed discussions of changes in family formation and their implications for the United States, and then Chapters 17 and 18 focus on notable trends in other countries.

Time Spent in Nonmarket Work

Existing estimates of time spent in nonmarket work—whether housework, childcare, or volunteer work—vary considerably for a number of reasons: they are based on different samples, the information may have been collected in different ways, and definitions of what is considered nonmarket work often differ as well.[1] For example, housework time may be more narrowly defined as time spent on activities performed in and around the household or may further include shopping and driving time.[2] As a second example, volunteer time may be narrowly counted as time devoted to formal organizations or may include informal activities like helping out neighbors. Another difference is that some studies collect information based on questions about people's recollections of how much time they spent in particular activities such as "How many hours did you spend doing laundry last week?" while other studies ask respondents to record in a "time diary" what they do during specific blocks of time. In the case of time spent in housework, it turns out that estimates obtained from questions based on recollections tend to be quite a bit higher.[3]

In 2003 the US government launched its first ever time use survey, the **American Time Use Survey (ATUS)**, following the lead of many other countries, including Canada, Australia, and a number of countries in the European Union.[4] In the ATUS time diary, reports are collected from one respondent per household using a subsample of households who were interviewed for the Current Population Survey (CPS). (The CPS is the US government survey used to collect data on unemployment and *paid* work and the source of much of the data presented in this book.) The majority of the current estimates of time spent in nonmarket work reported in the next sections are from the ATUS. Because these data have become available only relatively recently, we rely on other surveys to provide information about longer-term trends in time spent in these activities.

Time Spent in Housework

Let us begin by looking at Table 4-1, which provides detailed information on the current division of labor between women and men based on data from the 2014 ATUS. A useful feature of these data is that they show patterns in paid work and housework disaggregated by marital status and by employment status of the wife. As seen in Table 4-1, wives spent around 18 hours per week in core housework activities, such as laundry, cleaning, cooking, and yard work, compared with just under 11 hours for husbands. When household activities are more broadly defined to include time spent on grocery shopping and caring for household members, principally children, wives spent nearly 30 hours versus a bit more than 17 hours for husbands. Using either definition, wives spent 1.7 times (approximately 8 to 12 hours) more in household activities as husbands in 2014. Not surprisingly, time in unpaid housework is highest for nonemployed wives. Also, as we might expect, husbands of employed wives

---

[1]For a discussion of methodological issues, see F. Thomas Juster, Hiromi Ono, and Frank P. Stafford, "An Assessment of Alternative Measures of Time Use," *Sociological Methodology* 33 (2003): 19–54. For a summary of the major time use surveys, see Mark Aguiar, Erik Hurst, and Louikas Karabarbounis, "Recent Developments in the Economics of Time Use," *Annual Review of Economics* 4, no. 1 (July 2012): 373–97.

[2]See Suzanne Bianchi, Melissa A. Milkie, Liana C. Sayer, and John P. Robinson, "Is Anyone Doing the Housework? Trends in the Gender Division of Household Labor," *Social Forces* 79, no. 1 (September 2000): 1–39; and Anne E. Winkler, "Measuring Time Use in Households with More Than One Person," *Monthly Labor Review* 125, no. 2 (February 2002): 45–52.

[3]See, for instance, Winkler, "Measuring Time Use."

[4]A description of the ATUS can be found on the US Bureau of Labor Statistics' website, www.bls.gov/tus. Regarding international efforts, see National Research Council, *Time-Use Measurement and Research* (Washington, DC: National Academies Press, 2000); and Valeria Esquivel, "Sixteen Years after Beijing: What Are the New Policy Agendas for Time-Use Data Collection?" *Feminist Economics* 17, no. 4 (October 2011): 215–38.

TABLE 4-1	AVERAGE WEEKLY HOURS IN PAID AND UNPAID WORK, 2014					
	TIME IN PAID WORK		TIME IN UNPAID WORK			
	Market Work	Commute to Work	Housework	Grocery Shopping	Care of Household Members	Total
Women	24.1	1.9	15.8	3.0	6.6	25.4
Single	26.6	2.2	11.6	2.5	4.0	18.1
Married	22.8	1.7	18.3	3.4	8.0	29.7
Employed	34.6	2.6	14.7	3.1	6.7	24.5
Not Employed	0.0	0.0	25.3	3.9	10.4	39.6
Men	34.8	3.0	10.1	2.3	3.2	15.6
Single	28.9	2.3	9.1	2.3	1.1	12.5
Married	37.3	3.3	10.7	2.3	4.3	17.3
Wife Employed	38.1	3.4	11.6	2.4	4.4	18.4
Wife Not Employed	35.5	3.2	9.0	2.3	4.0	15.3
Gender Ratio of Time Use						
Women-to-Men	0.7	0.6	1.6	1.3	2.1	1.6
Married Women-to-Married Men	0.6	0.5	1.7	1.5	1.9	1.7

Notes: Figures are for respondents age 25–64. Single persons are not cohabiting.

Housework includes routine activities such as laundry, food preparation, and cleaning, as well as yard work, pet care, vehicle repair, interior and exterior upkeep, and household management.

Grocery shopping includes purchasing groceries, food, and gas.

Care of household members includes children and other adults.

Figures on housework, grocery shopping, and care of household members include travel time.

Wife's employment status is measured using information on usual hours worked.

Source: Authors' calculations from the 2014 American Time Use Survey.

spent a few more hours in housework than their counterparts who have nonemployed wives, though the difference was relatively modest.

How does the current situation (2014) shown in Table 4-1 compare to previous years? Data on trends from the 1960s through the early 2010s from various sources indicate a consistent set of trends regarding time spent in housework. They show that wives spent substantially less time doing housework in the 1970s than they had in the 1960s, while time spent by husbands in housework did not change much. Subsequently, from the late 1970s through the early 2010s, wives' time in housework decreased even further. In contrast, husbands' housework time increased modestly through the late 1980s, though it did not change appreciably thereafter.[5] As a result of these changes, married women's housework time fell substantially relative to their husbands'—from seven times that of married men in the mid-1960s to about one and

---

[5]Evidence is from Valerie Ramey, "Time Spent in Home Production in the Twentieth Century: New Estimates from Old Data," *Journal of Economic History* 69, no. 1 (2009): 1–47; Daniel S. Hamermesh, "Time Use," *NBER Reporter* no. 2 (2012); and Suzanne M. Bianchi, Liana C. Sayer, Melissa A. Milkie, and John P. Robinson, "Housework: Who Did, Does or Will Do It, and How Much Does It Matter?" *Social Forces* 91, no. 1 (September 2012): 55–63.

a half times as much in 2014 (as shown in Table 4-1).[6] Women also increased their market hours considerably over this period, largely as a result of the rise in the proportion of married women in the labor force but also because of an increase in hours of paid work among employed wives. (Trends in the labor force participation of married women will be discussed further in subsequent chapters.) As a result of both sets of changes, the difference in the allocation of time to market work and nonmarket work between wives and husbands narrowed considerably.[7]

There are a number of reasons why wives spent so much less time in housework in 2014 than in the 1960s. First, average family size has fallen. Second, norms regarding cleanliness have changed.[8] Third, one can point to dramatic changes in household technology and the increasing availability of substitutes for household production.[9] Most households today have numerous appliances including washing machines, dishwashers, microwaves, and food processors. These appliances considerably reduce the effort required for many basic housekeeping activities, as well as the time. Further, many goods and services that were previously produced at home are now often purchased. For instance, instead of taking the time to produce a home-cooked dinner, families increasingly purchase ready-to-use ingredients and foods at the supermarket or dine out at fast-food and casual restaurants.[10] Another strategy, albeit used by a relatively small share of families, is to hire firms or individuals to come to their homes to do regular household tasks, whether housecleaning or mowing the lawn. As might be expected, the research evidence indicates that family income matters, especially the wife's earnings, in determining whether a family purchases these types of market substitutes.[11]

An additional factor that likely contributed to the decrease in the time wives spend in nonmarket activities is the rise in their real wages, which increased the opportunity cost of their time spent in such activities. Indeed, a dynamic process may be going on in which rising market wages induce women to allocate more time to market work and less time to housework. As they do so, they accumulate more labor market experience, further increasing their wages and resulting in further decreases in their housework time.

For many of the same reasons listed so far—smaller family size, changes in household technology and market substitutes, and shifting norms—we would have

---

[6]The mid-1960s figure is from Bianchi, Sayer, Milkie, and Robinson, "Housework: Who Did, Does or Will Do It."

[7]There is also the question of whether the reallocation of wives' time between the home and the market came at the expense of a reduction in leisure time for them. Two studies suggest that this is not a concern. Examining trends from 1965 to the mid-2000s, Mark Aguiar and Erik Hurst found an *increase* in leisure time of about 5 to 6 hours per week for women as well as men in "Measuring Trends in Leisure: Evidence from Five Decades of Time Use Surveys," *Quarterly Journal of Economics* 122, no. 3 (August 2007): 969–1006. For roughly this same period, Valerie Ramey and Neville Francis found somewhat smaller increases in leisure time for both groups in "A Century of Work and Leisure," *American Economic Journal: Macroeconomics* 1, no. 2 (2009): 189–224. One of the first to raise this issue was Victor R. Fuchs, *Women's Quest for Economic Equality* (Cambridge, MA: Harvard University Press, 1988).

[8]Bianchi, Milkie, Sayer, and Robinson, "Is Anyone Doing the Housework?"

[9]Regarding the role of household technology, see Jeremy Greenwood, Ananth Seshadri, and Mehmet Yorukoglu, "Engines of Liberation," *Review of Economic Studies* 72, no.1 (January 2005): 109–33.

[10]For analysis, see Daniel Hamermesh, "Time to Eat: Household Production under Increasing Income Inequality," *American Journal of Agricultural Economics* 89, no. 4 (November 2007): 852–63.

[11]For evidence, see Philip N. Cohen, "Replacing Housework in the Service Economy: Gender, Class, Race-Ethnicity in Service Spending," *Gender and Society* 12, no. 2 (April 1998): 219–31; and Elena G. F. Stancanelli and Leslie S. Stratton, "Maids, Appliances and Couples' Housework: The Demand for Inputs to Domestic Production," *Economica* 81 (July 2014): 445–67. However, another study finds much weaker evidence that income matters; see Alexandra Killewald, "Opting Out and Buying Out: Wives' Earnings and Housework Time," *Journal of Marriage and Family* 73 (April 2011): 459–71.

expected husbands' housework time to have decreased as well. The fact that husbands' housework time actually increased during the 1980s suggests some reallocation of tasks between husbands and wives during this period (though as noted earlier, the increase did not continue after that). In fact, for this same period, there is even evidence of a reallocation of time between members of couples in which the wife was nonemployed. A possible explanation is that women's rising earnings potential may have altered the balance of bargaining power in the household, whether or not the wife was actually employed, and that wives used their increased bargaining power to obtain some reallocation of housework.[12] While there has been no further reallocation of housework time, husband's time in childcare has risen.

Recent research also suggests several other interesting patterns in the allocation of housework. For instance, based on Gary Becker's theory, we would expect to see that wives who bring home the majority of family earnings spend less time in housework than their counterparts who earn a smaller share of family earnings. However, a number of studies find evidence to the contrary, suggesting that long-held gender expectations of women's and men's proper roles continue to hold sway in determining the allocation of time to housework.[13]

Perhaps not surprisingly, gender differences in time spent on housework start long before young men and women first head their own households. Data from the early 2000s for the United States indicate that teenage girls spent 50 percent more time doing housework than teenage boys.[14] Indeed, girls participate more in housework than boys even in Denmark, for example, where arguably there is greater emphasis on gender equality than in the United States.[15]

Interesting differences are also evident in the allocation of housework between married spouses and cohabiting men and women. In both types of living arrangements, men spend less time on housework than women, but cohabiting men spend a larger share of time on it than married men.[16] Evidence also shows less specialization among partners in gay and lesbian couples.[17] As discussed further in Chapter 13, these patterns likely prevail, at least in part, because cohabiting opposite-sex couples have far fewer legal protections than married couples and, until fairly recently, same-sex couples lacked the option of marrying and were often denied benefits

---

[12]This point is made in Francine D. Blau, "Trends in the Well-Being of American Women, 1970–1995," *Journal of Economic Literature* 36, no. 1 (March 1998): 112–65.

[13]Studies finding evidence of a role for gender, apart from economic factors, in determining housework time include Michael Bittman, Paula England, Nancy Folbre, Liana Sayer, and George Matheson, "When Does Gender Trump Money? Bargaining and Time in Household Work," *American Journal of Sociology* 109, no. 1 (July 2003): 186–214; and Marianne Bertrand, Emir Kamenica, and Jessica Pan, "Gender Identity and Relative Income within Households," *Quarterly Journal of Economics* 130, no. 3 (2015): 571–614. However, others have questioned this finding. See, for instance, Oriel Sullivan, "An End to Gender Display through the Performance of Housework? A Review and Reassessment of the Quantitative Literature Using Insights from the Qualitative Literature," *Journal of Family Theory and Review* 3 (March 2011): 1–13.

[14]Shirley L. Porterfield and Anne E. Winkler, "Teen Time Use and Parental Education: Evidence from the CPS, MTF, and ATUS," *Monthly Labor Review* 130, no. 5 (May 2007): 37–56.

[15]Jens Bonk, "Children's Housework—Are Girls More Active Than Boys?" *Electronic International Journal of Time Use Research* 7, no. 1 (November 2010): 1-16, http://www.eijtur.org.

[16]Shannon N. Davis, Theodore N. Greenstein, and Jennifer P. Gerteisen Marks, "Effects of Union Type on Division of Household Labor: Do Cohabiting Men Really Perform More Housework?" *Journal of Family Issues* 28, no. 9 (September 2007): 1246–72.

[17]Lisa Giddings, John M. Nunley, Alyssa Schneebaum, and Joachim Zietz, "Birth Cohort and the Specialization Gap between Same-Sex and Different-Sex Couples," *Demography* 51, no. 2 (April 2014): 509–34. See also, Kenneth Matos, *Modern Families: Same and Different Sex Families Negotiating at Home* (Washington, DC: Work and Families Institute, 2015).

available to opposite-sex unmarried couples. Investment in homemaking and other "relationship-specific" capital is particularly costly to unmarried couples in the event that they break up. A notable development is that the "specialization gap" between gay and lesbian partners and their opposite-sex counterparts (both married and unmarried) has been found to be smaller for more recent cohorts (Generation Y, also known as Millennials) compared to the baby boom cohort. This change is attributed to husbands' and wives' reduced specialization in nonmarket and market work as discussed in Chapter 3 and earlier in this chapter, and the expansion of legal benefits to domestic partners and states' legalization of same-sex marriage.[18]

Time Spent with Children

Given the considerable interest in how much time parents spend with their children, particularly in light of women's rising labor force participation, we now turn to these patterns. A challenging aspect of looking at this issue is that it is not clear what activities should be included.[19] For instance, is going for a walk with a child nonmarket work or leisure? Further, the nature and "quality" of time parents spend with children vary depending on what else is going on and who else is around. During some of the time parents spend with children, they are directly engaged with them, for instance, playing a game, listening to them talk about their day, or feeding or bathing them. At other times, care consists of supervising the child while engaged in another primary activity, such as cooking, cleaning, or reading the newspaper, or while the parent and child are together in the car running errands. In the latter examples, the children are not the focus of the activity, so one might be inclined to ignore this dimension of time together. Still, value may be derived from having a parent in close proximity, even when she or he is primarily focused on other activities.

Keeping these measurement difficulties in mind, Table 4-2 provides figures on how much time wives and husbands spend in childcare in households that include children. The estimates presented are for time spent in "primary" childcare activities, when the parent is actively engaged with the child, and do not include time when they are merely "available."[20] Looking at the table, it should come as no surprise that it shows that nonemployed mothers spend more time with their children than employed mothers do. However, the difference is not as great as might have been expected. For example, the data in the table indicate that employed wives with at least one preschool-age child spent three-fourths as much time directly engaged with their children as their nonemployed counterparts.[21]

---

[18]Giddings, Nunley, Schneebaum, and Zietz, "Birth Cohort and the Specialization Gap." They also point to changes in reproductive technologies (e.g., in vitro) as another factor which has served to make these families more similar to opposite-sex counterparts with children.

[19]For an excellent discussion of these issues, see Nancy Folbre and Jayoung Yoon, "What Is Child Care? Lessons from Time-Use Surveys of Major English-Speaking Countries," *Review of Economics of the Household* 5, no. 3 (September 2007): 223–48.

[20]Figures on time spent in primary childcare differ somewhat across studies depending on what specific activities are included (e.g., basic care or more); the treatment of travel time; the age, marital status, and employment status of the respondent; and the age of the children. For details on the definition used here, see the note in Table 4-2.

[21]Suzanne M. Bianchi, John P. Robinson, and Melissa A. Milkie find a roughly similar figure (63 percent) for all mothers, while other studies have found figures just over 80 percent, with the variation due to such factors as the time use survey used, whether time use is calculated based on a survey of adults' or children's time use, and the precise definition of childcare time; see their book, *Changing Rhythms of American Family Life* (New York: Russell Sage Foundation, 2006), 74–78.

| TABLE 4-2 | PARENTS' AVERAGE WEEKLY HOURS IN PRIMARY CHILDCARE, BY PRESENCE OF HOUSEHOLD CHILDREN, 2014 |

	WITH AT LEAST ONE CHILD	WITH AT LEAST ONE PRESCHOOL-AGE CHILD
Married Women	10.0	18.1
Employed	8.1	16.0
Full-Time	7.5	15.7
Not Employed	14.0	20.8
Single Women	7.6	15.3
Employed	6.8	13.8
Full-Time	5.5	10.4
Not Employed	9.4	17.9
Married Men	5.2	9.1
Wife Employed	5.5	10.2
Full-Time	5.3	10.3
Wife Not Employed	4.6	7.5

Notes: Figures are for respondents age 25–64. Singles are not cohabiting.
Childcare time refers to primary time spent with children. Figures include routine activities, reading, playing, talking, organizing, attending events, looking after child as the principal activity, and associated travel time; figures exclude time spent in activities related to children's education and health.
Employment status is measured using information on usual hours worked.
Source: Authors' calculations from the 2014 American Time Use Survey.

Suzanne Bianchi, among others, has offered a number of plausible explanations for why the difference between employed and nonemployed mothers in time spent with children is relatively modest. For one thing, a considerable fraction of employed women work less than full time, full year. In addition, even women who are employed full time may be able to juggle their schedules in order to pick their children up after school or occasionally take an afternoon off from work. Indeed, as shown in Table 4-2, time spent in childcare by mothers with a preschool-age child is about the same for mothers who are employed full time as for all employed mothers (including those who work part time), about 16 hours for both. In addition, school-age children spend a good part of their day in school, and preschool has become quite common even for children with nonemployed mothers, reducing the amount of time for mothers and children to be together even when the mother is not employed. Employed mothers also take time from their own leisure activities and even sleep to spend time with children. All these factors reduce the difference in the amount of primary time that employed mothers spend with their children compared to their nonemployed counterparts.[22] Finally, it should be kept in mind that the figures reported in Table 4-2 are for primary time spent with children. When supervisory time (that is, time spent with children while engaged in another primary activity) is included, the gap between employed and nonemployed mothers is larger.[23]

---

[22]This discussion draws on Suzanne M. Bianchi, "Maternal Employment and Time with Children: Dramatic Change or Surprising Continuity?" *Demography* 37, no. 4 (November 2000): 401–14; and Bianchi, Robinson, and Milkie, *Changing Rhythms*, chap. 4.
[23]Bianchi, Robinson, and Milkie, *Changing Rhythms*, table 4.4.

Table 4-2 also compares the amount of time that married and single mothers spend in primary activities with their children. Not surprisingly, single mothers spend somewhat less time with their children since married mothers have the advantage of a second parent in the household with whom to better coordinate schedules to allow for greater time with children. For example, the figures show that, among employed mothers with preschool-age children, single mothers spent about 2 hours less per week with their children than their married counterparts (13.8 versus 16 hours).[24]

Other research provides information on trends in parents' childcare time from 1965 through the early 2010s. Mothers' time spent in childcare fell from 1965 to 1985 as they increasingly entered the labor force, but from 1985 through the early 2010s, mothers' time in childcare rose considerably. The rise in childcare time over this latter period occurred for both single and married mothers and for those who were employed as well as the nonemployed. Since 1985, fathers (principally those in two-parent families) have also increased their time with children, both overall and in routine activities (e.g., bathing, feeding).[25] Nevertheless, as can be seen in the 2014 ATUS data shown in Table 4-2, a substantial gender gap in time spent with children remains.[26] Moreover, even in families where both parents are employed full-time, in addition to spending more time caring for their children, mothers continue to shoulder a much greater share of the management and scheduling of children's activities.[27]

There is a growing educational divide in the United States on a range of dimensions—earnings, marriage, divorce, and nonmarital fertility—as well as the topic of this section, parental time with children. Indeed, mounting evidence shows that, especially since the mid-1990s, not only do more highly educated mothers and fathers spend more time directly engaged with their children than their less-educated counterparts but this gap has grown.[28] This finding is perhaps a bit surprising in light of the fact that more highly educated parents have higher employment rates and earn higher wages, so their opportunity cost of time spent with children is higher. What

---

[24]For a more detailed analysis and discussion, see Sarah M. Kendig and Suzanne M. Bianchi, "Single, Cohabiting, and Married Mothers' Time with Children," *Journal of Marriage and Family* 70 (December 2008): 1228–40; and Liana E. Fox, Wen-Jui Han, Christopher Ruhm, and Jane Waldfogel, "Time for Children: Trends in the Employment Patterns of Parents, 1967–2009," *Demography* 50, no. 1 (February 2013): 25–49.

[25]See Suzanne M. Bianchi, "Family Change and Time Allocation in American Families," *Annals of the American Academy of Political and Social Science* 638 (November 2011): 21–44; Sandra Hofferth and Yoonjoo Lee, "Family Structure and Trends in U.S. Fathers' Time with Children, 2003-2013," *Family Science* 6, no. 1 (2015): 318–29; and KimParker and Wendy Wang, "Americans' Time at Paid Work, Housework, Child Care, 1965 to 2011," in *Modern Parenthood: Roles of Moms and Dads Converge as They Balance Work and Family* (Washington, DC: Pew Research Center, March 2013), chap.5, www .pewresearch.org.

[26]Also, while the sample size for gay and lesbian couples is small, one study finds that parents' total time with children is the same, if not higher, in gay and lesbian families as for opposite-sex married families; see Kate C. Prickett, Alexa Martin-Storey, and Robert Crosnoe, "A Research Note on Time with Children in Different- and Same-Sex Two-Parent Families," *Demography* 52, no. 3 (2015): 905–18.

[27]Pew Research Center, "Raising Kids and Running a Household: How Working Parents Share the Load," November 4, 2015, www.pewresearch.org.

[28]For evidence and discussion, see Paula England and Anjula Srivastava, "Educational Differences in US Parents' Time Spent in Child Care: The Role of Culture and Cross-Spouse Influence," *Social Science Research* 42, no. 4 (July 2013): 71-88; Jonathan Guryan, Erik Hurst, and Melissa Kearney, "Parental Education and Parental Time with Children," *Journal of Economic Perspectives* 22, no. 3 (Summer 2008): 23–46; and Shelly Lundberg and Robert A. Pollak, "Cohabitation and the Uneven Retreat from Marriage in the United States, 1950–2010," in *Human Capital in History: The American Record*, eds. Leah Platt Boustan, Carola Frydman, and Robert A. Margo (Chicago: University of Chicago Press, 2014), chap. 7.

factors might explain a positive relationship between parents' education and time with children? One possible explanation has to do with differences in the amount of available time. More educated parents are able to spend their higher earnings on outsourcing household tasks, so they can replace this time with one-on-one time with children. Less educated mothers, on the other hand, do not have the income to purchase outside help. Moreover, less educated employed mothers often have less flexible schedules, as discussed further in Chapter 16, reducing the opportunity to take time off to devote to their children. Nonetheless, explanations that center on differences in time availability and income do not appear to adequately explain the growing educational divide in time spent with children. Evidence from economists and sociologists also suggests that highly educated parents—especially highly educated mothers—have increasingly come to view one-on-one time with children as a necessary "investment" in their children, alongside formal education and extracurricular activities. Sociologist Annette Lareau has labeled this child-rearing practice "concerted cultivation."[29] Regardless of the source of these differences, they affect children's longer-term outcomes.

While fathers in two-parent families are spending more time with their children, the rise in single-parent families means that an increasing number of fathers do not live in the same household with one or more of their children. As would be expected, fathers who do not live with their children are far less likely to interact with them, whether it is feeding, bathing, or playing with children under age 5 or eating with, helping with homework, or chauffeuring children ages 5 to 18. As just one example, while virtually all children who lived with their fathers ate a meal with him over the course of a month, among children who did not live with their fathers, 43 percent of those under age 5 and 53 percent of those ages 5 to 18 did not do so.[30]

To sum up, recent trends regarding the allocation of housework and market work between husbands and wives and of childcare between parents in two-parent families are promising. Still, the unequal division of labor continues and is highly likely to adversely affect employed women, in terms of the types of jobs they take, the hours that they work, and their earnings and career trajectory. While gender differences in the allocation of time continue to reflect long-standing gender norms, a recent study found that unsupportive workplace policies (e.g., lack of adequate leave, lack of flexible hours) amplify gendered norms.[31] On the positive side, their findings suggest that work–family policy may be effective in shifting gendered preferences and, in turn, reducing inequality in the allocation of time between husbands and wives.

Finally, in looking at the allocation of time between paid work and family, it is important not to lose sight of the particular challenges confronted by employed *single* mothers. Not only do they lack a partner in the household to help manage household tasks and care for children, but they also tend to have lower-paying, less

[29]See England and Srivastava, "Educational Differences;" Guryan et al, "Parental Education;" and Lundberg and Pollak, "Cohabitation." Regarding the notion of "concerted cultivation," see Annette Lareau, *Unequal Childhoods: Class, Race, and Family Life, with an Update a Decade Later* (Berkeley and Los Angeles: University of California Press, 2011).

[30]Jo Jones and William D. Mosher, "Fathers' Involvement with Their Children: United States, 2006–2010," *National Health Statistics Reports* 71 (December 20, 2013). See also Gretchen Livingston and Kim Parker, "A Tale of Two Fathers: More Are Active, but More Are Absent," Pew Research Center, June 15, 2011, www.pewresearch.org.

[31]David S. Pedulla and Sarah Thébaud, "Can We Finish the Revolution? Gender, Work–Family Ideals, and Institutional Constraint," *American Sociological Review* 80, no. 1 (February 2015): 116–39.

flexible jobs. Policies that can assist these and other workers in balancing the dual demands of paid work and family responsibilities are discussed in Chapter 16.

Time Spent in Volunteer Work

In addition to market work and housework, many people spend an appreciable amount of time on volunteer work. **Volunteer work** is defined as tasks performed without direct reward in money or in kind that mainly benefit others rather than the individuals themselves or their immediate family. The reasons why individuals volunteer vary.[32] True altruism (or conscience), contact with congenial people, dedication to a particular cause, desire for recognition, furthering one's business, and advancing one's own or a spouse's career or the well-being of one's loved ones all may play a part. Volunteer activities may also help those who are out of the labor force, typically women, get better jobs when they reenter. Such work provides opportunities to build their human capital and expand their social and professional networks. Although experience gained in volunteer work is probably not as valuable, in general, as that acquired on the job, women with demanding family responsibilities, such as caring for young children or elderly relatives, may value the more flexible schedule, and others may appreciate the greater ability to choose the type of work they do. Even high-earner individuals volunteer considerable time and effort, which might be surprising given the high opportunity cost of their time. Economists explain this by pointing to a concept called "**warm glow**"—the utility derived from charitable giving of any form. Results from lab experiments show that spending time volunteering provides greater "warm glow" than contributing an amount of money equal to the opportunity cost of that time.[33]

The fact that volunteer work is unpaid makes it distinct from paid work. A lack of pay, however, does not mean that volunteer work is unimportant to the functioning of the economy and the well-being of others or that participation is unrelated to individuals' self-interest. For instance, much business is transacted and valuable networking occurs in informal settings, such as at local Chamber of Commerce meetings. People participate in labor unions, at least in part, to improve their own working conditions or join their symphony's volunteer association to take advantage of special benefits such as free or reduced-price concerts. They are also more likely to participate in the PTA or scouting when they have children who are involved in these activities. Further, anything that enhances life in the community influences the well-being of the individuals themselves and of their families, at least indirectly, and often the connection is fairly close.

There is also the issue of distinguishing between volunteer work and leisure activities from which individuals derive gratification. Examples would be bringing meals to a sick neighbor or taking a Brownie troop to a museum. This problem is often solved by including only organized activities, but this tends to exclude some

---

[32]For discussions, see Richard B. Freeman, "Working for Nothing: The Supply of Volunteer Labor," *Journal of Labor Economics* 15, no. 1, pt. 2 (January 1997): S140–66; John Wilson and Marc Musick, "Doing Well by Doing Good: Volunteering and Occupational Achievement among American Women," *Sociological Quarterly* 44, no. 3 (August 2003): 433–50; Franz Hackl, Martin Halla, and Gerald J. Pruckner, "Volunteering and Income—The Fallacy of the Good Samaritan?" *Kyklos* 60, no. 1 (February 2007): 77–104; and Lionel Proteau and Francois-Charles Wolff, "On the Relational Motive for Volunteer Work," *Journal of Economic Psychology*, 29 (2008): 314–35.
[33]Alexander L. Brown, Jonathan Meer, and J. Forrest Williams, "Why Do People Volunteer? An Experimental Analysis of Preferences for Time Donations," Texas A&M University (September 2016).

TABLE 4-3   PARTICIPATION RATES IN VOLUNTEER WORK, 2015[a]

	WOMEN (%)	MEN (%)	TOTAL (%)
Total	27.8	21.8	24.9
Race/Ethnicity[b]			
White	29.5	23.1	26.4
Black	21.6	16.6	19.3
Asian	20.2	15.4	17.9
Hispanic Origin	17.9	13.0	15.5
Educational Attainment[c]			
Less than HS Diploma	9.5	6.6	8.1
HS Graduate Only	17.6	13.6	15.6
Some College	29.4	23.1	26.5
College Graduate	42.4	35.0	38.8
Employment Status			
Employed Full Time	29.9	23.6	26.3
Employed Part Time	34.8	24.3	31.1
Unemployed	28.2	18.7	23.3
Not in Labor Force	23.6	18.2	21.4

Notes: Figures are computed for individuals age 16 and over for period Sept. 1, 2014–Sept. 1, 2015.
[a]Figures on volunteers count those individuals who performed unpaid volunteer activities for an organization; figures exclude informal volunteer work such as helping a neighbor.
[b]The participation figures for race/ethnicity do not sum to 100% because the figures for "other races" are not included and because a person of Hispanic origin may be of any race.
[c]Data on educational attainment are computed for those age 25 and over.
Source: US Bureau of Labor Statistics, "Volunteering in the United States-2015," *News*, USDL-16-0363 (February 25, 2016), table 1, http://www.bls.gov/news.release/volun.toc.htm.

valid volunteer activities.[34] Thus, it is not surprising that estimates of the amount of volunteer work done vary widely, depending on the definition used, the questions asked, and the respondent who answers the questions.

Table 4-3 provides figures from a national survey conducted in 2015 on time adults spent volunteering for some type of formal organization, ranging from stacking shelves at a food pantry to serving as a board member.[35] Figures would be quite a bit higher if more informal volunteer activities, such as those described earlier, were included. These data indicate that 25 percent of all adults volunteered for a formal

---

[34]It has further been suggested that volunteering for a child's school-related, extracurricular, or sports activity might be regarded as an extension of home production (albeit technically outside the home). That is, just as parents invest time helping their children with homework (which would be counted as a type of home production), this is another way of investing time in children; see Eleanor Brown and Y. Zhang, "Is Volunteer Labor Part of Household Production? Evidence from Married Couples," *Review of Economics of the Household* 11, no. 3 (September 2013): 341–69.
[35]Data on volunteering are also available from the ATUS conducted by the Bureau of Labor Statistics and can be found on its website, www.bls.gov/tus.

organization. A notable gender difference seen in the table is that women volunteer at higher rates than men. In 2015, the rates were around 28 percent for women and 22 percent for men. This gender difference is true across all race and ethnicity and education groups shown in the table. Part of the explanation for this difference is that women are more likely to be part-time workers, a group with a much higher volunteer rate, though notably, even women who are employed full-time volunteer at a somewhat higher rate than their male counterparts.

Women and men also tend to differ in the kinds of volunteer work they do. Women contribute more time to health organizations and educational institutions, while men do more voluntary work for civic and political, as well as sport and recreational, organizations. There are, however, no substantial differences in the proportions of women and men involved in social welfare organizations and religious institutions.[36]

As may be seen in the table, rates of volunteerism also differ by race and ethnicity. In 2015, the participation rate in volunteer work for whites was 26 percent, while it was only 19 percent for African Americans and 16 percent for Hispanics. The lower figures for these groups are likely explained by the fact that volunteerism is greater, on average, for more highly educated and higher-income individuals. For example, as may be seen in the table, the participation rate for volunteer work was 39 percent for college graduates, considerably higher than the rate of 8 percent for those with less than high school.

An important question is whether, and to what extent, rates of volunteerism or time spent in volunteer activities decreased with women's entry into the labor force. Regrettably, consistent data are not available to assess long-term trends in volunteering. However, it is quite telling that for both employed and nonemployed women alike, they participate in volunteer activities at higher rates than men.

Estimating the Value of Nonmarket Production

Unpaid activities like housework and at-home childcare are valuable to households and to the larger society. At present, however, these contributions are not included in US **gross domestic product (GDP)**. GDP is the total money value of all the goods and services produced by factors of production within a country over a 1-year period. The consequences of the omission of nonmarket production from GDP are potentially serious. For instance, comparisons of GDP between countries are distorted to the extent that the relative sizes of household and market sectors differ. Further, within a country, the growth in GDP is overstated if women reduce home production as they work more in the labor market, as has been the case in the United States.[37] Related to the concept of an expanded measure of GDP, economists have also sought

---

[36]Stephanie Boraas, "Volunteerism in the United States," *Monthly Labor Review* 126, no. 8 (August 2003): 3–11.

[37]These distortions have been recognized for some time. For instance, in 1946, A. C. Pigou observed that "the services rendered by women enter into the dividend [Britain's measure of GDP at the time] when they are rendered in exchange for wages . . . but do not enter into it when they are rendered by mothers or wives. . . . Thus, if a man married his housekeeper or his cook, the national dividend is diminished." This quote is cited in Statistics Canada, "Households' Unpaid Work: Measurement and Valuation," *Studies in National Accounting* (December 1995), 3. For empirical evidence on the implications for married couples, see Christopher House, John Laitner, and Dmitriy Stolyarov, "Valuing Lost Home Production of Dual Earner Couples," *International Economic Review* 49, no. 2 (May 2008): 701–36.

to develop a more comprehensive measure of family well-being that not only takes into account money income but also incorporates the value of goods and services produced in the household. Such a measure could provide a more complete picture regarding the degree of income inequality across families, both at a point in time and over time.[38]

Estimating the value of nonmarket activities, and ultimately including this value in GDP, poses a number of challenges. Many of these difficulties are well known to forensic economists—economists called upon to estimate the value of lost household services in court cases involving wrongful death and permanent injury. Such estimates were needed in the aftermath of September 11, 2001, as discussed in the "September 11th Victim Compensation Fund" box. One problem, the lack of an ongoing national US time use survey, was surmounted in 2003 with the initiation of the Bureau of Labor Statistics' ATUS. However, a number of measurement difficulties remain. For one, there is the issue of what nonmarket activities should be included in an augmented measure of GDP. As in the earlier example, should taking a walk with children be counted fully as nonmarket work, or is it partly leisure? Also, there is the issue of whether childcare time should be defined to include only one-on-one time or should include supervisory time as well.[39]

Second, and perhaps even more challenging, is the lack of agreement regarding the preferable method of placing a value on nonmarket activities.[40] There are two fundamentally different methods, each with its own advantages and drawbacks: the opportunity cost approach and the market cost approach.

Economists, for the most part, tend to use the **opportunity cost approach**, which sets the value of unpaid work equal to the income the person could have earned in the labor market. It meshes well with the theory of labor supply, which will be discussed in detail in Chapter 6, in which individuals who participate in the labor force equate the value of an hour of nonmarket time to the market wage rate. For individuals who do not participate in the labor market, the value of nonmarket time must be at least as great as their potential market wage.

However, despite its theoretical appeal, a number of difficulties arise with this approach. First, there is the nontrivial problem of estimating a potential market wage for those who are out of the labor force. Second, although the market wage is known for those who are employed, the presumption that it accurately represents the value of nonmarket time may not be correct. Many workers do not have the option of working precisely as long as they wish but must work a specified number of hours or forgo an otherwise desirable job. Hence, they may not be able to divide their time so that the value of the last hour spent at home is exactly equal to their wage rate.

In addition to these problems, although correct application of the opportunity cost approach may identify the value of the nonmarket production to individuals and their families, it results in a higher value being placed on the nonmarket production of those whose market productivity is higher. So, for example, an hour spent scrubbing floors by a college graduate is valued more highly (at the value of her or his

---

[38]Harley Frazis and Jay Stewart, "How Does Household Production Affect Measured Income Inequality?" *Journal of Population Economics* 24 (2011): 3–22.

[39]Jooyeoun Suh and Nancy Folbre, "Valuing Unpaid Child Care in the U.S.: A Prototype Satellite Account Using the American Time Use Survey," *Review of Income and Wealth* 61, no. 1 (2015): 1–17.

[40]See National Research Council, *Beyond the Market: Designing Nonmarket Accounts for the United States* (Washington, DC: National Academies Press, 2005); and Nancy Folbre, *Valuing Children* (Cambridge, MA: Harvard University Press, 2008), chap. 7.

foregone wage) than an hour spent by a high school graduate in the same activity, even when they both do the task equally well.

The main alternative to the opportunity cost approach is the **market cost approach**, which sets the value of nonmarket production equal to the cost of hiring someone to do it. One way to estimate market cost is to first determine how much time is spent on each specific activity and then to use the wages of specialists such as cooks, home decorators, chauffeurs, and even child psychologists to estimate the value of nonmarket time. This is often referred to as the **specialist method**. One concern about this method is that it is unlikely that a typical homemaker can perform all these skills as competently as a specialist. For this reason, a report by the National Research Council recommends using this approach with adjustments for quality differences.[41] A simpler alternative is to value unpaid home work at the wage of a housekeeper. Regardless of the specific market-based measure, a common criticism is that this alternative fails to capture the value of "personal and emotional care" in much nonmarket work, such as caring for one's own children, thus yielding values of nonmarket work that are too low.[42]

Despite all these difficulties, some efforts have been made in the United States to adjust standard GDP for nonmarket work. Research using figures from 2010 indicates that by ignoring nonmarket output, US GDP is underestimated by nearly 25 percent when valued using a housekeeper's wage and by as much as 44 percent when childcare is defined broadly to include supervisory care and valued using a specialist method.[43] Estimates of GDP that include the value of nonmarket output could be used to supplement existing data on GDP, or GDP could even be redefined to include the value of unpaid work, though this would raise comparability issues with past GDP data.

Finally, another question that remains is whether including the value of nonmarket work in GDP would affect the status of women as a group. Some argue that the exclusion of unpaid work from GDP brands it as "unproductive." In this view, assigning a money value to housework would improve women's status because it would increase recognition for the activities of women in the home and validate their economic contributions.[44] Others dispute this contention and believe that the inclusion of housework in GDP would not fundamentally affect the status of women because it would neither make housewives economically independent nor raise the wages of women who perform these services for pay.[45]

Looking to the future, given that other economically advanced countries are estimating adjusted measures of GDP (along with the standard measure), it is likely that the United States will continue to explore alternative approaches. In light of the many methodological challenges, however, it may be some time before a standard method is widely accepted.

---

[41]National Research Council, *Beyond the Market.*

[42]Nancy Folbre and Julie A. Nelson emphasize that some nonmarket work has a caring component. "For Love or Money—Or Both?" *Journal of Economic Perspectives* 14, no. 4 (Fall 2000): 123–40. See also Nancy Folbre, *For Love and Money* (Cambridge, MA: Russell Sage Foundation, 2012), chap. 5.

[43]Figures are from Benjamin Bridgman, Andrew Dugan, Mikhael Lal, Matthew Osborne, and Shaunda Villones, "Accounting for Household Production in the National Accounts," *Survey of Current Business* (May 2012): 23–36; and Suh and Folbre, "Valuing Unpaid Child Care in the U.S." The opportunity cost method yields the highest of all estimates; see J. Steven Landefeld, Barbara M. Fraumeni, and Cindy M. Vojtech, "Accounting for Nonmarket Production: A Prototype Satellite Account Using the American Time Use Survey," *Review of Income and Wealth* 55, no. 2 (June 2009): 205–25, table 6.

[44]See Susan Himmelweit, "The Discovery of 'Unpaid Work': The Social Consequences of the Expansion of 'Work,'" *Feminist Economics* 1, no. 2 (Summer 1995): 1–19; and Nancy Folbre, *Who Pays for the Kids? Gender and the Structures of Constraint* (London: Routledge, 1994).

[45]Barbara R. Bergmann, "The Economic Risks of Being a Housewife," *American Economic Review* 71, no. 2 (May 1981): 81–86.

The September 11th Victim Compensation Fund of 2001: Just Compensation?

The terrorist attacks that occurred in the United States on September 11, 2001, took the lives of a diverse cross section of individuals: US citizens and noncitizens; males and females; old and young; spouses, significant others, parents, and children; food workers, investment bankers, flight crews, and nonemployed persons. In some instances, more than one family member was killed. In the wake of the attacks, Congress set up a special fund called the September 11th Victim Compensation Fund of 2001 to provide some measure of financial compensation for the families of the victims. Those who accepted awards from the fund had to agree not to sue the airlines involved or the US government. The US government appointed a "special master" to be in charge of the disbursement of monies. He faced the difficult task of deciding how much compensation each family would receive within the guidelines specified by Congress. The final ruling by the special master could not be disputed. Families were eligible to receive monies for the loss of their loved ones, independent of economic considerations (to reflect the loss of enjoyment of life and to compensate for the pain and suffering their loved ones experienced during the attacks). They were also to be compensated for the "presumed economic loss" of their loved ones, which is the focus here. The final rules, promulgated March 13, 2002, reflect input from a wide array of groups, including the National Organization for Women (NOW) Legal Defense and Education Fund.*

In the Victim Compensation Fund, economic loss was computed as lost income and benefits less consumption expenditures. For those who were employed at the time of the attack, income loss was calculated as lost future earnings potential. This amount is how much they *would have* earned, given their recent earnings stream, if they had been employed until the end of their projected work life. Early on, when the fund's rules were first set forth, the value of household work was not counted as lost income for *full-time* workers, while it was estimated at "replacement value" for homemakers and part-time workers. As noted in NOW's memo to the special master, excluding the value of household services for full-time workers seriously understates women's economic contribution because many women who work full-time for pay also work a "second shift" when they get home: they make dinner and clean up, do laundry, and take care of their children's needs. Men who work full-time also do some housework, but as we have seen, they spend far less time on it than women. The final rules gave the special master the discretion to include the value of lost household services for full-time workers as well. The replacement value of lost household services was calculated using information on average weekly hours for specific activities, valued at commercial wages.** As discussed in the text, this method likely provides an overestimate of these specific services since a specialist is typically more skilled at a particular task. However, there are a number of offsetting considerations. For one, this valuation approach does not take into account the value of the "managerial" function that many wives and mothers provide.*** Further, family members offer more than just household labor; their services include a "caring" component that cannot be readily quantified.

Another concern raised in the NOW memo was that the income loss for women workers was based on their lost earnings, which may be too low as a result of gender discrimination. The final rules did not make a specific adjustment for women's earnings in this regard, nor is this adjustment presently made in tort litigation involving wrongful death or permanent injury. However, in the final rules, estimates of men's average work life were used in calculating women's as well as men's economic loss. Because men's average work life estimates are longer than women's, this factor should work to many women's advantage. In addition, to the extent that women's lower earnings are the result of greater time and effort in household activities, the inclusion of household services in the economic loss estimate addresses this concern to some extent.

Apart from issues of gender equity, other equity concerns have been raised about the methodology

continues

used by the Victim Compensation Fund. For instance, the use of labor market earnings to estimate economic loss has made many uncomfortable because this method conferred substantially higher awards to families of high-level executives than to those working in lower-level positions (though both received identical compensation for noneconomic losses). Indeed, total awards varied from $250,000 to $6 million, principally as a result of differences in estimates of economic loss. However, it should be noted that the approach followed by the fund in this regard is quite standard in other cases in which an economic value is placed on loss of life or injury.****

Some concern also focused on the difficulties that long-term unmarried partners, whether opposite-sex or same-sex, faced in obtaining awards from the fund. State law determined who could seek compensation for the loss of a loved one. In 2003, the lesbian partner of one September 11 victim received monies from the fund, so at least some precedent was set; but other unmarried partners may have been deterred by the considerably lengthier hearings process required or by the publicity.*****

This discussion of the compensation awarded to the families of the victims of September 11 points to the fact that issues related to valuing housework have important practical applications. It also highlights the considerable challenges faced by those charged with the task of estimating such values.

*This material draws on Kenneth R. Feinberg, Camille S. Biros, Jordana Harris Feldman, Deborah E. Greenspan, and Jacqueline E. Zinns, Final Report of the Special Master for the September 11th Victim Compensation Fund of 2001 (Washington, DC: US Department of Justice, 2004); and Memo from NOW Legal Defense and Education Fund to Mr. Kenneth Feinberg (February 11, 2002). For the most updated information, see "September 11th Victim Compensation Fund," accessed August 11, 2016, https://www.vcf.gov/.
**Feinberg, Biros, Feldman, Greenspan, and Zinns, Final Report, n123.
***Thomas R. Ireland, "Economic Loss in the Case of a Full Time Mother and Homemaker: When Lost Services Are the Only Pecuniary Loss," Assessing Family Loss in Wrongful Death Litigation: The Special Roles of Lost Services and Personal Consumption, ed. Thomas R. Ireland and Thomas O. Depperschmidt (Tucson, AZ: Lawyers & Judges Publishing, 1999); and Anne E. Winkler and Thomas R. Ireland, "Time Spent in Household Management: Evidence and Implications," Journal of Family and Economic Issues 30, no. 3 (September 2009): 293–304.
****Figure is from "Judge Affirms 9/11 Fund; Finds Award Process Is Fair," Newsday, May 9, 2003. See also Steven Brill, "A Tragic Calculus," Newsweek, December 31, 2001, 28; and Thomas R. Ireland and John O. Ward, Assessing Damages in Injuries and Deaths of Minor Children (Tucson, AZ: Lawyers & Judges Publishing, 2001).
*****"U.S. Awards Lesbian 9/11 Compensation for Loss of Partner," Washington Post, January 23, 2003. See also Jennifer Barrett, "Shut Out," Newsweek, February 15, 2002.

The American Family in the Twenty-First Century

Although this chapter has focused primarily on opposite-sex married-couple families, it is important to discuss to what extent this type of family is still dominant in the United States, to what extent even this type of family has changed in recent decades, and what the increasingly common alternatives to such families are. The changes that have occurred in the United States did not happen in isolation but rather as part of a wave of similar changes in other economically advanced nations. Here we provide an overview of the developments in the United States, with a more detailed examination reserved for Chapter 13 and some discussion of trends in other countries in Chapters 17 and 18.

The most fundamental shift in the family in recent years relates to what has been termed a "retreat" from marriage.[46] Marriage rates have fallen considerably, from

[46]For an excellent overview of trends and explanations, see Frank F. Furstenberg, "Fifty Years of Family Change: From Consensus to Complexity," Annals of the American Academy of Political and Social Science 654 (July 2014): 12–30.

10.6 marriages per 1,000 population in 1970 to 6.9 in 2014, alongside an increase in unmarried, opposite-sex couples, often termed *cohabitors*. As of 2013, 57 percent of women between the ages of 15 and 44 had cohabited with a person of the opposite sex at some time in their lives.[47] Further, same-sex marriage is now legal throughout the United States. The state of marriage in the United States is discussed at length in the "State of Unions" box.

In addition, as we will discuss further in Chapter 13, the once strong link between marriage and childbearing has become substantially weaker. The proportion of births to unmarried mothers increased from slightly more than 1 in 10 births in 1970 to more than 2 in 5 by 2014, though at least 50 percent of these births go home to cohabiting couples.[48] Another notable change is the considerable rise in the divorce rate from the 1970s through the 1980s, although it subsequently leveled off and has declined somewhat since then. For all of these outcomes, there is a large and growing educational divide: on average, women with less education are less likely to marry, more likely to divorce, more likely to have unmarried births, and more likely to have first births at younger ages.

One consequence of these changes is that children's living arrangements are increasingly diverse. In 1970, 85.2 percent of children under age 18 lived in a two-parent family, while that was the case for just 68.7 percent of children in 2014, as shown Table 4-4.[49] Table 4-4 provides a detailed breakdown of children's living arrangements for that year. It shows that 58.4 percent of all children lived with two biological married parents, while another 3.6 percent lived with two biological parents who were unmarried. The table further shows that 5 percent of all children lived in a blended two-parent family, that is, with a biological parent and a step-parent; and in three-fourths of such families, they lived with a biological mother and a stepfather. Another one-fourth of all children lived in single-parent families, the vast majority of which were headed by single mothers; however, single fathers constituted a small but growing share of all families (3.9 percent). Finally, nearly 4 percent lived without a parent present, most often with a grandparent.[50]

The definitions used by the US Census Bureau to categorize family structure and children's living arrangements have failed to fully keep pace with these recent demographic changes. For instance, the government defines a **family** as two or more individuals living together who are related by blood, marriage, or adoption. Under this definition, a household consisting of an unmarried couple and their own children may be counted as a single-parent family. As rates of cohabitation have increased, government statistics have become increasingly misleading regarding the extent to which children live with one parent or both, though some recent efforts are being made to adjust government statistics to these changing realities. For instance, the US Census Bureau's Supplemental Poverty Measure, which became available in 2011, includes cohabitors and their relatives in the definition of family. The official poverty measure does not. As another example, same-same sex marriage was first legalized in Massachusetts in 2004, but it is only since fall 2014 that the US Census Bureau

---

[47]Unless otherwise noted, the statistics in this section draw on the data presented in Chapter 13.

[48]The figure regarding births to cohabiting couples is from Sheela Kennedy and Larry Bumpass, "Cohabitation and Children's Living Arrangements: New Estimates from the United States," *Demographic Research* 19 (2008): 1663–92.

[49]The 1970 figure is from US Census Bureau, "Living Arrangements of Children Under 18 Years Old: 1960 to Present," table CH-1, accessed August 15, 2016, www.census.gov.

[50]These changes are documented in the media, such as Natalie Angier, "The Changing American Family," *New York Times*, November 25, 2013.

TABLE 4-4 LIVING ARRANGEMENTS OF CHILDREN UNDER AGE 18, BY PRESENCE AND TYPE OF PARENTS, 2014 (%)

	2014
Living with Two Parents	68.7
With Both Biological Parents	62.0
Married Parents	58.4
Unmarried Parents	3.6
Blended Family (at least one parent is a step-parent)	5.1
Biological Mother and Stepfather	3.9
Biological Father and Stepmother	1.2
Other Two-Parent Family[a]	1.4
Single-Parent Family	27.5
With Mother Only	23.6
With Father Only	3.9
Without a Parent Present	3.8
Total	100.0

Notes: Total may not sum to 100 due to rounding.
[a]The majority of this group are children who live with at least one adoptive parent.
Source: US Census Bureau, "Children by Presence and Type of Parent(s), Race, and Hispanic Origin: 2014," Table C9, accessed June 15, 2016, www.census.gov.

began including married same-sex couples with opposite-sex married couples rather than grouping them with cohabitors.[51]

Another notable development is that families have become increasingly multigenerational. A larger fraction of young adults than in recent decades are staying in their parents' household longer or returning to it, a trend which began prior to the Great Recession. The nature of coresidence has also changed. One study of such families found that, in 2010, parents were much more likely to be financially supporting their adult children, while, in 1960, the reverse was true: children were more likely to be supporting their parents.[52]

The demographic mix (racial and ethnic composition) of the US population has also been changing. Changes in this mix are a consequence of shifts in immigration, in terms of source countries and the number of new entrants, as well as differences in birth rates among various groups in the US-born population. Another factor contributing to the growing diversity of the population is the rise in intermarriage.

---

[51]D'Vera Cohn, "Census Says It Will Count Same-Sex Marriages, but with Caveats," Pew Research Center, May 29, 2014, www.pewresearch.org.
[52]Joan R. Kahn, Frances Goldscheider, and Javier García-Manglano, "Growing Parental Economic Power in Parent–Adult Child Households: Coresidence and Financial Dependency in the United States, 1960–2010," *Demography* 50, no. 4 (2013): 1449–75. For figures, see Richard Fry, "More Millennials Living with Family Despite Improved Job Market," Pew Research Center, July 29, 2015, www.pewresearch.org. Another way that families are becoming more multigenerational is that a growing number of children are living in households that include grandparents; see Renee R. Ellis and Tavia Simmons, *Coresident Grandparents and Their Grandchildren*, US Census Bureau Report P20-576 (October 2014).

TABLE 4-5 DEMOGRAPHIC MAKEUP OF THE US POPULATION (%) 1990 AND 2015		
	1990	**2015**
Race Categories		
White	80.3	77.1
Black or African American	12.1	13.3
Asian	2.8	5.6
American Indian or Alaska Native	0.8	1.2
Native Hawaiian and Other Pacific Islander	0.1	0.2
Other[a]	3.9	n.a.
Two or More Races[b]	n.a.	2.6
Total	100.0	100.0
Ethnicity		
Hispanic	9.0	17.6
Non-Hispanic	91.0	82.4
Total	100.0	100.0
White, Non-Hispanic	75.6	61.6

Notes: In the US Census, race and ethnicity are separate categories; persons of Hispanic origin may be of any race.
[a]The 1990 survey included the option of checking "other race" and writing in a response; this category included multiethnic, multiracial, as well as some responses regarding Hispanc origin. While "other race" remained an option on the 2015 survey, the Census subsequently assigned these responses to one of the other race categories, as shown in the table.
[b]Starting with the 2000 census, individuals may select more than one race. This was not an option in 1990.
n.a. = not applicable.
Sources: US Census Bureau, "Race and Hispanic Origin," table 3, *1990 Census of Population: General Population Characteristics, United States*, accessed August 21, 2016, www.census.gov; and US Census Bureau, "Annual Estimates of the Resident Population by Sex, Race, and Hispanic Origin for the United States, and Counties: April 1, 2010 to July 1, 2015," accessed August 21, 2016, http://factfinder.census.gov.

Since the *Loving v. Virginia* Supreme Court decision of 1967, intermarriage across racial lines has been permitted in all US states, having been illegal in 16 states at that time. Estimates vary somewhat, but one recent study estimates that 15 percent of new marriages in 2010 were between spouses of different races or ethnicities, up from 7 percent in 1980.[53]

Table 4-5, which provides figures on the demographic makeup of the United States for 1990 and 2015, illustrates the impact of these changes. (In viewing the information in this table, it is important to keep in mind that the Census Bureau categorizes ethnicity – whether of Hispanic origin or Latino – separately from race.) Over this 25-year period, the share of the population identifying as Hispanic nearly doubled from 9 percent to 17.6 percent. The table also shows a rise in the share of Asians from 2.8 percent to 5.6 percent and a slight rise in the share of African

---

[53]This figure is from "The Rise of Intermarriage: Rates, Characteristics Vary by Race and Gender," Pew Research Center, February 16, 2012, www.pewresearch.org.

Americans, from 12.1 percent to 13.3 percent. There was a corresponding decline in the white non-Hispanic population, from 76 percent to 62 percent. In contrast, the share of the population that is white declined only slightly, from 80 percent to 77 percent, because it includes persons of Hispanic origin who select this race category. A majority of Hispanics self-identify as white, and the Hispanic share of the population has increased considerably.[54] Further indicative of changing demographics, July 2015 marked the first time that just slightly over 50 percent of all infants (children under age 1) were ethnic or racial minorities.[55]

With changes in the demographic composition of the United States, the US Census Bureau has periodically made changes to the racial and ethnic categorizations used in the decennial census and other government surveys.[56] For instance, prior to the 2000 census (as shown by the 1990 data in Table 4-5), individuals were limited to choosing a single category from the following race groups: white, black or African American, Asian, American Indian or Alaska native, Native Hawaiian or Other Pacific Islander, or "some other race."[57] A major criticism of this survey design was that individuals of multiracial backgrounds were forced to "check one box." Since the 2000 census, individuals may select as many of these categories as apply, rather than being restricted to choosing a single race. As shown in Table 4-5, 2.6 percent of individuals selected two or more races in 2015.[58]

The racial and ethnic categories may again undergo change. As the Census Bureau looks toward the 2020 census, it is considering a new combined race–ethnicity question because it has been found that persons of Hispanic origin are often unsure what category to choose when responding to the separate race question.[59] Some researchers argue that while this type of effort is a step in the right direction, these survey questions need more substantial revision to accurately and meaningfully capture the diversity of the US population.[60]

The previous discussion suggests that the American family in the early twenty-first century is rather different from that of the 1950s' characterization of an invariably white family, comprised of a homemaker-wife and breadwinner-husband with two

---

[54]Over 50 percent of persons of Hispanic origin identified their race as white in the 2010 census, while another one-third selected "some other race"; see Karen R. Humes, Nicholas A. Jones, and Roberto R. Ramirez, "Overview of Race and Hispanic Origin: 2010", *2010 US Census Briefs* C2010BR-02 (Washington, DC: US Census Bureau, March 2011). Also, research finds that the fraction of Hispanics who describe themselves as white is rising; see D'Vera Cohn, "Millions of Americans Changed their Racial or Ethnic Identity From One Census to the Next," Pew Research Center, May 5, 2014, www.pewresearch.org.

[55]D'vera Cohn, "It's Official: Minority Babies Are the Majority among the Nation's Infants, But Only Just," Pew Research Center, June 23, 2016, www.pewresearch.org. For an in-depth discussion, see Pew Research Center, "Race and Multiracial Americans in the U.S. Census," in *Multiracial in America: Proud, Diverse and Growing in Numbers*, June 11, 2015, chap. 1, www.pewresearch.org.

[56]For a graphical illustration of how Census Bureau categorizations changed from 1790 (the first census) to 2010, see US Census Bureau, "Measuring Race and Ethnicity across the Decades: 1790 to 2010," accessed July 26, 2016, www.census.gov.

[57]In 1990, as shown in Table 4-5, 3.9 percent of individuals chose "some other race," which permitted them to write in a response; write-in responses included "multiracial" and "multi-ethnic," as well as Hispanic ethnicities (although Hispanic ethnicity is a separate survey question).

[58]Individuals were still permitted to choose "some other race" and write in a response, as in 1990. In Table 4-5, this category is "NA" because the Census Bureau reassigned these responses to one of the other race categories, including "two or more races." See Humes, Jones, and Ramirez, "Overview of Race."

[59]For further discussion of this issue, see Pew Research Center, "Race and Multiracial Americans"; Sowmiya Ashok, "The Rise of the American 'Others,'" *Atlantic*, August 27, 2016; and Ana Gonzalez-Barrera and Mark Hugo Lopez, "Is Being Hispanic a Matter of Race, Ethnicity or Both?" Pew Research Center, June 15, 2015, www.pewresearch.org.

[60]For a detailed critique and a proposal, see Kenneth Prewitt, *What Is "Your" Race? The Census and Our Flawed Efforts to Classify Americans* (Princeton, NJ: Princeton University Press, 2014).

or three children and a dog as immortalized in television, movies, and American lore. A historical perspective indicates that this family was, to some extent, a demographic aberration. In fact, fertility rates were lower and the average age of marriage was higher in earlier times than in the 1950s, and divorce was, even then, by no means unheard of.[61] And racial and ethnic diversity existed at that time as well. Nonetheless, without a doubt, there has been substantial change in both how people live and how they make a living. These issues will be discussed further in subsequent chapters.

The State of Unions in the United States

During the last few years, it has been hard to read a newspaper or a magazine that does not have at least one article on some aspect of marriage. Part of the reason for this is that strengthening marriage has come to be viewed by some as an important solution to many of America's ills.* For instance, as discussed in Chapter 14, a number of academic studies, though not all, show that children do better in married families with both biological parents present than in single-parent families. Some people also advocate marriage as a potential antipoverty solution, as discussed further in Chapter 15. Finally, marriage has made headlines as gay and lesbian couples sought to have the same rights and privileges as opposite-sex couples. These efforts, bolstered by a dramatic change in public opinion, culminated in the Supreme Court decision that legalized same-sex marriage in all states in June 2015. In this box, we discuss the state of marriage as of 2016.

The US federal government and many state governments began actively promoting marriage (to opposite-sex couples) starting in the mid-1990s. For instance, a goal of the 1996 federal welfare legislation was to "encourage the formation and maintenance of two-parent families." Subsequently, in 2006 and then again in 2011, the federal government

reaffirmed its commitment to this goal, providing $150 million per year in grants toward efforts to promote marriage and responsible fatherhood.** These funds support activities including premarital education, mentoring, and parenting. Also with the goal of promoting marriage, several states, including Louisiana, Arizona, and Arkansas, enacted laws permitting an alternative, stricter form of marriage called "covenant marriage." Couples who choose to enter a covenant marriage must obtain marriage counseling prior to marrying, seek counseling if their marriage is in trouble, and provide a specific reason for divorce.*** At the federal level, changes were made in the individual income tax in the early 2000s to somewhat alleviate marriage penalties in the tax code. This policy change receives further attention in Chapter 15.

Turning to same-sex marriage, in 1996, the US Congress passed the **Defense of Marriage Act (DOMA)**, which defined marriage as the "legal union between one man and one woman" and defined a spouse as a husband or wife of the opposite sex. The act also specified that if a state were to permit same-sex marriage, other states did not have to provide legal recognition of such unions. Under DOMA, even same-sex couples who lived in a state that

continues

---

[61]Andrew J. Cherlin, "American Marriage in the Early Twenty-First Century," *The Future of Children* 15, no. 2 (Autumn 2005): 33–55; and Catherine A. Fitch and Steven Ruggles, "Historical Trends in Marriage Formation: The United States 1850–1990," in *The Ties That Bind: Perspectives on Marriage and Cohabitation*, ed. Linda Waite (New York: Aldine de Gruyter, 2000), 59–90.

legalized gay marriage were not eligible for federal benefits as married couples or spouses under federal programs such as Social Security. Reasons against same-sex marriage ranged from religious ones to the argument that it would diminish the significance of marriage and, in turn, reduce marriage rates.****

At the state level, states followed very different paths, though broad public sentiment in favor of same-sex marriage was generally rising, especially among younger cohorts. In 2000, Vermont was the first state to permit **civil unions** (a legal arrangement that provided same-sex couples with the same set of state rights as married couples without the label of "marriage"), while other states such as Oregon and Nevada recognized domestic partnerships, which was a step in the same direction. In 2004, Massachusetts became the first state to legalize same-sex marriage. By June 2013, 12 states and the District of Columbia had extended marriage to gay and lesbian couples. Moreover, as of that time, a majority—55 percent—of Americans favored same-sex marriage.***** Still, considerable opposition remained, as reflected by the fact that by this same date more than one-half of states had passed constitutional amendments to ban it.

The Supreme Court ruled on the first of two landmark decisions regarding same-sex marriage in June 2013. In *United States v. Windsor*, the court struck down DOMA, which meant that same-sex couples who were married in states that legalized same-sex marriage were now entitled to the same federal benefits as their opposite-sex married-couple counterparts living in the same state. While the court's decision in *Windsor* focused on the issue of whether the federal government was required to recognize state-level decisions on same-sex marriage, the language of the decision emphasized the dignity of same-sex relationships and the harm families in such relationships suffered from same-sex marriage bans. Over the next 2 years, the number of states allowing same-sex marriage increased from 12 (plus the District of Columbia) to 36 (plus the District of Columbia), most implemented under court order, with only 14 states with bans in place. Then, in June 2015, the Supreme Court ruled in *Obergefell v. Hodges* that same-sex marriage was legal in all states, thereby overturning the remaining state bans. In making this ruling, the United States joined nearly two dozen other countries, largely located in western Europe, which already permitted same-sex marriage******

*See, for instance, Wade F. Horn, "Wedding Bell Blues: Marriage and Welfare Reform," Brookings Review 19, no. 3 (Summer 2001): 3–42.
**See Administration of Children and Families, "Healthy Marriage and Responsible Fatherhood," accessed February 24, 2017, https://www.acf.hhs.gov/ofa/programs/healthy-marriage.
***Amanda J. Felkey, "Will You Covenant Marry Me? A Preliminary Look at a New Type of Marriage," Eastern Economic Journal 37 (2011): 367–89.
****Marcus Dillender investigated this argument but found no empirical support; see "The Death of Marriage?

The Effects of New Forms of Legal Recognition on Marriage Rates in the United States," Demography 51, no. 2 (April 2014): 561–85.
*****Pew Research Center, "Changing Attitudes on Gay Marriage," July 29, 2015, www.pewresearch.org.
******For a timeline of legalization by US states and information on legalization worldwide, see "A Timeline of Same-Sex Marriage in the United States," Boston Globe, January 9, 2016; and Pew Research Center, "Gay Marriage Around the World," June 26, 2015, www.pewresearch.org.

Conclusion

In this chapter, we have seen that, with women's rising labor force participation and the growth in dual-earner couples, the gender difference in the allocation of time in nonmarket work between husbands and wives has narrowed somewhat. The reduction in the gender difference in time spent in housework is largely a result of wives spending less time in this activity and, to a much lesser extent, husbands spending more time in it. Most noticeable is the increase in married fathers' time spent in childcare, not just in fun activities but in more routine tasks as well. Nonetheless, the situation is still far from equal. Looking forward, unless major changes take place in the availability and affordability of childcare and elder care and in the attitudes of men and women, women are likely to continue to shoulder the bulk of home responsibilities for quite some time.

Recent governmental efforts to collect time use data not only have illuminated gender differences in nonmarket work but also offer the opportunity to construct estimates of the value of time individuals spend in this activity. As we have seen, GDP is estimated to be considerably higher when the value of nonmarket work is included. Such estimates are an important reminder that much valuable economic activity is performed in the household, even if not reflected in standard government statistics.

Finally, this chapter pointed to important changes in the American family including the shift away from marriage and the rise in the fraction of unmarried births, though at least one-half of these births are to cohabiting couples. We also looked at the changing demographic makeup of the United States. In the next chapters, we will see that labor market outcomes differ considerably, not only by gender but also by race and ethnicity.

Questions for Review and Discussion

1. For a long time, economists did not include housework in their analyses. In what respect was this omission justified or not justified?

2. Why have women been so eager to increase their participation in the labor market, and why have men been so reluctant to increase their participation in housework?

3. Clearly nonmarket production has some value. Discuss the merits of estimating its value.

4. It is frequently pointed out that each method of valuing nonmarket production is far from perfect. Explain what the main advantages and deficiencies of each method are.

Internet-Based Data Exercise

Note: In doing this exercise, students should be aware that the precise names of documents and their location with a website may change over time. Visit the home of the American Time Use Survey (ATUS) at http://www.bls.gov/tus/. Read the ATUS FAQs.

1. To get a sense of how the ATUS time diary works, document how you spent your time during a prior weekday, from 1 p.m. to 7 p.m., using 15-minute blocks of time. (So, for instance, on a Tuesday, you would document how you spent your time on Monday from 10 a.m. to 10:15 a.m., etc.) Report on one activity during each time period. (The one exception, as in the ATUS, is that you can report secondary [supervisory] childcare time that occurs concurrently with another activity.) The final step is to convert your specific activities into the *narrow* categories outlined in Table A-1. For instance, if you did chores like cleaning

your house, this would be categorized as "housework," not the broad category "Household Activities."

a. Create a table (clearly labeled and sourced) of your time estimates. Compare your time estimates with those in Table A-1. Discuss the differences and the reasons for them. (And if you have an opportunity, compare your estimates with those of classmates.)

b. What specific issues did you encounter in completing the diary in terms of recall, multitasking, classification of activities, etc. What does your experience mean for time use data surveys?

Suggested Readings

Abraham, Katharine G., and Christopher Mackie, eds. *Beyond the Market: Designing Nonmarket Accounts for the United States*. Washington, DC: National Research Council, 2005.

Bianchi, Suzanne M., John P. Robinson, and Melissa A. Milkie. *Changing Rhythms of American Family Life*. New York: Russell Sage Foundation, 2006.

Cherlin, Andrew J. *The Marriage-Go-Round: The State of Marriage and the Family in America Today*. New York: Knopf, 2009.

Folbre, Nancy. *For Love and Money*. New York: Russell Sage Foundation, 2012.

Frey, William H. *Diversity Explosion: How New Racial Demographics Are Remaking America*. Washington, DC: Brookings Institution Press, 2014.

Furstenberg, Frank F. "Fifty Years of Family Change: From Consensus to Complexity." *Annals of the American Academy of Political and Social Science* 654 (July 2014): 12–30.

Hamermesh, Daniel S. "Time Use." *NBER Reporter*, no. 2 (2012).

Juster, F. Thomas, Hiromi Ono, and Frank P. Stafford. "An Assessment of Alternative Measures of Time Use." *Sociological Methodology* 33 (2003): 19–54.

Prewitt, Kenneth. *What Is "Your" Race? The Census and Our Flawed Efforts to Classify Americans*. Princeton, NJ: Princeton University Press, 2014.

Key Terms

American Time Use Survey (ATUS) (67)

volunteer work (75)

warm glow (75)

gross domestic product (GDP) (77)

opportunity cost approach (78)

market cost approach (79)

specialist method (79)

family (82)

Defense of Marriage Act (DOMA) (86)

civil union (87)

5

The Labor Force: Definitions and Trends

CHAPTER HIGHLIGHTS

- ■ The Labor Force: Some Definitions
- ■ Trends in Labor Force Participation
- ■ Trends in Labor Force Attachment of Women
- ■ Trends in Hours Worked
- ■ Trends in Gender Differences in Unemployment

The rapid growth in women's labor force participation is one of the most significant economic and social developments in the post–World War II period, in the United States and elsewhere. One reason for our interest in women's participation trends is that they underlie the transformation in gender roles that has occurred in much of the world in recent years. However, other reasons also motivate our examination of women's labor force participation.

First, the economic well-being of women and their families is significantly influenced by women's participation in the labor force and their earnings levels, given participation. Such issues have increased in importance with the rising incidence of female-headed families and the growing dependence of married-couple families on the contributions of employed wives. Second, the family bargaining models reviewed in Chapter 3 suggest that, in married-couple families, women's participation in the labor force and their level of earnings while employed affect their bargaining power and thereby the distribution of resources within marriage. This is likely the case among cohabiting couples as well. Third, changes in participation rates are of importance for women's wages in that they influence the average levels of labor market experience of women and, as we shall see in Chapter 9, experience is an important determinant of wages.

In this chapter, we first review the definitions of a number of labor force concepts and then summarize trends over time in female and male labor force participation and compare these trends across race and ethnic groups. Over the long term, that is from 1890 to the present, while female participation rates increased dramatically, male rates declined, albeit not as dramatically. As a consequence of changes, men's and women's labor force participation rates and their patterns of involvement in market work over the life cycle are becoming increasingly similar.

We also examine trends in gender differences in unemployment, a particularly prominent issue in the aftermath of the **Great Recession**, which began in December 2007 and ended in June 2009.[1] The Great Recession was the most severe downturn the United States had experienced since the Great Depression and was followed by a prolonged period of high unemployment and lower labor force participation. Even as late as 2012, for example, unemployment hovered in the 8 percent range. The unemployment rate did subsequently decline, averaging 5.3 percent in 2015.

In the next chapter, we develop some economic concepts for analyzing the labor supply decision and use them to provide a better understanding of the reasons for the remarkable influx of women into the labor market, as well as some of the other trends identified in this chapter.

The Labor Force: Some Definitions

Each month, the US Census Bureau conducts a survey to gather statistics on the labor force. These statistics are collected for the civilian noninstitutional population over age 16; thus, they exclude individuals who are in the active-duty military as well as those who are incarcerated[2] or in other institutions such as nursing homes. According to the official definition, the **labor force** includes all individuals 16 years of age and over who worked for pay or profit during the reference week or actively sought paid employment during the 4 weeks prior to the reference week. That is, the labor force is comprised of both the *employed* and the *unemployed*. Individuals who are neither employed nor unemployed are classified as **out of the labor force**.

The **employed** group includes all those who worked 1 hour per week or more as paid employees or were self-employed in their own business or profession or on their own farm. This definition includes those who worked **part-time**, fewer than 35 hours per week, as well as those who worked **full-time**, 35 hours or more. It also includes all those temporarily absent from paid employment because of bad weather, vacation, family leave, labor–management disputes, or personal reasons, whether or not they were paid. An exception to the emphasis on paid employment is that those who worked at least 15 hours as unpaid workers in an enterprise operated by a family member are also included.[3] The **unemployed** include those who do not have a job

---

[1]National Bureau of Economic Research, "US Business Cycle Expansions and Contractions," accessed February 21, 2017, http://www.nber.org/cycles/cyclesmain.html.

[2]US incarceration rates have been increasing, and there is a disproportionate incidence of incarceration among low-skilled black men; see Becky Pettit, *Invisible Men: Mass Incarceration and the Myth of Black Progress* (New York: Russell Sage Foundation, 2012).

[3]The labor force excludes people engaged in illegal activities such as prostitution and drug trafficking. Furthermore, employment ranging from babysitting to yard work, which is paid in cash and not reported for tax purposes (the so-called underground economy), is likely to be underreported in labor force statistics.

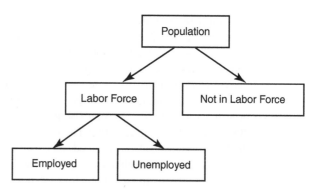

FIGURE 5-1 An Illustration of Labor Force Definitions

but who have made specific efforts to find a job within the past 4 weeks, as well as those not working but waiting to be called back to work or to report for a new job within 30 days. The relationships among these labor force concepts are illustrated in Figure 5-1.

The **labor force participation rate** of a particular group is equal to the number of its members who are in the labor force divided by the total number of the group in the population. Thus, for example, a labor force participation rate of 60 percent for women means that 60 percent of women 16 years of age and over are in the labor force. The **unemployment rate** of a particular group is equal to the number of individuals who are classified as unemployed divided by the size of the relevant labor force. An unemployment rate of 5 percent for women, for example, means that 5 percent of women who are in the labor force are unemployed.

A careful reading of the definition of the labor force makes it clear that being in the labor force is not synonymous with working. Individuals who work fewer than 15 hours a week as unpaid family workers and those who do only unpaid work in the household or as volunteer workers—no matter how many hours—are excluded. On the other hand, persons temporarily not working, or unemployed, are included in the labor force. In large part, this results from the emphasis in the official definition of the labor force on being employed in or actively seeking *market* work. Because women have tended to have primary responsibility for nonmarket work, they constitute a high proportion in the categories that are left out. Thus, as we saw in Chapter 4, their share of the labor force considerably understates their share of work. This was particularly true in earlier days when family enterprises were more common and when most married women were homemakers. Despite these reservations, women's labor force participation rate is an important indicator of women's status in a market economy.

Although the unemployment rate provides an important indicator of the health of the economy, it is an incomplete tool for fully assessing either economic hardship for workers or the loss of output for the economy. Measured unemployment rates fail to include individuals who would like a job but did not look for work during the prior 4 weeks. Instead, they are among those classified as out of the labor force. For this reason, the Bureau of Labor Statistics also provides supplemental data on alternative measures of labor market difficulty and underutilization that are broader than the official unemployment rate and include some individuals who are otherwise classified as not in the labor force. **Marginally attached workers** are those who are not currently working or looking for work but indicate that they want and are available for a job and have searched for work sometime in the last year (though not in the last 4 weeks). Marginally attached workers are considered to be the most likely individuals to resume their search and reenter the labor market when the economy picks up. **Discouraged workers** are a subset of marginally attached workers who specifically state that their reason for being out of the labor force is that they do not think labor market opportunities are available for them given their skills or express concerns about labor market discrimination.

The unemployment rate also fails to provide information about underemployed workers. One type of **underemployment** occurs when workers have to take jobs for which they are clearly overqualified. Examples would be an MBA taking a job as a sales clerk or a skilled automobile mechanic working as a janitor. Another type of underemployment occurs when individuals would prefer to work full-time but can only find part-time work. Individuals in this situation are classified as **part time for economic reasons** or sometimes called **involuntary part-time workers**.

Because the unemployment rate is so sensitive to the definition of who is counted among the unemployed, some economists also rely on broader measures of joblessness that include marginally attached workers and, in some cases, involuntary part-time workers, in addition to those officially classified as unemployed. This information is provided in government statistics on a supplemental basis along with the official unemployment rate.

A few other definitions are also used in this chapter and throughout the text. A **year-round** (or **full-year**) **worker** is defined as an individual who works 50 or more weeks per year (including paid vacation, etc.). Thus, a **full-time, year-round worker** is an individual employed 35 or more hours per week for 50 or more weeks per year. Often we are also interested in studying the behavior of individuals who are, for the most part, past college-going and in the preretirement years. These individuals are referred to as being of **prime working age**, typically defined as ages 25 to 54.

Trends in Labor Force Participation

In this section we review trends in female and male labor force participation rates and obtain an overview of just how substantial these changes have been, particularly for women. In the next chapter, we discuss the reasons for the observed changes.

Broad Labor Force Trends by Gender: 1890 to Present

Table 5-1 shows trends in labor force participation rates for selected years from 1890 to the present based on official government data.[4] As discussed at length in Chapter 2, the labor force participation rate for women reported for 1890 is arguably an underestimate because the official data for that year undercount the productive activity of women, particularly when they worked within the home and in family farms and

---

[4]We begin with 1890 because, until that year, census data contained few tabulations of the labor force participation and occupations of women. We omit 1910 because data on the labor force participation of women from the 1910 census are not comparable to other years. See Claudia Goldin, *Understanding the Gender Gap: An Economic History of American Women* (New York: Oxford University Press, 1990).

enterprises. Therefore, although Table 5-1 appears to suggest a continuous increase in female labor force participation since 1890, economic historian Claudia Goldin argues that women's labor force participation was more likely U-shaped, with the low point for women's labor force participation occurring around the 1920s.[5] Nonetheless, the official statistics are meaningful in that they track women's participation in market work outside the home fairly well, and, as we discussed in Chapter 2, work for pay outside the home particularly contributes to the status of women. In this chapter, we focus on the *official* statistics.

Prior to 1940, the increase in women's labor force participation was relatively slow. However, starting around 1940, female labor force participation rates began a strong, steady increase that continued over the next 50 years—see Table 5-1 and Figure 5-2. In 1940, 28 percent of women were in the labor force; by 1995, the figure had risen to nearly 60 percent and remained at roughly that level, before declining somewhat in the wake of the Great Recession.[6] Nonetheless, in 2015, female participation rates remained substantial at 57 percent, and nearly three-quarters of women between the ages of 25 and 54 were in the labor force. Overall, women constituted 47 percent of the labor force, up from 25 percent in 1940.

Table 5-1 also indicates the sizable effect that the mobilization for World War II had on female labor force participation. As men left their civilian jobs to join the armed forces, women entered the labor force in unprecedented numbers. Between 1940 and 1945, the female participation rate increased from 28 to 36 percent, a very substantial increase in such a short period of time. As suggested by the 1947 figure, some decline occurred in the immediate post–World War II period, but the upward trend in female participation quickly resumed and, as we have seen, continued through the mid-1990s.

In contrast to the long-term increase in labor force participation for women, Table 5-1 and Figure 5-2 show a decrease in male participation rates since the 1950s. While this trend has been less dramatic than the rise for women, its cumulative effects have been sizable, with male participation rates decreasing from 86 percent in 1950 to 73 percent in 2007 and 69 percent in 2015, with the sizable post-2007 dip again partly reflecting the effects of the Great Recession and its aftermath.

As a consequence of the opposing long-term trends in participation for women and men, the *difference* between the female and male participation rates has decreased sharply from 55 percentage points in 1940 to 12 percentage points in 2015. This growing *convergence* in female and male participation rates in the post–World War II period is illustrated in Figure 5-2.

Labor Force Trends by Race/Ethnicity

We gain a more in-depth picture of labor force participation patterns by examining them separately for different subgroups. Table 5-2 shows the trends in labor force participation since 1955 by race and Hispanic origin for years in which data are available.

---

[5]Claudia Goldin, "The U-Shaped Female Labor Force Function in Economic Development and Economics History," in *Investment in Women's Human Capital*, ed. T. Paul Schultz (Chicago: University of Chicago Press, 1995), 61–90.

[6]Caution must be taken in fully attributing the post-2007 decline in both women's and men's labor force participation rates to the Great Recession because the timing of the recession coincided with the start of the retirement of the enormous baby boom cohort. It also reflects a continuation of a longer-term decline in participation rates of prime-age women and, particularly, men; see Council of Economic Advisers, "The Labor Force Participation Rate since 2007: Causes and Policy Implications" (Washington, DC: White House, July 2014), https://obamawhitehouse.archives.gov.

| TABLE 5-1 | LABOR FORCE PARTICIPATION RATES OF MEN AND WOMEN, 1890–2015 |

YEAR	PERCENT OF MEN IN THE LABOR FORCE	PERCENT OF WOMEN IN THE LABOR FORCE
1890	84.3	18.2
1900	85.7	20.0
1920	84.6	22.7
1930	82.1	23.6
1940	82.5	27.9
1945	87.6	35.8
1947	86.8	31.5
1950	86.4	33.9
1960	83.3	37.7
1970	79.9	43.3
1980	77.4	51.5
1990	76.4	57.5
2000	74.8	59.9
2007	73.2	59.3
2010	71.2	58.6
2015	69.1	56.7

Notes: Based on the total population prior to 1950 and the civilian population thereafter. Rates are for individuals 14 years of age and over before 1947 and 16 years and over thereafter.

Sources: US Department of Commerce, Bureau of the Census, *Historical Statistics of the United States Colonial Times to 1970, Bicentennial Edition, Part 1,* 1975, 131–32; and *Employment and Earnings,* various issues.

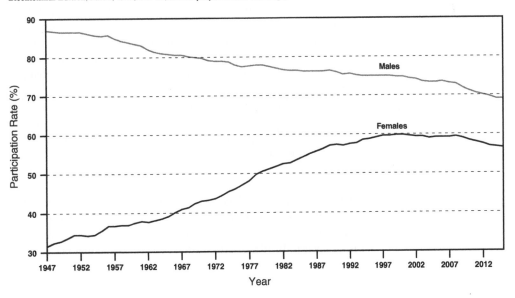

FIGURE 5-2 Trends in Female and Male Labor Force Participation Rates, 1947–2015

Source: Labor Force Statistics from the Current Population Survey available at www.bls.gov; and *Employment & Earnings,* various issues.

TABLE 5-2 LABOR FORCE PARTICIPATION RATES OF MEN AND WOMEN BY RACE AND HISPANIC ORIGIN, 1955–2015 (%)

YEAR	WHITES	BLACKS	HISPANICS	ASIANS
Men				
1955	85.4	85.0	n.a.	n.a.
1975	78.7	70.9	80.7	n.a.
1995	75.7	69.0	79.1	73.6[a]
2015	69.7	63.8	76.2	71.4
Women				
1955	34.5	46.1	n.a.	n.a.
1975	45.9	48.8	43.1	n.a.
1995	59.0	59.5	52.6	58.6[a]
2015	56.2	59.7	55.7	55.2

[a]Data are for 1996.

n.a. = not available

Notes: Civilian labor force includes population aged 16 and over. Hispanics may be of any race. For 2000 and beyond, data on whites are for white, non-Hispanics. Prior to 1975, other nonwhites are included with blacks. Prior to 2005, Pacific Islanders are included with Asians. Prior to 2005, persons who reported more than one race (white, black, or Asian) were included in the group they identified as the main race. Subsequently, whites, blacks, and Asians are defined as persons who selected this race group only; persons who selected more than one race group are not included.

Sources: US Department of Labor, Bureau of Labor Statistics, *Working Women: A Databook*, 1977, 44–45; US Department of Labor, *Handbook of Labor Statistics* (August 1989), 25–30; US Department of Labor, *Employment and Earnings* (various issues); and unpublished data from the Bureau of Labor Statistics. Asian data for 1996 are from US Census Bureau, Current Population Survey, available at http://www.census.gov/

Table 5-2 indicates that, over the long term, participation rates have risen for all groups of women except Asians (for whom we have data starting only in the mid-1990s) and that participation rates have increased substantially more for whites than for blacks.[7] Thus, while African American women traditionally had far higher labor force participation rates than white women, other data indicate that the black–white gap in participation had closed by the mid-1980s. Black women's participation again drew ahead of that of white women in the late 1990s due to a substantial increase in their participation rate during that time and remains slightly higher today. In contrast, Hispanic women's participation rates are consistently lower than those of white women in all years, although only slightly so in 2015. And, for years when data are available, Asian women's participation rate is about the same as or slightly lower than that of white women.

In looking at trends in labor force participation rates by race for men, we see that rates for both whites and blacks have fallen considerably since 1955, but the decline has been far more precipitous for black men, a policy concern that is discussed further in Chapter 6. In 1955, participation rates for white and black men were roughly

---

[7]The focus here is on long-term trends, but as we saw for overall labor force participation rates, rates declined slightly for all groups starting in 2007.

equal at 85 percent, while today the rate for blacks, at 64 percent, is considerably below the 70 percent rate for whites. In contrast, Hispanic men are much more likely to be in the labor force than white men, and Asian men's labor participation rates are slightly higher than those of white men.

Labor Force Trends over the Life Cycle

The growth in female labor force participation that has occurred since World War II has been accompanied by pronounced changes in the patterns of women's employment over the life cycle. This is illustrated in Figure 5-3, which shows women's participation rates by age. Before 1940, the typical female worker was young and single; most women tended to leave the labor force permanently upon marriage and childbearing. As Figure 5-3 shows, at that time, the peak age-specific participation rate occurred among women 20 to 24 years of age and declined for each successive age group after that.[8]

Over the next 20 years, older married women with school-age or grown children entered or reentered the labor force in increasing numbers, while little change occurred in the labor force participation rates of women between the ages of 20 and 34, who were more likely to have preschool-age children at home. These trends generated the M-shaped or double-peaked pattern shown for 1960 in the figure. As a result of the entry of older married women, the proportion of women workers who were married increased from 30 percent in 1940 to 54 percent in 1960. The World War II experience may have played a part in encouraging this shift in the behavior of married women because during the war, for the first time, large numbers of older married women worked outside the home.

Between 1960 and 1980, participation rates increased for all age groups of women; however, particularly notable was the increase in participation rates for women aged 20 to 34, which had not previously risen. The rise in participation rates for this group in part reflected declines in the birth rate and increases in the divorce rate over this period. Most notable, however, was the large increase in the participation rates of married women with small children. Among married women with children under 6 years old, only 19 percent worked outside the home in 1960 compared to 45 percent in 1980.

Looking at the age profile for 2000 (when many age groups attained their maximum rates), we see gains in labor force participation relative to 1980 for all women aged 20 and older. Subsequently, between 2000 and 2015, the profile shifted downward for all age groups under age 55, especially for teens. Nonetheless, in 2015 participation rates for women aged 25 and over remained high relative to 1980. Consistent with this trend, 61 percent of married mothers of children under 6 worked outside the home in 2015 compared to 45 percent in 1980. It used to be exceptional for women with small children to work outside the home, but now it is the norm.

As a result of these changes, the pattern of age-specific participation rates among women has come to more closely resemble the male pattern shown in Figure 5-4,

---

[8]Note that when labor force participation rates are changing, cross-sectional data on participation rates by age, as shown in Figure 5-3, may give a misleading impression of the actual experiences of individual women over the life cycle. For a comprehensive explanation of this issue, as well as an interesting analysis of cohort patterns of married women's participation, see Goldin, *Understanding the Gender Gap*, 21–23.

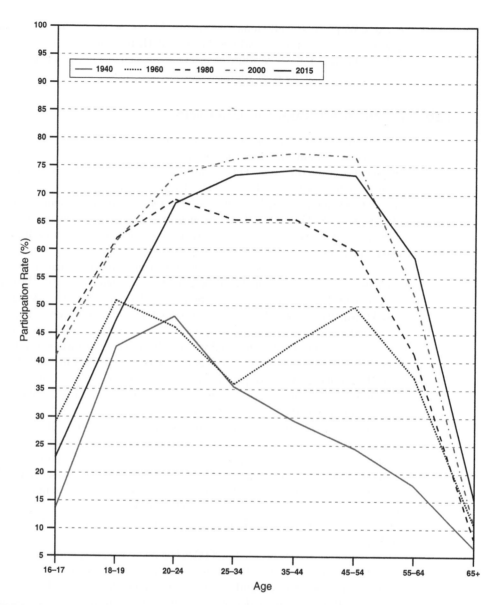

FIGURE 5-3 Labor Force Participation Rates of Women by Age

Source: US Department of Labor, Bureau of Labor Statistics, Employment and Earnings, Employment status of the civilian noninstitutional population by age, sex, and race, annual averages.

peaking in the prime working ages of 25 to 54. Figure 5-4 also shows that the long-term decline in male labor force participation rates that occurred during the post–World War II period was concentrated among younger men—teenagers and to a somewhat lesser extent those aged 20 to 24—and among older men aged 55 and over. Another important development for males is that, since the 1960s, smaller but notable decreases have also occurred in the participation rates of men in the prime working ages (25–54). This long-term trend continued after 2007, when noticeable participation declines occurred for this age group, as can be seen by comparing the profiles for 2007 and 2015. Nonetheless, participation rates for men in the prime working ages remain relatively high, at roughly 90 percent for 25- to 44-year-olds

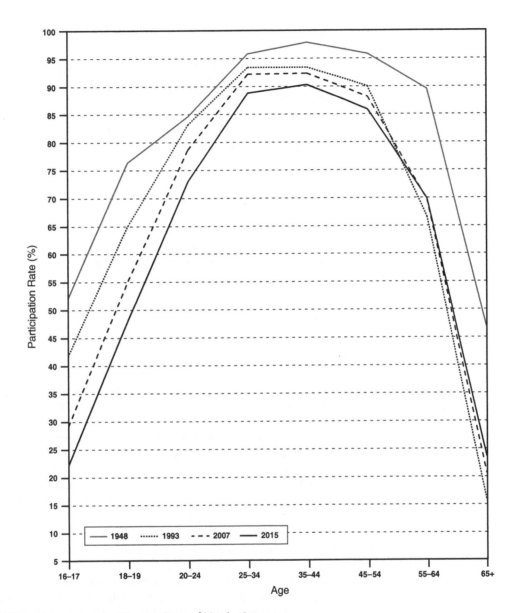

FIGURE 5-4 Labor Force Participation Rates of Men by Age

Source: US Department of Labor, Bureau of Labor Statistics, Employment and Earnings, Employment status of the civilian noninstitutional population by age, sex, and race, annual averages.

and 86 percent for 45- to 54-year-olds. In Chapter 6 we provide a more detailed discussion of factors behind these trends.[9]

Recent developments in participation rates for teens (ages 16–19) are fairly similar for both women and men. Participation rates have been declining over the long term for male teens and since around 2000 for female teens. Both groups experienced

[9]For further discussion, see Council of Economic Advisers, "The Long-Term Decline in Prime-Age Male Labor Participation" (June 2016), https://obamawhitehouse.archives.gov. There is considerable geographic variation in this pattern; see Gregor Aisch, Josh Katz, and David Leonhardt "Where Men Aren't Working," *New York Times*, December 11, 2014, nytimes.com.

a particularly sharp drop in labor force participation during the Great Recession, accentuating these long-term trends.

Finally, turning to older individuals, an interesting development is the reversal of the decline in the participation rate of older men (aged 55 and over). After decreasing throughout the post–World War II period, participation rates for this group bottomed out in the mid-1980s and then began to increase starting in the early 1990s,[10] a trend which continued even during the Great Recession. Participation rates of older women increased over the recession as well, also continuing longer-term trends.

Trends in Labor Force Attachment of Women

The changes in women's labor force participation rates by age since 1940, which we have just discussed, suggest that rising female participation rates have been associated with an increase in the **labor force attachment**, or the continuity of employment, of women over the life cycle.

One indicator of labor force attachment is the extent of women's employment over the course of the year. The share of women who remain attached to the labor force over a year period has increased considerably. For example, in 1970, 53 percent of women worked at some time during the year. Of these women with work experience, only 41 percent were employed full-time and year-round. By 2014, 58 percent of women worked at some time during the year, and 61 percent of them were employed full-time and year-round.[11] It has also been found that, although women typically take more time out of the workforce after childbirth than men, the difference has been narrowing.[12]

As we shall see in greater detail in Chapter 9, work experience is an important determinant of labor market earnings. The lesser amount of work experience of women compared to men has traditionally been cited as an important reason for their lower earnings. It is not immediately obvious, however, whether the increases in women's labor force participation that occurred in the post–World War II period would be associated with increases or decreases in the *average* amount of work experience of the female labor force. The size of the labor force is increased by entries into the labor force and decreased by exits from the labor force. Thus, both *increases* in flows of *entrants* and *decreases* in flows of *exits* contribute to the growth of the female labor force. On the one hand, a growing number of new entrants, with little or no work experience, negatively affects the average labor market experience of women workers. On the other hand, the growing tendency for women to remain in the labor force more continuously has a positive effect.

---

[10]US Department of Labor, Bureau of Labor Statistics, "Spotlight on Statistics: Older Workers" (July 2008), www.bls.gov; and Alicia H. Munnell and Steven A. Sass, "The Labor Supply of Older American Men," in *Labor Supply in the New Century*, ed. Katharine Bradbury, Christopher L. Foote, and Robert K. Triest (Boston: Federal Reserve Bank of Boston, 2008).

[11]US Department of Labor, Bureau of Labor Statistics, "Work Experience of the Population—2010," news release, December 18, 2012, accessed December 18, 2012 www.bls.gov; and US Department of Labor, Bureau of Labor Statistics, "Work Experience of the Population—2014," news release, December 9, 2015, accessed June 28, 2016, www.bls.gov.

[12]This was mainly due to increased participation of mothers rather than decreased participation of fathers. See Judith Dey, "How Has Labor Force Participation among Young Moms and Dads Changed? A Comparison of Two Cohorts," *Beyond the Numbers* 3, no. 19 (September 2014), accessed July 1, 2016, www.bls.gov.

What has been the net effect of women's increased labor force participation on their average experience? Unfortunately, data on work experience are not routinely collected in government surveys. However, estimates are made from time to time based on special surveys that explicitly ask respondents about their labor market experience, as well as less directly from information on labor force entry and exit rates. The evidence suggests that, between 1960 and 1980, rising female labor force participation rates were associated with a slight decrease in average levels of work experience among women workers, but since then, notable gains in women's average experience levels have occurred.[13] These trends are discussed in greater detail in Chapter 9.

Trends in Hours Worked

The main focus of this chapter is on labor force participation. However, another important dimension of the labor supply decision is *hours worked*. In Chapter 4, we considered trends in the allocation of time of women and men between housework and market work. Here we focus on trends in work hours among the employed. Hours worked can be measured as hours worked per day, per week, or annually. One particularly notable difference between women and men workers is in part-time employment: women are much more likely than men to be employed part-time, although the gender difference has declined a bit as the share of men working part-time has increased. Recall that part-time work is defined as working fewer than 35 hours per week. In 2015, 25 percent of employed women usually worked part-time, roughly the same as in 1970 when 26 percent did so. A considerably smaller share of men, 12.4 percent, worked part-time in 2015, up from 8.5 percent in 1970.[14]

Considering hours worked more broadly and over a longer period of time, one striking trend is that the full-time workweek declined from 55 to 60 hours at the turn of the twentieth century to about 40 hours in the 1940s and remains at about that level today.[15] Similarly, the average number of hours worked per week (including both full- and part-time workers) has shown considerable stability for both male and female workers; male workers have averaged about 43 hours per week since the 1940s, while women workers have averaged about 37 hours since at least the 1970s.[16] The lower figure for women in part reflects their continued greater likelihood of working part-time than men. In addition, although, as already noted, the proportion

---

[13]Goldin, *Understanding the Gender Gap*, 37–41; James P. Smith and Michael P. Ward, "Time Series Changes in the Female Labor Force," *Journal of Labor Economics* 3, no. 1, pt. 2 (January 1985), S59–90; and Francine D. Blau and Lawrence M. Kahn, "The Gender Wage Gap: Extent, Trends, and Explanations," *Journal of Economic Literature* (forthcoming).

[14]US Bureau of Labor Statistics, Household Data Annual Averages, 2015, Table 8, "Employed and Unemployed Full- and Part-Time Workers by Age, Sex, Race, and Hispanic or Latino Ethnicity," accessed June 28, 2016, http://www.bls.gov/cps/cpsaat08.htm; and US Department of Labor, Bureau of Labor Statistics, *Women in the Labor Force: A Databook* (December 2014), accessed June 28, 2016, www.bls.gov.

[15]Thomas J. Kniesner, "The Full-Time Work Week in the U.S.: 1900–1970," *Industrial and Labor Relations Review* 30, no. 1 (October 1976): 3–15; and Jerry A. Jacobs and Kathleen Gerson, *The Time Divide: Work, Family, and Gender Inequality* (Cambridge, MA: Harvard University Press, 2004). Valerie Ramey and Neville Francis point to an important distinction between average hours *per worker*, the figure cited in the text, and hours *per person in the working-age population*. This latter concept is useful for estimating trends in leisure for the full working-age population; see "A Century of Work and Leisure," *American Journal of Economics: Macroeconomics* 1, no. 2 (July 2009): 189–224.

[16]Jacobs and Gerson, *The Time Divide*.

of employed women working full-time and year-round has increased, even among this group, women tend to work fewer hours than men.

Trends in annual work hours are more difficult to measure than trends in labor force participation because they may be influenced by workers' difficulty in obtaining a job (as reflected in time spent unemployed or out of the labor force), decisions to work part-time or part-year, and how paid vacation time is counted. Not surprisingly then, there has been some controversy about these trends and how they should be measured, with some studies finding little change in annual hours for women and men and others finding modest positive or negative trends.[17]

While in the aggregate relatively little change has occurred in weekly and annual work hours in the post–World War II period, an important development is that trends in work hours of both men and women have diverged by skill level, with a rising trend for more highly skilled workers and a declining trend for the less skilled.[18] For instance, the length of the workweek generally decreased for employees with less than a high school education, while it rose for those who completed 4 or more years of college, as well as for those in professional, managerial, and technical occupations. As discussed in subsequent chapters, the increase in work hours in some highly skilled occupations, combined with an increased return to long work hours, appears to have disadvantaged women relative to men in the labor market—increasing the gender wage gap, creating a barrier to women's participation in some occupations, and intensifying work–family conflicts.[19]

This increase in work hours for some individuals, combined with the fact that many Americans are single parents with responsibility for children or are members of a dual-earner family, leads to more families facing a growing "time squeeze," a topic discussed further in Chapter 16.

Trends in Gender Differences in Unemployment

Those participating in the labor force are not always able to find employment, as has been made all too clear during the Great Recession and its aftermath. Therefore, although our main focus in this chapter is on labor force participation, we review trends in gender differences in unemployment here.

Figure 5-5 shows female and male unemployment rates with periods of recession indicated. Recession dating is based on the level of economic activity. Recessions are periods of declining economic activity and are followed by expansions or periods of rising economic activity. As may be seen in the figure, it generally takes some time for unemployment rates to rebound following the official end of a recession. While this is generally the case, the lag between the end of the recession and the reduction

[17]For a review, see Jacobs and Gerson, *The Time Divide*.
[18]Jacobs and Gerson, *The Time Divide*; Peter Kuhn and Fernando Lozano, "The Expanding Workweek? Understanding Trends in Long Work Hours among U.S. Men, 1979–2006," *Journal of Labor Economics* 26, no. 2 (April 2008): 311–43; and Heather Boushey and Bridget Ansel, *Overworked America: The Economic Causes and Consequences of Long Work Hours*, Washington Center for Equitable Growth (May 16, 2016), accessed July 1, 2016, equitablegrowth.org.
[19]See, for example, Claudia Goldin, "A Grand Gender Convergence: Its Last Chapter," *American Economic Review* 104, no. 4 (May 2014): 1091–1119; Boushey and Ansel *Overworked America*; and Youngjoo Cha and Kim A. Weeden, "Overwork and the Slow Convergence in the Gender Gap in Wages," *American Sociological Review* 79, no. 3 (June 2014): 457–84.

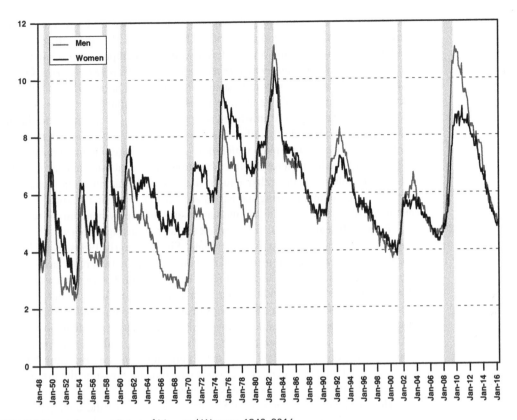

FIGURE 5-5 Unemployment Rates of Men and Women, 1948–2016

Notes: Unemployment data are seasonally adjusted. Vertical gray bars indicate the official dates of recessions as determined by the National Bureau of Economic Research (NBER).

Sources: Unemployment data are for ages 16+ from the Bureau of Labor Statistics, Labor Force Statistics, based on CPS data, available at www.bls.gov (accessed April 9, 2016); NBER dating from Federal Reserve Economic Data, available at research.stlouisfed.org/fred2 (accessed July 7, 2016).

in unemployment may be longer in some recessions than in others. This lag was particularly pronounced following the Great Recession, an extremely severe downturn.

As shown in Figure 5-5, the gender difference in the unemployment rates of men and women has changed over time. Although women traditionally had *higher* unemployment rates than men, since the early 1980s, women's unemployment rates have tended to be about the same as men's. The one important exception to this pattern is during and after recessions, when the unemployment rate is high. In this situation, women's unemployment rates are *lower* than men's, as was the case during the Great Recession.[20] The change in the gender gap in unemployment rates over time is the net result of various factors working in opposing directions.

First, despite increases over time, *women continue to have lower labor force attachment* than men. On the one hand, the larger proportion of entrants and reentrants among women in the labor force tends to increase female unemployment relative to male unemployment because many will experience a period of unemployment as they search for jobs. On the other hand, the weaker labor force attachment of women

---

[20]US Bureau of Labor Statistics, "Spotlight on Statistics: The Recession of 2007–2009" (February 12, 2012), accessed February 17, 2012, www.bls.gov/spotlight.

means that they are more likely than men to exit the labor force when they lose their jobs and hence to be counted as out of the labor force rather than unemployed. Particularly in recessions, this works to lower women's unemployment relative to men's.

Second, there are *gender differences in occupations and industries.* On the one hand, men are more heavily represented in blue-collar jobs and in durable manufacturing, sectors with above-average layoff and unemployment rates. Women are more likely to be employed in white-collar jobs, which experience lower layoff and unemployment rates. On the other hand, women are also disproportionately represented in service occupations, which have above-average unemployment rates. On balance, the gender differences in occupations and industries appear to lower the female unemployment rate relative to the male rate. The fact that blue-collar jobs and durable-goods manufacturing industries are subject to greater cyclical variation in employment tends to particularly increase men's unemployment during recessions.

Prior to the early 1980s, the net result of these opposing forces was that women's unemployment rates were higher than men's. Since the early 1980s, as we have seen, the balance has shifted and men's and women's unemployment rates have been about the same, except during periods of high unemployment. Factors that contributed to this convergence in male and female unemployment rates likely include rising labor force attachment of women and perhaps declining labor force attachment of men,[21] decreasing demand for manufacturing workers and increasing demand for workers in services due to structural changes in the economy, and a declining number of young people competing with women for entry-level jobs as the baby bust cohort entered the job market. As of 2007, prior to the Great Recession, the average female unemployment rate was 4.5 percent, very close to the male rate of 4.7 percent.

However, as shown in Figure 5-5, the gender gap in the unemployment rate remains sensitive to cyclical swings in the business cycle, with male unemployment rates rising *relative* to female rates during recessions. And during the more recent recessions since the early 1980s, the male rate actually rose above the female rate. The greatest gender difference occurred in May 2009, just before the official end of the Great Recession (June 2009), when the seasonally adjusted rates for men and women stood at 10.6 and 8.0 percent, respectively, a 2.6 percentage point difference.

The very large gender gap in unemployment rates during the Great Recession led to the oft-used description by the media of a "mancession." However, as we have seen, the pattern of gender differences in unemployment during the Great Recession was broadly similar to the pattern in prior economic downturns since 1980. It was simply the depth of the Great Recession that magnified the size of the gender differences.[22] Also in line with previous recessions, as the economic recovery continued, gender parity in unemployment rates reasserted itself. By January 2012, the male and female unemployment rates were the same at 8.3 percent and, as may be seen in the figure, continued at roughly similar levels subsequently. So, for example, in 2015, the unemployment rate was 5.2 percent for women and 5.4 percent for men.[23]

---

[21]Stefania Albanesi and Ayşegül Şahin, "The Gender Unemployment Gap," *Federal Reserve Bank of New York Staff Reports*, no. 613 (April 2013), accessed July 1, 2016, newyorkfed.org. These authors conclude that "the rise in female labor force attachment and the decline in male attachment can mostly account for the closing of the gender unemployment gap;" quote is from abstract.

[22]This is consistent with Hilary W. Hoynes, Douglas L. Miller, and Jessamyn Schaller's finding that there has been remarkable stability in the pattern of unemployment and job opportunity cycles across demographic groups over recessions since at least the late 1970s; see "Who Suffers during Recessions?" *Journal of Economic Perspectives* 26, no. 3 (Summer 2012): 27–48.

[23]Figures are from the US Department of Labor, Bureau of Labor Statistics, "2016 Employment & Earnings Online," accessed June 29, 2016, www.bls.gov.

Differences in unemployment rates across a number of other demographic categories remain quite sizable, even when the economy is strong. Particularly notable are the extremely high unemployment rates of African Americans. Among both men and women, unemployment rates are about twice as high for blacks as for whites, even during good economic times. Thus, the black–white difference in unemployment rates, already substantial, widens even further when the economy is sluggish or in a recession.[24] The large black–white difference in unemployment rates may be seen in Figure 5-6, which shows unemployment rates for blacks and whites in 2011, when the *overall* unemployment rate was still quite high at 8.9 percent in the aftermath of the Great Recession, and, for 2015, when the economy had rebounded and the *overall* unemployment rate was again relatively low at 5.3 percent.

Possible explanations for the higher unemployment rates of blacks include lower average levels of education and skills, a lack of jobs located in or near communities

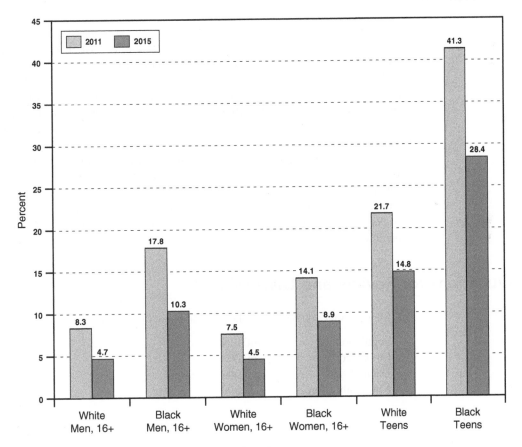

FIGURE 5-6 Unemployment Rates by Race for 2011 and 2015

Source: US Bureau of Labor Statistics, Labor Force Statistics from the CPS, available at www.bls.gov (accessed March 29, 2016)

---

[24]Kenneth A. Couch and Robert Fairlie, "Last Hired, First Fired? Black–White Unemployment and the Business Cycle," *Demography* 47, no. 1 (February 2010): 227–47.

where many of them live, and employment discrimination.[25] The higher incarceration rates of young black men also contribute to the race difference in unemployment rates since ex-offenders have difficulty finding employment.[26] For some of the same reasons, Hispanics also tend to have higher unemployment rates than whites, although the difference is generally smaller than the difference between blacks and whites.

Another group with considerably higher unemployment rates in both good times and bad is teens. And young workers are especially hard hit by economic downturns, including the Great Recession. Figure 5-6 shows that black teens had especially high rates, with 41.3 percent unemployed in 2011, 2 years after the official end of the Great Recession. By 2015, the rate had fallen considerably but remained at 28 percent (twice as high as that for white teens).

Conclusion

We began by reviewing the trends in male and female participation rates. We found that while measured female labor force participation rates have increased dramatically over the course of the past century, particularly since 1940, male participation rates have declined, albeit at a slower pace. As a result of both of these developments, the *difference* between the female and male participation rates has decreased sharply from 55 percentage points in 1940 to 12 percentage points in 2015, and the pattern of women's involvement in market work over the life cycle now looks very similar to men's.

However, after decades of substantial increase, growth in female labor force participation stalled in the 1990s, and overall female participation rates have remained roughly constant, even declining a bit, especially during and in the wake of the Great Recession. The reasons for these and other trends identified here will be considered in the next chapter after we have developed the requisite tools based on economic theory.

Questions for Review and Discussion

1. Suppose that you have the following information for country X:

Population:	100,000
Employed:	60,000
Unemployed:	3,000
Not in labor force:	37,000

---

[25]Ronald B. Mincy, ed., *Black Males Left Behind* (Washington, DC: Urban Institute Press, 2006). Measured unemployment rates tend to understate the employment difficulties of blacks because a higher fraction of blacks than whites are not captured in this statistic as they have given up on job search and hence are "not in the labor force." Moreover, blacks are more likely to be incarcerated and not included in the statistics; see Pettit, *Invisible Men;* and Justin Wolfers, David Leonhardt, and Kevin Quealy, "1.5 Million Missing Black Men," *New York Times,* April 20, 2015, nytimes.com.

[26]See Harry J. Holzer, Paul Offner, and Elaine Sorensen, "Declining Employment among Young Black Less-Educated Men: The Role of Incarceration and Child Support," *Journal of Policy Analysis and Management* 24, no. 2 (Spring 2005): 329–50.

a. Calculate the size of the labor force, the labor force participation rate, and the unemployment rate.

b. Provide examples of individuals who would be classified as "not in the labor force."

c. What economic factors might shift a woman from "not in the labor force" to "in the labor force"? Discuss.

d. Suppose an economic downturn occurred. How would you expect this change to affect the number of employed, the number of unemployed, and the number classified as "not in the labor force"? Explain.

2. Referring back to Chapter 2, explain why the official data for women's labor force participation in 1890 given in Table 5-1 provide a misleading impression of the relationship between women's labor force participation and economic development.

3. Why is the unemployment rate considered by some to be an incomplete measure of economic hardship and lost output? What alternative measures are provided by the Bureau of Labor Statistics, and what issue does each address?

4. Do you expect that sometime in the future labor force participation rates of women will resume their increase? Discuss.

Internet-Based Data Exercise

In doing this exercise, students should be aware that the precise names of documents and their location within a website may change over time.

1. The US Bureau of Labor Statistics is the primary source of US government data on labor force statistics. These figures are reported monthly in the BLS Economic News Release titled "The Employment Situation."

    Visit the home page of the US Bureau of Labor Statistics at http://www.bls.gov/.

    Find "The Employment Situation." For all questions, provide answers based on data for the most recent month (seasonally adjusted, if available):

    a. Using Table A-1, confirm that you understand how to calculate the labor force participation rate and the unemployment rate using the definitions provided at the start of this chapter. Show your work.

    b. Using Table A-1, find the current unemployment rate. How does it compare to the rate 1 year ago? What are the current rates for women and men over 16 years of age?

    c. Table A-4 provides current labor force statistics by educational attainment. What patterns do you see, and what might explain them?

    d. Table A-15 provides statistics on labor force underutilization. What is the current range of estimates of unemployment (lowest to highest)? Which measures do you think are most useful, and why?

2. A key online Bureau of Labor Statistics publication is called "Employment & Earnings Online." Visit the home page at http://www.bls.gov/opub/ee/. Click on

"Household Data from the Current Population Survey." Under data for "Annual Average Household Data," look for Table 27, "Unemployed Persons by Reason for Unemployment, Sex, and Age."

a. For the most recent year available, what is the percent distribution of the unemployed by reason (e.g., job leaver, job loser, etc.) for each of these groups: men (ages 20+), women (ages 20+), and teens (16–19)?

b. What notable patterns do you see? What might explain these patterns?

Suggested Readings

Boushey, Heather, and Bridget Ansel. *Overworked America: The Economic Causes and Consequences of Long Work Hours.* Washington Center for Equitable Growth. May 16, 2016.

Council of Economic Advisors, Office of the President. "The Labor Force Participation Rate since 2007: Causes and Policy Implications." July 2014. https://obamawhitehouse.archives.gov .

Hoynes, Hilary W., Douglas L. Miller, and Jessamyn Schaller, "Who Suffers During Recessions?" *Journal of Economic Perspectives* 26, no. 3 (Summer 2012): 27–48.

Jacobs, Jerry A., and Kathleen Gerson. *The Time Divide: Work, Family, and Gender Inequality.* Cambridge, MA: Harvard University Press, 2004.

Juhn, Chinhui, and Simon Potter. "Changes in Labor Force Participation in the United States." *Journal of Economic Perspectives* 20, no. 3 (Summer 2006): 27–46.

Mincy, Ronald B., ed. *Black Males Left Behind.* Washington, DC: Urban Institute Press, 2006.

Petitt, Becky. *Invisible Men: Mass Incarceration and the Myth of Black Progress.* New York: Russell Sage Foundation, 2012.

US Bureau of Labor Statistics, "How the Government Measures Unemployment." Current Population Survey (CPS) Technical Documentation. June 2014. http://www.bls.gov/cps/cps_htgm.pdf.

Key Terms

Great Recession (91)

labor force (91)

out of the labor force (91)

employed (91)

part-time (91)

full-time (91)

unemployed (91)

labor force participation rate (92)

unemployment rate (92)

marginally attached workers (92)

discouraged workers (93)

underemployment (93)

part time for economic reasons (93)

involuntary part-time workers (93)

year-round or full-year worker (93)

full-time, year-round worker (93)

prime working age (93)

labor force attachment (100)

The Labor Supply Decision

In the previous chapter, we identified significant trends in female and male labor force participation. In this chapter, we develop some economic concepts for analyzing these trends and use them to provide a better understanding of the reasons for the remarkable influx of women into the labor market. We also use economic theory to analyze the reasons behind the decrease in male labor force participation and conclude with an examination of factors contributing to differences in labor force participation trends between blacks and whites.

The Labor Supply Decision

In Chapters 3 and 4, we examined the division of housework and market work between husband and wife. Here we focus upon the closely related question of how an individual, whether married or single, decides on the allocation of his or her time between the home and the labor market. We again use a neoclassical model and assume that the individual's goal is to maximize utility or satisfaction.[1] A brief preview of our conclusions may be helpful in understanding the more detailed analysis that follows.

The economic model suggests that individuals decide whether or not to participate in the labor force by comparing the value of their time in the market given by their hourly wage rate (w) to the value they place on their time spent at home (w^*). If the value of market time is greater than that of home time ($w > w^*$), they choose to participate in the labor force. Alternatively, if the value of nonmarket or home time is greater than or equal to that of market time ($w^* \geq w$), they choose to remain out of the labor force. In this section, we trace out the reasoning behind this decision rule.

Individuals are viewed as deriving utility from the consumption of **commodities** (goods and services) that are produced using inputs of market goods and nonmarket time.[2] For example, the commodity, a family dinner, is produced using inputs of market goods (groceries, cooking equipment, etc.) and the individual's own time in preparing the meal. In order to keep this model reasonably simple, we make the following three additional assumptions.

First, we assume that all income earned in the labor market is spent on market goods. This assumption avoids the need to consider the determinants of savings and means that we may use the terms **market income** and (the money value of) **market goods** interchangeably.

Second, we assume that all nonmarket time is spent in the production of commodities, whether the output is a loaf of bread, a clean house, a healthy child, or a game of tennis. This approach not only avoids the need for analyzing a three-way choice among market work, housework, and leisure but also makes the often difficult distinction between nonmarket work (including volunteer work) and leisure unnecessary.[3] We do not wish to suggest, however, that in reality no difference separates the two. Indeed, one of the concerns about the impact of married women's increased labor force participation on their well-being is that it has not been accompanied by a comparable reallocation of household chores. As a result, women are often saddled with the "double burden" of home and market work. Working a "double shift" may reduce the leisure time available to women, impede their ability to compete with men in the labor market, or both. Data on time spent in housework and childcare were presented in Chapter 4.

Third, we focus here on the individual rather than on the family as a whole. This focus is quite realistic when the individual is the only adult in the family. However, as we saw in Chapter 3, where more than one adult is present, the division of

---

[1]As before, the underpinnings of the analysis are derived from the work of Nobel laureate Gary S. Becker, see "A Theory of the Allocation of Time," *Economic Journal* 75, no. 299 (September 1965): 493–517; and Jacob Mincer, see "Labor Force Participation of Married Women," in *Aspects of Labor Economics*, ed. H. Gregg Lewis, Universities National Bureau of Economic Research Conference Studies 14 (Princeton, NJ: Princeton University Press, 1962), 63–97. Nobel laureate James Heckman and Reuben Gronau, among others, have made significant contributions to the development of statistical techniques for estimating the theoretical relationships.

[2]Students who have read the appendix to Chapter 3, where a graphical analysis of specialization and exchange was presented, will recognize the basic approach employed here as quite similar. However, in this analysis, we do not need to make the rigid distinction between home goods (produced exclusively with inputs of home time) and market goods (produced entirely with market-purchased goods). Indeed, we can recognize not only that market goods and nonmarket time are both inputs into the production of commodities but also that more than one way may be used to produce the same commodity.

[3]Market work is relatively easy to distinguish as any activity that results in a material, usually monetary, reward. However, it is quite problematic to determine whether preparing a gourmet meal, going to a meeting of young professionals, growing flowers, or taking a child to the zoo is work or leisure.

labor among them, and thus the labor supply decision of each, is reasonably expected to be a family decision. We do not introduce all the complexities of family decision-making here because it would cause the exposition to become unduly complex. We do, however, view the individual in a family context by taking into account the impact of the earnings of other family members on each person's labor supply decision; but the labor supply of other members of the household is taken as given and assumed not to be influenced by the individual's own choice. This assumption is probably not too unreasonable when we consider women's labor supply decisions since, in most American families, husbands are still likely to remain in the labor market full-time regardless of their wives' participation decision.[4]

Now that we have reviewed some of the assumptions of the model, we are ready to turn to an analysis of the labor supply decision itself. In the model, both market goods and nonmarket time are used in the production of the commodities from which the individual derives satisfaction. Therefore, the goal of the individual is to select his or her utility-maximizing combination of market goods and nonmarket time. Because market goods are purchased with income earned through market work and all time available is spent either on market work or on nonmarket activities, this choice of the utility-maximizing combination of market goods and nonmarket time is the basis of the labor supply decision. In making this choice, the individual must take into account both the options that are open to him or her, given by the *budget constraint* shown in panel a of Figure 6-1, and his or her preferences expressed in the set of *indifference curves* shown in panel b of Figure 6-1. Let us trace out this decision for the hypothetical case of a married woman named Mary.

The Budget Constraint

The **budget constraint** in panel a shows the various combinations of nonmarket time and market goods from which Mary can choose, given her market wage rate and the nonlabor income available to her. The **wage (*w*)** is the amount of money an individual earns for each hour he or she works; that is, the wage is an hourly rate of pay. **Nonlabor income** is any income an individual receives, apart from his or her own labor market earnings. The amount of nonlabor income is therefore unrelated to the amount of time the individual devotes to the labor market. Nonlabor income may include the earnings of a spouse as well as any income received from interest, dividends, or rental property. For simplicity, government transfer payments, such as welfare or unemployment insurance, may also be considered nonlabor income, although the amount of income received from such sources is in fact influenced by the amount of time a person supplies to the labor market. Hours of **nonmarket time** are measured from left to right along the horizontal axis.

We assume that Mary has a total of 16 hours available to her in a day to allocate between market and nonmarket activities (allowing 8 hours for nondiscretionary activities like sleeping). Since any of this time that Mary does not spend in nonmarket activities is spent in the market, hours of **market time** are measured from right to left along the horizontal axis.

---

[4]An indicator of this is that the responsiveness of husbands' labor supply decisions to their wives' wages tends to be quite low; wives' labor supply decisions are much more responsive to their husbands' wages. See, for example, Francine D. Blau and Lawrence M. Kahn, "Changes in the Labor Supply Behavior of Married Women: 1980–2000," *Journal of Labor Economics* 25, no. 3 (July 2007): 393–438; for additional results on men, see their March 2005 NBER Working Paper 11230 by the same title.

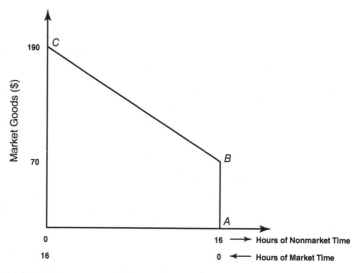

(a) THE BUDGET CONSTRAINT

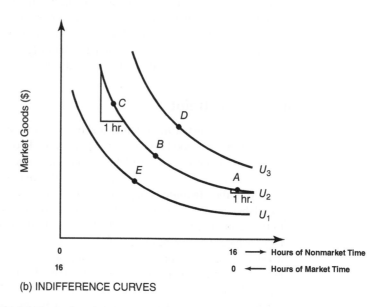

(b) INDIFFERENCE CURVES

FIGURE 6-1 The Budget Constraint and the Indifference Curves

Mary's nonlabor income is $70 a day. The vertical segment *AB* of the budget constraint shows that Mary has this income available to her even if she supplies no time to the labor market. She may increase her money income by participating in the labor force. For each additional hour she supplies to the market, she must give up an hour of nonmarket time. In return she receives $7.50, her hourly market wage (*w*). Thus, segment *CB* is negatively sloped. Its slope is equal to −7.50 or −*w*. If Mary devotes all her time to the market, her total earnings will be $120 ($7.5 × 16). Her total daily income, including her nonlabor income, will be $190 ($120 + $70).

Indifference Curves

In panel b, we represent Mary's preferences for market goods and nonmarket time. As discussed previously, we can incorporate the family context of decision-making into the budget constraint by including the income of other family members as part of the individual's nonlabor income. This issue is more difficult when we consider preferences because preferences among family members may differ and the process of arriving at family decisions is complex. Therefore, we focus on *individual* (rather than family) preferences. However, it is important to recognize that this is only an approximation. In fact, we expect that the individual's decisions are made in the context of the family and that the preferences of other family members are taken into account in the decision-making process. Bearing this point in mind, we now take a closer look at the representation of Mary's preferences in panel b.

Suppose Mary is told that she could have the combination of market goods and nonmarket time represented by point B. She is then asked to find various other combinations of market goods and nonmarket time from which she would get exactly the same amount of satisfaction or utility and identifies the combinations represented by points A and C. These and other points, which represent equal satisfaction, can all be connected into one **indifference curve**, so named because Mary is indifferent about being at various points on the curve. Thus, each indifference curve indicates the various combinations of market goods and nonmarket time that provide Mary with the same amount of utility or satisfaction.

However, Mary has not just one indifference curve but a whole set of higher and lower curves (an **indifference map**). A point like D on indifference curve U_3 is clearly preferable to B because it offers more of both market goods and nonmarket time. Thus, by extension, all points on U_3 are preferred to all points on U_2. Similarly, B is preferred to E, and, thus, all the points on U_2 are preferred to all the points on U_1.[5] As we move out from the origin in a northeasterly direction, consumption possibilities, and thus potential satisfaction, increase.

Indifference curves are generally assumed to be convex to the origin. That is, they become flatter as we move from left to right and steeper as we move from right to left. This shape occurs because it is believed that individuals generally value additional units of relatively scarcer commodities more highly than additional units of relatively more plentiful ones. At point A, where nonmarket time is relatively plentiful and market goods are relatively scarce, Mary would be willing to exchange an hour of nonmarket time for a relatively small amount of income (market goods) and still feel equally well off. However, at a point like C, where market goods are relatively plentiful and nonmarket time is relatively scarce, it would take a lot of income (market goods) to induce her to give up an additional hour of scarce nonmarket time.

It is interesting to consider more closely the way in which an individual like Mary may substitute market goods for nonmarket time (or vice versa) along an indifference curve while still remaining equally well off. It is important to recognize that we assume she does not derive satisfaction directly from market goods and

---

[5]It should be clear that indifference curves can never intersect. All points on any one curve represent an equal amount of utility, while any point above (below) represents a larger (smaller) amount of utility. At the point where two curves intersect, they represent the same utility. Yet at all other points they do not. This is a logical impossibility.

nonmarket time. Rather, she values them only insofar as they can be used to produce commodities.[6] Broadly speaking, two types of substitution are involved: substitution in consumption and substitution in production.

SUBSTITUTION IN CONSUMPTION Some commodities are relatively goods-intensive to produce. That is, they are produced using relatively large amounts of market goods and relatively little nonmarket time. Examples include buying expensive furniture and clothing or recreational activities such as dining at an elegant restaurant or flying to the Caribbean for a short vacation.

Other commodities are relatively *time-intensive*. That is, they are produced using relatively greater amounts of nonmarket time and relatively fewer inputs of market goods. Examples of these commodities include recreational activities like hiking, birdwatching, or taking a cycling trip. Also, as anyone who has spent time caring for children can attest, small children are a relatively time-intensive "commodity."

Substitution in consumption involves choosing among commodities so as to substitute goods-intensive commodities for time-intensive ones or time-intensive commodities for goods-intensive ones. When such substitutions are made along a given indifference curve, the implication is that the individual is indifferent between the two alternatives. So, for example, an individual may be indifferent between a goods-intensive vacation like staying for a short time at an expensive resort or a more time-intensive one of spending a longer period hiking and backpacking. Or, more broadly, an individual might be indifferent between having a large family of time-intensive children and spending more time in recreational activities that are more goods-intensive.

SUBSTITUTION IN PRODUCTION In many instances, the same commodity can be produced using a relatively time-intensive technique or a relatively goods-intensive technique. For example, a meal may be prepared from scratch at home, made using convenience foods, or purchased at a restaurant. A clean house may be produced by individuals doing the work themselves or by hiring cleaning help. A small child may be cared for entirely by a parent or by a babysitter for a few hours a day or may spend all day at a childcare center.

Substitution in production involves choosing among various ways of producing the same commodity so as to substitute goods-intensive production techniques for time-intensive ones or time-intensive production techniques for goods-intensive ones. Again, when such substitutions are made along a given indifference curve, the implication is that the individual is indifferent between the two alternatives. Examples here include those already described: preparing a meal at home versus eating out, hiring cleaning help versus doing it oneself, taking a child to a childcare center versus taking care of the child oneself.

SUBSTITUTION BETWEEN MARKET GOODS AND NONMARKET TIME As an individual like Mary moves from point A to point B to point C along indifference curve U_2 in Figure 6-1, she is likely to exploit opportunities for substitution in both consumption and production. That is, she will substitute goods-intensive

---

[6]The indifference curves used in this chapter are a graphical representation of what has been termed the individual's *indirect utility function*; see Becker, "A Theory of the Allocation of Time." Students who read the appendix to Chapter 3 will recognize that we took a different approach in the analysis presented there and simply assumed that families derive utility *directly* from market and home goods.

commodities for time-intensive commodities in consumption and goods-intensive for time-intensive production techniques. As she continues to do so, she will exhaust many of the obvious possibilities. It will take larger increments of market goods to induce her to part with her scarcer nonmarket time, which explains why indifference curves are believed to get steeper as we move from right to left.

Comparing *across* individuals, the steepness of the indifference curve is influenced by how easy or difficult it is for them to substitute market goods for nonmarket time while remaining equally well off. This ease or difficulty, in turn, will depend on their opportunities for substituting one for the other in consumption or production or both. For example, those who enjoy hiking a great deal will not easily be induced to decrease the time they spend on it. They will have steeper indifference curves, reflecting that they have greater difficulty in substituting market goods for nonmarket time in consumption than those who care less for such time-intensive activities.

Similarly, we would expect those whose services are in greater demand in the home (say, because small children are present) to have steeper indifference curves, reflecting their greater difficulty in substituting market goods for nonmarket time in production. Tastes and preferences will be a factor here, too. People who feel strongly that children should be cared for full-time by their own parent and that alternative care is an extremely poor substitute will have steeper indifference curves than those who believe that adequate alternative care can be provided.

This analysis assumes a degree of substitutability between market goods and nonmarket time.[7] However, some commodities cannot be purchased in the market. Various personal services and management tasks provided in the home may be of this nature. Similarly, some commodities available in the market cannot be produced at home. Examples range from sophisticated medical care and advanced education to means of transportation and communication, insurance, and many consumer durables. Nonetheless, it is highly likely that, when all commodities are aggregated together (as in the indifference curves shown in Figure 6-1), some substitution possibilities between market goods and nonmarket time exist. The ease or difficulty of substitution is then represented by the steepness of the indifference curves.

TASTES Beyond considerations of this kind, economists generally do not analyze the determinants of individuals' preferences for income (market goods) versus nonmarket time. However, it is important to point out that individuals do not operate in a social vacuum. Their tastes and behaviors are undoubtedly influenced by social attitudes and norms.[8] For example, the willingness of a woman to substitute purchased services for her own time in childcare is undoubtedly influenced by the social acceptability of doing so. Yet it is probably true that attitudes follow behavior to some extent as well. Therefore, it is likely, for example, that it is more acceptable for mothers of small children to work outside the home than it used to be in part because it is more common for them to do so.

A woman's relative preference for income (market goods) versus nonmarket time also reflects a variety of other factors not generally emphasized by economists. As we saw in Chapter 3, women may value earning their own income for the economic

[7]For an interesting discussion, see Nancy Folbre and Julie A. Nelson, "For Love or Money—Or Both?" *Journal of Economic Perspectives* 14, no. 4 (Fall 2000): 123–40.

[8]The importance of social norms is particularly emphasized by Clair Brown, "An Institutional Model of Wives' Work Decisions," *Industrial Relations* 24, no. 2 (Spring 1985): 182–204.

independence it brings and to enhance their relative bargaining power in the family. In addition, an increasing number of women value career success in much the same way their male counterparts do, which also affects the shape of their indifference curves.

Although such considerations do not invalidate the use of this model in analyzing women's labor supply decisions, they do serve to make us aware that the term *preferences* (or tastes), as economists use it, covers a lot of ground. This awareness is particularly important as we attempt to explain women's rising labor force participation over time.

While, as noted, economists have tended not to analyze the determinants of tastes or of gender differences in tastes, more recently these topics have been the subject of a growing body of research. Perhaps not surprisingly, the evidence suggests that family background influences tastes. For example, in families where mothers have less traditional attitudes about gender roles, daughters and sons tend to share these views. Women also seem to be influenced by the work behavior of the mothers of their friends when they were teenagers, suggesting the influence of peers when growing up.[9] Moreover, the work behavior of mothers not only influences their daughters, but also their daughters-in-law: the *wives* of men whose mothers worked are themselves more likely to work. One explanation is that if a son is raised by a mother with less traditional attitudes, he may be more favorably disposed toward his wife working or perhaps more willing to share housework chores, thus facilitating his wife's employment.[10]

Research on immigrant women's labor force participation rates, which shows that these rates are influenced by patterns in their countries of origin, also points to the role of family background and cultural factors in influencing tastes.[11] Specifically, women migrating from countries with relatively high female labor force participation rates have higher labor supply in the United States than women coming from countries with lower female participation rates. Further, even though both groups assimilate toward native-born women's labor supply patterns as they spend more time in the United States, the gap in their labor supply tends to persist. Similarly, the labor supply behavior of the US-born daughters of immigrants (the second generation) has been found to be positively associated with both female participation rates in their parents' country of origin and the participation patterns of immigrants from those origin countries in their parents' generation.[12] Nonetheless, here too there is considerable assimilation of the second generation to native-born patterns.

---

[9]Lídia Farré and Francis Vella, "The Intergenerational Transmission of Gender Role Attitudes and Its Implications for Female Labor Force Participation," *Economica* 80, no. 318 (April 2013): 219–47; and Claudia Olivetti, Eleonora Patacchini, and Yves Zenou, "Mothers, Friends and Gender Identity," NBER Working Paper 19610 (National Bureau of Economic Research, Cambridge, MA, November 2013).

[10]Raquel Fernández, Alessandra Fogli, and Claudia Olivetti, "Mothers and Sons: Preference Formation and Female Labor Force Dynamics" *Quarterly Journal of Economics* 119, no. 4 (November 2004): 1249–99.

[11]Francine D. Blau, Lawrence M. Kahn, and Kerry L. Papps, "Gender, Source Country Characteristics and Labor Market Assimilation among Immigrants," *Review of Economics and Statistics* 93, no. 1 (February 2011): 43–58; and Heather Antecol, "An Examination of Cross-Country Differences in the Gender Gap in Labor Force Participation Rates," *Labour Economics* 7, no. 4 (July 2000): 409–26.

[12]Racquel Fernández and Alessandra Fogli, "Culture: An Empirical Investigation of Beliefs, Work, and Fertility," *American Economic Journal: Macroeconomics* 1, no. 1 (January 2009): 146–77; Francine D. Blau, Lawrence M. Kahn, Albert Yung-Hsu Liu, and Kerry L. Papps, "The Transmission of Women's Fertility, Human Capital, and Work Orientation across Immigrant Generations," *Journal of Population Economics* 26, no. 2 (April 2013): 405–35.

The Labor Force Participation Decision

Let us suppose that Mary's indifference curves and her budget constraint are those shown in panel a of Figure 6-2. Mary will maximize utility or satisfaction at point Y where her budget constraint just touches the highest attainable indifference curve, U_2. At Y, the amount of income needed to induce her to give up an additional hour of nonmarket time, given by the slope of the indifference curve at Y, exactly equals the market wage she is offered for that hour, given by the slope of the budget constraint. That is, the budget constraint is *tangent* to the indifference curve at Y. Mary,

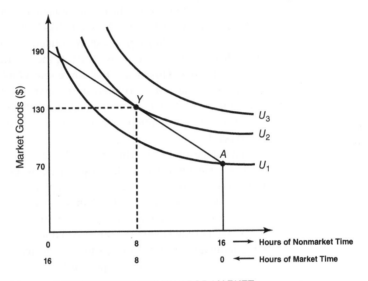

(a) $w > w^*$ PARTICIPATES IN THE LABOR MARKET

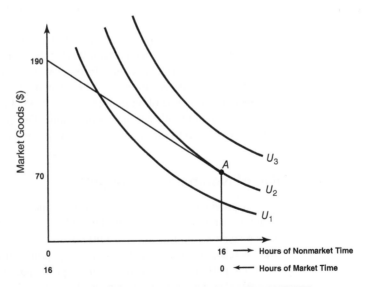

(b) $w < w^*$ DOES NOT PARTICIPATE IN THE LABOR MARKET

FIGURE 6-2 The Labor Force Participation Decision

therefore, supplies 8 hours per day to the market and spends 8 hours on nonmarket activities. Her daily earnings of $60 ($7.50 × 8) plus her daily nonlabor income of $70 give her (and her family) a total income of $130 per day.

It is interesting to consider in greater detail why Mary does not select point A, where she would supply no time to the labor market. At A, where indifference curve U_1 intersects the budget constraint, the curve is *flatter* than the negatively sloped portion of the budget constraint (which passes through point A and point 190 on the market goods axis). This means that, at point A, Mary values her nonmarket time *less* than the wage the market is willing to pay her for it. Therefore, she will certainly choose to supply some time to the market.

Another woman, Joyce, faces the same budget constraint as Mary but has steeper indifference curves (shown in Figure 6-2b). Perhaps she has more young children to care for than Mary. In Joyce's case, the budget constraint touches the highest attainable indifference curve at point A. At A, the indifference curve is steeper than the budget constraint. This means that Joyce sets a *higher* value on her nonmarket time than the wage rate she is offered in the market. She will maximize her utility by remaining out of the labor force, spending all 16 hours available to her on nonmarket activities. Her consumption of market goods will be limited to her nonlabor income of $70 per day.

The slope of the indifference curve at 0 hours of market work (point A in Figure 6-2a and b) is termed the **reservation wage** or the **value of nonmarket time** (**w***). It is equal to the value an individual places on nonmarket time at 0 work hours. If the market wage (w) is greater than the value of nonmarket time (i.e., $w > w^*$), as in panel a, the individual will choose to participate in the labor market. If the value of nonmarket time is greater than or equal to the market wage ($w^* \geq w$), as in panel b, the individual will choose not to participate. This decision rule can be summarized by the following simple equations:

$$w > w^* \Rightarrow \text{in the labor force}$$
$$w^* \geq w \Rightarrow \text{out of the labor force}$$

This economic analysis suggests that factors that increase the value of market time (w) tend to increase the probability that the individual will choose to participate in the labor force, all else equal. In other words, labor force participation is *positively related* to the wage or the value of market time. On the other hand, factors that increase the value of nonmarket time (w*) tend to lower the probability of labor force participation, other things being equal. Therefore, labor force participation is *negatively related* to the value of nonmarket time or home time.

The Value of Nonmarket Time (w*)

As our previous discussion suggests, the value of nonmarket time is influenced by tastes and preferences and by the demands placed on an individual's nonmarket time. Given some adherence to the traditional division of labor in most families, factors that increase housework and caregiving responsibilities, like the presence of small children, particularly influence women's participation decisions.

Another factor that influences the value placed on nonmarket time is the availability of income from sources other than the individual's own work efforts. Figure 6-3 shows the impact of changes in nonlabor income on the labor force

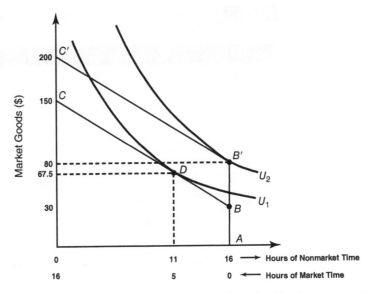

FIGURE 6-3 The Impact of Nonlabor Income on Labor Force Participation

participation decision. Let us suppose that the figure represents the budget constraint and indifference curves for Susan, a married woman with two small children. Suppose that her husband is unemployed and that initially her budget constraint is *ABC*. This represents $30 of nonlabor income (from interest on some bonds the family owns) and her market wage of $7.50. She maximizes utility at point *D*, where she supplies 5 hours a day to the market and earns $37.50. This brings the family's total daily income to $67.50. Now suppose Susan's husband finds a job. When his earnings ($50) are added to the interest received from the bonds ($30), her nonlabor income becomes $80. Her new budget constraint is *AB'C'*. Note that segment *B'C'* is parallel to segment *BC*. This is because Susan's market wage rate, which is the slope of segment *BC*, remains unchanged at $7.50.

At the higher income level, Susan's consumption possibilities increase, and she is able to reach a higher indifference curve. She maximizes utility at *B'*, where she has more of both market goods and nonmarket time and supplies less time to the market; in fact, in this example, she withdraws from the labor force entirely. This example represents the impact of the **income effect**. Ordinarily, when individuals' incomes go up, they demand more of all commodities from which they derive utility. To the extent that nonmarket time is used to produce these commodities, an increase in income will increase the value of nonmarket time and result in less time spent in the labor market. The income effect will be relatively large when the demand for time-intensive commodities increases sharply with income. The individual then needs to transfer more time from market to nonmarket activities in order to produce them. This shift is likely to occur when market goods are not considered to be good substitutes for home-produced items. So Susan, whose wage rate has not changed while her income increased, may choose to spend more time caring for her children. Of course, an increase in nonlabor income will not cause all women to withdraw from the labor force as Susan did. But an increase in nonlabor income may induce some women to exit the labor force, and thus, an increase in nonlabor income lowers the *probability* of labor force participation.

TABLE 6-1 | LABOR FORCE PARTICIPATION RATES OF WOMEN WITH CHILDREN UNDER AGE 18 BY MARITAL STATUS, 1960 AND 2015

Marital Status	Total	AGE OF YOUNGEST CHILD	
		6 to 17	Under 6
1960			
Never Married	n.a.	n.a.	n.a.
Married, Husband Present	27.6	39.0	18.6
Other Ever-Married	56.0	65.9	40.5
2015			
Never Married	72.2	77.6	68.5
Married, Husband Present	67.6	72.4	61.3
Other Ever-Married	78.2	80.5	72.4

Notes: Data are for March of each year and include women 16 years of age and over in 2015, and 14 years of age and over in 1960; n.a. = Not available.

Sources: US Census Bureau, *Statistical Abstract of the United States*: 1995, Table 638; and unpublished data from the Bureau of Labor Statistics.

Table 6-1 illustrates the impact of the value of nonmarket time (w^*) on women's labor force participation decisions more generally, using data on participation rates of women with children in 1960 and 2015 by marital status and age of children. (No data are available for never-married mothers in 1960.)

Let's begin by considering the relationship of labor force participation to marital status. Marital status reflects in part the availability and level of alternative sources of income. Thus, we see that, within children's age categories, women who are married, with spouse present, are generally less likely to work outside the home than either never-married or other ever-married women. (*Other ever-married* women are divorced, widowed, or separated from their husbands.) Further evidence for the importance of the value of home time is provided by studies that find that married women's labor force participation is negatively related to their husband's income, all else equal.[13] Recall that we expect an increase in the wife's nonlabor income to raise the value of her nonmarket time (w^*).

Looking at data for 2015, Table 6-1 indicates that married women's participation rates are closer to those of never-married women than they are to other ever-married women. One reason for this is that never-married mothers tend to be a less educated group than either married or other ever-married women, on average, and their lower education levels tend to depress their participation rates, all else equal. (We discuss the effect of education on labor force participation in greater detail later in this chapter.) Indeed, as we shall see shortly, the participation difference between married and never-married mothers has fluctuated over time, with married mothers actually having higher participation rates than never-married mothers in the 1980s and early 1990s.

---

[13]See, for example, Richard Blundell and Thomas MaCurdy, "Labor Supply: A Review of Alternative Approaches," in *Handbook of Labor Economics*, vol. 3A, ed. Orley Ashenfelter and David Card (Amsterdam: Elsevier, 1999), 1559–1695.

Now, look at the impact of children on women's labor force participation. This may be discerned by comparing the participation rates of women with small children (children under 6) to the rates for women with school-age children (children 6–17), within each marital status category. We see that the presence of small children has a negative effect on women's labor force participation, no doubt because small children greatly increase the value of time spent at home. Statistical analyses that control for other determinants of labor force participation generally find that children have a negative effect on female labor supply, with larger negative effects for younger children.[14] Also consistent with a negative relationship between the value of home time and women's labor supply is research that finds that, among women with children, having a child with a disability reduces a woman's labor supply compared to other mothers.[15]

While we have emphasized that children have a negative effect on women's labor supply through their impact on the value of home time, it is possible the causation, at least to some extent, runs in the opposite direction. That is, women who are more committed to the labor market or who have more attractive labor market opportunities may choose to have fewer children. It is difficult to distinguish between these two possible explanations regarding the negative association between women's labor supply and the presence and number of children, but research that has addressed the issue of causation generally suggests that children do indeed have a negative effect on women's labor supply.[16]

Table 6-1 also illustrates some interesting trends in the impact of marital status and children on women's labor force participation. First, the negative effect of children on women's labor supply appears to have decreased considerably since 1960. Although the presence of small children is strongly negatively associated with women's labor force participation in each year, women with small children were considerably more likely to work outside the home in 2015 than in 1960. For example, in 2015, 61 percent of married women with children under 6 years old were in the labor force compared to only 19 percent in 1960. Participation rates have also increased dramatically for women with older children: 72 percent of married women with children between the ages of 6 and 17 were labor force participants in 2015 compared to 39 percent in 1960.[17]

---

[14]See, for example, Blau and Kahn, "Changes in the Labor Supply Behavior of Married Women."

[15]Nada Wasi, Bernard van den Berg, and Thomas C. Buchmueller, "Heterogeneous Effects of Child Disability on Maternal Labor Supply: Evidence from the 2000 US Census," *Labour Economics* 19, no. 1 (January 2012): 139–54.

[16]In order to identify the causal effect of children on labor supply, it is necessary to find a variable that determines the number of children but does not directly influence labor supply. For an interesting approach using variation in the sex composition of the first two children as well as twin births as predictors of fertility, see Joshua D. Angrist and William N. Evans, "Children and Their Parents' Labor Supply: Evidence from Exogenous Variation in Family Size," *American Economic Review* 88, no. 3 (June 1998): 450–77; and Joyce P. Jacobsen, James Wishart Pearce III, and Joshua L. Rosenbloom, "The Effects of Childbearing on Married Women's Labor Supply and Earnings: Using Twin Births as a Natural Experiment," *Journal of Human Resources* 34, no. 3 (Summer 1999): 449–74.

[17]Statistical analyses controlling for other factors affecting the labor force participation of wives generally confirm that children exert a smaller negative influence on wives' participation than in earlier years; see, for example, Arleen Leibowitz and Jacob Klerman, "Explaining Changes in Married Mothers' Employment Over Time," *Demography* 32, no. 3 (August 1995): 365–78; Diane J. Macunovich, "Reversals in the Patterns of Women's Labor Supply in the United States, 1977–2009," *Monthly Labor Review* 133, no. 11 (November 2010): 16–36; and Heather Boushey, "'Opting Out'? The Effect of Children on Women's Employment in the United States," *Feminist Economics* 14, no. 1 (January 2008): 1–36. However, Saul D. Hoffman reports more mixed results; see "The Changing Impact of Marriage and Children on Women's Labor Force Participation" *Monthly Labor Review* 132, no. 2 (February 2009): 3–14.

The rising participation rates of mothers represent an increase in the *attachment* of women to the labor force over the life cycle. This attachment is dramatically illustrated by data on how quickly women return to the labor force after a first birth. In the early 1960s, 44 percent of first-time mothers worked during pregnancy and, of this group, only 17 percent returned to work within 3 months and just 21 percent within 6 months. By the first decade of the 2000s, 66 percent of first-time mothers worked during pregnancy and, of this group, fully 59 percent returned to work within 3 months and nearly three-quarters (73 percent) within 6 months.[18]

Second, the differences in participation rates by marital status are also considerably smaller today than they were in 1960. That is, married women's participation rates in each presence-of-children category are considerably closer to those of ever-married women in 2015 than they were in 1960. In addition, research has found that, within the group of married women, wives' participation decisions are less sensitive to their husbands' income than they were in the past.[19] In other words, the negative effect of having a high-earning husband on the labor force participation rates of today's wives is much smaller than it used to be. In this way too, married women's behavior is now more similar to that of their nonmarried counterparts.

Figure 6-4 shows trends in participation rates of women with children under age 18 by marital status in more detail. This figure shows that for all three groups—never-married, married, and other ever-married mothers—there have been long-term increases in labor force participation rates but that the timing and magnitude of these changes varied considerably.

From 1960 to the early 1990s, the main story is the dramatic rise in married women's participation rates relative to other groups. In 1960 participation rates of married mothers were 28 percentage points lower than those of other ever-married mothers, but by 1992 married women's participation rates lagged by only 5 percentage points. Data on never-married mothers have been available only since 1975. At that time their participation rates were about the same as those of married mothers; however, by 1992 married mothers were *considerably more* (15 percentage points more) likely to be in the labor force than never-married mothers.

After 1990, the growth in labor force participation rates of married mothers slowed, and by the mid-1990s their participation rates began to level off and eventually declined somewhat. In contrast, over the 1990s, participation rates increased sharply among never-married and other ever-married mothers,[20] although the participation rates of these groups too began to level off and decline a bit after the early 2000s. Nevertheless, participation rates of never-married and, especially, other ever-married mothers continue to be higher than those of married mothers. The factors behind these recent trends are explored further later in this chapter.

---

[18]Linda Laughlin, "Maternity Leave and Employment Patterns of First-Time Mothers: 1961–2008," US Census Bureau, Washington, DC (October 2011). The "early 1960s" refers to 1961–1965, and the "first decade of the 2000s" refers to 2006–2008 for the prebirth data and 2005–2007 for the postbirth data. See also Judith Dey, "How Has Labor Force Participation among Young Moms and Dads Changed? A Comparison of Two Cohorts," *Beyond the Numbers* 3, no. 19 (September 2014), accessed July 1, 2016, www.bls.gov.

[19]Blau and Kahn, "Changes in the Labor Supply Behavior of Married Women"; and Bradley T. Heim, "The Incredible Shrinking Elasticities: Married Female Labor Supply, 1978–2002," *Journal of Human Resources* 42, no. 4 (Fall 2007): 881–918.

[20]Rebecca M. Blank, "Distinguished Lecture on Economics in Government—Fighting Poverty: Lessons from Recent U.S. History," *Journal of Economic Perspectives* 14, no. 2 (Spring 2000): 3–19; and Bruce D. Meyer and Dan T. Rosenbaum, "Making Single Mothers Work: Recent Tax and Welfare Policy and Its Effects," *National Tax Journal* 53 (December 2000): 1027–62.

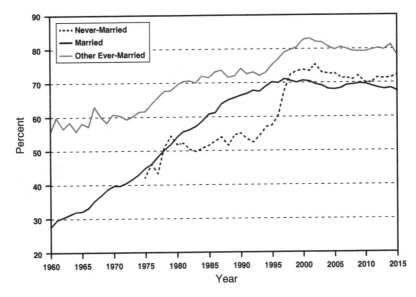

FIGURE 6-4 Labor Force Participation Rates of Women With Children Under Age 18, 1960–2015

Sources: *Statistical Abstract of the United States*, 2004 (Table 597), 2008 (Table 580), and 2012 (Table 599), and Proquest Statistical Abstract of the United States 2016 (Table 617) from https://rowman.com/ISBN/9781598887938/ProQuest-Statistical-Abstract-of-the-United-States-2016 (accessed May-2016); BLS Bulletin 2340 (August 1989); Bernan Press, Handbook of US Labor Statistics, 1st ed. (1997); and unpublished data from the BLS.

Even though most attention has been focused on the effect of the presence of children on women's labor supply, some research has examined the impact of children on male labor supply. Perhaps not surprisingly given traditional gender roles, fatherhood has been found to *increase* the labor supply of men. What may be surprising, however, is that men have been found to increase their labor supply more in response to the birth of sons than daughters.[21] Although, as discussed in Chapter 17, preference for male children is quite pronounced in a number of Asian countries including India and China, this and other recent research suggest it is by no means entirely absent in the United States.[22]

The Value of Market Time (*w*)

In addition to the impact of the value of nonmarket time, the labor force participation decision is influenced by the labor market opportunities an individual faces, particularly the wage rate available in the labor market. To see this effect in greater detail, let us consider the case of Ellen, who initially faces the budget constraint *ABC*, shown in Figure 6-5. Her potential market wage is $8.00 per hour, while her

---

[21]Shelly Lundberg and Elaina Rose, "The Effects of Sons and Daughters on Men's Labor Supply and Wages," *Review of Economics and Statistics* 84, no. 2 (May 2002): 251–68.

[22]For example, the birth or expected birth of a son has been found to increase the probability that unmarried biological parents will marry and the presence of sons to reduce the probability that married couples will divorce. Studies also find that in families with at least two children, the probability of having another child is higher in all-girl families than in all-boy families. See Gordon B. Dahl and Enrico Moretti, "The Demand for Sons: Evidence from Divorce, Fertility, and Shotgun Marriage," *Review of Economic Studies* 75, no. 4 (October 2008): 1085–120; and Shelly Lundberg and Elaina Rose, "Child Gender and the Transition to Marriage," *Demography* 40, no. 2 (May 2003): 333–49.

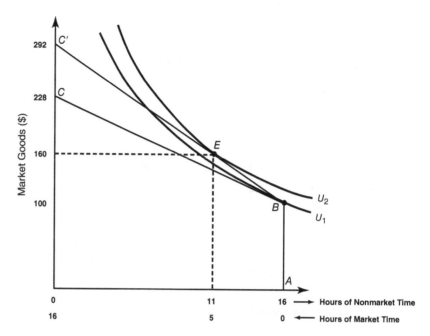

FIGURE 6-5 Impact of the (Potential) Market Wage on Labor Force Participation

nonlabor income (say, equal to her husband's earnings) is $100 per day. Given her tastes (represented by her indifference curves), she maximizes utility at point B, where she devotes all her time to nonmarket activities. Note that at point B the indifference curve (U_1) is steeper than the budget line (BC)—Ellen's value of nonmarket time (w^*) is higher than the wage rate offered to her by the market (w).

Now suppose that Ellen's market opportunities improve and her potential market wage increases to $12.00. Her new budget constraint is ABC'. Segment AB of her budget constraint remains unchanged because it is still the case that if she remains out of the labor market entirely, she (and her family) will receive $100 a day of nonlabor income. However, BC' is steeper than BC because she now receives $12.00 for each hour she supplies to the market rather than $8.00. Another way to see this is to realize that C' must lie above C because if Ellen devotes all her time to market work, her total income at a wage of $12.00 per hour ($292) will be higher than it would have been at a wage of $8.00 per hour ($228).

At the higher wage, the budget constraint (BC') is now steeper than the indifference curve at point B—the market wage (w) is greater than the value of nonmarket time (w^*), and Ellen maximizes her utility at point E on indifference curve U_2, where she supplies 5 hours to the market. Therefore, Ellen now chooses to participate in the labor force.

This example illustrates the **substitution effect**. An increase in the wage rate, all else equal, raises the opportunity cost of time spent in nonmarket activities and, hence, the "price" of nonmarket time. Individuals are expected to respond by supplying more time to the market and substituting market goods for nonmarket time in consumption or production. Because the wage increase clearly enables Ellen to reach a higher indifference curve, we may conclude that she feels better off with the combination of commodities represented by point E, even though she has less nonmarket time available at E than at B.

Published data are not readily available on participation rates of individuals by the wage they could potentially earn in the labor market. However, some indication of the impact of the potential market wage on labor force participation may be gained by examining the association between educational attainment and labor force participation. As we shall see in greater detail in Chapter 8, education is strongly positively associated with labor market earnings. A common interpretation of this empirical relationship is that education increases market productivity and hence market earnings. The positive association between education and labor market earnings leads us to expect education to be positively associated with labor force participation. One qualification worth noting, however, is that, especially for women, the positive effect of education on labor force participation may be reduced to the extent that additional education also raises the productivity of women's nonmarket time. For example, the time that more educated mothers spend with their children could potentially contribute more to their children's achievement levels than the time spent by less educated mothers.[23]

Nonetheless, as may be seen in panel a of Figure 6-6, a positive relationship exists between education and labor force participation among women. (Women with higher levels of education are more likely to be in the labor force.) We may interpret this positive relationship between education and labor force participation as reflecting a positive relationship between wages and labor force participation, although it may also reflect self-selection: women who plan to spend a relatively high proportion of their adult years in the labor force are more likely to invest in their education. It is also the case that the jobs held by more educated individuals usually offer greater **nonpecuniary** (or nonmonetary) **benefits**—such as a more pleasant environment, more challenging work, more prestige—as well as higher wages. Consideration of such job features serves to emphasize that the value of market work should ideally take into account nonpecuniary as well as pecuniary aspects of the job.

The most striking pattern shown in Figure 6-6a is that the positive relationship between participation and education for women grew considerably stronger between 1970 and 2015. This in part reflects the considerably smaller increase in the participation rate of women who did not complete high school compared to the other education groups, but also the larger participation gains for women with some college and 4 or more years of college compared to high school graduates.

Panel b of Figure 6-6 show a similar positive relationship between labor force participation and education for men in 2015. Here too we see that this represents a strengthening of this relationship between 1970 and 2015; indeed, for men, the positive association between participation and education was fairly muted in 1970. One important gender difference, is that, in contrast to the participation increases for women, the labor force participation of men *fell* for all education groups. This decrease was particularly pronounced for less educated men and smallest for male college graduates.

At the same time that the labor force participation rates of less educated men and women decreased relative to their more educated counterparts, their relative labor market wages also fell. As explained in more detail in Chapter 10, wage inequality has increased in the United States and in many other economically advanced nations. The wages of less-skilled workers have decreased relative to their more highly skilled counterparts. Some evidence indicates that the declining

---

[23]Interestingly, more educated parents (mothers and fathers) spend more time with their children than less educated parents do, all else equal; see Jonathan Guryan, Erik Hurst, and Melissa Kearney, "Parental Education and Parental Time with Children," *Journal of Economic Perspectives* 22, no. 3 (Summer 2008): 23–46.

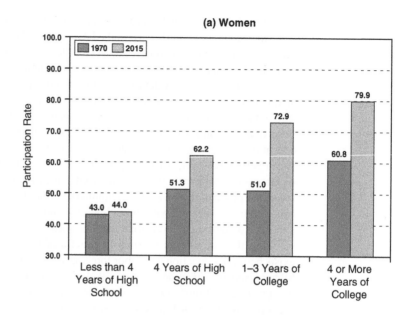

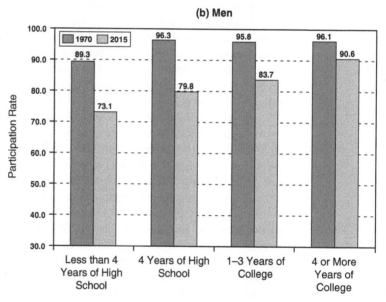

FIGURE 6-6 Labor Force Participation by Education, 1970 and 2015, Ages 25-64

Source: US Department of Labor, *Handbook of Labor Statistics,* and author's tabulations from the 2015 microdata file of the March Current Population Survey.

relative labor force participation of less educated women and men is due at least in part to their declining market wage opportunities.[24] The widening wage gap between more educated and less educated women and men is considered in more detail in Chapter 8. In addition to the negative effect of declining relative

---

[24]Chinhui Juhn, "Decline of Male Labor Market Participation: The Role of Declining Market Opportunities," *Quarterly Journal of Economics* 107, no. 1 (February 1992): 79–121; and Chinhui Juhn and Kevin M. Murphy, "Wage Inequality and Family Labor Supply," *Journal of Labor Economics* 15, no. 1, pt. 1 (January 1997): 72–97.

participation and wages on the economic status of less educated women, single headship increased considerably more for this group than for their more highly educated counterparts. This development also adversely affected their economic status.[25] Chapter 14 discusses the considerable economic disadvantages faced by such families.

The Hours Decision

The impact of a change in the wage rate on the number of *hours* supplied to the market by those who are already labor force participants is a bit more complex than the impact of a wage change on *labor force participation*. This complexity is illustrated in Figure 6-7. As we saw in Figure 6-5, an increase in the wage rate corresponds to an outward rotation of the budget constraint because more market goods can now be purchased for every hour worked. This is shown as a rotation from *CD* to *CD'* in Figure 6-7. In both panels a and b, the individual initially maximizes utility at point *A* on indifference curve U_1. At a higher wage, he or she is able to reach a higher indifference curve and selects point *B* on indifference curve U_2, resulting in either an increase, (shown in panel a) or a decrease (shown in panel b) in hours supplied to the market.[26] These outcomes illustrate that, *for labor force participants*, an increase in the wage rate produces two distinct effects.

On the one hand, the increase in the wage is like an increase in income. For any given amount of time supplied to the market *greater than 0 hours*, income is higher along *CD'* than along *CD*. This gives rise to an *income effect* that, other things equal, increases the demand not only for most market goods, but also for nonmarket time and, hence, lowers hours supplied to the market. On the other hand, the increase in the wage also raises the opportunity cost of nonmarket time, resulting in a *substitution effect* that, all else equal, causes a reduction in nonmarket time and an increase in the supply of hours to the market.

Thus, when the wage rate rises, the substitution effect operates to increase labor hours supplied, but the income effect operates to reduce labor hours supplied. The net effect is theoretically indeterminate. If the substitution effect dominates the income effect, work hours increase (panel a). If the income effect dominates the substitution effect, work hours decrease (panel b). Again, recall that *a wage increase unambiguously raises the probability of labor force participation* because, in this case, there is only a positive substitution effect; no offsetting income effect occurs.

Empirical Evidence on the Responsiveness of Labor Supply to Wages and Income

Our consideration of the labor supply decision suggests that both the wages that workers can earn in the labor market and the nonlabor income available to them should influence their labor supply decisions. This is what economic theory predicts, but what has actually been found when economists have looked at the data?

---

[25]Francine D. Blau, "Trends in the Well-Being of American Women: 1970–1995," *Journal of Economic Literature* 36, no. 1 (March 1998): 112–65; and Sara McLanahan, "Diverging Destinies: How Children Are Faring under the Second Demographic Transition," *Demography* 41, no. 4 (November 2004): 607–27.
[26]The diagrammatic representation of the effect of a wage change on work hours is shown in greater detail in Appendix 6A.

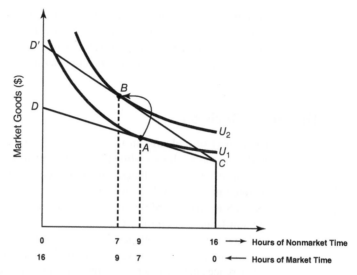

(a) THE SUBSTITUTION EFFECT DOMINATES THE INCOME EFFECT

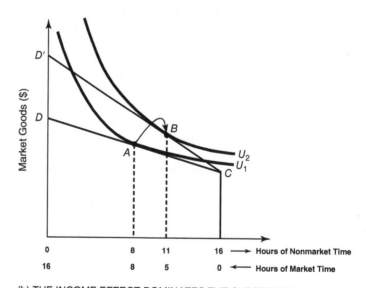

(b) THE INCOME EFFECT DOMINATES THE SUBSTITUTION EFFECT

FIGURE 6-7 Impact of the Market Wage on Labor Hours

How responsive is labor supply really to an individual's wages and nonlabor income? Does this responsiveness differ between women and men? Has this responsiveness changed over time?

The research to date especially focuses on married women because, given traditional gender roles, their labor supply behavior is most likely to be affected by the family context. As explained in greater detail in the "Labor Supply Elasticities" box, economists measure the magnitude of this responsiveness by the **elasticity**. The **wage elasticity** measures the responsiveness of an individual's labor supply to a change in his or her own wage. The **income elasticity** measures the responsiveness of an individual's labor supply to a change in his or her nonlabor income. For married individuals, especially wives, the largest source of nonlabor income is generally their spouses' wages (or income). Thus, much of the research on the impact of nonlabor income focuses on how a change in a husband's wage (or income) affects his wife's labor supply. The effect of a change in a wife's wage (or income) on her husband's labor supply has also been examined.

As a baseline, let us begin by considering research findings for the 1970s and 1980s. An extensive survey of the labor supply literature, with most of the data in the studies cited coming from that period, found that men's wage elasticity was 0.08, while women's wage elasticity was much larger, at 0.78.[27] For nonlabor income, the evidence was a bit more mixed but again suggested that women's labor supply was more responsive to changes in their husbands' wage than vice versa. For example, one study found that in 1980 the elasticity of married women's labor supply to their husband's wage was about −0.4, while the elasticity of married men's labor supply to their wife's wage was considerably smaller in absolute value, with estimates ranging from −0.01 to 0.04.[28]

These empirical findings suggest that, at least circa 1980, women's labor supply was considerably more sensitive to their own wages and to their spouse's wage or income than was men's. This gender difference is likely related to the traditional division of labor in the family. As Jacob Mincer pointed out in important early work, women may be seen as substituting among market work, home production, and leisure, while men may be viewed as substituting only or primarily between market work and leisure.[29] Although it is possible to substitute market goods for nonmarket time in leisure activities, these possibilities are relatively limited. In contrast, because purchased goods and services are in many cases useful substitutes for nonmarket time in producing the commodities the family wants, women have closer substitutes for time spent in market work than men do. Thus, changes in market wages are expected to have a larger substitution effect on women's labor supply, yielding a larger wage elasticity for them than for men.[30] One might also reason that, given traditional gender roles, women would generally be perceived as the secondary earner within the family and, thus, that their labor supply would be

---

[27]These were the medians across the studies surveyed; see Blundell and MaCurdy, "Labor Supply."

[28]See Blau and Kahn, "Changes in the Labor Supply Behavior of Married Women" (and additional results in their NBER Working Paper No. 11230). For men, these elasticities were also not always statistically significant. See also Paul J. Devereux, "Changes in Relative Wages and Family Labor Supply," *Journal of Human Resources* 39, no. 3 (Summer 2004): 696–722.

[29]Mincer, "Labor Force Participation of Married Women."

[30]Another reason for the gender difference in wage elasticities that is also related to the traditional division of labor is that many more women than men are out of the labor force. Thus, when the dependent variable is annual hours, women's wage elasticity reflects both (1) the responsiveness to a change in the wage of the participation decision as well as (2) the responsiveness to a change in the wage of the hours worked decision. For men, there is usually only the latter effect. Evidence suggests that the participation elasticity tends to be quite large, while the responsiveness of hours worked of labor force participants to a wage change tends to be fairly small, thus contributing to women's larger wage elasticity compared to men's. See James J. Heckman, "What Has Been Learned about Labor Supply in the Past Twenty Years," *American Economic Review* 83, no. 2 (May 1993): 116–21. Nonetheless, even for the hours worked decision of labor force participants, married women's responsiveness to wages and nonlabor income tends to exceed men's. Readers should also note that the discussion in the text abstracts from issues of complementarity and substitutability of the home and work time of husband and wife. There is some evidence of complementarity for older couples, which we discuss later when we consider trends in male participation.

more responsive to changes in their husband's wage than vice versa. An interesting extension of this reasoning is that, to the extent that the traditional division of labor is breaking down and men and women are more equally sharing home and market responsibilities, we would expect women's labor supply elasticities to become more similar to men's over time.

A similar conclusion is reached by Claudia Goldin who provides an insightful analysis of changes in women's labor supply elasticities over the twentieth century.[31] She reports that, around 1900, when relatively few attractive labor market options were available to women and there was considerable stigma against wives working, married women's labor supply was largely determined by their husbands' labor market opportunities, rather than their own. That is, married women might increase hours worked substantially if their husband became unemployed or if his wage fell sharply but not respond very much, if at all, when their own potential market wage rose. However, as women's education levels increased and white-collar employment opportunities became available to them, the stigma against married women working diminished. As a consequence, women's responsiveness to their own labor market opportunities (e.g., a higher wage for themselves) increased, while their responsiveness to changes in their husband's income decreased. Goldin further reasoned that, as divorce rates rose and women's jobs increasingly became careers as opposed to merely a means to earn income, not only should the effect of husbands' income continue to decline but wives' labor supply would eventually become less responsive to changes in their own wages as well. That is, as women became more strongly attached to the labor force and more committed to their careers, they would be less likely to move in and out of the labor force or greatly change their hours worked in response to changes in their wages. Putting this somewhat differently, they would begin to behave more like men.

The expectation that women's labor supply behavior would become more similar to men's has indeed been realized, although significant gender differences remain. Francine Blau and Lawrence Kahn found that, between 1980 and 2000, women's wage elasticity fell from around 0.8 to about 0.4, while their responsiveness to their husbands' wage declined in absolute value from around −0.4 to about −0.2 (i.e., each elasticity was cut roughly in half).[32] Recent evidence for the 2000s suggests this decline did not continue; there was a slight increase in the absolute value of both elasticities during this period, but it is nonetheless the case that both elasticities remain considerably below their values in earlier years.[33] Goldin sees the substantial long-term changes that have occurred so far as manifestations of a "quiet revolution" in which most women, like most men, have come to view their employment as part of a long-term career, rather than as a series of disconnected jobs.[34]

---

[31]Claudia Goldin, *Understanding the Gender Gap: An Economic History of American Women* (New York: Oxford University Press, 1990), chap. 5.

[32]Blau and Kahn, "Changes in the Labor Supply Behavior of Married Women." They obtain a range of elasticities for each year based on various specifications of the labor supply equations. Thus, more precisely, they found that women's own wage elasticity fell by 50 to 56 percent, while their income (husband's wage) elasticity declined by 38 to 47 percent in absolute value. See also Heim, "The Incredible Shrinking Elasticities."

[33]Macunovich, "Reversals in the Patterns of Women's Labor Supply."

[34]Claudia Goldin, "The Quiet Revolution That Transformed Women's Employment, Education, and Family," *American Economic Review* 96, no. 2 (May 2006): 1–20.

Labor Supply Elasticities

Economists use a concept called **elasticity** to describe how one variable responds to a change in another variable. Is this response very large or relatively small? In the case of labor supply analysis, economists focus on two specific elasticities: **wage elasticity** and **income elasticity**. The wage elasticity measures the responsiveness of an individual's labor supply to a change in his or her own wage. The income elasticity measures the responsiveness of an individual's labor supply to a change in his or her nonlabor income (for married couples, this is often their spouse's income or wage). Elasticities are useful because they provide information not only about the direction of a change, for example, that an increase in the wage increases hours worked, but also about the *magnitude* or size of the change.

Specifically, the *wage elasticity of labor supply* is defined as the percentage change in hours worked by an individual induced by a 1 percent increase in an individual's own wage.

$$\text{Wage Elasticity:} \frac{\%\text{ change in hours worked}}{\%\text{ change in wages}}$$

The *income elasticity of labor supply* is defined as the percentage change in hours worked by an individual induced by a 1 percent increase in an individual's nonlabor income.

$$\text{Income Elasticity:} \frac{\%\text{ change in hours worked}}{\%\text{ change in nonlabor income}}$$

Let us suppose that a study finds that the wage elasticity of married women is 0.78. To understand what this means, we can rewrite this as 0.78/1. This figure tells us that a 1 percent increase in wages (the denominator) leads to a 0.78 percent increase in hours worked (the numerator). Let us say the same study finds that the wage elasticity of labor supply of married men is 0.08. This is clearly a considerably smaller response than that for married women—for married men, a 1 percent increase in wages induces only a 0.08 percent increase in hours worked.

Our consideration of the labor supply decision leads us to expect the income elasticity of labor supply to be negative. That is, an *increase* in nonlabor income (e.g., spouse's income) is expected to *reduce* work hours. For example, an income elasticity of −0.4 for married women means that a 1 percent increase in nonlabor income leads to a 0.4 percent decrease in hours worked. An income elasticity of −0.01 for married men means that a 1 percent increase in nonlabor income leads to only a 0.01 percent decrease in hours worked.

When an elasticity exceeds 1 (in absolute value*), we say that the relationship is relatively "elastic." When an elasticity is less than 1 (in absolute value), we say that the relationship is relatively "inelastic." When an elasticity is just equal to 1 (in absolute value), we say that the relationship is "unit elastic," with the magnitude of the response (a 1 percent change) exactly equal to the magnitude of the change

continues

in the variable that caused it (a 1 percent change). In these examples, the wage and income elasticities are inelastic for both married men and married women, although women's elasticities are considerably larger than men's in absolute value.

---

*Absolute value *refers to the value of a number, regardless of its sign. For example, the absolute value of both −2 and 2 is 2.*

Economic Conditions

Fluctuations in economic conditions also affect labor force participation. These effects are likely to be largest among so-called secondary workers. Economists view the response of labor force participation to changes in the level of economic activity as being the net result of two opposing effects.

The **added worker effect** predicts that during economic downturns, if the primary earner becomes unemployed, other family members may enter (or postpone their exit from) the labor force in order to maintain family income. The decline in their nonlabor income due to the unemployment of the primary earner lowers the value of other family members' nonmarket time (w^*). (This effect is shown as a movement from point B' to point D in Figure 6-3.) Such individuals may leave the labor force when economic conditions improve and the primary earner is again employed on a regular basis.

At the same time, the **discouraged worker effect** holds that during times of high unemployment, when individuals lose their jobs, they may become discouraged and drop out of the labor force after a fruitless period of job search. Others who are out of the labor force may postpone labor force entry until economic conditions improve. Discouragement is due to the decline in the *expected* reward to market work (w)[35] because of the difficulty of locating an acceptable job. (This effect is shown as a movement from point E to point B in Figure 6-5.) As economic conditions improve, previously discouraged workers may renew their job search and enter the labor force.

Both of these effects can operate at the same time for different households. The *net* effect of economic conditions on labor force participation rates depends on whether the discouraged or added worker effect predominates in the aggregate. This is an empirical question. Research suggests that the discouraged worker effect is dominant. Thus, the labor force tends to shrink or grow less rapidly in recessions and to expand or grow more rapidly during upturns in the economy.[36] The dominance of the discouraged worker effect is consistent with trends in labor force participation during the Great Recession and its aftermath that we reviewed in Chapter 5. As we saw in Figure 5-2, both male and female labor force participation rates declined between 2007 and 2015. Moreover, in our discussion of Figures 5-3 and 5-4, we noted that the participation rates of teenagers declined particularly sharply over this period.

However, now that the recovery from the recession has been ongoing for a number of years, the absence of a rebound (uptick) in male and female participation rates is

---

[35]The expected reward to market work is equal to p (the probability of finding an acceptable job) multiplied by w (the wage given a job is obtained) or ($p \times w$).

[36]For some evidence, see Luca Benati, "Some Empirical Evidence on the 'Discouraged Worker' Effect," *Economics Letters* 70, no. 3 (2001): 387–95. This does not rule out an added worker effect, it just means that the discouraged worker effect generally dominates. For evidence on the added worker effect, see Martha A. Starr, "Gender, Added-Worker Effects, and the 2007–2009 Recession: Looking within the Household," *Review of Economics of the Household* 12, no. 2 (June 2014): 209–35.

both puzzling and a source of concern. These continued low participation rates may be because, as argued in an analysis by President Obama's Council of Economic Advisors, the post-2007 decline in labor force participation reflected both shorter-term cyclical and long-term factors.[37] To the extent the decline was due to cyclical factors, the particular severity of the Great Recession may have lowered participation to a greater extent than occurred in previous downturns. With respect to long-term factors, the large cohort of baby boomers (those born between 1946 and 1964) began aging out of the prime working ages (25–54) at right around the same time as the Great Recession. This demographic shift places downward pressure on the overall labor force participation rate because, as we have seen, older individuals participate in the labor force at lower rates. In addition, as the data in Chapter 5 show, male labor force participation rates have been gradually declining since the 1950s and there were also some small decreases in participation rates for prime-age women even prior to the recession. These longer-term trends, particularly the male declines, might have been expected to continue even in the absence of the recession. Declining participation rates of prime-age males and the stalling and slight downturn in women's participation rates are in themselves significant and concerning developments that are examined later in this chapter.

Some Applications of the Theory: Taxes, Childcare Costs, and Labor Supply

Taxes and the Decision to Work

Not all money earned is actually at the disposal of the worker. Some of it has to be paid out in taxes. Because earnings are taxed and the value of home production is not, labor force participation among married women is discouraged. Two features of the US income tax system particularly discourage married women's labor force participation: the tax system is progressive (additional increments of income are taxed at higher rates), and these tax rates are applied to family, not individual, income. (This issue is discussed in greater depth in Chapter 15.) One consequence is that married women, often regarded as secondary earners within the family, face a relatively high tax rate on the first dollar of their labor market earnings since it is "added on" to their husbands' earnings in calculating taxes. In general, we expect that the higher the tax rate (the lower the after-tax wage), the more likely a woman is to decide not to participate in the labor force.

This point may be illustrated by Figure 6-5. Suppose Joan earns $12.00 per hour and faces budget constraint ABC'. If she has to pay out, say, one-third (33.3 percent) of her income in taxes, her after-tax wage (or hourly take-home pay) will be only $8.00. This situation is represented by budget constraint ABC. At this lower wage, Joan chooses to stay out of the labor market.[38]

Some empirical evidence on the impact of taxes on labor supply is provided by research on the effect of the **Earned Income Tax Credit (EITC)** on the labor force participation of single and married women in families with children. As explained

---

[37]Council of Economic Advisors, Office of the President, "The Labor Force Participation Rate since 2007: Causes and Policy Implications" (July 2014), https://obamawhitehouse.archives.gov.

[38]We simplified the representation of a progressive tax by using Figure 6-5 in that we show only one tax rate—the one Joan faces given her level of family income—and assume that additional hours worked do not push her into a higher tax bracket. In fact, as long as individuals are below the maximum rate, it is possible that as they work more hours their higher total income will push them into a higher tax bracket. Thus, the after-tax budget constraint may be "kinked," its slope becoming flatter each time the individual enters a higher tax bracket.

in greater detail in Chapter 15, the EITC, which is part of the federal tax code, targets low-earning families with children and subsidizes their earnings through a refundable tax credit. Consider Dawn, a low-earner single mother. For individuals like Dawn, the amount of the EITC increases with additional hours worked. This is in effect a wage subsidy, raising their wage rate and hence their probability of participating in the labor force. Again looking at Figure 6-5, this increase in the wage rate corresponds to a change in the budget constraint from *ABC* to *ABC'* and, hence, encourages labor force participation. The EITC has been found to strongly promote employment among low-earner single mothers. It has been estimated that nearly 60 percent of the very large increase in the employment of single mother from 1984 to 1996 was due to the expansion of the EITC alone.[39]

However, since the EITC is targeted on low-earning families, it is gradually phased out as total family earnings rise.[40] For instance, consider the situation of a low-income married couple with children. Depending on the level of the husband's earnings, the EITC could either encourage or discourage the labor force participation of a wife in such a family. In the case where the husband has very low earnings, his wife's participation is encouraged by the wage subsidy provided by the EITC for which the family is still eligible. (This is similar to the case of Dawn.) However, at higher levels of the husband's income, the decrease in the EITC with additional hours worked is like a decrease in the wage of a secondary worker contemplating labor force entry—as in the case of Joan. In such families, employment of wives will be discouraged. Evidence suggests that, on net, the EITC modestly discourages labor force participation by wives in low-earning families, decreasing their participation by about 1 percentage point.[41] Still, given the EITC's considerable positive effect on the labor force participation of single mothers, the policy on net promotes women's labor force participation.

Government Subsidies of Childcare and Women's Labor Force Participation

The negative effect of young children on their mothers' labor force participation has diminished, but young children are still a significant deterrent to the entry of their mothers into the labor market. Childcare subsidies by the government could lower the cost of childcare. What would be the expected effect on women's labor supply? We can use economic theory to see that a reduction in childcare costs is expected to increase women's labor force participation.

Recall that so far we have assumed that individuals do not value market goods and nonmarket time in and of themselves but rather because they can be used to produce the commodities people do value. This framework yields valuable insights

[39]Bruce D. Meyer and Dan T. Rosenbaum, "Welfare, the Earned Income Tax Credit, and the Labor Supply of Single Mothers," *Quarterly Journal of Economics* 116, no. 3 (August 2001): 1063–1114. See also Nada Eissa and Jeffrey B. Liebman, "Labor Supply Response to the Earned Income Tax Credit," *Quarterly Journal of Economics* 111, no. 2 (May 1996): 606–37.

[40]For a comprehensive diagrammatic representation of the impact of the EITC on the individual's budget constraint, including the phase-out range, see Ronald G. Ehrenberg and Robert S. Smith, *Modern Labor Economics: Theory and Evidence*, 12th ed. (Upper Saddle River, NJ: Pearson, 2015), chap. 6.

[41]Nada Eissa and Hilary Williamson Hoynes, "Taxes and the Labor Market Participation of Married Couples: The Earned Income Tax Credit," *Journal of Public Economics* 88, issues 9–10 (August 2004): 1931–58. A recent review of the evidence confirms the findings of earlier research that the labor supply effects of the EITC are positive for single mothers and smaller and negative for married mothers; see Austin Nichols and Jesse Rothstein, "The Earned Income Tax Credit (EITC)," in *Economics of Means-Tested Transfer Programs in the United States*, vol. 1, ed. Robert Moffitt (Chicago: University of Chicago Press, 2016), 137–218.

into the possibilities of substitution in consumption and in production, which help determine the steepness of the indifference curves. However, to examine the impact of the cost of childcare explicitly, it is more convenient to simply assume that the indifference curves represent the individual's preferences for market goods (income) versus nonmarket time.

Suppose Figure 6-5 represents the situation of Nancy, a woman with small children. To examine the impact of childcare costs, it is helpful to think of the hourly cost of childcare that Nancy must pay if she works as similar to a tax on her market earnings. If the budget constraint shows the wage Nancy receives after childcare costs are subtracted out, it is clear that a decrease in childcare costs is equivalent to an increase in her wage rate. For example, suppose Nancy can earn $14.00 an hour but must pay $6.00 an hour in childcare costs. This results in a *net* wage of $8.00 per hour ($14.00 − $6.00 = 8.00), given by segment *BC*. At this wage, she chooses not to participate in the labor market. However, if her childcare costs were to fall to $2.00 per hour due to a subsidy, her net wage rises to $12.00 per hour ($14.00 − $2.00 = $12.00), given by segment *BC'* and she would participate.

In this example, the decrease in childcare costs results in Nancy deciding to enter the labor force. In general, we would expect the availability of childcare at a lower price to increase the labor force participation rate of women with small children. The empirical evidence supports this expectation.[42] For example, one study that examined the effect of receiving a childcare subsidy on the employment of single mothers found a substantial positive effect, ranging from 13 to 33 percentage points.[43] Some evidence also suggests that provision of free public kindergarten (which is like a large public subsidy of childcare costs for 5-year-olds) had a substantial positive effect on the labor supply of mothers of 5-year-olds.[44]

A decline in childcare costs is also likely to have long-run effects on women's labor supply and wages. Because women would experience shorter (and possibly fewer) labor force interruptions, they would accumulate longer and more continuous labor market experience. This is expected to enhance their career progression and increase their earnings, which would in turn further reinforce the tendency to spend more time in the labor market.[45] Therefore, in the long run, a reduction in childcare costs is likely not only to raise women's labor force participation but also to enhance

[42]For a review of the evidence on the negative relationship between childcare costs and mother's labor force participation, see Taryn W. Morrissey, "Child Care and Parent Labor Force Participation: A Review of the Research Literature," *Review of Economics of the Household*, March 23, 2016, http://link.springer.com/article/10.1007/s11150-016-9331-3.

[43]David Blau and Erdal Tekin, "The Determinants and Consequences of Child Care Subsidies for Single Mothers in the USA," *Journal of Population Economics* 20, no. 4 (October 2007): 719–41. A positive effect of a subsidy has been identified for Canada as well; see Michael Baker, Jonathan Gruber, and Kevin Milligan, "Universal Child Care, Maternal Labor Supply, and Family Well-Being," *Journal of Political Economy* 116, no. 4 (August 2008): 709–45.

[44]Jonah Gelbach, "Public Schooling for Young Children and Maternal Labor Supply," *American Economic Review* 92, no. 1 (March 2002): 307–22. However, another study focusing on the introduction of universal preschool in three states found little effect on the labor supply of most women; see Maria Donovan Fitzpatrick, "Preschoolers Enrolled and Mothers at Work? The Effects of Universal Prekindergarten," *Journal of Labor Economics* 28, no. 1 (January 2010): 51–85.

[45]For evidence that current work experience increases the probability of future participation due to its effect on wages, see Zvi Eckstein and Kenneth I. Wolpin, "Dynamic Labour Force Participation of Married Women and Endogenous Work Experience," *Review of Economic Studies* 56, no. 3 (July 1989): 375–90. Evidence that rising labor market returns to experience between the 1970s and the 1990s contributed to the observed increase in the labor force participation of married women is provided in Claudia Olivetti, "Changes in Women's Aggregate Hours of Work: The Role of Returns to Experience," *Review of Economic Dynamics* 9, no. 4 (October 2006): 557–87.

their occupational attainment and earnings. Thus, childcare subsidies could contribute to a reduction in labor market inequality between men and women. Whether such subsidies are desirable on other grounds is considered in greater detail in Chapter 16.

Other Factors Affecting Childcare Costs and Women's Labor Force Participation

Childcare costs and thus the decision to work are influenced not only by government subsidies but also by other alternatives to mothers' own caregiving time, including the availability and cost of housekeeping and childcare services and the proximity of family who can potentially help out. Two studies provide evidence of the potential importance of each of these factors.

The first study looked at the relationship between the supply of low-skilled immigrants in a city and the *labor supply* of high-wage women in that city. Low-skilled immigrants tend to provide in-home care more inexpensively and offer more flexible hours compared to native-born workers. This study found that a higher concentration of low-skilled immigration in a city increased the labor supply of high-wage, high-skilled women. In addition, it found that these women decreased the time they spent in household work and increased their expenditures on housekeeping services, suggesting that they had employed substitutes for their time in these activities to facilitate their increased labor supply.[46]

The second study focused on the availability of relatives to help with childcare. In particular, the study looked at whether married mothers of young children lived in close geographical proximity to their mothers or mothers-in-law. Nearby family not only increases the availability of regularly scheduled childcare during work hours but also may help with irregular or unanticipated childcare. (The researchers call the latter an insurance aspect of proximity.) This study found that having a mother or mother-in-law nearby was indeed associated with significantly higher labor force participation of these mothers of young children.[47]

Analyzing the Long-Term Growth in Women's Labor Force Participation

In the remaining sections of this chapter we apply the theoretical model of labor supply to analyze some of the major trends in labor force participation described in Chapter 5. In this section, we provide an overview of the factors responsible for the *long-term* increase in women's labor force participation over the twentieth century. We conclude this section with a box that looks closely at the ways in which World War II contributed to both the short- and long-term increases in women's labor force participation. In the next section, we consider the period since the mid-1990s—when women's participation rates first plateaued and then declined a bit. Next, we consider explanations for the long-term decrease in men's labor force participation rates and

[46]Patricia Cortés and José Tessada, "Low-Skilled Immigration and the Labor Supply of Highly-Skilled Women," *American Economic Journal: Applied Economics* 3, no. 3 (July 2011): 88–123.
[47]Janice Compton and Robert A. Pollak, "Family Proximity, Childcare, and Women's Labor Force Attachment," *Journal of Urban Economics* 79 (January 2014): 72–90.

conclude with an examination of some of the reasons for differences in labor force participation trends of blacks and whites.

Why did female labor force participation rise over the course of the twentieth century? Drawing upon the analysis presented earlier in this chapter, the obvious answer is a rise in the wage rate (w), a decrease in the value of nonmarket time (w^*), or a combination of both. Considerable evidence shows various developments that would be expected to cause each of these effects, as well as complex interactions that reinforce the original results.[48]

Factors Influencing the Value of Market Time (w)

A variety of factors caused the real (inflation-adjusted) wages of women (w) to increase over time. The result was an outward rotation of the budget constraint, as shown in Figure 6-5. Under these circumstances, more women are expected to find that the wage offered to them by the market exceeds the value of their nonmarket time and, hence, choose to enter the labor force.[49] This process does not require that women's wages increase relative to men's wages. During the 1950s and 1960s, both men's and women's real wages were rising and the gender gap remained roughly constant. For much of the period since the early 1970s, however, men's real wages were stagnant or declining, while women's real wages have increased since 1980. During this time, the gender pay gap narrowed.

RISING QUALIFICATIONS: EDUCATION AND EXPERIENCE   As women obtained more education, the wage rate they were able to earn by working in the market went up, and they were more likely to work outside the home. At the same time, once women were more inclined to work for pay, they sought more schooling, and also more market-oriented fields of study, in order to obtain better-paying jobs.

The magnitude of this phenomenon can be gauged by the enormous increase in the proportion of the population that has graduated from high school or obtained college degrees. Between 1940 and 2015, the proportion of women who completed at least 4 years of high school increased from 26 to 89 percent and the proportion of men, from 23 to 88 percent. During this same period, the proportion of women who completed 4 or more years of college increased from 3.8 to 32.7 percent, and for men the proportion rose from 5.5 to 32.3 percent.[50]

The statistics for higher education reflect the fact that, traditionally, more young men than young women completed college and pursued graduate study. However, this gender differential began to decline in the late 1960s. Since that time, women have greatly increased their share of college, graduate, and professional degrees, as well as their representation in traditionally male fields of study. Hence, although men's educational attainment has also increased, gender differences in higher education in

---

[48]See Goldin, *Understanding the Gender Gap*, chap. 5, for an interesting econometric analysis of the trends in labor force participation.

[49]Considerable evidence links the growth in female labor force participation to rising wages for women; see, for example, Juhn and Murphy, "Wage Inequality and Family Labor Supply"; Blau and Kahn, "Changes in the Labor Supply Behavior of Married Women"; and Christian Bredemeier and Falko Juessen, "Assortative Mating and Female Labor Supply," *Journal of Labor Economics* 31, no. 3 (July 2013): 603–31.

[50]The statistics presented on educational attainment here, which are from the *Statistical Abstract of the United States* (2016), differ somewhat from those presented later in Chapter 8. This discrepancy is due to the age range, which is 25 years or over here but ages 25–64 in Chapter 8.

the general population have narrowed substantially; in fact, since the 1980s, young women have been more likely to graduate college than young men. Data on these trends and explanations for them are presented in Chapter 8.

THE DEMAND FOR FEMALE LABOR   It is also the case that, first with industrialization and then with the shift to an increasingly service-based economy, the demand for workers in traditionally female clerical and service jobs increased, and this caused their wages to be higher than they otherwise would have been.[51] As discussed in Chapter 2, married women were barred from clerical employment by many large firms in the 1920s and 1930s, and they did not fully benefit from this expansion in demand until these marriage bars were abandoned in the 1950s.[52] It is also quite likely that antidiscrimination legislation has increased the demand for women in traditionally male jobs since its passage in the mid-1960s. In addition to the labor market offering women higher wages, the reward to labor market experience rose during the latter part of the twentieth century, as the demand for skill grew. This further increased women's incentives to remain attached to the labor market.[53]

OVERALL PRODUCTIVITY INCREASES   Female as well as male workers benefited from increases in labor productivity due to growth over time in the capital stock and **technological change** (invention, innovation, and diffusion), which exerted upward pressure on wages, all else equal.

Factors Influencing the Value of Nonmarket Time (w*)

It would be a mistake, however, to ascribe the impetus for the influx of women into the labor market entirely to higher wage rates and increases in demand for women workers and thus to overlook those changes that influenced the relative value of nonmarket time (w*). Even though changes in w* are not directly measurable, a review of the changes in the various factors influencing w* suggests that their net effect was to decrease the value of nonmarket time. In any case it is clear the value of nonmarket time did decline *relative to* market time, thus causing the proportion of women working for pay to increase.

AVAILABILITY OF MARKET SUBSTITUTES AND HOUSEHOLD APPLIANCES AND THE ROLE OF TECHNOLOGICAL CHANGE   Among the most obvious changes was the increase in the availability of **market substitutes**, goods and services previously produced in the home that become available for purchase in the market. For instance, fruits and vegetables that used to be grown in the family garden became

---

[51]Valerie Oppenheimer, *The Female Labor Force in the United States: Demographic and Economic Factors Governing Its Growth and Changing Composition* (Westport, CT: Greenwood Press, 1976; originally published 1970); Goldin, *Understanding the Gender Gap*; Mary C. Brinton, "Gendered Offices: A Comparative-Historical Examination of Clerical Work in Japan and the U.S.," in *The Political Economy of Low Fertility: Japan in Comparative Perspective*, ed. Frances McCall Rosenbluth (Stanford, CA: Stanford University Press, 2007), 87–111; and Francine D. Blau and Lawrence M. Kahn, "The US Gender Pay Gap in the 1990s," *Industrial and Labor Relations Review* 60, no. 1 (October 2006): 45–66.

[52]Goldin, *Understanding the Gender Gap*. Both Oppenheimer and Goldin attribute the increased willingness of employers to hire older married women in the 1950s to a decrease in the supply of young, single female workers, caused by the small size of the cohort born during the 1930s, coupled with the decline in the marriage age that occurred during the 1950s.

[53]Olivetti, "Changes in Women's Aggregate Hours."

increasingly available at the grocery store, fresh, canned, or frozen, and often conveniently packaged for immediate use. Similarly, in earlier years yarn was spun and clothes were sewn at home, but increasingly clothes became available for purchase off the rack. For young children, nursery schools and, later, day-care centers became more prevalent, while hospitals increasingly cared for the sick, and various types of care for the infirm and aged became more common. These are only a few examples of commodities or services that in earlier days were produced with large inputs of home time but that today require mainly expenditures of money.

At the same time, important technological innovations, including indoor plumbing and electrification, eased the burden of housework, and technological change also made available a growing number of household appliances, ranging from vacuum cleaners, washing machines, and refrigerators to dishwashers and microwave ovens, which made housework easier and less time-consuming.[54]

Technological changes in other areas were beneficial as well. In the first half of the twentieth century, medical advances reduced pregnancy-related conditions that could result in severe or prolonged disablement, and the development and commercialization of infant formula provided an effective substitute for breast milk.[55] Later, in the 1960s, the development and dissemination of more effective contraceptive techniques, most importantly the birth control pill, gave women greater control not only over their fertility but also over the timing of births, allowing them to reduce the educational and labor force disruptions caused by childbearing and child-rearing.[56]

Thus, we see that the growing number of market substitutes and household appliances and other changes spurred by technological advances made doing housework and bearing and rearing children less time-consuming. As a result, the value of women's nonmarket time (w^*) decreased. This change is illustrated in Figure 6-2 by the flatter indifference curves shown in panel a compared to the steeper indifference curves shown in panel b. As may be seen in Figure 6-2, this reduction in the value of their nonmarket time caused women's labor force participation to increase. At the same time, women's rising labor force participation tended to increase the demand for market goods and services that substitute for their time in the home or make housework tasks easier, further encouraging the development and production of such products.

DEMOGRAPHIC TRENDS   Another important change that influenced relative preferences for home versus market time was the long-run decline in the birth rate, from 30.1 births per 1,000 population in 1910 to 12.5 per 1,000 by 2014. Because the rearing of young children, generally considered to be women's responsibility, is extremely time-intensive, especially in the absence of adequate provision for their care outside the home, presence of children has traditionally been one of the strongest barriers to women's entry into the labor market. As already described, only since

---

[54]For evidence on the impact of the increased availability of consumer durables on female labor force participation, see Jeremy Greenwood, Ananth Seshadri, and Mehmet Yorukoglu, "Engines of Liberation," *Review of Economic Studies* 72, no. 1 (January 2005): 109–33.

[55]Stefania Albanesi and Claudia Olivetti, "Gender Roles and Medical Progress," *Journal of Political Economy* 124, no. 3 (June 2016): 650–95.

[56]Claudia Goldin and Lawrence F. Katz, "The Power of the Pill: Oral Contraceptives and Women's Career and Marriage Decisions," *Journal of Political Economy* 110, no. 4 (August 2002): 730–70; and Martha J. Bailey, "More Power to the Pill: The Impact of Contraceptive Freedom on Women's Lifecycle Labor Supply," *Quarterly Journal of Economics* 121, no. 1 (February 2006): 289–320.

the 1960s have mothers of preschoolers worked outside the home to any significant extent, and even now their participation remains lower than that of mothers with school-age children.[57]

Not only is the period during which young children are present in the home more protracted as their numbers rise, but the longer the woman is at home, the more her skills are likely to depreciate, and the greater the probability she is to remain out permanently. Women are, of course, aware of this cost and to some extent adjust family size to their work plans, as well as vice versa.

Just as women's labor force participation is influenced by, and in turn influences, their fertility, the same is true of marital stability. The divorce rate per 1,000 population per year went from 0.9 in 1910 to 3.2 in 2014. The divorce rate influences women's labor force participation in part due to its impact on the composition of the female population: divorced women have considerably less nonlabor income than married women and are thus more likely to participate in the labor force. However, married women's behavior is affected by rising divorce rates as well. As married women become aware of the increasing probability of divorce, their labor force participation increases as a means of safeguarding their standard of living in case of a marital breakup.[58] This behavior may further increase the divorce rate in that a two-earner couple can more readily afford to get divorced. A woman can count on her own income, rather than being completely dependent on the often uncertain support of her ex-husband; and the man is less likely to need to spend resources to fully support his ex-wife.

CHANGING ROLE OF HUSBAND'S INCOME Not all changes have operated in the direction of lowering the value of nonmarket time. In particular, the earnings of men increased more rapidly than the cost of living for most of the twentieth century. As their husbands' real income goes up, all else equal, married women's labor force participation is reduced due to the income effect (see Figure 6-3). For women, however, the positive substitution effect of their own rising real wages tends to more than offset the negative income effect due to the increasing real incomes of their husbands.[59] Also, as we have seen, perhaps due to changing gender roles, the responsiveness of married women's participation to their husbands' income has declined over time. Moreover, since the 1970s, men's real wages have been stagnating overall, and those of the less educated and unskilled have declined in real terms. Given these trends, along with the decline in the responsiveness of wives' participation to husbands' income discussed earlier, this factor has had relatively little effect on women's labor supply trends in recent years.[60]

---

[57]The impact of fertility trends on the growth in female labor force participation has been confirmed in a number of studies; for a recent example, see Bredemeier and Juessen, "Assortative Mating and Female Labor Supply."

[58]William R. Johnson and Jonathan Skinner, "Labor Supply and Marital Separation," *American Economic Review* 76, no. 3 (June 1986): 455–69. The terms under which divorce is available can also affect the labor supply of married women; see Betsey Stevenson, "Divorce Law and Women's Labor Supply," *Journal of Empirical Legal Studies* 5, no. 4 (December 2008): 853–73.

[59]This was first pointed out by Mincer in "Labor Force Participation of Married Women."

[60]In fact, the married women with the largest increase in market hours since 1950 were those with high-wage husbands; see Juhn and Murphy, "Wage Inequality and Family Labor Supply"; and Ellen R. McGrattan and Richard Rogerson, "Changes in the Distribution of Family Hours Worked since 1950," in *Frontiers of Family Economics*, vol. 1, ed. Peter Rupert (Bingley, UK; Cambridge, MA: Emerald Group Publishing, 2008), 115–38. For more recent evidence focused on the post-1970 period, see Bredemeier and Juessen, "Assortative Mating and Female Labor Supply."

TASTES Over time, the development of many desirable market products, such as automobiles, air conditioning, high-definition televisions, personal computers, and smartphones, that could not be produced in the home likely increased people's preferences for market-produced goods and reduced the relative value placed on nonmarket time.[61] Such changes in tastes may be related to broader trends such as the growing urbanization of the population. The movement from farm to city reduced the opportunity for household production and increased the convenience of market purchases as well as access to market work. Even leisure activities changed from those that mainly required time—hiking, swimming in the waterhole, and chatting on the front porch—to others that required substantial expenditures, such as going to the theater, concerts, and sporting events; watching television at home on a high-definition TV; and listening to music on a smartphone.

More broadly, it is likely that changes in social attitudes and tastes across a variety of dimensions played a role in the increases in married women's labor force participation rates. This is suggested by a large number of studies that find that measured factors, like wages, husband's income, education, and presence of children, can only partially explain the observed increases in married women's labor force participation since 1970.[62] A role for attitudes is further suggested by the finding that female labor force participation expanded from the mid-1970s to the mid-1990s, when gender role attitudes were consistently becoming more egalitarian, but then stagnated subsequently when attitudes did not change further.[63]

It is also entirely possible that the trend toward rising female participation rates itself contributed to further changes in tastes and roles. It was probably far more difficult for women to enter the labor force in the past when it was the exception rather than today when it is the rule. In addition, shifting cultural norms, encouraged in part by the example of more women working in the market, led women to place a higher value on the independence and autonomy that their own earnings bring; and, increasingly, many women value career success in much the same way as their male counterparts. Finally, to the extent that people want to keep up with the Joneses in their consumption standards, it generally takes two paychecks to keep pace today.[64]

---

[61]This factor is particularly emphasized by Brown, "An Institutional Model of Wives' Work Decisions."
[62]See, for example, Juhn and Murphy, "Wage Inequality and Family Labor Supply"; John Pencavel, "The Market Work Behavior and Wages of Women: 1975–94," *Journal of Human Resources* 33, no. 4 (Fall 1998): 771–804; and Blau and Kahn, "Changes in the Labor Supply Behavior of Married Women." In addition, as we have seen, women's responsiveness to their own wages, the presence of small children, and their husbands' income also changed, reflecting changes in attitudes.
[63]David Cotter, Joan M. Hermsen, and Reeve Vanneman, "The End of the Gender Revolution? Gender Role Attitudes from 1977 to 2008," *American Journal of Sociology* 117, no. 4 (July 2011): 259–89; and Nicole M. Fortin, "Gender Role Attitudes and Women's Labor Market Participation: Opting-Out, AIDS, and the Persistent Appeal of Housewifery," in "Economics of Gender," special issue *Annals of Economics and Statistics* 117/118 (June 2015): 379–401. For a longer-term analysis of the role of culture, see Raquel Fernández, "Cultural Change as Learning: the Evolution of Female Labor Force Participation over a Century," *American Economic Review* 103, no. 1 (February 2013): 472–500.
[64]For evidence suggesting that women's labor force participation decisions are influenced by those of other women, see David Neumark and Andrew Postlewaite, "Relative Income Concerns and the Rise in Married Women's Employment," *Journal of Public Economics* 70, no. 1 (October 1998): 157–83.

The World War II Experience: Women's Surge in Labor Force Participation

As we saw in Table 5-1 in Chapter 5, a sharp rise in the female labor force participation rate occurred during World War II, particularly among married women. The female participation rate declined in the immediate post–World War II period, but it remained above prewar levels and began its long-term rise shortly after that. In this box we explain these changes by considering factors influencing the value of market time (w) and nonmarket time (w^*). Overall, the World War II experience illustrates the importance of both economic and social factors in causing changes in female labor force participation.

As men were mobilized to serve in the armed forces and the need for civilian production workers to produce military goods rose at the same time, the demand for women to fill the available positions increased greatly. This surge in labor market opportunities, including relatively high-paying, traditionally male jobs, drove up the potential market wages of women. At the same time, married women were urged to work outside the home to contribute to the war effort, raising the nonpecuniary benefits of market work for them and lowering their subjective assessment of the value of nonmarket time. In addition, the birth rate, already relatively low in the Depression years of the 1930s, remained low during the war because many young men were away in the armed forces. In addition, many of the women whose husbands joined the military experienced a decrease in their nonlabor income because working for "Uncle Sam" often did not pay as much as civilian employment. (On the other hand, those whose husbands had been unemployed before joining the military might have experienced an increase in income.)

A further factor that worked to lower the value of home time for married women was that the government and some employers opened day-care centers for children of employed mothers.* Even though not enough places were available to accommodate all the children whose mothers were employed, this action increased both the supply and the acceptability of alternative care of children, at least for the duration of the war.

Thus, the combination of an increase in the value of market time and a reduction in the value of nonmarket time induced a large increase in the proportion of women working outside the home during the war.

In the immediate postwar period, each of these factors was reversed, helping to bring about the observed decline in women's participation rates. As men returned from the war, many were able to reclaim their former jobs from the women who held them during the war. For example, many union contracts reserved their former jobs for men who had left them for military service. Even in the absence of union agreements, some employers voluntarily restored veterans' jobs because they felt it was the appropriate recompense for the veterans' wartime contribution. Moreover, whether or not a returning veteran claimed a specific job held by a woman during the war, the influx of returning males into the labor market likely lowered the demand for women workers. Also, the increase in husbands' earnings as they resumed civilian employment boosted wives' nonlabor income.

In addition, social values changed and the employment of married women outside the home was once again frowned upon, now that the wartime emergency was over. Indeed, after enduring the major dislocations of the Great Depression of the 1930s followed by a world war of unprecedented proportions, there may have been a keen desire to return to "normalcy," including traditional gender roles. This swing in attitudes also likely played a part in producing the upsurge in birth rates during the postwar period—the post–World War II baby boom (1946–1964). Finally, when the wartime labor shortage was over, day-care centers were perceived to be no longer needed and were closed.

These changes combined to lower the benefits of market work relative to the value of home time and to reduce women's labor force participation rate in the immediate post–World War II period.

The operation of the long-term factors discussed earlier meant that the female labor force participation rate immediately following the war, while lower

continues

than the wartime peak, exceeded prewar levels. The long-term rise in participation rates that followed was primarily due to fundamental economic and social factors. Yet the wartime experience may have hastened this process by helping to break down the attitudinal barriers to married women's employment outside the home and giving many women a taste of the benefits of earning their own income. Historian William H. Chafe argues that the notion that woman's appropriate sphere was in the home was so deeply embedded that it took a cataclysmic event like World War II to break down this normative barrier.** Moreover, although data indicate that more than half of the female wartime entrants left the labor force by the end of the decade,*** this means that a substantial number also *remained*. And, in line with Chafe's argument, there may have also been *longer-term* effects of the war on social views of women's roles or on the subsequent behavior of young women who were employed during the war and later returned to the labor force after dropping out for a time. A recent study suggests that there was indeed a significant longer-term effect of the war: in states with greater mobilization of men during the war, women worked more both immediately after the war and in 1950.****

*During the 1941–1943 period, the US federal government provided matching funds to induce states to provide day-care centers. An estimated 1.6 million children attended these programs. The best-known centers established by large private employers were those by Curtiss-Wright in Buffalo and by Kaiser in Portland. See Bernard Greenblatt, The Changing Role of Family and State in Child Development (San Francisco: Jossey Bass, 1977), 58–60.

**William H. Chafe, The American Woman: Her Changing Social, Economic, and Political Role, 1920–1970 (Oxford: Oxford University Press, 1972). See also Dorothy Sue Cobble, "Recapturing Working-Class Feminism: Union Women in the Postwar Era," in Not June Cleaver: Women and Gender in Postwar America, 1945–1960, ed. Joanne

Meyerowitz (Philadelphia: Temple University Press, 1994), 57–83.

***Claudia Goldin, "The Role of World War II in the Rise of Women's Work," American Economic Review 81, no. 4 (September 1991): 741–56.

****Daron Acemoglu, David H. Autor, and David Lyle, "Women, War, and Wages: The Effect of Female Labor Supply on the Wage Structure at Midcentury," Journal of Political Economy 112, no. 3 (June 2004): 497–551; see also Claudia Goldin and Claudia Olivetti, "Shocking Labor Supply: A Reassessment of the Role of World War II on Women's Labor Supply," American Economic Review: Papers & Proceedings 103, no. 3 (May 2013): 257–62.

Recent Trends in Women's Labor Force Participation: Has the Engine of Growth Stalled?

As we have seen, the post–World War II period ushered in a half-century of strong and sustained growth in female labor force participation. Since the mid-1990s, however, female participation rates have plateaued and even decreased slightly. Has the engine of growth stalled? If so, why? Will the engine restart in the foreseeable future? In this section, we consider these questions and summarize what is known about them, although, unfortunately, at this point we lack definitive answers.

At the center of both the long-term increase in female participation rates and the more recent stalling of that increase are the labor supply decisions of married women, once the overwhelming majority and still the largest segment of the adult female population. The expansion of the female labor force was a reflection of the shifting roles of married women as first married women with older, school-age children entered the labor force in increasing numbers and later married mothers of younger, preschool children joined them. Participation rates of unmarried mothers also increased, reflecting a shifting role for mothers of all marital statuses. As we saw in Figure 6-4, the growth in participation rates for married mothers began to slow in the 1990s, and by the mid-1990s their participation rates began to level off and eventually declined somewhat. There was a somewhat different picture for single mothers who experienced substantial growth in participation rates in the 1990s, but by the early 2000s their participation rates also began to flatten and decline.

Regarding these developments, we know the most about the reasons for the increase in participation rates of single mothers in the 1990s. Analyses suggest that the increasing participation of this group reflects the impact of important changes in government policy combined with a buoyant economy.[65] Starting in the 1990s, the United States experienced its longest economic expansion during peacetime—10 years—which lasted from March 1991 to March 2001. An expanding economy disproportionately benefits less-skilled individuals and the 1990s expansion benefited single-female family heads, who tend to be low-skilled. As explained further in Chapter 15, two government policies reinforced the positive effects of the booming economy on the employment of this group. First, changes in welfare policies, including a new work requirement for welfare recipients, led to an increase in single mothers' labor force participation and contributed to a substantial decline in the welfare rolls. Second, the EITC was expanded several times in the 1990s. These expansions raised the wage subsidy received by low-income single mothers and thus, as explained earlier, increased their incentive to work outside the home.

The reasons for the subsequent plateauing and declining participation rates for single mothers since the early 2000s are less well understood.[66] Certainly economic conditions have been less favorable. The economy fell into a moderate recession in March 2001, which lasted through November of that year, and then experienced its deepest downturn since the Great Depression of the 1930s with the onset of the Great Recession, which began in December 2007 and lasted through June 2009. Both recessions were followed by "jobless recoveries," that is, periods during which the economy was again expanding but job growth was disappointing and employment difficulties remained. Nonetheless, it seems unlikely that weak economic conditions provide the full explanation. As may be seen in Figure 6-4, participation rates for never-married and other ever-married mothers began to decline prior to the onset of the Great Recession and have changed little in the last few years (apart from year-to-year fluctuations).

Also not well understood is the plateauing and subsequent small decline in the participation rates of married mothers during the 1990s and early 2000s.[67] Again, one factor to be considered is prevailing labor market conditions. But they cannot provide a full explanation for the stagnation in participation rates of married mothers that dates to the mid-1990s, a period of buoyant economic conditions.[68] Furthermore, the participation rates of married mothers, like those of single mothers, are showing no sign of rising as the recovery from the Great Recession proceeds.

If not economic conditions, then what might explain the stagnation in married women's participation rates? It does not appear to be how their husbands were faring: it has been

---

[65]This discussion draws on Blank, "Fighting Poverty"; and Rebecca Blank, "Evaluating Welfare Reform in the United States," *Journal of Economic Literature* 60, no. 4 (December 2002): 1105–66. See also Meyer and Rosenbaum, "Making Single Mothers Work"; and Eissa and Liebman, "Labor Supply Response to the Earned Income Tax Credit."

[66]For an analysis of the trends over the 2000–2007 period, see Robert A. Moffitt, "The U.S. Employment–Population Reversal in the 2000s: Facts and Explanations," *Brookings Papers on Economic Activity* (Fall 2012): 201–64. Moffitt concludes that the declines in employment–population ratios for women over this period, which were concentrated among the unmarried, are not well explained by measured variables.

[67]For discussion and analyses of the trends, see Blau and Kahn, "Changes in the Labor Supply Behavior of Married Women"; Macunovich, "Reversals in the Patterns of Women's Labor Supply"; Moffitt, "The U.S. Employment–Population Reversal in the 2000s"; and Katharine Bradbury and Jane Katz, "Women's Rise: A Work in Progress," *Regional Review* 14, no. 3 (Q1 2005): 58–67.

[68]For evidence on the 2001 recession and its aftermath, see Boushey, "'Opting Out'?"

found that husbands' improved income growth in the 1990s and early 2000s relative to the 1980s played only a small role in explaining wives' slowdown in participation growth.[69] This finding is consistent with evidence discussed earlier that the dominant economic factor explaining the *increase* in married women's labor force participation in prior decades was their *own* labor market opportunities, not changes in their husbands' incomes.

Some media attention has suggested that married mothers, especially highly educated ones, might be increasingly "opting out" of the labor force,[70] but a number of pieces of evidence dispute this conclusion, as discussed at greater length in Chapter 16. For one things, as we have seen, the negative effect of children on married women's participation has, if anything, decreased. Moreover, Figure 6-4 indicates that participation rates have also declined for single mothers since 2000.

A further possible factor is changes (or lack thereof) in gender role attitudes. As noted previously, there has been little change in such attitudes since the mid-1990s, the period when women's labor force participation rates began to plateau.[71] While it is difficult to firmly establish causation, this juxtaposition is intriguing. It is possible that the lack of further changes in gender role attitudes contributed to the flattening of growth in women's labor force participation, although the lack of movement in attitudes may itself be due, at least in part, to the flatlining of the participation trends.

Just as the plateauing and even declines in women's labor force participation for both married and single mothers remain something of a puzzle, it is also not known whether the engine of growth will restart in the foreseeable future. The fairly lengthy period of stagnation in overall female participation rates and in participation rates of married mothers that we have already experienced—20 years and counting—suggests the answer may be *no*. Moreover, one might argue that, now that nearly three-quarters of women aged 25–54 are in the labor force, it may be reasonable to expect that female labor force participation rates will not increase much further. Perhaps the labor force already includes the types of women who can most readily participate and have the greatest incentives to do so.

However, a comparison with other economically advanced countries provides useful insights and suggests there may be room for further increases in US women's labor force participation rates. Interestingly, as recently as 1990, the United States had one of the higher female participation rates among economically advanced countries—it ranked 6th out of a set of 22 such countries in that year. By 2010, however, it had lost considerable ground and ranked 17th. One major difference between the United States and other economically advanced countries, which likely helps to explain the decline in the US ranking, is that most other countries offer more generous parental leave programs (in both length of the leave and benefits received), and many require employers to provide greater part-time options.[72] A recent study

---

[69]Blau and Kahn, "Changes in the Labor Supply Behavior of Married Women"; and Macunovich, "Reversals in the Patterns of Women's Labor Supply."

[70]Lisa Belkin wrote the best-known article that first suggested this trend and, in turn, popularized the phrase "opt out"; see "The Opt-Out Revolution," *New York Times*, October 26, 2003.

[71]For evidence on the attitudinal trends that suggests that they are not explained by education, demographic factors, or broad ideological changes in American society, see Cotter, Hermsen, and Vanneman, "End of the Gender Revolution?" For an effort to capture their contribution to women's participation slowdown, see Fortin, "Gender Role Attitudes and Women's Labor Market Participation."

[72]Francine D. Blau and Lawrence M. Kahn, "Female Labor Supply: Why Is the US Falling Behind?" *American Economic Review, Papers and Proceedings* 103, no. 3 (May 2013): 251–56—data are for women aged 25–54; see also Ariane Hegewisch and Janet C. Gornick, *Statutory Routes to Workplace Flexibility in Cross-National Perspective* (Washington, DC: Institute for Women's Policy Research, 2008). Note too that most of these other countries use a system of individual taxation that is more encouraging of the labor force participation of secondary workers than a system where the family is the unit of taxation, as we have in the United States; see Chapter 18.

finds that the greater expansion of family-friendly policies in these other countries accounts for a substantial portion (nearly 30 percent) of the decrease in US women's labor force participation rates relative to these other countries over this period.[73] This research suggests that work–family issues may be a factor in the US stagnation in participation rates. However, one qualification, discussed further in Chapter 18, is that, while more expansive family-friendly policies may promote women's labor force participation, they come at the risk of channeling women into "mommy track" jobs that tend to be associated with fewer opportunities for advancement and lower pay. Consistent with this, the study found that US women were more likely than women in these other countries to have full-time jobs and to work as managers or professionals. Nonetheless, given the very low level of mandated parental leave in the United States (12 weeks of unpaid leave), there may be room for expansion in generosity here without encountering such adverse effects. The issues surrounding parental leave in the United States are addressed in greater detail in Chapter 16.

The Bureau of Labor Statistics (BLS) forms projections of labor force participation rates, and it is interesting to consider its forecasts. Currently, it expects the overall labor force participation rate of women (aged 16 and over) to be 56 percent in 2024; this is a bit below its current value of 57 percent and nearly 4 percentage points below its late 1990s' peak of 60 percent.[74] These BLS projections bring in a factor we mentioned in connection with our discussion of the discouraged worker effect, the aging of the population. As the very large baby boom generation ages out of the prime working ages of 25–54, downward pressure is exerted on the labor force participation rates of both men and women. In addition, importantly, the projections assume that it is unlikely that the labor force participation rate of women, even in the prime ages, will again achieve the significant increases registered in the years prior to 1990.

Analyzing Trends in Men's Labor Force Participation

The long-term changes in men's labor force participation patterns, while less dramatic than women's, are nonetheless quite significant. Overall, and for each age group, male labor force participation rates have been declining (see Figures 5-2 and 5-4).

The sizable long-term decline in the participation rates of younger men, particularly teens, is mainly due to their tendency to remain in school longer. This trend in turn reflects the increasing skills demanded by our advanced economy. Young people's behavior is especially affected because expenditures on education are more profitable to the individual when they are made relatively early in the life cycle, resulting in a longer period over which to reap the returns to this investment in the form of higher earnings. Moreover, with rising real incomes, families are able to keep their children in school longer not only because they can better afford to pay the bills but also because they can better afford to forgo the contribution their children might otherwise make to family income. As we noted in Chapter 5, this long-term trend was amplified by the impact of the Great Recession, which was accompanied by sharp declines in participation rates of teens.

The long-term decrease in participation rates of older males is often viewed as evidence of the dominance of the income effect over the substitution effect for this

---

[73]Blau and Kahn, "Female Labor Supply: Why is the U.S. Falling Behind?."
[74]Mitra Toossi, "Labor Force Projections to 2024: The Labor Force Is Growing, but Slowly," *Monthly Labor Review* (December 2015): 1–33, available at bls.gov; see also, Council of Economic Advisors, "The Labor Force Participation Rate Since 2007."

group. As real wages rose over the course of the last century, men's demand for non-market time increased. This is suggested by the decline (and subsequent stability) of the average full-time workweek discussed in Chapter 5. The increased propensity of men to retire at earlier ages is also seen as part of this pattern. In addition, the provision of Social Security and the growing coverage of private pension schemes, while in part a transfer of income from earlier to later years, created an income effect that encouraged older males to retire.[75]

Interestingly, as noted in Chapter 5, the long-term decline in older men's labor force participation rates ceased in the mid-1980s, and, since the late 1990s, rates have increased modestly.[76] One reason for this development relates to the growth in the labor force participation of older women. While, in general, husbands and wives appear to substitute their time in household activities, there is evidence of complementarity of time use among older couples, with couples tending to make joint retirement decisions. Since husbands are on average 3 years older than their wives, they have responded to the higher likelihood of their wives being employed by remaining in the labor force longer themselves.[77] There have also been significant changes in the Social Security program that have increased the benefits that older individuals can receive while continuing to work and thus made employment more attractive.[78] In addition, changes in private pension schemes have made the exact amount of benefit payments individuals receive after retirement more uncertain.[79] During the Great Recession, many older Americans found that the value of these pensions and other savings had declined. This may be one reason why, despite overall decreases in participation rates of men during the Great Recession, participation rates of men aged 55–64 held steady and those of men 65 and over actually increased.[80] Finally, with the growth of service employment and changes in the nature of jobs in the manufacturing sector, jobs have become less physically demanding, making them more attractive to older individuals.

---

[75]See Patricia M. Anderson, Alan L. Gustman, and Thomas L. Steinmeier, "Trends in Male Labor Force Participation and Retirement: Some Evidence on the Role of Pensions and Social Security in the 1970s and 1980s," *Journal of Labor Economics* 17, no. 4, pt. 1 (October 1999): 757–83.

[76]For an excellent analysis of recent and longer-term trends in the labor force participation of older men, see Alicia H. Munnell and Steven A. Sass, "The Labor Supply of Older American Men," in *Labor Supply in the New Century*, ed. Katharine Bradbury, Christopher L. Foote, and Robert K. Triest (Boston: Federal Reserve Bank of Boston, 2008), 83–138. Our discussion draws heavily on this article. Gary Burtless and Barry P. Bosworth find that the increase in labor force participation of older individuals was prevalent across most industrialized countries and, in general, was not slowed by the Great Recession; see "Impact of the Great Recession on Retirement Trends in Industrialized Countries," Brookings Institution (December 16, 2013), brookings.edu.

[77]Tammy Schirle, "Why Have the Labor Force Participation Rates of Older Men Increased since the Mid-1990s?" *Journal of Labor Economics* 26, no. 4 (October 2008): 549–94. See also Munnell and Sass, "The Labor Supply of Older American Men."

[78]Chief among these is the liberalization of the Social Security "earnings test" (the earnings limit for receiving benefits) and its complete elimination for beneficiaries older than the full retirement age. For more explanation and a summary of additional changes in the program, see Munnell and Sass, "The Labor Supply of Older American Men."

[79]Specifically, there has been a decline in the share of workers covered by defined benefit programs and a corresponding increase in the share covered by defined contribution programs. For a comprehensive explanation and assessment, see Munnell and Sass, "The Labor Supply of Older American Men"; and BLS, "Spotlight on Statistics: Older Workers: Are There More Older people in the Workplace?" (July 2008), http://www.bls.gov/spotlight/2008/older_workers/.

[80]For an analysis of the impact of the Great Recession on retirement security and behavior, see Alicia H. Munnell and Matthew S. Rutledge, "The Effects of the Great Recession on the Retirement Security of Older Workers," *Annals of the American Academy of Political and Social Science* 650, no. 1 (November 2013): 124–42.

The same factors that have influenced the labor force participation of younger and older men have also affected the participation of women in these age groups. As shown in Figure 5-3, the long-term increase in the participation rates for women over 65 has been quite modest, although, like their male counterparts, their participation rate also increased in the aftermath of the Great Recession. In addition, the participation of younger women (teens) has declined since 1980 as greater numbers of them remain in school for longer periods. Also, like their male counterparts, their participation rates fell quite sharply during and after the Great Recession.

Returning to trends in male participation rates, of considerable concern is the long-term decline in the participation rate of prime-age males (aged 25–54) shown in Figure 5-4. So, for example, participation rates of prime-age males fell from a peak of 98 percent in 1954 to 88 percent in 2015, a decrease of 10 percentage points. Although this decline is smaller than the declines for younger and older men, it is notable because this is the age group at which workers are at their most productive and are most likely to be actively engaged in the labor force. Referring to this trend, President Obama's Council of Economic Advisors observed that it "has outsized implications for individual well-being as well as for broader economic growth. A large body of evidence has linked joblessness to worse economic prospects in the future, lower overall well-being and happiness, and higher mortality, as well as negative consequences for families and communities." Moreover, the decline in participation among this group has been sharper in the United States than in other economically advanced countries.[81]

This decrease appears closely connected to falling relative demand for less-skilled workers, which depressed their relative wages.[82] This linkage is suggested by Figure 6-6b, which shows that men's participation rates decreased most markedly for less educated males. Another contributing factor is the expansion of government programs that provide disability income to men below conventional retirement age.[83] In the absence of such programs, more men with disabilities would probably be forced to seek employment. Less-skilled men are disproportionately affected by the provision of disability income because the opportunity cost of leaving the labor force is smaller for low-wage workers.

Another factor that has received growing attention is the substantial increase in incarceration in the United States and its impact on labor market outcomes. One estimate indicates that, in 2008, between 6 and 7 percent of the prime-age male population had been incarcerated at some point in their lives.[84] Individuals who have been incarcerated face diminished labor market opportunities, including higher

---

[81]Council of Economic Advisors, Office of the President, "The Long-Term Decline in Prime-Age Male Labor Force Participation," June 2016, https://obamawhitehouse.archives.gov; quotation is from p. 2.

[82]Council of Economic Advisors, "The Long-Term Decline in Prime-Age Male Labor Force Participation." For important early work, see Juhn, "Decline of Male Labor Market Participation." For the 2000s, see Moffitt, "The U.S. Employment–Population Reversal." For a useful analysis of participation and other labor force developments for men, see David Autor and Melanie Wasserman, *Wayward Sons: The Emerging Gender Gap in Labor Markets and Education* (Washington, DC: Third Way, April 2013), www.thirdway.org.

[83]Donald Parsons, "The Decline in Male Labor Force Participation," *Journal of Political Economy* 88, no. 1 (February 1980): 117–34; and David H. Autor and Mark G. Duggan, "The Rise in the Disability Rolls and the Decline in Unemployment," *Quarterly Journal of Economics* 118, no. 1 (February 2003): 157–205. These programs expanded first in the 1960s and 1970s and then again since the mid-1980s.

[84]Council of Economic Advisors, "The Long-Term Decline in Prime-Age Male Labor Force Participation." For fuller discussions of the rise in incarceration and its impacts, see Bruce Western, Jeremy Travis, and Steve Redburn, eds., *The Growth of Incarceration in the United States: Exploring Causes and Consequences* (Washington, DC: National Research Council, 2014). This rise has particularly affected African American men, as discussed in the next section.

unemployment rates and lower wages, upon their release. Workers may also face difficulties even if they were arrested but not convicted or have a misdemeanor on their record.[85]

Finally, it is possible that part of the explanation for prime-age men's declining participation rate may be women's increased employment outside of the home. As the two-earner family becomes the norm, the additional income may induce some (albeit still relatively few) males to leave the labor force for periods of time, say, to care for small children or to retool for a midlife career change.[86]

Will the long-term downward trend in male labor force participation rates continue in the future? The answer to this question is not completely clear. The participation rates for teens may rebound somewhat as the effects of the Great Recession continue to dissipate. And the downward trend in labor force participation rates for older men has not only stopped but there have even been modest increases since the 1990s. Whether participation rates of prime-aged males will continue falling is difficult to predict and may depend on the labor market opportunities available to them. The BLS projects that *overall* male labor force participation rates (ages 16 years and over) will be 66.2 percent in 2024—nearly 3 percentage points below the rate of 69.1 percent in 2015. This may well be reasonable given the trends we have discussed in this section, especially when we additionally factor in the downward pressure caused by the aging of the baby boom cohort that we discussed previously. Alternatively, it is possible that, with improved educational opportunities and greater government provision of job training and job search assistance, prospects for this group could be improved, especially given that the United States lags relative to other countries.

Black and White Participation Differentials: Serious Employment Problems for Black Men

As we saw in Table 5-2, since the 1950s, black male participation rates have declined faster than those of white males, while black female participation rates have increased at a slower pace than those of white females (though the period from 1995 to 2000 is a recent exception). The result is that now black male participation rates are considerably below those of white males, while black female participation rates, which used to greatly exceed those of white women, are now only a few percentage points higher.

---

[85]See Steven Raphael, *The New Scarlet Letter? Negotiating the U.S. Labor Market with a Criminal Record* (Kalamazoo, MI: UpJohn Institute for Employment Research, 2014); Maya Rhodan, "A Misdemeanor Conviction Is Not a Big Deal, Right? Think Again," *New York Times*, March 1, 2015; and Gary Fields and John R. Emshwiller, "As Arrest Records Rise, Americans Find Consequences Can Last a Lifetime," *Wall Street Journal*, August 18, 2014. In 2012, the US Equal Employment Opportunity Committee established new guidelines; see "What You Should Know about the EEOC and Arrest and Conviction Records," accessed July 12, 2016, https://www.eeoc.gov. Many states are also revising their laws; see, for instance, Alison Knezevich, "New State Laws to Help Marylanders Clear Arrest Records," *Baltimore Sun*, September 26, 2015.

[86]Fathers represent a small but growing share of at-home parents, increasing from 10 percent of this group in 1989 to 16 percent in 2012; see Gretchen Livingston, "Growing Number of Dads Home with the Kids: Biggest Increase among Those Caring for Family," Pew Research Center's Social and Demographic Trends project, June 2014. Nonetheless, even relatively recent analyses find little evidence of responsiveness of husbands' labor supply decisions to their wives' wages in the prime working ages; see, for example, Blau and Kahn, "Changes in the Labor Supply Behavior of Married Women."

Focusing first on the more serious employment problems of black men, one explanation for the differential trend in black and white participation rates is that, since blacks obtain less education, on average, and are more likely to drop out of high school than whites, they are disproportionately negatively affected by the overall trends toward lower participation among less educated individuals. However, even when comparing participation rates of less-skilled white and black men, these trends are less favorable for blacks. This observation suggests that while declining labor market opportunities for the less educated in general may explain a portion of the race trends in male participation, other factors also play a role.[87] One such factor may be the expansion of government disability programs. Because black men are less educated, on average, they would be particularly affected by the expansion of these programs—and, to the extent that, due to discrimination, their wages are lower than those of white men with similar education, the attractiveness of these programs to them is further increased. Higher rates of unemployment also likely reduce African Americans' labor force participation due to discouragement. Black unemployment rates tend to be twice as high as those of whites. Even 2015, for example, when the overall unemployment rate had rebounded to 5.3 percent, the black male unemployment rate stood at 10.3 percent. (As we saw in Chapter 5, black women also face unemployment rates that are nearly double those of their white counterparts.)

Two other factors have also been identified in recent research as contributing to the decrease in the employment of less educated, young black men (ages 16–34) relative to their white counterparts.[88] One is the dramatic increase in incarceration rates, discussed previously, which rose more rapidly for blacks than whites. Individuals who are incarcerated are not included in statistics on labor force participation and employment, implying that such statistics may understate the employment problems faced by blacks. However, ex-offenders are included in the statistics and are likely to have poorer employment prospects than nonoffenders due both to the negative effect of incarceration itself (e.g., loss of work experience) and to employer reluctance to hire ex-offenders.[89] As mentioned earlier, arrests and misdemeanor convictions may cause employment difficulties as well. Another factor that may contribute to relatively lower employment rates of less educated young African American men is the stronger enforcement of child support laws in recent years. Although this policy may be desirable on other grounds, mandated child support payments are equivalent to a "tax" on the income of noncustodial fathers. This "tax" is expected to reduce work incentives, especially for those with low incomes. Here again, young African

---

[87]Juhn, "Decline of Male Labor Market Participation"; and Chinhui Juhn, "Black–White Employment Differential in a Tight Labor Market," in *Prosperity for All? The Economic Boom and African Americans*, ed. Robert Cherry and William M. Rodgers III (New York: Russell Sage Foundation, 2000), 88–109. For overviews of the employment problems of black men, see Harry J. Holzer, "The Labor Market and Young Black Men: Updating Moynihan's Perspective," *Annals of the American Academy of Political and Social Science* 621 (January 2009): 47–69; and Ronald B. Mincy, ed., *Black Males Left Behind* (Washington, DC: Urban Institute Press, 2006).

[88]Harry J. Holzer, Paul Offner, and Elaine Sorensen, "Declining Employment among Young Black Less-Educated Men: The Role of Incarceration and Child Support," *Journal of Policy Analysis and Management* 24, no. 2 (Spring 2005): 329–50; see also Steven Rafael, "The Socioeconomic Status of Black Males: The Increasing Importance of Incarceration," in *Poverty, the Distribution of Income, and Public Policy*, ed. Alan J. Auerbach, David Card, and John M. Quigley (New York: Russell Sage Foundation, 2006), 319–58; and Becky Pettit, *Invisible Men: Mass Incarceration and the Myth of Black Progress* (New York: Russell Sage Foundation, 2012).

[89]Devah Pager presents convincing evidence from an audit study not only of the negative effects of a criminal record on employment opportunities but also of employer discrimination against black men compared to whites with the same offender status; see "The Mark of a Criminal Record," *American Journal of Sociology* 108, no. 5 (March 2003): 937–75.

American males are likely to be disproportionately affected, both because they are a low-income group and because female headship is much more pronounced in the black than in the white community.

The relative participation picture for black women, who have traditionally had higher participation rates than white women, is considerably more favorable than that for black men. Currently, black women have slightly higher participation rates than those of white women.[90] Nonetheless, labor force participation growth has been considerably faster for white women than black women since the mid-1950s, converting what had been a large participation edge for black women into just a small advantage. Indeed, as we noted in Chapter 5, white women had completely closed the race gap in participation by the mid-1980s. Since 1995, however, the labor force participation rates of African American women have again drawn slightly ahead of those of white women, largely as a result of an increase in participation among less educated black women during the 1990s.[91] This increase was likely tied to the growth in participation rates of single mothers during this period that we discussed previously because within each education category black women are more likely to be single-family heads than are white women.[92] In addition, given their extremely high unemployment rates, blacks as a group are likely to have benefited disproportionately from the decline in unemployment that occurred over the late 1990s. Notably, however, as with other groups, improved economic conditions following the Great Recession have not yet boosted black women's participation rates.

Conclusion

In this chapter, our review and application of the economic theory of labor supply has enhanced our understanding of the determinants of some major trends in labor force participation rates of both men and women and helped to explain trends in black–white differences in participation. As we have seen, economic theory does not have all the answers but provides valuable insights into the sources of these trends, as well as the impact of a number of government policies.

Questions for Review and Discussion

*Indicates that the question can be answered using an indifference curve framework as well as verbally. Consult with your instructor about the appropriate approach for your class.

1. Explain the reasons why men's labor force participation decreased. Do any of these factors have a negative effect on women's labor force participation as well?

2. Use economic theory (economic reasoning) to explain why the labor force participation rate for married women and never-married women might differ.*

---

[90]For an analysis of the race difference, see Leah Platt Boustan and William J. Collins, "The Origin and Persistence of Black–White Differences in Women's Labor Force Participation," in *Human Capital in History: The American Record*, ed. Leah Boustan, Carola Frydman, and Robert A. Margo (Chicago: University of Chicago Press, 2014), 205–40.

[91]See Francine D. Blau, Marianne A. Ferber, and Anne E. Winkler, *The Economics of Women, Men, and Work*, 4th ed. (Upper Saddle River, NJ: Prentice Hall, 2002), table 4-5, 127.

[92]Blau, "Trends in the Well-Being of American Women."

3. Suppose the government were to provide a $2-per-hour subsidy for families with an employed mother who purchases childcare.

   a. Consider a mother with a preschool-age child who is currently not employed. How would this subsidy affect her decision to work, all else equal?*

   b. Consider a mother with a preschool-age child who is currently employed. How would this subsidy affect the number of hours that she chooses to work (assuming she can vary them), all else equal?*

4. Now suppose that the government provides a subsidy of $300 per month for all families with children. Answer parts a and b of question 3 again under this scenario. How would your answers to question 3 change? Explain fully.*

5. Do you expect that sometime in the future labor force participation rates for men and women will be equal? Discuss.

Suggested Readings

Autor, David, and Melanie Wasserman. "Wayward Sons: The Emerging Gender Gap in Labor Markets and Education." Washington, DC: Third Way, April 2013. www .thirdway.org.

Bailey, Martha, and Tom DiPrete. "Five Decades of Remarkable, but Slowing, Change in U.S. Women's Economic and Social Status and Political Participation." In "A Half Century of Change in the Lives of American Women." Special issue, *The Russell Sage Foundation Journal of the Social Sciences* 2, no. 4 (2016): 1–32.

Blau, Francine D., and Lawrence M. Kahn. "Changes in the Labor Supply Behavior of Married Women: 1980–2000." *Journal of Labor Economics* 25, no. 3 (July 2007): 393–438.

Boustan, Leah Platt, and William J. Collins. "The Origin and Persistence of Black–White Differences in Women's Labor Force Participation." In *Human Capital in History: The American Record*, edited by Leah Boustan, Carola Frydman, and Robert A. Margo, 205–40. Chicago: University of Chicago Press, 2014.

Council of Economic Advisors, Office of the President. "The Labor Force Participation Rate since 2007: Causes and Policy Implications." July 2014, https:// obamawhitehouse.archives.gov.

Council of Economic Advisors, Office of the President. "The Long-Term Decline in Prime-Age Male Labor Force Participation." June 2016, https://obamawhitehouse .archives.gov.

Goldin, Claudia. "The Quiet Revolution That Transformed Women's Employment, Education, and Family." *American Economic Review* 96, no. 2 (May 2006): 1–20.

Holzer, Harry J. "The Labor Market and Young Black Men: Updating Moynihan's Perspective." *Annals of the American Academy of Political and Social Science* 621 (January 2009): 47–69.

Mincy, Ronald B., ed. *Black Males Left Behind*. Washington, DC: Urban Institute Press, 2006.

Munnell, Alicia H., and Steven A. Sass. "The Labor Supply of Older American Men." In *Labor Supply in the New Century*, edited by Katharine Bradbury, Christopher L. Foote, and Robert K. Triest, 83–138. Boston: Federal Reserve Bank of Boston, 2008.

Key Terms

commodities (110)

market income (110)

market goods (110)

budget constraint (111)

wage (*w*) (111)

nonlabor income (111)

nonmarket time (111)

market time (111)

indifference curve (113)

indifference map (113)

substitution in consumption (114)

substitution in production (114)

reservation wage (118)

value of nonmarket time (*w**) (118)

income effect (119)

substitution effect (124)

nonpecuniary benefits (125)

elasticity (128, 131)

wage elasticity (128, 131)

income elasticity (129, 131)

added worker effect (132)

discouraged worker effect (132)

Earned Income Tax Credit (EITC) (133)

technological change (138)

market substitutes (138)

APPENDIX 6A

The Income and Substitution Effects: A Closer Look

As discussed in Chapter 6, for labor force participants, an increase in the wage rate causes an uncertain effect on hours supplied, all else equal. This is illustrated in greater detail in Figure 6-8. The *overall* effect of the wage change is shown (in panels a and b) by the move from point *A* to point *C*. It may be broken down into two distinct components, attributable to the income and substitution effects.

The income effect is represented by a hypothetical increase in income just large enough to get the individual to the higher indifference curve, U_2, leaving the wage rate unchanged. This shift takes the individual from point *A* to point *B*. For the reasons discussed earlier, the effect of the increase in income, all else equal, is unambiguously to reduce labor hours supplied to the market. The substitution effect is given by the impact of a hypothetical change in the wage (the slope of the budget constraint) along a given indifference curve, U_2, resulting in a move from *B* to *C*. The substitution effect of an increase in the opportunity cost (or price) of nonmarket time, all else equal, is unambiguously to increase labor hours supplied.

As may be seen in panel a, if the substitution effect is large relative to the income effect, *the substitution effect dominates the income effect* and the wage

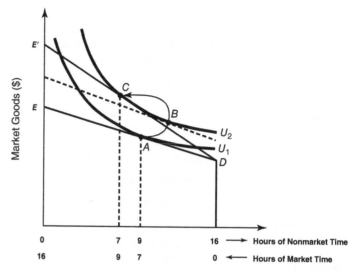

(a) THE SUBSTITUTION EFFECT DOMINATES THE INCOME EFFECT

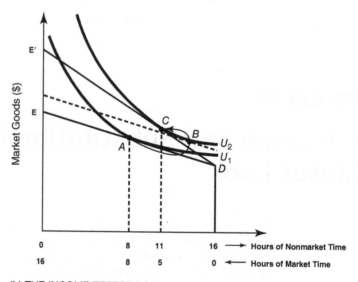

(b) THE INCOME EFFECT DOMINATES THE SUBSTITUTION EFFECT

FIGURE 6-8 Impact of the Market Wage on Labor Hours: A Closer Look

increase results in an *increase* in hours worked. Alternatively, as seen in panel b, if the income effect is large relative to the substitution effect, *the income effect dominates the substitution effect* and the wage increase results in a *decrease* in hours worked.

PART III

Labor Market Outcomes: Theory, Evidence, and Policy

Evidence on Gender Differences in Labor Market Outcomes

CHAPTER HIGHLIGHTS

- Gender Differences in Occupations
- The Gender Pay Ratio
- Gender Differences in Union Membership
- Gender Differences in Self-Employment
- Gender Differences in Nonstandard Work

As we saw in Chapters 5 and 6, there has been a large increase in women's labor force participation since World War II. This increase, in conjunction with a decline in male labor force participation rates, resulted in a narrowing of gender differentials in labor force participation rates. Further, as women have become more committed to market work, their labor force attachment has increased and they have worked more continuously over the life cycle. We now turn to the question of how women fare in the labor market.

In this chapter, we first review the extent of gender differences in the two main indicators of labor market status—occupational attainment and earnings. Next, we summarize gender differences regarding three additional dimensions of employment: unionization, self-employment, and the extent of nonstandard versus regular employment. As we shall see, despite important recent gains, substantial differences between men and women remain. Our major focus in this chapter is simply to describe the extent of and trends in these gender differences in labor market outcomes. In subsequent chapters, we consider explanations.

Gender Differences in Occupations

One of the most salient differences in women's and men's labor market outcomes for as long as we have had data has been the pronounced differences in men's and women's occupations. These differences have drawn considerable attention in part because occupational differences are strongly associated with gender differences in wages. That mechanism will be explored in Chapter 10. When considering the occupations of men and women, we can get a general idea of the extent of the differences by comparing the distribution of male and female workers across the 10 **major occupations** for which the government provides data. However, to fully grasp the magnitude of the dissimilarities, we need to examine gender differences at the level of the more than 400 **detailed occupations** for which the government also provides data.[1] We do both in this section.

Overview of Gender Differences in Occupations

The distribution of female and male workers across major occupations for 1970 and 2015 is shown in Table 7-1. We first describe the gender differences in 2015 and then briefly summarize some of the important changes that have occurred since 1970.

TABLE 7-1 DISTRIBUTION OF MEN AND WOMEN BY MAJOR OCCUPATION, 1970 AND 2015

Occupation	1970		2015	
	Men (%)	Women (%)	Men (%)	Women (%)
Management, Business, and Financial Operations Occupations	13.6	4.7	17.2	15.1
Professional and Related Occupations	13.2	16.8	18.3	27.8
Service Occupations	9.5	19.7	14.2	21.1
Sales and Related Occupations	10.1	10.9	10.1	11.1
Office and Administrative Support Occupations	8.0	31.2	6.3	18.5
Farming, Fishing, and Forestry Occupations	1.9	0.5	1.0	0.4
Construction and Extraction Occupations	9.1	0.3	9.4	0.3
Installation, Maintenance, and Repair Occupations	6.9	0.3	6.1	0.3
Production Occupations	16.7	13.2	7.7	3.5
Transportation and Material Moving Occupations	10.9	2.3	9.8	2.0
Total Employed	100.0	100.0	100.0	100.0

Notes: Data refer to civilian workers 16 years of age and over. There were substantial changes in the census occupational categories in 2000. The 1970 data were converted to the 2000 occupational codes using a crosswalk developed in Francine D. Blau, Peter Brummund, and Albert Yung-Hsu Liu, "Trends in Occupational Segregation by Gender 1970–2009: Adjusting for the Impact of Changes in the Occupational Coding System," *Demography*, 50, no. 2 (April 2013): 471–92. In addition, due to a change in the occupational classification system, data for 2015 are not strictly comparable with earlier years.
Source: 2015 data from US Department of Labor, Bureau of Labor Statistics, 2016 *Employment & Earnings Online*, Annual Averages, table 10, "Employed Persons by Occupation, Race, Hispanic or Latino Ethnicity, and Sex," accessed March 2016, http://www.bls.gov/cps/cpsaat10.htm. The 1970 data are authors' tabulations from the 1970 microdata file of US Census (accessed from Integrated Public Use Microdata Series).

---

[1]A listing of most of the detailed categories included in each major occupation is provided by the US Department of Labor, Bureau of Labor Statistics at 2016 Employment & Earnings Online, Annual Averages, table 11, http://www.bls.gov/opub/ee/2016/cps/annavg11_2015.pdf.

Traditionally, and to a considerable extent today, women are concentrated in *office and administrative support occupations;* these tend to be mid- to lower-paying jobs. Nineteen percent of women workers were in such jobs compared to only 6 percent of men in 2015. This category includes jobs like secretaries and administrative assistants, customer service representatives, and various types of clerks.

Women are also more heavily concentrated in *service occupations* than men. In 2015, 21 percent of women were in such jobs compared to 14 percent of men. Service occupations tend to be lower-paying. Examples include childcare workers, waiters and waitresses, janitors and maids, but also some higher-paying jobs like firefighter and police officer.

Women are also considerably more likely than men to be in *professional occupations.* These tend to be occupations which require higher levels of education and receive relatively higher pay, although traditionally male professions, like engineer, physician, and lawyer, tend to pay better than traditionally female occupations, like elementary and secondary school teacher, registered nurse, and social worker. In 2015, 28 percent of women were in such jobs compared to 18 percent of men.

Men, on the other hand, are considerably more likely than women to be in *blue-collar occupations.* One-third of male workers were employed in such jobs in 2015 compared to just 6 percent of women. Blue-collar occupations span higher-paying skilled production, craft, and repair work, as well as lower-paying semiskilled and unskilled manual jobs. The blue-collar categories include (1) *construction and extraction occupations* such as electricians, carpenters, plumbers, and highway maintenance workers; (2) *installation, maintenance, and repair occupations* such as automotive mechanics, computer repairers, and telecommunications line installers; (3) *production occupations* such as bakers, machinists, laundry and dry-cleaning workers, and sewing machine operators; and (4) *transportation and material-moving occupations* such as truck, taxi, and bus drivers; aircraft pilots and flight engineers; parking lot attendants; and trash and recycling collectors.

Gender differences in the remaining broad occupations listed in Table 7-1 are quite a bit smaller. A slightly higher share of men than of women are employed in *management, business, and financial occupations*: 17 percent of men compared to 15 percent of women in 2015. Examples of jobs in this high-paying category include chief executives, marketing and sales managers, education administrators, accountants and auditors, and purchasing agents. And the share of men and women in *sales occupations* is roughly equal. There is considerable variation in pay for sales jobs, including lower-paying occupations, such as cashier or retail clerk in a discount store, as well as higher-paying jobs, such as financial services sales agents or car salesperson.[2]

Some notable changes have occurred over time in the extent of gender differences in occupations. These changes can be seen by comparing the percentage of women in a given occupation in 2015 with their percentage in 1970. For instance, women are considerably less concentrated in office and administrative support occupations today than they were in 1970 when nearly one third (31 percent) held such jobs (down to 19 percent in 2015). The decline in women's employment in this area was matched by an increase in their representation in managerial and professional jobs, both of which are generally higher-paying. As shown in Table 7-1, the

---

[2]There is also a small gender difference in the occupation of farming, fishing, and forestry, but it is not discussed in the text given the small size of this category; just 1 percent of employed men and 0.4 percent of employed women are in these jobs.

representation of women in managerial occupations increased sharply: only 5 percent of women were in such jobs in 1970 compared to 15 percent in 2015. In 1970, less than one in five managers was a woman; by 2015 this was true of two in five. In addition, women moved into professional jobs at a faster rate than men between 1970 and 2015, increasing their already higher representation in these occupations. (As we shall see, during this time they also made substantial inroads into traditionally male-dominated professions.) Finally, gender differences in employment in services are smaller now than they were in 1970 as women's concentration in service jobs has remained roughly stable while men's has increased.

The industries in which men and women work also differ considerably. As may be seen in Table 7-2, in 2015, men were more heavily concentrated in construction, manufacturing, and transportation and utilities than women—33 percent of men worked in those industries compared to 10 percent of women.[3] In contrast, women were considerably more likely to be employed in education and health services—36 percent of women were in these industries compared to 11 percent of men. As discussed in Chapter 5, these differences in employment by industry affect how women fare relative to men in recessions, as was particularly noticeable during the Great Recession. Male workers were particularly hard hit by the recession itself as jobs in construction and manufacturing took a particularly hard hit, and women, who were less

TABLE 7-2   DISTRIBUTION OF MEN AND WOMEN BY MAJOR INDUSTRY, 2015

INDUSTRY	MEN (%)	WOMEN (%)
Agriculture, Forestry, Fishing, and Hunting	2.3	0.9
Mining	1.0	0.2
Construction	11.4	1.3
Manufacturing	13.8	6.4
Wholesale and Retail Trade	14.2	13.1
Transportation and Utilities	7.6	2.5
Information	2.3	1.7
Financial Activities	6.0	7.7
Professional and Business Services	13.0	10.3
Education and Health Services	10.8	36.0
Leisure and Hospitality	8.5	10.1
Other Services	4.4	5.4
Public Administration	4.8	4.5
Total Employed	100.0	100.0

Note: Data refer to civilian workers 16 years of age and over.
Sources: US Department of Labor, Bureau of Labor Statistics, 2016 *Employment & Earnings Online*, Annual Averages, table 17, "Employed Persons by Industry, Sex, Race, and Occupation," accessed March 2016, http://www.bls.gov/cps/cpsaat17.htm.

---

[3]Men were also more heavily represented in agriculture and mining than women, but those two industries accounted for only a small share of all workers.

concentrated in these areas, fared better. However, in the aftermath of the recession, financially strapped state and local governments cut jobs; and since women disproportionately hold such government jobs (including positions in the education sector), they experienced a larger adverse effect and thus a slower employment recovery.[4]

To some extent, these differences in distribution by industry reflect gender differences in occupations. For example, as we have seen, men are more likely to hold blue-collar jobs than women, and a high proportion of such jobs are in construction, manufacturing, and transportation. Women are considerably more likely than men to be elementary and secondary school teachers, and those jobs are in the education industry. However, substantial differences exist in the employment of men and women by firm or industry even *within* occupational categories,[5] further contributing to the observed industry differences by gender.

It is also instructive to consider occupational differences by race and ethnicity as well as by gender. Table 7-3 provides data separately for non-Hispanic whites and for black, Asian, and Hispanic workers. As explained in Chapter 1, since many Hispanics self-identify as white, the inclusion of this sizable disadvantaged group among whites would present a distorted picture of the relative status of minority groups. Thus, where data are available, we use non-Hispanic whites as the comparison group. African Americans and Hispanics were less likely than non-Hispanic whites of the same sex to be employed in higher-paying managerial and professional positions and were overrepresented (relative to whites) in service jobs, which tend to be lower-paying. Black and Hispanic men were also more heavily concentrated than whites in transportation jobs, and a particularly high share of Hispanic men worked in construction occupations. The occupational distribution of Asian men and women compares much more favorably to that of whites than is the case for the other minority groups. Asian women were about as likely as white women to be employed in managerial jobs and professional jobs, while Asian men were a bit less likely than whites to be employed in management jobs but considerably more likely to be employed as professionals. Asian men were less likely than white men to be in blue-collar occupations, although Asian women were more likely than white women to be in production occupations. These occupational differences across racial and ethnic groups are related to educational differences between them. As we shall see in Chapter 8, on average, blacks and Hispanics tend to be less well educated than non-Hispanic whites, while Asians tend to be better educated.

Despite these differences in occupations across racial and ethnic groups, *within each group* the broad outlines of occupational differences by gender show considerable similarities. A common pattern is that women are heavily overrepresented in office and administrative support and more likely than men to be in service occupations. And, except among Asians, women are more likely than men to be in professional jobs. At the

---

[4]See "The Recession of 2007–2009," *BLS Spotlight on Statistics* (February 2012), accessed March 2012, www.bls.gov/spotlight; and Institute for Women's Policy Research, *Is the Recovery Starting for Women? Slow Job Growth in October for Both Women and Men* (Washington, DC: Institute for Women's Policy Research, updated November 2011), www.iwpr.org.

[5]See, for example, early work by Francine D. Blau, *Equal Pay in the Office* (Lexington, MA: Lexington Books, 1977); later research by Erica L. Groshen, "The Structure of the Female/Male Wage Differential: Is It Who You Are, What You Do, or Where You Work?" *Journal of Human Resources* 26, no. 3 (Summer 1991): 457–72; and Kimberly Bayard, Judith Hellerstein, David Neumark, and Kenneth Troske, "New Evidence on Sex Segregation and Sex Difference in Wages from Matched Employee–Employer Data," *Journal of Labor Economics* 21, no. 4 (October 2003): 887–922. For historical evidence, see Claudia Goldin, *Understanding the Gender Gap: An Economic History of American Women* (New York: Oxford University Press, 1990).

TABLE 7-3 DISTRIBUTION OF WORKERS BY OCCUPATION, RACE, HISPANIC ORIGIN, AND GENDER, 2015

Occupation	NON-HISPANIC WHITES		BLACKS		ASIANS		HISPANICS	
	Men (%)	Women (%)	Men (%)	Women (%)	Men (%)	Women (%)	Men (%)	Women (%)
Management, Business, and Financial Operations Occupations	20.4	16.8	10.9	11.7	17.1	17.5	9.1	9.7
Professional and Related Occupations	20.1	30.7	14.0	23.6	35.1	32.6	8.7	16.9
Service Occupations	11.5	17.4	21.6	27.7	12.7	20.0	19.9	31.8
Sales and Related Occupations	11.0	11.0	8.1	10.7	10.2	10.2	7.8	12.2
Office and Administrative Support Occupations	5.7	19.1	9.3	18.5	6.8	13.0	6.5	18.2
Farming, Fishing, and Forestry Occupations	0.8	0.3	0.5	0.1	0.2	0.2	2.6	1.2
Construction and Extraction Occupations	8.4	0.3	6.2	0.2	2.1	0.1	17.6	0.6
Installation, Maintenance, and Repair Occupations	6.5	0.3	4.8	0.2	3.2	0.2	6.5	0.3
Production Occupations	7.2	2.7	8.4	4.1	6.6	5.4	9.1	5.9
Transportation and Material-Moving Occupations	8.4	1.6	16.3	3.2	6.0	0.8	12.2	3.2
Total Employed	100.0	100.0	100.0	100.0	100.0	100.0	100.0	100.0

Notes: Data refer to civilian workers 16 years of age and older. Hispanics may be of any race.
Sources: US Department of Labor, Bureau of Labor Statistics, 2016 *Employment & Earnings Online*, Annual Averages, table 10, "Employed Persons by Occupation, Race, Hispanic or Latino Ethnicity, and Sex," accessed March 2016, http://www.bls.gov/cps/cpsaat10.htm, and unpublished data on non-Hispanic whites from the Bureau of Labor Statistics.

same time, women tend to be underrepresented in blue-collar occupations compared to men, although minority women are more likely to work in production jobs than white women. One difference, however, is that while white women are less well represented in managerial positions than white men, among minorities, male and female representation in this category is fairly similar. Another difference is that black and Hispanic women are *more* likely than black and Hispanic men to be sales workers, while among whites and Asians, representation in this category is the same for both sexes.

So far, we have discussed gender differences in occupational distributions for broadly defined occupational categories, but data on these major occupations do not reveal the full extent of occupational differences by gender. As we mentioned earlier, information is, in fact, available on the large set of detailed occupations that underlie these broad categories. The precise number varies over time but, as already noted, is generally well in excess of 400. Women's representation in these detailed occupations varies considerably more than it does for the major occupation categories. This is illustrated in Table 7-4, which shows percent female (i.e., the percentage of workers in the occupation who are women) for a selection of professional occupations, chosen because we tend to be familiar with the nature and function of the various professions and because both men and women are substantially represented in the category as a whole. Data are presented for 1970 and 2015. Overall, the data indicate

TABLE 7-4 PERCENT FEMALE IN SELECTED PROFESSIONAL AND RELATED OCCUPATIONS, 1970 AND 2015[a]

OCCUPATIONS	1970	2015
Predominantly Male in 1970		
Architects, Except Naval	4.9	25.7
Biological Scientists	27.1	42.6
Chemists and Materials Scientists	13.2	36.1
Clergy	3.1	20.6
Computer Systems Analysts	15.8	34.2
Computer Programmers	23.3	21.0
Dentists	4.6	25.9
Engineering Occupations[a]		
Aerospace Engineers	1.8	11.3
Chemical Engineers	1.5	14.7
Civil Engineers	1.9	12.6
Electrical and Electronics Engineers	1.9	12.5
Industrial Engineers, Including Health and Safety	3.2	20.2
Mechanical Engineers	1.2	8.3
Lawyers	6.6	34.5
Pharmacists	13.9	57.0
Physicians and Surgeons	10.5	37.9
Integrated in 1970		
Psychologists	31.5	70.3
Public Relations Specialists	34.7	61.3
Teaching Occupations[a]		
Postsecondary Teachers	30.9	46.5
Predominantly Female in 1970		
Dietitians and Nutritionists	91.4	94.6
Librarians	82.0	83.0
Registered Nurses	96.8	89.4
Social Workers	68.2	83.8
Teaching Occupations[a]		
Preschool and Kindergarten Teachers	96.6	96.8
Elementary and Middle School Teachers	79.7	80.7
Secondary School Teachers	49.1	59.2

[a]Occupations listed here do not include all those in this category.

Notes: An occupation was classified as predominantly male, predominantly female, or integrated with reference to the female share of total employment in 1970 (38 percent). An occupation was predominantly male if the proportion female was less than 28 percent (38 − 10 = 28), predominantly female if the proportion female was more than 48 percent (38 + 10 = 48), and integrated if the proportion female was in the 28-48 percent range. Data refer to civilian workers 16 years of age and over. There were substantial changes in the census occupational categories in 2000. The 1970 data were converted to the 2000 occupational codes using a crosswalk developed in Francine D. Blau, Peter Brummund, and Albert Yung-Hsu Liu, "Trends in Occupational Segregation by Gender 1970–2009: Adjusting for the Impact of Changes in the Occupational Coding System," *Demography*, 50, no. 2 (April 2013): 471–92. In addition, due to a change in the occupational classification system, data for 2015 are not strictly comparable with earlier years.

Sources: 1970: authors' tabulations from the 1970 microdata file of US Census (accessed from Integrated Public Use Microdata Series), 2015: US Department of Labor, Bureau of Labor Statistics, 2016 *Employment & Earnings Online*, Annual Averages, table 11, "Employed Persons by Detailed Occupation, Sex, Race, and Hispanic or Latino Ethnicity," accessed March 2016, http://www.bls.gov/cps/cpsaat11.htm.

considerable differences in the employment of women and men by occupation *within* the professional category in both years, although there was considerable progress for women in entering traditionally male professions over the period.

In Table 7-4, we classified the selected professional specialty occupations in terms of their sex composition in 1970. We labeled them as **predominantly male occupations**, **predominantly female occupations**, or **integrated occupations** with reference to women's share of total employment in 1970. Women's share of total employment was 38 percent in that year, so if occupational employment were unrelated to sex, we would expect the female share of each occupation to be close to 38 percent. To classify occupations, we categorized an occupation as predominantly male or female if its female share differed by more than 10 percentage points from women's overall employment share (38 percent). Specifically, an occupation was considered predominantly male (that is, women were substantially *underrepresented* in the occupation) if the percent female was less than 28 percent. An occupation was considered predominantly female (that is, women were substantially *overrepresented* in the occupation) if the percent female was more than 48 percent. Occupations with a female share between 28 and 48 percent were considered integrated.

As may be seen in the table, using this classification scheme, only three out of the 26 occupations listed were integrated in 1970. The rest were sex-segregated and generally highly segregated; that is, they employed either a very low or a very high share of women. So, for example, women comprised 80 percent or more of workers in five of the professions shown in the table—dietitians and nutritionists, librarians, preschool and kindergarten teachers, elementary and middle school teachers, and registered nurses. At the same time, men comprised 80 percent or more of workers in 14 of the occupations listed. These occupations included lawyers, physicians, dentists, architects, computer systems analysts, all the categories of engineers listed, and the clergy. It is also notable that the predominantly male occupations tended to be higher-paying than the predominantly female occupations.

The data in Table 7-4 also indicate that gender segregation by occupation was still the norm in 2015. We can see this by comparing women's share in each professional occupation with women's overall employment share in 2015, which stood at 47 percent. If, as before we categorize an occupation as predominantly male or female if its female share differs by more than 10 percentage points from women's overall employment share, we see that most occupations are still predominantly male (the female share is less than 37 percent) or still predominantly female (the female share is greater than 57 percent). Again, only a small number of occupations—four—are integrated, that is have a female share that falls between 37 and 57 percentage points.

Nonetheless, the table also indicates important progress as women have made considerable inroads into traditionally male professions since 1970. For instance, by 2015 women constituted more than 20 percent of workers in the majority of previously highly segregated male occupations. Most of the occupations where women continue to substantially lag behind are in the broad category of **STEM fields** (science, technology, engineering, and math), which includes engineers and computer programmers. It is worth noting, however, that women do not lag behind in all sciences; biological science is 43 percent female.[6]

---

[6]For an overview of women's participation in STEM occupations and changes over time, see Liana Christin Landivar, *Disparities in STEM Employment by Sex, Race, and Hispanic Origin*, American Community Survey Reports ACS-24 (September 2013), www.census.gov.

The table also shows that, in general, men have entered female professions to a far lesser extent than women have entered male professions. Only one of the female professions listed, nursing, has seen an increase in male representation: 11 percent of nurses are now male compared to just 3 percent in 1970.[7] The table also shows that two occupations, psychologists and public relations specialists, have flipped from predominantly male to predominantly female (and pharmacist, with 57 percent female, is right at the top of our definition of integrated for 2015). This occupational structure is still problematic since these jobs remain segregated, although with the opposite sex composition.

Measuring Occupational Segregation

One way to assess the magnitude of differences in the distribution of women and men across occupational categories that is particularly helpful in summarizing gender differences across the large number of detailed occupational categories is to use a summary measure, the extent of **occupational segregation**. One widely used measure is the **index of segregation**.[8] It gives the percentage of female (or male) workers who would have to change jobs in order for the occupational distribution of the two groups to be the same. The index would equal 0 if the distribution of men and women across occupational categories were identical; it would equal 100 if all occupations were either completely male or completely female.

Researchers have calculated the index of segregation for various years using a detailed breakdown of all occupations. These studies show that, for much of the twentieth century, occupational segregation was well in excess of 60 percent. Significant declines in the index began in the 1970s, and we shall consider this important trend in greater detail later. Nonetheless, as may be seen in Figure 7-1, the extent of occupational segregation remains substantial: the segregation index was estimated to be 51 percent in 2009, indicating that more than half of women (or men) would have had to change their jobs for the occupational distribution of the two groups to be the same. Moreover, measures based on these detailed census occupational categories likely underestimate the full extent of employment segregation by sex. For one thing, job categories used by employers are far more detailed than the census occupational categories, and such finer breakdowns would likely reveal more segregation. In addition, researchers have found that particular firms often employ mostly men or mostly women in an occupation, even in occupations where both sexes are fairly well represented at the market-wide level. Restaurants, for instance, commonly employ only waiters or only waitresses but not both. Or women may be well represented as sales workers in clothing stores but not in stores selling electronics, computers, and televisions.[9]

---

[7]For an overview of male participation in nursing occupations and changes over time, see *Men in Nursing Occupations*, American Community Survey Highlight Report (February 2013), www.census.gov.

[8]Otis Dudley Duncan and Beverly Duncan, "A Methodological Analysis of Segregation Indexes," *American Sociological Review* 20, no. 2 (1955): 210–17. The index of occupational segregation by sex is defined as

$$\text{Segregation index} = \frac{1}{2}\sum_{i}\left|M_i - F_i\right|$$

where M_i = the percentage of males in the labor force employed in occupation i and F_i = the percentage of females in the labor force employed in occupation i.

[9]Blau, *Equal Pay*; Groshen, "Structure of the Female/Male Wage Differential"; and Bayard et al., "New Evidence on Sex Segregation."

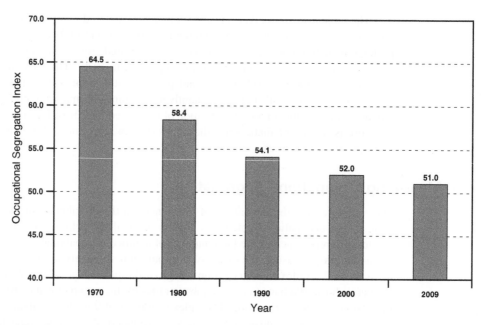

FIGURE 7-1 Trends in Occupational Segregation by Sex, 1970–2009

Source: Francine D. Blau, Peter Brummund, and Albert Yung-Hsu Liu, "Trends in Occupational Segregation by Gender 1970–2009: Adjusting for the Impact of Changes in the Occupational Coding System," *Demography* 50, no.2 (April 2013): 471–92, Table 2.

Hierarchies within Occupations

Not only do men and women tend to work in different occupations but they also tend to be employed at different levels of the hierarchy *within* occupations. So, for example, although women have markedly increased their share of managerial jobs, their representation in top positions is still sparse. According to a report by *Catalyst* on S&P 500 companies in 2015, women were fairly well represented among first- and mid-level managers at 36.4 percent. Women's representation stood at 25.1 percent among executive or senior-level managers and was just 9.5 percent of those in top earner positions. And, at the very top, only 4.2 percent of CEOs were women. (This works out to only 21 of the 500 firms being headed by women.) While these latter figures, especially, remain quite low, they represent a substantial increase since 1995; in that year women comprised just 1.2 percent of top earners and there was only one woman CEO.[10]

These types of disparities prompt the claim that women face a glass ceiling or a set of subtle barriers impeding their efforts to move up the hierarchy. We return to this issue in Chapter 10, where we more closely examine the evidence on women's representation at the upper levels of management as well as possible explanations for the observed gender differences.

Evaluating the Extent of Occupational Segregation

However segregation is measured, and whatever the numerical value of the index, how can any figure in excess of 0 and short of 100 be classified as modest or excessive?

---

[10]Catalyst, "Women in S&P 500 Companies," updated July 2016, http://www.catalyst.org/; and *2002 Catalyst Census of Women Corporate Officers and Top Earners in the Fortune 500* (New York: Catalyst, 2002); note that the earlier figures are for the Fortune 500 firms and thus not completely comparable to current figures based on firms included in the S&P 500.

The answer depends, in part, on one's perception of how great the differences are in men's and women's talents, tastes, and motivation and how relevant they are to their occupational distribution and achievements.

On one side are those who argue that occupational segregation is natural and appropriate. In this view, efforts to change the existing situation will merely lead to economic inefficiency and personal frustration. Its proponents emphasize the similarities among individuals within each sex and the differences between the two groups. Those who emphasize the similarities between men and women and the variations among individuals within each sex group are on the other side. In this view, if men and women were not constrained by gender stereotyping and various barriers to individual choice but were free to follow their own inclinations, they would be far less concentrated in separate occupations. In this case, removing existing barriers would increase efficiency and decrease frustration because individuals could seek work more suited to their particular aptitudes.

However, even if the present level of occupational segregation is deemed excessive, it would be unreasonable to conclude that the optimal situation would necessarily be a precisely proportional distribution of men and women. Apart from whatever innate differences may exist, past socialization and the prevalent allocation of household responsibilities would make such an outcome unlikely for some time to come.

In addition, the rate of change is limited by the time it takes for new people to be trained and hired. Large numbers of people cannot be expected to change jobs on short notice, as the computation of the segregation index perhaps implies. The most that could reasonably be expected is that the underrepresented group would be more highly represented among new hires, to the extent that they are qualified for the available positions, than among those presently employed in the occupation—at best, a slow process.

Trends in Occupational Segregation by Sex

The same issues confronted in measuring current occupational segregation arise in determining the extent to which it has changed over time. However, in addition to concerns over how detailed the categories are and whether women are included in the upper ranks of occupational hierarchies, there is the further difficulty of making meaningful comparisons as definitions of occupations themselves change over time. The main difficulty is that the definition and number of occupational categories often undergo significant changes. For example, if the Census Bureau rigidly adhered to the occupational categories of an earlier era, jobs such as computer systems analyst and computer programmer would not be included. Thus, regardless of the best efforts of those who compile the data and the researchers who use them, data are not entirely comparable over the years and are less so as the years get further apart.

Despite these data difficulties, results from numerous studies provide convincing evidence that the degree of occupational segregation by sex was substantial and largely constant (at well over 60 percent) from 1900 to 1970.[11] However, starting in 1970, there were significant decreases in occupational segregation. As

---

[11]See Edward Gross, "Plus Ça Change? The Sexual Structure of Occupations over Time," *Social Problems* 16, no. 2 (Fall 1968): 198–208; Jerry A. Jacobs, "Long-Term Trends in Occupational Segregation by Sex," *American Journal of Sociology* 95, no. 1 (July 1989): 160–73; and Francine D. Blau and Wallace E. Hendricks, "Occupational Segregation by Sex: Trends and Prospects," *Journal of Human Resources* 14, no. 2 (Spring 1979): 197–210.

may be seen in Figure 7-1, the index fell by 6.1 percentage points over the 1970s. As the figure shows, the index continued to decline thereafter but at a diminished pace with each successive decade.[12] The index fell by 4.3 percentage points in the 1980s, 2.1 percentage points in the 1990s, and only 1 percentage point in the 2000s. Nonetheless, although the level of occupational segregation remains considerable at 51 percent, the cumulative reduction of nearly 14 percentage points in the segregation index between 1970 and 2009 constitutes substantial change.[13]

Changes in the extent of segregation result from two factors: (1) changes in the *sex composition* of individual occupations as a result of the integration of previously male or female jobs and (2) shifts in the *occupational mix* of the economy, as the size of some occupations increases while the size of others decreases. When we think about changes in occupational segregation, we generally have changes in the sex composition of jobs in mind as women enter previously predominantly male occupations or men enter formerly predominantly female occupations. However, changes in occupation mix can also be important. For instance, if integrated occupations experience large employment growth while more segregated occupations shrink, the index of segregation will fall, all else equal.

Research suggests that the decrease in occupational segregation over the past four decades was mainly due to changes in the sex composition of occupations. Moreover, the major factor causing this change in sex composition was the movement of women into formerly predominantly male jobs; there was little reverse movement of men into formerly female jobs. Women were especially successful in entering formerly male white-collar occupations, particularly professional and managerial occupations. Examples of the gains for women in the professional category are shown in Table 7-4, where we see that women significantly increased their representation in a number of formerly highly segregated male professions. Another area of substantial recent female gains is the military; the removal of the remaining restrictions on women's access to some military occupations, including combat positions, as of 2016, is described in the "Women in the Military" box.

During this period, shifts in the occupational mix of the economy played a lesser role but, on net, also served to decrease segregation. Segregated jobs that declined in relative importance include a number of predominantly female administrative support occupations and predominantly male production occupations. During the early 2000s, the impact of these trends was somewhat offset, however, by growth

---

[12]The data in the figure are for the 2000 census occupational classification system and a comparable set of occupations in each of the years and are from Francine D. Blau, Peter Brummund, and Albert Yung-Hsu Liu, "Trends in Occupational Segregation by Gender 1970–2009: Adjusting for the Impact of Changes in the Occupational Coding System," *Demography* 50, no. 2 (April 2013): 471–92. See also Patricia Simpson and Deborah Anderson, "Continuing Progress? Trends in Occupational Segregation over the 1970s and 1980s," *Feminist Economics* 4, no. 3 (Fall 1998): 29–71; and David A. Cotter, Joann M. DeFiore, Joan M. Hermsen, Brenda Marsteller Kowalewski, and Reeve Vanneman, "Occupational Gender Desegregation in the 1980s," *Work and Occupations* 22, no. 3 (1995): 3–21. Andrea Beller was among the first to call attention to the decline in occupational segregation that began in the 1970s; see "Changes in the Sex Composition of U.S. Occupations, 1960–1981," *Journal of Human Resources* 20, no. 2 (Spring 1985): 235–50.

[13]Another interesting trend is that gender segregation by workplace—the extent to which women and men work in different firms—also declined between 1990 and 2000; see Judith Hellerstein, David Neumark, and Melissa McInerney, "Changes in Workplace Segregation in the United States between 1990 and 2000: Evidence from Matched Employer–Employee Data," in *The Analysis of Firms and Employees: Quantitative and Qualitative Approaches*, ed. Stefan Bender, Julia Lane, Kathryn L. Shaw, Fredrik Andersson, and Till Von Wachter (Chicago: University of Chicago Press, 2008), 163–96.

in some sex-segregated female service jobs, including a number of occupations in health care, household employment, and personal services.[14]

Despite recent gains, numerous predominantly single-sex occupations remain. Many of the predominantly male jobs are blue-collar occupations: examples of these include carpenters, electricians, plumbers, sheet metal workers, and automotive service technicians and mechanics—all occupations in which women comprise less than 5 percent of workers. Female-dominated categories include, in addition to the traditionally female professions noted earlier, a number of jobs in the administrative support and service areas, such as secretaries and administrative assistants, receptionists and information clerks, childcare workers, and hairdressers—all occupations where women comprise more than 90 percent of workers.[15]

Recent reductions in occupational segregation have differed by education, so not all women have benefited to the same degree. More substantial progress was made by highly educated women, who succeeded in moving into formerly male managerial and professional occupations. Gains were smaller for less educated women, reflecting the slower progress in integrating blue-collar occupations.[16] The finding that gender differences in occupations narrowed less among the less educated is yet another piece of evidence of increasing differences in trends and outcomes by educational attainment. As discussed in Chapter 6, the labor force participation rates of less educated women and men fell substantially relative to the more highly educated; and, as we shall see in Chapter 8, their wages also declined relative to the more highly educated. In addition, single-headed families increased considerably more among less educated women than among their more highly educated counterparts; as discussed in Chapter 14, such families face considerable economic difficulties.

In considering the overall long-term decrease in occupational segregation, it is also important to consider whether the observed trends reflect real improvements in opportunities for women. In some cases, firms have responded to government pressures by placing women in token management positions, that is, those that involve little responsibility and little contact with higher levels of management. In other instances, jobs became increasingly female when skill requirements declined because of technological changes. In the latter case, integration may turn out to be a short-run phenomenon as resegregation occurs and women increasingly come to dominate such jobs. One example of this phenomenon is the case of insurance adjusters and examiners. One study found that although women dramatically increased their share of this occupation after 1970, they were employed primarily as "inside adjusters" whose decision-making was, to a considerable extent, computerized and involved little discretion. "Outside adjusters," a better-paid and more prestigious job, remained largely male. In yet other instances, women may gain access to a sector of an occupation that was always low-paying. For example, the same study found that even though the representation of women among bus drivers increased substantially after 1970, men

[14]This analysis of the trends is from Blau, Brummund, and Liu, "Trends in Occupational Segregation."
[15]See the listing of sex composition by detailed occupation at US Department of Labor, Bureau of Labor Statistics, "2016 Employment & Earnings Online," "Annual Averages," table 11, http://www.bls.gov/opub/ee/2016/cps/annavg11_2015.pdf; and Blau, Brummund, and Liu, "Trends in Occupational Segregation."
[16]Blau, Brummund, and Liu, "Trends in Occupational Segregation"; Francine D. Blau, Peter Brummund, and Albert Yung-Hsu Liu, "Erratum to: Trends in Occupational Segregation by Gender 1970–2009: Adjusting for the Impact of Changes in the Occupational Coding System," *Demography* 50, no. 2 (April 2013): 493–94; and Jerry A. Jacobs, "The Sex Segregation of Occupations: Prospects for the 21st Century," in *Handbook of Gender and Work*, ed. Gary N. Powell (Newbury Park, CA: Sage Publications, 1999), 125–41.

Women in the Military: No Positions Are Off Limits as of 2016

While, as we have seen, women remain underrepresented in some occupations and at the upper rungs of various hierarchies, December 2015 marks a date of historic change for the US military. On that date, Secretary of Defense Ashton B. Carter announced that, effective January 2016, for the first time, all military occupations and positions would be open to women, including all combat positions: "There will be no exceptions. . . . They'll be allowed to drive tanks, fire mortars and lead infantry soldiers into combat. They'll be able to serve as Army Rangers and Green Berets, Navy SEALs, Marine Corps infantry, Air Force parajumpers and everything else that was previously open only to men." In announcing the new policy, Carter argued that it was necessary to ensure that the United States remained the world's most powerful military force.* Carter's announcement marks the culmination of shifts in policies across all branches of the military to eliminate gender barriers. For instance, in 2013, prior US secretary of defense Leon Panetta announced the elimination of the military's official ban on women in combat, though he gave the services time to set forth plans on how to implement the change.

Among the reasons for this shift, many came to view this restriction as outdated and unfair. Women were permitted to *serve* in combat zones and often found themselves under fire and engaged in combat. But they were barred from officially holding many combat positions. This included positions in the infantry, which are crucial to moving up in the command structure.** As of 2016, women were 17 percent of officers and 15 percent of enlisted service members, but only three out of 38 four-star generals and admirals (8 percent) were women.***

This decision has raised a long-simmering issue—should young women be required to register for the draft? Opening all military roles to women—and, notably, all combat roles—implicitly calls into question the rationale expressed in a 1981 Supreme Court decision that found that women did not have to register. The court observed that since women were not permitted to participate in the front lines of combat, they should not face the same requirement as men to register for the draft. As of 2016, this issue was under consideration in the US Congress and is likely to be debated for some time to come.****

---

*Matthew Rosenberg and Dave Philipps, "All Combat Roles Now Open to Women, Defense Secretary Says," New York Times, *December 3, 2015, nytimes.com; and Cheryl Pellerin,* "Carter Opens All Military Occupations, Positions to Women," US Department of Defense *DoD News, December 3, 2015, www.defense.gov.*
**See Tanya L. Domi, *"Women in Combat: Policy Catches Up with Reality,"* New York Times, *February 8, 2013, nytimes.com.*

***Michael S. Schmidt, "First Woman Nominated to Lead U.S. Combatant Command," New York Times, *March 18, 2016, nytimes.com.*
****Jennifer Steinhauer, "Senate Votes to Require Women to Register for the Draft," New York Times, *June 14, 2016, nytimes. com; and Dan Lamothe, "Why the Pentagon Opening all Combat Roles to Women Could Subject Them to a Military Draft,"* Washington Post, *December 4, 2015), washingtonpost.com.*

---

continued to comprise the majority of full-time workers in metropolitan transportation systems, whereas women were concentrated among part-time school bus drivers.[17]

Resegregation may also be due to **occupational tipping**. Occupational tipping occurs when the female share in an occupation becomes so high that men exit (or avoid entering) the occupation because they prefer not to work in an occupation with too many women.[18]

---

[17]These examples are from Barbara F. Reskin and Patricia A. Roos, *Job Queues, Gender Queues: Explaining Women's Inroads into Male Occupations* (Philadelphia: Temple University Press, 1990).
[18]See Jessica Y. Pan, "Gender Segregation in Occupations: The Role of Tipping and Social Interactions," *Journal of Labor Economics,* 33, no. 2 (April 2015): 365–408. See also Paula England, Paul Allison, Su Li, Noah Mark, Jennifer Thompson, Michelle Budig, and Han Sun, "Why Are Some Academic Fields Tipping toward Female? The Sex Composition of U.S. Fields of Doctoral Degree Receipt, 1971–2002," *Sociology of Education* 80, no. 1 (January 2007): 23–42.

At the same time, it is important to point out that women are expected to benefit from the increase in the demand for female labor that results when they are able to enter additional occupations from which they were previously excluded, even when the new jobs are qualitatively similar to those formerly available to them. This is because an increase in the demand for female workers is expected to increase their relative wages, all else equal. Moreover, despite concerns raised about occupational resegregation, tipping, and tokenism, it is most likely that much of the observed decline in occupational segregation does indeed represent enhanced labor market opportunities for women—that is, increased access to higher-earning or otherwise more desirable occupations.

The Gender Pay Ratio

For many years, the single best-known statistic relevant to the economic status of women in this country was probably that women who worked full-time, year-round earned about 59 cents to every dollar earned by men full-time, year-round workers.[19] One reason for the public awareness of this figure was that the gender pay ratio persisted at that level for two decades, with only modest fluctuations and no significant trend. (The **gender pay ratio** is equal to female earnings divided by male earnings.) This is shown in Table 7-5 and Figure 7-2, which indicate that the gender pay ratio based on annual data hovered close to the 59 percent figure throughout the 1960s and 1970s.[20] And the ratio had actually been somewhat higher in the 1950s than it was in these decades. However, the gender earnings ratio began to rise in the early 1980s. And, between 1981 and 2015 it increased substantially, from 59 to 80 percent.[21] Nonetheless, a substantial gender pay gap remains and is often in the news today, as we discuss in the "Gender Pay Gap" box.

In addition to information on full-time, year-round workers, Table 7-5 and Figure 7-2 also show the gender earnings ratio calculated using data on the usual weekly earnings of full-time workers. For a variety of reasons, the earnings ratio computed on the basis of weekly earnings is generally higher than the annual figure.[22] Of more interest, however, is that the data for weekly earnings also show an upward trend, in this case dating from the late 1970s. Between 1978 and 2015, the earnings ratio, defined in these terms, increased from 61 to 81 percent.

Looking more closely at the trends in Figure 7-2, we see a substantial and steady increase in the gender pay ratio (or a narrowing of the **gender pay gap**, which is

---

[19]The focus on full-time, year-round workers is an effort to adjust published government data on annual earnings for gender differences in hours and weeks worked. However, because even women who are employed full-time tend to work fewer hours per week than male full-time workers, a finer adjustment for hours would raise the earnings ratio; see June O'Neill, "Women & Wages," *American Enterprise* 1, no. 6 (November/December 1990): 25–33.

[20]Data are for median earnings, which is what is available in the government data series used. The definition of the *median* is that half the cases fall above it and half below. In this case, half the individuals have higher earnings and half have lower. The *mean*, or arithmetic mean, is calculated by adding up the total earnings of all the individuals concerned and dividing by their number. Because a relatively small number of persons report extremely high earnings, the mean tends to be higher than the median.

[21]Focusing on all workers, rather than simply those employed full-time and year-round, Francine D. Blau and Andrea H. Beller report evidence of some earnings gains for women during the 1970s, after adjustment for hours and weeks worked; see "Trends in Earnings Differentials by Gender, 1971–1981," *Industrial and Labor Relations Review* 41, no. 4 (July 1988): 513–29.

[22]For example, annual earnings include overtime pay and bonuses, and men tend to receive greater amounts of this type of pay; see Nancy Rytina, "Comparing Annual and Weekly Earnings from the Current Population Survey," *Monthly Labor Review* 106 (April 1983): 32–38.

TABLE 7-5 FEMALE-TO-MALE EARNINGS RATIOS OF FULL-TIME WORKERS, SELECTED YEARS, 1955–2015

YEAR	ANNUAL EARNINGS OF FULL-TIME YEAR-ROUND WORKERS[a] (%)	USUAL WEEKLY EARNINGS OF FULL-TIME WORKERS[b] (%)
1955	64.4	
1960	60.7	
1965	59.9	
1970	59.4	62.3
1975	58.8	62.0
1980	60.2	64.2
1985	64.6	68.1
1990	71.6	71.9
1995	71.4	75.5
2000	73.7	76.9
2005	77.0	81.0
2010	76.9	81.2
2015	79.6	81.1

[a]Workers aged 15 and over. Prior to 1979, workers aged 14 and over.
[b]Workers aged 16 and over.

Sources for Table 7-5 and Figure 7-2: Annual Earnings Data: US Census Bureau, *Current Population Reports*, P60, "Income of Persons in the United States," various years, accessed November 2012, http://www2.census.gov/ prod2/popscan/; US Census Bureau, *Current Population Reports*, P60, "Income and Poverty in the United States: 2014," table A-4, accessed September 2016, http://www.census.gov/content/dam/Census/library/publications/2016/ demo/p60-256.pdf; Weekly Earnings Data: Earl F. Mellor, "Investigating the Differences in Weekly Earnings of Women and Men," *Monthly Labor Review* 107, no. 6 (June 1984); US Bureau of Labor Statistics, Report 1058, *Highlights of Women's Earnings in 2014*, table 13, accessed June 2016, http://www.bls.gov/opub/reports/womens-earnings/archive/highlights-of-womens-earnings-in-2014.pdf; US Department of Labor, Bureau of Labor Statistics, 2016 *Employment & Earnings Online*, Annual Averages," table 37, "Median Weekly Earnings of Full-Time Wage and Salary Workers by Selected Characteristics," accessed September 2016, http://www.bls.gov/cps/cpsaat37.htm.

equal to 100 – the gender pay ratio) over the 1980s. This increase continued beyond the 1980s; however, the pace of the increase in the ratio in both earnings series slowed, and both series behaved more erratically.

Evidence on changes in the gender pay ratio over the life cycle is shown in Table 7-6 for the 1970 to 2014 period. Data are presented on the mean earnings ratios of full-time, year-round workers for four age groups: 25–34, 35–44, 45–54, and 55–64. (The age range 25–64 was selected because individuals in this age group have generally completed their formal schooling but not yet retired from paid employment.) The table indicates that, for example, in 1970 the ratio was 64.9 percent for 25- to 34-year-olds. Reading down this column, we see that the ratio increased over time and that, by 2014, 25- to 34-year-old women were earning 83.5 percent of what men in that age group earned.

Looking down the other columns in Table 7-6, we see that the gender pay ratio for each age group increased substantially starting in the 1980s. This is similar to the pattern we observed for the overall gender pay ratio. The separate data by age in Table 7-6 indicate that the earnings ratio began to rise as early as the 1970s for younger women (especially the youngest group aged 25–34) but that, even for this group, the 1980s gains were considerably larger. Younger women also experienced

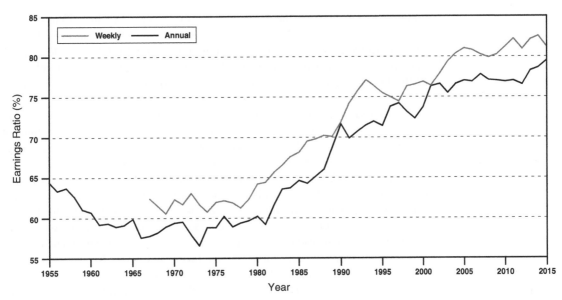

FIGURE 7-2 Gender Earnings Ratios of Full-Time Workers 1955–2015

Source: See Table 7–5

TABLE 7-6 FEMALE-TO-MALE RATIOS OF MEAN EARNINGS FOR FULL-TIME, YEAR-ROUND WORKERS BY AGE, 1970–2014

AGE	1970	1980	1990	2000	2010	2011	2014
25-34	64.9	68.5	76.9	76.9	83.0	83.8	83.5
35-44	53.9	55.3	64.4	66.7	73.3	74.0	75.1
45-54	56.3	52.0	58.2	60.3	68.7	67.1	67.4
55-64	60.3	54.9	57.1	54.7	64.8	67.5	71.1

Sources: 1970: June O'Neill, "Women & Wages," *American Enterprise* 1 (November/December 1990), 29; 1980 and 1990: US Census Bureau, Consumer Income Series P-60, Money Income of Households, Families, and Persons in the United States, 1981 and 1991; 2000-2014: US Census Bureau, Historical Income Tables - People, Table P-32, "Educational Attainment—Full-Time, Year-Round Workers 18 Years Old and Over by Mean Earnings, Age, and Sex: 1991 to 2014" accessed June 2016 https://www2.census.gov/programs-surveys/cps/tables/time-series/historical-income-people/p32.xls.

the largest cumulative increases: between 1970 and 2014, the earnings ratio rose by roughly 20 percentage points for both 25- to 34-year-olds and 35- to 44-year-olds but by only about 11 percentage points for 45- to 54-year-olds and 55- to 64-year-olds.

The increase in the earnings ratio that occurred for each age group suggests that one mechanism by which women have narrowed the aggregate gender earnings gap is the entry of new cohorts of women who have higher relative earnings than their predecessors. (For example, those who were aged 25–34 in 1990 had a considerably higher earnings ratio than 25- to 34-year-olds did in 1980.) These higher earnings ratios may reflect higher educational attainment, the choice of more lucrative majors and occupations, greater commitment to market work, and perhaps less discrimination against them as well.

The data in Table 7-6 may also be used to see what happens to the gender pay ratio of a particular cohort of women as they age. To do this, we follow the progress of individual "birth" cohorts by looking diagonally down the rows of the table. For example, we may compare the pay ratio for 25- to 34-year-olds in 1970 to the ratio for 35- to 44-year-olds 10 years later in 1980. We have shaded the entries in the table that trace out the experience of this cohort until they were 55–64 years old in 2000. Similarly, we have shaded the entries for the cohort that was 25–34 in 1980 and 55–64 in 2010. These are the only two cohorts whose work life may be fully observed in the table, but we can also see portions of the work life of a number of other cohorts.[23]

Looking across the diagonal entries in Table 7-6 for the youngest cohort (aged 24–34), we tend to see a falloff in the pay ratio as the cohort ages, although the magnitude of that decline varies and indeed does not always occur. Declines in relative earnings with age tend to be less pronounced at older ages (say, comparing 35- to 44-year-olds to 45- to 54-year-olds a decade later). To the extent that a decrease in the gender earnings ratio with age does occur, it is likely due, in part, to women accumulating less work experience than men, on average, as they age because, particularly in the past but even today, they are more likely to interrupt their labor force attachment for family-related reasons. It may also reflect greater barriers to women's advancement at higher levels of the job hierarchy, an issue we discuss further in Chapter 10 when we consider evidence on the glass ceiling. The stronger evidence of declines in the ratio between ages 25–34 and 35–44, which correspond to the primary childbearing years, may particularly reflect the negative effects of family-related workforce interruptions for this age group. However, these are also important ages for climbing the job hierarchy, so they may reflect lesser progress for women than men along this dimension as well.

Reviewing the changes in the earnings ratio between ages 25–34 and 35–44 for the various cohorts shown in the table tentatively suggests that, while the pattern is not completely uniform, the falloff in relative earnings for young women as they age may not be as large today as it was previously.[24] Possible explanations for this pattern are that more recent cohorts of young women are more firmly attached to the labor force and may also encounter less discrimination than their predecessors in moving up the ranks.

Figure 7-3 provides information on the earnings of workers by level of educational attainment. Although education has a strong positive effect on the earnings of both men and women, men continue to earn substantially more than women within each educational category. In 1974 and indeed through much of the 1970s, the gender gap was so large that it was often noted that female college graduates earned less than male high school dropouts. While differences remain, as was the case for the overall earnings gap and the earnings differentials by age, the gender gap within educational categories has also narrowed considerably over time. And, as we shall see in Chapter 8, the earnings of female college graduates have pulled considerably ahead of their less educated male counterparts.

Figure 7-3 also highlights another trend that has been getting increasing attention and to which we shall return in Chapters 9 and 10. It appears that the gender earnings

---

[23]One caution to bear in mind is that comparisons of this type may be influenced by which men and women choose to seek paid employment in each year and by their relative success in locating jobs. Due to this problem of "selection bias," we cannot be completely certain that data on those who are employed accurately measure shifts in labor market opportunities for all women. Nobel laureate James J. Heckman greatly increased economists' understanding of problems of this type; see, for example, "Sample Selection Bias as a Specification Error," *Econometrica* 47, no. 1 (January 1979): 153–61.

[24]Increases in women's rate of age-related wage growth relative to men's may account for as much as one-third of the narrowing of the gender wage gap (controlling for education) between 1960 and 2000; see Catherine Weinberger and Peter Kuhn, "Changing Levels or Changing Slopes? The Narrowing of the U.S. Gender Earnings Gap, 1959–1999," *Industrial and Labor Relations Review* 63, no. 3 (April 2010): 384–406. This suggests that the remainder is due to across-cohort gains of the type discussed above (i.e., comparing age groups over time).

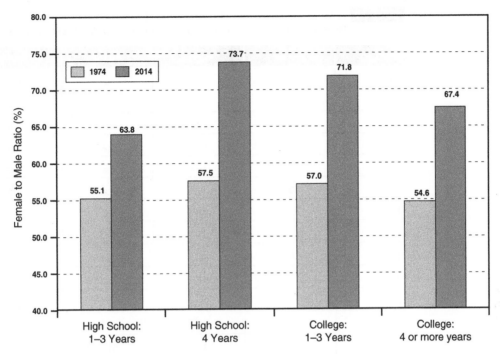

FIGURE 7-3 Ratio of Female-to-Male Mean Earnings by Education for Workers 18 Years Old and Over, 1974 and 2014

Notes: Definitions of educational categories are not exactly comparable for the two years. In 2014, mean earnings for 1-3 years of college is computed as a weighted average of the means for "some college, no degree" and "associate degree."
Sources: 1974: US Census Bureau Historical Income Tables-People Series, Table P-35, from www.census.gov/hhes/www/income/data/historical/people/, accessed August 2012; 2014: CPS 2012 Annual Social and Economic Supplement, Table PINC-04, accessed June 2016, https://www.census.gov/data/tables/time-series/demo/income-poverty/cps-pinc/pinc-04.2014.html.

ratio has increased to a lesser degree for the most highly skilled women, represented here by those with 4 or more years of college, compared to those with lesser skills (in Figure 7-3, specifically those who completed high school or just some college).[25] This finding may be related to increasing employer demands for workers in some highly skilled occupations to work long hours and to increasing rewards for such "over-work."[26] To the extent that men work these longer hours and reap the financial reward of doing so rather than women, this damps down any increase in the gender ratio that might otherwise occur. Figure 7-3 also suggests that the gender earnings ratio of the least skilled (those with 1–3 years of high school) has also lagged behind, though this finding may be due to the definition of skill used here (education level) since other research does not indicate this same lack of progress using a different measure.[27]

[25]See, Francine D. Blau and Lawrence M. Kahn, "The Gender Wage Gap: Extent, Trends, and Explanations," NBER Working Paper 21913 (January 2016) (*Journal of Economic Literature* forthcoming) and Patricia Cortés and Jessica Pan, "When Time Binds: Returns to Working Long Hours and the Gender Wage Gap among the Highly Skilled," IZA Discussion Paper No. 9846 (March 2016).
[26]Claudia Goldin, "A Grand Gender Convergence: Its Last Chapter." *American Economic Review* 104, no. 4 (May 2014): 1091-1119; Youngjoo Cha and Kim A. Weeden, "Overwork and the Slow Convergence in the Gender Gap in Wages," *American Sociological Review* 79, no. 3 (June 2014): 457–84; and Cortés and Pan, "When Time Binds." For an overview of the explanations for the gender gap, see, Blau and Kahn, "The Gender Wage Gap."
[27]Blau and Kahn, "'The Gender Wage Gap," for example, do not find slower progress for the least skilled; they measure skill by wages and look at gender wages differentials for workers at various points in the wage distribution.

| TABLE 7-7 | FEMALE-TO-MALE RATIOS OF MEDIAN EARNINGS BY RACE AND HISPANIC ORIGIN FOR FULL-TIME, YEAR-ROUND WORKERS, 1955–2014 |

YEAR	WHITES	BLACKS	ASIANS	HISPANICS
1955	65.3	55.1	n.a.	n.a.
1960	60.6	62.2	n.a.	n.a.
1965	57.9	62.5	n.a.	n.a.
1970	58.7	69.8	n.a.	n.a.
1975	57.6	74.6	n.a.	68.3
1980	58.9	78.8	n.a.	71.4
1985	63.0	81.9	n.a.	76.6
1990	67.6	85.4	79.7	81.9
1995	68.8	84.6	78.8	84.3
2000	72.3	83.3	75.1	86.9
2005	73.5	90.0	76.4	90.5
2010	77.5	87.4	79.9	89.2
2014	75.4	81.7	81.9	87.7

Notes: Prior to 1970, data are for income rather than earnings. Data for 1980 onward refer to workers 15 years of age and older, and those for 1955–1975 refer to workers 14 years of age and older. Hispanic individuals may be of any race. Prior to 1970, blacks include blacks and other nonwhites; prior to 2005, Asians include Asians and Pacific Islanders. Beginning in 1990, data on whites are for white, non-Hispanics. After 2000, individuals were able to report more than one race. In this table, *whites* are defined as persons who selected this race group only, *blacks* are defined as persons who selected black alone or in combination with other races, *Asians* are defined as persons who selected Asian alone or in combination with other races.

n.a. = not available.

Sources: 1955–1965: US Census Bureau, *Current Population Reports*, Consumer Income Series P-60, various issues; 1970 and beyond: US Census Bureau, "Historical Income Tables—People," table P-40 "Women's Earnings as a Percentage of Men's Earnings by Race and Hispanic Origin," accessed June 2016, https://www2.census.gov/programs-surveys/cps/tables/time-series/historical-income-people/p40.xls.

Table 7-7 reviews the trends in the median earnings of women relative to men separately by race and Hispanic origin. Within each group, women earned less than men in 2014, but the gender pay ratio was higher for all minority groups compared to (non-Hispanic) whites. While the ratio stood at 75 percent among whites, it was 82 percent for African Americans and Asians and 88 percent for Hispanics. Not surprisingly, the trends in earnings ratios by gender among whites (non-Hispanic whites after 1990) roughly mirror the overall trends because whites still comprise a substantial majority of the population. For whites, the gender ratio declined from 1955 to 1965, changed little from 1965 to 1980, and then increased at a rapid pace through 1990. Thereafter, progress was slower and more erratic. In contrast, the gender earnings ratio among African Americans increased consistently starting in the mid-1950s, increasing 27 percentage points by 2014. A sizable increase in the gender earnings ratio (16 percentage points) is also apparent among Hispanics since the mid-1970s when data first became available for this group. The data on Asians do not show a clear trend; however, data for this group have been available only since 1990.[28]

---

[28]Trends for this group should be regarded with some caution because underlying sample sizes are small and, prior to 2005, the data on Asians in the table (based on available government data) also included Pacific Islanders.

TABLE 7-8   MINORITY-TO-WHITE RATIOS OF MEDIAN EARNINGS BY GENDER FOR FULL-TIME, YEAR-ROUND WORKERS, 1955–2014

	BLACK-TO-WHITE RATIOS		ASIAN-TO-WHITE RATIOS		HISPANIC-TO-WHITE RATIOS	
Year	Males	Females	Males	Females	Males	Females
1955	60.9	51.4	n.a.	n.a.	n.a.	n.a.
1960	66.1	67.8	n.a.	n.a.	n.a.	n.a.
1965	62.8	67.9	n.a.	n.a.	n.a.	n.a.
1970	69.0	82.2	n.a.	n.a.	n.a.	n.a.
1975	74.4	96.3	n.a.	n.a.	72.1	85.6
1980	70.7	94.6	n.a.	n.a.	70.8	85.8
1985	69.7	90.6	n.a.	n.a.	68.0	82.7
1990	70.1	88.6	88.8	104.8	63.5	77.0
1995	71.0	87.3	91.8	105.1	59.2	72.6
2000	73.0	84.1	98.3	102.1	57.6	69.2
2005	71.0	87.0	101.4	105.5	57.6	71.0
2010	71.1	80.1	99.0	102.1	60.8	70.0
2014	73.2	79.4	101.9	110.6	62.3	72.4

Notes: Prior to 1970, data are for income rather than earnings. Data for 1980 onward refer to workers 15 years of age and older, and those for 1955–1975 refer to workers 14 years of age and older. Hispanic individuals may be of any race. Prior to 1970, blacks include blacks and other nonwhites; prior to 2005, Asians include Asians and Pacific Islanders. Beginning in 1990, data on whites are for white, non-Hispanics. After 2000, individuals were able to report more than one race. In this table, *whites* are defined as persons who selected this race group only, *blacks* are defined as persons who selected black alone or in combination with other races, *Asians* are defined as persons who selected Asian alone or in combination with other races.

n.a. = not available.

Sources: 1955–1965: US Census Bureau, *Current Population Reports*, Consumer Income Series P-60, various issues; 1970 and beyond: US Census Bureau, "Historical Income Tables—People," table P-38 "Full-Time, Year-Round Workers by Median Earnings and Sex," accessed June 2016, https://www.census.gov/data/tables/time-series/demo/income-poverty/historical-income-people.html.

Table 7-8 provides earnings comparisons for male and female minority group members relative to their white counterparts—non-Hispanics whites after 1990 when this breakdown became available, but for all whites in prior years.

In terms of the racial and ethnic differences shown in the table, we see that blacks and Hispanics of both sexes earned less than whites in 2014, but the differential was smaller among women than among men.[29] In that year, black males earned 73 percent of white males' earnings, and the figure for Hispanic males was 62 percent. These figures were considerably lower than the earnings ratios of 79 percent for black women and 72 percent for Hispanic women, both compared to white women. In contrast, the median earnings of Asian men have been about the same as those of white men since 2000, and Asian women's earnings have consistently

---

[29]For a review of trends in the black–white gap in labor market outcomes and their sources, see Derek Neal, "Black–White Labour Market Inequality in the United States," in *The New Palgrave Dictionary of Economics*, 2nd ed., ed. Steven Durlauf and Lawrence Blume (London: Palgrave Macmillan, 2008), also *The New Palgrave Dictionary of Economics Online*, accessed January 19, 2009, http://www.dictionaryofeconomics.com/article?id=pde2008_B000306.

been higher than their white counterparts' since data became available for this group in 1990. The higher ratios for Asians than for other minorities likely reflects the educational attainment advantage of Asians compared to whites, which will be discussed in Chapter 8.

The earnings ratio for black women relative to white women increased substantially from the mid-1950s, when it stood at only 51 percent, to the mid-1970s, when it was 96 percent. During this period, black men also gained relative to white men, although not as rapidly, from 61 percent of white men's earnings in 1955 to 74 percent in 1975. Unfortunately, there has been no further convergence in earnings for black women or men since then and, on the contrary, a noticeable decline for black women compared to their 1975 high point.

Some caution is warranted in interpreting the trends for black males in Table 7-8 because the data are based on the measured earnings of employed individuals. As discussed in Chapters 5 and 6, the participation and employment rates of black males relative to white males have decreased substantially since the 1950s, and it is likely that those who dropped out of the labor force were the individuals with the least favorable labor market opportunities. As we also noted in earlier chapters, incarceration rates are higher for blacks than whites and have been increasing; incarcerated individuals are also not included in Table 7-8. If blacks with the lowest earnings potential are leaving the labor force at a faster rate than comparable whites or are otherwise not counted (e.g., due to incarceration), observed black–white earnings ratios may rise (or show less of a decline) than is actually the case, simply because of a change in the composition of employed blacks, rather than due to a true improvement in their labor market opportunities. Research suggests that this factor is important, but the general outlines of the trends shown in Table 7-8 remain.[30]

A similar issue potentially affects trends in the black–white earnings ratio among women because, although black women traditionally had higher labor force participation rates than white women, the black–white participation gap has narrowed considerably since the 1950s. However, the participation decision of women is considerably more complex than men's, and researchers find it more difficult to estimate the likely effects of shifting participation patterns on the black–white earnings ratio for women.[31] Earnings trends by race will be considered further in Chapter 10.

Earnings ratios for Hispanics relative to whites are considerably lower than black–white ratios for both men and women. Moreover, they have been declining since the mid-1970s, when these data first became available. One reason for this decrease may be that a large and growing proportion of Hispanics are recent

---

[30]This is another example of selection bias; and again, James Heckman was the first to call attention to it in this context in his work with Richard Butler, "The Impact of the Economy and State on the Economic Status of Black Americans: A Critical Review," in *Equal Rights and Industrial Relations*, ed. Farrell E. Bloch (Madison, WI: Industrial Relations Research Association, 1977), 235–81. Other work includes, for example, Chinhui Juhn, "Labor Market Dropouts and Trends in the Wages of Black and White Men," *Industrial and Labor Relations Review* 56, no. 4 (July 2003): 643–63; and Amitabh Chandra, "Labor-Market Dropouts and the Racial Wage Gap: 1940–90," *American Economic Review* 90, no. 2 (May 2000): 333–38.
[31]For an insightful consideration of the selection issues, see Derek Neal, "The Measured Black–White Wage Gap among Women Is Too Small," supplement, *Journal of Political Economy* 112 (February 2004): S1–S28. For a study of trends, see Francine D. Blau and Andrea H. Beller, "Black–White Earnings over the 1970s and 1980s, Gender Differences in Trends," *Review of Economics and Statistics* 74, no. 2 (May 1992): 276–86. For an interesting historical analysis, see Martha J. Bailey and William J. Collins, "The Wage Gains of African-American Women in the 1940s," *Journal of Economic History* 66, no. 3 (September 2006): 737–77.

immigrants to the United States. Hence their earnings are reduced because they tend to be relatively young, may not speak English well, and face other difficulties in adjusting to their new environment. Of course, discrimination may also play a role in Hispanic–white earnings differences, just as it may for black–white differences.

The Gender Pay Gap in the News

We are bombarded in the press with a multitude of figures regarding how much women earn relative to men. Compounding this information overload is often inaccurate or misleading interpretations of the data. Here we provide a source and context for two figures that have received particular media attention.

The most common figure cited is based on the median earnings of year-round, full-time workers. It is readily available from the Census Bureau website and, as shown in Table 7-5, was 80 percent in 2015. While this figure *does* pertain to men and women who work full-time and year-round, it is important to bear in mind that they may well differ, on average, in their age, experience, educational attainment, seniority, occupation, industry, and other characteristics related to earnings. This caveat is often neglected, and the lower earnings of women for this broad group are sometimes interpreted as an indicator of discrimination. As we shall see in more detail in Chapter 10, it is necessary to account for differences in measured qualifications in assessing the extent of discrimination, and even then it may be difficult to reach definitive conclusions.

Another figure that has received substantial media attention is the 2010 finding by a market research company that in 147 out of 150 of the biggest cities in the United States, the median full-time salaries of single, young women were 8% *higher* than those of single, young men.* Should we take this statistic to mean that discrimination has been virtually eliminated, as some commentators have concluded? This inference does not appear to be warranted.

First, this finding applies only to a very specific group: unmarried women under 30 who do not have children and who live in cities. Moreover, as with the 79 percent figure discussed earlier, the gender comparison does not standardize for differences between the women and men in the sample. As the study's author pointed out, the women in the sample were much more likely than the men to have graduated college or obtained an advanced degree, and this was, no doubt, an important factor explaining their higher earnings. Second, it represents women's and men's earnings at the start of their careers. Hence, it does not reflect pay differences that may arise later as a result of gender differences in promotions and advancement. As we see in Table 7-6, the gender earnings ratio tends to decrease with age. Finally, the statistic compares men and women who do not have children. As we shall see in Chapter 9, research indicates that mothers incur a wage penalty compared to other women, even when they have the same measured qualifications, such as education and experience. No such wage penalty is found for fathers; indeed, researchers generally find a wage premium for them, meaning that they earn more than other men with similar qualifications. Thus, family status has very different labor market implications for women and men, even with the same human capital. While it is not necessarily the case that these gender differences in the impact of family status on wages are entirely due to discrimination, their magnitude and sources are worthy of serious consideration.

Identifying the sources of the gender pay gap, and particularly whether or not labor market discrimination plays a role, is a complex undertaking and involves more than an inspection of one or two statistics, including either or both of the two discussed here. To begin with, it is important to be clear about what economists mean by labor market discrimination. **Labor market discrimination** exists when employers treat men and women differently, even when they have the same qualifications, such as educational attainment and years of labor market experience.

continues

Measuring discrimination is challenging on a number of dimensions. On the one hand, worker qualifications may be difficult to measure, and some qualifications that employers regard as important may not be available in the data sets used by researchers. On the other hand, differential treatment of men and women, or the anticipation of it, may adversely influence a woman's decisions, including her decisions about the level and type of qualifications to acquire, as well as her subsequent labor market choices.

Our careful review of the available evidence in Chapter 10 suggests that discrimination against women in the labor market does exist and, while it may not be as severe as in the past, it continues to represent more than an occasional anomaly.

The study is by James Chung of Reach Advisors and is a follow-up of earlier research from Queens College, New York, that reached similar conclusions. Our discussion is based on an article by Belinda Luscombe, "Workplace Salaries:

At Last, Women on Top," Time, September 1, 2010, accessed November 3, 2012, http://www.time.com/time/business/article/0,8599,2015274,00.html.

Gender Differences in Union Membership

Gender differences in union membership have received considerable attention because unions confer a range of benefits on their members, with the most cited benefit being a **union wage advantage** (the difference between the wages of union and nonunion members). The union wage advantage has averaged about 17 to 18 percent since the early 1970s.[32]

Traditionally, men were much more likely to be union members than women, and the gender gap in unionization rates was extremely large. (The **unionization rate** is the share of workers who are union members.) But, as shown in Table 7-9, this gender difference has declined dramatically since the 1950s. The gender gap in unionization rates was nearly 17 percentage points in 1956 and had fallen to less than 1 percentage point by 2015. As may be seen in Figure 7-4, as a consequence of these changes, 46 percent of union members are now women, up from less than 20 percent in the mid-1950s. This is only a couple of percentage points below women's share of the labor force.

The declining gender gap in unionization rates is closely tied to the precipitous decline in unionization that occurred for the labor force as a whole. In the mid-1950s, over a quarter of all workers were union members; in 2015 just 11 percent were. The decrease in unionization has been especially pronounced for men; their unionization rate dropped from 32 to 12 percent. Women's rate, while initially quite a bit lower, has *declined* far less, decreasing only from 16 to 11 percent. As a result, the gender *difference* in unionization rates has virtually disappeared.

While debate continues about the precise causes of the decline in private sector unionization, most agree that the shift in industrial structure away from more heavily unionized sectors, such as manufacturing, is an important contributing factor.[33]

---

[32]See David G. Blanchflower and Alex Bryson, "What Effect Do Unions Have on Wages Now and Would Freeman and Medoff Be Surprised?" in *What Do Unions Do? A Twenty-Year Perspective*, ed. James T. Bennett and Bruce E. Kaufman (New Brunswick, NJ: Transaction Publishers, 2007), 79–113. The earlier study referred to in the book title is Richard B. Freeman and James L. Medoff, *What Do Unions Do?* (New York: Basic Books, 1984).

[33]Other explanations include firms' increased opposition to unions, differential growth in traditionally union and nonunion sectors, and changes in legal and institutional factors that may have affected union organizing activity. See Henry Farber and Bruce Western, "Round Up the Usual Suspects: The Decline of Unions in the Private Sector, 1973–98," *Journal of Labor Research* 2, no. 2 (Summer 2001): 63–88.

TABLE 7-9 TRENDS IN UNION MEMBERSHIP FOR SELECTED YEARS, 1956–2015

Year	UNION MEMBERS AS A PERCENT OF EMPLOYED WORKERS		
	Men	Women	Total
1956	32.2	15.7	27.0
1966	30.7	13.1	24.4
1970	32.9	16.9	26.8
1980	25.1	14.7	20.7
1990	19.3	12.6	16.1
2000	15.2	11.5	13.5
2010	12.6	11.1	11.9
2015			
All	11.5	10.6	11.1
Whites	11.2	10.2	10.8
Blacks	14.5	12.8	13.6
Asians	8.9	10.7	9.8
Hispanics	9.6	9.2	9.4

Notes: Data for 1955 and 1956 refer to unions only. The remaining years include unions and associations. For 2015, race refers to those who selected this race group only. Persons whose ethnicity is Hispanic may be of any race.
Sources for Table 7-9 and Figure 7-4: US Department of Labor, Bureau of Labor Statistics, "Earnings and Other Characteristics of Organized Workers," Bulletin 2105 (May 1980), table 2, 2; Linda H. LeGrande, "Women in Labor Organizations: Their Ranks Are Increasing," *Monthly Labor Review* 101, no. 8 (August 1978): table 1, 9; "Employment and Training Report of the President (1981)," table A-16, 144–46; *Employment and Earnings* 38, no. 1 (January 1991): 228; US Department of Labor, Bureau of Labor Statistics, "Union Members in 2000," USDL 01-21 (January 2001), "Union Members-2011," USDL-12-0094 (January 2012), and US Department of Labor, Bureau of Labor Statistics, 2016 *Employment & Earnings Online*, Annual Averages, table 40, "Union Affiliation of Employed Wage and Salary Workers by Selected Characteristics," accessed March 2016, http://www.bls.gov/cps/cpsaat40.htm.

Since these sectors were largely the bastions of men, this shift has had a much larger negative effect on men's unionization rates than women's. Not only did women lose fewer union jobs due to the decline in manufacturing but a much larger share of female union workers are employed in the public sector, typically in the fields of health, education, and public administration, where unionization rates actually *rose* during the 1970s and unions have held their own subsequently. One consequence of the divergent trends in public and private sector unionization is that in 2015 nearly one-half of all union workers were employed in the public sector compared to just 17 percent in 1973.[34]

---

[34]Figures are from Barry Hirsch and David Macpherson, "Union Membership and Coverage Database from the CPS," available at www.unionstats.com. For useful discussions, see Janelle Jones, John Schmitt, and Nicole Woo, "Women, Working Families, and Unions," Center for Economic and Policy Research (June 2014), accessed January 18, 2016, www.cepr.net; Ruth Milkman, "Two Worlds of Unionism: Women and the New Labor Movement," in *The Sex of Class: Women Transforming American Labor*, ed. Dorothy Sue Cobble (Ithaca, NY: Cornell University Press, 2007), 63–80; and Henry S. Farber, "Union Membership in the United States: The Divergence between the Public and Private Sectors," in *Collective Bargaining in Education: Negotiating Change in Today's Schools*, ed. Joan Hannaway and Andrew Rotherham (Cambridge, MA: Harvard Education Press, 2006), 27–52.

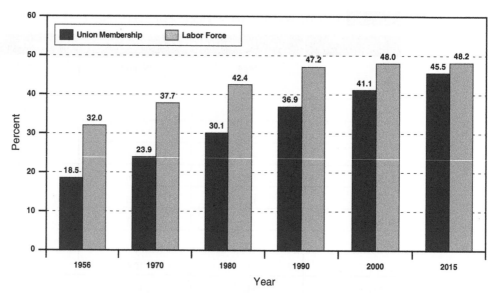

FIGURE 7-4 Women's Share of All Employed Workers and Share of Union Membership, 1956–2015

Notes: Data for 1955 and 1956 refer to unions only. The remaining years include unions and associations. For 2015, race refers to those who selected this race group only. Persons whose ethnicity is Hispanic may be of any race.
Source: See Table 7-9 for sources.

While the gender gap in union membership has declined, as is the case for other sectors—academia, government, and the private sector—women are considerably less likely to hold union leadership positions than men, especially top posts at the national level. As just one example, in 2016 only 11 out of 53 (21 percent) of AFL-CIO executive council members were women.[35] Factors likely impeding women's advancement up the career ladder in union organizations are similar to those in other sectors of the economy. We examine these issues further in our discussion of the glass ceiling in Chapter 10.

Gender Differences in Self-Employment

Self-employed workers are defined as those who work for themselves (typically unincorporated businesses) plus those who head their own larger businesses (typically incorporated).[36] They may be distinguished from the much larger group of **wage and salary workers** who are employees; that is, they work for another individual or a business in exchange for compensation. As may be seen in Table 7-10, in 2015 just over 9 percent of workers were self-employed, down from a recent high of 10.4 percent in 2005, shortly before the onset of the Great Recession.

---

[35]"AFL-CIO, Executive Council Members," accessed September 2016, www.aflcio.org. The AFL-CIO is the largest union federation in the United States. For further discussion about women in leadership, see Gill Kirton and Geraldine Healy, *Gender and Leadership in Unions*, Routledge Research in Employment Relations (New York and Abingdon, UK: Routledge, 2012).

[36]Self-employment is one of a number of measures of entrepreneurship, including new business starts and the number of small businesses; see Maria Minniti, "Gender Issues in Entrepreneurship," *Foundations and Trends in Entrepreneurship* 5, nos. 7–8 (2009): 497–621.

TABLE 7-10 SELF-EMPLOYMENT RATES OF WOMEN AND MEN IN THE NONAGRICULTURAL SECTOR, SELECTED YEARS, 1996–2015

Year	SELF-EMPLOYMENT RATE (%)		
	Total	Women	Men
1996	10.9	7.4	13.7
2000	10.0	6.9	12.6
2005	10.4	7.0	13.2
2010	9.8	6.8	12.4
2015	9.3	6.5	11.7

Notes: Includes individuals 16 years of age and older who work 15+ hours per week. Figures were calculated by Robert W. Fairlie of University of California, Santa Cruz, using data from the monthly Current Population Survey. The self-employed include workers in both unincorporated and incorporated businesses.
Source: Unpublished data from Robert W. Fairlie, http://people.ucsc.edu/~rfairlie/

Table 7-10 further provides a breakdown of the self-employment rate for women and men for the 1996–2015 period.[37] (The **self-employment rate** refers to the percentage of workers who are self-employed.) As of 2015, men's self-employment rate stood considerably higher than women's rate, at 11.7 percent compared to 6.5 percent for women. The gender gap in self-employment rates has been relatively stable in recent decades. In 2015, it was 5.2 percentage points, only slightly smaller than the 1996 gap of 6.3 percentage points.

There are some factors that might make self-employment particularly attractive to women. It may provide greater flexibility to combine work and family responsibilities and could be a potential avenue of escape from a glass ceiling that limits women's advancement in the wage and salary sector.[38] Self-employment has also been suggested as a possible route out of poverty for low-income women, and, in fact, a modest amount of financial and technical assistance is available to low-income women for starting their own businesses.[39] While such considerations may influence female decisions about self-employment, as we have seen, thus far the self-employment gender gap has not been narrowing.

Higher rates of self-employment for men have also been found for an extensive set of racial and ethnic groups. However, self-employment rates for women and men vary considerably by race and ethnicity. For instance, in 2012, the rate for Asian women was nearly three times higher than that for black women. More generally, rates of self-employment among African Americans, both men and women, remain among the lowest of any group. Part of the reason for the race difference is that blacks

---

[37]Data were provided by Robert W. Fairlie; see http://people.ucsc.edu/~rfairlie. For trends using slightly different definitions of self-employment, see Steven F. Hipple, "Self-Employment in the United States," *Monthly Labor Review* (September 2010): 17–32; and Kristen Roche, "Female Self-Employment in the United States: An Update to 2012," *Monthly Labor Review* (October 2014): 1–5.

[38]For a comprehensive review, see Minniti, "Gender Issues in Entrepreneurship"; for evidence on the attractiveness to women of the greater flexibility offered by self-employment, see Allison J. Wellington, "Self-Employment: The New Solution for Balancing Family and Career," *Labour Economics* 13, no 3 (June 2006): 357–86.

[39]See Shaila Dewan, "Microcredit for Americans," *New York Times*, October 28, 2013; Margaret Sherrard Sherrarden, Cynthia K. Sanders, and Michael Sherraden, *Kitchen Capitalism: Microenterprise in Low-Income Households* (Albany: State University of New York Press, 2004); and Magnus Lofstrom, "Does Self-Employment Increase the Economic Well-Being of Low-Skilled Workers?" *Small Business Economics* 40, no. 4 (May 2013): 933-52. The success of such programs in developing countries is discussed in Chapter 17.

have fewer assets and less access to credit. Further, business ownership tends to "run in the family," and, since black women and men are less likely to have a self-employed parent, they are also less likely to be self-employed themselves, all else equal.[40]

Research generally finds that female self-employed workers earn less than their wage and salary counterparts with the same qualifications.[41] However, one study suggests that this aggregate finding may mask differential effects by occupation, depending on women's reasons for entry into self-employment.[42] Women in professional occupations appear to earn a premium from self-employment, even after accounting for marital status and children. This is consistent with the notion that, for these women, self-employment reflects an expansion in career opportunities. In contrast, self-employed women in nonprofessional occupations, including those providing childcare services, experience an earnings penalty. For many in this latter group, self-employment may serve as a means to increase workplace flexibility. For men the evidence is more mixed, with some studies finding that self-employment boosts earnings but one detailed analysis reporting a negative effect.[43] All told, the available evidence on earnings suggests that many women, and possibly some men, may forgo some income in exchange for greater freedom in determining their own hours and working conditions. Hence the lower earnings of the self-employed may be considered a compensating differential.[44]

Gender Differences in Nonstandard Work

Nonstandard work has received increased attention in the media, especially as a very small but rising number of individuals participate in what has come to be called the **"online gig" economy**—a new part of the economy in which technology brings together workers who do short stints ("gigs") with customers. Prime examples are Uber, the well-known ride-sharing service, and TaskRabbit, a popular errand service.[45] This type of employment is part of a broader category called alternative or **nonstandard work**. Nonstandard work typically refers to arrangements where the "time, place, or quantity of work is unpredictable" or where the employment is arranged by an intermediary.[46]

---

[40]For recent data, see Roche, "Female Self-Employment." For further discussion, see Robert W. Fairlie and Alicia M. Robb, *Race and Entrepreneurial Success: Black-, Asian-, and White-Owned Businesses in the United States* (Cambridge, MA: MIT Press, 2008); and Magnus Lofstrom and Timothy Bates, "African American's Pursuit of Self-Employment," *Small Business Economics 40, no. 1 (January 2013): 73–86.*

[41]See Minniti, "Gender Issues in Entrepreneurship"; and Michele J. Budig, "Gender, Self-Employment, and Earnings: The Interlocking Structures of Family and Professional Status," *Gender and Society* 20, no. 6 (December 2006): 725–53.

[42]Budig, "Gender, Self-Employment, and Earnings."

[43]Marianne A. Ferber and Jane Waldfogel, among others, find that self-employed men earn more than their wage and salary counterparts but present some evidence that this result is due to unobserved heterogeneity; see "The Long-Term Consequences of Nontraditional Employment," *Monthly Labor Review* 121, no. 6 (May 1998): 3–12. After accounting for selection into self-employment, Barton H. Hamilton finds evidence of lower earnings for self-employed men; see "Does Entrepreneurship Pay? An Empirical Analysis of the Returns to Self-Employment," *Journal of Political Economy* 108, no. 3 (June 2000): 604–31.

[44]In addition, self-employed workers tend to have lower retirement benefits and are less likely than their wage and salary worker counterparts to have health care coverage in their own right. See Roche, "Female Self-Employment."

[45]Jane Dokko, Megan Mumford, and Diane Whitmore Schanzenbach, "Workers and the Online Gig Economy," The Hamilton Project (Washington, DC: Brookings Institution, December 2015); and Sarah A. Donovan, David H. Bradley, and Jon O. Shimabukuro, *What Does the Gig Economy Mean for Workers?* (Washington, DC: Congressional Research Service, February 5, 2016).

[46]While definitions vary slightly, this type of employment may also be called "contingent work" or "alternative employment." See the section titled "Concepts and Definitions" in US Bureau of Labor Statistics, "Contingent and Alternative Employment Arrangements: February 2005."

While definitions of nonstandard workers vary, surveys conducted by the **US Bureau of Labor Statistics (BLS)** in 1995 and 2005 focused on four broad categories of workers for whom this type of employment was their main job.[47] The first category, **temporary workers (temps)**, are individuals who do not have a direct contract with their employer but work for a temporary help agency.[48] The second category is **independent contractors**, individuals who provide a good or service directly to a firm and are most often self-employed.[49] Examples are freelance writers and management consultants. The third category is **on-call workers** such as substitute teachers and construction workers supplied by a union hiring hall. Finally, the fourth category is **contract workers**; these are workers who are employed by firms that provide them or their services to other companies under contract. These workers supply such varied services as cleaning, security, landscaping, or computer programming.[50] Using these definitions, a 2005 BLS survey found that nearly 11 percent of all employed workers held one of these types of employment as their main job. Women comprised 40 percent of all such workers and slightly over one-half of all temps. Women and men were about equally represented among on-call workers, and men comprised around two-thirds of all contract workers and independent contractors.[51]

Unfortunately, the next official BLS survey is not planned until 2017. Thus, evidence on aggregate trends in nonstandard work is limited. A recent study that used similar definitions to the BLS survey, albeit for a much smaller sample, provided updated figures for 2015. This study found that 15.8 percent of all employed workers were in one of these four categories for their main job, which translates into a substantial increase in the share of nonstandard workers (from 11 to 15.8 percent) over the 10-year period from 2005 to 2015.[52] However, other recent research finds little change to a modest increase in the share of such workers.[53] The fielding of the new BLS survey should provide firmer conclusions about the most recent trends.

In evaluating estimates of the share of nonstandard workers, it is useful to keep in mind, as noted earlier, that there is not a single strict definition.[54] For instance, there

---

[47]As we shall discuss shortly, typically, "gig" employment supplements earnings but is not the individual's main job or source of earnings.

[48]Perhaps surprisingly, the majority of temps are now in manufacturing employment; see Susan N. Houseman and Carolyn J. Heinrich, "Temporary Help Employment in Recession and Recovery," Upjohn Institute Upjohn Institute Working Paper 15-227 (Kalamazoo, MI: W.E. Upjohn Institute for Employment Research, 2015).

[49]However, self-employed business operators, such as shop owners or restaurateurs, are not included among independent contractors.

[50]To be included under alternative employment arrangements, contract workers had to report that they usually had only one customer and worked at the customer's worksite. These characteristics distinguish contract workers from those employed by companies that carry out work assignments, such as advertising agencies, equipment manufacturers, lawyers, or economics "think tanks"; see Anne E. Polivka, "Contingent and Alternative Work Arrangements, Defined," *Monthly Labor Review* 119 (October 1996): 3–9.

[51]All figures in this paragraph are from US Bureau of Labor Statistics, "Contingent and Alternative Employment Arrangements."

[52]The methodology and findings of the 2015 survey are reported in Lawrence F. Katz and Alan B. Krueger, "The Rise and Nature of Alternative Work Arrangements in the United States, 1995–2015," NBER Working Paper 22667 (National Bureau of Economic Research, Cambridge, MA, September 2016).

[53]See, for instance, General Accounting Office, "Contingent Workforce: Size, Characteristics, Earnings and Benefits," GAO-15-168R (April 2015), http://www.gao.gov; Annette Bernhardt, "Labor Standards and the Reorganization of Work: Gaps in Data and Research," Institute for Research on Labor and Employment Working Paper 100-14 (University of California-Berkeley, January 2014); and Peter H. Cappellini and J. R. Keller, "A Study of the Extent and Potential Causes of Alternative Employment Arrangements," *ILR Review* 66 no. 4 (July 2013): 874–901.

[54]General Accounting Office, "Contingent Workforce."

is some question about whether or not to include part-time workers. Some individuals hold part-time positions only briefly, perhaps because, as discussed in Chapter 6, they cannot find full-time employment. It might make sense to include such individuals among nonstandard workers. However, other individuals not only voluntarily choose such jobs but also hold them for long stretches of time, so it does not seem appropriate to include them in the nonstandard group. Another group that might, perhaps, be included are nonstandard workers in academia, such as those who hold adjunct and instructor positions.[55] Finally, as noted above, the BLS estimates only count those who hold nonstandard employment as their *main* job. However, research on the online gig economy finds that most "gig workers," including Uber drivers, are using this employment to supplement their wages and salaries from other jobs (they would therefore not be counted).[56]

While the gig economy has received much popular attention, available evidence indicates that only around .4 to .6 percent of all workers hold such jobs. By far, the largest employer is Uber.[57] Interestingly, a recent study of the Uber market found that around 14 percent of its drivers are women, a figure that is actually somewhat higher than the percentage of taxi drivers who are women.[58]

In terms of labor market outcomes, as would be expected, pay and benefits differ depending on the type of nonstandard work. Evidence indicates that independent contractors and contract workers (the more heavily male categories) earn more than those in traditional employment with similar qualifications and job characteristics.[59] This is not the case for on-call workers and temps (the more heavily female categories) who tend to earn less even controlling for measured characteristics.[60] Also, although those in nonstandard work are less likely than those in regular employment to be covered by employer-provided health insurance and pensions, among those in nonstandard work, contract workers are more likely to receive these benefits, and independent contractors tend to have coverage from other sources. Thus, women are at a disadvantage in terms of both pay and benefits to the extent they are underrepresented among contract workers and independent contractors.[61]

---

[55]This group constitutes a large and growing share of faculty. For instance, from academic year 1993–1994 to 2013–2014, the percentage of full-time faculty with a tenure-track position fell from 56 to 48 percent. Moreover, in 2013–2014 only 43 percent of full-time women employed in academia held tenured or tenure-track positions compared to 57 percent of men. See National Center for Education Statistics, "Digest of Education Statistics," *2014*, table 316.80, www.nces.ed.gov.

[56]Jonathan V. Hall and Alan B. Krueger, "An Analysis of the Labor Market for Uber's Driver-Partners in the United States," NBER Working Paper 22843 (National Bureau of Economic Research, Cambridge, MA, November 2016); and Eric Morth, "Gig Economy Attracts Many Workers, Few Full-Time Jobs," *Wall Street Journal*, February 18, 2016.

[57]Katz and Krueger, "Rise and Nature of Alternative Work." An issue that has come to the fore, in large part due to the rise of Uber and other similar services, is whether gig workers such as Uber drivers are entitled to labor protections such as overtime pay and worker's compensation. Their labor "classification" is not clear. Uber drivers, for instance, are similar to traditional workers because they work for someone else—in this case an intermediary who matches workers to customers—and their employer sets the fares. But the fact that they have autonomy over their own schedules makes them more akin to independent contractors. See Seth D. Harris and Alan B. Krueger, "The Gig Economy How to Modernize the Rules of Work to Fit the Times," *Milken Institute Review*, 2nd quarter (May 2016): 7–24.

[58]Hall and Krueger, "An Analysis of the Labor Market for Uber's Driver-Partners."

[59]Arne L. Kalleberg, Barbara F. Reskin, and Ken Hudson, "Bad Jobs in America: Standard and Nonstandard Employment Relations and Job Quality in the United States," *American Sociological Review* 65, no. 2 (April 2000): 256–78.

[60]See Kalleberg, Reskin, and Hudson, "Bad Jobs in America," and General Accounting Office, "Contingent Workforce."

[61]See US Bureau of Labor Statistics, "Contingent and Alternative Arrangements," table 9. Similar evidence is found in General Accounting Office, "Contingent Workforce."

Workers may be attracted to nonstandard work for a variety of reasons, including the flexibility and autonomy such jobs may offer and the prospect of higher wages (at least for independent contractors and contract workers). And, as we have seen, technology has facilitated the expansion of some types of nonstandard employment. However, some workers take nonstandard jobs because they are unable to locate regular employment. In this respect it is notable that more than four-fifths of independent contractors stated in a survey that they preferred their current work arrangement, while just one-third of temporary help workers did so.[62] This again suggests that women are concentrated in the less desirable types of nonstandard work.

Conclusion

In this chapter, we presented data on gender differentials in occupations and earnings for women overall as well as for various subgroups. Although gender differences in occupations and earnings remain substantial, both have declined significantly. Substantial reductions in occupational segregation by sex date back to 1970, and particular progress occurred over the 1970s and 1980s. The overall gender earnings gap for full-time workers started to narrow around 1980. The trend toward earnings convergence between men and women was particularly dramatic during the 1980s and has been slower and more uneven since then. Women were also traditionally less likely than men to be union workers, but that gender difference has been virtually eliminated as unionization rates have fallen more precipitously for men than women. Women are also considerably less likely to be self-employed than men, and that gender difference has shown little sign of narrowing. And while some evidence suggests that women are less likely than men to be nonstandard workers, they are concentrated in the lower-paying and less desirable types of nonstandard employment. The following chapters thoroughly investigate the possible explanations for a number of the gender differences described here, particularly focusing on wages and employment.

Questions for Review and Discussion

1. Why have women been eager to move into men's occupations? Why do you think men generally show less enthusiasm about moving into women's occupations?

2. Consider the following hypothetical information about the occupational distribution in country Y. Assume that 100 employed men and 100 employed women work in either occupation A or occupation B.

	EMPLOYED WOMEN (%)	EMPLOYED MEN (%)
Occupation A	70	20
Occupation B	30	80
Total	100	100

---

[62]See US Department of Labor, Bureau of Labor Statistics, "Contingent and Alternative Employment," table 11. 2010 data from a different survey show a similar pattern; see General Accounting Office, "Contingent Workforce."

a. Calculate the index of occupational segregation by sex using the formula given in footnote 8 of this chapter.

b. Explain exactly what the number you obtained means in light of the verbal definition of the segregation index.

3. Calculate the segregation index for 2015 for the 10 major occupational categories shown in Table 7-1. Why is the figure you obtain lower than the values that are obtained when a large set of detailed occupations are considered as in Figure 7-1?

4. Explain why the female–male earnings ratio is likely to be higher for full-time, year-round workers than for all workers.

5. What has been the trend in the gender gap in unionization rates? How have differences in the sectors where men and women are employed contributed to the trends?

6. It is noted in the text that there are a number of reasons why women might find self-employment attractive—what are those reasons? Yet women are less likely to be self-employed than men—why do you think that is the case?

7. What is nonstandard work? Which types of nonstandard work are women especially likely to be concentrated in? Is nonstandard work positively or negatively associated with workers' wages?

Internet-Based Data Exercise

In doing this exercise, students should be aware that the precise names of documents and their location within a website may change over time.

1. The US Census Bureau is the primary source of government data on many topics included in this text, including income, education, and poverty.

   Visit the home page of the US Census Bureau at http://www.census.gov.

   Click on "Income." On the income page, look for the most recent document titled "Income and Poverty in the United States" (or a similar title). Find "Table 1," which provides income and earnings summary measures by selected characteristics.

   a. What are the most recent estimates of median earnings for full-time, year-round women and men workers?

   b. How does the current female–male earnings ratio compare to figures in Table 7-5?

   c. Calculate the female–male earnings ratio using data on female householders (no husband present) and male householders (no wife present). Offer likely reasons why this ratio is higher than your answer in b. (We will examine these types of families further in later chapters.)

2. The US Bureau of Labor Statistics is the primary source of government data on labor force statistics. A key online Bureau of Labor Statistics publication is

called *Employment and Earnings*. Visit the home page at http://www.bls.gov/opub/ee/. Click on "Household Survey Data." Under data for "Annual Averages," look for Table 39, "Median Weekly Earnings of Full-Time Wage and Salary Workers by Detailed Occupation and Sex."

a. For the broad occupation categories listed in Table 7-1, create your own table (fully labeled with a complete source) that compares median weekly earnings for women and men for the most recent year available.

b. Discuss the patterns that you see in light of the textbook discussion in Chapter 7.

Suggested Readings

Bennett, James T., and Bruce E. Kaufman, eds. *What Do Unions Do? The Evidence Twenty Years Later*. New Brunswick, NJ: Transaction Publishers, 2007.

Blau, Francine D., Peter Brummund, and Albert Yung-Hsu Liu. "Trends in Occupational Segregation by Gender 1970–2009: Adjusting for the Impact of Changes in the Occupational Coding System." *Demography* 50, no. 2 (April 2013): 471–92.

Blau, Francine D., and Lawrence M. Kahn. "Gender Differences in Pay." *Journal of Economic Perspectives* 14, no. 4 (Autumn 2000): 75–99.

Blau, Francine D., and Lawrence M. Kahn. "The Gender Wage Gap: Extent, Trends, and Sources." NBER Working Paper 21913 (National Bureau of Economic Research, Cambridge, MA, January 2016) (*Journal of Economic Literature*, forthcoming).

Carré, Francoise, Marianne A. Ferber, Lonnie Golden, and Steve Herzenberg, eds. *Nonstandard Work: The Nature and Challenges of Changing Employment Arrangements* Champaign, IL: Industrial Relations Research Association, 2000.

Cobble, Dorothy Sue, ed. *The Sex of Class: Women Transforming American Labor*. Ithaca, NY: ILR Press, 2007.

Fairlie, Robert W., and Alicia M. Robb. *Race and Entrepreneurial Success: Black-, Asian-, and White-Owned Businesses in the United States*. Cambridge, MA: MIT Press, 2008.

Gleason, Sandra E. *The Shadow Workforce. Perspectives on Contingent Work in the United States, Japan, and Europe*. Kalamazoo, MI: Upjohn Institute for Employment Research, 2015.

Hegewisch, Ariane, Marc Bendick, Jr., Barbara Gault, and Heidi Hartmann. *Narrowing the Wage Gap by Improving Women's Access to Good Middle-Skill Jobs*. Washington, DC: Institute for Women's Policy Research, 2016, available at www.iwpr.org.

Kalleberg, Arne L. *Good Jobs, Bad Jobs: The Rise of Polarized and Precarious Employment Systems in the United States, 1970s–2000s*. New York: Russell Sage Foundation, 2011.

Kirton, Gill, and Geraldine Healy. *Gender and Leadership in Unions*. Routledge Research in Employment Relations. New York and Abingdon, UK: Routledge, 2012.

Minniti, Maria. "Gender Issues in Entrepreneurship." *Foundations and Trends in Entrepreneurship* 5, nos. 7–8 (2009): 497–621.

Stainback, Kevin, and Donald Tomaskovic-Devey. *Documenting Desegregation: Racial and Gender Segregation in Private-Sector Employment since the Civil Rights Act*. New York: Russell Sage Foundation, 2012.

Key Terms

major occupations (158)

detailed occupations (158)

predominantly male occupation (164)

predominantly female occupation (164)

integrated occupation (164)

STEM fields (164)

occupational segregation (165)

index of segregation (165)

occupational tipping (170)

gender pay ratio (171)

gender pay gap (171)

labor market discrimination (179)

union wage advantage (180)

unionization rate (180)

self-employed workers (182)

wage and salary workers (182)

self-employment rate (183)

"online gig" economy (184)

nonstandard work (184)

US Bureau of Labor Statistics (BLS) (185)

temporary workers (temps) (185)

independent contractors (185)

on-call workers (185)

contract workers (185)

Gender Differences in Educational Attainment: Theory and Evidence

8

CHAPTER HIGHLIGHTS

- Supply and Demand Explanations: An Overview
- What Is Human Capital?
- Gender Differences in Levels of Educational Attainment
- Gender Differences in High School Coursework and College Field of Study
- The Educational Investment Decision
- The Rising College Wage or Earnings Premium
- Education and Productivity
- Gender Differences in Educational Investment Decisions: The Human Capital Explanation
- Gender Differences in Educational Investment Decisions: Social Influences and Anticipation of Discrimination
- The Impact of Title IX—Sports, Academics, Sexual Harassment, and Sexual Violence
- Explaining Women's Rising Educational Attainment

In this and the next chapter, we present supply-side explanations for the gender differences in occupations and earnings described in Chapter 7. In our consideration of supply-side explanations, we place considerable emphasis on human capital analysis, which is the supply-side approach that has received the most attention in the economics literature. In this chapter, we focus on the determinants of the decision to invest in formal education and ask why, in earlier years, men were more likely to invest in higher education than women and why, in more recent decades, there has been a reversal of that pattern (i.e., women are now more likely to invest in higher education than men). We also highlight gender differences in fields of study, which have fallen over time but remain important. In Chapter 9, we continue our examination of supply-side explanations by studying gender differences in another type of human capital, on-the-job training, and look into other supply-side factors that may produce gender differences in economic outcomes. In Chapter 10 we examine the empirical evidence related to the underlying sources of gender differences in outcomes. In addition to supply-side factors, the evidence points to a role for demand-side factors or labor market discrimination. After establishing that labor market discrimination accounts for at least some of the observed gender differences, in Chapter 11 we review economic theories of discrimination. Finally, in Chapter 12, we review policy interventions to counter labor market discrimination. It is our view that the human capital and discrimination explanations are not mutually exclusive and that both provide valuable insights into the sources of male–female differences in labor market outcomes.

Supply and Demand Explanations: An Overview

Supply-side explanations for gender differences in earnings and occupations focus on the observation that men and women may come to the labor market with different qualifications, such as education, formal training, or experience, and with different preferences or tastes. An example of a gender difference in qualifications would be a woman with a college degree in English and a man with a college degree in engineering. Or, as another example, a woman might move in and out of the labor force as her family situation changes, whereas a man's labor force attachment might be more continuous. Gender differences in preferences might mean, for example, that one group or the other shows greater tolerance for an unpleasant, unhealthy, or dangerous work environment; for longer work hours or inflexible work schedules; or for physical strain or risk and is more willing to accept these working conditions in return for higher wages. To the extent that such differences in men's and women's qualifications and preferences exist, they could cause women to earn less and to be concentrated in different, often lower-paying, occupations.

Before considering the role of supply-side factors in this and the next chapter, one issue that arises is whether such differences in qualifications should be viewed as the result of the voluntary choices men and women make or as the outcome of what has been termed *prelabor market* or *societal discrimination*. **Societal discrimination** denotes the multitude of social influences that cause women to make decisions that adversely influence their status in the labor market. Because we are all products of our environments to a greater or lesser extent, it is often difficult to draw the line between voluntary choice and this type of discrimination.

This distinction may in part reflect disciplinary boundaries. Economists tend to view individual decisions as determined by economic incentives and individual preferences (or tastes). They generally do not analyze the formation of preferences, and choices are generally viewed as being at least to some extent voluntary. In contrast, sociologists and social psychologists are more apt to examine the role of socialization and social structural factors in producing what economists classify as individual preferences.[1] Thus, within the context of sociology or social psychology, individual choices are more likely to be seen as stemming from social conditioning or constraints rather than as being voluntary.

The tendency to emphasize the role of choice versus societal discrimination may also reflect an implicit value judgment. Those who are reasonably content with the status quo of gender differences in economic outcomes tend to speak mainly of voluntary choices, whereas those who raise concerns about gender inequality in pay and occupations are more inclined to focus on the role of discrimination, either societal discrimination or labor market discrimination.

We tend toward the view that at least some of the gender differences in qualifications that currently exist stem from societal discrimination, although we acknowledge that, particularly in the past and to a lesser extent today, many individuals regarded this type of gender differentiation as perfectly appropriate. The important point is that even if societal discrimination is a problem, it is essentially different from **labor market discrimination**, and a different set of policies is required to address it. Labor market discrimination exists when two equally qualified individuals are treated differently in the labor market solely on the basis of their gender (or other characteristic unrelated to their qualifications or productivity). As we have noted, labor market discrimination and relevant policies are the focus of subsequent chapters.

It is also important to recognize that distinguishing between supply- and demand-side factors is not always clear-cut. Labor market discrimination can affect women's economic status *indirectly* by reducing their incentives to invest in themselves and to acquire particular job qualifications. Thus, gender differences in qualifications such as education may reflect not only the voluntary choices of men and women and the impact of societal discrimination but also the indirect effects of labor market discrimination.

What Is Human Capital?

Within the economics literature, the human capital model provides the major supply-side explanation for gender differentials in economic outcomes, although gender differences in psychological attributes, including attitudes and preferences (which we discuss in Chapter 9), are getting increasing attention. The human capital model helps explain why some individuals invest in college and others do not, as well as why individuals choose varying fields of study. Also, as we shall see in Chapter 9, it explains why individuals invest in different amounts of on-the-job training.

Most of us are familiar with the notion of investments in physical capital. For example, businesspeople expend resources today to build new plants or to purchase new machinery. This augments their firms' productive capabilities and increases output in the future. They make such decisions based upon a comparison of the expected costs and benefits of these investments. Important early work by Nobel laureates Theodore Schultz and Gary Becker and by Jacob Mincer pointed out that individuals and their families make analogous decisions regarding human capital

---

[1]Sociologists might question the appropriateness of the term *discrimination* in the context of gender socialization. We use it here only to the extent that the socialization process adversely affects the labor market success of young women.

investments.[2] **Human capital** is the stock of skills and knowledge that workers possess. A **human capital investment** is akin to a physical capital investment; it reflects an augmentation of an individual's stock of skills and knowledge. In this case, an individual invests resources today in order to increase his or her productivity and earnings in the future. Examples of human capital investments include not only formal education but also on-the-job training, job search, and geographic migration.

Although the analogy between physical and human capital is compelling, some differences between the two are important. Chiefly, an individual's human capital investment decisions will be influenced to a greater extent by nonpecuniary (nonmonetary) considerations than is typically the case for physical capital investment decisions. Some people enjoy going to school; others do not. Some find indoor, white-collar work attractive; others would prefer to do manual work in the fresh air. Another important difference is that, in the absence of government intervention, it is generally more difficult to borrow to finance human capital investments than to finance physical capital investments, due to a lack of collateral. These differences between physical and human capital illustrate the general point that although labor markets are similar to other markets, they are not identical to them—in large part because labor services cannot be separated from the individuals who provide them. This distinction does not invalidate the use of economic analysis in the study of labor markets, but it does require us to be aware of the significant differences between labor markets and other markets.

We first focus upon the pecuniary aspects of the human capital investment decision and then consider how nonpecuniary factors might influence the analysis. We emphasize two major kinds of human capital investments: formal schooling (in this chapter) and on-the-job training (in the next chapter). According to the pioneering work of Jacob Mincer and Solomon Polachek, and others who followed, gender differences in these areas—in both the amount and the type of investments made—can produce substantial differences in the pay and occupations of men and women in the labor market.[3]

Gender Differences in Levels of Educational Attainment

In 2015, gender differences in educational attainment were not large in the United States. As a point of comparison, gender differences are considerably smaller than educational differences between minorities and whites in the United States, and they are also smaller than gender differences in educational attainment in many parts of the developing world. The major development in recent decades has been a *reversal* of the male advantage in higher education. This trend is shown in Figure 8-1, which provides figures on the educational attainment of the population aged 25 to 64 in 1970 and 2015.

---

[2]See, for example, Theodore W. Schultz, "Investment in Human Capital," *American Economic Review* 51, no. 1 (March 1960): 1–17; Gary S. Becker, *Human Capital: A Theoretical and Empirical Analysis, with Special Reference to Education*, 3rd ed. (Chicago: University of Chicago Press, 1993); and Jacob Mincer, "On-the-Job Training: Costs, Returns, and Some Implications," *Journal of Political Economy* 70, no. 5, pt. 2 (October 1962): 50–79.
[3]Jacob Mincer and Solomon W. Polachek, "Family Investments in Human Capital: Earnings of Women," *Journal of Political Economy* 82, no. 2, pt. 2 (March/April 1974): 76–108; and Solomon W. Polachek, "Occupational Self-Selection: A Human Capital Approach to Sex Differences in Occupational Structure," *Review of Economics and Statistics* 63, no. 1 (February 1981): 60–69.

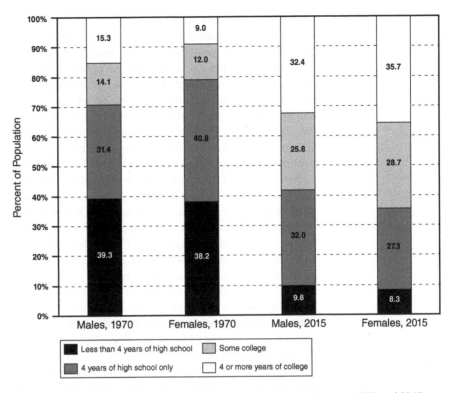

FIGURE 8-1 Educational Attainment of the Population by Gender (Percent): 1970 and 2015 (Ages 25–64)

Notes: In making the 1970 and 2015 data compatible, we follow the suggestions of David A. Jaeger, "Reconciling the Old and New Census Bureau Education Questions: Recommendations for Researchers," *Journal of Business and Economic Statistics* 15, no. 3 (July 1997): 300-09. In particular, individuals with a high school degree and those with 4 years of high school but no degree are both coded as having 4 years of high school only.
Source: Tabulated from the 1970 and 2015 microdata files of the March CPS.

We begin by reviewing patterns of educational attainment for women and men at the lower end of the educational distribution—high school dropouts and those who have completed only high school. Overall, the figure shows rising educational attainment for both men and women. This shift is indicated by a falling share of the population that has not graduated from high school for both groups. For women, there has also been a considerable decline in the share with high school only. The figure also shows that in both 1970 and 2015 a somewhat higher proportion of men than women had less than 4 years of high school—but these gender differences were small. However, data like those in Figure 8-1 understate the gender difference in the share of high school dropouts because they do not include the incarcerated, who tend to be less educated and are overwhelmingly male. This understatement is larger in 2015 than in 1970 due to an increase in incarceration rates.[4] Further, the category "4 years of high school only" increasingly includes individuals who earned GED certificates, many of whom earned this certificate while in prison. (Individuals who have been incarcerated are included in the data once they are released.) Evidence suggests that

---

[4]The Current Population Survey, the source of these data, surveys the civilian, noninstitutional population, thus excluding incarcerated persons. For more on statistical issues raised by incarceration and its rising rates, particularly for black men, see Becky Pettit, *Invisible Men: Mass Incarceration and the Myth of Black Progress* (New York: Russell Sage Foundation, 2012).

the GED certificate is worth less than a high school diploma in the labor market,[5] so grouping certificate earners with high school graduates (increasingly) overstates men's educational qualifications at the lower end of the educational distribution.

A further troubling recent trend, which is not adequately reflected in Figure 8-1 due to the broad age range and the data problems mentioned earlier, is that overall high school graduation rates of young people stagnated between 1970 and 2000, halting what had previously been a steady upward trend in secondary education in the United States throughout the twentieth century.[6] While in the late 1960s the United States ranked first in high school graduation rates among countries in the Organisation for Economic Co-operation and Development (OECD), by 2000 it ranked 13th out of 19 OECD countries. Since 2000, the upward trend in high school completion has resumed; but graduation rates in other countries also increased, and, as a result, the US rate remained well below the OECD average in 2010.[7]

Figure 8-1 also points to another dimension of rising educational attainment for the full population (those aged 25–64): a large increase in the share of women and men who completed 4 years of college. This increase is a consequence of notable gains in women's and men's rates of college-going. The data in this figure also reflect a reversal in the shares of women and men receiving bachelor's degrees. Traditionally, men were considerably more likely than women to get a college education or higher degree.[8] For example, in the 1960s and early 1970s, women received only about 40 percent of bachelor's degrees.[9] Therefore, it is not surprising that the data for the full population in Figure 8-1 show that, in 1970, a higher share of men (15.3 percent) than women (9 percent) had completed 4 or more years of college. However, by 1980 young women had caught up to young men in college graduation rates, and in subsequent years they surpassed them. Young women are now substantially *more* likely to graduate college than young men—they received 57 percent of bachelor's degrees in 2014, for example. And, as shown in Figure 8-1, by 2015, for the full population (aged 25–64), the proportion of women who had completed 4 or more years of college was slightly (3.3 percentage points) *higher* than the proportion of men. This gender difference favoring women in the full population will increase further as more recent cohorts, which are increasingly comprised of women who are more highly educated than men, continue to replace earlier cohorts, in which men

---

[5]Indeed, labor market outcomes for GED recipients are more similar to those for high school dropouts than high school graduates; see James J. Heckman and Paul A. LaFontaine, "The American High School Graduation Rate: Trends and Levels," *Review of Economics and Statistics* 92, no. 2 (May 2010): 244–62; and James J. Heckman and Paul LaFontaine, "Bias Corrected Estimates of GED Returns," *Journal of Labor Economics* 24, no. 3 (July 2006): 661–700.

[6]See Heckman and LaFontaine, "The American High School Graduation Rate"; and Richard J. Murnane, "U.S. High School Graduation Rates: Patterns and Explanations," *Journal of Economic Literature* 51, no. 2 (June 2013): 370–422. These authors measure high school graduation rates comparably for each year by excluding GEDs from graduates; they also exclude recent immigrants from the sample. The earlier strong growth in the high school graduation rate and its economic importance are documented in Claudia Goldin and Lawrence F. Katz, *The Race between Education and Technology* (Cambridge, MA: Harvard University Press, 2008).

[7]These figures are from Murnane, "U.S. High School Graduation Rates." For the recent trend, see also Richard Fry and Kim Parker, "Record Shares of Young Adults Have Finished Both High School and College," Pew Research Center, November 5, 2012, accessed November 10, 2012, www.pewsocialtrends.org.

[8]Interestingly, in the early part of the twentieth century, while men earned the majority of bachelor's degrees, the ratio of male to female undergraduates in the United States was closer to parity than it would be in mid-century; see Claudia Goldin, Lawrence F. Katz, and Ilyana Kuziemko, "The Homecoming of American College Women: The Reversal of the College Gender Gap," *Journal of Economic Perspectives* 20, no. 4 (Fall 2006): 133–56.

[9]Figures on degrees awarded are presented in Table 8-2.

had the educational advantage. Similar developments are taking place in other economically advanced countries, with female educational attainment now surpassing, or about to surpass, male educational attainment in most of these countries.[10]

Although the increase in higher education is impressive, as in the case of high school completion, there are some troubling signs that the growth in college graduation rates is not adequate for the United States to keep up with other economically advanced countries. The United States ranks 14th among 37 OECD countries in the percentage of 25- to 34-year-olds with higher education, after having been one of the world leaders in the past.[11] Growth in college graduation rates has been particularly sluggish for males, though on a positive note there is some recent evidence that college graduation rates are picking up, even for young men.[12] One significant international difference that may play a role in the United States' relatively low ranking is financial access to college. The United States does not provide as much financial support for higher education as other economically advanced countries, and the odds that a young person in the United States will be in higher education if his or her parents have low levels of education are among the lowest in the OECD.[13] Moreover, not only is the gap between the share of students from high-income and poor families who earn bachelor's degrees large in the United States but it has risen sharply in recent decades. For example, for the cohort born between 1961 and 1964, the share of individuals from the richest quartile of families who completed college was 36 percent compared to 5 percent from the poorest quartile; for the cohort born between 1979 and 1982, 54 percent of individuals from the richest families completed college compared to 9 percent from the poorest.[14]

Table 8-1 provides a breakdown of educational attainment for the population aged 25 to 64 by race and Hispanic origin. The patterns by gender for non-Hispanic whites, blacks, and Hispanics are broadly similar. At the lower end of the educational distribution, with the exception of Asians, women are less likely to be high school dropouts than men, although gender differences are fairly small. (We again note that gender differences at this end of the educational distribution are likely understated in the data.) At the upper end of the educational distribution, again with the exception of Asians, women are more likely to have completed college; the gender

---

[10]The gender patterns are also similar, with men overrepresented among dropouts from secondary school and women overrepresented among students and graduates in higher education; see Tuomas Pekkarinen, "Gender Differences in Education," *Nordic Economic Policy Review 1* (2012): 165–97.

[11]OECD, "Country Note—United States," *Education at a Glance: OECD Indicators 2012*, September 11, 2012, accessed November 12, 2012, http://www.oecd.org. For an analysis of the US trends, see Goldin and Katz, *The Race between Education and Technology*.

[12]After hovering in the 27 to 28 percent range since the mid-1990s, the share of 25- to 29-year-olds who completed college degrees increased from 28 to 33 percent between 2006 and 2012; see Fry and Parker, "Record Shares of Young Adults Have Finished Both High School and College." See also Catherine Rampell, "Data Reveal a Rise in College Degrees Among Americans," *New York Times*, June 12, 2013, nytimes.org.

[13]In the United States, 62 percent of the expenditure on higher education comes from private sources compared to 30 percent on average for the OECD countries; see OECD, "Country Note—United States."

[14]For evidence on the extent and widening of inequality in postsecondary education in the United States, see Martha J. Bailey and Susan M. Dynarski, "Inequality in Postsecondary Education" in *Whither Opportunity: Rising Inequality, Schools, and Children's Life Chances*, ed. Greg Duncan and Richard Murnane (New York: Russell Sage Foundation, 2011), 117–32. Data in the text are from Bailey and Dynarski as cited in Jason DeParle, "For Poor, Leap to College Often Ends in a Hard Fall," *New York Times*, December 23, 2012, www.nytimes.com. For an excellent summary of growing differences in educational success between high- and lower-income students along a number of dimensions, see Sean F. Reardon, "No Rich Child Left Behind," *New York Times*, April 27, 2013, opinionator.blogs.nytimes.com.

TABLE 8-1   EDUCATIONAL ATTAINMENT OF THE POPULATION BY GENDER, RACE, AND HISPANIC ORIGIN, 2015 (AGES 25–64)

	NON-HISPANIC WHITES		BLACKS		HISPANICS		ASIANS	
	Males (%)	Females (%)	Males (%)	Females (%)	Males (%)	Females (%)	Males (%)	Females (%)
Less than 4 Years of High School	4.9	3.9	9.3	7.9	30.4	26.9	6.1	7.5
4 years of High School Only	31.0	25.7	39.8	32.6	34.7	32.0	18.6	19.5
Some College	27.3	29.9	29.7	34.0	20.6	23.5	16.4	17.1
4 or More Years of College	36.8	40.6	21.3	25.5	14.3	17.7	59.0	55.9
Total	100.0	100.0	100.0	100.0	100.0	100.0	100.0	100.0

Notes: Whites are defined as white only; blacks are defined as black only as well as black in combination with another race; Asians are defined as Asian only as well as Asian in combination with another non-black race. Hispanics may be of any race. As in Figure 8-1, the category of 4 years of high school only includes those with a high school degree as well as those with 4 years of high school but no degree.
Source: Tabulated from the 2015 microdata file of the March Current Population Survey (CPS).

gap is about 3 to 4 percentage points.[15] The major gender difference by racial group is that Asian men are better educated than Asian women, while women have the educational advantage for all other groups examined.

Differences are larger when we compare educational attainment across groups. Blacks and Hispanics had lower educational attainment than (non-Hispanic) whites: they were less likely to have completed high school and less likely to have graduated from college. The differences between blacks and whites were considerably smaller than the differences between Hispanics and whites, reflecting a substantial increase in the relative educational attainment of the black population since the 1960s. The large influx of immigrants with low levels of education explains some of the sizable Hispanic–white difference in educational attainment. However, the numbers also reflect higher high school dropout rates even for native-born Hispanic students.[16] In contrast to other minorities, Asians had *higher* educational attainment than whites, with an especially high proportion of both women and men—well over half—graduating college.

Table 8-2 shows the trends in higher education for the full population in greater detail and highlights the rising educational attainment of women compared to men. As mentioned earlier, during the 1960s and early 1970s, women received just two out of five bachelor's degrees. Table 8-2 indicates that this was about the same as their share in 1930—30 to 40 years earlier. By 1980, however, women were receiving about half of bachelor's degrees. And, as we noted previously, in subsequent years they not only caught up to men but surpassed them. In 2014, 57 percent of bachelor's degrees were awarded to women, and the female share has stood at this level since the late 1990s. Women comprised an even larger share, 60 percent, of master's

---

[15]For a study of historical trends in the gender education gap among blacks, see Anne McDaniel, Thomas A. DiPrete, Claudia Buchmann, and Uri Shwed, "The Black Gender Gap in Educational Attainment: Historical Trends and Racial Comparisons," *Demography* 48, no. 3 (2011): 889–914.
[16]Heckman and LaFontaine, "The American High School Graduation Rate"; and Murnane, "U.S. High School Graduation Rates." Murnane reports that, while there was little convergence in high school graduation rates for blacks and Hispanics relative to non-Hispanic whites between 1970 and 2000, there were gains for both groups between 2000 and 2010.

| TABLE 8-2 | DEGREES AWARDED TO WOMEN BY LEVEL, 1929–1930 TO 2013–2014 (SELECTED YEARS) |

YEARS	ASSOCIATE (%)	BACHELOR'S (%)	MASTER'S (%)	PH.D. (%)	FIRST PROFESSIONAL (%)
1929–1930	n.a.	39.9[a]	40.4	15.4	n.a.
1960–1961	n.a.	38.5	31.7	10.5	2.7
1970–1971	42.9	43.4	40.1	14.3	6.3
1980–1981	54.7	49.8	50.3	31.1	26.6
1990–1991	58.8	53.9	53.6	37.0	39.1
2000–2001	60.0	57.3	58.5	44.9	46.2
2010–2011	61.7	57.2	60.1	51.4[a]	49.0
2013–2014	61.1	57.1	59.9	51.8[a]	49.1

[a]Includes first professional degrees.
n.a., not available.
Source: 1929–2000 data: U.S. Department of Education, National Center for Education Statistics, *Digest of Education Statistics, 2007*, Table 258; 2010 data: U.S. Department of Education, National Center for Education Statistics, *Digest of Education Statistics, 2012*, Table 310, and Table 322, from http://nces.ed.gov/programs/digest/2012menu_tables.asp (accessed June 2016); 2013 data: U.S. Department of Education, National Center for Education Statistics, *Digest of Education Statistics, 2015*, Table 318.10, and Table 324.50, from http://nces.ed.gov/programs/digest/current_tables.asp (accessed June 2016).

degrees in that year. Similarly, although women received 43 percent of associate degrees in the early 1970s, they received a majority of such degrees by the 1980s and 61 percent in 2014.[17] Women were also awarded about half of doctorate (Ph.D.) and first professional degrees in 2014, up from 11 percent of Ph.D.s and just 3 percent of first professional degrees in 1961. First professional degrees are those awarded in postcollege professional training programs, including medicine, law, dentistry, pharmacy, veterinary medicine, and theology.[18]

Women's higher share of bachelor's degrees reflects two notable educational differences between women and men. First, women are more likely to attend college than men: in 2010, among young people aged 18 to 24, 47 percent of women were enrolled in either college or graduate school compared to 39 percent of men. Second, a substantial share of students who begin college do not graduate, but women are more successful than men in this regard as well. For example, among first-time students seeking bachelor's degrees who started full time at a 4-year college in 2004, a higher percentage of women (61 percent) than men (56 percent) obtained a bachelor's degree within 6 years.[19]

---

[17]Within the postsecondary sector, women are disproportionately represented in for-profit schools compared to public and nonprofit institutions, as is also true for older and low-income students and disadvantaged minorities. For an analysis of the strengths and weaknesses of such institutions, see David J. Deming, Claudia Goldin, and Lawrence F. Katz, "The For-Profit Postsecondary School Sector: Nimble Critters or Agile Predators?" *Journal of Economic Perspectives* 26, no. 1 (Winter 2012): 139–64.
[18]Master's degrees in business are also generally thought of as first professional degrees; however, the Department of Education, which provides the data for Table 8-2, includes them with master's degrees. In Figure 8-2, we include master's degrees in business with first professional degrees.
[19]Institute of Education Sciences, National Center for Education Statistics, *Higher Education: Gaps in Access and Persistence Study, Executive Summary*, p. v, accessed November 8, 2012, http://nces.ed.gov.

Gender Differences in High School Coursework and College Field of Study

The figures on educational attainment reveal only part of the story of gender differences in formal schooling. Beginning in high school, male and female students tended to differ in the types of courses taken and fields of specialization. This difference was especially true in the past and remains the case to some extent even today, especially at the college level.

At the high school level, in the past, girls achieved higher class rank than boys and did better than boys in reading, but they took fewer courses in mathematics and natural sciences and lagged substantially behind boys in math achievement test scores.[20] In recent years, girls not only continue to have higher grade point averages but have widened their lead in reading and, most notably, narrowed the test score gap with boys in math. A government report found that by the early 2000s "overall, females' high school academic programs in mathematics and science are at least as challenging as those taken by males."[21] Gender differences in high school math coursework have especially important implications for college graduates. Taking more high school math has been found to increase the wages of female college graduates, as well as their likelihood of entering technical and nontraditional fields.[22]

As illustrated in Table 8-3, differences between men and women in fields of specialization at the *college level* are more substantial and persistent than in high school, although here too the gender difference has narrowed considerably since the mid-1960s. The setup of the table is similar to our consideration of gender composition of professional occupations in Chapter 7 (see Table 7-4). We classify fields based on their sex composition in 1965–1966. A field is considered integrated if the female share is within 10 percentage points of women's overall share of bachelor's degrees in 1965–1966 (42 percent). It is considered predominantly male if women were substantially underrepresented in the field or the percent female was less than 32 percent ($42 - 10 = 32$) and predominantly female if women were substantially overrepresented in the field or the percent female was more than 52 percent ($42 + 10 = 52$). As in the case of the professional occupations we examined in Chapter 7, using this classification system, most fields were either predominantly male or predominantly female in 1965–1966; only four of the 18 fields listed were integrated.

As may be seen in Table 8-3, there was a trend toward greater gender integration as women increased their representation in initially predominantly male and

---

[20]Goldin, Katz, and Kuziemko, "The Homecoming of American College Women."

[21]Catherine E. Freeman, "Trends in Educational Equity of Girls and Women" (NCES 2005–016), US Department of Education, National Center for Education Statistics (Washington, DC: US Government Printing Office, 2004), 7. See also Goldin, Katz, and Kuziemko, "The Homecoming of American College Women"; and Christianne Corbett, Catherine Hill, and Andresse St. Rose, *Where the Girls Are: The Facts about Gender Equity in Education* (Washington, DC: AAUW Educational Foundation, May 2008), http://www.aauw.org. One study found that, from the 1980s to the early 2000s, there was a growing female advantage in obtaining A's in secondary school and that the most important factor accounting for this trend was the increasing expectation of girls relative to boys of attending graduate or professional school; see Nicole M. Fortin, Philip Oreopoulos, and Shelley Phipps, "Leaving Boys Behind: Gender Disparities in High Academic Achievement," *Journal of Human Resources* 50, no. 3 (Summer 2015): 549–79.

[22]See Charles Brown and Mary Corcoran, "Sex-Based Differences in School Content and the Male/Female Wage Gap," *Journal of Labor Economics* 15, no. 3, pt. 1 (July 1997): 431–65; and Phillip B. Levine and David J. Zimmerman, "The Benefit of Additional High-School Math and Science Classes of Young Men and Women," *Journal of Business and Economic Statistics* 13, no. 2 (April 1995): 137–49.

TABLE 8-3 BACHELOR'S DEGREES AWARDED TO WOMEN BY FIELD, 1965–1966, AND 2013–2014 (SELECTED FIELDS)

DISCIPLINE	1965–1966 (%)	2013–2014 (%)
Predominantly Male in 1965–1966		
Agriculture and Natural Resources	2.7	50.9
Architecture and Related Services	4.0	43.4
Biological Sciences/Life Sciences	28.2	58.5
Business Management, Administrative Sciences, and Marketing	8.5	47.4
Computer and Information Sciences	13.0[a]	18.0
Engineering	0.4	18.4
Economics	9.8	30.5
Physical Sciences and Science Technologies	13.6	39.3
Integrated in 1965–1966		
History	34.6	39.7
Mathematics	33.3	43.0
Psychology	41.0	76.7
Social Sciences	35.0	49.0
Predominantly Female in 1965–1966		
Education	75.3	79.4
English and English Literature	66.2	68.6
Foreign Languages	70.7	69.2
Health	76.9	84.4
Home Economics	97.5	96.1
Sociology	59.6	68.7

[a]Data are for 1969, the earliest year available.

Notes: A field was classified as predominantly male, predominantly female, or integrated with reference to the share of bachelor's degrees awarded to women in 1965–66 (42 percent). A field was predominantly male if percent female was less than 32 percent (42−10=32); predominantly female if percent female was more than 52 percent (42+10=52); and integrated if percent female was in the 32-52 percent range.

Source: 1965–66 data: U.S. Department of Health, Education, and Welfare, Office of Education, *Earned Degrees Conferred: 1965–66*; U.S. Department of Education, National Center for Education Statistics, *Digest of Education Statistics, 1995*, Table 236; 2013–14 data: U.S. Department of Education, National Center for Education Statistics, *Digest of Education Statistics, 2015*, Table 318.30, from http://nces.ed.gov/programs/digest/current_tables.asp (accessed June 2016).

integrated occupations. Research has found that these gains were most rapid through the mid-1980s and slowed after that.[23] Similarly, the dramatic increase in the percentage of women receiving first professional degrees, which we saw in Table 8-2,

---

[23]Paula England and Su Li, "Desegregation Stalled: The Changing Gender Composition of College Majors, 1971–2002," *Gender and Society* 20, no. 5 (October 2006): 657–77; and Jerry A. Jacobs, "Gender and Academic Specialties: Trends among Recipients of College Degrees in the 1980s," *Sociology of Education* 68, no. 2 (April 1995): 81–98.

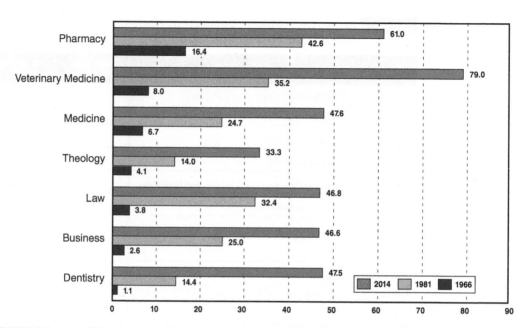

FIGURE 8-2 Percent of First Professional Degrees Awarded to Women by Field, 1966, 1981, and 2014 (Selected Fields)

Notes: Business refers to masters degress in business. Data for Pharmacy in 1966 come from academic year 1967–1968.
Sources: US Department of Health, Education and Welfare, Office of Education, *Earned Degrees Conferred:* 1965-66; U.S. Department of Education, National Center for Educational Statistics, *Digest of Education Statistics*, 1983 and 2015, from http://nces.ed.gov/programs/digest/current_tables.asp (accessed June 2016).

reflects large gains in their representation among students in traditionally male fields, such as medicine, law, and business (a specific breakdown is shown in Figure 8-2).

Nonetheless, women remain extremely underrepresented in some college fields relative to their proportion of total bachelor's degrees (57 percent in 2014). They comprised fewer than one in five graduates in computer and information sciences and engineering and were also underrepresented in other areas including economics (31 percent of majors, a figure discussed further in the "Where Are the Women Economics Majors" box), physical sciences and science technologies (39 percent of majors), and mathematics (43 percent of majors). These are mostly STEM (science, technology, engineering, and mathematics) fields, although it is worth noting that women are well represented in biological sciences, for example. The underrepresentation of women in STEM has generated considerable concern, in part because these occupations are among the highest-paying. Further, attracting talented individuals into these areas, both women and men, is believed to be important if the United States is to remain competitive in high-tech fields.[24] At the same time, in 2014 women comprised the vast majority—about 80 percent or more—of graduates in education, health, and home economics and were also heavily represented among

---

[24]See, for example, David Beede, Tiffany Julian, David Langdon, George McKittrick, Beethika Khan, and Mark Doms, *Women in STEM: A Gender Gap to Innovation*, US Department of Commerce, Economics, and Statistics Administration (August 2011), accessed November 8, 2012, http://www.esa.doc.gov; and Christianne Corbett and Catherine Hill, "Graduating to a Pay Gap: The Earnings of Women and Men One Year after College Graduation," AAUW, Washington, DC, (October 2012), accessed November 9, 2012, http://www.aauw.org.

graduates in English and English literature, foreign languages, psychology (which was previously integrated), and sociology.

In summary, traditionally, girls were somewhat more likely than boys to complete high school, but higher proportions of men than women completed 4 or more years of college. Further, girls took fewer math and science courses than boys in high school, and college men and women differed greatly in their fields of study. Much has changed. Girls do retain an edge in high school completion, but the other gender differences we have enumerated have been narrowed, eliminated, or even reversed in recent years. The high school academic programs of girls and boys in math and science now tend to be equally challenging; young women are actually more likely to get a college degree than young men; and, while gender differences in fields of study at the college level persist, they are much smaller than they were in the past. Despite these positive developments, education gaps between women and men continue to affect labor market outcomes. For more recent cohorts, the gender differences in fields of study that remain are of concern because they negatively affect women's earnings and occupational attainment. Moreover, recent cohorts are just one segment of the female labor force. Women workers from earlier cohorts completed their education at a time when the gender difference in college attendance was considerably larger (and favored men) and when there were much greater gender differences in fields of study.

We now turn to the explanation provided by the human capital model for the historic tendency of women to acquire less education than men as well as the continuing differences in the fields of specialization chosen. We then consider some of the other factors that may account for these differences. We follow this with an examination of the reasons why women caught up to and then surpassed men in college attendance in more recent cohorts.

The Educational Investment Decision

We begin by considering an individual's decision of whether or not to invest in formal education, as illustrated in Figure 8-3. Here we consider Daniel's choice between going to college and ending his formal education with high school. Initially, we focus solely upon the pecuniary costs and benefits of investing in education, although later we consider nonpecuniary costs and benefits as well. The investment decision entails a comparison between the expected **experience-earnings profiles** (the annual earnings at each level of labor market experience) associated with each type of schooling.

In this case, Daniel expects his profile to be *DF* if he enters the labor market after completing high school. Alternatively, if he goes on to college, he will incur out-of-pocket expenses on tuition and books of *OA* dollars per year (negative "earnings") for the 4-year period. (He does not anticipate taking a job while he goes to school.) Upon graduation, he expects to earn *OE'* dollars. The investment in a college education is believed to increase his productivity and, hence, his earnings above what he could have earned if he entered the labor force directly after high school (*OD*). His experience-earnings profile, if he goes to college, is *ABCEG*.

As indicated in Figure 8-3, the earnings of both high school and college graduates are expected to increase with labor market experience over much of the individual's work life. Human capital theory attributes this increase to the productivity-enhancing effects of on-the-job training, which we discuss in Chapter 9. Note that Figure 8-3

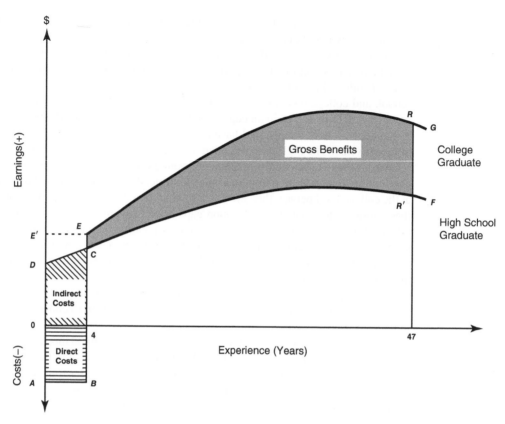

FIGURE 8-3 The Educational Investment Decision

shows the college graduate's profile as rising more steeply than the high school graduate's. As we shall see later in this chapter, this has indeed been found to be the case empirically and suggests that college graduates acquire more training informally on the job as well as formally in school.

Now let us consider how Daniel can use the information in Figure 8-3 to make his investment decision. To do so he considers both the incremental costs and the incremental benefits associated with graduating from college. He must take into account two types of costs of schooling. **Direct costs** are expenditures on items such as tuition, fees, and books. Less obvious, but no less important than direct costs, are the earnings foregone during the time an individual is in school. These **indirect costs** correspond to the opportunity costs of time spent in schooling. We assumed that Daniel does not work for pay while attending college, but even if he did, his forgone earnings are still likely to be substantial—college students are seldom employed for as many hours or for as high a wage as workers not enrolled in school. The full costs of a college education are equal to the sum of the direct and indirect costs, or area *ABCD*.

The gross benefits of a college education are equal to the excess of the expected earnings of a college graduate over those of a high school graduate over the individual's work life. Other things being equal, the size of these benefits depends on the length of the individual's expected work life. If Daniel expects to work for 43 years after college until retirement at age 65, his gross benefits are equal to the shaded area *CERR'*.

For Daniel to decide in favor of a college education (on an economic basis), the *gross benefits* of this investment must exceed the costs; that is, the *net benefits* must be positive. Further, gross benefits must exceed costs by an amount sufficient to give him an adequate return on his investment. Individuals may differ on the rate of return required to induce them to undertake this investment, but all are likely to require a positive rate of return.

For one thing, instead of investing resources in his human capital, Daniel could have put his money into a savings account or invested it in other assets. Those alternatives provide a positive rate of return, and thus, his human capital investment must also do so in order to be competitive. More fundamentally, Daniel, like most people, prefers income (and the opportunity to spend it) now to income (and the opportunity to spend it) later. To induce him to delay his gratification and receive his income later rather than sooner, the labor market has to offer him (and others like him) an inducement in the form of a positive rate of return. In Daniel's case, the investment does appear profitable, although we cannot tell simply by looking at the diagram because even though the benefit area appears to exceed the cost area, we do not know what the resulting rate of return is or whether Daniel will find it acceptable. If indeed he deems the investment sufficiently profitable, he is likely to decide to go on to college.

As explained in the "Calculating the Net Present Value" box, it is possible to express the present value of an income or cost stream today by discounting future income or costs by the interest rate. Based on such a calculation, an individual would undertake the investment in education if the present value of benefits is greater than the present value of costs.

Calculating the Net Present Value of a Human Capital Investment

To determine whether to undertake a human capital investment, such as acquiring an additional year of education or specialized training, we calculate the benefits (B), typically measured as the increased earnings in the coming years due to the investment, and costs (C) in *present value* terms. **Present value** (PV) tells us the value *today* of an earnings stream to be received in the future. The difference between the present value of benefits, $PV(B)$, and the present value of costs, $PV(C)$, is called **net present value** (NPV). If NPV is positive, an individual would undertake the investment.

Decision rule: If $PV(B) - PV(C) > 0$, then undertake the investment.

The key principle to keep in mind is that $1 in your pocket today is worth more to you than the promise of $1 tomorrow. The reason is that if you have $1 today, you can put it in the bank (or in stocks, bonds, or other financial instruments) and earn a positive return on it. So any promise to pay money in the future must also offer a similar return. And, again, more fundamentally, this is because people value money and the opportunity to spend it now more highly than waiting to receive money in the future. (This is why the interest rate is sometimes called the *reward to waiting*.)

Present value is the reverse of the concept of future value, which may be more familiar. Let us first recall how to calculate **future value**, how much a specified dollar amount today is worth at a future date

$$\text{Future value} = (FV) = PV(1 + r)^t$$

continues

where r is the market interest rate (or the rate of return on the investment), FV is the future value, PV is the present value, and t is the time period being considered (1 = next year, 2 = 2 years from now, etc.).

If we assume we have $1 today (our $PV = \$1$), $r = .05$, and $t = 1$ (next year), then $FV = \$1.05$. Or if we want to know the value of $1 in 2 years, the formula tells us the answer is $1.10.

Now consider the case in which we can earn $1 next year and want to know its value *today*. To determine this, all we need to do is rewrite the earlier equation as

$$\text{Present value}(PV_t) = \frac{FV_t}{(1+r)^t}$$

If we assume we will receive $1 next year ($FV$ is $1), $r = .05$, and $t = 1$ (next year), then the present value of $1 received next year is $.95 today. If we want to know the value of $1 received 2 years from now, then we would use the same formula as previously, where $t = 2$ (or $.91). Note that when used to express a future value in present value terms, the interest rate (r) is referred to as the **discount rate**. The discount rate can be thought of as the return that could be earned on an alternative investment.

Let us look at an example to better understand how to calculate the net present value of an educational investment. Suppose Denise, age 50, is considering whether to obtain 1 year of specialized training. To decide whether she should make this investment, she needs to know about the costs (both indirect and direct), the benefits (the increase in her future earnings due to this investment), how long she expects to work after the training (and hence reap the benefits), and the discount rate. Her net present value calculation is

$$NPV = -C + \frac{B_1}{1+r} + \frac{B_2}{(1+r)^2} + \frac{B_3}{(1+r)^3} + \ldots + \frac{B_T}{(1+r)^T}$$

where C = today's costs, B = benefits, r = discount rate, and T = end of work life.

Suppose Denise's direct costs for tuition, books, and supplies are $8,000 and her indirect costs, measured as the salary foregone during the 1 year of training, are $20,000. Thus, her total costs (C), assumed to be incurred during the current year, are $28,000. (Because the costs are all incurred in the current year, they are not discounted.) Once Denise receives the training, she will earn an additional $6,000 per year thereafter. Thus, all the Bs in this equation are $6,000. Let us further suppose that Denise plans to work for 10 years after the training and then retire and that the discount rate is 5 percent. Therefore, Denise performs the following present value calculation:

$$NPV = -\$28,000 + \frac{\$6,000}{(1+.05)^1} + \frac{\$6,000}{(1+.05)^2} + \frac{\$6,000}{(1+.05)^3} + \frac{\$6,000}{(1+.05)^4}$$

$$+ \frac{\$6,000}{(1+.05)^5} + \frac{\$6,000}{(1+.05)^6} + \frac{\$6,000}{(1+.05)^7} + \frac{\$6,000}{(1+.05)^8}$$

$$+ \frac{\$6,000}{(1+.05)^9} + \frac{\$6,000}{(1+.05)^{10}} = \$18,330.41$$

continues

Since Denise's *NPV* exceeds 0, it makes economic sense for Denise to invest in the training.

Alternatively, one can solve for the discount rate that exactly equates the present value of costs to the present value of benefits (most easily calculated using a spreadsheet program like Excel). If this rate, called the **internal rate of return**, represents an adequate rate of return for the individual (for Denise, the internal rate of return would have to equal or exceed the discount rate of 5 percent), then the individual will choose to make the educational investment.

An additional factor that affects the returns to college and thus the investment decision is the economic conditions that prevail at the time the decision is made. On the one hand, a weak economy may boost the returns to college and thus college enrollment. This is because the opportunity cost of attending college is lower when the economy is weak (as a consequence of a lower probability of getting a job and reduced foregone earnings during the investment period). On the other hand, financial resources like parental income may be negatively affected by a weak economy, making it more difficult for families to send children to college. Most studies find that a weak economy (a time of higher unemployment rates) does increase school enrollment, including in community college, college, and graduate school.[25]

A large literature in economics documents a positive return to individuals' investments in education.[26] Investigations of this return generally focus on estimating the **college wage premium** or the **college earnings premium**, that is, how much a college-educated worker earns compared to a high school–educated worker.[27] However, when tuition data are available, one can further calculate the return to education, which takes both costs and benefits into account, as in Figure 8-3. One 2012 study of the return to a bachelor's degree found that the real cost of tuition has increased (and this increase has received considerable attention in the media). However, the benefits of a college education in terms of higher earnings have also risen substantially. Someone starting college in 2010 was expected to earn $450,000 more than a high school graduate over his or her working life compared to $260,000 more in 1980 (adjusting for inflation and assuming a discount rate of 5 percent). (We present additional evidence on the rising relative earnings of college graduates shortly.) Taking into account costs (including tuition and foregone earnings) and benefits, the return to a college education was estimated to be above 15 percent and to have been

---

[25]See, for example, Julian R. Betts and Laurel L. McFarland, "Safe Port in a Storm: The Impact of Labor Market Conditions on Community College Enrollments," *Journal of Human Resources* 30, no. 4 (Fall 1995): 741–65; Ernest Boffy-Ramirez, Benjamin Hansen, and Hani Mansour, "The Effect of Business Cycles on Educational Attainment," unpublished working paper, University of Colorado Denver (May 13, 2013), https://papers.ssrn.com/sol3/papers.cfm?abstract_id=2294146; and Lisa B. Kahn, "The Long-Term Labor Market Consequences of Graduating from College in a Bad Economy," *Labour Economics* 17, no. 2 (April 2010): 303–16.

[26]There are a number of issues in estimating the returns to schooling; for insightful discussions, see David Card, "The Causal Effect of Education on Earnings," in *Handbook of Labor Economics*, vol. 3, ed. Orley Ashenfelter and David Card (Amsterdam: Elsevier, 1999), 1801–63; and James J. Heckman, Lance J. Lochner, and Petra E. Todd, "Earnings Functions and Rates of Return," *Journal of Human Capital* 2, no. 1 (Spring 2008): 1–31.

[27]Both *wages* and *earnings* refer to income received from labor or work activities. The wage is income received per hour; earnings measure income received over a longer period of time, generally annually. Either may be used to measure the college premium. Also, depending on the purpose, the college premium may be measured as a difference (found by subtracting high school from college earnings) or as a ratio (college earnings divided by high school earnings).

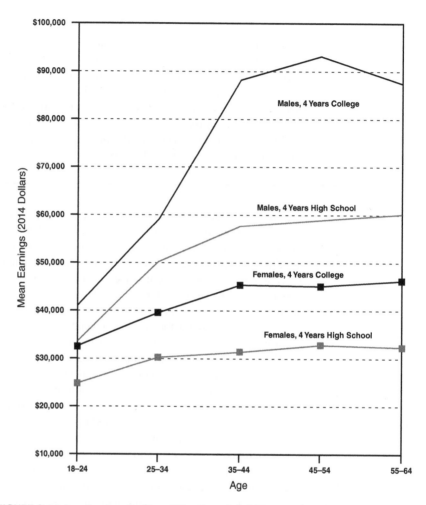

FIGURE 8-4A Age-Earnings Profiles of Year-Round, Full-Time Workers by Gender and Education, 1974 (2014 Dollars)

relatively constant since the early 1980s.[28] According to the authors, this is more than double the average return experienced in the stock market over the last 60 years (6.8 percent) and more than five times the return to such investments as corporate bonds (2.9 percent) or long-term government bonds (2.2 percent).

College graduates fare better not only with respect to wages and earnings but also in terms of their considerably higher probability of being employed. For example, although younger workers in general were hard hit by the recent Great Recession, the college-educated fared much better than their less educated counterparts. In 2010, when the unemployment rate was still extremely high at 9.6 percent, 88 percent of

---

[28]Michael Greenstone and Adam Looney, "Regardless of the Cost, College Still Matters," Brookings Institution (October 5, 2012), http://www.brookings.edu. These estimates use the actual "sticker price" for tuition in the calculations of the cost of college, but such estimates may overstate the actual increase in costs because they do not account for increases in financial aid. Greenstone and Looney note that according to the College Board, the actual cost of a 4-year degree had remained relatively constant over the previous 15 years. A wider range of studies finds that the rate of return to college ranges between 7 and 15 percent, but even at the lower end, it exceeds the rate of return from alternative investments. For further discussion, see Philip Oreopoulos and Uros Petronijevic, "Who Benefits from College? A Review of Research on the Returns to Higher Education," *The Future of Children* 23, no. 1 (Spring 2013): 41–65.

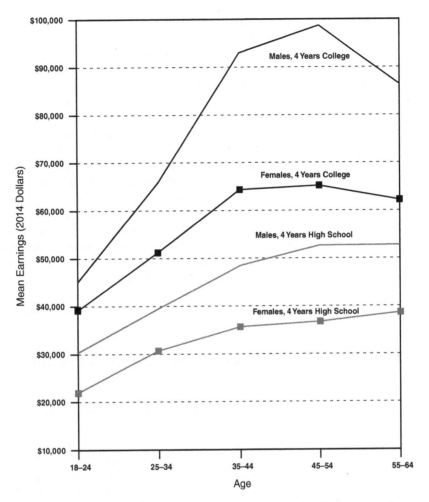

FIGURE 8-4B Age-Earnings Profiles of Year-Round, Full-Time Workers by Gender and Education, 2014 (2014 Dollars)

Sources: US Census Bureau Historical Income Tables - People, Table P-32 "Educational Attainment—Full-Time, Year-Round Workers 18 Years Old and Over by Mean Earnings, Age, and Sex: 1991 to 2014," and Table P-35 "Years of School Completed—Full-Time, Year-Round Workers 18 Years Old and Over by Mean Earnings, Age, and Sex: 1974 to 1979" from https://www.census.gov/data/tables/time-series/demo/income-poverty/historical-income-people.html (accessed June 2016).

young adults (aged 23–24) with a college degree were employed. This may be compared to 79 percent of those with some college, 64 percent with a high school diploma, and just 43 percent without a high school diploma.[29] This does not mean that college graduates do not experience any significant adverse effects in economic downturns. Indeed, it has been found that those who graduate college in a bad economy suffer significant long-term negative wage effects compared to those who graduate during better economic conditions.[30] Nonetheless, given the higher lifetime earnings and employment probabilities of college graduates compared to their less educated counterparts, college is still a good investment.

The empirical relationship between education and earnings is illustrated in Figures 8-4(a) and (b), which shows age-earnings profiles of high school and college

---

[29]Michael Greenstone and Adam Looney, "How Do Recent College Grads Really Stack Up? Employment and Earnings for Graduates of the Great Recession," Brookings Institution (June 3, 2011), http://www.hamiltonproject.org.

[30]Kahn, "The Long-Term Labor Market Consequences of Graduating from College in a Bad Economy."

graduates for 1974 and 2014. These profiles, based on actual data, are strikingly similar to the hypothetical profiles presented earlier in Figure 8-3. In both years the earnings of college graduates lie above those of high school graduates of the same sex, and, moreover, the earnings profiles of college graduates of both sexes are steeper than those of their high school counterparts. However, the figures do show important gender differences. Within each education group, women earn less than men, and their earnings profiles tend to be flatter than men's. We consider possible reasons for these gender differences in this and subsequent chapters.

Despite the general similarity of the profiles in 1974 and 2014, there have been some changes that illustrate important labor market developments in recent decades. Earnings are shown in 2014 dollars for both years (i.e., they are adjusted for inflation), so levels of earnings and differences across groups are comparable between the years. One striking difference between the mid-1970s and 2014 is that, for each sex, the college wage or earnings premium (the gap between the high school and college profiles) rose. This increase is part of a trend toward rising returns to skills like education over this period.[31] We consider the rising college wage premium in more detail in the next section. (As noted earlier, the gap between the high school and college profiles focuses only on earnings differentials, that is, the gross benefits to college depicted in Figure 8-1, and does not take into account the costs of college.)

The Rising College Wage or Earnings Premium

In recent decades, among both men and women, college graduates experienced more favorable trends in earnings than those with less education. Among men, these differences in earnings trends were associated with substantial *declines* in real wages for the less educated. Among women, real wages either declined slightly or grew considerably more slowly for the less educated.

These trends may be seen in Table 8-4 and Figure 8-5. Table 8-4 gives the mean earnings of year-round, full-time workers in other educational categories *relative* to those of high school graduates for 1974 (before the sharp rise in the returns to education) and 2014. It shows that the earnings of those who did not complete high school decreased relative to those of high school graduates, while the relative earnings of college graduates increased considerably. For instance, in 2014, women and men with a college degree or more earned nearly twice as much as high school graduates compared to about 50 percent more in 1974. Those with some college also increased their earnings relative to high school graduates but to a lesser extent than college graduates did. The fact that the ratios of each educational category's earnings relative to high school graduates are fairly similar for men and women in both years in Table 8-4 suggests that the rate of return to education (if costs were also factored in) is also fairly similar. However, some more detailed research discussed in a subsequent section on "Explaining Women's Rising Educational Attainment" suggests that women may, in fact, get a higher return to education than men.[32]

---

[31]For analyses of the rising returns to education and skills, see Claudia Goldin and Lawrence F. Katz, *The Race between Education and Technology* (Cambridge, MA: Harvard University Press, 2008); and David H. Autor, Lawrence F. Katz, and Melissa S. Kearney "Trends in U.S. Wage Inequality: Revising the Revisionists," *Review of Economics and Statistics* 90, no. 2 (May 2008): 300–23.

[32]By detailed analyses, we mean statistical analyses of the rate of return to education that control for other factors that may be correlated with wages, such as age or experience, race, and ethnicity.

TABLE 8-4 MEAN EARNINGS OF EDUCATION GROUPS RELATIVE TO HIGH SCHOOL GRADUATES, 1974 AND 2014 (%)

Education	1974		2014	
	Men	Women	Men	Women
High school				
1–3 years	88.9	85.3	84.0	76.9
4 years	100.0	100.0	100.0	100.0
College				
1–3 years	113.6	112.6	120.8	117.7
4 or more years	155.0	147.2	210.0	192.1

Notes: Data refer to year-round, full-time workers 18 years of age and older. Definitions of educational categories are not exactly comparable for the 2 years. In 2014, mean earnings for 1–3 years of college is computed as a weighted average of the means for "some college, no degree" and "associate degree." Due to small sample size, the earnings of high school dropouts in 2014 are calculated based on an average of 2013 and 2014 real earnings.
Source: US Census Bureau Historical Income Tables - People, Table P-32, from https://www.census.gov/data/tables/time-series/demo/income-poverty/historical-income-people.html (accessed June 2016).

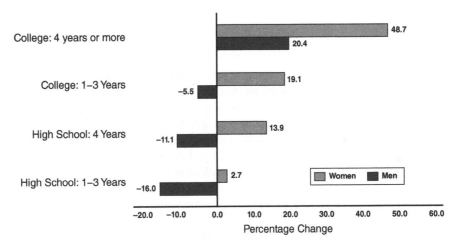

FIGURE 8-5 Percent Change in Real Mean Earnings of Men and Women by Education for Year-Round, Full-time Workers, 1974–2014

Notes: Data refer to year-round, full-time workers 18 years of age and older. Definitions of educational categories are not exactly comparable for the 2 years. In 2014, mean earnings for 1-3 years of college is computed as a weighted average of the means for "some college, no degree" and "associate degree." Adjusted for inflation using the Consumer Price Index for All Urban Areas (CPI-U-RS). Due to small sample size, the earnings of high school dropouts for 2014 are calculated as an average of 2013 and 2014 real earnings.
Sources: US Census Bureau Historical Income Tables - People, Table P-32 and Table P-35, from https://www.census.gov/data/tables/time-series/demo/income-poverty/historical-income-people.html (accessed June 2016).

Figure 8-5 shows the consequences of the widening earnings gaps by education for trends in real earnings of education groups over this same period (1974–2014). For both men and women, more highly educated workers did considerably better in terms of real earnings changes. Among men, only college graduates experienced an increase in real earnings, with real earnings increases of 20 percent; for other education groups real earnings *decreased*. The largest decline was for high school dropouts, whose real earnings fell by 16 percent over the period. In terms of real wage growth, women fared better than their male counterparts within each educational category. However, for women as well as men, the college-educated did a great deal better than their less educated counterparts. Real earnings increased by 3 percent for female dropouts but rose by 49 percent for female college graduates.

The deteriorating earnings situation of less educated women and men shown in Figure 8-5 tells only part of the story of the declining economic status of the less educated in the United States. To be included in these tabulations, an individual must not only be employed but work year-round and full-time. As we saw in Chapter 6, the labor force participation rates of less educated women and men have decreased relative to their more highly educated counterparts since 1970. Among women, this trend reflects considerably smaller increases in participation rates for those with less than 4 years of high school in comparison to substantial increases (over the period as a whole) for those with higher levels of education. Among men, decreases in participation rates occurred among all education groups, but the declines were especially precipitous among those who did not complete high school. A final piece of the story is the rising incidence of families headed by single mothers that we shall examine in Chapter 14. This increase, which was particularly pronounced among the less educated, places them and their families at even greater economic disadvantage.

Education and Productivity

Human capital theory postulates that earnings rise with additional education because of the productivity-enhancing effects of education. Intuitively, it seems reasonable that education imparts a variety of skills and knowledge that could be useful on the job, ranging from specific skills, such as computer programming and accounting, to general skills, such as reasoning ability, writing skills, and proficiency in solving mathematical problems. Educational institutions may also teach behaviors that are valued on the job, such as punctuality, following instructions, and habits of predictability and dependability.

An alternative interpretation of the observed positive relationship between education and earnings that has been suggested is that education functions solely as a **signal**. This theory, advanced by Nobel laureate Michael Spence,[33] postulates that employers have imperfect information on worker productivity and, thus, seek ways to distinguish more productive applicants from less productive applicants before hiring them. At the same time, it is assumed that more able (productive) individuals find the (psychic and monetary) costs of acquiring additional schooling lower than the less able, perhaps because they find their studies less arduous or because they are awarded scholarships. If the more able incur lower costs, an educational investment may be profitable for them when it would not be for the less able. In an extreme version of the signaling model, education is rewarded *solely* because it *signals* higher productivity to the employer and *not* because of any skills it imparts.

This theoretical disagreement between the human capital and signaling models has proved difficult to resolve empirically. The issue is a particularly thorny one—*not* whether or not more education is correlated with higher productivity and earnings

---

[33]See Michael Spence, "Job Market Signaling," *Quarterly Journal of Economics* 87, no. 3 (August 1973): 205–21.

but *why*. From the individual's perspective, however, it does not matter whether education raises earnings by increasing productivity or by signaling greater ability. Thus, the decision-making process illustrated in Figure 8-3 would be unaffected.

Nonetheless, one potential consequence of the signaling model for gender differences in labor market outcomes is worth noting. If employers believe that a given level of education signals lower productivity for a woman than for a man, women may need to have higher educational credentials than men to obtain the same job. For example, suppose an employer who is hiring for entry-level management positions believes that a bachelor's degree signals a lower commitment to the labor market for women than for men. The employer may require a woman to have, say, an MBA in order to obtain employment, while being willing to hire a man with only a bachelor's degree. This is quite similar to the notion of **statistical discrimination** discussed in Chapter 11.

Gender Differences in Educational Investment Decisions: The Human Capital Explanation

Does our analysis of the human capital investment decision suggest any reasons why men and women might decide to acquire different amounts or types of formal education? According to the analysis we have presented, the major factors to consider are the expected costs and benefits of the investment. Thus, we will want to consider why men and women might differ in terms of costs or benefits. The definitions of costs and benefits may be extended to include nonpecuniary, as well as pecuniary, costs and benefits, and we do so later.

The major factor emphasized by human capital theorists as producing gender differences in human capital investments like education is **expected work life**. Given traditional gender roles in the family, many women anticipate shorter, more disrupted work lives than men; in turn, from an economic standpoint, it makes sense for them to invest in fewer years of education. Further, it will not pay for them to make the types of human capital investments that require a sustained, high-level commitment to the labor force to make them profitable and that depreciate rapidly during periods of work interruptions. For example, this consideration might lead them to avoid some fields of study like engineering or science or costly professional training.

The impact of these factors is illustrated in Figure 8-6, which reproduces the earnings profiles shown in Figure 8-3. Note that the horizontal axis now refers to potential experience or the total time elapsed since completing high school. We present it this way in order to represent periods of time out of the labor force on the diagram.

A career-oriented woman who anticipates working the same number of years as Daniel will find it equally profitable to invest in a college education, assuming she faces similar costs and has the opportunity to reap the same returns. However, a woman who expects to spend fewer years in the labor market will find her benefits correspondingly reduced.

Suppose Adele plans to be in the labor force for a time—6 years—after college and then to drop out for 10 years, say, for child-rearing. If she, like Daniel, expects to retire at age 65, her expected work life is 33 years in comparison with his 43 years. Her shorter work life reduces the benefits of her human capital investment because she does not earn income during the time she spends out of the labor force. Further, it is generally believed that skills depreciate during time spent out of the labor force

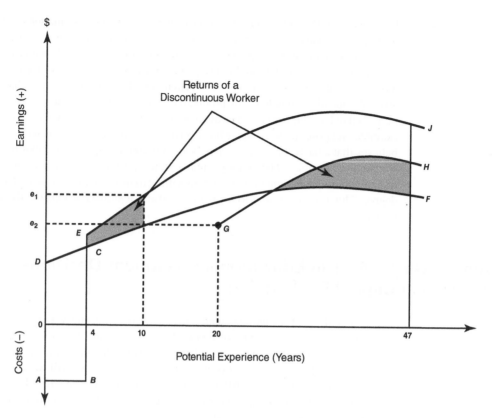

FIGURE 8-6 The Impact of Expected Work Life on the Educational Investment Decision

because they are not used. It is thus expected that, upon her return to the labor force after an interruption of 10 years, Adele's earnings of e_2 will be less in real terms than she was making when she left (e_1) and that she will be faced with profile *GH* rather than profile *EJ*. We show profile *GH* as approaching *EJ* over time, as Adele retools or becomes less rusty. Nonetheless, her time out of the labor force costs her a reduction in earnings over the remainder of her working life. In this example, the benefits of the investment in a college education, the sum of the two shaded areas, may not be large enough to make it worthwhile in relation to the costs.

A complication that we do not show in Figure 8-6 is that a break in experience would also affect *DF*, the high school earnings profile. Specifically, a portion of the *DF* line would be shifted down to represent Adele's options after she returns from her workforce interruption. However, taking this consideration into account is unlikely to affect our conclusion that a workforce interruption reduces the returns to investing in a college education because a major factor reducing the returns to the investment in college is simply the interruption itself and the loss of returns for that period. In addition, because the skills of high school graduates are less than those of college graduates, the loss due to depreciation is likely to also be less for them. Thus, we omit this shift in *DF* from Figure 8-6 to keep our diagram as simple as possible while still capturing the major points.

One factor that might somewhat offset the conclusions we have arrived at in considering Figure 8-6 is that education may increase productivity in some nonmarket activities as well as in market work. For example, the time that more highly educated parents spend with their children may have a larger positive effect on their offsprings' cognitive ability than the time of less educated parents. Were we to factor in these potential benefits in the home, the loss of returns due to labor force withdrawals would be reduced. However, it is unlikely that our conclusion would be altered: higher anticipated time spent out of the labor force is likely to lower the amount of educational investments that the individual finds profitable.

Thus, the human capital model shows how an adherence to traditional gender roles in the family can explain why, in the past, women were less likely than men to pursue college and graduate study. It also suggests one reason for the increase in women's college attendance. As we saw in Chapters 5 and 6, women have increased their labor force participation substantially. As young women anticipate longer and more continuous working lives, it will be profitable for them to increase their investment in formal education. Furthermore, Figure 8-6 suggests that once women decide to acquire higher education, for whatever reason, their attachment to the labor force is reinforced because the opportunity cost of time spent out of the labor force is increased.

Although our application of the human capital model suggests a plausible explanation for the historical tendency of men to be more likely to pursue college and graduate study, it does not explain why in the past women were considerably *more* likely than men to complete high school. For example, in 1900, only two-thirds as many young men as young women graduated from high school. A likely explanation for this difference is that the opportunity cost of remaining in high school was lower for the young women than their male counterparts because their potential labor market earnings were less. As job opportunities for young men who did not finish high school declined, so too did the gender differential in high school completion.

The human capital model also suggests a possible explanation for gender differences in fields of specialization, focusing on expectations of workforce disruptions. In some fields, such as science and engineering, technological change progresses rapidly. A woman returning from a labor force interruption will have to contend not only with her depreciation of skills over the interim but also with the advancement of the field during her absence. On the other hand, in fields such as teaching history or English, the pace of change is slower. A woman returning from a workforce interruption is likely to find that her earnings fall less steeply. Women anticipating traditional gender roles are, therefore, expected to avoid fields where the rate of technological change is rapid and to concentrate in fields where the cost of workforce interruptions is lower.[34] Thus, women's increasing labor force attachment may partially explain their increased representation in traditionally male fields of study.

Another factor that has received attention as contributing to gender differences in college majors is mathematical ability.[35] Although a gender gap in math scores remains, it has declined as the high school coursework of young men and women has

---

[34]This insight was developed by Solomon W. Polachek; see "Sex Differences in College Major," *Industrial and Labor Relations Review* 31, no. 4 (July 1978): 498–508; and "Occupational Self-Selection." For a consideration of issues related to skills obsolescence, see the contributions in Andries de Grip, Jasper van Loo, Ken Mayhew, eds., *The Economics of Skills Obsolescence*, Research in Labor Economics, Vol. 21 (Bingley, UK: Emerald Group Publishing, 2002). Another issue is that some fields more easily accommodate part-time work, thus facilitating reentry.

[35]For an early study, see Morton Paglin and Anthony M. Rufolo, "Heterogeneous Human Capital, Occupational Choice, and Male–Female Earnings Differences," *Journal of Labor Economics* 8, no. 1, pt. 1 (January 1990): 123–44.

grown more similar. For example, in 1977, girls' SAT math scores lagged 46 points below boys' scores, on average. By the mid-1990s, the gender difference was 35 points, though it has declined only slightly since that time, standing at 31 points in 2014.[36] While math test scores could be a factor in explaining differences in majors, research suggests that the math score differences are too small to account for the sizable gender differences in majors in STEM fields.[37] Consistent with this, a study of college students found that most of the gender differences in majors were due to differences between men and women in the types of courses they expected to enjoy and the greater weight placed by women on nonpecuniary (versus pecuniary—that is, monetary) workplace outcomes. Gender differences in beliefs about academic ability explained only a small and insignificant part of the gap.[38] The "Where are the Women Economics Majors?" box explores some of factors influencing gender differences in majors in more detail.

Whatever the reasons for them, gender differences in college major are strongly related to the wages of college graduates and help account for the male–female wage differential among this group. We consider this issue further in Chapter 10. This also implies that the growing similarity in college majors between men and women has contributed to the narrowing of the gender wage gap for college graduates over time.[39]

Where Are the Women Economics Majors?*

This question was raised in 2013 by then-American Economic Association president, Claudia Goldin, professor of economics at Harvard. She noted that at the top 100 universities, as ranked by *US News and World Report*, women were about one-third of economics majors in 2011, a figure little changed from 20 years prior. (Table 8-3 of this text shows roughly this figure for 2014.) Of course, this figure varies to some degree by institution.

Why are there relatively so few women economics majors? One explanation Goldin offers is that in principles of economics courses women

continues

---

[36]Findings for 2014 also indicate that the SAT critical reading score of boys exceeds that of girls, though this difference (4 points) is much smaller, and the writing score of girls is higher than that of boys (by 11 points). See "2014 College-Bound Seniors: Total Group Profile Report," College Board, October 7, 2014. In a similar vein, Goldin, Katz, and Kuziemko in "The Homecoming of American College Women" present evidence that girls narrowed the gender gap in high school math achievement tests between 1972 and 1992.

[37]See Janet S. Hyde, Sara M. Lindberg, Marcia C. Linn, Amy B. Ellis, and Caroline C. Williams, "Gender Similarities Characterize Math Performance," *Science* 321 (July 25, 2008): 494–95, www .sciencemag.org; Stephen J. Ceci, Donna K. Ginther, Shulamit Kahn, and Wendy M. Williams, "Women in Academic Science: A Changing Landscape," *Psychological Science* 15, no. 3 (November 2014): 75–141; and Allison Mann and Thomas A. DiPrete, "Trends in Gender Segregation in the Choice of Science and Engineering Majors," *Social Science Research* 42, no. 6 (November 2013): 1519–41.

[38]Basit Zafar, "College Major Choice and the Gender Gap," *Journal of Human Resources 48,* no. 3 (Summer 2013): 545–95.

[39]See Corbett and Hill, "Graduating to a Pay Gap"; Judith A. McDonald and Robert J. Thornton, "Do New Male and Female College Graduates Receive Unequal Pay?" *Journal of Human Resources* 42, no. 1 (Winter 2007): 32–48. For earlier research, see Brown and Corcoran, "Sex-Based Differences"; and Eric Eide, "College Major Choice and Changes in the Gender Wage Gap," *Contemporary Economic Policy* 12, no. 2 (April 1994): 55–64.

and men respond differently to the major signal given—the final letter grade. She found that in response to earning a grade of A, female students are somewhat *more* likely than male students to pursue an economics major. However, in response to a grade of B (and even more so in response to a grade of C), female students are much *less* likely than their male counterparts to continue on in economics. The problem may be wider than economics. STEM courses, like economics, that offer students higher-paying jobs on graduation, also tend to grade lower on average than courses in other fields. For example, one study found that science departments grade an average of .4 points lower (on a 4-point scale) than humanities departments.**

Why might women shy away from economics, particularly if they do not do well in the principles course? One factor that Goldin does not believe accounts for the gender difference in majors is a gender difference in math ability. She argues that the math ability differences between men and women at college entry are "small and, in many cases, nonexistent or in women's favor." She does however point to a gender gap in confidence, with women having less confidence in their abilities. Also, she finds that men tend to choose economics as their major before going to college and are more likely to stick with it once on campus. Another explanation has to do with course content. The typical principles of economics course may not adequately demonstrate the breadth of applications for economics. Economics training is valuable well beyond the narrow purview of finance and business, as demonstrated in this textbook.

There are some additional factors, not considered by Goldin, which might explain why women shy away from economics if they do not do well in the principles course. One is that female students, on average, tend to earn higher overall grade point averages (GPAs) than their male counterparts. This may mean that they are more likely to be choosing between economics and other possible majors where they are earning higher grades. It is also possible that women need a stronger "signal" (that is, grade) than male students to be induced to enter economics (and STEM more generally) because they anticipate barriers associated with entering a predominantly male field and fear doing so unless they are demonstrably highly qualified.

Why does the number of women economics majors matter? For one, women and minorities (another underrepresented group among economics majors) offer a different perspective based on their life experiences. If talented women and minorities are not choosing to major or pursue a career in economics for reasons other than personal preference, their good ideas will remain untapped. Second, many—though not all—individuals who go on to pursue a Ph.D. in economics begin as undergraduate majors. Thus, entry into the major (or lack thereof) affects the "pipeline" into the ranks of assistant to associate to, the highest rank, full professor. To put this in perspective, in 2014, women comprised only 23 percent of full professors at non–Ph.D.-granting economics departments and just 12 percent at Ph.D.-granting economics departments.*** If we cannot turn economics students into economics majors, the academic glass ceiling will remain firmly in place in this field.

---

*This box draws on "Notes on Women and the Economics Undergraduate Major" by Claudia Goldin, published in CSWEP News (Summer 2013), a publication of the Committee on the Status of Women in the Economics Profession (CSWEP), which is a standing committee of the American Economic Association; and Claudia Goldin, "Will More of Our Daughters Grow up to be Economists?" Bloomberg View (17 October 2013). http://www.ohio.com/editorial/claudia-goldin-will-more-of-our-daughters-grow-up-to-be-economists-1.437694. The quotation is from Bloomberg View.

**For further discussion of Goldin's results and related research, see Catherine Rampell, "Women Should Embrace the B's in College to Make More Later," Washington Post, March 10, 2014, www.washingtonpost.com. The information on GPAs is from a study cited by Rampell, Stuart Rojstaczer, and Christopher Healy, "Grading in American Colleges and Universities," Teachers College Record, March 4, 2010, available at www.tcrecord.org.

***Marjorie McElroy, "2014 Annual Report of the Committee on the Status of Women in the Economics Profession," CSWEP News no. 1 (2015), tables 5 and 6.

Gender Differences in Educational Investment Decisions: Social Influences and Anticipation of Discrimination

Although expected working life is a factor that has been particularly emphasized by human capital theorists, a variety of other factors may also contribute to gender differences in educational attainment and field of specialization. In the past, there was overt discrimination against women by educational institutions, and we review this practice in the "Historical Background" box. While, fortunately, overt barriers to women's participation in higher education have largely been eliminated, a variety of social influences may well have contributed to gender differences in educational attainment in the past as well as to the continuing gender differences in fields of study that we see today.[40] We consider a number of such factors in this section, including differences in the way girls and boys are socialized, biased evaluations of male and female performance, and various subtle barriers to female success. These types of factors may be considered manifestations of societal discrimination.

Before turning to the specific factors, let us examine how social influences may impact women's decision-making. To do this, it is useful to consider the nonpecuniary as well as the pecuniary costs and benefits of human capital investments. Societal influences may raise the costs or lower the benefits of specific types of education for women relative to men, particularly in male-dominated fields. For instance, as discussed at greater length shortly, the negative reactions of some family and friends may raise the nonpecuniary costs of entering such "male" fields, while the expected benefits of this field may be lowered to the extent that the faculty are predominantly male and are more encouraging and supportive of male than of female students. To the extent that women anticipate or encounter such higher costs or lower benefits, their returns to investing in education in these areas are reduced, and they may choose not to enter these fields. Moreover, if women anticipate that they will encounter labor market discrimination upon completion of their studies, their benefits and hence their returns are additionally decreased, further deterring their entry into these fields.

Historical Background: Overt Discrimination by Educational Institutions

While now largely eliminated, overt discrimination against women in admission to college and professional school was pervasive in the not-too-distant past. Such discrimination placed serious limits on the educational options of older women, and thus its impact continues to be reflected in the *current* occupational distribution and wages of these women. Moreover, such discrimination not only limited the educational opportunities of the women directly affected by these barriers but also contributed to a dearth of female role models for subsequent generations.

continues

---

[40]For an interesting discussion of barriers to women's advancement in the sciences and of policies that might improve their representation, see Jo Handelsman, Nancy Cantor, Molly Carnes, Denice Denton, Eve Fine, Barbara Grosz, Virginia Hinshaw, Cora Marrett, Sue Rosser, Donna Shalala, and Jennifer Sheridan, "Policy Forum: More Women in Science," *Science* 309 (August 19, 2005): 1190–91, www.sciencemag.org.

While options for higher education for American men date back to the colonial period,* American women were excluded from higher education until 1837 when Oberlin College, founded a few years previously, opened its doors to women and Mount Holyoke, a female seminary, was established.** Women did not gain entrance to medical school until 1847, and it was not until 1915 that the American Medical Association accepted women members. As late as 1869, the US Supreme Court upheld the refusal of the Illinois State Bar to admit women. One of the justices declared that "the natural and proper timidity and delicacy which belongs to the female sex evidently unfit it for many of the occupations of civil life." Nonetheless, a year later, in 1870, the first woman did succeed in graduating from an American law school.

Even after these "firsts," women were not universally admitted to all institutions of higher education in all fields for a long time. The prestigious Harvard

Medical School did not admit women until 1945, while Harvard Law School excluded women until 1950. Similarly, many highly respected undergraduate institutions, such as Princeton and Yale, remained male-only until the late 1960s or early 1970s. Others, such as Harvard, granted women access to classes and some facilities but officially restricted them to a separate college.

Moreover, the opening of doors to women did not necessarily mean that the doors opened as widely for women as for men. Often women continued to be discriminated against in admissions and financial aid policies long after they gained formal admittance. In some cases, women were held to higher standards than men; in others, overt or informal quotas limited the number of places available to them.*** Often course requirements for male and female high school students were different, and, at all levels, gender-based counseling was prevalent.

*The oldest institution of higher education, Harvard University, was founded in 1636 and, the second oldest, the College of William and Mary, was founded in 1693; see http://www.hno.harvard.edu/guide/intro/index.html and http://www.wm.edu/about/wmataglance/index.php.
** The chemist and educator Mary Lyon, who founded Mount Holyoke Female Seminary, famously said, "Go where no one else will go, do what no one else will do." See https://new.oberlin.edu/about/history.dot and https://www.mtholyoke.edu/about/; the quotation is from https://www.mtholyoke.edu/marylyon/legacy. Unless otherwise indicated, the remaining information on admissions of

women in this box is from Michelle Patterson and Laurie Engleberg, "Women in Male-Dominated Professions," in Women Working: Theories and Facts in Perspective, ed. Ann H. Stromberg and Shirley Harkess (Mountain View, CA: Mayfield, 1978), 266–92; the quotation in the text is from p. 277.
***See, for example, Ann Sutherland Harris, "The Second Sex in Academe," AAUP Bulletin 56, no. 3 (Fall 1970): 283–95; and Mary Frank Fox, "Women and Higher Education: Gender Differences in the Status of Students and Scholars," in Women: A Feminist Perspective, 3rd ed., ed. Jo Freeman (Palo Alto, CA: Mayfield, 1984), pp. 217–35.

Socialization

Socialization is the name given to the process by which the influence of family, friends, teachers, and the media shapes an individual's attitudes and behavior.[41] The socialization process influences the self-esteem of men and women, as well as their perceptions of gender-appropriate competencies and behavior. Girls may be socialized to emphasize

[41]See, for example, Francine D. Blau, Mary C. Brinton, and David B. Grusky, "The Declining Significance of Gender?" in The Declining Significance of Gender? ed. Francine D. Blau, Mary C. Brinton, and David B. Grusky (New York: Russell Sage Foundation, 2006), 3–34. For a classic explication of the impact of this process on gender differences, see Margaret M. Marini and Mary C. Brinton, "Sex Stereotyping in Occupational Socialization," in Sex Segregation in the Work Place: Trends, Explanations, and Remedies, ed. Barbara Reskin (Washington, DC: National Academies Press, 1984), 192–232. In recent years increasing attention has focused on the role of social networks in influencing behavior and outcomes, see for example, Nicholas A. Christakis and James H. Fowler, CONNECTED: The Surprising Power of Our Social Networks and How They Shape Our Lives (Little, Brown & Company, 2009).

appropriate "feminine" traits, such as being subordinate, nurturing, and emotional, while boys may be socialized to emphasize "masculine" traits, such as dominance, competitiveness, and rationality. Or, as another example, socialization may affect boys' and girls' perceptions of their mathematical abilities or the appropriateness of their interest in this subject. Having internalized the idea of what is properly "female," women may then avoid male fields because they perceive a nonpecuniary cost to acting in an "unfeminine" manner or because they feel unequipped to do so. In the latter case, they might expect to be less successful in the field, thus lowering their anticipated benefits. Similarly, if women are raised to believe that they lack competence in "masculine" subjects like math and science, this belief would raise their perceived costs and lower their perceived benefits to entry into fields emphasizing this knowledge. Men may see traditionally female fields as inappropriate for similar reasons.

The socialization process also helps shape the role boys and girls expect work to occupy in their lives. We have already seen how gender differences in the expected importance of market work in their lives may influence men's and women's educational investment decisions, in the past deterring women from investing in college. Negative attitudes of family, teachers, or friends toward women's college attendance may have also reduced their college attendance by comprising a nonpecuniary cost that lowered their subjective evaluation of the net value of this investment. The socialization process may also contribute to gender differences in occupational orientation, which are also likely to be important. Boys and girls may be taught from an early age to aspire to and train for gender-appropriate lines of work. Here too, disapproval by or lack of support from family, teachers, or friends may be a factor discouraging girls and women from venturing into nontraditional areas.

It is likely that gender differences in socialization have diminished with the growing social acceptance of women's employment outside the home and their participation in what were formerly viewed as male occupations, but it is unlikely that such gender differences have disappeared entirely.

Biased Evaluations

Even women's possession of "male" traits or competencies and their willingness to display them may not guarantee them equal success. Studies have found that, among both female and male college students, identical papers were given higher ratings on dimensions such as value, persuasiveness, profundity, writing style, and competence when respondents believed the author to be male rather than female. Similar findings are obtained in studies asking both women and men to evaluate the qualifications of applicants for employment.[42] Peers too may underestimate the performance of female colleagues.[43] The expectation of inferior performance may eventually cause that inferior performance. Even if it does not, it would lower the expected benefits to investments in educational credentials in these areas.

---

[42]We review one such study in Chapter 10 that involved evaluations of the application of college seniors applying for a science laboratory manager position; see Corinne A. Moss-Racusin, John F. Dovidio, Victoria L. Brescoll, Mark J. Graham, and Jo Handelsman, "Science Faculty's Subtle Gender Biases Favor Male Students," *Proceedings of the National Academy of Sciences* 109, no. 41 (2012): 16474–79, accessed December 16, 2012, http://www.pnas.org/content/early/2012/09/14/1211286109.full.pdf. For discussions and evidence, see Alice H. Eagly and Linda L. Carli, *Through the Labyrinth* (Cambridge, MA: Harvard Business School Press, 2007), and Virginia Valian, *Why So Slow? The Advancement of Women* (Cambridge, MA: MIT Press, 1998), 125–44.

[43]Daniel Z. Grunspan, "Males Under-Estimate Academic Performance of Their Female Peers in Undergraduate Biology Classrooms." *PLoS One* 11, no. 2 (February 10, 2016): e0148405.

Subtle Barriers: Role Models, Mentoring, and Networking

Although *overt* barriers to women in higher education have been eliminated, as discussed in the "Historical Background" box, *subtle* barriers to their success in the study of traditionally male fields remain a problem. As we explain in Chapter 11, such **subtle barriers** also block women's progress in the workplace.

Simply the fact that a field is predominantly male can discourage young women from attempting to enter it. In this way, past discrimination may continue to have an impact on young women today. Lacking contact with or firsthand knowledge of successful women, young women may assume (perhaps erroneously) that they too would be unable to succeed. Even if they believe that times have changed and that their prospects for success are better than indicated by the present low representation of women, the scarcity of women may still pose problems for them, limiting their eventual success and lowering their benefits to entering predominantly male fields.

For example, without older women to serve as **role models**, female entrants lack adequate information about acceptable (or successful) modes of behavior and dress. They also lack access to the knowledge acquired by older women about successful strategies for managing their careers and for combining work roles and family responsibilities. Thus, they are forced to be pioneers, and blazing a new trail is undoubtedly more difficult than following along a well-established path.

Women students may also be excluded from informal relationships that enhance the chances of career success. Older individuals who are well established in the field (mentors) often take promising young students (protégés) under their wing—informally socializing them into the norms of the field, giving them access to the latest research in the area, and tying them into their network of professional contacts. The **mentor–protégé relationship** is generally the result of the older individual identifying with the younger person. Male mentors may simply not identify with young women. The potential mentor may also fear that a close relationship with a young woman would be misunderstood by his colleagues or his wife. Thus, women students are likely to be at a disadvantage in predominantly male fields. Their problems will be further aggravated if male students neglect to include them in their **informal network**. Such informal contacts among students include study groups and discussions over lunches, sports, coffee breaks, or a Friday afternoon beer, where important information about coursework, the field, and career opportunities is often exchanged.

Thus, women often lack the support and encouragement, as well as the access to information and job opportunities, provided by informal contacts between teachers and students and among students, as well as female role models to emulate. The absence of these opportunities raises the nonpecuniary costs to them in comparison with otherwise similar male students, lowering their incentives to enter traditionally male fields. It may also result in their being less successful than comparable men when they complete their studies. To the extent that women students foresee this, their entry into predominantly male fields is further discouraged.

Although it is widely believed that a lack of female role models and mentors is a significant problem for women students, it is difficult to obtain quantitative evidence since many factors may influence whether one has a mentor of the same sex. One recent study provides particularly persuasive evidence of the impact of faculty gender using data on college students who had been randomly assigned to professors for a number of required standardized courses. The study found that having a female professor had a strong positive effect on female students' performance in math and science classes, their likelihood of taking future math and science courses, and their likelihood of graduating with a STEM degree. The effects were largest for female students with very strong math skills, the most likely candidates for careers in science.[44] In the same vein, another study of undergraduates found that the percentage of female faculty at their undergraduate college or university was positively related to the probability that female students attained an advanced degree. And a study of economics Ph.D. students found that additional female faculty had beneficial effects for female students on completion rates and time to completion of the Ph.D.[45]

Further evidence from our own profession of economics suggests the value of mentoring and networking for faculty as well as students. A study based on random assignment into a mentoring program found positive results on the academic productivity of female junior faculty (assistant professors) who participated in a 2-day mentoring program that also emphasized networking among the participants.[46]

The Impact of Title IX—Sports, Academics, Sexual Harassment, and Sexual Violence

To remedy discrimination in educational institutions, in 1972 Congress passed **Title IX** of the Educational Amendments to the Civil Rights Act of 1964. Title IX prohibits discrimination on the basis of sex in any educational program or activity receiving federal financial assistance and covers admissions, financial aid, and access to programs and activities, as well as employment of teachers and other personnel. Discrimination on the basis of sex also includes sexual harassment and sexual violence. Here we discuss some notable, but by no means all of the, provisions of Title IX, first focusing on impacts on sports, academics, and access to education and then turning to prohibitions against sexual harassment and sexual violence.

At the high school level, all courses and programs, including sports, must be available to both males and females. At the university level, Title IX provisions include nondiscrimination in admissions, faculty hiring, and participation in sports programs and equal availability of scholarships and fellowships, assistantships, research opportunities, and housing. Private, single-sex undergraduate schools are exempt from the nondiscrimination in admission requirements; however, once any women (or men) are admitted, no discrimination in admissions is permitted. Even though enforcement has not always been rigorous, it is likely that this legislation contributed to the substantial changes in the participation of women in higher education and in fields of study that we have reviewed.

Title IX has had a particularly dramatic impact on high school and collegiate athletics. Since its passage, support and facilities for women athletes have greatly increased, as has women's participation in athletic programs at both the high school

---

[44]See Scott E. Carrell, Marianne E. Page, and James E. West, "Sex and Science: How Professor Gender Perpetuates the Gender Gap," *Quarterly Journal of Economics* 125, no. 3 (August 2010): 1101–44. Gender of professor was found to have little impact on male students.
[45]Donna S. Rothstein, "Do Female Faculty Influence Female Students' Educational and Labor Market Attainments?" *Industrial and Labor Relations Review* 48, no. 3 (April 1995): 515–30; and David Neumark and Rosella Gardecki, "Women Helping Women? Role-Model and Mentoring Effects on Female Ph.D. Students in Economics," *Journal of Human Resources* 33, no. 1 (Winter 1998): 220–46.
[46]Francine D. Blau, Janet M. Currie, Rachel T. A. Croson, and Donna K. Ginther, "Can Mentoring Help Female Assistant Professors? Interim Results from a Randomized Trial," *American Economic Review: Papers and Proceedings* 100, no. 2 (May 2010): 348–52.

and the college levels.[47] Some research suggests that athletics has a positive effect on girls who participate. For example, looking across states, it has been found that in states where girls had a greater opportunity to play high school sports, female college attendance, labor force participation, and participation in previously male-dominated, typically high-skilled occupations were also higher.[48]

Title IX has been credited with revolutionizing women's sports. US women's participation in the Olympics offers one measure of this. At the 1972 Olympics (the year Title IX was passed), US women were only sparsely represented and won just 23 medals compared to US men's 71. In contrast, at the 2016 Olympics in Rio, the United States fielded more women than men, and the overall medal tally was one greater for women than men. The gender disparity was particularly striking for gold medals: US women won 27 gold metals compared to 18 for US men.[49]

The implementation of Title IX in athletics has not, however, been without controversy. The chief concern is that efforts to comply with the legislation, particularly at the collegiate level, have come at the expense of men's sports. However, research suggests that "institutions were more likely to add female teams or participants than to cut male teams or participants in order to move closer to compliance."[50] Indeed, the participation of both men and women in collegiate sports has increased since the early 1980s.[51]

Another controversial issue that has arisen is the desirability and legality of single-sex education. Some claim that, due to classroom issues, such as the tendency for males to dominate class discussion, women may benefit from single-sex schooling. (Similar arguments provide support for predominantly black institutions.) Some also believe boys may be adversely affected by the distractions of having girls in the classroom.

From a legal perspective, different issues are raised depending on whether the educational institution involved is publicly funded. As we have seen, single-sex, privately funded institutions are exempt from Title IX's admission requirements. However, constitutional issues come into play in single-sex, publicly funded schools. At the college level, a 1996 Supreme Court case found that the exclusion of qualified women from the Virginia Military Institute (VMI), a state-run, all-male military college, was not permissible. Writing for the majority, Justice Ruth Bader Ginsburg explained that the state must demonstrate an "exceedingly persuasive justification" for any official action that treats men and women differently. "The justification must be genuine, not hypothesized or invented *post hoc* in response to litigation. . . . And it must not rely on overbroad generalizations about the different talents, capacities, or preferences of males and females." This decision resulted in the admission of

---

[47]Betsy Stevenson, "Title IX and the Evolution of High School Sports," *Contemporary Economic Policy* 25, no. 4 (October 2007): 486–505; and Welch Suggs, *A Place on the Team: The Triumph and Tragedy of Title IX* (Princeton, NJ: Princeton University Press, 2005).

[48]Betsy Stevenson, "Beyond the Classroom: Using Title IX to Measure the Return to High School Sports," *Review of Economics and Statistics* 92, no. 2 (May 2010): 284–301.

[49]Greg Myre, "U.S. Women Will Rule in Rio (You Can Thank Title IX)," The Torch (NPR's Olympics Coverage), August 4, 2016, www.npr.org; and Jera Longman, "For Those Keeping Score, American Women Dominated in Rio," *New York Times*, August 22, 2016, nytimes.com.

[50]Deborah J. Anderson and John J. Cheslock, "Institutional Strategies to Achieve Gender Equity in Intercollegiate Athletics: Does Title IX Harm Male Athletes?" *American Economic Review* 94, no. 2 (May 2004): 307–11.

[51]National Coalition for Women and Girls in Education (NCWGE), *Title IX at 40: Working to Ensure Gender Equity in Education* (Washington, DC: NCWGE, 2012), www.ncwge.org; and John J. Cheslock, *Who's Playing College Sports? Money, Race, and Gender*, Women's Sports Foundation Research Report (September 2008), www.WomensSportsFoundation.org.

women into VMI and a similar institution, the Citadel in South Carolina, that was not explicitly involved in the case.[52]

Private colleges were not affected by the Supreme Court decision. However, all-male private colleges are nonetheless now quite rare, with only four in operation in 2016. All-female private colleges are much more prevalent, with 44 in 2015, though this figure was down considerably from 233 in 1960.[53]

Considerable controversy also continues to surround the issue of single-sex public schools at the elementary and high school levels. Despite concerns by some critics that single-sex schools are in violation of Title IX, the number of single-sex public schools is growing; it is estimated that in 1995 there were only two single-sex public schools and that by 2011–2012 there were 116. In addition, an increasing number of coeducational public schools offer some single-sex classrooms.[54] The benefits of single-sex classrooms are the subject of heated debate, not only in terms of whether or not such arrangements promote academic success but also regarding whether or not they reinforce gender stereotypes.[55]

Finally, as noted at the outset, discrimination under Title IX also includes sexual harassment and sexual violence, which means that both actions are prohibited under Title IX. (As discussed in Chapter 12, sexual harassment in the workplace is illegal under Title VII of the Civil Rights Act of 1964.) Schools are required to respond promptly and effectively to address sexual harassment and violence. As a result of a number of high-profile cases in the mid-2010s, the treatment of these issues by schools has received increasing attention and the US Department of Education has pursued active investigations of institutions of higher education over their handling of reported incidents.[56] While estimates vary considerably, in large part due to the definitions used, a 2015 survey found that 23 percent of undergraduate women (and 5 percent of undergraduate men) reported that they were victims of nonconsensual sexual contact. The high incidence rate reported points to the fact that schools continue to struggle with finding the best way to address sexual violence on campus.[57]

---

[52]Linda Greenhouse, "Military College Can't Bar Women, High Court Rules," *New York Times*, June 27, 1996, A1, B8.

[53]"All-Male Colleges: Only 4 Remain," July 1, 2016, NICHE, articles.niche.com; and Jasmine Garsd, "Are Women's Colleges Doomed? What Sweet Briar's Demise Tells Us," March 26, 2015, nprED, www. npr.org. See also, Leslie Miller-Bernal and Susan L. Poulson, "The State of Women's Colleges Today," in *Challenged by Coeducation: Women's Colleges Since the 1960s*, ed. Leslie Miller-Bernal and Susan L. Poulson (Nashville, TN: Vanderbilt University Press, 2007), 375–88. For an analysis of the shift from single-sex to coeducation, see Claudia Goldin and Lawrence F. Katz, "Putting the 'Co' in Education: Timing, Reasons, and Consequences of College Coeducation from 1835 to the Present," *Journal of Human Capital* 5, no. 4 (Winter 2011): 377–417.

[54]See the National Association for Single Sex Public Education (NASSPE) website at www.singlesex-schools.org.

[55]For a study that points to the negatives of single-sex schooling, see Diane F. Halpern, Lise Eliot, Rebecca S. Bigler, Richard A. Fabes, Laura D. Hanish, Janet Hyde, Lynn S. Liben, and Carol Lynn Martin, "The Pseudoscience of Single-Sex Schooling," *Science* 333, no. 6050 (September 23, 2011): 1706–07. For a more positive perspective, see Hyunjoon Park, Jere Behrman, and Jaesung Choi, "Single-Sex Education: Positive Effects," *Science* 335, no. 6065 (January 13, 2012): 165–66.

[56]See US Department of Education, Office for Civil Rights, "Know Your Rights: Title IX Prohibits Sexual Harassment and Sexual Violence Where You Go to School," http://www2.ed.gov; and Sara Lipka, "How to Use The Chronicle's Title IX Tracker, and What We've Learned," *The Chronicle of Higher Education*, June 2, 2016, www.chronicle.com.

[57]Nick Anderson and Susan Svrluga, "What a Massive Sexual Assault Survey Found at 27 Top U.S. Universities," *Washington Post*, September 21, 2015, www.washingtonpost.com; and Allie Bidwell, "Campus Sexual Assault: More Awareness Hasn't Solved Root Issues," *U.S. News & World Report*, May 20, 2015, www.usnews.com.

Explaining Women's Rising Educational Attainment

Whatever the past barriers to women's access to higher education or the remaining gender differences in fields of study, the increase in women's representation in college and postgraduate study that we documented earlier in this chapter is truly remarkable. How do we explain this change that began in earnest in the 1970s? One particularly puzzling feature of the recent trends is that not only did women become half of those receiving bachelor's degrees in 1980, but their representation continued to increase thereafter. In 2014, women received 57 percent of bachelor's degrees, and the female share had stood at this level since the late 1990s. So, women are now *more* likely to go to college than men. While these developments are still not fully understood, we can point to a number of factors that have contributed to the increase in women's college attendance and, in some cases, encouraged women's college attendance to exceed men's.

As we noted previously, the increase in women's expected work life is undoubtedly a central factor explaining the increase in women's college attendance. Looking at Figure 8-6, we see that as women anticipated spending longer periods in the labor market, the return to women's investment in higher education increased and with it their motivation to obtain higher levels of education and more market-oriented education (i.e., fields of study and types of training with higher market payoffs). And, indeed, the data suggest that women graduating from college in recent decades spend considerably less time out of the labor force than earlier cohorts. We saw, for example, in Chapter 6 that the labor force participation rates of female college graduates are quite high, 80 percent in 2015, up from 61 percent in 1970. In contrast, participation rates remain quite a bit lower for female high school graduates and have increased less since 1970. In 2015, 62 percent of this group participated in the labor force, up from 51 percent in 1970. Evidence of college-educated women's strong labor force attachment is also provided by a study of the work experience of women who graduated in 1981 from one of 34 highly selective colleges and universities. In the 15 or so years following their completion of college or more advanced schooling, fully 58 percent of the women surveyed were never out of the job market for more than 6 months in total. Overall, the group had spent a total of just 1.6 years out of the labor force, on average, or 11 percent of their potential working years.[58]

Expanding labor market opportunities for college women also likely played a role. Due to the passage of antidiscrimination legislation, which we discuss in Chapter 12, as well as shifting social attitudes toward women's work roles and capabilities, there has been a growth in opportunities for women in traditionally male occupations. Moreover, this increase in opportunities principally benefited college-educated women. As we saw in Chapter 7, occupational segregation by sex particularly declined in managerial and professional jobs, high-earning occupations likely to provide opportunities for college women. In contrast, occupational segregation has declined very little in blue-collar occupations, thereby providing fewer new opportunities for less educated women.

---

[58]Claudia Goldin, "Working It Out," *New York Times*, March 15, 2006, www.nytimes.org. For an interesting study focusing on three cohorts of Harvard/Radcliffe graduates, see Claudia Goldin and Lawrence F. Katz, "Transitions: Career and Family Life Cycles of the Educational Elite," *American Economic Review* 98, no. 2 (May 2008): 363–69.

There has also been an increase in the returns to education for women as well as men since 1980 due in part to technological change that has benefited more highly educated workers relative to their less-skilled counterparts.[59] This means that the gap between the college and high school profiles shown in Figure 8-3 has increased, raising the return to college education for both men and women. Moreover, not only have returns to education increased, but some research suggests that the *returns* to education are higher for women than for men, and this appears to have been the case for a considerable period of time.[60] This means that, in this respect at least, women have a greater incentive to invest in a college education than men. This may help explain why women are now more likely to go to college than men, especially now that their expected work life has become more similar to men's.

Two additional factors may have contributed to the ability of women to *respond* to these increasing economic incentives to go on to higher education and reinforced those incentives. First is the development of oral contraception, otherwise known as **the pill**, and especially its growing availability to young, unmarried women beginning in the late 1960s and early 1970s. The availability of the pill was associated with and facilitated a delay in marriage and childbearing, which in turn enabled women to pursue professional training after college. According to the authors of one major study, the pill led to important *direct* and *indirect* effects on women's career investments. The direct effect of the pill was that it increased the reliability of contraception and the ease of using it, thereby enabling women to postpone marrying and starting a family and more confidently embark on a lengthy professional education. The indirect effect of the pill was that, because it encouraged the delay of marriage for *all* young people (not just those acquiring professional training), a woman who postponed marriage to pursue professional studies would find a larger pool of eligible bachelors to choose from. Had this not occurred, a woman who put off marriage for professional studies would have faced a much smaller pool of potential mates and, given this smaller selection, might have had to settle for a less desirable match if she wanted to marry. This would have raised the cost to women of professional study.[61] Second, passage and enforcement of Title IX, which specifically banned discrimination by educational institutions, likely led to changes in admission and other practices of educational institutions that facilitated and encouraged women's increased participation in higher education.

For both women and men, a college education not only boosts their own income but also results in **family-related income gains**. One source of these family-related income gains is that college-educated individuals (male and female) tend to marry others with the same level of education. As a result, the college-educated not only reap the gains to their own higher education but also reap the benefits of having a higher-earning spouse. Since husbands are still the higher-earning partner in most

[59]For an excellent long-term analysis, see Goldin and Katz, *The Race between Education and Technology.*
[60]Christopher Dougherty, "Why Are the Returns to Schooling Higher for Women than for Men?" *Journal of Human Resources* 40, no. 4 (Fall 2005): 969–88. See also Brian A. Jacob, "Where the Boys Aren't: Non-Cognitive Skills, Returns to School and the Gender Gap in Higher Education," *Economics of Education Review* 21, no. 6, pt. B. (2002): 589–98. However, another study casts doubt on this finding when a problem with the data used in most studies (the Current Population Survey)—topcoding—is corrected; see William H. J. Hubbard, "The Phantom Gender Difference in the College Wage Premium," *Journal of Human Resources* 46, no. 3 (Summer 2011): 568–86.
[61]Claudia Goldin and Lawrence F. Katz, "The Power of the Pill: Oral Contraceptives and Women's Career and Marriage Decisions," *Journal of Political Economy* 110, no. 4 (August 2002): 730–70. See also Martha J. Bailey, "More Power to the Pill: The Impact of Contraceptive Freedom on Women's Life-cycle Labor Supply," *Quarterly Journal of Economics* 121, no. 1 (February 2006): 289–320.

families, gains due to having a higher-earning spouse are likely to be larger for women than for men. Another factor, one that is of particular importance for women, is that college-educated women have lower divorce rates and a lower incidence of out-of-wedlock births. This means that they are less likely than their less educated counterparts to become lower-income, single-family heads. Taking these factors together, one study finds that family-related income gains increased more for women than for men, suggesting that this may be at least part of the reason for the dramatic increase in women's college completion rates.[62]

Finally, girls may have lower nonpecuniary costs of investing in college than boys. That is, investing in education may entail less disutility for girls than boys. These lower costs may explain why, with the elimination of social and labor market barriers, women's college attendance has not only increased but come to surpass men's rates. For one thing, as discussed earlier, girls have traditionally excelled relative to boys in secondary school academic performance and continue to do so today. They also appear more willing to put in effort; boys spend much less time doing homework than girls. In addition, boys have a much higher incidence of school disciplinary and behavior problems, ranging from more minor infractions to school suspensions and participation in criminal activity. Boys are also two to three times more likely to be diagnosed with attention deficit hyperactivity disorder (ADHD). The reasons for these gender differences have not been fully determined, but one factor may be the later maturation of boys.[63] In addition, boys seem to be more adversely affected than girls in their behavior and school achievement by growing up in disadvantaged conditions.[64] Regardless of their sources, a recent study points out, "the slower social development and more serious behavioral problems of boys . . . allowed girls to leapfrog over them in the race to college."[65]

While the explanations we have considered help to explain why girls and women are making considerable advances, catching up to and surpassing their male counterparts, they do raise the question of why men's level of educational attainment has not grown more, particularly in light of the rising college wage premium and the continued high return to investing in college. The answer to this question is not fully known. One factor appears to be that, as we noted previously, boys seem to be more adversely affected than girls by growing up in economically disadvantaged families. For example, research finds that boys raised in such families have relatively lower levels of academic achievement (as measured by test scores and high school graduation rates) than girls reared in a similar environment and relatively more behavioral issues, as measured by school absences and suspensions. Moreover, poor

---

[62]Thomas A DiPrete and Claudia Buchmann, "Gender-Specific Trends in the Value of Education and the Emerging Gender Gap in College Completion," *Demography* 43, no. 1 (February 2006): 1–24. These are gains in family income adjusted for family size.

[63]This is drawn primarily from Goldin, Katz, and Kuziemko, "The Homecoming of American College Women." See also Jacob, "Where the Boys Aren't." Gary S. Becker, William H. J. Hubbard, and Kevin M. Murphy conclude that gender differences in these types of noncognitive skills are the principal explanation for the worldwide trend toward women overtaking men in higher education—they emphasize women's lower dispersion of noncognitive skills; see "Explaining the Worldwide Boom in Higher Education of Women," *Journal of Human Capital* 4, no. 3 (September 2010): 203–41. The finding on gender differences in time teens spend on homework is from Shirley L. Porterfield and Anne E. Winkler, "Teen Time Use and Parental Education: Evidence from the CPS, MTF, and ATUS," *Monthly Labor Review* 130, no. 5 (May 2007): 37–56.

[64]For a useful summary with references to the research literature, see Jeff Guo, "Poor Boys Are Falling Behind Poor Girls, and It's Deeply Troubling," Wonkblog, *Washington Post*, November 23, 2015, washingtonpost.com.

[65]Goldin, Katz, and Kuziemko, "The Homecoming of American College Women," 154.

school quality appears to amplify these differential impacts.[66] The difficulties faced by boys, especially those from economically disadvantaged families, and what can be done to improve their economic prospects is the subject of active research. This is an important issue not only for the well-being of boys and the men they will become but for women as well. As we shall see in Chapter 13, men's economic circumstances impact marriage rates and rates of female headship.

Conclusion

In this chapter, we examined gender differences in one of the principal human capital factors that determine individuals' occupations and earnings, their investment in formal education. We saw that while, traditionally, men had the edge in college graduation, now women are more likely than men to obtain a bachelor's or master's degree and have reached parity in Ph.D.s and first professional degrees. While some gender differences in fields of study remain, this is undeniably a dramatic development. We have applied economic theory to better understand why women lagged behind men in higher education in the past and why they caught up to and then surpassed men. In the next chapter we turn to another extremely important type of human capital investment, on-the-job training, and consider other supply-side factors that may contribute to the gender gap in occupations and earnings.

Questions for Review and Discussion

*Indicates that the question can be answered using a diagram illustrating the individual's human capital investment decision as well as verbally. Consult with your instructor about the appropriate approach for your class.

1. What are the main economic factors that underlie the decision to invest in a college education? Explain in detail.*

2. Carefully explain how the following hypothetical situations would affect the cost–benefit decision of whether it is worthwhile to invest in college.

   a. It is increasingly the case that full-time undergraduate students need 5 years to complete all of the requirements for a bachelor's degree.*

   b. The real earnings of college-trained workers increase, while those of high school–trained workers decrease.*

3. Why did women, in the past, frequently invest less in a college education than men? What changed this tendency?*

---

[66]David Autor, David Figlio, Krzysztof Karbownik, Jeffrey Roth, and Melanie Wasserman, "Family Disadvantage and the Gender Gap in Behavioral and Educational Outcomes," NBER Working Paper 22267 (National Bureau of Economic Research, Cambridge, MA, May 2016); and David Autor, David Figlio, Krzysztof Karbownik, Jeffrey Roth, and Melanie Wasserman, "School Quality and the Gender Gap in Educational Achievement," NBER Working Paper 21908 (National Bureau of Economic Research, Cambridge, MA, January 2016). Moreover, not only do boys have more behavior issues than girls, but even when boys and girls exhibit the same behaviors in school, one study finds that teachers respond more negatively to the boys; see Jayanti Owens, "Early Childhood Behavior Problems and the Gender Gap in Educational Attainment in the United States," *Sociology of Education* 89, no. 3 (2016): 236–58.

4. To what extent and how did economic factors influence the following?

   a. Your decision to attend college.

   b. Your choice of major.

   c. Your plans to go on or not to go on to graduate work.

   Would you expect any of these considerations to differ between men and women, and if so, why?

5. This problem revisits Denise's net present value calculation regarding the decision to invest in specialized training, which was discussed in the box entitled "Calculating the Net Present Value of a Human Capital Investment." (Consult with your instructor to find out if you are responsible for this material.) The calculation performed in the box (referred to subsequently as the "initial calculation") was based on a set of assumptions. Recalculate the net present value of Denise's training investment for the following situations: [*Hint*: You can use a spreadsheet program like Excel to calculate net present value.]

   a. The discount rate is .10 instead of .05. (All other parts of the initial calculation remain the same). What does this tell you about the effect of an increase in the discount rate on the training decision, all else equal?

   b. Salary foregone during training is $30,000 instead of $20,000. (All other parts of the initial calculation remain the same.) What does this tell you about the effect of an increase in training costs on the training decision, all else equal?

   c. Additional earnings from training are expected to be $5,000 per year instead of $6,000. (All other parts of the initial calculation remain the same.) What does this tell you about the effect of a reduction in annual benefits on the training decision, all else equal?

   d. Expected work life after training falls from 10 to 5 years. (All other parts of the initial calculation remain the same.) What does this tell you about the effect of a shorter work life on the training decision, all else equal?

6. Girls (and women) are doing relatively better than boys (and men) in terms of level of educational attainment. Explain the reasons for this development.

7. Think about the factors that affected your own decision to go to college (or, if you prefer, think about the decision of someone you know well). What role did societal discrimination, role models/mentors, expected family plans, and other social factors discussed in this chapter play in the decision?

Internet Data-Based Exercise

The US Census Bureau is the primary source of government data on many topics included in this text, including income, education, and poverty.

Visit the home page of the US Census Bureau at http://www.census.gov.

Click on "Income." On the income page, look for the most recent document titled "Income and Poverty in the United States" (or a similar title). Look for tables based on this document. Find Table PINC-03, "Educational Attainment—People 25 Years Old and Over, by Total Money Earnings, Work Experience, Age, Race, Hispanic Origin, and Sex."

a. Compare mean earnings for *female* workers (all races) aged 25–34 who worked full-time year-round for the following education groups: high school graduates (including the GED), some college (no degree), and a bachelor's degree (only). Do the same for *male* workers.

b. Referring to your answers in a, discuss the earnings consequences of not (fully) completing a four year college degree.

Suggested Readings

Bailey, Martha J., and Susan M. Dynarski. "Inequality in Postsecondary Education." In *Whither Opportunity: Rising Inequality, Schools, and Children's Life Chances*, edited by Greg Duncan and Richard Murnane, 117–32. New York: Russell Sage Foundation, 2011.

Bradbury, Bruce, Miles Corak, Jane Waldfogel, and Elizabeth Washbrook. *Too Many Children Left Behind: The U.S. Achievement Gap in Comparative Perspective*. New York: Russell Sage Foundation, 2015.

Corbett, Christianne, and Catherine Hill. *Graduating to a Pay Gap: The Earnings of Women and Men One Year after College Graduation*. Washington, DC: AAUW. October 2012. Accessed November 9, 2012. http://www.aauw.org.

Corbett, Christianne, Catherine Hill, and Andresse St. Rose. *Where the Girls Are: The Facts about Gender Equity in Education*. Washington, DC: AAUW Educational Foundation. May 2008. Accessed November 9, 2012. http://www.aauw.org.

DiPrete, Thomas A., and Claudia Buchmann. *The Rise of Women: The Growing Gender Gap in Education and What It Means for American Schools*. New York: Russell Sage Foundation, 2013.

Duncan, Greg J., and Richard Murnane, eds. *Wither Opportunity: Rising Inequality, Schools, and Children's Life Chances*. New York: Russell Sage Foundation, 2011.

Goldin, Claudia, and Lawrence F. Katz. *The Race between Education and Technology*. Cambridge, MA: Harvard University Press, 2008.

Goldin, Claudia, Lawrence F. Katz, and Ilyana Kuziemko. "The Homecoming of American College Women: The Reversal of the College Gender Gap." *Journal of Economic Perspectives* 20, no. 4 (Fall 2006): 133–56.

King, Jacqueline E. *Gender Equity in Higher Education: 2006*. Washington, DC: American Council on Education, Center for Policy Analysis, 2006.

Stevenson, Betsey. "Title IX and the Evolution of High School Sports." *Contemporary Economic Policy* 25, no. 4 (October 2007): 486–505.

Tobias, Sheila, and Victor Piercey. *Banishing Math Anxiety*. Seattle, WA: Kendall Hunt Publishing, 2012.

Key Terms

societal discrimination (192)

labor market discrimination (193)

human capital (194)

human capital investment (194)

experience-earnings profiles (203)

direct costs (204)

indirect costs (204)

present value (205)

net present value (205)

future value (205)

discount rate (206)

internal rate of return (207)

college wage (earnings) premium (207)

signal (212)

statistical discrimination (213)

expected work life (213)

socialization (219)

subtle barriers (221)

role models (221)

mentor–protégé relationship (221)

informal network (221)

Title IX (222)

the pill (226)

family-related income gains (226)

Other Supply-Side Sources of Gender Differences in Labor Market Outcomes

In this chapter, we continue our consideration of supply-side explanations for gender differences in occupations and earnings. The last chapter focused on investments in education. Here, we consider a second major type of human capital investment, on-the-job training. We first examine the determinants of the decision to invest in on-the-job training and analyze the sources of gender differences in this decision. Then, we apply these concepts to understanding gender differences in occupations and earnings. While differences in human capital are likely an important part of the story, we also point to the high wage penalty for temporal flexibility (the ability to adjust work schedules) in some occupations, which may help to explain observed gender wage differences among workers in those jobs and possibly influence the occupational choices of women as well. Next, we look at a topic that is especially important for women, the effect of family and parenthood on earnings. In the remaining sections of the chapter, we consider gender differences in psychological attributes (also frequently referred to as "noncognitive skills" or "soft skills") that may produce gender differences in labor market outcomes and take a closer look at what might explain gender differences in math test scores.

On-the-Job Training and Labor Market Experience

One of the major insights of human capital theory is the observation that individuals can increase their productivity not only through their investments in formal education but also through **on-the-job training**, that is by learning important work skills while they are on the job.[1] Sometimes workers learn these skills by participating in formal training programs sponsored by employers. More often, they benefit from informal instruction provided by supervisors or coworkers and even grow more proficient at their jobs simply through repetition and trial and error. Human capital theory suggests that the weaker attachment to the labor force of women who follow traditional gender roles means that they will acquire less of this valuable on-the-job training. As will be discussed in Chapter 11, women may also be denied equal access to this type of training due to employer discrimination.

Gender Differences in Labor Market Experience

Before developing these ideas further, let us look at the actual extent of gender differences in work experience. **Work experience** has two dimensions: **general labor market experience** (sometimes referred to simply as "work experience"), which refers to the cumulative length of time a worker has spent in the labor force, and **tenure**, which refers to the length of time that a worker spends with a specific firm. (If one were to sum up a worker's tenure at all firms, this would be equal to the worker's general labor market experience.) While information on tenure is regularly collected by government agencies, this is not the case for general labor market experience. Instead, for the latter dimension, we must piece together information from various special surveys and other estimates.

The available data on general labor market experience indicate that, on average, women have less work experience than men but that gender differences have narrowed considerably since 1980. Prior to 1980 (between 1960 and 1980), the

---

[1]See, for example, Gary S. Becker, *Human Capital: A Theoretical and Empirical Analysis, with Special Reference to Education*, 3rd ed. (Chicago: University of Chicago Press, 1993); Jacob Mincer, "On-the-Job Training: Costs, Returns and Some Implications," *Journal of Political Economy* 70, no. 5, pt. 2 (October 1962): 50–79; and Walter Oi, "Labor as a Quasi-Fixed Factor," *Journal of Political Economy* 70, no. 6 (December 1962): 538–55. Analyses of the gender pay gap build on the pioneering work of Jacob Mincer and Solomon W. Polachek, "Family Investments in Human Capital: Earnings of Women," *Journal of Political Economy* 82, no. 2, pt. 2 (March/April 1974): 76–108.

average level of experience for all women workers fell slightly.[2] This was the case even though, during that time, women's labor force attachment *rose* and employed women increased their average labor market experience *within* each age group. The *average* level of experience for all women workers nonetheless fell slightly because of the large increases in labor force participation of *younger* women (including those in the prime childbearing/child-rearing years) during that time (as discussed in Chapter 5). Even with women in each age group working more years than previously, because younger women have less experience than older women, this change in age mix resulted in a small decline in average experience for women as a whole.[3] Yet, it is precisely this pattern of growing labor force attachment of women during the childbearing years that would subsequently cause women's average experience to increase.

Beginning in the 1980s, overall female experience levels unambiguously began to rise and the gender experience gap—the difference in average years of labor market experience between women and men—began to fall.[4] In 1981, women workers averaged 13.5 years of full-time work experience compared to 20.3 years for men—a gender experience gap of 6.8 years. By 2011 (the most recent year for which this information is available), women averaged 16.4 years of full-time experience compared to 17.8 years for men—a gender gap of only 1.4 years.[5]

The gender difference in tenure (time with a *specific* employer) has declined as well. So, for example, in 1966, men's median tenure was 2.4 years more than women's. By 2014, the gender tenure gap had fallen to only .2 years. And the share of long-term workers, those with tenure of 10 or more years, was only slightly higher for men (34 percent) than for women (33 percent).[6]

---

[2]Average years of work experience for working women were 13.25 (1960), 12.97 (1970), and 12.22 (1980), see Claudia Goldin, *Understanding the Gender Gap: An Economic History of American Women* (New York: Oxford University Press, 1990), 41. These figures are Goldin's calculations based on data from James P. Smith and Michael P. Ward, *Women's Wages and Work in the Twentieth Century*, R-3119-NICHD, Santa Monica, CA: Rand Corporation, 1984.

[3]Goldin, *Understanding the Gender Gap*, 41. There was an increase in women's average experience between 1950 and 1960 (from 11.57 [1950] to 13.25 [1960]), also due to changes in the age distribution of employed women.

[4]A number of studies report rising relative experience levels for women in the 1980s; see, for example, June O'Neill and Solomon W. Polachek, "Why the Gender Gap in Wages Narrowed in the 1980s," *Journal of Labor Economics* 11, no. 1, pt. 1 (January 1993): 205–28; and Francine D. Blau and Lawrence M. Kahn, "Swimming Upstream: Trends in the Gender Wage Differential in the 1980s," *Journal of Labor Economics*, 15, no. 1, pt. 1 (January 1997): 1–42.

[5]Data are for full-time workers and are from Francine D. Blau and Lawrence M. Kahn, "The Gender Wage Gap: Extent, Trends, and Sources," NBER Working Paper 21913 (National Bureau of Economic Research, Cambridge, MA, January 2016) (*Journal of Economic Literature*, forthcoming). Blau and Kahn note that the very small experience gap in 2011 may be partly due to the negative effect of the Great Recession on male experience levels. In 1999 the gender gap in full-time experience was 3.8 years, and in 2007 (the year prior to the Great Recession) it was 2.6 years. As we have seen, just 4 years later it was 1.4 years.

[6]US Department of Labor, Bureau of Labor Statistics, *Job Tenure of Workers, January 1966, Special Labor Force Report* 77 (1967); and US Department of Labor, Bureau of Labor Statistics, "Employee Tenure in 2014," *news release*, September 18, 2014, http://www.bls.gov. Note median tenure data are for workers aged 16 and over; data on the share of long tenure are for workers aged 25 and over. The increasing labor force attachment of married mothers contributed to increases in women's tenure relative to men's, especially as tenure declined for men and never-married women; see Matissa N. Hollister and Kristin E. Smith, "Unmasking the Conflicting Trends in Job Tenure by Gender in the United States, 1983–2008," *American Sociological Review* 79, no. 1 (February 2014): 159–81.

To summarize, the data indicate that women have, on average, less work experience than men but that the differences between men and women in labor market experience, both general experience and experience on their current job (tenure), have narrowed considerably since 1980. We examine next how, according to the human capital model, gender differences in labor force attachment and experience could lower women's pay and cause differences in occupational choices between men and women. By the same token, this analysis implies that improvements in women's relative experience levels compared to men should boost their earnings and occupational attainment.

The On-the-Job Training Investment Decision

We begin with an analysis of the training investment decision itself and then consider gender differences in this decision. On-the-job training may be divided into two types:

- General training
- Firm-specific training

General training increases the individual's productivity to the same extent in all (or a large number of) firms. For example, an individual may learn to use computer software or operate office equipment that is widely used by many firms. On the other hand, **firm-specific training**, as its name implies, increases the individual's productivity only at the firm that provides the training. For example, one may learn how to get things done within a particular bureaucracy or deal with the idiosyncrasies of a particular computer application or piece of equipment. Most training probably combines elements of both general and firm-specific training. However, for simplicity, we assume that training may be classified as being entirely general or entirely firm-specific.

General Training

General training is, by definition, completely transferable from the firm providing the training to other firms. Employers will presumably not be willing to foot any part of the bill for such training because, in a competitive labor market, they have no way of making sure they will be able to collect any of the returns on their investment. This is because, after workers obtain training, employers must pay them what they are worth elsewhere, or they will simply leave the firm. Thus, if general training is to occur, employees must be willing to bear all the costs since they will reap all the returns. As in the case of formal education, an individual decides whether to invest in general training by comparing the costs and benefits.

Let us consider Lisa's investment decision, illustrated in Figure 9-1. She will contrast the experience-earnings profile she can expect if she takes a job with no training (UU') to the profile she can expect if she receives general training (GG'). On-the-job training, although often informal, still entails costs just as does formal schooling. Some of these costs may be direct. For example, in the cases with formal programs, expenses are incurred for instructors or for materials used in the training. Another portion of the costs is indirect as the worker and his or her

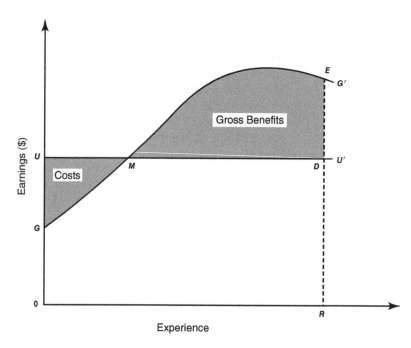

FIGURE 9-1 The On-the-Job Training Investment Decision: General Training

coworkers or supervisor transfer their attention from daily production to training activities. Such expenses arise even when, as is frequently the case, no formal program is in place. The resulting decline in output represents the opportunity cost to the firm of the training activity.

How does Lisa go about "paying" such costs if she decides to invest in general training? She does so by accepting a wage below what she could obtain elsewhere. This lower wage corresponds to her productivity (net of training costs) to the firm during the training period. The costs of the investment in general training are given by the area *UGM*. As Lisa becomes more skilled, her earnings catch up to and eventually surpass what she could earn without training. Assuming a total of *OR* years of labor market experience over her work life, her gross benefits will be equal to the area *MED*. As in the case of formal schooling, she is likely to undertake the investment if gross benefits exceed costs by a sufficient amount to yield the desired rate of return (as appears to be the case in Figure 9-1).

Firm-Specific Training

Figure 9-2 illustrates Don's decision of whether to invest in firm-specific training. His productivity on the job is shown by the profile *GG'*. It is also what his earnings profile would be in the case of general training. However, because firm-specific training is not transferable, Don will not be willing to bear all the costs of the training; his ability to reap the returns depends on continued employment at the firm that initially provided the training. If he were to lose his job, his investment would be wiped out. (The earnings profile available to him at another firm is *UU'*.) If Don paid for all his training, he would experience a strong incentive to remain with his employer, but his employer would have no particular reason to accord him any special protection from layoffs.

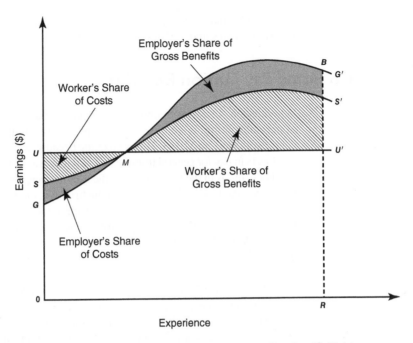

FIGURE 9-2 The On-the-Job Training Investment Decision: Firm-Specific Training

Similarly, his employer is unwilling to shoulder all the costs of firm-specific training because if Don were to quit, the firm would lose its investment. If the employer were to pay all the costs and receive all the returns, Don's profile would be UU'. He would have no special incentive to remain with the firm because he would be earning no more than he could get elsewhere. A temporary shift in demand that resulted in higher wages in another industry or even just more favorable working conditions at another firm might be sufficient to lure him away.

The solution is for the worker and the employer to share the costs of, and returns to, firm-specific training. In this case, the specifically trained worker's profile is SS'. The worker (Don) has an incentive to remain with the firm after completing training because he earns more there than he can get elsewhere (given by profile UU'). The firm also has an incentive to retain a worker who has completed specific training, even in the face of, say, a dip in the demand for its product. This incentive results because the specifically trained worker (Don in this case) is actually being paid less than his productivity—after point M, SS' lies below GG'.

This analysis of firm-specific training has two important implications. First, a relatively permanent attachment is likely to develop between the firm and the specifically trained worker. Such workers are less likely either to quit or to be laid off their jobs than untrained or generally trained workers. Second, because employers pay part of the costs of firm-specific training, they will be concerned about the expected quit rates of workers they are considering hiring into jobs where such training is important. (This point is developed further later.)

As Figures 9-1 and 9-2 suggest, earnings will increase with experience for workers who have invested in training. Considerable empirical evidence does indeed show a positive relationship between labor market experience and earnings for workers of both sexes. Although the return to experience was lower for women than for men in the 1960s and 1970s, the return to experience for women subsequently increased relative to men's and, in later decades, little gender difference was found.[7]

Why Do Firms Pay Tuition Benefits?

One situation where we do observe employers partially or even fully covering the costs of general training is the case where employers reimburse tuition for a general set of coursework (e.g., an MBA). This is puzzling because, as we have seen, we do not expect employers to pay for general training that will increase workers' productivity by as much in other firms as in the firm providing the training. Such general training is not expected to increase the workers' attachment to the firm and, on the contrary, might be expected to increase worker turnover by increasing their attractiveness to other firms. One reason that employers may nonetheless pay for tuition benefits is that offering a tuition benefit may enable the firm to attract higher-quality (more productive) employees who value the option of using the tuition program. In addition, perhaps surprisingly, most of the evidence finds that tuition investment programs are associated with *lower* turnover of workers, and indeed firms cite increased employee retention as a motivation for offering such programs. There are a number of possible reasons for these higher retention rates.

One reason is that the availability of the tuition benefit may attract workers who are not only more productive but also have lower quit propensities (i.e., are less prone to quit). Such workers may particularly value a benefit of this type.[8] Moreover, the tuition benefit may encourage those workers who utilize the program to stay on the job longer than they otherwise might in order to continue making use of the benefit.[9]

A final possible reason for higher retention rates at firms providing tuition benefits is that tuition reimbursement may be offered in conjunction with other training that is firm-specific in nature (i.e., as a complement to firm-specific training rather than as a substitute for it). If this is the case, on net, the "package" of training offered by the firm may be firm-specific, that is, may increase the worker's productivity more at the firm providing the training than at other firms, thus providing an incentive for the worker to remain with the firm.[10]

To sum up, this discussion points to the fact that employer-subsidized tuition assistance provides benefits to the firm by enabling it to attract more productive workers

---

[7]For evidence of higher returns to experience for men in earlier years, see, for example, Mincer and Polachek, "Family Investments in Human Capital." For studies pointing to a reduction or elimination of this gender difference over the 1980s and 1990s, see, for example, O'Neill and Polachek, "Why the Gender Gap in Wages Narrowed in the 1980s"; Blau and Kahn, "Swimming Upstream"; and Francine D. Blau and Lawrence M. Kahn, "The U.S. Gender Pay Gap in the 1990s," NBER Working Paper 10853 (National Bureau of Economic Research, Cambridge, MA, October 2004)—these data are not available in the published version of this paper in the *ILR Review*.

[8]Peter Cappelli, "Why Do Employers Pay for College?" *Journal of Econometrics* 121, nos. 1–2 (July–August 2004): 213–41; and Colleen Flaherty Manchester, "General Skills and Employee Mobility: How Tuition Reimbursement Increases Retention through Sorting and Participation," *Industrial and Labor Relations Review* 65, no. 4 (October 2012): 951–74.

[9]This could be a considerable period of time since most employers prohibit access to tuition benefits for new hires, often waiting a year or more to make these benefits available. Moreover, obtaining a post-secondary degree is a time-consuming process, especially for those who work at the same time. See, Cappelli, "Why Do Employers Pay for College?"

[10]Colleen Flaherty Manchester, "The Effect of Tuition Reimbursement on Turnover: A Case Study Analysis," in *The Analysis of Firms and Employees: Quantitative and Qualitative Approaches*, ed. Fredrik Andersson, Julia Lane, and Kathryn Shaw (Chicago: University of Chicago Press, 2008), 197–228; and Daron Acemoglu and Jorn Steffen Pischke, "The Structure of Wages and Investment in General Training," *Journal of Political Economy* 107, no. 3 (June 1999): 539–72.

and by encouraging higher worker retention rates (lower turnover). There are a number of plausible reasons for these higher retention rates, even though they might initially appear to conflict with expectations based on the standard on-the-job training model.

Experience and Productivity

Human capital theory suggests that the reason earnings tend to increase with experience in the labor market is that on-the-job training augments worker productivity. However, critics of the human capital explanation argue that it is not clear that the productivity-enhancing effects of on-the-job training actually *cause* these higher earnings.[11] Particular controversy has centered on the reward to tenure with the firm: whether tenure boosts earnings above and beyond the return to general labor market experience and, if it does, whether this is due to the productivity-enhancing effects of firm-specific training.

For example, the rise in earnings with tenure may simply reflect the widespread use of **seniority arrangements**, which appear to govern wage setting to some extent in the nonunion as well as in the union sector. (*Seniority arrangements* refer to employer policies mandating pay increases based on seniority—length of time with the firm, regardless of merit/productivity.) Of course, this reasoning does not explain why firms would adhere to this practice if more senior workers were not also generally more productive.

Another alternative to the human capital explanation is that upward-sloping earnings profiles, which reward experience with the firm (tenure), raise workers' productivity because employees are motivated to work hard so as to remain with the firm until retirement and, thus, reap the higher earnings that come with longer tenure.[12] This relationship is in the interest of both workers and firms because the resulting increased productivity makes possible both higher earnings and higher profits. Note that, in this model, even though workers are induced to put forth extra effort and are thus more productive, their higher productivity is *not* due to training and their productivity does *not* rise with firm tenure.

It is difficult to obtain data to shed light on whether the returns to tenure are due to human capital or an alternative explanation because information on actual productivity of workers is seldom available.[13] Moreover, while there is considerable consensus in the empirical literature that there is a substantial positive return to general labor market experience, there is more disagreement about the magnitude of the contribution to wage growth of the return to tenure.[14]

---

[11]For an early critique, see James L. Medoff and Katherine G. Abraham, "Are Those Paid More Really More Productive? The Case of Experience," *Journal of Human Resources* 16, no. 2 (Spring 1981): 186–216.

[12]This theoretical model was developed by Edward P. Lazear, "Why Is There Mandatory Retirement?" *Journal of Political Economy* 87 (December 1979): 1261–84.

[13]For an interesting study providing evidence supportive of a role for tenure in increasing productivity (based on productivity data), see Kathryn Shaw and Edward P. Lazear, "Tenure and Output," *Labour Economics* 15, no. 4 (August 2008): 704–23.

[14]One possibility is that the estimated return to tenure is just a statistical artifact because "good matches" between workers and firms tend to last longer; see Katherine G. Abraham and Henry Farber, "Job Duration, Seniority, and Earnings," *American Economic Review* 77, no. 3 (June 1987): 278–97. For a useful summary and more recent findings, see Moshe Buchinsky, Denis Fougère, Francis Kramarz, and Rusty Tchernis, "Interfirm Mobility, Wages and the Returns to Seniority and Experience in the U.S.," *Review of Economic Studies* 77, no. 3 (July 2010): 972–1001. One analysis of factors explaining earnings growth over the career finds that general skill accumulation is the most important factor; however, job seniority (tenure) and job mobility also play a role; see Joseph G. Altonji, Anthony Smith, and Ivan Vidangos, "Modeling Earnings Dynamics," *Econometrica* 81, no.4 (July 2013): 1395–1454.

From the perspective of the individual, the factors influencing the investment decision are not affected by the reasons for the upward-sloping tenure-earnings profile. It is the magnitude of costs versus benefits that is the individual's principal concern. Even if the upward-sloping tenure-earnings profile reflects an incentive structure offered to the worker by a particular firm, the situation is similar to firm-specific training in that the higher earnings will only be available to the worker if he or she remains at that firm.

Gender Differences in Training Investment Decisions

Expected Work Life

As in the case of investments in education, human capital theory provides insights into gender differences in training investment decisions. Specifically, as we shall see, adherence to traditional gender roles, as reflected by women's shorter expected work lives and greater labor market intermittency, lowers women's incentives to invest.

The impact of women's shorter, more disrupted work lives is illustrated in Figure 9-3. Let us assume TT' represents the earnings profile of a worker with general training who works continuously in the labor market. Here we see that, just as in the case of formal education, the gross return to on-the-job training depends upon the number of years over which the return is earned. Jane, who plans to be in the labor market for a shorter period of time than Lisa, will find the investment in on-the-job training less profitable. For example, suppose she expects to work R' years and then return after an interruption of $R''-R'$ years. Her benefits are reduced by the time spent out of the labor force when her earnings are zero. Further, it is expected that, due to depreciation of skills, the workforce interruption will lower

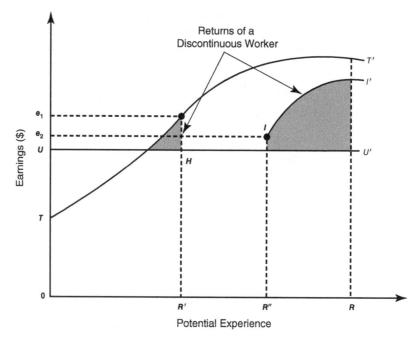

FIGURE 9-3 The Impact of Expected Work Life on the Training Investment Decision

her earnings profile when she returns from the profile of a continuous worker (TT') to the postinterruption profile (II'), resulting in a further loss of benefits. Although we have again shown the postinterruption profile II' as approaching the profile of a continuous worker TT', a lifetime loss in earnings still occurs.

Jane's gross return to her investment in general training is equal to the sum of the two shaded areas, considerably less than Lisa's return shown in Figure 9-1. Given these reductions in benefits, women following traditional gender roles are likely to find it less profitable to make large investments in general training than will career-oriented men or women. Moreover, as we noted in our discussion of field of educational specialization, if occupations differ in the amount of depreciation associated with them, women who anticipate discontinuous work lives are likely to be attracted to fields in which such depreciation is relatively small.[15]

Figure 9-3 may also be used to illustrate the consequences of the shorter and more discontinuous labor force participation of women following a traditional path for their incentives to invest in *firm-specific* training. Assume now that TT' is the earnings profile of a worker who obtained firm-specific training. The impact of work interruptions is potentially even more serious in this case, depending crucially on whether a woman is able to return to her initial employer.

Suppose Jennifer left the labor force for a substantial period of time and is unable to get her old job back. The firm-specific skills she acquired are useless in other firms. Her earnings upon her return to the labor force will be only U dollars (the earnings of an individual without training), and her new earnings profile will be UU' (the profile of an individual without training). The returns to Jennifer's previous investment in firm-specific training were completely wiped out by her withdrawal from the labor force! That is, the second shaded area shown in Figure 9-3 is eliminated, although she will still receive some returns for the brief period before she leaves the labor force. (She could start investing in training again, but the point remains that she will receive no returns from her earlier firm-specific training when she reenters the labor force.)

Thus, human capital theory suggests that individuals—most often women—who anticipate workforce interruptions, especially of long or uncertain duration, will particularly avoid jobs where firm-specific training is important. Of course, in our example, this conclusion depended on our assumption that Jennifer could not return to her original employer. However, unless an individual is guaranteed reemployment after an absence, she must always face this risk. In the past, provision of parental leave by employers was voluntary and many did not provide it, even in the case of relatively short leaves of fixed duration. That is why policies such as the Family and Medical Leave Act (FMLA) of 1993, discussed in Chapter 16, are critical to fostering investments in women's firm-specific human capital. The FMLA mandates that employers provide 12 weeks of unpaid leave, along with a guarantee of the same or an equivalent position when the worker returns to the firm.

Considerable empirical evidence supports the prediction of the human capital model that women will receive less on-the-job training than men, although much of the research on this topic used data from an earlier period in which women's

---

[15]This argument was initially developed by Solomon W. Polachek, "Occupational Self-Selection: A Human Capital Approach to Sex Differences in Occupational Structure," *Review of Economics and Statistics* 63, no. 1 (February 1981): 60–69. For a consideration of issues related to skills obsolescence, see the contributions in Andries de Grip, Jasper van Loo, and Ken Mayhew, eds., *The Economics of Skills Obsolescence,* Research in Labor Economics Vol. 21 (Bingley, UK: Emerald Group Publishing, 2002).

labor force attachment was lower.[16] This finding is consistent with employer and worker decisions based on a lower expected probability of women remaining with the firm or in the workforce. Interestingly, however, one study conducted using data for this period that explicitly examined the determinants of obtaining training found that, even though women's higher probability of turnover could explain some of the gender training difference, a major portion remained unexplained even after this and other determinants of training were taken into account.[17] This finding suggests that differences in the amount of training men and women acquire may not be fully explained by the factors emphasized in the human capital model and that discrimination (discussed in the next section) potentially plays a role.

As women's labor force attachment and career orientation have increased, so has the profitability of on-the-job training investments for them, both general and firm-specific. This suggests that some of the reduction in occupational segregation by sex that we reviewed in Chapter 7 may be due to women's greater willingness to enter jobs that require considerable amounts of training, as well as the greater willingness of employers to hire them into such jobs. Moreover, as more women are employed in jobs where they receive on-the-job training, the opportunity cost of workforce interruptions is increased and their labor force attachment is further reinforced. The most important factor in the case of firm-specific training is attachment to a particular firm. Such an attachment most likely requires that women keep any workforce interruptions within the limits of their employers' leave policy and raises the question of what such policies should be. We consider leave policies in Chapter 16.

Discrimination

The explanation for gender differences in on-the-job training investment decisions suggested by human capital theory stresses differences between men and women in anticipated labor force participation over the life cycle. It is, however, important to point out that, just as in the case of men's and women's formal education decisions, societal discrimination may also be a factor increasing the (pecuniary and nonpecuniary) costs or decreasing the (pecuniary and nonpecuniary) returns to entry into traditionally male fields. Further, labor market discrimination, which is discussed in greater detail in upcoming chapters, may also play a part in reducing women's representation in jobs where training is important. That is, overt or subtle discrimination on the part of employers, coworkers, or customers may prove an obstacle to women gaining access to jobs in such areas or reduce the pay of those who are able to obtain employment.

Firm-specific training provides a particular rationale for employer discrimination that may be important. As illustrated in Figure 9-2, the employer is expected to share some of the costs of firm-specific training. The returns to the firm's (as well as to the worker's) investment depend on how long the individual remains with the firm. Thus, if employers believe that women are less likely to stay at the firm than men,

---

[16]See, for example, Joseph G. Altonji and James R. Spletzer, "Worker Characteristics, Job Characteristics, and the Receipt of On-the-Job Training," *Industrial and Labor Relations Review* 45, no. 1 (October 1991): 58–79; John Barron and Dan A. Black, "Gender Differences in Training, Capital and Wages," *Journal of Human Resources* 28, no. 2 (Spring 1993): 342–64; and Reed Neil Olsen and Edwin A. Sexton, "Gender Differences in the Returns to and the Acquisition of On-the-Job Training," *Industrial Relations* 35, no. 1 (January 1996): 59–77.

[17]Anne Beeson Royalty, "The Effects of Job Turnover on the Training of Men and Women," *Industrial and Labor Relations Review* 49, no. 3 (April 1996): 506–21.

on average, they may prefer men for jobs that require considerable specific training. Employers' differential treatment of men and women on the basis of their perceptions of average gender differences in productivity or job stability has been termed **statistical discrimination** and will be discussed further in Chapter 11. Such behavior on the part of employers can restrict opportunities for career-oriented as well as non-career-oriented women, if employers cannot easily distinguish between them.

Finally, labor market discrimination may indirectly lower women's incentives to invest in themselves by decreasing the rewards for doing so. The possibility of such *feedback effects* is considered in greater detail in Chapter 11.

Occupations and Earnings

The analysis of gender differences in occupations and earnings based on the human capital model is quite straightforward. It is assumed that, given the traditional division of labor in the family, most women do indeed anticipate shorter and less continuous work careers than men. Thus, women are expected to select occupations requiring less investment in education and on-the-job training than those chosen by men. They will particularly avoid jobs in which firm-specific training is important, and employers will be reluctant to hire them for such jobs. Further, they will seek jobs where depreciation of earnings for time spent out of the labor force is minimal.

Hypothetical earnings profiles for predominantly male and predominantly female jobs are shown in Figure 9-4. For simplicity, we assume all workers have the same amount of formal schooling. Earnings profiles in predominantly male jobs are expected to slope steeply upward, as does profile MM', because men are expected to undertake substantial investments in on-the-job training. Women, on the other hand, are expected to choose the flatter profile FF', representing smaller amounts of investment in on-the-job training. The existence of the crossover point, H, is crucial to this argument. Before H, profile FF' lies above profile MM'. It is argued that women choose higher earnings now in preference to higher earnings in the future because they do not expect to be in the labor market long enough for the larger human capital investment to pay off. Thus, we see that the human capital analysis of on-the-job training decisions, in conjunction with our previous discussion of formal education, can provide an explanation for the occupational segregation by gender detailed in Chapter 7.

The human capital analysis can also provide an explanation for gender differences in earnings. As we saw in Chapter 8, the human capital model can explain past differences in college graduation by women and men (which have now reversed), as well as differences in fields of specialization (which persist today). For given levels of formal education, our consideration of on-the-job training investments also gives us reasons to expect women to earn less, on average. The crucial factors behind gender differences in pay are gender differences in labor market experience and the associated gender differences in on-the-job training.

Figure 9-4 illustrates the relationship between experience and earnings for women and men with the same levels of education. (For simplicity, we abstract from gender differences in fields of specialization.) Mean female earnings are $\bar{E}_f$ dollars and are less than male mean earnings of $\bar{E}_m$ dollars. Why do women earn less? First, on average they have less labor market experience than men—$\bar{X}_f$ is less than $\bar{X}_m$. Because earnings tend to increase with experience, women's lesser experience decreases their earnings relative to men's. Second, as we have just seen, men are

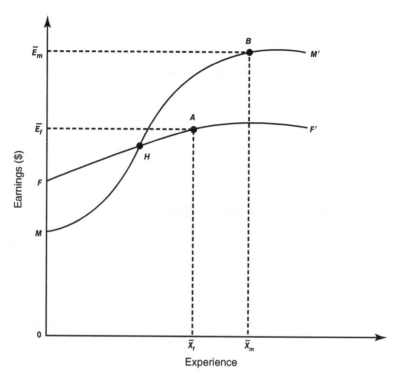

FIGURE 9-4 On-the-Job Training and Sex Differences in Occupations and Earnings

expected to undertake more substantial investments in on-the-job training and hence to have steeper earnings profiles. This means that they experience larger increases in earnings for additional years of experience. After crossover point *H*, this difference in returns produces a widening gap between male and female earnings with increasing labor market experience.

Temporal Flexibility and the Gender Wage Gap

Recent work by Claudia Goldin points to the impact of **temporal flexibility** (or the lack thereof) as an alternative to gender differences in human capital (or discrimination) for explaining the gender wage gap. *Temporal flexibility* refers to the flexibility of work schedules as they pertain to hours worked per day and per week, where the work is performed, and the need to work specific days and times.[18] Goldin's main focus is on hours and, in particular, on the disproportionate rewards in some occupations and firms for working long hours and particular hours (e.g., a lawyer being available for face time during the standard business day or a lawyer working extremely long hours right before a case comes to trial). Such pressures are likely to

---

[18]Claudia Goldin, "A Grand Convergence: Its Last Chapter," *American Economic Review* 104, no. 4 (May 2014): 1091–1119; and for a useful summary in less technical terms, Claudia Goldin, "How to Achieve Gender Equality," *Milken Institute Review* Q3 (July 2015): 24–33. For an empirical analysis of the impact of long hours on trends in the gender wage gap, see Youngjoo Cha and Kim A. Weeden, "Overwork and the Slow Convergence in the Gender Gap in Wages," *American Sociological Review* 79, no. 3 (June 2014): 457–84.

be particularly acute in a number of highly skilled occupations like law and management. Goldin sees gender pay differences as arising because of differences across workplaces in the value of long hours. The result is what economists term a **compensating differential**. Workers willing to provide longer hours or cover certain time periods receive a wage premium; workers who are not willing to do so incur a wage penalty. Given the traditional gender division of labor within the home, which, as we found in Chapter 4, persists to some extent today, women are more likely than men to value flexibility and hence to bear a wage penalty. While Goldin's main focus is on hours of work, as she notes, workforce interruptions can also be analyzed in a similar way. She suggests this is why even brief interruptions may have quite negative effects on women's wages in some fields.

Goldin points to the importance of occupational characteristics that make providing temporal flexibility extremely costly in some sectors and relatively inexpensive in others. The wage penalty for flexibility is likely to be high in jobs that require meeting deadlines (time pressure), being in contact with others to perform the job, maintaining and establishing interpersonal relationships, adhering to preset schedules, and doing work for which other workers are not close substitutes. As an example, long hours may be required of lawyers at large, high-powered firms who have to meet the needs of clients with complex cases that require ongoing, close attention by a single individual and cannot be readily handed over to other employees. The trade-off is working in a different department at the same firm (or at a smaller firm) where the legal work is more general in nature, the continuity of the employment relationship matters less, and the pay is lower. While there will be a pay difference between lawyers in the different work settings due to the compensating differential, the level of human capital of both lawyers may be the same.

A contrast to law is provided by the field of pharmacy, where most workers are employed by large firms and computerization facilitates substitutability across workers and thus flexibility in work hours and scheduling. In this field the penalties for part-time or part-year work are small, as is the gender wage gap.[19]

The Goldin analysis suggests that rewards to long hours in some settings, as well as penalties to workforce interruptions, are susceptible to other interpretations than human capital. Goldin highlights the costs of providing flexibility in some workplaces. Another interesting perspective, which provides an alternative to both the human capital and Goldin's explanations as an interpretation of long hours, is signaling—a concept we discussed in Chapter 8 in the context of the returns to education. In this case, employers may use longer hours and workforce continuity as a signal or a screen to identify workers with a greater willingness to work hard, as well as greater motivation and commitment.[20] Related to this argument, employers may engage in statistical discrimination against the "type" of worker who puts a high value on flexibility, believing that on average such workers are less productive. The concept of statistical discrimination is discussed in greater detail in Chapter 11.

Goldin's work suggests a link between occupations that demand long hours and a gender gap in wages within such jobs. Although not considered by Goldin, it seems

---

[19]Claudia Goldin and Lawrence F. Katz, "A Most Egalitarian Profession: Pharmacy and the Evolution of a Family Friendly Occupation," *Journal of Labor Economics* 34, no. 3 (July 2016): 705–46.

[20]For an example of a model related to the legal profession where employers use hours as a screen, see Renée M. Landers, James B. Rebitzer, and Lowell J. Taylor, "Rat Race Redux: Adverse Selection in the Determination of Work Hours in Law Firms," *American Economic Review* 86, no. 3 (1996): 329–48.

plausible that the requirement of long hours in an occupation may also contribute to occupational segregation as women, particularly mothers or those who would like to have children, may avoid such jobs. Some support for this reasoning is provided in a study that found that mothers were more likely to leave predominantly male occupations when they had been working 50 hours or more per week but that this was not the case for men or for women who did not have children present.[21]

Family-Related Earnings Gaps

Traditional gender roles, which result in women being viewed as the secondary earner in the family, may work to produce differences in economic outcomes in a variety of ways beyond their impact on human capital investments.[22] In the following sections, we first consider a number of ways in which adherence to traditional gender roles in the family could reduce women's wages relative to men's. We then examine the evidence on how various dimensions of family—marriage, children, and employment of a spouse—affect women's and men's wages (compared to others of the same sex) and discuss the underlying factors that contribute to such differentials.

Traditional Gender Roles and Gender Wage Gaps

How do traditional gender roles—particularly women being viewed as the secondary earner in the family—potentially impact gender wage differentials? There are a number of ways in which this could occur, and we describe them in the following sections. However, as with the human capital investment decisions we discussed earlier, it is important to bear in mind that women's decisions concerning the priority they place on their own versus their husbands' careers, the amount of housework they do, the adaptations they make in response to family responsibilities, and so on may reflect social pressures as well as voluntary choices. Moreover, to the extent that women face discrimination in the labor market that decreases their wages relative to their husbands', traditional gender roles in the family are reinforced. This is the case because discrimination lowers the opportunity cost to wives of sacrificing their career objectives to family demands relative to their husbands' opportunity cost. Finally, as discussed, the lack of temporal flexibility in many work settings imposes constraints on women as they seek to balance family responsibilities.

WOMEN'S GREATER RESPONSIBILITY FOR HOUSEWORK AND CAREGIVING
Women's generally greater nonmarket responsibilities could impact labor market outcomes for women and men in a number of ways. The longer hours that married women and mothers tend to spend in these activities may reduce the effort that they put into their market jobs and thus decrease their hourly wages compared to men

---

[21]Young Cha, "Overwork and the Persistence of Gender Segregation in Occupations," *Gender & Society* 27, no. 2 (2013): 158–84.

[22]One study found that wives in dual-earner couples who have the "secondary" career in their family tend to earn lower wages than those who have the "primary" career, even controlling for any differences in levels of education or actual work experience and the presence of children; see Anne E. Winkler and David C. Rose, "Career Hierarchy in Dual-Earner Families," in *Research in Labor Economics*, ed. Solomon W. Polachek (Greenwich, CT: JAI Press, 2000), 147–72.

with similar qualifications.[23] Indeed, it has been found that additional hours spent on housework by workers are associated with lower wages, all else equal.[24]

In addition to the possibility that responsibility for housework reduces work effort, it may also result in women trading off earnings for other aspects of the job that are desirable to them. They may, for example, seek jobs with greater temporal flexibility (e.g., shorter or more convenient hours) or closer proximity to home, or they may take a lower-paying, less-demanding position or a job that does not require a lot of work-related travel. In other cases, when women, particularly mothers, are in jobs with inflexible hours, they may have greater absenteeism, for example, when they take time off to care for a sick child or to take their child to an appointment. Their job performance ratings and wages may consequently suffer.[25]

GENDER DIFFERENCES IN QUITTING   Gender differences in quit behavior can also differentially impact the labor market outcomes of men and women. For example, it is often claimed that, due to family responsibilities, women workers have higher quit rates than men workers, making employers reluctant to invest in their job-related skills. As we shall see in Chapter 11, this turns out not to be the case. While some evidence suggests that women workers may have higher quit rates on average than men, most of this gender difference is due to the types of jobs they are in and the worker's personal characteristics. That is, all else equal, women are no more likely to quit than their male counterparts. However, consistent with women placing a greater priority on family responsibilities to the detriment of their labor market outcomes, evidence indicates that women are more likely to quit their jobs for *family-related reasons*. These types of quits negatively affect subsequent earnings as workers lose seniority and firm-specific training. Men are more likely to quit for *job-related reasons*; such quits tend to positively affect subsequent earnings as workers are bid away to higher-paying opportunities.[26]

GENDER AND THE LOCATION OF THE FAMILY   To the extent that families place priority on the husband's, rather than on the wife's, career in determining the location of the family, her earnings are likely to be decreased. She may be a "tied mover," relocating when it is not advantageous for her to leave a job where she has accumulated considerable seniority and firm-specific training. Alternatively, she

---

[23]See Gary S. Becker, "The Allocation of Effort, Specific Human Capital, and the Differences between Men and Women in Earnings and Occupations," *Journal of Labor Economics* 3, no. 1, pt. 2 (January 1985): 33–58.

[24]For evidence that housework reduces wages, see Joni Hersch and Leslie S. Stratton, "Housework, Fixed Effects and Wages of Married Workers," *Journal of Human Resources* 32, no. 2 (Spring 1997): 285–307; and Joni Hersch, "Home Production and Wages: Evidence from the American Time Use Survey," *Review of Economics of the Household* 7, no. 2 (June 2009): 159–78.

[25]Deborah J. Anderson, Melissa Binder, and Kate Krause, "The Motherhood Wage Penalty Revisited: Experience, Heterogeneity, Work Effort and Work-Schedule Flexibility," *Industrial and Labor Relations Review* 56, no. 2 (January 2003): 273–94; and Leslie S. Stratton, "Why Does More Housework Lower Women's Wages? Testing Hypotheses Involving Job Effort and Hours Flexibility," *Social Science Quarterly* 82, no. 1 (March 2001): 67–76.

[26]Kristen Keith and Abagail McWilliams, "The Wage Effects of Cumulative Job Mobility," *Industrial and Labor Relations Review* 49, no. 1 (October 1995): 121–37; and Sylvia Fuller, "Job Mobility and Wage Trajectories for Men and Women in the United States," *American Sociological Review* 73 (February 2008): 158–83. One study found that the gender difference in the reason for quits was concentrated among workers with a high school education or less, with little gender difference for those who had attended college; see Anne Beeson Royalty, "Job-to-Job and Job-to-Nonemployment Turnover by Gender and Education Level," *Journal of Labor Economics* 16, no. 2 (April 1998): 392–443.

may be a "tied stayer," unable to relocate despite good opportunities elsewhere.[27] Anticipation of a lesser ability to determine the geographic location of the family may also lead women to select occupations in which jobs are likely to be readily obtained in any labor market, thus constraining their occupational choices. For example, even as women have entered higher-level, traditionally male occupations in recent years, their entry into more geographically dispersed occupations (e.g., physicians, accountants, pharmacists, and managers) has been considerably greater than their entry into those that tend to be more geographically clustered (e.g., specialized engineers and physical scientists, occupations that are likely to be located near national laboratories).[28]

Some couples do try to accommodate the careers of both spouses and make a joint location decision, but doing so may limit the career prospects of both partners. One solution might be to live in a big city that would offer more job opportunities for both spouses, and in fact, big cities are home to an increasing share of highly educated couples. At present, it is not yet clear whether this growing fraction is a result of decisions by highly educated married couples to locate in a big city or whether such cities are simply desirable locations for highly educated individuals, whether unmarried or married.[29]

Wage Penalties and Premiums Associated with Marriage and Parenthood

Further evidence suggesting that women's nonmarket responsibilities may negatively affect their labor market outcomes is provided by the differential effects that marriage and parenthood have on men's and women's wages. We consider the male marriage premium and the motherhood wage penalty in the following sections.

MALE MARRIAGE PREMIUM   Considerable evidence suggests that men's earnings rise with marriage. It is likely that this **male marriage premium** is primarily due to the benefits husbands reap from specialization in the family: to the extent their wives have primary responsibility for the home and children, husbands can devote greater attention to their jobs. Further, with one career as the primary focus of the family, both spouses can concentrate on making that career as successful as possible. The positive association between men's wages and marriage may also reflect the personal characteristics of married men, such as a greater ability to get along with others, that make them more likely both to marry and to be successful at work. Related to this is that, given traditional gender roles, women may select spouses with higher earning potential.[30] To the extent that married men simply differ from unmarried men on personal characteristics that are positively related

[27]See, early work by Jacob Mincer, "Family Migration Decisions," *Journal of Political Economy* 86, no. 5 (October 1978): 749–73; and Thomas J. Cooke, Paul Boyle, and Kenneth Couch, "A Longitudinal Analysis of Family Migration and the Gender Gap in Earnings in the United States and Great Britain," *Demography* 46, no. 1 (February 2009): 147–67.

[28]Alan Benson, "Re-thinking the Two-Body Problem: The Segregation of Women into Geographically-Flexible Occupations," *Demography* 51, no. 5 (October 2014): 1619–39.

[29]Dora Costa and Matthew E. Kahn provide evidence that "power couples" choose to locate in big cities in "Power Couples: Changes in the Locational Choice of the College-Educated, 1940–1990," *Quarterly Journal of Economics* 115, no. 4 (November 2000): 1287–1315; while Janice Compton and Robert A. Pollak question this conclusion in "Why Are Power Couples Increasingly Concentrated in Large Metropolitan Areas?" *Journal of Labor Economics* 25, no. 3 (July 2007): 475–512.

[30]We consider the economic determinants of marriage in more detail in Chapter 13.

to wages, the observed positive relationship between marriage and male wages may not be causal. However, the majority of evidence suggests that marriage does cause men's wages to be higher.[31]

The presence of children also appears to boost men's earnings, presumably because fatherhood increases their incentive to work harder to support the family.[32] Some evidence suggests that this effect is greater for fathers of male compared to female children, implying some preference for boys.[33]

MOTHERHOOD WAGE PENALTY The effect of family on women's earnings is quite different from the case for men. For one, married women do not receive a premium compared to unmarried women. Further, considerable evidence shows that mothers earn less than women without children, a finding commonly known as the **motherhood wage penalty**.[34] Much of the explanation for this penalty is that mothers tend to have lesser levels of labor market experience, either because of time out of the labor force or time spent in part-time work, which tends to be associated with lower wages and lower returns to experience. But what raises particular attention is that the motherhood penalty exists even for mothers with the same labor market experience and education as nonmothers.[35] A variety of explanations have been offered, and it may well be that all play a role to some degree.

One factor that likely contributes to the motherhood wage penalty is that some mothers are not able to return to their previous employer after childbirth but instead must change firms, especially if their employer does not provide adequate maternity leave. Women in this situation lose out on the benefits of firm-specific training and potential rewards from an especially good initial job match.[36] This explanation has likely become less important since the passage of the 1993 FMLA, which provides 12 weeks of unpaid family leave. Nevertheless, as discussed further in Chapter 16, many workers are not covered by the legislation or a similar policy provided by their employer and so may have no alternative but to start over with a new firm after the

---

[31]For a comprehensive review of studies on the marriage premium for men, see David C. Ribar, "What Do Social Scientists Know About the Benefits of Marriage? A Review of Quantitative Methodologies," IZA Discussion Paper 998 (IZA, Bonn, Germany, January 2004). One study using data from Norway has challenged the view that marriage is causal; it finds that men who eventually marry choose higher-paying occupations even *before* they marry; see Trond Petersen, Andrew M. Penner, and Geir Høgsnes, "The Male Marital Wage Premium: Sorting Versus Differential Pay," *Industrial and Labor Relations Review* 64, no. 2 (2011): 283–304.

[32]Shelly J. Lundberg and Elaina Rose, "Parenthood and the Earnings of Married Men and Women," *Labour Economics* 7, no. 6 (November 2000): 689–710; and Michelle J. Budig, *The Fatherhood Bonus & the Motherhood Penalty: Parenthood and the Gender Gap in Pay* (Washington, DC: Third Way, September 2, 2014), www.thirdway.org.

[33]Shelly J. Lundberg and Elaina Rose, "The Effects of Sons and Daughters on Men's Labor Supply and Wages," *Review of Economics and Statistics* 84, no. 2 (May 2002): 251–68.

[34]For a review of the evidence across a number of countries, see Wendy Sigle-Rushton and Jane Waldfogel, "Motherhood and Women's Earnings in Anglo-American, Continental European, and Nordic Countries," *Feminist Economics* 13, no. 2 (April 2007): 55–91. For a study on the United States, see Budig, *The Fatherhood Bonus & the Motherhood Penalty.*

[35]One exception is a study by Jeremy Staff and Jeylan T. Mortimer which focuses exclusively on women at the start of their careers, defined as ages 19 to 31. After accounting for finely grained information on cumulative work experience, they find no remaining gap; see "Explaining the Motherhood Wage Penalty During the Early Occupational Career," *Demography* 49 (2012): 1–21.

[36]Jane Waldfogel points to this issue and the potential benefits of adequate family leave, in "Working Mothers Then and Now: A Cross Cohort Analysis of the Effects of Maternity Leave on Women's Pay," in *Gender and Family Issues in the Workplace*, ed. Francine D. Blau and Ronald Ehrenberg (New York, Russell Sage Foundation, 1997), 92–126. The rest of the explanations offered here are nicely summarized in Sigle-Rushton and Waldfogel, "Motherhood and Women's Earnings."

birth of a child. Moreover, women may choose to stay out of the labor force for longer than the 12-week leave time allowed by the law or any additional leave time offered by their employer.

The motherhood penalty may also arise from the fact that women, even those employed full-time, continue to bear primary responsibility for the household and children. In the preceding section, we discussed why this might lower the earnings of women in general, and this would be particularly true of mothers since they have greater household responsibilities. This might also lead women to change firms (or occupations) to find positions that are more compatible with the demands of motherhood, and such jobs may provide flexibility at the cost of lower earnings. This possibility was suggested by our earlier discussion of temporal flexibility.

There may also be labor market discrimination against mothers. Such discrimination is suggested by a study that finds that women, but not men, face differential treatment based on parental status. In this study, the researchers first conducted a laboratory experiment in which they asked student evaluators to assess résumés of equally qualified same-sex (female or male) job applicants who differed only as to whether they were parents or not. Mothers were perceived by the student evaluators as less competent and less committed to paid work than nonmothers, and the evaluators recommended lower starting salaries for them. In contrast, student evaluators did not penalize men for being fathers and, indeed, perceived them to be more committed and recommended higher starting salaries for them. The researchers further confirmed the real-world implications of their findings from the lab experiment using a field experiment. (We discuss laboratory and field experiments further later in this chapter in the section on "Gender Differences in Psychological Attributes.") They sent résumés and cover letters from fictional, equally qualified, same-sex applicants to employers advertising for job openings. Strikingly, they found that prospective employers called mothers back only about half as often as nonmothers, while fathers were not disadvantaged in the hiring process.[37]

Why might employers discriminate against mothers relative to nonmothers? One possibility is that that they perceive mothers as a group to be less productive, on average, due to the types of factors we have previously discussed—their greater responsibility for housework, constraints on work schedules and travel, and so on. Employers may respond by discriminating against mothers based on their perceptions of average differences in productivity between mothers and nonmothers. This is another example of statistical discrimination, a discrimination model we consider further in Chapter 11. As we noted previously, statistical discrimination results in all members of a group—in this case mothers—being penalized, even those as equally committed and career-oriented as nonmothers.

Finally, it is important to note that parenthood may not directly *cause* wages for mothers to be lower. Rather, women (and men) who become parents may have different attributes from those who do not have children. For instance, it may be the case that women who are especially career-oriented are more likely to remain childless.[38]

---

[37]Shelley J. Correll, Stephen Benard, and In Paik, "Getting a Job: Is There a Motherhood Penalty?" *American Journal of Sociology* 112, no. 5 (2007): 1297–1338. Parental status was subtly indicated by including information on the application such as PTA coordinator for a parent and fundraiser for a neighborhood association for a nonparent. The field experiment potion of this study used an "audit study" methodology; this method is explained further in Chapter 10.

[38]Lundberg and Rose, "Parenthood and the Earnings of Married Men and Women."

Gender Differences in Psychological Attributes

Traditionally, when labor economists have sought to explain labor market behavior and outcomes, they have relied on what might be termed economic variables—that is variables that have been identified as important in economic models. This has been in large part the approach we have taken in this book. So, for example, when analyzing labor supply behavior, the impact of wages and nonlabor income is emphasized. And, as we shall see in Chapter 13, these same factors are believed to play a role in explaining a number of demographic decisions like marriage, divorce, and fertility rates. When the focus is on explaining wage and occupational outcomes, the impact of human capital investments (education and on-the-job training) and the possible role of labor market discrimination are emphasized. When information is available, the role of cognitive skills, as measured by IQ and academic achievement tests, has also been considered.

In recent years, however, labor economists have become increasingly interested in the effect of psychological attributes on labor market outcomes and behavior. This trend has been driven by a number of factors, but perhaps most important is that, although considerable evidence supports the importance of traditional economic variables in explaining labor market behavior and outcomes, there is almost always a sizeable component of any behavior or outcome that is not explained by economic variables. This has led researchers to reach out beyond the confines of traditional economic models for explanations.

A leader in this approach is Nobel laureate James Heckman, who has been a strong advocate for the importance of what he terms "soft skills" in influencing the behavior and outcomes economists analyze. Heckman and Tim Kautz define **soft skills** as "personality traits, goals, motivations, and preferences that are valued in the labor market, in school, and in many other domains."[39] Other oft-used synonyms are **noncognitive skills** and **psychological attributes**. Here we use the latter term, *psychological attributes*, because much of this research has its origins in psychology.[40] In this section, we discuss some psychological attributes that research suggests systematically differ between women and men and that are believed to influence labor market outcomes—these include gender differences in attitudes toward negotiation, competition, and risk and in what are known as the "Big Five" personality traits in psychology (as defined later in this section).

In considering gender differences in psychological attributes, a number of cautions must be borne in mind. First, even if men and women do differ on average, it is not possible at this point to know what has caused the observed gender differences—the role of nature, nurture, or both, a topic we discussed in Chapter 2. Social influences could have caused or at least contributed to the observed gender differences, and therefore, one should not assume that all observed average differences between men and women on various psychological traits are entirely due to biological factors.

---

[39]James J. Heckman and Tim Kautz, "Hard Evidence on Soft Skills," Adam Smith Lecture, *Labour Economics*, 19, no. 4 (August 2012): 451–64; quotation is from p. 451. This is an excellent overview and summary of the role of both cognitive and noncognitive skills in influencing important outcomes.

[40]For two excellent reviews of the evidence on gender differences in psychological attributes and preferences, see Marianne Bertrand, "New Perspectives on Gender," in *Handbook of Labor Economics*, vol. 4b, ed. Orley C. Ashenfelter and David Card (Amsterdam: Elsevier, 2010), 1545–92; and Rachel Croson and Uri Gneezy, "Gender Differences in Preferences," *Journal of Economic Literature* 47 no. 2 (June 2009): 448–74. In using the term *psychological attributes*, we follow Bertrand.

Moreover, whatever their origin (nature or nurture), gender differences may still be malleable—so, for example, women may be encouraged to negotiate and offered tips on improving their skills.[41]

Second, gender differences in all psychological attributes do not necessarily favor men. For example, there is some evidence that women have better interpersonal or "people" skills than men; people skills are related to sociability and include being adept at various tasks that require interacting with people, such as working with a team, teaching or training others, persuading or influencing others, caring for clients, and listening to colleagues. Such interpersonal skills have been found to be an advantage in many settings.[42] Another area where differences favor women is that, as we saw in the preceding chapter, the greater behavioral problems of boys appear to contribute to their lower rate of college-going.[43] Also, it should be noted that a particular psychological attribute—like men's willingness to compete or lower risk aversion—may be an advantage in some settings but a disadvantage in others.

Third, most of the evidence on gender differences in psychological attributes, and their effect on labor market outcomes, has been gleaned from **laboratory (lab) experiments**. In a lab experiment, an outcome is observed after subjects (often undergraduates) are randomly assigned to "treatment" and "control" groups and other environmental influences are carefully controlled. One question that often comes up is the generalizability of such findings to the real world. **Field experiments** are performed in the real world and "blend experimental methods with field-based research, relaxing certain controls over environmental influences to better simulate real-world interactions."[44] So, for example, in this approach, as we earlier saw applied to investigating the motherhood penalty, a researcher might send out fictitious résumés to employers, where the résumés are effectively the same except for a variable like gender and employers are randomly selected to receive a résumé from a male or a female. Field experiments might be regarded as providing more generalizable results, but even in this case, there may be questions about how well the researcher can set up the experiment to duplicate what would occur in a real-world setting.[45]

Fourth, and perhaps most importantly, it is essential not to let the study of gender differences in various traits lead to the stereotyping of girls and boys or men and women. Regardless of the source of observed gender differences—nature, nurture, or both—there is generally considerable variation among men and women around the average. Stereotypical views may thus adversely impact behavior and outcomes for both women and men who do not conform to the stereotypes. So, for example, highly qualified individuals may be discouraged from entering a particular profession because they belong to a group that is, on average, less qualified for it. In addition, as we shall see in our discussion of "stereotype threat" and mathematics in

---

[41]A number of programs have been or are being developed to do this, see Jessica Bennett, "How to Attack the Gender Wage Gap? Speak Up," *New York Times*, December 15, 2012, www.nytimes.com.
[42]Lex Borghans, Bas ter Weel, and Bruce Weinberg, "People Skills and the Labor Market Outcomes of Underrepresented Groups," *Industrial and Labor Relations Review* 67, no. 2 (April 2014): 287–334.
[43]For further discussion and evidence, see Bertrand, "New Perspectives on Gender."
[44]Devah Pager, "The Use of Field Experiments for Studies of Employment Discrimination: Contributions, Critiques, and Directions for the Future," *Annals of the American Academy of Political and Social Science* 609 (2007): 103–33; quotation is from p. 109.
[45]One of the critiques concerns questions about appropriate matching (in this case, are the résumés truly identical). For reviews of the issues in the use of this method, see Glenn W. Harrison and John A. List, "Field Experiments," *Journal of Economic Literature* 52, no. 4 (December 2004): 1009–55; and Pager, "The Use of Field Experiments."

the next section, the stereotypes themselves may adversely affect the performance of individuals, further compounding their negative effects.

Attitudes toward Negotiating

Researchers have found that men's and women's propensity to negotiate differs, with women feeling much more apprehensive about negotiating and being much less likely to do so. This means that women may be less likely than men to negotiate over salaries, raises, or promotions, thus reducing their pay relative to men's. A comprehensive examination of the gender gap in negotiating attributes the gender difference to social factors that hold women back.[46] As one of the leading researchers in the field, Linda Babcock, explains, "this reluctance to promote their own interests [that is, to negotiate] is not an innate quality or a genetic blind spot in women. As a society, we teach little girls . . . that it's not nice or feminine or appropriate for them to focus on what they want and pursue their self-interest—and we don't like it when they do."[47] Women are socialized to feel that they are being pushy or overbearing if they pursue their own goals in the face of conflict with others (including, say, employers or coworkers). Consistent with the notion that the female gender role is seen as incongruent with negotiating, it has been found that gender differences in negotiating outcomes are reduced when women negotiate on behalf of *another individual* rather than on their *own behalf.* The reason for this difference is that when women negotiate on behalf of others, this behavior is consistent with gender norms about their expected caring role, and thus they are more likely to be successful.[48] Further, women have likely learned as a result of a variety of personal experiences that asserting their own needs can trigger a negative response from others.

A recent study based on a field experiment suggests that gender differences in negotiating behavior may also be sensitive to the cues given. The study examined the response of applicants to two different job advertisements—one that explicitly stated that wages were negotiable and another that left this ambiguous. The researchers found that men were more likely to negotiate than women when there was no *explicit* statement that wages were negotiable. However, when it was explicitly stated that wages were negotiable, the gender difference disappeared and even reversed.[49] These findings suggest that if employers provided more explicit statements about when negotiation is expected, it could help to reduce women's hesitation about engaging in negotiating.

---

[46]In this section, we draw on Linda Babcock and Sara Laschever, *Women Don't Ask: Negotiation and the Gender Divide* (Princeton, NJ: Princeton University Press, 2003); Hannah Riley Bowles, "Psychological Perspectives on Gender in Negotiation," in *The Sage Handbook of Gender and Psychology*, ed. Michelle K. Ryan and Nyla R. Branscombe (Los Angeles: Sage, 2013), 465–83; and Hannah R. Bowles, Linda Babcock, and Lei Lai, "Social Incentives for Sex Differences in the Propensity to Initiate Negotiation: Sometimes It Does Hurt to Ask," *Organizational Behavior and Human Decision Processes* 103, no. 1 (May 2007): 84–103. For useful advice on negotiating, see Linda Babcock and Sara Laschever, *Ask for It: How Women Can Use the Power of Negotiation to Get What They Really Want* (New York: Bantam Books, 2008).

[47]Linda Babcock, "Women, Repeat This: Don't Ask, Don't Get," *New York Times*, April 6, 2008, www.nytimes.com.

[48]Jens Mazei, Joachim Hüffmeier, Philipp Alexander Freund, Alice F. Stuhlmacher, Lena Bilke, and Guido Hertel, "A Meta-Analysis on Gender Differences in Negotiation Outcomes and Their Moderators," *Psychological Bulletin* 141, no. 1 (January 2015): 85–104.

[49]Andreas Leibbrandt and John A. List, "Do Women Avoid Salary Negotiations? Evidence from a Large-Scale Natural Field Experiment," *Management Science* 61, no. 9 (September 2015): 2016–24.

While it is likely desirable to enhance women's negotiating skills and reduce the gender difference in negotiating, it is also important to realize that there are limitations to what may be achieved by doing so. First, research suggests that women who negotiate may elicit negative responses from others, making negotiation problematic for them, even if they are successful and possibly even reducing their probability of success. For example, in a series of laboratory experiments, study participants were asked to evaluate managers based on a transcript or a video of a job placement interview. The researchers found that the study participants were disinclined to want to work with female managers who initiated negotiations for higher compensation but the same behavior by male managers had little effect on their willingness to work with them.[50] Second, negotiation is a form of bargaining and, as such, the outcome is influenced by the alternatives available to the individual. To the extent that women face discrimination in the labor market that lowers their wages relative to men's, the expected gain from the negotiation process will be smaller than for their male counterparts.

Attitudes toward Competition

There is some evidence from laboratory experiments that men are more competitively inclined than women. For example, in one study subjects were given a task (adding up sets of two-digit numbers) for which there was no gender difference in actual performance. When given a choice between a noncompetitive compensation scheme (a piece rate—payment based on the number of problems correctly solved) and a competitive compensation scheme (a tournament where only the highest scorer out of a group of four was compensated), men overwhelmingly selected the tournament, while very few women did so. Interestingly, while high-scoring women lost out financially by shying away from competition, low-performing men actually competed too much from a payoff-maximizing perspective.[51] The gender difference in attitudes toward competition could be a disadvantage for women in the labor market, potentially lowering their relative pay and leading them to avoid certain occupations or business settings to their economic detriment. However, the research findings also suggest that men may compete more than is optimal in certain circumstances (as did the low-performing men in the experiment).

Evidence from outside the laboratory that women shy away from competitive environments is indicated by a field experiment that randomly assigned job seekers into viewing advertisements for administrative assistant positions with different compensation schemes. Individuals then decided whether or not to apply for the job. Consistent with the results of lab experiments, the more *heavily* the compensation package tilted toward rewarding the individual's performance *relative* to a coworker's performance, the more the applicant pool shifted to being more male-dominated. However, there were factors that attenuated the gender difference. There was little or no gender difference when compensation was *only slightly* (rather than *heavily*) based on individual performance relative to a coworker's performance or when the job was to be performed in teams. Further, the nature of the job—whether perceived as female or male—mattered. When the position was

---

[50]Bowles, Babcock, and Lai, "Social Incentives for Sex Differences in the Propensity to Initiate Negotiation."

[51]Muriel Niederle and Lise Vesterlund, "Do Women Shy Away from Competition?" *Quarterly Journal of Economics* 122, no. 3 (August 2007): 1067–1101.

perceived as predominantly female (involving general tasks in the predominately female job of administrative assistant), there was no gender difference in application propensity related to compensation scheme. However, a difference emerged when the job was perceived as male (the administrative assistant tasks were focused around sports).[52]

Also of interest is a study that compared the results of lab experiments testing for gender differences in preferences for competition in two different cultures. Consistent with the results for Western cultures, in a traditional patriarchal society (i.e., the Maasai of Tanzania), men opted to compete at roughly twice the rate of women. However, in a matrilineal/matrilocal society where inheritance and residence are determined by the female lineage (i.e., the Khasi of India), women chose the competitive environment more often than men and even chose to compete a bit more often than Maasai men did.[53] The findings of this study strongly suggest that men's and women's attitudes toward competition are influenced by broader social factors.

Attitudes toward Risk

Attitudes toward risk involve the willingness of individuals to accept risk (uncertain payoffs). An individual is said to be **risk-averse** if he or she prefers a certain outcome to an uncertain one with a higher expected payoff. The more risk-averse an individual is, the more he or she will seek to avoid risk or the higher the premium he or she will demand to take on risk. Much of the research based on laboratory experiments suggests that women are more risk-averse than men.[54]

Gender differences in attitudes toward risk may contribute to gender differences in labor market outcomes in that some occupations have relatively stable earnings, while others have more risky (variable) earnings. All else equal, occupations with more variable earnings are expected to pay a compensating wage differential to induce workers to accept the higher levels of risk. Thus, women's greater risk aversion could lower their earnings relative to men if they avoid such risky occupations.[55]

Gender differences in risk aversion could also affect performance of women compared to men in some occupations, like manager or financial advisor. Interestingly, while women are found to be more risk-averse among persons drawn from

[52]Jeffrey A. Flory, Andreas Leibbrandt, and John A. List, "Do Competitive Work Places Deter Female Workers? A Large-Scale Natural Field Experiment on Gender Differences in Job-Entry Decisions," *Review of Economic Studies* 82, no. 1 (January 2015): 122–55. To explain individual relative performance, the applicants were told in one of the treatments, for example, that "You will be paired with one other person we are also currently hiring into the same position. The base wage for the position is \$13.50/hr plus a bonus, which translates to an additional \$3/hr, if you perform better than this co-worker. Thus, the wage is either \$13.50/hr or \$16.50/hr, depending on which of you does best." Quotation is from p. 45.

[53]Uri Gneezy, Kenneth L. Leonard, and John A. List, "Gender Differences in Competition: Evidence from a Matrilineal and a Patriarchal Society," *Econometrica* 77, no. 5 (September 2009): 1637–64. For some fascinating evidence that gender differences in math abilities may differ across matrilineal versus patrilineal societies, see Moshe Hoffman, Uri Gneezy, and John A. List, "Nurture Affects Gender Differences in Spatial Abilities," *Proceedings of the National Academy of Sciences* 108, no. 36 (September 2011): 14786–88.

[54]Croson and Gneezy, "Gender Differences in Preferences." However, another review challenges this conclusion, finding the results to be more mixed, with some studies reporting higher female average risk-taking and others finding little evidence of a male advantage (as gauged by statistical significance); see Julie A. Nelson, "Are Women Really More Risk-Averse Than Men? A Re-Analysis of the Literature Using Expanded Methods," *Journal of Economic Surveys* 29, no. 3 (July 2015): 566–85.

[55]Bertrand, "New Perspectives on Gender."

the general population or among university students, studies that focus on managers and professionals have found little or no evidence of gender differences in financial risk preferences. For example, one study of mutual fund managers found that funds managed by men and women did not differ in risk or performance. Similarly, male and female managers and entrepreneurs displayed similar risk propensities. It is not possible to know whether these findings are due to the type of selection we have just discussed (with more risk-taking people of both sexes choosing to enter or remain in these fields) or learning (people who initially differ in their risk propensities may learn from their professional environment).[56] These findings suggest that while women's relative aversion to risk may lower their relative earnings due to occupational sorting, this factor probably does not help to explain *within*-occupational earnings differences (or at least not within these specific occupations). Further, to the extent these finding are due to learning, it suggests that attitudes toward risk can be shaped by environment.

Gender Differences in the "Big Five" Personality Traits

There is also evidence of some gender differences in what are known in psychology as the Big Five personality traits. These traits are openness to experience, conscientiousness, extroversion, agreeableness, and neuroticism (the opposite of emotional stability). (A helpful acronym to remember them is OCEAN). One of the most consistent gender differences has been found for agreeableness, with women being found to be more agreeable than men.[57] *Agreeableness* refers to being more trusting, straightforward, altruistic (warm), compliant, modest, and sympathetic—it is the opposite of antagonistic or disagreeable.

Perhaps not surprisingly, since the workplace can be a "dog-eat-dog" environment, a study that used statistical analysis to examine the relationship between agreeableness and earnings found that men earned a premium for being disagreeable. Interestingly, however, this attribute was not found to be related to women's wages, either positively or negatively. The gender difference in agreeableness thereby contributed to the gender earnings gap both because men were considerably more disagreeable than women and because only men were rewarded for this trait.[58] Another study also found broadly similar results regarding the effect of agreeableness. Although, in this case, both men and women were rewarded for being disagreeable, the reward was *much larger* for men than women.[59]

Taken together, the results of both studies on disagreeableness show a gender gap in the rewards to this personality trait and hint at a double bind for women—that is, confronting them with a choice between two undesirable courses of action. The same could be said of the findings for negotiating discussed earlier: if women do not negotiate or are not disagreeable, they may face lower pay for those reasons; but if they do negotiate or are disagreeable, they may elicit a negative response or at least one that is less positive than their male counterparts enjoy.

---

[56]Croson and Gneezy, "Gender Differences in Preferences."
[57]Bertrand, "New Perspectives on Gender." For a precise definition of each trait, see Gerrit Mueller and Erik J. S. Plug, "Earnings Effects of Personality," *Industrial and Labor Relations Review* 60, no. 1 (October 2006): 3–22.
[58]Mueller and Plug, "Earnings Effects of Personality."
[59]Timothy A. Judge, "Do Nice Guys—and Gals—Really Finish Last?" *Journal of Personality and Social Psychology* 102, no. 2 (February 2012): 390–407.

A Closer Look at Gender Differences in Math Test Scores

As we discussed in Chapter 8, gender differences in math scores in the United States have been greatly reduced. Indeed, some evidence indicates that boys no longer have higher average math test scores during their high school years than girls.[60] However, there is continuing evidence of a gender difference at top performance levels, with males outnumbering females in the very high ranges of science and math test scores and females outnumbering males at the very high ranges of reading and language test scores.[61] The male advantage at the upper end of test scores has been cited as a factor in the underrepresentation of women in STEM (science, technology, engineering, and mathematics) fields, although this has been the focus of considerable debate. This debate entered the national stage in 2005 when then-Harvard president, Lawrence Summers suggested in a speech at an academic conference that one possible reason for the underrepresentation of women among the tenured faculty in science and engineering at top universities was gender differences in "availability of aptitude at the high end."[62] While the role of this factor in women's representation in STEM fields has been hotly contested,[63] the issue has focused considerable attention on what explains the continuing gender difference in math test scores. While math test scores are regarded as a measure of *cognitive* ability, evidence suggests that a host of other factors also play a role. These include social influences and psychological attributes like competition, discussed earlier. Also, as we shall see, some research indicates that just the very stereotyping of an activity (e.g., telling students that males generally score better on the test) may influence test outcomes.

Evidence that social influences matter in influencing math test scores comes from a variety of sources. One study looked at gender patterns in math and reading test scores across US states and regions. The study found that in all states and regions, while the average math scores on standardized tests of boys and girls were roughly equal, boys were disproportionately represented at the top of test scores in math and science, while girls were disproportionately represented at the top in reading test scores. However, the study found that the *extent* of the gender difference among the top performers varied considerably across states and regions. This finding alone suggests environmental factors play a role. Moreover, it found that in states where boys were more heavily represented among top scorers in math and

---

[60]See, for example, Janet S Hyde, Sara M. Lindberg, Marcia C. Linn, Amy B. Ellis, and Caroline C. Williams, "Gender Similarities Characterize Math Performance," *Science* 321 (July 2008): 494–95, www.sciencemag.org; and Devin G. Pope and Justin R. Sydnor, "Geographic Variation in the Gender Differences in Test Scores," *Journal of Economic Perspectives* 24, no. 2 (Spring 2010): 95–108. However, Roland G. Fryer and Steven D. Levitt continue to find a gender gap at the high school level; see "An Empirical Analysis of the Gender Gap in Mathematics," *American Economic Journal: Applied Economics* 2, no. 2 (April 2010): 210–40.

[61]See Pope and Sydnor, "Geographic Variation in the Gender Differences in Test Scores" and the literature cited therein.

[62]Lawrence H. Summers, Remarks at NBER Conference on Diversifying the Science & Engineering Workforce, Cambridge, MA, January 14, 2005, accessed December 16, 2012, http://www.harvard.edu/president/speeches/summers_2005/nber.php.

[63]For example, while Hyde et al., "Gender Similarities Characterize Math Performance," note the slightly greater variance of male test scores in their data, they say that gender differences along this dimension "are insufficient to explain lopsided gender patterns in participation in some STEM fields." This conclusion is echoed in an extensive review of the literature on the access and performance of women in mathematically intensive fields by Stephen J. Ceci, Donna K. Ginther, Shulamit Kahn, and Wendy M. Williams, "Women in Academic Science: A Changing Landscape," *Psychological Science* 15, no. 3 (November 2014): 75–141.

science, girls were more heavily represented among top scorers in reading. This finding suggests that sex stereotyping is going on in some states, with boys and girls being differentially treated in some way(s) that contribute to the gender imbalance in test scores at the upper end.[64]

International comparisons are also instructive in shedding light on the nature and sources of the gender difference in math scores in the United States, particularly the role of social influences. While girls' average math scores are below boys' in many countries, the gender difference in scores varies considerably across countries. In some countries, such as Sweden and Norway, there is no gender gap in math scores, and in Iceland girls' mean scores are higher than those of boys. Similarly, there is considerable variation in the proportion of girls compared to boys scoring at the highest levels (above 95 or 99 percent) of each country's test score distribution. For example, in Iceland more girls scored at the highest levels than boys.

The importance of social factors is further suggested by a recent analysis of data from a variety of countries that found that girls' math scores—whether measured at the means or based on performance at the highest levels—were positively related to indicators of country-level gender equity (such as the World Economic Forum's Gender Gap Index).[65] This finding suggests that social influences likely play an important role in determining the gender math gap and may well affect gender differences in math scores in the United States.

The importance of social factors is also suggested by the considerable international variation found in a study that examined girls' participation in the most difficult math competition for young people. The data in this study suggest that different cultures place different emphasis on the value of mathematics and that these differences affect girls' participation. For example, the United States has participated in the International Mathematical Olympiad since 1974, and between 1974 and 2008 the various six-person teams fielded by the United States have included a total of 3 girls, compared to 9 for Bulgaria, 10 for East Germany/Germany, and 13 for the Soviet Union/Russia. As a further indicator of the importance of culture, this study found that half of recent US team members were immigrants or the children of immigrants from countries where, according to the authors of the study, mathematics is more highly valued than it is in the United States.[66] A role for social influence or culture is also suggested by a study of multiple countries that found that the gender gap in math performance of the children of immigrants (the second generation) in

[64]See Pope and Sydnor, "Geographic Variation." There is also some evidence from a study of Israeli schools that teachers may discriminate against girls in their grading of math tests (judged by comparing the average grades of boys and girls on a "non-blind" classroom exam to the means for these groups on a "blind" national exam marked anonymously). The authors use this comparison to identify biased teachers and track the long-term results of having such biased teachers on student outcomes. See Victor Lavy and Edith Sand, "On the Origins of Gender Human Capital Gaps: Short and Long Term Consequences of Teachers' Stereotypical Biases," NBER Working Paper 20909 (National Bureau of Economic Research, Cambridge, MA, January 2015).

[65]The examples cited in the text and this finding are from Luigi Guiso, Ferdinando Monte, Paola Sapienza, and Luigi Zingales, "Education Forum: Culture, Gender, and Math," *Science* 320 (May 30, 2008): 1164–65, www.sciencemag.org. In "An Empirical Analysis of the Gender Gap in Mathematics," Fryer and Levitt report that the finding that the gender math gap is linked to measures of gender equality is sensitive to the inclusion of Muslim countries where, although women have very low status, there is little or no gender gap in math.

[66]Titu Andreescu, Joseph A. Gallian, Jonathan M. Kane, and Janet E. Mertz, "Cross-Cultural Analysis of Students with Exceptional Talent in Mathematical Problem Solving," *Notices of the American Mathematical Society* 55, no. 10 (November 2008): 1248–60; and Sara Rimer, "Math Skills Suffer in U.S., Study Finds," *New York Times*, October 10, 2008, www.nytimes.org.

the host country was influenced by the degree of gender equality (as measured by a gender-equity index) in the parents' country of origin: the greater the degree of gender equality in the parents' country of origin, the higher the math performance of girls relative to boys in the host country.[67]

Gender differences in psychological attributes also likely contribute to gender differences in math scores. Earlier we discussed gender differences in attitudes toward competition and evidence that women shy away from competition. There is also evidence that women respond differently (and less favorably) than men to competitive pressure. Thus, the competitive pressures associated with test-taking may "magnify and potentially distort underlying gender differences in skills," particularly in an area like mathematics where there is a strong belief that men are better at it.[68] The evidence discussed in the box "Women, Math, and Stereotype Threat" further indicates how men's and women's math test scores may be influenced by such gender stereotypes.

Women, Math, and Stereotype Threat

Research by psychologists Diane M. Quinn, Steven J. Spencer, and Claude M. Steele suggests that cultural stereotypes, such as the belief that girls and women have better verbal skills while boys and men are better at mathematics and science, may negatively affect girls' performance on math exams. Quinn explains how such "stereotype threat" situations can adversely affect girls' test performance and summarizes some of their findings:

In the case of gender and math, imagine a boy and girl sitting down to take the SAT for the first time. They have equivalent math experience. Taking the SAT is a tense, sometimes frustrating experience for both of them. However, as the girl is taking the test she has an extra worry to contend with that the boy does not: A stereotype that she, as a girl, has inferior math skills. As she experiences frustration and difficulty with the problems, she has the burden of knowing that her difficulty could be judged as proof of the veracity of the stereotype.

The boy has none of these doubts or thoughts to interrupt his performance. It is important to note that in this situation neither the girl nor the boy have to believe that the stereotype is true. . . . Just the knowledge of the stereotype itself is enough to affect performance in the situation. How do we know this occurs?

My colleagues and I have tested the stereotype threat hypothesis in a series of studies. . . . In all of our experiments we bring university men and women matched for equivalent math backgrounds and interest into the laboratory. In the first of these studies we simply gave participants an easy or difficult math test. We found that women only performed worse than men on the difficult math test. To demonstrate that it was the threat of the stereotype that caused this underperformance, we gave a second group of men and women the same difficult math test. In order to make stereotypes about math explicit, half of the participants were told that the test had shown gender differences in

continues

---

[67]Natalia Nollenberger, Núria Rodríguez-Planas, and Almudena Sevilla, "The Math Gender Gap: The Role of Culture," *American Economic Review* 106, no. 5 (May 2016): 257–61.
[68]Muriel Niederle and Lise Vesterlund, "Explaining the Gender Gap in Math Test Scores: The Role of Competition," *Journal of Economic Perspectives* 24, no. 2 (Spring 2010): 129–44; the quotation is from p. 140. They cite evidence on test-taking from Evren Örs, Frederic Palomino, and Eloic Peyrache, "Performance Gender-Gap: Does Competition Matter?" *Journal of Labor Economics* 31, no. 3 (July 2013): 443–99.

the past. In order to eliminate a stereotype based interpretation of the situation, the other half of the participants were told that the test had been shown to be gender fair—that men and women performed equally on this test. In line with our predictions, when the stereotype was not applicable to the situation, when men and women were simply told that they were taking a gender fair test, men and women performed equally on the test. When told that the exact same test had shown gender differences in the past, women scored lower on the test than men. Just a simple change in the situation—a different line in the instructions—changed an outcome that many believed intractable. . . . We have also conducted studies where we have a condition in which we do not mention gender at all—we simply describe the math test as a standardized test. In this situation, women also score lower on the test than men, suggesting that standardized mathematical testing situations are implicitly stereotype threat situations . . .

When we look at what women and men are actually doing when working on the difficult test, we found that women and men primarily used the same strategies to solve the problems, however,

women in stereotype threat situations were less likely to think of any way to solve a problem. That is, women were more likely to "blank out" or "choke" on a problem when they were in a stereotype threat condition. Thus research results so far point to the following scenario: When women with a strong interest and identification with math are in a situation in which their math skills could be negatively judged, their performance is undermined by the cognitive activation of gender stereotypes combined with some feelings of stress or anxiety. Women are not alone in being affected by negative stereotypes. Research on stereotype threat has demonstrated its effect on African-Americans and Latinos in intellectual situations, on the elderly in memory testing situations and even on White men in sports situations.*

Quinn also offers some suggestions to reduce stereotype threat and level the playing field for all students. For instance, stereotype threat is likely to be reduced when women (or minorities) are reassured that everyone struggles with difficult concepts and are assured that the exam is fair. Even small measures, such as these, may make a real difference.

---

*Reprinted from Diane M. Quinn, "Women, Math, and Stereotype Threat," Newsletter of the American Economic Association Committee on the Status of Women in the Economics Profession (Winter 2004): 10–11, www.cswep. org. Reprinted by permission of the author. See also Diane M. Quinn and Steven Spencer, "The Interference of Stereotype Threat on Women's Generation of Mathematical Problem-Solving Strategies," Journal of Social Issues 57, no. 1 (Spring 2001): 55–71; and Steven J. Spencer, Claude M. Steele, and Diane M. Quinn, "Stereotype Threat and Women's Math Performance," Journal of Experimental Social Psychology 35, no. 1 (1999): 4–28.

Conclusion

In this chapter, we considered additional supply-side explanations for gender differences in occupations and earnings. We began by examining a major component of human capital, investment in on-the-job training, and its contribution to gender differences in labor market outcomes. We also discussed how high rewards to long hours in some occupations may contribute to a gender wage gap, given an unequal gender division of labor in the home. Next, we considered how, given the traditional role of women as secondary earners in many families, family-related factors can produce gender differences in occupations and earnings and also examined the reasons for the male marriage premium and the motherhood wage penalty. Then, we turned to an area that is receiving growing attention in economics, that is, the relationship between psychological attributes and labor market outcomes. Here we explored evidence on gender differences in psychological attributes and their potential implications for gender differences in earnings and occupations. Finally, we concluded by taking a closer look at the factors that might explain ongoing gender differences in math scores, pointing to the potential role of gender differences in competition and stereotype threat, as well as the role of social factors.

Although the evidence from the preceding chapter and this one suggests that supply-side factors are important, they are only part of the story. Discrimination against women in the labor market is also an important factor, to which we turn in the following chapters.

Questions for Review and Discussion

*Indicates that the question can be answered using a diagram illustrating the individual's human capital investment decision as well as verbally. Consult with your instructor about the appropriate approach for your class.

1. As a future worker, explain the potential costs and benefits to you of obtaining highly specialized training from a particular firm.*

2. What are the main reasons why women frequently invested less in on-the-job training than men? What changed this tendency?* What government or employer policies would be likely to accelerate this change?

3. It is claimed that employers are reluctant to hire women for some jobs because of their higher expected quit rates. Assuming women are more likely to quit, use human capital theory to explain what kind of jobs an employer would be especially reluctant to hire women for. Explain the reasons for the employer's reluctance.* How valid do you think such employer assumptions about women are today?

4. Do the effects of marriage and children have different effects on women's and men's wages and, if so, why?

5. What is your attitude toward negotiating? How might the research discussed here inform your future behavior or the behavior of others to whom you might be giving advice?

Suggested Readings

Babcock, Linda, and Sara Laschever. *Ask for It: How Women Can Use the Power of Negotiation to Get What They Really Want.* New York: Bantam Books, 2008.

Bertrand, Marianne. "New Perspectives on Gender." In *Handbook of Labor Economics*, vol. 4b, edited by Orley C. Ashenfelter and David Card, 1545–92. Amsterdam: Elsevier, 2010.

Blau, Francine D., and Lawrence M. Kahn. "Gender Differences in Pay." *Journal of Economic Perspectives* 14, no. 4 (Fall 2000): 75–99.

Blau, Francine D., and Lawrence M. Kahn. "The Gender Wage Gap: Extent, Trends, and Sources." NBER Working Paper 21913. National Bureau of Economic Research, Cambridge, MA, January 2016 (*Journal of Economic Literature* forthcoming).

Bowles, Hannah Riley. "Psychological Perspectives on Gender in Negotiation." In *The Sage Handbook of Gender and Psychology*, edited by Michelle K. Ryan and Nyla R. Branscombe, 465–83. Los Angeles: Sage, 2013.

Croson, Rachel, and Uri Gneezy. "Gender Differences in Preferences." *Journal of Economic Literature* 47 no. 2 (June 2009): 448–74.

Fryer, Roland G., and Steven D. Levitt. "An Empirical Analysis of the Gender Gap in Mathematics." *American Economic Journal: Applied Economics* 2, no. 2 (April 2010): 210–40.

Goldin, Claudia. "A Grand Convergence: Its Last Chapter." *American Economic Review* 104, no. 4 (May 2014): 1091–1119.

Goldin, Claudia. "How to Achieve Gender Equality." *Milken Institute Review* Q3 (July 2015): 24–33.

Niederle, Muriel, and Lise Vesterlund. "Explaining the Gender Gap in Math Test Scores: The Role of Competition." *Journal of Economic Perspectives* 24, no. 2 (Spring 2010): 129–44.

Pope, Devin G., and Justin R. Sydnor. "Geographic Variation in the Gender Differences in Test Scores." *Journal of Economic Perspectives* 24, no. 2 (Spring 2010): 95–108.

Sigle-Rushton, Wendy, and Jane Waldfogel. "Motherhood and Women's Earnings in Anglo-American, Continental European, and Nordic Countries." *Feminist Economics* 13, no. 2 (April 2007): 55–91.

Tobias, Sheila. *Overcoming Math Anxiety: Revised and Expanded*. New York: W. W. Norton, 1995.

Waldfogel, Jane. "Understanding the 'Family Gap' in Pay for Women with Children." *Journal of Economic Perspectives* 12, no. 1 (Winter 1998): 157–70.

Key Terms

on-the-job training (233)

work experience (233)

general labor market experience (233)

tenure (233)

general training (235)

firm-specific training (235)

seniority arrangements (239)

statistical discrimination (243)

temporal flexibility (244)

compensating differential (245)

male marriage premium (248)

motherhood wage penalty (249)

soft skills/psychological attributes/noncognitive (251)

laboratory (lab) experiments (252)

field experiments (252)

risk-averse (255)

Evidence on the Sources of Gender Differences in Earnings and Occupations: Supply-Side Factors Versus Labor Market Discrimination

CHAPTER HIGHLIGHTS

- ◼ Labor Market Discrimination: A Definition
- ◼ Analyzing the Sources of Gender Differences in Labor Market Outcomes
- ◼ Empirical Evidence on the Sources of Gender Differences in Earnings
- ◼ The Declining Gender Pay Gap
- ◼ Empirical Evidence on the Causes and Consequences of Gender Differences in Occupations
- ◼ Is There a Glass Ceiling?

In the preceding chapters, we reviewed supply-side explanations, including the insights offered by human capital theory, that might help to explain the gender differences in earnings and occupational attainment that were described in Chapter 7. Part of the explanation for observed gender differences may also come from the demand side, as a result of labor market discrimination. In this chapter, we define what economists mean by labor market discrimination and then examine empirical evidence to assess the relative importance of supply-side factors (including human capital) versus demand-side factors (labor market discrimination) in explaining the observed gender differences in labor market outcomes. First, we look at gender differences in earnings and investigate both the sources of the gender pay gap at a point in time and the reasons why the gender pay gap has narrowed over time. Next, we look at gender differences in occupations, considering both the causes of occupational differences and their consequences for gender differences in pay. When we consider the role of discrimination, our focus is on gender discrimination. However, the empirical methods used for measuring discrimination that we present here are equally applicable to assessing discrimination based on other factors, such as race, ethnicity, age, disability, or sexual orientation. As we shall see, both supply-side factors and labor market discrimination play a role in explaining gender differences in labor market outcomes. The evidence on discrimination motivates our review in Chapter 11 of the theoretical explanations offered by economists to explain the existence and persistence of such discrimination. Concern about labor market discrimination is partly a question of equity or fairness. However, there is also an issue of misallocation of resources when workers are not hired, promoted, or rewarded on the basis of their qualifications. Thus, both equity and efficiency concerns provide important rationales for government intervention to combat labor market discrimination. In Chapter 12, we review the government's antidiscrimination policies and examine their possible effects. Supply-side factors, which are also important, include gender differences that stem from women's role within the family. This provides the motivation for our examination of government and employer work–family policies in Chapter 16.

Labor Market Discrimination: A Definition

Labor market discrimination exists when two equally qualified individuals are treated differently in the labor market solely on the basis of their gender (race, ethnicity, age, disability, sexual orientation, etc.).[1] As we saw in Chapter 1, in the absence of discrimination, profit-maximizing employers in a competitive labor market pay workers in accordance with their productivity. For similar reasons, they also find it in their economic self-interest to make other personnel decisions, such as hiring, placement, or promotion, on the same objective basis. An individual's gender (or race, ethnicity, age, disability, sexual orientation, etc.) would be an irrelevant consideration.

If labor market discrimination nonetheless exists, it is expected to adversely affect the economic status of women *directly* by producing differences in labor market outcomes between men and women that are *not* accounted for by differences in their productivity-related characteristics or qualifications. That is, men and women who, in the absence of discrimination, would be equally productive and would receive the same pay (or be in the same occupation) do not receive equal rewards. Such gender disparities may occur because women are paid less than their marginal product[2] due to discrimination. However, it may also be the case that labor market discrimination *directly* lowers women's productivity as well as their pay, as

---

[1]This definition is derived from the work of Gary S. Becker, *The Economics of Discrimination*, 2nd ed. (Chicago: University of Chicago Press, 1971).
[2]*Marginal product* is the increase in output of a firm that results from the hiring of an additional worker, all other factors remaining constant.

when a woman is denied access to an employer-sponsored training program or when customers are reluctant to patronize a female salesperson.

Labor market discrimination may also *indirectly* lower women's pay or occupational attainment. If discriminatory differences in *treatment* of equally qualified men and women are widespread and persistent, the behavior of women themselves may be adversely affected. As we saw in the preceding chapter, productivity differences among workers reflect, in part, the decisions they make whether to continue their schooling, participate in a training program, remain continuously in the labor market, and so on. Faced with discrimination in the labor market that lowers the returns to such human capital investments, women have less incentive to undertake them. To the extent that such *indirect* or **feedback effects** of labor market discrimination exist, they are also expected to adversely affect the economic outcomes of women compared to men.

Most of the empirical work on labor market discrimination has focused on the more readily measured *direct* effects of discrimination on pay or occupational differences between equally well-qualified (or potentially equally productive) men and women. We follow that emphasis in this chapter, focusing on the direct effects of discrimination and taking as given any gender differences in qualifications. However, it is important to recognize that the *full* impact of discrimination also includes any feedback effects on women's behavior that result in their being less well qualified than men.[3]

Analyzing the Sources of Gender Differences in Labor Market Outcomes

In the following sections, we analyze the sources of earnings and occupational differences between men and women. We seek to shed light on the following types of questions. To what extent are gender differences in labor market outcomes due to gender differences in qualifications or (potential) productivity? Which qualifications are particularly important, and has their importance changed over time? Are gender differences in labor market outcomes *fully* explained by gender differences in qualifications or (potential) productivity? If not, how large is the unexplained portion of the gender differential? It is this differential that is commonly used as an estimate of the impact of labor market discrimination. Unfortunately, as we shall see, though the questions are relatively straightforward, the answers are not so easily obtained. Nonetheless, much can be learned from empirical analyses of gender differences in labor market outcomes.

Empirical Evidence on the Sources of Gender Differences in Earnings

Economists and other social scientists have extensively studied the sources of the earnings gap between men and women workers. Estimates vary depending on the data used, the method of analysis, and the types of qualifications examined.

---

[3]Note that the argument is not that *all* differences in qualifications between men and women are due to the indirect effects of discrimination but, rather, that *some* of these differences may be a response to such discrimination.

However, virtually all studies find that a substantial portion of the gender pay gap cannot be explained by gender differences in qualifications.[4]

Evidence from Statistical Analyses: Labor Market-wide Evidence

One standard method of analyzing gender differences in earnings is to investigate them using statistical methods applied to survey data (an example of survey data is the government's Current Population Survey, discussed in earlier chapters). This method may be used to decompose the **gender wage gap** (or **gender wage differential**) into two parts: the part of the gender difference that is due to differences in human capital or other qualifications (the **explained gap**) and the part that *cannot* be explained by these factors (the **unexplained gap**). As we noted previously, the unexplained gap is commonly used as an estimate of the impact of labor market discrimination, although, as we shall see, the matter is not quite so simple. Putting this in the form of an equation, we have

Gender Wage Gap =

Explained Gap (Portion explained by measured differences in qualifications)

+

Unexplained Gap (Portion unexplained, reflects discrimination and unmeasured differences in characteristics)

In Table 10-1, we present findings from a representative study by Francine Blau and Lawrence Kahn of the sources of the gender wage gap in 2010.[5] The Blau-Kahn analysis is based on data from the Panel Study of Income Dynamics (PSID), which contains information on actual labor market experience for a large, nationally representative sample. This is important because, as we saw in Chapter 9, information on labor market experience is important in analyzing gender wage differences. The sample consists of full-time workers, aged 18 to 65, who worked at least half the year (26 weeks). The restriction to full-time workers with substantial work experience over the year is designed to focus on male and female workers who are as similar as possible.[6]

---

[4]For summaries of this literature, see, for example, Francine D. Blau and Lawrence M. Kahn, "The Gender Wage Gap: Extent, Trends, and Sources," NBER Working Paper 21913 (National Bureau of Economic Research, Cambridge, MA, January 2016) (*Journal of Economic Literature*, forthcoming); Francine D. Blau and Lawrence M. Kahn, "Women's Work and Wages," in *The New Palgrave Dictionary of Economics*, 2nd ed., ed. Steven N. Durlauf and Lawrence E. Blume (London: Palgrave Macmillan, 2008), 762–72, http://www.dictionaryofeconomics.com/dictionary; Joni Hersch, "Sex Discrimination in the Labor Market," *Foundations and Trends in Microeconomics* 2, no. 4 (2006): 281–361; and Joseph G. Altonji and Rebecca M. Blank, "Race and Gender in the Labor Market," in *Handbook of Labor Economics*, vol. 3C, ed. Orley C. Ashenfelter and David Card (Amsterdam: North-Holland, 1999), 3143–3259. For a review of the evolution of empirical work on discrimination, including the difficulty of distinguishing between taste-based and statistical discrimination, see Jonathan Guryan and Kerwin Kofi Charles, "Taste-Based or Statistical Discrimination: The Economics of Discrimination Returns to Its Roots," *Economic Journal* 123, no. 572 (November 2013): F417–32.
[5]Blau and Kahn, "The Gender Wage Gap."
[6]In addition to gender differences in qualifications and the extent of discrimination, the gender earnings differential may be affected by the self-selection of women and men into the labor force and into full-time employment. In other words, those choosing to participate—or to work full-time for at least half the year—may differ from those who choose to remain outside the labor force or to work part-time in terms of both their measured and unmeasured characteristics. One possibility is that labor force participants are a positively selected group of those who received higher wage offers. Similarly, full-time workers may be more highly qualified and more committed to market work. For further consideration of the selection issue, see Blau and Kahn, "The Gender Wage Gap"; and Casey B. Mulligan and Yona Rubinstein, "Selection, Investment, and Women's Relative Wages," *Quarterly Journal of Economics* 123, no. 3 (August 2008): 1061–1110. Research on the earnings differential between white and black women has found that, if self-selection is not accounted for, the race gap is underestimated; see Derek Neal, "The Measured Black–White Wage Gap among Women Is Too Small," *Journal of Political Economy* 112, no. 1, pt. 2 (February 2004): S1–28.

TABLE 10-1 CONTRIBUTION TO THE WAGE DIFFERENTIAL BETWEEN MEN AND WOMEN OF DIFFERENCES IN MEASURED CHARACTERISTICS, 2010

CHARACTERISTICS	PERCENT EXPLAINED
Educational Attainment	−5.9
Labor Force Experience	14.1
Race	4.3
Region	0.3
Occupational Category	32.9
Industry Category	17.6
Union Status	−1.3
Unexplained	38.0
Total	100.0
[Wage Differential (%)]	[20.7]

Source: Francine D. Blau and Lawrence M. Kahn, "The Gender Wage Gap: Extent, Trends, and Explanations," NBER Working Paper 21913 (January 2016) [*Journal of Economic Literature*, forthcoming], Table 4.

Table 10-1 shows the contribution of each type of variable included in the analysis to explaining the gender wage differential (or gender wage gap), which is 20.7 percent in this sample—see the last line of the table. The method used to obtain these estimates is explained in detail in Appendix 10A. The explanatory variables considered include indicators of human capital (education and experience), as well as measures of occupation, industry, and union status. Race and region are also included as control variables but account for very little of the wage gap.

As would be expected based on our discussion in Chapter 9, women had less labor market experience than men in 2010. The gender difference in full-time experience was 1.4 years and, although smaller than in previous years, still explained a noticeable share of the gender wage differential. As shown in Table 10-1, experience accounted for 14 percent of the gender wage differential.[7]

In contrast, women in this sample had *more* education than men, which (as indicated by the negative sign in the table) worked to *lower* the gender wage gap by 6 percent of the wage differential. In other words, gender differences in educational attainment do *not* help to explain the gender wage gap but rather work in the opposite direction. As we saw in Chapter 8, women are now better educated than men in the full population in that a higher share of women have at least a college degree, so it is not surprising that this would be true among men and women in the labor force.

Finally, as we would expect based on the data presented in Chapter 7, gender differences in occupation and industry are substantial and help to explain a considerable portion of the gender wage gap. Recall that men are more likely to be in blue-collar jobs and a number of traditionally male occupations in the professional category and to work in the mining, construction, durable manufacturing, and transportation and utilities industries. Women are more likely to be in clerical and service occupations,

---

[7]Although women do have a bit more part-time experience than men, part-time experience is found to have a very low payoff in terms of current wages.

as well as a number of traditionally female professions, and to work in the education and health services industries. In the analysis, the authors accounted for 21 separate occupations and 15 separate industries. Taken together, gender differences in occupation and industry explained 51 percent of the gender wage gap—33 percent for occupation and 18 percent for industry.

Union status is another factor considered, though it plays an extremely small role. This is to be expected since, as we saw in Chapter 7, although men used to be much more highly unionized than women, the gender gap in unionization has virtually disappeared. In the published government statistics, men remain slightly more likely to be unionized than women; in the data set and sample used in the analysis in Table 10-1 women were slightly more likely to be unionized than men (hence the negative sign in the table). But the gender difference in both cases is very small.

Although these findings suggest that gender differences in productivity-related characteristics are important, they also indicate that this factor is only part of the story. The portion of the wage differential that is *not* explained by productivity-related characteristics (qualifications) serves as an estimate of labor market discrimination. In this case, 38 percent of the gender gap cannot be explained even when gender differences in education, experience, industries, occupations, and union status are taken into account. The portion of the pay gap that remains unexplained is potentially due to discrimination, though, as we shall see shortly, the matter is not quite so simple.

Another way to interpret the results of this study is to focus on the **gender wage ratio** (female wages divided by male wages); this draws in part on data not presented in the table. The actual ("unadjusted") gender wage ratio in 2010 was 79.4 percent; that is, women's wages were, on average, 79 percent of men's wages.[8] If women had the same human capital characteristics (i.e., education and experience), industry and occupational distributions, and union coverage as men, the "adjusted" ratio would have risen to 91.6 percent of men's wages. Thus, although measured characteristics are important, women still earn less than otherwise similar men when all measured characteristics are taken into account.

Biases in the Unexplained Gap as an Estimate of Discrimination

How conclusive are estimates of the unexplained gap, like that from the study considered in the previous section, as indicators of labor market discrimination? Certainly not entirely so; a number of problems associated with these types of analyses may result in either upward or downward biases in the estimate of discrimination.[9]

One difficulty is that we lack information on all the possible qualifications of individuals that are associated with their (potential) productivity. Some of the factors that affect earnings, such as motivation, work effort, or willingness to compete, cannot easily be quantified. Others (e.g., college major, math score) may be unavailable in a particular data set. Hence, in general, it is not possible to include all relevant

---

[8]Note that the unadjusted gender wage ratio is equal to (100 minus the unadjusted wage differential) or 79.4 ≈ (100 − 20.7)—with a small difference due to rounding.

[9]For a consideration of these issues, see Ronald Oaxaca, "Male–Female Wage Differences in Urban Labor Markets," *International Economic Review* 14, no. 3 (October 1973): 693–709; and Alan Blinder, "Wage Discrimination: Reduced Form and Structural Estimates," *Journal of Human Resources* 8, no. 4 (Fall 1973): 436–55. The type of statistical analysis presented in Table 10-1 is often called a Oaxaca-Blinder decomposition.

job qualifications in a study of gender differences in wages. For instance, although the study reported in Table 10-1 accounts for differences between men and women in many important work-related factors, it lacks data on others that are also potentially relevant. If men are more highly qualified with respect to the factors that are omitted from the analysis, the extent of labor market discrimination is overestimated by the unexplained gap. This is because some portion of the "unexplained" gender differential in Table 10-1 may, in fact, be due to men being more competitive or to gender differences in college major, for example. However, it is also possible that women are more highly qualified in some respects not taken into account. They may possess greater interpersonal skills, for example. In that case, discrimination would be *underestimated*. In general, more attention has been focused on the possibility that discrimination may be overestimated due to omitted factors.[10]

There are other considerations that could cause discrimination to be *underestimated*. One factor is that some of the lower qualifications of women may themselves be a direct result of labor market discrimination. For example, qualified women may be excluded from particular jobs due to discrimination in hiring or promotion. The results reported in Table 10-1 include controls for variables such as occupation, industry, and unionism, which could themselves be affected by such discrimination. To the extent that studies of discrimination control for qualifications that themselves reflect the direct effects of discrimination, the impact of discrimination on the pay gap will be *underestimated*. The unexplained gap would be considerably larger if we had not controlled for occupation, industry, and unionism in Table 10-1. Indeed, according to estimates based on the Blau-Kahn study, the adjusted wage ratio would fall from 91.6 to 82.1 percent if these variables were excluded and only education, experience, race, and region were controlled for.

Analyses of the type presented in Table 10-1 also neglect the feedback effects of labor market discrimination on the behavior and choices of women. For example, to the extent that women receive lower returns to labor market experience than men, they have less incentive to accumulate experience. As another example, women may be less likely to pursue college study in traditionally male fields if they believe they will encounter job discrimination in these areas.

Evidence on Possible Sources of the Unexplained Gender Wage Gap

While the existence of an unexplained pay gap in traditional statistical analyses is consistent with discrimination against women in the labor market, as we have seen, this does not mean that the full unexplained gap may be attributed to discrimination. In this section, we consider some of the factors *apart from discrimination* that may contribute to an unexplained pay gap between men and women in conventional analyses.

Some of the unexplained gap may be due to the impact of childbearing. As we saw in Chapter 9, research suggests a negative effect of children on women's wages

---

[10]This problem is a bit less serious than it appears at first glance because the included factors likely capture some of the effects of those that cannot be controlled for because of lack of information. For example, it is likely that more highly educated individuals are more able, on average, than the less educated or, as another example, that college major is correlated with current occupation. See Arthur Goldberger, "Reverse Regression and Salary Discrimination," *Journal of Human Resources* 19, no. 3 (Summer 1984): 293–318.

that is not simply due to the workforce interruptions associated with childbearing.[11] This negative effect may reflect a variety of factors including losses in the returns to firm-specific training for some women who permanently leave their employer when they have a child, the extra caregiving and housework burdens many mothers shoulder, and decisions by mothers to accept lower wages for greater job flexibility. On the other hand, as we also saw in Chapter 9, there is some evidence that mothers face discrimination relative to nonmothers. Moreover, our earlier discussion of feedback effects suggests that the division of labor in the family may itself be influenced by the market opportunities available to women and men in the labor market.

Another possible source of the unexplained wage gap is the gender differences in psychological attributes (soft skills) such as attitudes toward negotiation, competition, and risk, which generally favor men, and interpersonal skills, which generally favor women; these were discussed at length in Chapter 9. These types of variables, while potentially important, are not generally available in standard survey data sets including the data set used in the Blau-Kahn study examined here. Women's lesser willingness to compete, for instance, could negatively affect their performance and wages compared to men in certain settings. Or, as another example, men might earn higher wages than women because they are more willing to negotiate with their employers. Further, women have been found in attitudinal surveys to place a lesser value on money and work than men do. This preference has been found to lower their wages relative to men's.[12] However, some caution must be used in broadly attributing the unexplained gap to these types of factors. For one thing, not all gender differences in psychological attributes and preferences favor men. As noted earlier, interpersonal skills are an important soft skill, and women tend to have better interpersonal skills than men.[13] There may also be feedback effects from differential treatment in the labor market to psychological attributes and preferences. For example, women's lesser focus on wages or reluctance to negotiate may be a result of anticipated discrimination. Perhaps most importantly, as we discussed in Chapter 9, much of the evidence on psychological attributes (soft skills) comes from laboratory experiments. While such studies are of interest, they do not readily map into a particular share of the pay gap that may be attributed to these factors. A recent review of the subset of studies that applied statistical methods to survey data that *included* measures of psychological attributes concluded that such factors could account for only a small to moderate share of the gender wage gap.[14] Statistical techniques have also been used to look at the effect of sexual orientation on earnings, as summarized in the "Sexual Orientation and Gender Identity" box.

---

[11]Complex issues are involved in measuring this effect because it may be that children reduce women's productivity and hence their earnings, but it may also be the case that less productive women choose to have more children. For a review of the empirical findings, see Hersch, "Sex Discrimination in the Labor Market."

[12]Nicole M. Fortin, "The Gender Wage Gap among Young Adults in the United States: The Importance of Money Versus People," *Journal of Human Resources* 43, no. 4 (Fall 2008): 884–918. The measure of the value placed on money and work that was used in this study was based on respondents' answers to questions about the importance in selecting a career of *Making of lots of money* and *The chance to be a leader* and about the importance in life of *Being successful at work* and *Having lots of money* (p. 888).

[13]Lex Borghans, Bas ter Weel, and Bruce Weinberg, "People Skills and the Labor Market Outcomes of Underrepresented Groups," *Industrial and Labor Relations Review* 67, no. 2 (April 2014): 287–334.

[14]Blau and Kahn, "The Gender Wage Gap."

The Effect of Sexual Orientation and Gender Identity on Earnings

Statistical techniques similar to those used to analyze the gender wage gap have also been employed to study discrimination on the basis of sexual orientation. This research has generally found that gay men earn less than heterosexual men, both married and unmarried, while lesbians earn more than married and unmarried heterosexual women (although less than either heterosexual or gay men).* One reason for this is probably that gay men and lesbians are less likely to pursue a traditional division of labor with their partners than heterosexual men and women.** In most states in the United States, they were not, until very recently, permitted to marry, and their inability to form a legally sanctioned union made specialization more risky for them. Therefore, gay men did not expect to reap the same benefits from specialization as married men and had lower incentives to specialize in market activities. Similarly, lesbian women may be more career-oriented than heterosexual women who are married or expect to marry, and they may even benefit to the extent that employers view unmarried women as more career-oriented. Of course now that same-sex marriage is legal in all states, based on the 2015 Supreme Court decision in *Obergefell v. Hodges*, these patterns may begin to change.

At the same time, the finding that gay men earn less than heterosexual men with similar qualifications is certainly also consistent with discrimination. Even the earnings premium lesbians receive compared to heterosexual women with the same measured qualifications might conceal some discrimination against them based on their sexual orientation. If lesbians have traits that lead to higher productivity that are unmeasured in standard analyses, such as greater career orientation, then their observed wages, though higher than those of heterosexual women, may not fully reflect their higher average productivity. In addition, discrimination may lower the potential wages of both gay men and lesbians by leading them to trade off high-wage jobs in some occupations for positions that are more accepting of them.

A very interesting analysis of the experience of transgender individuals presents further evidence on gender discrimination in the labor market and sheds light on the economic consequences of such transitions. The study, based on a special survey, examined the labor market outcomes of transgender individuals, that is, people who changed their gender, generally with hormone therapy and surgery. The study found that the average earnings of individuals who changed their gender from female to male *increased* slightly, while the average earnings of individuals who changed their gender from male to female *fell* by nearly one-third. The authors note that their findings are consistent with subjective reports that "for many male-to-female workers, becoming a woman often brings a loss of authority, harassment, and termination, but that for many female-to-male workers, becoming a man often brings an increase in respect and authority."***

*For evidence of a sexual orientation effect, see Dan A. Black, Hoda R. Makar, Seth G. Sanders, and Lowell Taylor, "The Effects of Sexual Orientation on Earnings," Industrial and Labor Relations Review 56, no. 3 (April 2003): 449–69; John M. Blandford, "The Nexus of Sexual Orientation and Gender in the Determination of Earnings," Industrial and Labor Relations Review 56, no. 4 (July 2003): 622–42; and M. V. Lee Badgett, "Testimony on HR 2015, The Employment Non-Discrimination Act of 2007," US House of Representatives, Committee on Education and Labor, Subcommittee on Health, Employment, Labor, and Pensions, September 5, 2007, http://www.policyarchive.org/handle/10207/18053. For an extensive review, see Marieka Klawitter, "Meta-Analysis of the Effects of Sexual Orientation on Earnings," Industrial Relations 54, no. 1 (January 2015): 4–32.

**Dan A. Black, Seth G. Sanders, and Lowell J. Taylor, "The Economics of Lesbian and Gay Families," Journal of Economic Perspectives 21, no. 2 (Spring 2007): 53–70.

***Kristen Schilt and Matthew Wiswall, "Before and After: Gender Transitions, Human Capital, and Workplace Experiences," The B.E. Journal of Economic Analysis & Policy 8, no. 1 (2008): Article 39, available at http://www.bepress.com/bejeap/vol8/iss1/art39/. The quotation is from the abstract.

Further Evidence from Statistical Analyses: A Look at Subgroups of College Graduates, Lawyers, and MBAs

In this section, we examine a number of studies that apply the same statistical techniques as those already discussed but focus on subgroups, including college graduates, lawyers, and MBAs. By focusing on more homogeneous subgroups of workers than labor market-wide studies, such studies minimize gender differences in unmeasured characteristics and thereby yield more convincing evidence of labor market discrimination. Such analyses also provide deeper insights into the supply-side sources of gender differentials that may vary by profession (MBAs or lawyers) or for subgroups like college graduates.

We look first at a study of recent college graduates that examined gender wage differences in 2009 among those who had graduated 1 year earlier.[15] Since these recent graduates were relatively young (average age 23) and most were single and did not have children, their wages are less likely to be affected by unmeasured differences in labor market experience or family roles that might otherwise confound the analysis. Thus, this is a particularly useful sample for studying discrimination.[16] Moreover, the researchers had data on a number of important productivity-related factors that are not typically available in national data sets—college major, college grade point average, and type of educational institution attended (private vs. public institution, very selective institution)—as well as current labor market variables like occupation, hours worked, and employment sector, and personal characteristics like age and marital status.

On average, women earned 18 percent less than men, even in this group of new graduates. College major was an important factor explaining this difference, with men more likely to have majored in relatively higher-paying fields like engineering and computer science and women more likely to have majored in fields like education and the social sciences that tend to lead to lower-paying jobs.[17] Occupational differences also contributed to the gender pay gap. Overall, men were more likely to work in higher-paying occupations, including business and management occupations, computer and physical science occupations, and engineering. Women were more likely to work in lower-paying occupations, including business support occupations and as administrative assistants, teachers, social service professionals, and nurses and other health care providers. The underrepresentation of women in STEM (science, technology, engineering, and mathematics) majors and occupations is particularly striking in light of our discussion of this sector in previous chapters. When college major, occupation, and other variables were controlled for, the gender pay

---

[15]Christianne Corbett and Catherine Hill, *Graduating to a Pay Gap: the Earnings of Women and Men One Year after College Graduation* (Washington, DC: AAUW, 2012), www.aauw.org. See also Dan A. Black, Amelia M. Haviland, Seth G. Sanders, and Lowell J. Taylor, "Gender Wage Disparities among the Highly Educated," *Journal of Human Resources* 43, no. 3 (Summer 2008): 630–59; and Joseph G. Altonji, Erica Blom, and Costas Meghir, "Heterogeneity in Human Capital Investments: High School Curriculum, College Major, and Careers," *Annual Review of Economics* 4 (2012): 185–223. Also of interest is an examination of three cohorts of Harvard graduates by Claudia Goldin and Lawrence F. Katz, "Transitions: Career and Family Life Cycles of the Educational Elite," *American Economic Review* 98, no. 2 (May 2008): 363–69.

[16]It is possible, however, that the anticipation of future gender differences in experience or responsibility for children could affect current outcomes.

[17]Altonji, Blom, and Meghir also found college major to be an important factor in explaining the gender wage difference, accounting for slightly over half the gap; see "Heterogeneity in Human Capital Investments."

gap was substantially reduced, but researchers still found an unexplained pay gap of 7 percent between men and women. This is a sizeable gap potentially due to discrimination. Moreover, since these are young people, it is likely that the gap will increase as they age, to the extent that men fare better in terms of raises and promotions.

Two other studies examined the gender gap among women and men with professional degrees in law and business. As in the prior study, they also had a detailed set of control variables that are not generally found in broader labor market studies. These studies suggest that career–family trade-offs contribute importantly to gender pay differences among lawyers and MBAs. They further show that even if one accounts for variables related to family/parental status, like workforce interruptions and fewer weeks or hours worked, unexplained gender earnings differences remain.

The first study focused on two cohorts of graduates of the University of Michigan Law School 15 years after graduation; the first cohort was surveyed between 1987 and 1993 and the second between 1994 and 2000.[18] The results for the two cohorts were quite similar. The gap in pay between women and men was found to be relatively small at the outset of their careers, but 15 years later men earned over 50 percent more. Some of this difference reflected choices that workers themselves made, including the greater propensity of women lawyers to currently work shorter hours and to have worked part-time in the past or to have taken some time out after childbirth. However, even after accounting for such differences, as well as an extensive list of worker qualifications and other factors, including grades while in law school, detailed work history data, and information about type and size of employer, men still earned 11 percent more.

The second study examined earnings of MBAs who graduated between 1990 and 2006 from the Booth School of Business of the University of Chicago (they were surveyed in 2006–2007). Like the study of lawyers, the researchers reported a relatively small gender differential at the outset of the career. However, averaged across the full set of MBA graduates (individuals who had been out for 1–16 years), men earned 33 percent more than women. The study found that this gender gap could largely be explained by career–family trade-offs, including workforce interruptions by women (as a result of childbearing) and fewer weekly hours worked by women (as mothers sought more flexibility). In fact, the study found that there were large wage penalties for taking *any* time out from work. Some of the difference was also due to men's slight academic advantage in their prior MBA programs (higher GPA and more finance courses taken). While this study points to the sizeable role that family plays in explaining the gender earnings gap among MBAs, even after accounting for this and other factors, men still earned nearly 7 percent more.[19]

While one must be cautious in interpreting the unexplained gaps identified in these studies as entirely due to discrimination for the reasons we discussed previously, these findings are consistent with discrimination against highly educated

---

[18]Mary C. Noonan, Mary E. Corcoran, and Paul Courant, "Pay Differences among the Highly Trained: Cohort Differences in the Sex Gap in Lawyers' Earnings," *Social Forces* 84, no. 2 (December 2005): 853–72.

[19]Marianne Bertrand, Claudia Goldin, and Lawrence F. Katz, "Dynamics of the Gender Gap for Young Professionals in the Financial and Corporate Sectors," *American Economic Journal: Applied Economics* 2, no. 3 (July 2010): 228–55. The gender gap was calculated by evaluating the regression coefficient on the female dummy in Table 3, specification 6; this was the authors' preferred specification and the most highly specified regression that did not include a control for "reason for choosing job," which we felt inappropriate to include in a regression estimating the unexplained gap potentially due to discrimination.

women. On the other hand, they also point to the importance of various supply-side factors, including the underrepresentation of women in the more lucrative STEM fields and the negative impact of career/work trade-offs on the gender gap in earnings. Work–family problems may differ by field, and there is some evidence, based on a sample of Harvard graduates, that female MBAs have a more difficult time combining career and family than female physicians, Ph.D.s, and lawyers. Fifteen years after graduating from college, women who had earned an MBA had the lowest share working full-time and full-year and had taken the greatest amount of time off from employment compared to M.D.s, J.D.s, and Ph.D.s. They also faced larger earnings penalties to career interruptions. At present the reasons for these differences are not fully understood, although MBAs may have less workplace flexibility.[20]

More generally, as discussed at length in Chapter 9, Claudia Goldin points to women's greater demand for **temporal flexibility** (that is, flexibility in work schedules) as producing a gender wage gap among skilled workers in some occupations. For a sample of college graduates in the 95 highest-earning occupations, Goldin found that an index of occupational characteristics associated with high costs of flexibility was positively related to (i.e., increased) the gender wage gap in the occupation (after adjusting for other factors). In terms of particular occupations, she found business occupations and law had high values on the inflexibility index and high rewards for working longer hours, while technology and science jobs scored much lower on the inflexibility measure and had smaller rewards for working longer hours. The situation in business and law may in part reflect the importance of working closely with clients in those fields.[21] In sharp contrast to business and law, Goldin points to pharmacy. As discussed earlier in Chapter 9, this is an occupation in which industry developments and technological factors greatly reduced the costs of flexibility, and the gender pay gap fell accordingly.[22]

Evidence on Discrimination from Experiments

Given the problems with traditional statistical studies, researchers have been interested in uncovering alternative sources of evidence on discrimination. One approach that provides particularly persuasive evidence of discrimination is experiments, either naturally occurring labor market events that may be seen and analyzed as if they were experiments (e.g., blind vs. nonblind musical auditions, as we shall discuss) or actual experiments in which the researcher manipulates the treatment so as to test for discrimination. The advantage of experimental studies is that they

---

[20]Goldin and Katz, "Transitions." For a study emphasizing the importance of career–family trade-offs in contributing to the underrepresentation of women in science, see Stephen J. Ceci and Wendy M. Williams, "Understanding Current Causes of Women's Underrepresentation in Science," *Proceedings of the National Academy of Sciences* 108, no. 8 (2011): 3157–62.

[21]Claudia Goldin, "A Grand Convergence: Its Last Chapter," *American Economic Review* 104, no. 4 (May 2014): 1091–1119; and for a useful summary in less technical terms, Claudia Goldin, "How to Achieve Gender Equality," *Milken Institute Review* Q3 (July 2015): 24–33. For empirical analyses of the impact of long hours on trends in the gender wage gap, see Youngjoo Cha and Kim A. Weeden, "Overwork and the Slow Convergence in the Gender Gap in Wages," *American Sociological Review* 79, no. 3 (June 2014): 457–84; and Patricia Cortés and Jessica Pan, "Women Time Binds: Returns to Working Long Hours and the Gender Wage Gap among the Highly Skilled," IZA Working Paper 9846 (IZA, Bonn, Germany, March 2016).

[22]Goldin, "A Grand Convergence"; see also Claudia Goldin and Lawrence F. Katz, "A Most Egalitarian Profession: Pharmacy and the Evolution of a Family Friendly Occupation," *Journal of Labor Economics* 34, no. 3 (July 2016): 705–46.

offer estimates of the role of discrimination that are potentially less contaminated by unmeasured factors.

The first study we consider investigated the impact of the decision of symphony orchestras to adopt "blind" auditions for musicians in which a screen is used to conceal the identity of the candidate.[23] The adoption of the screen created what might be considered a natural experiment (i.e., an experiment not set up by the researchers themselves) that enabled the researchers to investigate what happened when those judging the auditions were unable to determine the sex of the musician auditioning. They found that the adoption of the screen substantially increased the probability that a woman would advance out of preliminary rounds and be the winner in the final round. The switch to blind auditions was found to explain one-quarter of the increase in the percentage female in the top five symphony orchestras in the United States, from less than 5 percent of all musicians in 1970 to 25 percent in 1996.

A second study conducted an actual experiment, in this case what is termed a "hiring audit." Male and female pseudo–job seekers were given similar résumés and sent to apply for jobs waiting on tables at the same set of 65 Philadelphia restaurants.[24] The results provided statistically significant evidence of discrimination against women in high-priced restaurants where earnings of workers are generally higher. In these restaurants, a female applicant's probability of getting an interview was 40 percentage points lower than a male's and her probability of getting an offer was 50 percentage points lower.

A third experimental study, also a hiring audit, sheds light on bias in a very different domain, science. Science faculty from the fields of biology, chemistry, and physics at six large, research-intensive universities were asked to provide feedback on the application materials of senior undergraduate students who all ultimately intended to go to graduate school and had recently applied for a science laboratory manager position. The faculty participants believed they were evaluating a real student who would subsequently receive the faculty participants' ratings as feedback to help their career development. Participants were randomly assigned to receive an application from either a female student or a male student; all other information was otherwise set up to be identical. Faculty participants rated the male applicant as significantly more competent and suitable for the position than the (identical) female applicant. Participants also selected a starting salary for male applicants that was almost $4,000 higher than the salary offered to female applicants and offered more career mentoring to the male applicants. Female faculty were equally likely to exhibit bias against the female students as male faculty.[25]

A fourth study implemented a laboratory experiment. In the experiment, some subjects (employers) hired other subjects (applicants) to perform an arithmetic task that men and women perform equally well, on average. The findings are consistent with negative stereotyping of women in math-related areas. The study found that

[23]Claudia Goldin and Cecilia Rouse, "Orchestrating Impartiality: The Impact of 'Blind' Auditions on Female Musicians," *American Economic Review* 90, no. 4 (September 2000): 715–41. See also Blair Tindall, "Call Me Madame Maestro," *New York Times*, January 14, 2005, www.nytimes.com.

[24]David Neumark, with the assistance of Roy J. Blank and Kyle D. Van Nort, "Sex Discrimination in Hiring in the Restaurant Industry: An Audit Study," *Quarterly Journal of Economics* 111, no. 3 (August, 1996): 915–42.

[25]Corinne A. Moss-Racusin, John F. Dovidio, Victoria L. Brescoll, Mark J. Graham, and Jo Handelsman, "Science Faculty's Subtle Gender Biases Favor Male Students," *Proceedings of the National Academy of Sciences* 109, no. 41 (2012): 16474–79, accessed December 16, 2012, http://www.pnas.org/content/early/2012/09/14/1211286109.full.pdf.

when employers had no information about applicants other than physical appearance (which permitted them to distinguish women from men), both male and female employers were twice as likely to hire a man as a woman. The extent of gender discrimination in hiring was similar when applicants self-reported their expected performance, largely because men tended to overestimate future performance and women slightly underestimated theirs. Gender discrimination in hiring was reduced, *but not fully eliminated* (women remained less likely to be hired), when employers were provided with full information about applicants' previous performance on the arithmetic task.[26] This study points to the importance of objective information in reducing the differential treatment of women and men applicants but also to the persistence of some degree of discrimination even in the face of such information.

Finally, we point to the results of a study summarized in Chapter 9 that suggests that women, but not men, face discrimination based on their parental status. Using both laboratory and field experiments, the researchers found that the participants had less favorable views regarding the résumés of equally qualified mothers relative to those of nonmothers, while fathers were not disadvantaged relative to nonfathers.[27]

Evidence on Discrimination from Court Cases

Evidence that labor market discrimination exists is also provided by the many employment discrimination cases in which employers were found guilty of discrimination in pay or reached out-of-court settlements with the plaintiffs. A number of employment practices that explicitly discriminated against women used to be quite prevalent, including marriage bars restricting the employment of married women, which we discussed in Chapter 2,[28] and the intentional segregation of women into separate job categories with lower pay scales.[29] Although such overt practices no longer exist, recent court cases provide evidence that employment practices that produce discriminatory outcomes for women are still present. Moreover, these cases give some examples of the types of workplace issues and practices that have been alleged. We illustrate with some recent settlements.

In 2010, there was a $175 million settlement of a class action case against Novartis Pharmaceuticals Corporation by current and former female sales representatives who alleged discrimination in pay, promotions, and other working conditions. Plaintiffs claimed that Novartis was a male-dominated company that denied advancement to female sales representatives and was unresponsive to their complaints. Some plaintiffs also alleged sexual harassment and testified that if clients made sexual advances, they were expected to accept.[30]

Other examples may be drawn from three cases that involve the financial services industry. In 2008, there was a $33 million settlement of a sex discrimination lawsuit against Smith Barney charging discrimination against female financial consultants.

---

[26]Ernesto Reuben, Paola Sapienza, and Luigi Zingales, "How Stereotypes Impair Women's Careers in Science," *Proceedings of the National Academy of Sciences* 111, no. 12 (March 25, 2014): 4403–08.
[27]Shelley J. Correll, Stephen Benard, and In Paik, "Getting a Job: Is There a Motherhood Penalty?" *American Journal of Sociology* 112, no. 5 (2007): 1297–1338.
[28]Claudia Goldin, *Understanding the Gender Gap: An Economic History of American Women* (New York: Oxford University Press, 1990).
[29]See, for example, Bowe v. Colgate-Palmolive Co., 416 F. 2d 711 (7th Cir., 1969), and IUE v. Westinghouse Electric Co., 631 F. 2d 1094 (3rd Cir., 1980).
[30]Kevin P. McGowan, "Court OKs $175 Million Settlement of Novartis Sex Bias Claims," *Bloomberg BNA*, November 30, 2010, accessed December 17, 2012, http://www.bna.com/court-oks-175-n5510/.

The complaint charged that Smith Barney routinely assigned smaller and less valuable accounts to female brokers (including those who outperformed their male counterparts) and thereby lowered their pay, provided women with less sales and administrative support than it provided to men, and maintained "a corporate culture hostile to female professionals."[31] Similarly, in a sex discrimination lawsuit against Morgan Stanley, which was settled in 2004 for $54 million, the plaintiffs claimed that the firm underpaid and did not promote women. Allegations of sexist practices included claims that Morgan Stanley withheld raises and desirable assignments from women who took maternity leave and that it condoned a hostile workplace where men made sexist comments and organized trips to topless bars and strip clubs.[32] Finally, in a third case, allegations made by female brokers in a 2013 sex discrimination lawsuit against Bank of America were quite similar. They alleged being underpaid and that they did not receive their fair share of the more lucrative accounts. In this case, the female brokers received a $39 million settlement.[33]

Evidence on Discrimination: An Assessment

Where do these findings, taken as a whole, leave us? They suggest that pinpointing the exact portion of the pay gap that is due to labor market discrimination is difficult. Nonetheless, the findings of traditional, labor market-wide statistical studies, using data on all full-time workers, provide strong evidence of pay differences between men and women that are *not* accounted for by gender differences in measured qualifications, even when the list of qualifications is quite extensive. The inference from these results is backed up by the findings of statistical studies that focus on more homogeneous subgroups like lawyers and MBAs. Studies conducted using an experimental approach, including hiring audits and lab experiments, provide further substantiation. Finally, as further suggestive evidence, we point to the large payouts resulting from court cases in which discrimination was alleged. All told, there is overwhelming evidence that discrimination does indeed exist. Although precisely estimating its magnitude is difficult, the evidence suggests that the *direct* effects of labor market discrimination may explain as much as 40 percent of the overall pay differential between full-time employed men and women, controlling for education, experience, occupation and industry, and considerably more when occupation and industry are not controlled for.

The Declining Gender Pay Gap

In this section, we focus on explanations for the decrease in the gender wage gap that, as we saw in Chapter 7, began around 1980. In doing so, we again focus on the two sets of factors we have considered in the previous sections to understand

[31]"Women Employees Sue Smith Barney for Sex Discrimination," news release, March 31, 2005, accessed April 2, 2013, http://www.genderlawsuitagainstsmithbarney.com/press_release_01.htm; and "Court Grants Final Approval to $33 Million Gender Class Action Settlement with Smith Barney," news release, August 13, 2008, accessed April 2, 2013, http://www.genderlawsuitagainstsmithbarney.com/press-release-03.htm.
[32]"Sex Suit Costs Morgan Stanley $54M," July 12, 2004, www.cbsnews.com. See also Patrick McGeehan, "Discrimination on Wall St.? Run the Numbers and Weep," *New York Times*, July 14, 2004, C1, C7.
[33]Jonathon Stempel and Nate Raymond, "U.S. Court OKs Bank of America $39 Million Gender Bias Deal," Reuters, December 27, 2013, www.reuters.com.

gender differences in earnings: supply-side factors (including human capital) and labor market discrimination. We also consider another factor that is particularly relevant to changes in the gender pay gap *over time*, that is, changes that have occurred in the overall US wage structure. **Wage structure** refers to the returns that the labor market offers for various skills and for employment in various industries or occupations. The focus on wage structure is desirable because it is useful to see the declining gender pay gap in the context of the other dramatic shift in earnings patterns that has taken place in recent decades—rising **wage inequality**, or a widening dispersion in the distribution of earnings. Before turning to explanations for the declining gender pay gap, we review what has been happening to US wage inequality.

The Context: Widening Wage Inequality

US wage inequality has been rising since around 1980 and now stands at very high levels by historical standards and in comparison to other economically advanced countries. Increases in wage inequality have occurred among both women and men.[34] The rise in inequality reflects changes in wage structure—specifically an *increase* in the **returns to skills** or the rewards that the labor market gives for various worker skills and for employment in various industries or occupations. When the returns to skills and sector increase, wage inequality also rises. For instance, consider an individual with a 4-year college education. As we saw in Chapter 8 (see Table 8-4), the wage (or earnings) premium associated with a college education is considerably higher today than it was in earlier years, reflecting an increase in the returns to this skill. There is not full consensus on the reasons for the increase in the returns to education and to skills more generally (education is just one example, although a particularly important one), but research points to factors on both the demand and supply sides as playing a role.[35]

On the demand side, there has been an increase in the relative demand for skills, driven primarily by technological change. For example, the development of personal computers and related information technologies has increased the demand for college-educated workers, while increased computer use has largely been a substitute for less-skilled workers, reducing the demand for less-skilled workers.[36] Some research also suggests that growing international trade has had a similar effect, reducing

---

[34]For summaries of these trends, see, for example, Rebecca M. Blank, *Changing Inequality* (Berkeley: University of California Press, 2011); Francine D. Blau, "Trends in the Well-Being of American Women: 1970–95," *Journal of Economic Literature* 36, no. 1 (March 1998): 112–65; and David H. Autor, Lawrence F. Katz, and Melissa S. Kearney, "Trends in U.S. Wage Inequality in the 1990s: Revising the Revisionists," *Review of Economics and Statistics* 90, no. 2 (May 2008): 300–23.

[35]This discussion draws on Lawrence F. Katz and David H. Autor, "Changes in the Wage Structure and Earnings Inequality," in *Handbook of Labor Economics*, vol. 3A, ed. Orley C. Ashenfelter and David Card (Amsterdam: Elsevier, 1999), 1463–1555; Claudia Goldin and Lawrence M. Katz, *The Race between Education and Technology* (Cambridge, MA: Belknap Press of Harvard University Press, 2008); and Autor, Katz, and Kearney, "Trends in U.S. Wage Inequality."

[36]In explaining the trends since the 1990s, David H. Autor, Lawrence F. Katz, and Melissa S. Kearney have postulated a more complex situation, with computers complementary to nonroutine cognitive (high-education) tasks, substitutable for routine (middle-education) tasks, and having little impact on nonroutine manual (low-education) tasks. This is consistent with the observed empirical pattern in which wage inequality in the top half of the distribution has been rising since 1980 but inequality in the bottom half of the distribution has not increased since the late 1980s. See "The Polarization of the U.S. Labor Market," *American Economic Review* 96, no. 2 (May 2006): 189–94. See also, Autor, Katz, and Kearney, "Trends in U.S. Wage Inequality."

the demand for less-skilled US workers, although its role appears to be smaller than technological change.

Supply-side shifts also appear important in explaining the trends in the college wage premium. There was a sharp slowdown in the growth in the supply of college-educated workers after 1980. So, as the relative demand for more educated workers increased steadily, the growth in the supply of educated workers did not keep pace.[37] This meant that the rightward shift in the demand curve was larger than the rightward shift in the supply curve, and the college wage premium rose.

Some also point to rising immigration as contributing to the widening wage gap between higher- and lower-skilled workers by increasing the supply of the less-skilled, although there is less agreement about the importance of this factor.[38] In addition, institutional factors including the decline in unionism, which we discussed in Chapter 7, and the decreasing real value of the minimum wage also likely contributed.[39] As described in "The Minimum Wage" box, in the context of rising wage inequality, increasing public attention has focused on the decreasing real value of the minimum wage and policies to increase it. Raising the minimum wage also has the potential to reduce the gender wage gap because, as a relatively low-paid group, women are more likely than men to be earning wages that would be boosted by a higher minimum. Higher minimum wages may also reduce family poverty (particularly in conjunction with the Earned Income Tax Credit); this issue is considered in Chapter 15. Of course, in judging the minimum wage as a policy approach, possible adverse employment effects must be considered; as noted in the box, the evidence on this is mixed.

Determinants of Trends in the Gender Wage Gap

As we have seen, the evidence suggests that both human capital and other supply-side factors and labor market discrimination likely play a role in explaining the gender wage gap. Following this reasoning, we would expect the gender wage gap to decline if (1) women increase their qualifications relative to men's or (2) labor market discrimination against women decreases.

The human capital and discrimination explanations for the gender wage gap imply a role for a third factor that affects trends in the gap, one which we mentioned earlier, and that is changes in wage structure (the returns to skills and employment in various industries or occupations).[40] Based on the human capital analysis and

---

[37]See, especially, Goldin and Katz, *Race between Education and Technology.*

[38]See, for example, George J. Borjas, "The Labor Demand Curve *Is* Downward Sloping: Reexamining the Impact of Immigration on the Labor Market," *Quarterly Journal of Economics* 118 no. 4 (November 2003): 1335–74; and David Card, "Immigration and inequality," *American Economic Review* 99 no. 2 (May 2009): 1–21. For reviews, see Francine D. Blau and Christopher Mackie, eds., *The Economic and Fiscal Consequences of Immigration* (Washington, DC: National Academies Press, 2016), and Francine D. Blau and Lawrence M. Kahn, "Immigration and the Distribution of Incomes," in *The Handbook on the Economics of International Migration*, ed. Barry R. Chiswick and Paul W. Miller (Amsterdam: Elsevier, 2015), 793–843.

[39]John DiNardo, Nicole M. Fortin, and Thomas Lemieux, "Labor Market Institutions and the Distribution of Wages, 1973–1992: A Semiparametric Approach," *Econometrica* 64, no. 5 (September 1996): 1001–44: See, also, Thomas Lemieux, "The Changing Nature of Wage Inequality," *Journal of Population Economics* 21, no. 1 (January 2008): 21–48.

[40]See Blau and Kahn, "The Gender Wage Gap"; Francine D. Blau and Lawrence M. Kahn, "Swimming Upstream: Trends in the Gender Wage Differential in the 1980s," *Journal of Labor Economics* 15, no. 1, pt. 1 (January 1997): 1–42; and Francine D. Blau and Lawrence M. Kahn. "The U.S. Gender Pay Gap in the 1990s: Slowing Convergence," *Industrial and Labor Relations Review* 60, no. 1 (October 2006): 45–66.

The Minimum Wage: What Is It?*

The campaign for a $15 minimum wage by fast-food and other low-wage workers dominated headlines in 2015 and 2016. One reason this issue garnered considerable attention is because the federal **minimum wage** had stood at $7.25 since 2009. As a point of comparison, the value of the minimum wage in 1968 (when it was at its historic peak) was equivalent to $10.90 in 2015, after adjusting for inflation. Further, in 1968 its value stood at around 50 percent of the national median wage; in 2015 it was just under 40 percent of that level.**

The federal minimum wage was established in 1938 under the **Fair Labor Standards Act**. It is a **wage floor**; that is, it is the legal minimum price that firms can pay per hour for workers covered by the law. Workers who are not covered include exempt workers such as executives and administrators. A large group of low-wage workers who are covered by the law but not paid the federal minimum wage are tipped workers. These are workers who regularly receive more than $30 per month in tips. Employers can pay these workers a "tipped wage" that is below the federal minimum (though employers are required to supplement it so that the wage paid is at least equal to the federal minimum).

As of 2016, 29 states and the District of Columbia had adopted state minimum wages that were higher than $7.25. In addition, many localities, starting with Seattle and San Francisco in 2015, adopted city-wide minimum wages of $15; and in 2016 California became the first state in the nation to adopt a $15 state-wide minimum wage. The new minimum wage is typically implemented over several years, rather than being immediately increased. In the case of California, for instance, it will not be fully phased in until 2022. Also, the California law permits a delay in the phase-in for smaller firms and has a clause that stalls the increase during an economic downturn.***

Another related concept often linked to the minimum wage or used synonymously with a high minimum wage is a **living wage**. A living wage does not have a fixed definition, but one definition is that it be "equal to the hourly rate that an individual must earn to support their family, if they are the sole provider and are working full-time (2080 hours per year)."**** This is not to be confused with local "**living wage laws**" that prevail in many cities. Living wage laws have also been adopted to address concerns about the adequacy of worker's wages but address it in a different way. While the specifics of these laws vary, they typically require that workers covered by city contracts (e.g., a city hires janitorial workers) must be paid a wage that is higher than the prevailing minimum wage; its value is often tied to the poverty line. The first city to adopt such an ordinance was Baltimore in 1994.

Understanding the details of minimum wage policies, including the geographic scope, eligibility coverage, and implementation, is useful in understanding the overall labor market context in which employment outcomes, the gender wage gap, and the family poverty rate are determined.

---

*For more information on the federal and state minimum wages, go to www.dol.gov. For an updated list of cities with minimum wages see Berkeley Labor Center, http://laborcenter.berkeley.edu (accessed June 30, 2016). There is a voluminous academic literature on the impact of the minimum wage on employment, poverty, and a host of outcomes. For reviews of the research, see David Neumark, "The Effects of Minimum Wages on Employment," FRBSB Economic Letter (San Francisco: Federal Reserve Bank, December 2015), and Andrajit Dube; "Keeping Up with a Changing Economy: Indexing the Minimum Wage," US Senate Committee on Health, Education, Labor & Pensions Hearing (March 14, 2013); for influential early work, see David C. Card and Alan B. Krueger, Myth and Measurement: The New Economics of the Minimum Wage (Princeton, NJ: Princeton University Press, 1995). For discussions of local living and minimum wages, see Andrajit Dube, "Proposal 13: Designing Thoughtful Minimum Wage Policy at the State and Local Levels," Hamilton Project (Washington, DC: Brookings Institution, 2014); and David Neumark, Matthew Thompson, and Leslie Koyle, "The Effects of Living Wage Laws on Low-Wage Workers and Low-Income Families: What Do We Know Now?" IZA Journal of Policy 1 no. 11 (2012).

**The 1968 figure was adjusted for inflation using the Consumer Price Index; see US Bureau of Labor Statistics, accessed July 3, 2016, www.bls.gov. The comparison with median earnings is from Dube, "Proposal 13."

***While these policies enjoy considerable support, they have raised some concerns as well. See, for instance, Noam Scheiber and Ian Lovett, "$15-an-Hour Minimum Wage in California? Plan Has Some Worried," New York Times, March 28, 2016; and Alan Krueger, "The Minimum Wage: How Much Is Too Much? New York Times, October 9, 2015.

****The quoted definition is from the MIT "Living Wage Calculator," "Living Wage Calculation for New York," accessed March 1, 2017, livingwage@mit.edu./states/36. The MIT Living Wage Calculator provides separate calculations for each state to reflect variation in basic expenses such as shelter and food. For details on the methodology, see Carey Anne Nadeau, "Living Wage Calculator User's Guide / Technical Notes 2015 Update," accessed March 1, 2017, livingwage@mit.edu.

discrimination models, we expect men and women to have different qualifications and to be employed in different occupations and industries. This means that changes in the returns to qualifications (skills) and sectors (occupations and industries) will have *different* effects on women's and men's wages and, thus, can potentially influence trends in the gender wage gap.

For example, despite important recent gains, women still have less experience than men, on average. If the labor market return to experience (i.e., the increase in wages associated with each additional year of experience) rises over time, women will be *increasingly* disadvantaged by their lesser amount of experience. As another example, despite recent decreases in occupational segregation, women and men continue to be employed in different occupations and industries. This implies that an increase in the rewards for employment in "male" occupations or industries will also place women at an *increasing* disadvantage. Thus, we may add point (3) if wage structure (the returns to skill and sector) changes to more highly reward qualifications and sectors where men are better endowed than women, the gender wage gap will increase.

In fact, the increases in overall wage inequality in the labor market, particularly in the 1980s, resulted from precisely such increases in the market rewards to skill and to employment in high-wage male sectors. This means that women as a group were essentially "swimming upstream" in a labor market growing increasingly unfavorable for workers with below-average skills—in this case, below-average experience—and for workers employed in disproportionately female occupations and industries.

Explaining the Decline in the Gender Wage Gap

How can we explain the *decrease* in the gender wage gap in recent decades in the face of *rising* labor market returns to skill and sector that worked against women as a group? The study we have reviewed by Francine Blau and Lawrence Kahn sheds light on this question.[41]

For the sample of full-time workers described earlier, Blau and Kahn examined the effect of changes in women's and men's measured characteristics—experience, education, occupation, industry, and union status—and changes in wage structure on trends in the gender wage gap. They also investigated the role of changes in the unexplained gap, that is, the part of the change in the gender gap that cannot be explained by measured factors.

RESULTS OF THE BLAU–KAHN STUDY This study found that one important factor contributing to the narrowing of the gender wage gap is that women full-time workers *improved their qualifications relative to men*.[42] Thus, although women

---

[41]Results cited in this discussion are from Blau and Kahn, "The Gender Wage Gap," and Blau and Kahn, "The U.S. Gender Pay Gap in the 1990s"; see also Blau and Kahn, "Swimming Upstream." Other research on the convergence of the gender gap includes, for example, Marigee Bacolod and Bernardo S. Blum, "Two Sides of the Same Coin: U.S. 'Residual Inequality' and the Gender Gap," *Journal of Human Resources* 45, no. 1 (Winter 2010): 197–242; and Mulligan and Rubinstein, "Selection, Investment, and Women's Relative Wages."

[42]For evidence regarding the relationship between access to the birth control pill over the 1960s and 1970s and subsequent increases in women's human capital investments and wages, see Martha J. Bailey, Brad Hershbein, and Amalia R. Miller, "The Opt-In Revolution? Contraception and the Gender Gap in Wages," *American Economic Journal: Applied Economics* 4, no. 3 (July 2012): 225–54.

continued to have less labor market experience than men, on average, they *narrowed the gender difference in experience*. The gender gap in full-time experience fell from 7 years in 1981 to 1.4 years in 2011.[43] In the case of education, women not only closed the gap with men but *surpassed men in educational attainment*. In 1981, the incidence of a college or advanced degree was 5 percentage points higher among employed men than women; by 2011, women workers were 1 percentage point *more* likely to have a college or advanced degree than men workers. *Shifts in women's occupations* played an important role too; the employment of women in higher-skilled, higher-paying professional and managerial jobs rose, while their concentration in lower-paying clerical and service jobs fell. Women's wages also increased relative to men's because of the *decrease in the gender gap in unionization* that occurred during this time. This was because the decline in unionization (discussed in Chapter 7) had a larger negative wage effect on male than female workers; men, who were traditionally much more likely than women to be unionized, experienced a larger decrease in unionization than women.

Another major factor that worked to decrease the gender wage gap substantially, especially during the 1980s, was a *decrease in the unexplained portion of the gender differential*, that is, a decline in the pay difference between men and women with the same measured characteristics (i.e., experience, education, occupation, industry, and union status). Although the unexplained gap (and thus changes in it) are often ascribed to labor market discrimination, as discussed earlier in this chapter in the section on "Biases in the Unexplained Gap as an Estimate of Discrimination," we cannot overlook the role of (changes in) a number of unmeasured labor market factors in influencing the unexplained gap. In the section on "Understanding the Decline in the Unexplained Portion of the Gender Pay Gap" below, we consider in detail the possible reasons for the decrease in the unexplained gap during this period.

Taken together (1) increases in women's qualifications and (2) decreases in the unexplained gap worked to reduce the gender wage gap substantially. Working in the opposite direction, however, were (3) changes in wage structure (or returns to skills and sector) that favored men over women, especially during the 1980s. Of particular importance were a rise in the return to experience (recall that women have less of it) and increases in returns to employment in predominantly male occupations and industries. The effect of these adverse shifts in labor market returns by themselves would have *increased* the gender wage gap substantially. Thus, in order for the gender wage gap to *decline*, the factors favorably affecting women's wages (improved qualifications and decreases in the unexplained gap) needed to be large enough to more than offset the impact of unfavorable shifts in wage structure. This was indeed the case, so the gender wage gap declined.

UNDERSTANDING THE DECLINE IN THE UNEXPLAINED PORTION OF THE GENDER PAY GAP What can we say about the reasons for the decrease in the unexplained gender wage gap that occurred during this period? Such a shift may reflect a decline in *labor market discrimination* against women, and evidence suggests this is part of the explanation. However, as discussed earlier, the unexplained

---

[43]See also June O'Neill and Solomon W. Polachek, "Why the Gender Gap in Wages Narrowed in the 1980s," *Journal of Labor Economics* 11, no. 1, pt. 1 (January 1993): 205–28; and Catherine Weinberger and Peter Kuhn, "Changing Levels or Changing Slopes? The Narrowing of the U.S. Gender Earnings Gap, 1959–1999," *Industrial and Labor Relations Review* 63, no. 3 (April 2010): 384–406.

gap might also be at least partly attributed to unmeasured factors. In the context of changes over time in the gender wage gap, this means that the decline in the unexplained gap could also be due to an upgrading of women's *unmeasured labor market skills*, a shift in *labor market demand* favoring women over men, or changes in the *composition of the labor force* due to the pattern of labor force entries or exits. Indeed, all of these factors, including declines in discrimination, may have played a role, and all appear credible during this period.

First, it is likely that discrimination against women declined. One rationale that employers have traditionally given for discriminating against women is that women as a group are less strongly attached to the labor force and to their jobs than men. (We consider this idea further in our discussion of statistical discrimination in the next chapter.) It is likely that such views have eroded, at least to some extent, as women have become more firmly attached to the labor force. Further, in the presence of feedback effects, employers' revised views can generate additional increases in women's wages by raising their returns to investments in job qualifications and skills—both measured and unmeasured. Another possible reason for a decline in discrimination against women is that changes in attitudes may have made discriminatory tastes or prejudices increasingly less socially acceptable.

Second, since women improved the relative level of their *measured* skills, like full-time job experience and education, as well as their employment in higher-skilled managerial and professional jobs, it is plausible that they also enhanced their *unmeasured* skills compared to men. By *unmeasured skills* we mean skills that are not measured (or observed) in standard data sets used in statistical analyses like this one. But, in some cases, information on "unmeasured" skills may be available from other sources. For example, as we saw in Chapter 8, gender differences in college major—found to be strongly related to the gender wage gap among college graduates—have decreased, and gender differences in SAT math scores have declined as well. Further, as we saw in the section on "Evidence on Possible Sources of the Unexplained Gender Wage Gap" earlier in this chapter, the lower value that women have traditionally placed on money and work is a factor that has been linked to women's lower pay. It has been found that men's and women's attitudes toward money and work have become more similar in recent years and that this helps to explain the decrease in the gender wage gap.[44]

Third, the underlying labor market demand shifts that widened overall wage inequality appear to have favored women relative to men in certain ways and, thus, also likely contributed to a decrease in the unexplained gender gap identified in the present analysis and other similar types of studies.[45] Overall, manufacturing employment declined, particularly in the 1980s. In addition, some evidence indicates that technological change produced within-industry demand shifts that favored white-collar relative to blue-collar workers in general.[46] Given that men

---

[44]Fortin, "The Gender Wage Gap."

[45]For examples of studies emphasizing the importance of demand shifts in explaining the trends, see, for example, Finis Welch, "Growth in Women's Relative Wages and in Inequality among Men: One Phenomenon or Two?" *American Economic Review* 90, no. 2 (May 2000): 444–49; Bacolod and Blum, "Two Sides of the Same Coin"; Blau and Kahn, "The U.S. Gender Pay Gap in the 1990s"; and Blau and Kahn, "Swimming Upstream."

[46]Eli Berman, John Bound, and Zvi Griliches, "Changes in the Demand of Skilled Labor Within U.S. Manufacturing Industries: Evidence from the Annual Survey of Manufacturing," *Quarterly Journal of Economics* 109, no. 2 (May 1994): 367–97.

have tended to hold a disproportionate share of manufacturing and blue-collar jobs, these shifts would be expected to benefit women relative to men. Increased computer use, a key aspect of technological change, also seems to favor women compared to men. For one, women are more likely than men to use computers at work, and computers also restructure work in ways that de-emphasize physical strength.[47] In addition, with the spread of computers, some evidence suggests that interpersonal interactions have become more important because teamwork is more important in occupations with greater computer use. Since women's interpersonal skills tend to exceed men's, on average, this factor is believed to have increased women's wages relative to men's.[48] Alongside these developments, there has also been an increase in the labor market return to cognitive skills and a corresponding decrease in the return to motor skills. This has also boosted women's wages relative to men's because women tend to be more highly represented in occupations where cognitive skills are important while men are more likely to be in jobs that emphasize motor skills.[49]

A final factor contributing to the considerable narrowing of the "unexplained" gender wage gap was favorable shifts in the composition of the female labor force. The female labor force expanded, particularly during the 1980s, and some evidence suggests that the women who entered the labor force tended to be those with relatively high (unmeasured) skills. These skills improved the quality of the female labor force and thus contributed to the narrowing of the gender wage gap.[50]

Minorities Fared Less Well in Narrowing the Wage Gap with Whites

The experience of blacks in recent decades stands in sharp contrast to that of women. As we saw in Chapter 7, while the black–white earnings gap declined after the passage of civil rights legislation in the mid-1960s, it changed little after the mid- to late 1970s. Some research suggests that changes in wage structure may provide at least a partial explanation for the stalling of progress of African Americans. On average, blacks have lower educational attainment than whites (although the race gap in education has declined) and, as a consequence, blacks are more adversely affected than whites by declining relative wages for less educated workers. Some evidence also indicates that the decline in blue-collar jobs in manufacturing particularly negatively affected black males. Growth in incarceration rates, which has disproportionately affected blacks, has also been cited as a factor. For black women, although their exit from extremely low-paying, private household employment was an important factor in narrowing the race gap in earlier years, this factor was no longer relevant by the 1980s, when their representation in these jobs approached levels for whites. Despite these interesting insights, the full explanation

---

[47]Alan B. Krueger, "How Computers Have Changed the Wage Structure: Evidence from Microdata, 1984–1989," *Quarterly Journal of Economics* 108, no. 1 (February 1993): 33–60; and Bruce Weinberg, "Computer Use and the Demand for Female Workers," *Industrial and Labor Relations Review* 53, no. 2 (January 2000): 290–308. The growing importance of "brains" relative to "brawn" as a factor narrowing the gender pay gap is particularly emphasized by Welch, "Growth in Women's Relative Wages."
[48]Borghans, ter Weel, and Weinberg, "People Skills."
[49]Bacolod and Blum, "Two Sides of the Same Coin."
[50]Blau and Kahn, "The U.S. Gender Pay Gap in the 1990s." The authors find that female labor force entrants were less skilled during the 1990s than the 1980s, perhaps as a result of the entry of many relatively low-skilled, female single-family heads. See also Mulligan and Rubinstein, "Selection, Investment, and Women's Relative Wages," who place greater emphasis on the role of selection in narrowing the gender wage gap.

for the unfortunate lack of progress in narrowing the race gap in earnings since the 1970s remains elusive.[51]

The data presented in Chapter 7 also indicate that the wages of Hispanic women and men have fallen relative to those of whites of the same sex since data became available for this group in the mid-1970s. Education gaps between Hispanics and whites are considerably larger than those between blacks and whites, so it is likely that Hispanics were more negatively affected by the declining relative wages of less educated workers. In addition, as noted in Chapter 7, a large and growing proportion of Hispanics are recent immigrants to the United States; hence, the earnings of Hispanics are reduced, on average, because new immigrants tend to be relatively young, may not speak English well, and are likely to face other difficulties in adjusting to their new environment. This negative effect was exacerbated by the fact that the economic status of immigrants has deteriorated relative to that of the native-born.[52]

Empirical Evidence on the Causes and Consequences of Gender Differences in Occupations

As we saw in Chapter 7, not only do women earn less than men but they also tend to be concentrated in different occupations. In this and the next section, we address two sets of questions:

- What are the *consequences* for women of occupational segregation? In particular, what is its relationship to the pay gap between men and women?

- What are the *causes* of gender differences in occupational distributions? Specifically, what role does labor market discrimination play? Does the evidence indicate a "glass ceiling" that limits the upward mobility of women?

From a policy perspective, an understanding of the consequences of segregation is crucial for assessing its importance, and an analysis of its causes helps us to determine the most effective tools for attacking it.

---

[51]For a useful overview of black–white differences, see Derek Neal, "Black–White Labour Market Inequality in the United States," in *The New Palgrave Dictionary of Economics*, 2nd ed., ed. Steven Durlauf and Lawrence Blume (London: Palgrave Macmillan, 2008). For an analysis of black–white trends for males and females, see Valerie Wilson and William M. Rodgers III, "Black–White Wage Gaps Expand with Rising Wage Inequality," Economic Policy Institute, September 19, 2016, accessed November 9, 2016, http://www.epi.org. For studies on males, see, for example, John V. Winters and Barry T. Hirsch, "An Anatomy of Racial and Ethnic Trends in Male Earnings," *Review of Income and Wealth* 60, no. 4 (December 2014): 930–47; Chinhui Juhn, Kevin M. Murphy, and Brooks Pierce, "Accounting for the Slowdown in Black–White Wage Convergence," in *Workers and Their Wages*, ed. Marvin Kosters (Washington, DC: AEI Press, 1991), 107–43 (this study is especially important for clarifying the role of changes in wage structure); and Derek Neal and Armin Rick, "The Prison Boom and the Lack of Black Progress after Smith and Welch," NBER Working Paper 20283 (National Bureau of Economic Research, Cambridge, MA, July 2014). For studies on females, see Martha T. Bailey and William J. Collins, "The Wage Gains of African-American Women in the 1940s," *Journal of Economic History*, 66, no. 3 (September 2006): 737–77; and Francine D. Blau and Andrea H. Beller, "Black–White Earnings over the 1970s and 1980s, Gender Differences in Trends," *Review of Economics and Statistics* 74, no. 2 (May 1992): 276–86.

[52]For analyses of Hispanic and immigrant earnings, see Maury B. Gittleman and David R. Howell, "Changes in the Structure and Quality of Jobs in the United States: Effects by Race and Gender, 1973–1990," *Industrial and Labor Relations Review* 48, no. 3 (April 1995): 420–40; Gregory DeFreitas, *Inequality at Work: Hispanics in the U.S. Labor Force* (Oxford: Oxford University Press, 1991); and George J. Borjas, "The Slowdown in the Economic Assimilation of Immigrants: Aging and Cohort Effects Revisited Again," *Journal of Human Capital* 9, no. 44 (2015): 483–517.

Consequences of Occupational Segregation

In Chapter 7, we saw that women are concentrated in clerical and service jobs, whereas men are more likely than women to work in blue-collar occupations, including the higher-paying, skilled jobs in this category. Similarly, although the representation of women in the professional category actually exceeds men's, men are more likely to work in lucrative professions such as lawyer or physician and in high-paying STEM fields like computer science and engineering, whereas women are more often employed in relatively lower-paying ones such as elementary and secondary school teaching and nursing. Such observations suggest that women are concentrated in relatively low-paying occupations compared to men with similar skills and that this gender difference in occupations helps to explain the male–female pay gap.

On the other hand, it is possible that the requirements or skills of male and female jobs may help to account for pay differences between them. For example, male jobs may tend to require more education and training than female jobs or call for the exercise of skills, such as supervisory responsibility, that are more valuable to the employer. Also, some may require more physical strength, inconvenient hours, and so on.

Such characteristics are important, but occupational differences between men and women appear to be a significant factor in explaining the earnings gap, even when productivity-related characteristics of workers are held constant. The findings reported in Table 10-1, for example, suggest that differences in the employment of men and women across the 21 occupational categories included in the study account for 33 percent of the pay difference between men and women, controlling for education, experience, and other factors. A substantial body of research that takes into account a much larger number of detailed occupational categories—over 400—finds a negative relationship between percent female in an occupation (the share of those in the occupation who are female) and the wage of the occupation, even after controlling for the measured qualifications of workers. In other words, predominantly female jobs pay less than predominantly male jobs for both men and women, all else equal.[53] Moreover, even *within* female-dominated occupations, women tend to earn less than their male counterparts, and they tend to move up the career ranks more slowly. This phenomenon has been termed a **glass escalator** for men.[54] Women, in contrast, may experience a phenomenon known as a glass ceiling—a set of subtle factors that inhibit their rise in predominantly male jobs or to the higher ranks of hierarchies more generally. We discuss this concept at length shortly.

---

[53]See, for example, Asaf Levanon, Paula England, and Paul Allison, "Occupational Feminization and Pay: Assessing Causal Dynamics Using 1950–2000 U.S. Census Data," *Social Forces* 88, no. 2 (December 2009): 865–981; and Stephanie Boraas and William M. Rodgers III, "How Does Gender Play a Role in the Earnings Gap? An Update," *Monthly Labor Review* 126, no. 3 (March 2003): 9–15. For some earlier work, see David A. Macpherson and Barry T. Hirsch, "Wages and Gender Composition, Why Do Women's Jobs Pay Less?" *Journal of Labor Economics* 13, no. 3 (July 1995): 426–71; and Elaine Sorensen, "The Crowding Hypothesis and Comparable Worth Issue," *Journal of Human Resources* 25, no. 1 (Winter 1990): 55–89.

[54]This term was coined by Christine L. Williams, "The Glass Escalator: Hidden Advantages for Men in the 'Female' Professions," *Social Problems* 39, no. 3 (August 1992): 253–67. In reflecting on this concept 20 years later, Williams emphasizes that it is most applicable to white men employed in occupations and positions with stable employment; see Christine L. Williams, "The Glass Escalator, Revisited: Gender Inequality in Neoliberal Times," *Gender & Society* 27, no. 5 (October 2013): 609–29. For empirical evidence, see Michelle J. Budig, "Male Advantage and the Gender Composition of Jobs: Who Rides the Glass Escalator?" *Social Problems* 49, no. 2 (May 2002): 258–77.

One category of predominantly female employment that has gotten increasing attention is paid care work. It is comprised of workers in industries and occupations providing care services. Such occupations are those in which "concern for the well-being of others is likely to affect the quality of services provided"—including occupations like nurse, teacher, college professor, childcare worker, licensed practical nurse, and health aide.[55] Care work is an expanding and disproportionately female sector. Its growth is propelled by the increase in female labor force participation, which has increased the need for childcare, as well as the aging of the population, which has raised the demand for caregiving services for the elderly, among other factors. Research suggests that there is a wage penalty associated with care work. For example, one study found that care work pays less than other occupations in statistical analyses that control for worker education and experience and a number of occupation and industry characteristics, including percent female in the occupation.[56]

While evidence suggests that predominantly female occupations pay less, all else equal (and that wages may be even lower in care work), it has been suggested that the negative effect of predominantly female occupations on wages is likely underestimated. Although the census regularly collects data on some 400 occupations, employers use considerably finer breakdowns of occupations and job titles in classifying workers, as discussed in Chapter 7. It is likely that, were wage information on such extremely detailed categories available for the economy as a whole, an even higher proportion of the pay gap would be attributed to occupational segregation. Moreover, employment segregation takes other forms in addition to occupational segregation. Within the same occupational category, women tend to be employed in low-wage firms and industries. In the study reported in Table 10-1, for example, gender differences in industry and union status together account for an additional 25 percent of the gender gap. More generally, a substantial body of research finds evidence of negative effects on women's wages of segregation by industry and firm, even within the same occupation.[57]

When evaluating the negative consequences of occupational segregation for women, it is important to bear in mind that the focus on earnings does not take into account any adverse nonpecuniary (nonmonetary) consequences of such segregation. For one, it is likely that occupational segregation reinforces cultural notions of exaggerated differences between men and women in capabilities, preferences, and social and economic roles. For instance, women's overrepresentation in paid care work perpetuates the idea that women, not men, are nurturers. Such beliefs may adversely affect the opportunities and outcomes of all women, even those in predominantly male jobs.

---

[55]See, the contributions in Nancy Folbre, ed., *For Love and Money: Care Provision in the United States* (New York: Russell Sage Foundation, 2012), especially Nancy Folbre, "Introduction," xi–xvii, and Candace Howes, Carrie Leana, and Kristin Smith, "Paid Care Work," 65–91; quotation is from p. 66.

[56]Paula England, Michelle Budig, and Nancy Folbre, "Wages of Virtue: The Relative Pay of Care Work," *Social Problems* 49, no. 4 (November 2002): 455–73. A more recent study by Barry T. Hirsch and Julia Manzella finds smaller, although still negative, effects; see, "Who Cares and Does It Matter? Measuring Wage Penalties for Caring Work," *Research in Labor Economics* 41 (2014): 213–75.

[57]For an early study, see, Francine D. Blau, *Equal Pay in the Office* (Lexington, MA: Lexington Books, 1977). For more recent evidence, see Erica L. Groshen, "The Structure of the Female/Male Wage Differential: Is It Who You Are, What You Do, or Where You Work?" *Journal of Human Resources* 26, no. 3 (Summer 1991): 457–72; and Kimberly Bayard, Judith Hellerstein, David Neumark, and Kenneth Troske, "New Evidence on Sex Segregation and Sex Difference in Wages from Matched Employee–Employer Data," *Journal of Labor Economics* 21, no. 4 (October 2003): 887–923.

Causes of Occupational Segregation

As with earnings differences, the causes of occupational segregation may be classified into supply-side versus demand-side factors. Only the latter—differences in treatment—represent *direct* labor market discrimination. Of course, here again, the anticipation of, or experience with, labor market discrimination may indirectly influence women's choices via feedback effects.

As we explained in Chapter 9, human capital theory suggests that to the extent women generally anticipate shorter and less continuous work lives than men, it is in their economic self-interest to choose predominantly female occupations, which presumably require smaller human capital investments and have lower wage penalties for time spent out of the labor market. We also discussed other supply-side factors that could influence women's occupational choices, including the constraints placed by traditional gender roles on women's ability to work long hours, travel extensively as part of their jobs, and relocate to new labor markets, as well as gender differences in psychological attributes. In Chapter 8, we considered the role of the socialization process and various subtle barriers that may impede women's access to training in traditionally male fields. On the demand side, employers may contribute to occupational segregation by discriminating against equally qualified women in hiring, job placement, access to training programs, and promotion for traditionally male jobs. It is highly likely that both supply- and demand-side factors play a role in producing the occupational segregation by sex that we observe in the labor market, although precisely quantifying their relative effects is difficult.

There is some evidence suggesting that discrimination may be a factor in gender differences in occupations; however, the literature on this topic is much sparser than for gender differences in wages, and moreover, much of it is not very current. Some persuasive evidence of the importance of discrimination in past years comes from descriptions of institutional barriers that historically excluded women from particular pursuits or impeded their upward progression.[58] Of course, this may have relevance to the present in that it contributed to a dearth of mentors and role models in predominantly male occupations for women entering the labor market in subsequent years. Of particular relevance to the present is that many studies, although not all, find that women are less likely to be promoted, all else equal.[59] And one suggestive finding is that a major portion of the gender difference in on-the-job training remains unexplained, even after gender differences in the probability of worker turnover and other variables are taken into account.[60] This finding suggests that women

---

[58]See Barbara F. Reskin and Heidi I. Hartmann, eds., *Women's Work, Men's Work: Sex Segregation on the Job* (Washington, DC: National Academies Press, 1986); and Patricia A. Roos and Barbara F. Reskin, "Institutional Factors Contributing to Occupational Sex Segregation," in *Sex Segregation in the Workplace: Trends, Explanations, Remedies*, ed. Barbara Reskin (Washington, DC: National Academies Press, 1984), 235–60.

[59]For examples of studies that find evidence of lower promotion rates, see Francine D. Blau and Jed DeVaro, "New Evidence on Gender Differences in Promotion Rates: An Empirical Analysis of a Sample of New Hires," *Industrial Relations* 46, no. 3 (July 2007): 511–50; Deborah A. Cobb-Clark, "Getting Ahead: The Determinants of and Payoffs to Internal Promotion for Young U.S. Men and Women," in *Worker Wellbeing in a Changing Labor Market*, ed. Solomon W. Polachek, *Research in Labor Economics*, vol. 20 (Amsterdam: Elsevier Science, JAI, 2001), 339–72; and Kristin McCue, "Promotions and Wage Growth," *Journal of Labor Economics* 14, no. 2 (1996): 175–209. For an example of a study that does not find evidence of lower promotion rates, see Joni Hersch and W. Kip Viscusi, "Gender Differences in Promotions and Wages," *Industrial Relations* 35, no. 4 (October 1996): 461–72.

[60]Anne Beeson Royalty, "The Effects of Job Turnover on the Training of Men and Women," *Industrial and Labor Relations Review* 49, no. 3 (April 1996): 506–21. See also John M. Barron, Dan A. Black, and Mark A. Lowenstein, "Gender Differences in Training, Capital and Wages," *Journal of Human Resources* 28, no. 2 (1993): 342–64.

may encounter discrimination in access to on-the-job training, impeding their entry into the types of jobs where such training is important.

Although such findings regarding promotion and training are consistent with discrimination, it is important to note that they suffer from the same types of problems raised earlier in our analysis of the determinants of the gender wage gap. They may overstate discrimination if other important nondiscriminatory factors are omitted from the analysis, such as tastes for particular types of work and availability for travel, which could help to account for the observed gender differences. On the other hand, discrimination would be understated to the extent some of the variables that are controlled for, such as initial job title in a study of promotions, reflect the impact of labor market discrimination.

Given these types of concerns, it is not possible to use these findings to ascribe a specific portion of gender differences in occupations to the choices individual men and women make versus labor market discrimination (i.e., to supply-side vs. demand-side factors).[61] However, as in the case of our review of evidence on the pay gap, the evidence suggests that both are important. And, as in the case of pay differences, evidence of discrimination may be found not only in statistical analyses but also in experimental studies and in discrimination cases in which employers were found guilty of gender discrimination or settled the cases out of court.

Is There a Glass Ceiling?

The foregoing consideration of gender differences in occupations raises the question of whether a class ceiling exists in the labor market. The **glass ceiling** is the name given to the set of subtle barriers believed by many to inhibit women and minorities from reaching the upper echelons of corporate America, government, unions, and academia. To the extent such barriers exist, they constitute a form of labor market discrimination.[62] Substantial disparities in the representation of women at the upper levels of most hierarchies are easy to document. As our preceding discussion suggests, however, the reasons for them are harder to pin down.

Let us begin by considering the extent of gender differences in the representation of women at the top echelons across a number of areas. The extremely low representation of women in the senior ranks of management was already noted in Chapter 7. As we saw, although women are now about 40 percent of managers, overall, they comprise only about a quarter of senior-level managers in S&P 500 companies. At the very top, only 4.2 percent (or 21) of CEOs were women, although this represents a substantial increase from just 1 woman CEO in 1995.[63] As we saw in Chapter 7, women were also underrepresented among the highest-paid executives

---

[61]For additional evidence on and discussion of the sources of gender differences in occupations, see Barbara F. Reskin and Denise D. Bielby, "A Sociological Perspective on Gender and Career Outcomes," *Journal of Economic Perspectives* 19, no. 1 (Winter 2005): 71–86; Alice H. Eagly and Linda L. Carli, *Through the Labyrinth: The Truth about How Women Become Leaders* (Cambridge, MA: Harvard Business School Press, 2007); and Virginia Valian, *Why So Slow? The Advancement of Women* (Cambridge, MA: MIT Press, 1998).

[62]For insightful examinations of this issue and related questions, see Eagly and Carli, *Through the Labyrinth*; and Valian, *Why So Slow?*

[63]Catalyst, "Women in S&P 500 Companies," updated July 2016, http://www.catalyst.org/, and *2002 Catalyst Census of Women Corporate Officers and Top Earners in the Fortune 500* (New York: Catalyst); note that the earlier CEO figure is for the Fortune 500 firms and is thus not completely comparable to the current figure for the S&P 500.

and corporate board members. The underrepresentation of women at the highest levels is similar in government. For example, in 2016, women comprised 20 percent of US senators, 19 percent of members of the US House of Representatives, 12 percent of governors, and 24 percent of state legislators.[64] As another example, in the union sector, women are also underrepresented in the top echelons. As just one example, in 2016 only 21 percent of AFL-CIO executive council members were women.[65] Finally, the status of women in academia follows a similar pattern. Despite considerable growth in the representation of women among college and university faculty at all levels of the hierarchy, women are still more highly represented at the lower echelons. In academic year 2014–2015, women constituted 61 percent of instructors, 56 percent of lecturers, and 51 percent of assistant professors (at the lower ranks) compared to 44 percent of associate and 30 percent of full professors (at the upper ranks).[66]

We focus our attention on the underrepresentation of women in top-level management positions, a topic of broad concern.[67] One issue that comes up in considering this issue here as elsewhere is that it is difficult to determine whether the scarcity of women at the top is simply due to the fact that women are relative newcomers and it takes time to move up through the ranks (what is called the **pipeline argument**) or whether it represents particular barriers to women's advancement. The pipeline argument is certainly credible. Women received only 5 percent of master's degrees in business in 1970, a figure little changed from 1960. While their representation in these programs grew sharply thereafter, reaching 25 percent in 1981 and 47 percent in 2014, a lag is to be expected in woman's representation in top-level positions. Thus, it is difficult to ascertain whether progress to date has been adequate, particularly given the absence of information on available candidates for such jobs as well as on norms regarding the typical speed of movement up the corporate ladder. Nonetheless, given that the growth of women in top-level managerial jobs has been so much slower than the expansion in female receipt of MBA degrees, which, again, dates back to the 1970s, it seems reasonable to conclude that the pipeline effect can only partly explain the low representation of women at the top.[68]

Work–family conflicts provide another plausible nondiscriminatory explanation for the scarcity of women in top corporate jobs. Consistent with this, a survey of top executives at 10 major US firms with global operations found that, while 90 percent of

---

[64]For data on women's representation in elective office, see http://www.cawp.rutgers.edu. In Chapter 17, we discuss US women's political participation in an international context.

[65]"AFL-CIO, Executive Council Members," accessed September 2016, www.aflcio.org. The American Federation of Labor-Congress of Industrial Organizations (AFL-CIO) is the largest union federation in the United States.

[66]American Association of University Professors (March–April 2016), table 12, "Distribution of Faculty, by Rank, Gender, Category, and Affiliation, 2014–15 (Percent)," accessed June 2016, http://www.aaup .org. For evidence on the economics profession, see the annual reports of the Committee on the Status of Women in the Economics Profession, https://www.aeaweb.org/about-aea/committees/cswep/.

[67]We draw on the excellent consideration of this issue in Marianne Bertrand, "CEOs," *Annual Review of Economics* 1, no. 1 (April 2009): 121–50. See also the insightful contributions in Matt L. Huffman, ed., "Gender and Race Inequality in Management: Critical Issues, New Evidence," special issue, *Annals of the American Academy of Political and Social Science* 639 (January 2012).

[68]This is Bertrand's assessment; see "CEOs." The 1970 figure cited in the text is from Bertrand, and the rest of the statistics are from Figure 8-2 in Chapter 8. Note that these figures refer to master's degrees in business (which is broader than MBAs). Data on women's share of MBAs assembled by the Association to Advance Collegiate Schools of Business put the female share lower, at 37 percent in 2012–2013; see "Women's Share of MBAs Earned in the U.S.," Catalyst, accessed November 11, 2016, www.catalyst .org.

male executives had children, only 65 percent of female executives did. And although the majority of both the male and the female executives were married or in a couple relationship, this was true of a considerably higher proportion of men (94 percent) than of women (79 percent). Another indication of the greater work–family conflict female executives face is that, among those who were married or in a couple relationship, nearly 75 percent of the women had a spouse/partner who was employed full-time; in contrast, 75 percent of the men had a spouse/partner who was *not* employed outside the home.[69] The study of graduates from a top MBA program reviewed earlier also suggests that work–family issues are important. The study finds that women were more likely than men to have taken time out since graduation and, moreover, that there were huge wage penalties for taking *any* time out. As one of the authors of the study, Marianne Bertrand, notes, this is "consistent with the view that a continuous commitment to the workforce is pretty much a sine qua non [an essential] condition to make it to the very top in corporate America."[70]

It seems likely that pipeline effects and work–family conflicts account for some of the extremely low representation of women at the very top of corporate America. This does not, however, rule out a role for discrimination or other subtle barriers in limiting women's opportunities. Notably, the study of top corporate executives discussed earlier found that while women are less likely to have children than men at all levels of the corporate hierarchy, reflecting the challenges of balancing work and family, women at the very top echelons were actually more likely to have children than women at the lower echelons.[71] This finding suggests that the presence of children and the associated demands are not the full explanation for women's underrepresentation higher up the ladder. The possibility of discrimination is also suggested by a study that found that the gender gap in executive compensation is smaller when there is a larger number of women on the compensation committee of the board (the group that sets executive compensation).[72] In a similar vein, another study found that an increase in the share of female top managers was associated with subsequent increases in the share of women in mid-level management positions.[73]

What are the economic consequences of women's lower representation at the top? A 2001 study of gender differences in pay among the five highest-paid executives in S&P 1500 firms suggests that they are substantial.[74] It was found that the 2.5 percent of executives in the sample who were women earned 45 percent less than

---

[69]The Families and Work Institute, Catalyst, and the Boston College Center for Work and Family, "Leaders in a Global Economy: A Study of Executive Women and Men," January 2003, http://familiesandwork .org/site/research/summary/globalsumm.pdf. As the study points out, although there has been considerable speculation in the press about "trophy husbands" of high-level female executives based on anecdotal evidence, in these data only 17 percent of the women had husbands who were not employed, just slightly more than the average of 11 percent for all employed married women.

[70]Bertrand, Goldin, and Katz, "Dynamics of the Gender Gap for Young Professionals"; the quotation is from Bertrand, "CEOs," 127.

[71]Families and Work Institute, Catalyst, and Boston College Center for Work and Family, "Leaders in a Global Economy."

[72]Taekjin Shin, "The Gender Gap in Executive Compensation: The Role of Female Directors and Chief Executive Officers," in Huffman, ed., *Gender and Race Inequality in Management*. There is also some evidence that greater representation of women in high-level management narrows the overall gender wage gap among workers; see Philip N. Cohen and Matt L. Huffman, "Working for the Woman? Female Managers and the Gender Wage Gap," *American Sociological Review* 72, no. 5 (October 2007): 681–704.

[73]Fidan Ana Kurtulus and Donald Tomaskovic-Devey, "Do Female Top Managers Help Women to Advance? A Panel Study Using EEO-1 Records," in Huffman, ed., *Gender and Race Inequality in Management*.

[74]Data are for the 1992–1997 period; see Marianne Bertrand and Kevin F. Hallock, "The Gender Gap in Top Corporate Jobs," *Industrial and Labor Relations Review* 55, no. 1 (October 2001): 3–21.

their male counterparts. Female executives were younger and thus had less seniority, a factor contributing to the gender pay difference. However, three-quarters of the gender pay gap was due to the fact that women managed smaller companies and were less likely to be the CEO, chair, or president of their company.

Additional studies focusing on the labor market as a whole (not just the business sector) are also consistent with a glass ceiling, one that has perhaps been getting more difficult to break through over time.[75] For example, the research by Francine Blau and Lawrence Kahn, which we drew on for Table 10-1, also examined the gender wage gap at various points in the wage distribution. They found that the gender wage gap was larger at the top of the wage distribution (90th percentile) than at the middle (50th percentile) or the bottom (10th percentile) and that the wage gap had also declined less at the top over the preceding 20 years than it had at the middle and the bottom. Moreover, the larger gap at the top and the slower progress for those in this group remained even after adjusting for gender differences in qualifications, as in Table 10-1.[76] Of course, studies like this one are subject to the caveats we raised earlier about interpreting an unexplained gender wage gap as evidence of discrimination.

In reviewing the evidence about gender differences in pay and representation at the top, it is important to recognize that, to the extent discrimination plays a role, it need not manifest itself through overt and conscious behavior.[77] The barriers women face are often subtle and difficult to document, let alone to remove. For example, recruiting practices may involve the use of personal contacts from an "old boys' network" that leaves women "out of the loop." Women may also remain outsiders to a "male" workplace culture. A prime example is that, because sports have traditionally been a male domain, successful women are often those who learn to play golf and talk sports.[78] As a final example, women may be disadvantaged by a perception that men make better bosses. A survey of female executives from Fortune 1000 companies by *Catalyst* found that 40 percent believed that men have difficulty being managed by women.[79] Or, as reported in another study, although "women, more than men, manifest leadership styles associated with effective performance as leaders . . . more people prefer male than female bosses."[80]

There may also be stereotyped views about women's qualifications and preferences that result in well-qualified women receiving fewer opportunities. For example,

---

[75]See the studies reviewed in Blau and Kahn, "Gender Wage Gap."

[76]Blau and Kahn, "The Gender Wage Gap." In an earlier study, Blau and Kahn found evidence consistent with a greater negative effect of glass ceiling barriers on women's wages in the 1990s than in the 1980s, They speculated that women's gains in the1980s placed more of them into the higher-level positions where glass ceiling barriers might then hinder their further upward progression; see Blau and Kahn, "The U.S. Gender Pay Gap in the 1990s."

[77]Heather A. Haveman and Lauren S. Beresford argue that gender roles and norms explain most of the gender difference in representation at the top; see "If You're So Smart, Why Aren't You the Boss? Explaining the Persistent Vertical Gender Gap in Management," in Huffman, ed., *Gender and Race Inequality in Management*.

[78]Tory Johnson, "Sports in the Office: How to Make Sure You Have Your Bases Covered," accessed April 3, 2013, https://cisternonline.experience.com/alumnus/article?channel_id=career_management& source_page=editor_picks&article_id=article_1196100376020.

[79]See Catalyst, "Women in U.S. Corporate Leadership" (New York: Catalyst, 2003), 6. Alice H. Eagly and Steven J. Karau argue that a perceived incongruity between the female gender role and leadership roles results in women being viewed less favorably than men as potential leaders and being evaluated less favorably than men for behavior that fits with a leadership role; see "Role Congruity Theory of Prejudice Toward Female Leaders," *Psychological Review* 109, no. 3 (July 2002): 573–98.

[80]Alice H. Eagly, "Female Leadership Advantage and Disadvantage: Resolving the Contradictions," *Psychology of Women Quarterly* 31, no. 1 (March 2007): 1–12.

many people believe that women are not aggressive enough, are unwilling to relocate for higher positions, and, when they have families, are less committed to their jobs than their male counterparts. A number of additional preconceptions may especially limit women's access to top-level jobs in the increasingly important arena of international business. Among these are that international clients are not as comfortable doing business with women as with men.[81]

Conclusion

In this chapter, we considered the factors that explain gender differences in earnings and occupations, particularly focusing on the role of supply-side factors versus labor market discrimination. Disentangling the two is difficult because, among other reasons, labor market discrimination against a particular group is likely to be detrimental, not only directly but also indirectly through feedback effects on their accumulation of human capital. We also examined the reasons for the decrease in the gender pay gap that has occurred since 1980.

Empirical studies have used available evidence on differences in the characteristics of male and female workers to explain the pay gap and the differences in occupational distributions between the two groups. Productivity-related factors, including gender differences in experience, occupations, and industries have been found to be important for the pay gap; but they have not been able to account for all of the gender differences in wages, leaving an unexplained gap that is potentially due to discrimination, although other unmeasured factors may play a role. Similarly, the observed decline in the gender pay gap that began in the 1980s has been due in part to changes in measured productivity factors but also in part to a decrease in the unexplained gap and thus possibly a decline in discrimination. There is also some evidence of unexplained gender differences in occupations, as we saw in our close examination of women in management. Taken together, these results suggest that while supply-side factors are important, discrimination also likely plays a role, thus providing a motivation for our consideration of economic models focused on explaining discrimination (discussed in Chapter 11) and policies to combat discrimination (discussed in Chapter 12).

Questions for Review and Discussion

1. Generally speaking (without referring to any formulas), how do economists measure the extent of labor market discrimination against women using statistical techniques? What important qualifications need to be noted about such estimates? Do such studies indicate that discrimination against women in the labor market continues to exist?

2. What factors explain why some researchers conclude that labor market discrimination against women is small, while others come to a different conclusion? [*Hint*: You may also want to consult the box on the gender pay gap in Chapter 7.]

---

[81]Catalyst, "Passport to Opportunity: U.S. Women in Global Business," news release, October 18, 2000.

3. What measured factors have been found to be most important in explaining pay differences between men and women?

4. It has been found that female MBAs have a more difficult time combining career and family than female physicians, Ph.D.s, and lawyers. Why do you think combining career and family may be especially difficult for MBAs? What kind of policies might address this problem?

5. Suppose you are given data about a firm, indicating that the average wage of male employees is $15.00/hour and the average wage of female employees is $10.50/hour. Define *labor market discrimination* against women. Do the preceding data *prove* that the firm discriminates against women? What kind of additional information would you need to determine whether such discrimination exists?

6. What has happened to wage inequality since 1980? What factors account for the change?

7. Economists point to three major factors behind trends in the gender wage gap. Discuss each, and explain the role each played in the narrowing of the gender wage gap since 1980.

8. Based on the research findings discussed in this chapter, can you conclude that discrimination against women in the labor market has definitely declined? Why or why not? Explain fully.

9. Using paid care work as an example, explain the relationship between occupational segregation and the gender wage gap.

Suggested Readings

Bailey, Martha, and Tom DiPrete. "Five Decades of Remarkable, but Slowing, Change in U.S. Women's Economic and Social Status and Political Participation." In "A Half Century of Change in the Lives of American Women," special issue, *The Russell Sage Foundation Journal of the Social Sciences* 2, no. 4 (August 2016): 1–32.

Bertrand, Marianne, and Esther Duflo. "Field Experiments on Discrimination." NBER Working Paper 22014 (National Bureau of Economic Research, Cambridge, MA, February 2016) (in *Handbook of Field Experiments*, edited by Abhijit Banerjee and Esther Duflo. Amsterdam: North Holland, forthcoming).

Blank, Rebecca M. *Changing Inequality.* Berkeley: University of California Press, 2011.

Blau, Francine D., and Lawrence M. Kahn. "Gender Differences in Pay." *Journal of Economic Perspectives* 14, no. 4 (Fall 2000): 75–99.

Blau, Francine D., and Lawrence M. Kahn. "The Gender Wage Gap: Extent, Trends, and Sources." NBER Working Paper 21913 (National Bureau of Economic Research, Cambridge, MA, January 2016) (*Journal of Economic Literature*, forthcoming).

Blau, Francine D., Mary C. Brinton, and David B. Grusky, eds. *The Declining Significance of Gender?* New York: Russell Sage Foundation, 2006.

Darity, William A., Jr., and Patrick L. Mason. "Evidence on Discrimination in Employment: Codes of Color, Codes of Gender." *Journal of Economic Perspectives* 12, no. 2 (Spring 1998): 63–90.

Eagly, Alice H., and Linda L. Carli. *Through the Labyrinth: The Truth about How Women Become Leaders*. Cambridge, MA: Harvard Business School Press, 2007.

Fiske, Susan T. "Stereotyping, Prejudice, and Discrimination." In *Handbook of Social Psychology*, edited by D. T. Gilbert, S. T. Fiske, and G. Lindzey, 357–411. New York: McGraw-Hill, 1998.

Folbre, Nancy, ed. *For Love and Money: Care Provision in the United States*. New York: Russell Sage Foundation, 2012.

Goldin, Claudia. "A Grand Convergence: Its Last Chapter." *American Economic Review* 104, no. 4 (May 2014): 1091–1119.

Goldin, Claudia. "How to Achieve Gender Equality." *Milken Institute Review* Q3 (July 2015): 24–33.

Goldin, Caudia, and Lawrence F. Katz. *The Race between Education and Technology*. Cambridge, MA: Belknap Press of Harvard University Press, 2008.

Hersch, Joni. "Sex Discrimination in the Labor Market." *Foundations and Trends in Microeconomics* 2, no. 4 (2006): 281–361.

Huffman, Matt L., ed. *"Gender and Race Inequality in Management: Critical Issues, New Evidence."* Annals of the American Academy of Political and Social Science 639 (January 2012).

Neal, Derek. "Black–White Labour Market Inequality in the United States." In *The New Palgrave Dictionary of Economics*, 2nd ed., edited by Steven Durlauf and Lawrence Blume. London: Palgrave Macmillan, 2008.

Reskin, Barbara F., and Denise D. Bielby. "A Sociological Perspective on Gender and Career Outcomes." *Journal of Economic Perspectives* 19, no. 1 (Winter 2005): 71–86.

Valian, Virginia. *Why So Slow? The Advancement of Women*. Cambridge, MA: MIT Press, 1998.

Wilson, Valerie, and William M. Rodgers III. *Black–White Wage Gaps Expand with Rising Wage Inequality*. Washington, DC: Economic Policy Institute, September 19, 2016. Accessed November 9, 2016. http://www.epi.org.

Key Terms

labor market discrimination (264)

feedback effects (265)

gender wage gap (266)

gender wage differential (266)

explained gap (266)

unexplained gap (266)

gender wage ratio (268)

temporal flexibility (274)

wage structure (278)

wage inequality (278)

returns to skills (278)

minimum wage (280)

Fair Labor Standards Act (280)

wage floor (280)

living wage (280)

living wage laws (280)

glass escalator (286)

glass ceiling (289)

pipeline argument (290)

work–family conflicts (290)

dependent variable (296)

explanatory variable (296)

least squares regression analysis (297)

multiple regression analysis (297)

APPENDIX 10A

Regression Analysis and Empirical Estimates of Labor Market Discrimination

In Table 10-1, we presented empirical estimates of the sources of the gender wage differential. In this appendix,[82] we explain in more detail how economists arrive at such estimates, with special focus on the issue of labor market discrimination. The goal is to be able to "decompose" the gender wage gap into a portion due to measured productivity-related characteristics and a portion that cannot be explained by differences in characteristics and is, therefore, potentially due to labor market discrimination.

The starting point of such analyses is the estimation of a wage regression, which expresses wages as a function of factors such as experience and education. For simplicity, let us begin with the case in which there is only one explanatory variable, experience. Figure 10-1 shows a hypothetical scatter of points, "observations," for individual women, with each point representing one woman's wage rate and experience.

To better understand how wages are determined, we would like to use this information to estimate the effect of an additional year of work experience on wages. As can be seen, if we were to fit a straight line to the points in Figure 10-1, it would be an upward-sloping line, suggesting that wages increase with additional years of labor market experience.

Before considering the technique that we would use to estimate the line shown in the figure, let us begin with the following equation that models the general relationship between wages and experience:

$$\text{WAGE}_i = a_0 + a_1 X_i + e_i$$

In this equation, WAGE represents the wage rate of individual i and is called the **dependent variable**. The independent or **explanatory variable** is X, which represents the individual's level of experience. The regression coefficients, a_0 and a_1, specify the relationship between the dependent and explanatory variable: a_0 is the intercept of the line on the y-axis and a_1 is the slope of the line. The intercept gives the wage rate corresponding to zero years of work experience, that is, for a new entrant into the labor market. The slope of the line tells us how much wages increase for each additional year of experience. The last term, e, is a random error term. It is included because we do not expect each observation to lie along the straight line; random factors unrelated to experience are also likely to influence wages. (We shall see later that other factors that are systematically related to wages, such as education, can be incorporated in multiple regression analysis.)

How do we find the straight line that best fits the points in the figure? This amounts to estimating a_0 and a_1. The statistical technique generally used is called

---

[82]In formulating this section, we benefited from reviewing Ronald G. Ehrenberg and Robert S. Smith, *Modern Labor Economics,* 6th ed. (Reading, MA: Addison Wesley, 1996), appendix 1A, 17–24; and Mark Killingsworth, "Where Does the Pay Gap Come From?" Class Handout for Economics 375, Women in the Economy, Rutgers University. For a more detailed treatment of regression analysis, see a statistics or econometrics textbook.

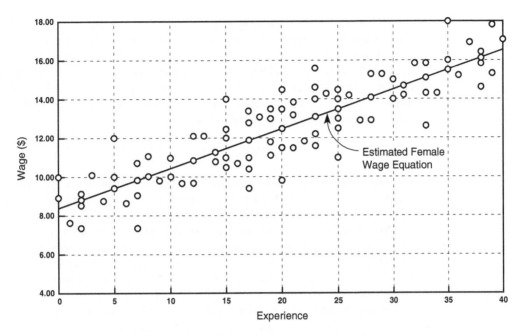

FIGURE 10-1 Scatter Plot and Regression Line for Women's Wages

least squares regression analysis. It is estimated by finding the line that minimizes the sum of the squared deviations (vertical differences) of each point from the line.

If we estimate a least squares regression using the points in Figure 10-1, we obtain the following estimated line:

$$\text{WAGE}_i = 8.5 + 0.2X_i$$

The estimate of $a_0 = 8.5$ and the estimate of $a_1 = 0.2$ mean that a new entrant into the labor market is expected to earn \$8.50 per hour, and an individual's wages are expected to increase by \$0.20 with each additional year of experience.

At least two potential problems arise with this estimate. First, the hypothetical and the actual earnings profiles we showed in Chapters 8 and 9 were not straight lines but rather curved lines, which suggests that even though earnings rise with experience, the rate of increase tends to fall over time. Such a relationship can readily be estimated using regression analysis, and in fact, most studies by economists allow for this.[83] We, however, will stick to a straight line as in Figure 10-1 to simplify our exposition.

Second, economic theory tells us that a number of other explanatory variables besides experience are important determinants of wages. These additional explanatory variables can be incorporated by using **multiple regression analysis**. We illustrate multiple regression analysis by adding education as an explanatory variable. Our wage equation now becomes

$$\text{WAGE}_i = a_0' + a_1'X_i \times a_2'ED_i + e_i'$$

---

[83]To do this, we include experience squared (X^2), in addition to X, as an explanatory variable in the regression.

ED is a variable measuring years of schooling completed. Each regression coefficient now tells us the impact of a unit change in each explanatory variable on the dependent variable, *holding the other explanatory variable constant*. So, for example, a_1' gives the effect of an additional year of experience on wages, holding education constant. Thus, the regression coefficients a_0' and a_1' are not necessarily equal to a_0 and a_1 because their interpretation has changed. The new relationship estimated by multiple regression analysis is found to be

$$\text{WAGE}_i = 2 + 0.3X_i + 0.5Ed_i$$

That is, we find that, holding education constant, each additional year of experience raises wages by $0.30 and, holding experience constant, each additional year of education raises wages by $0.50.

Note that including education changed our estimate of the effect of experience. This change occurs because education is *correlated* with experience: given the trend toward rising educational attainment, younger women have higher levels of education, on average, but less experience than older women. The estimated experience coefficient in the simple regression (the one that includes only experience) is *smaller* than that in the multiple regression because the positive effect of experience on earnings is offset somewhat by the tendency of older people (with higher levels of experience) to be less well educated. Thus, education is an important *omitted variable*, and not taking it into account results in a *biased* estimate of the effect of experience; specifically, the estimated effect of experience is *biased downward* when education is omitted from the regression.

The results obtained with multiple regression analysis for the relationship between wages and experience can still be summarized in a simple diagram if we evaluate them at a specific level or specific levels of education, as shown in Figure 10-2 for *ED* = 12 (high school graduates) and *ED* = 16 (college graduates).

Now that the basics of regression analysis are clear, we can consider how it is used to obtain statistical estimates of the contribution of measured variables like experience and the extent of labor market discrimination. We first do this in terms of a diagram and then present a general formula.

Figure 10-3 shows hypothetical male and female wage regression lines for college graduates. By focusing on one education group, we can proceed in terms of simple regression with one explanatory variable, experience. As may be seen in the figure, women's average wages, $\bar{w}_f$, are lower than men's average wages, $\bar{w}_m$. At the same time, women have less experience on average, $\bar{x}_f$, than men do, $\bar{x}_m$. How much of the difference in average wages between men and women, $\bar{w}_m - \bar{w}_f$, is due to the gender difference in average levels of experience, $\bar{x}_m - \bar{x}_f$, and how much cannot be explained by this difference in qualifications? This "unexplained" portion is our estimate of discrimination.

We begin by observing that the female regression line lies below the male line and that it is also flatter. This comparison shows that women earn less than men with the same experience both because they earn less at the outset of their careers than men do (the intercept of the female line is below the intercept of the male line) and because they receive a smaller return than men for each additional year of experience (the female line is flatter than the male line). We would like our estimate of discrimination to capture both these differences.

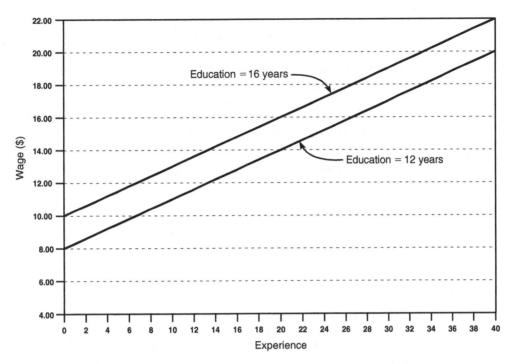

FIGURE 10-2 The Estimated Relationship between Wages and Experience for Women Evaluated at 12 and 16 Years of Education

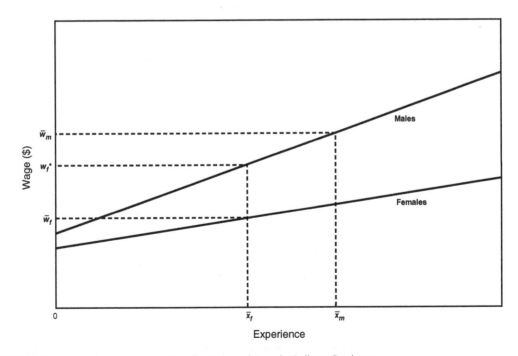

FIGURE 10-3 Hypothetical Regression Lines for Male and Female College Graduates

To estimate how much of the gender wage gap is due to gender differences in experience, we ask what women's wages would be if women were rewarded the same way as men for their experience. Reading off the male regression line, we see that a man with $\bar{x}_f$ years of experience would receive a wage of w_f^*. Thus, the portion of the gender wage gap attributable to women's lower average level of experience is $\bar{w}_m - w_f^*$. The remainder, $w_f^* - \bar{w}_f$, is unexplained and potentially due to discrimination. The unexplained portion of the gender gap is due to gender differences in the estimated coefficients of the wage regression (a_0 and a_1).

We can express this relationship mathematically as follows:

Gender wage difference = Difference due to qualifications + Unexplained difference

$$\bar{w}_m - \bar{w}_f \quad = \quad \left(\bar{w}_m - \bar{w}_f^* \right) \quad + \quad \left(\bar{w}_f^* - \bar{w}_f \right)$$

where

$$\bar{w}_m = a_{0m} + a_{1m} \times \bar{x}_m$$
$$\bar{w}_f = a_{0f} + a_{1f} \times \bar{x}_f$$
$$\bar{w}_f^* = a_{0m} + a_{1m} \times \bar{x}_f$$

In the preceding equations, a_{0m} and a_{1m} are the intercept and slope of the male regression and a_{0f} and a_{1f} are the intercept and slope of the female regression.

The portion of the wage difference that is due to differences in qualifications, in this case experience, is $\left(\bar{w}_m - \bar{w}_f^* \right)$. It is obtained by evaluating both men's and women's average levels of experience using the male regression coefficients. The unexplained portion of the gender difference is estimated by the difference between what women's wages are when their average experience is evaluated using the male regression versus when they are evaluated using the female regression. This approach can readily be applied in the multiple regression context and underlies estimates such as those presented in Table 10-1.[84]

---

[84]Our ability to perform this decomposition is aided by the property of least squares regression that the regression line passes through the means of the dependent and explanatory variables. Thus, the point $\left(\bar{w}_f, \bar{x}_f \right)$ will lie on the female regression line and the point $\left(\bar{w}_m, \bar{x}_m \right)$ will lie on the male regression line. This analysis is known as a *Oaxaca-Blinder Decomposition*, after the economists who were the first to use it; see Oaxaca, "Male–Female Wage Differentials," and Blinder, "Wage Discrimination."

Labor Market Discrimination: Theory

11

CHAPTER HIGHLIGHTS

- Theories of Labor Market Discrimination: An Overview
- Tastes for Discrimination
- Subtle Barriers
- Statistical Discrimination
- The Overcrowding Model
- Institutional Models
- Feedback Effects

In the preceding chapter, we examined the empirical evidence regarding the role of supply-side factors versus labor market discrimination in producing the gender differences in earnings and occupational attainment that we observe in the labor market. As we have seen, the available evidence suggests that both supply-side influences and discrimination are responsible for gender differences in economic outcomes. In this chapter, we consider economic models that have been offered to explain the existence and persistence of **labor market discrimination**—the situation where two equally qualified individuals are treated differently in the labor market solely on the basis of their gender. As mentioned in Chapter 10, although our focus is on gender discrimination, the models reviewed here are equally applicable to discrimination based on other factors, such as race, ethnicity, age, disability, or sexual orientation. In fact, most of the models of discrimination we discuss were initially developed to explain racial discrimination. In Chapter 12, we turn to the potential role for government to address discrimination and then review the major policies in place and examine their effects on labor market outcomes.

Theories of Labor Market Discrimination: An Overview

Economists have developed a variety of models that are used to analyze discrimination. At this point, we do not know which of these approaches most accurately describes the labor market. Indeed, for the most part, the explanations offered by these models are *not* mutually exclusive, and each may shed some light on how labor market discrimination affects women's economic outcomes. We focus on the following theoretical explanations: tastes for discrimination (among employees, employers, or customers), statistical discrimination, the overcrowding model, and institutional models (including dual labor markets). We also discuss how discrimination against women need not be an overt, conscious process on the part of discriminators but rather may be subtle and even unconscious and how subtle barriers may impede women's progress in the labor market.

Unless otherwise indicated, the analyses presented here assume that male and female workers are equally well qualified and, in the absence of discrimination, would be equally productive (have the same **marginal product**, MP) and receive the same pay. (MP is the increase in output of a firm that results from the hiring of an additional worker, all other factors remaining constant.) We know that this assumption is not an accurate description of reality—gender differences in qualifications exist and explain some of the pay gap. However, this assumption is appropriate because models of discrimination are efforts to explain the portion of the pay gap that is *not* due to differences in qualifications; that is, they are intended to explain pay differences between men and women who are (potentially) equally productive. We say "potentially" equally productive because, while in some situations discrimination results in women being paid less than their MP, in others discrimination itself lowers women's productivity relative to the nondiscriminatory situation.

Tastes for Discrimination

The foundation for the neoclassical analysis of labor market discrimination was laid by Nobel laureate Gary Becker.[1] Becker conceptualized discrimination as a personal prejudice, or what he termed a *taste* against associating with a particular group. In his model, employers, coworkers, and customers may all potentially display such **tastes for discrimination**. In contrast to the case of racial discrimination that Becker initially analyzed, it may at first seem odd to hypothesize that men would not like to associate with women when, in fact, men and women generally live together in

---

[1]Gary S. Becker, *The Economics of Discrimination*, 2nd ed. (1957; repr., Chicago: University of Chicago Press, 1971). In our presentation of the tastes for discrimination model, we incorporate some of the insights of another Nobel prize winner, Kenneth Arrow; see "The Theory of Discrimination," in *Discrimination in Labor Markets*, ed. Orley Ashenfelter and Albert Rees (Princeton, NJ: Princeton University Press, 1973), 3–33. For a summary and appreciation of Becker's contribution, see Christopher J. Flinn, "Gary Becker's Contributions to the Analysis of Discrimination," *Journal of Demographic Economics* 81, no. 1 (March 2015): 45–50. For a review of the evolution of empirical work on discrimination, including the difficulty of distinguishing between taste-based and statistical discrimination, see Jonathan Guryan and Kerwin Kofi Charles, "Taste-Based or Statistical Discrimination: The Economics of Discrimination Returns to Its Roots," *Economic Journal* 123, no. 572 (November 2013): F417–32. For a review of theory and evidence on race discrimination, see Kevin Lang and Jee Yeon K. Lehmann, "Racial Discrimination in the Labor Market: Theory and Empirics," *Journal of Economic Literature* 50, no. 4 (December 2012): 959–1006.

families. The issue for gender may be more one of socially appropriate roles than of the desire to maintain social distance, as Becker postulated was the case with race.[2]

Employers who show no reservations about hiring women as secretaries or administrative assistants may be reluctant to employ them as plumbers. Men who are willing to work with women in complementary or subordinate positions may dislike interacting with them as equals or superiors. Customers who are delighted to purchase pantyhose from female clerks may avoid women who sell cars or work as attorneys. If such discriminatory tastes reflect a dislike for interacting with women in these positions, rather than beliefs that women are less qualified than men for traditionally male pursuits, they are appropriately analyzed as a taste for discrimination.[3] The possibility that women are treated differently because they are perceived as a group to be less qualified or less productive is considered in the section on "Statistical Discrimination."

In order for such discriminatory tastes to result in negative consequences for women's earnings and employment, tastes must actually influence people's behavior. According to Becker, individuals with tastes for discrimination against women act as if there were nonpecuniary costs of associating with women. A **nonpecuniary cost** is a nonmonetary cost, such as the feeling of distaste experienced when an individual has to associate with a woman who holds what is viewed as a socially inappropriate role.[4] The *strength* of the individual's discriminatory taste is measured by his or her **discrimination coefficient** (i.e., the size of these costs in money terms). We now examine the consequences of discrimination based on employer, employee, and customer tastes for discrimination (or prejudices).

Employer Discrimination

In the case of **employer discrimination**, an employer who has a taste for discrimination against women will act as if there is a nonpecuniary cost of employing women equal in dollar terms to d_r (the discrimination coefficient). To this employer, the costs of employing a man will be his wage, w_m, but the *full* costs of employing a woman will be her wage *plus* the discrimination coefficient ($w_f + d_r$). A discriminating employer will hire a woman only if the full cost of employing her ($w_f + d_r$) is no greater than the cost of employing a man (w_m) and will be indifferent between hiring a man or a woman if the full cost of a woman exactly equals the cost for a man. This implies that the discriminating employer will hire a woman only at a lower wage than a man ($w_f = w_m - d_r$). The lower female wage exactly compensates the employer for the disutility of hiring a woman (d_r). Further, if we assume that men and women are equally productive, that is, their *MP*s are the same, and that men are paid in accordance with their productivity, then women will be hired only if they are paid less than their productivity.[5]

---

[2]The notion of socially appropriate roles may also be a factor in racial discrimination, as when blacks experience little difficulty in gaining access to menial or lower-level jobs but encounter discrimination in obtaining higher-level positions.

[3]However, as we shall see, such discriminatory preferences on the part of workers or customers for men will cause women to be less productive from the point of view of the employer.

[4]Throughout, we assume that employers, coworkers, or customers have tastes for discrimination against women. It is also possible that they have positive preferences for employing, working with, or buying from men. This may be termed *nepotism*. See Matthew Goldberg, "Discrimination, Nepotism, and Long-Run Wage Differentials," *Quarterly Journal of Economics* 97, no. 2 (May 1982): 307–19, for an interesting analysis of the consequences of nepotism for the persistence of discrimination in the long run.

[5]That is, if w_m = MP, where MP is equal to the marginal productivity of men (or women), then women will be paid $w_m - d_r$, which is less than their productivity.

Becker's analysis showed that the consequences of this situation for female workers depend on the prevalence and size of discriminatory tastes among employers, as well as on the number of women seeking employment. Nondiscriminatory employers are willing to hire men and women at the same wage rate (i.e., their discrimination coefficient equals 0). When the number of such nondiscriminatory employers is relatively large or relatively few women are seeking employment, women workers may all be absorbed by the nondiscriminatory firms. In this case, no discriminatory pay differential occurs based on gender, even though some employers have tastes for discrimination against women.

However, if discriminatory tastes are widespread or the number of women seeking employment is relatively large, some women will have to find jobs at discriminatory firms. These women obtain such employment only if w_f is less than w_m. If we assume that the labor market is competitive, all employers will pay the (same) going rate established in the market for workers of a particular sex. No employer would be willing to pay more than the going rate because additional workers are always available at that wage. No worker will accept less than the going rate because jobs at other firms are always available to him or her at that wage. In equilibrium, then, the market wage differential between men and women must be large enough so that all the women who are looking for employment are able to obtain it—including those who must find work at discriminatory firms. Thus, the more prevalent and the stronger employers' discriminatory tastes against women and the larger the number of women seeking employment, the larger will be the marketwide wage gap ($w_m - w_f$) between men and women.

This model of employer tastes for discrimination is consistent with some of the inequalities between men and women that we observe in the labor market. Under this model, a wage differential may exist between equally qualified male and female workers because discriminatory employers will hire women workers only at a wage discount.[6] Further, because less discriminatory employers will hire more women workers than more discriminatory employers, male and female workers may be segregated by firm—as also appears to be the case. Finally, if, as seems likely, employer tastes for discrimination vary across occupations, occupational segregation by sex can also occur.

However, one problem that economists have identified with this model is that discrimination is not costless to the employer who forgoes the opportunity to hire more of the lower-priced female labor and less of the higher-priced male labor. Therefore, less discriminatory firms should have lower costs of production. Such a competitive advantage would enable them to expand and drive the more discriminatory firms out of business in the long run. As the less discriminatory firms expand, the demand for female labor would be increased and the male–female pay gap would be reduced. If there were enough *entirely* nondiscriminatory firms to absorb all the women workers, the gender pay gap would be eliminated. Hence, the question is how discrimination, which represents a departure from pure profit-maximizing behavior, can withstand the impact of competitive pressures.

---

[6]Some researchers have proposed testing the employer discrimination model by comparing the gender pay gap between self-employed workers and employees. The claim is that if *employer* discrimination is responsible for the pay differential, female self-employed workers should fare relatively better than female employees, all else equal. See Victor R. Fuchs, "Differences in Hourly Earnings between Men and Women," *Monthly Labor Review* 94, no. 5 (May 1971): 9–15; and Robert L. Moore, "Employer Discrimination: Evidence from Self-Employed Workers," *Review of Economics and Statistics* 65, no. 3 (August 1983): 496–501. Although such studies do not support the employer discrimination model, they do not provide an ideal test because self-employment and wage and salary employment differ in a number of important dimensions. For one thing, self-employment requires access to capital, and there may be discrimination against women by lenders. Discrimination by customers is another possibility.

One answer is that discrimination may result from a lack of such competitive pressures in the economy. For this reason, Becker hypothesized that, on average, discrimination would be less severe in competitive than in monopolistic industries, and some research supports this prediction. For example, with the deregulation of the banking industry beginning in the mid-1970s, the gender pay gap in banking declined and the representation of women in managerial positions increased.[7] These findings suggest that employers in banking were able to discriminate in part due to the monopolistic nature of the industry but that their ability to do so was reduced when competition was increased by deregulation.

Also consistent with Becker's reasoning is another study that finds that, among plants with high levels of product market power (and hence an ability to exercise their tastes for discrimination in the Becker model), those employing relatively more women were more profitable.[8] This correlation suggests that, among these firms, there is some discrimination against women and that less discriminatory firms benefit from the lower costs of production resulting from hiring more women and thus have higher profits.

Finally, unions may also, to some extent, be considered a barrier to competition in that wages may be set above the competitive level in the union sector. Unions are also more likely to arise in less competitive industries, and, as we saw in Chapter 7, it is indeed the case that historically women were less highly represented in unionized employment, although such gender differences have now been virtually eliminated. Thus, historically women did not benefit from the wage advantage of unionism to the same extent as men.[9] For this reason, as we saw in Chapter 10, declining gender *differences* in union representation have boosted the wages of women relative to men.

It has also been suggested that monopsony power by employers in the *labor market* plays a role in producing and perpetuating the gender pay differential. **Monopsony power** means that a firm has some power to set the wages of its workers, akin to the better-known concept of monopoly power, which means that a firm has some ability to set the price of its product. Firms can gain some degree of monopsony power in a number of ways.

One way in which a firm gains monopsony power is when it is a large buyer of labor relative to the size of a particular market. To see how monopsony power can adversely affect women in this situation, consider the not uncommon case of a one-university town. In the past, when the husband's job prospects usually determined the location of the family, the faculty wife with a Ph.D. had little choice but to take whatever the university offered her—most considered themselves fortunate if they were able to obtain employment at all. Even the growing numbers of egalitarian Ph.D. couples cannot entirely avoid this problem. Although an increasing number of two-career couples, in academia and elsewhere, work in different locations and see each other, say, on weekends, most seek jobs in the same location. In order to

[7]Sandra E. Black and Philip E. Strahan, "The Division of Spoils: Rent-Sharing and Discrimination in a Regulated Labor Market," *American Economic Review* 91, no. 4 (September 2001): 814–31. See also Sandra E. Black and Elizabeth Brainerd, "Importing Equality? The Effects of Globalization on Gender Discrimination," *Industrial and Labor Relations Review* 57, no. 4 (July 2004): 540–59; and Orley Ashenfelter and Timothy Hannan, "Sex Discrimination and Product Market Competition: The Case of the Banking Industry," *Quarterly Journal of Economics* 101, no. 1 (February 1986): 149–73.

[8]Judith K. Hellerstein, David Neumark, and Kenneth Troske, "Market Forces and Sex Discrimination," *Journal of Human Resources* 37, no. 2 (Spring 2002): 353–80.

[9]For an analysis of the impact of unions on gender pay differences during the period when men had the edge in unionization, see William E. Even and David A. Macpherson, "The Decline of Private-Sector Unionism and the Gender Wage Gap," *Journal of Human Resources* 28, no. 2 (Spring 1993): 279–96.

change jobs, such couples must find *two* acceptable alternatives in a single location. This will obviously be harder to do than to find *one* desirable alternative. Thus, Ph.D. couples will have fewer options than those with only one Ph.D. in the family. (Similar problems can arise for two-career couples in other fields.) This situation gives the employer a degree of monopsony power and is likely to lower the pay of both members of the couple relative to Ph.D.s who can relocate more easily. Among such Ph.D. couples, both the husband's and the wife's salary may be adversely affected.[10]

The monopsony model has also been offered as a general explanation for the gender pay gap. Some argue that employers hold greater monopsony power over women than men due to factors such as occupational segregation that may limit women's options. Further, as we saw in Chapter 9, women who adopt more traditional gender roles will tend to seek jobs that are closer to home, thus potentially giving their employers some degree of monopsony power.[11]

Consideration of job search suggests that another way in which firms may gain monopsony power is if workers lack perfect information about employment opportunities.[12] In a competitive labor market with perfect information, even a slightly higher wage at another firm will induce workers to move to that better opportunity. However, when information is imperfect, workers must search among employers for a good job match, thus incurring "search costs." These costs include the opportunity cost of the time spent looking for a job, as well as out-of-pocket costs for printing up a résumé, transportation expenses to employment interviews, and so on. Because search is costly, workers will be less mobile across firms than they would be if information was perfectly and costlessly available, and it will take larger wage premiums at other firms to bid them away. Thus, it is argued that the presence of search costs gives employers some degree of monopsony power over workers. If we further assume that some employers discriminate against women and are not willing to hire them, we see that women will face higher search costs than men. As a consequence, employers can exploit this greater monopsony power over women and offer them lower wages than men. Thus, when information is imperfect and search costs exist, it is more credible that employer discrimination can persist in the long run.[13]

Evolving views of the nature of prejudice may also shed light on the persistence of discrimination in the long run. As we noted in our discussion of a possible glass

---

[10]For early evidence consistent with monopsony in one academic institution, see Marianne A. Ferber and Jane W. Loeb, "Professors, Performance and Rewards," *Industrial Relations* 13, no. 1 (February 1974): 67–77.

[11]Janice F. Madden, *The Economics of Sex Discrimination* (Lexington, MA: Lexington Books, 1973). See also Alan Manning, "The Equal Pay Act As an Experiment to Test Theories of the Labour Market," *Economica* 63, no. 250 (May 1996): 191–212.

[12]We draw heavily here on the insights provided by Dan A. Black in "Discrimination in an Equilibrium Search Model," *Journal of Labor Economics* 13, no. 2 (April 1995): 309–34.

[13]For evidence consistent with the monopsony model as an explanation for gender wage differentials, see Michael R. Ransom and Ronald L. Oaxaca, "New Market Power Models and Sex Differences in Pay," *Journal of Labor Economics* 28, no. 2 (April 2010): 267–89; Michael R. Ransom and David P. Sims, "Estimating the Firm's Labor Supply Curve in a 'New Monopsony' Framework: Schoolteachers in Missouri," *Journal of Labor Economics* 28, no. 2 (2010): 331–55; and Douglas A. Webber, "Firm-Level Monopsony and the Gender Pay Gap." *Industrial Relations* 55, no. 2 (April 2016): 323–45. However, a number of studies that look at quit/separation behavior—indicators of mobility—find no evidence that men's quits are more sensitive to wages than women's (as required by the monopsony model); see, e.g., Francine D. Blau and Lawrence M. Kahn, "Race and Sex Differences in Quits by Young Workers," *Industrial and Labor Relations Review* 34, no. 4 (July 1981): 563–77; Audrey Light and Manuelita Ureta, "Early-Career Work Experience and Gender Wage Differentials," *Journal of Labor Economics* 13 no. 1 (January 1995): 121–54; and Alan Manning, *Monopsony in Motion: Imperfect Competition in Labor Markets* (Princeton, NJ: Princeton University Press, 2003).

ceiling curtailing women's upward progress in Chapter 10, discrimination against women need not be overt or even conscious. Social cognition theory, developed by social psychologists, suggests that unconscious biases can cause people to "think, feel, and behave in ways that oppose their explicitly expressed views, and even, explicitly known self-interests,"[14] For example, they may automatically categorize others and treat them in a manner consistent with the stereotypes they hold about the social category to which the individuals belong. They may also tend to remember evidence that is consistent with their preexisting stereotypes and ignore, discount, or forget evidence that undermines them.[15] So, for example, a manager might sincerely profess a belief in gender equity but still tend to undervalue the qualifications of female job applicants, based on unconscious biases. Or such an individual might tend to remember when female employees leave for family-related reasons but dismiss as exceptional examples of female employees who remain committed workers after having a child. This type of thinking has been termed **implicit discrimination**; such discrimination may be less likely to be eliminated by competitive forces, or, at a minimum, the impact of competitive forces may operate more uncertainly and slowly.[16]

Finally, models of statistical discrimination, developed after Becker's work, suggest another possible reason for the persistence of discrimination in the labor market: employers are motivated to discriminate against women not simply by personal prejudice but rather by actual or perceived differences between male and female workers in productivity or behavior. We consider such models of statistical discrimination later in the section on "Statistical Discrimination." Before turning to such models, however, we consider two other possible sources of discrimination in the Becker model. A major insight of Becker's was the realization that, even if employers themselves have no tastes for discrimination against women, profit-maximizing behavior by employers may result in gender discrimination in the labor market if employees or customers have such tastes. No conflict arises here with profit maximization by employers. Hence, there is no economic reason why this type of discrimination cannot continue.[17] We now consider the possibility of employee and customer discrimination.

Employee Discrimination

In the case of **employee discrimination**, a male employee who has a taste for discrimination against women will act as if there is a nonpecuniary cost of working with women equal to his discrimination coefficient, d_e. This is the premium he must be paid to induce him to work with women. Thus, if a discriminating male worker would receive w_m if he did not work with a woman, he would only be willing to work with a woman at a higher wage ($w_m + d_e$). This higher wage is analogous to the

[14]Marianne Bertrand, Dolly Chugh, and Sendhil Mullainathan, "Implicit Discrimination," *American Economic Review* 95, no. 2 (May 2005): 94–98; quotation is from p. 94.

[15]See Barbara F. Reskin, "The Proximate Causes of Employment Discrimination," *Contemporary Sociology* 29, no. 2 (March 2000): 319–28; Susan T. Fiske, "Stereotyping, Prejudice, and Discrimination," in *Handbook of Social Psychology*, ed. D. T. Gilbert, S. T. Fiske, and G. Lindzey (New York: McGraw-Hill: 1998), 357–411; and Francine D. Blau, Mary C. Brinton, and David B. Grusky, "The Declining Significance of Gender?" in *The Declining Significance of Gender?* ed. Francine D. Blau, Mary C. Brinton, and David B. Grusky (New York: Russell Sage Foundation, 2006), 3–34.

[16]Bertrand, Chugh, and Mullainathan, "Implicit Discrimination," suggested this term.

[17]Lawrence M. Kahn presents a model that shows that customer discrimination can produce persistent discriminatory wage differentials in "Customer Discrimination and Affirmative Action," *Economic Inquiry* 29, no. 3 (July 1991): 555–71.

compensating wage differential that economists expect workers to be offered for unpleasant or unsafe working conditions.

What will be the profit-maximizing employer's response to this situation? One solution would be for the employer to hire a sex-segregated (either all-male or all-female) workforce and thereby eliminate the necessity of paying a premium to male workers for associating with female workers. If all employers responded in this way (but had no taste for discrimination themselves), male and female workers would be paid the same wage rate, although they would work in segregated settings.

However, as pointed out by Kenneth Arrow, complete segregation may not be profitable when there are substantial costs of adjustment in altering the current workforce.[18] For example, suppose an employer has an all-male work group and is thinking of hiring women to tap into a new supply of labor. As we have seen, discriminatory male employees will require a wage premium to work with women. Thus, adding female employees to the existing all-male workforce would increase wage costs. An option would be to fire the existing male workers and replace them with female workers. However, the hiring of new workers entails recruiting and screening costs for the firm, as well as costs for firm-specific training if such skills are needed. Where such adjustment costs are present, changing from an all-male to an all-female workforce is costly, and employers may be reluctant to do so. Thus, an employer may choose to add some female workers to the existing all-male work group and pay the higher wages the men demand to work with women. The result will be a gender wage differential. There is also likely to be a tendency toward segregation due to the costs of introducing women into the work group (that is, the need to pay men higher wages).

Historically, there have been large increases in female labor force participation rates and in the availability of women for traditionally predominantly male occupations. This meant that women, as relatively new entrants, found men already in place in many sectors. Further, as we saw in Chapter 2, women were heavily concentrated in a few predominantly female occupations even when they constituted just a small proportion of the labor force. Regardless of the various factors initially causing the segregation of some occupations as predominantly male, adjustment costs in conjunction with employee tastes for discrimination could, as described in the Arrow analysis, result in a gender wage differential combined with a tendency toward segregation.

Given employee tastes for discrimination and adjustment costs, market-wide wage differences between male and female workers may result. Again, the size of the wage differential depends on the distribution and intensity of, in this case, *employees'* discriminatory tastes, as well as the relative number of women seeking employment. If employees with no taste for discrimination against women represent a large proportion of male workers or relatively few women are seeking jobs, then it may be possible for all the women to work with nondiscriminatory men; and no pay differential would occur.

However, if discriminatory tastes are widespread or relatively large numbers of women are seeking jobs, some of the women will have to work with discriminating male workers. Those males will require higher compensation to induce them to work with women. The result will be a wage differential between male and female workers, on average, because some males will receive this higher pay. Moreover, it is also

---

[18]Arrow, "The Theory of Discrimination."

possible that women will be paid less to compensate. In addition, more variation will occur in male workers' wage rates than would otherwise be the case. For instance, discriminating male workers who do not work with women do not need to be paid a wage premium, nor do nondiscriminating males, regardless of whether or not they are employed with women.

In an empirical test of this prediction, one study compared the wages of men and women (within the same narrowly defined white-collar occupations) in sex-integrated and sex-segregated firms. The study found that, contrary to what was expected on the basis of the employee discrimination model, men earned *more* in sex-segregated (predominantly male) firms than in integrated firms, and women earned *more* when they worked with men than when they worked only with other women. Women earned less than men on average because they were more concentrated in the lower-paying firms.[19] These findings are more consistent with a situation in which high-wage (e.g., monopolistic or unionized) employers are better able to indulge their preferences for hiring men than one in which the pay differentials are due to employee discrimination. There may, however, be other cases in which employee discrimination has played an important role.

If such employee tastes for discrimination do in fact exist and if they vary by occupation, employee discrimination may be a factor causing occupational segregation as well as pay differentials. For example, one reason why women may not be hired for supervisory and managerial positions may be that even male employees who do not mind working with women do not like being supervised by them. This could create a barrier to the employment of women in such jobs.[20]

Barbara Bergmann and William Darity have suggested that employee discrimination may adversely affect the morale and productivity of discriminating male workers who are forced to work with women, a possibility not initially considered by Becker.[21] This possibility would make employers reluctant to hire women, especially when their male employees require considerable firm-specific training and are hard to replace. Further, if employers do hire women under such circumstances, they may pay them less to compensate for the reduction in the productivity of the discriminating male employees. In a sense, a woman's marginal productivity is lower than a man's because adding her to the workforce causes a decline in the productivity of previously hired male workers. Adding another male worker causes no such decline in output.

Two other proposed models of discrimination suggest additional motivations for male employees to discriminate against female coworkers and provide possible reasons why men may resist female inroads into traditionally male occupations

[19]Francine D. Blau, *Equal Pay in the Office* (Lexington, MA: Lexington Books, 1977). See also Erica L. Groshen, "The Structure of the Female/Male Wage Differential: Is It Who You Are, What You Do, or Where You Work?" *Journal of Human Resources* 26, no. 3 (Summer 1991): 457–72; and Kimberly Bayard, Judith Hellerstein, David Neumark, and Kenneth Troske, "New Evidence on Sex Segregation and Sex Difference in Wages from Matched Employee–Employer Data," *Journal of Labor Economics* 21, no. 4 (October 2003): 887–923.

[20]However, one study found that *both* male and female employees earned *less* when they had a female supervisor, which is not consistent with employee discrimination against female supervisors and suggests rather that the presence of a female supervisor is associated with less favorable characteristics of the job. See Donna S. Rothstein, "Supervisor Gender and the Early Labor Market Outcomes of Young Workers," in *Gender and Family Issues in the Workplace*, ed. Francine D. Blau and Ronald G. Ehrenberg (New York: Russell Sage, 1997): 210–55.

[21]Barbara R. Bergmann and William A. Darity Jr., "Social Relations in the Workplace and Employer Discrimination," in *Proceedings of the Thirty-Third Annual Meetings of the Industrial Relations Research Association* (Madison: University of Wisconsin, 1981), 155–62.

beyond simply a taste for discrimination (or personal prejudice). In both cases, men believe they will be negatively affected if women enter their traditionally male occupation. In George A. Akerlof and Rachel E. Kranton's **identity model**, occupations are associated with societal notions of "male" and "female." In this model, men oppose the entry of women into traditionally male jobs out of concern that they will lose their male identity or sense of self.[22] In Claudia Goldin's **pollution theory of discrimination**, the entry of women into traditionally male jobs is seen by male incumbents as reducing the prestige of the occupation, based on general social perceptions that women are, on average, less productive.[23]

A final way in which employee discrimination could depress women workers' pay, also not initially considered by Becker, is that it could directly reduce the productivity of women in comparison with men. This is most likely to be a problem in traditionally male fields where the majority of workers are male. For example, on-the-job training frequently occurs informally as supervisors or coworkers demonstrate how things are done and give advice and assistance. When male employees have tastes for discrimination against women, they may be reluctant to teach them these important skills. Consequently, with less training women may be less productive.

Customer Discrimination

In the case of **customer discrimination**, customers or clients who have tastes for discrimination against women will act as if there is a nonpecuniary cost associated with purchasing a good or a service from a woman equal to their discrimination coefficient, d_c. That is, they will behave as if the full price of the good or service is $p + d_c$ if sold or provided by a woman but only p if sold or provided by a man. Then, at the going market price, women will sell less. Alternatively, in order to sell as much as a comparable male, a woman would have to charge a lower price ($p - d_c$). Discrimination, this time on the part of possible customers or clients, results in potentially equally productive women being less productive (in terms of revenue brought in) than comparable males. They are, thus, less desirable employees and receive lower pay. If, as we speculated earlier, such customer discrimination exists in some areas but not in others, occupational segregation may also result.

Subtle Barriers

As we noted previously, discrimination against women is not always or even usually conscious and overt. In Chapter 8, we outlined subtle barriers that may limit women's pursuit of higher education, particularly in traditionally male fields. Such **subtle barriers** may also operate in the labor market, as suggested by our discussion of the glass ceiling in Chapter 10. For instance, as in educational institutions, women in the workplace may have fewer *role models* available to them, participate

---

[22]George A. Akerlof and Rachel E. Kranton, "Economics and Identity," *Quarterly Journal of Economics* 115, no. 3 (August 2000): 715–53.
[23]Claudia Goldin, "A Pollution Theory of Discrimination: Male and Female Differences in Occupations and Earnings," in *Human Capital in History: The American Record*, ed. Leah Platt Boustan, Carola Frydman, and Robert A. Margo (Chicago: University of Chicago Press, 2014), 313–48.

less in the beneficial *mentor-protégé* relationships that often develop between senior and junior workers and may be excluded from the *informal networks* that tend to arise among peers. As a result, they will be denied access to important job-related information, skills, and contacts, as well as the informal support systems that male workers generally enjoy. In these cases, although women are *potentially* equally productive, this type of subtle discrimination reduces both their productivity and their pay.

Discrimination may also result from the perception that a woman would not "fit in" with the group as well as a man would, and evaluations of a female employee's competence may be tainted by gender stereotypes of appropriate female behavior. Discrimination by employers, employees, and customers may also be reinforced by habitual behavior that has the effect of disadvantaging women, even though its link to discriminatory outcomes may not be apparent at first. A good example of this is the role that all-male clubs traditionally served for business executives, high-level professionals, and civic leaders.[24] While some mistakenly perceive such clubs as "social" in their orientation, there is increased recognition that much business is transacted and many professional contacts are made in these settings. For this reason, many clubs, under legal pressure or voluntarily, have opened their doors to women. In addition, although no federal law prohibits gender discrimination by private clubs, a number of major cities and several states have banned the exclusion of women by business-oriented private clubs.[25]

The issue of women's admission to all-male clubs is by no means entirely one of the past. In 2002, a firestorm of negative media attention surrounded the male-only membership restriction of the exclusive Augusta National Golf Club, the private club which hosts the Masters Tournament. (The club excluded blacks until 1990.) Despite considerable media attention and controversy that lasted over a decade, it was not until August 2012 that this club effectively ended its all-male policy by inviting its first two female members, former secretary of state Condoleezza Rice and leading South Carolina businesswoman Darla Moore. The backstory behind this decision highlights the business role of some ostensibly private social clubs. In 2012, Virginia Rometty became the first female CEO of IBM, which was one of the three principal sponsors of the Masters Tournament. She was not invited to become a member of the Augusta National Golf Club even though the four previous IBM CEOs (all males) had been. After initially standing firm on its male-only policy, Augusta National relented and invited Rice and Moore (but not Rometty) to become members. It was only in 2014 that Rometty became the third woman to join the club.[26]

---

[24]For further discussion on this issue, including the legal status of male-only private clubs, see Jennifer Jolly-Ryan, "Teed Off about Private Club Discrimination on the Taxpayer's Dime: Tax Exemptions and Other Government Privileges to Discriminatory Private Clubs," *William & Mary Journal of Women and the Law* 13, no. 1 (2006), accessed December 23, 2012, http://scholarship.law.wm.edu/wmjowl/vol13/iss1/6/. See also Robin L. Bartlett and Timothy I. Miller, "Executive Earnings by Gender: A Case Study," *Social Science Quarterly* 69, no. 4 (December 1988): 892–909.

[25]Jason De Rusha, "Good Question: Why Can Some Clubs Discriminate?" August 20, 2012, CBS Minnesota, accessed December 23, 2012, http://minnesota.cbslocal.com/2012/08/20/good-question-why-can-some-clubs-discriminate/.

[26]Karen Crouse, "Augusta National Adds First Two Female Members," *New York Times*, August 10, 2012, www.nytimes.com; Chris Isidore, "Augusta National Admits IBM CEO as 3rd Female Member," CNN Money, November 14, 2014, money.cnn.com. There continue to be other male-only golf clubs where at least a portion of the facilities are restricted to men; see Brian Reid, "Male-Only Golf Enclaves: It's Not Just Augusta," *Forbes* (April 9, 2012), www.forbes.com; Teddy Greenstein, "Are All-Male Golf Clubs Necessarily a Bad Thing?" *Chicago Tribune*, May 19, 2016, www.chicagotribune.com.

Statistical Discrimination

As noted earlier, models of **statistical discrimination** developed by Edmund Phelps and others[27] attribute a different motivation to employers for discrimination, one that is potentially more consistent with profit maximization and, thus, with the persistence of discrimination in the long run. Statistical discrimination occurs when employers believe that, *on average*, women are less productive or less stable employees and treat *individual* women as if they conform to the average. Statistical discrimination models assume that employers are constantly faced with the need for decision-making under conditions of incomplete information and uncertainty. Even if they carefully study the qualifications of applicants, they never know for certain how individuals will perform on the job or how long they will stay with the firm after being hired. Mistakes can be costly, especially when substantial hiring and training costs are involved. Promotion decisions entail similar risks, although in this case employers have additional firsthand information on past job performance with the firm.

Perceptions of Average Gender Differences Can Result in a Pay Gap

In light of these uncertainties, it is not surprising that employers often use any readily accessible information that may be correlated with productivity or job stability in making difficult personnel decisions. If they believe that, *on average*, women are less productive or less stable employees, *statistical discrimination* against *individual* women may result. That is, employers may judge the individual woman on the basis of their beliefs about group averages. The result may be discrimination against women in pay or in hiring and promotion.

For example, suppose an employer is screening applicants for an entry-level managerial position and that the two major qualifications considered are level of education and grades. Assume further that the employer believes that at the same level of qualifications (e.g., an MBA with an A average), women as a group will be less likely to remain with the firm than men. Then, for a given level of qualifications, the employer would hire a woman only at a lower wage or, perhaps, simply hire a man rather than a woman for the job. More careful screening of applicants might enable the employer to distinguish more from less career-oriented women (e.g., a consideration of the candidate's employment record while a student or of her extracurricular activities while in school), but it may not be cost-effective for the employer to invest the additional resources necessary for this screening.

Judged on the basis of statements employers themselves make, such beliefs regarding differences in average ability or behavior by sex are quite common. For example, employers are often concerned that women do not take their careers as seriously as men and fear that they will quit their jobs when they have children. Other perceptions of average differences in behavior or performance of men and women were noted in our consideration of issues related to the glass ceiling in Chapter 10.

---

[27]Edmund S. Phelps, "The Statistical Theory of Racism and Sexism," *American Economic Review* 62, no. 4 (September 1972): 659–61. For an influential development of the concept, see Dennis J. Aigner and Glen G. Cain, "Statistical Theories of Discrimination in Labor Markets," *Industrial and Labor Relations Review* 30, no. 2 (January 1977): 175–87.

If such employer beliefs are simply incorrect or exaggerated or reflect time lags in adjusting to a new reality, actions based on them are clearly unfair and constitute labor market discrimination as we define it. That is, they generate wage and occupation differences between men and women that are not accounted for by (potential) productivity differences. If such views are not simply rationalizations for personal prejudice, it might be expected that, over time, they will yield to new information. However, this process may be more sluggish than one would like, and in the meantime employers make less than optimal choices. Moreover, as noted previously, some discrimination may be unconscious and, thus, less susceptible to change by new information.

The situation is different, and a bit more complicated, if the employer views *are* indeed correct *on average*. Employers make the best choices possible with imperfect knowledge, and, in a sense, at the market-wide level, labor market discrimination does not exist in this case: any resulting wage and employment differences between men and women, on average, would be accounted for by *average* productivity differences.

Yet the consequences for *individual* women are far from satisfactory. A particular woman who would be as productive and as stable an employee as her male counterpart is denied employment or paid a lower wage because of the average characteristics of her group. It is clear from a *normative* perspective that basing employment decisions on a characteristic such as sex is unfair. Indeed, the practice of judging an *individual* on the basis of *group* characteristics rather than on his or her own merits seems the very essence of stereotyping and discrimination. Such behavior is certainly not legal under the antidiscrimination laws and regulations that we discuss in Chapter 12. Yet it most likely still plays a role in employer thinking. Moreover, statistical discrimination, which is based on employers' *correct* assessment of average gender differences, is not likely to be eroded by the forces of competition.

Statistical Discrimination and Feedback Effects

As Nobel laureate Kenneth Arrow pointed out, the consequences of statistical discrimination are particularly pernicious when accompanied by *feedback effects*.[28] For example, if employers' views of female job instability lead them to give women less firm-specific training and to assign them to jobs where the costs of turnover are minimized, women experience little incentive to stay with the employer and may respond by exhibiting exactly the unstable behavior that employers expect. Employers' perceptions are confirmed, and they see no reason to change their discriminatory behavior. Yet if employers believe women to be stable workers and hire them into positions that reward such stability, they might well be stable workers!

Hence, where statistical discrimination is accompanied by feedback effects, employer behavior that is based on *initially* incorrect assessments of average gender differences may persist in the long run and be fairly impervious to competitive pressures.

Empirical Evidence on Gender Differences in Quitting

Some indication that such feedback effects are important is provided by studies of male and female quitting—an issue mentioned in Chapter 9. This issue is important because the view that women are more likely to quit their jobs than men tends to be

---

[28]Arrow, "The Theory of Discrimination."

fairly widespread among employers. A number of studies find that although women are *on average* more likely to quit their jobs than men, most of this difference can be explained by the types of jobs women are in and their individual characteristics.[29] These findings suggest that, when a woman worker is confronted with the same incentives to remain on the job in terms of wages, advancement opportunities, and so on, she is no more likely to quit than a comparable male worker. Indeed, it is unclear that even the average gender difference in quitting still prevails. Research using data from as far back as the late 1980s, for example, found little difference between men and women in average turnover rates.[30] Thus, there appears to be little rationale for differential treatment of women and men by employers based on perceptions of gender differences in quit behavior.

The Overcrowding Model

The **overcrowding model**, developed by Barbara Bergmann, is of interest because it gives a more central role to occupational segregation in causing a wage differential between men and women than the discrimination models we have considered so far.[31] Bergmann's overcrowding model demonstrates that, regardless of the reason for segregation (e.g., socialization, personal preferences, or labor market discrimination), the *consequence* may be a male–female pay differential. This differential will occur if demand (job opportunities) in the female sector is small relative to the supply of women available for such work. The overcrowding model is consistent with the evidence presented in Chapter 10 that, all else equal, earnings tend to be lower for both women and men in predominantly female than in predominantly male jobs.[32] The fact that men in predominantly female occupations receive lower wages than men in predominantly male occupations is not necessarily inconsistent with the overcrowding hypothesis. Although men as a group are obviously not excluded from the male sector, some of them may, nonetheless, enter female occupations because they have a strong preference or particular skills for this type of work. Or they may simply be unlucky or poorly informed about alternative opportunities. In such circumstances, some men will accept the lower wages paid in female jobs. However, this lower pay is primarily caused by the many

---

[29]See, for example, Nachum Sicherman, "Gender Differences in Departures from a Large Firm," *Industrial and Labor Relations Review* 49, no. 3 (April 1996): 484–505; and Anne Beeson Royalty, "Job-to-Job and Job-to-Nonemployment Turnover by Gender and Education Level," *Journal of Labor Economics* 16, no. 2 (April 1998): 392–443; for an early study, see, Blau and Kahn, "Race and Sex Differences in Quits."

[30]Royalty, "Job-to-Job and Job-to-Nonemployment Turnover." Moreover, while some research suggests that employers might have had greater difficulty *predicting* the quit behavior of women than the quit behavior of men for earlier cohorts, this was not found to be the case for women born after 1950; see Audrey Light and Manuelita Ureta, "Panel Estimates of Male and Female Job Turnover Behavior: Can Female Nonquitters Be Identified?" *Journal of Labor Economics* 10, no. 2 (April 1992): 156–81.

[31]Barbara R. Bergmann, "Occupational Segregation, Wages and Profits When Employers Discriminate by Race or Sex," *Eastern Economic Journal* 1, nos. 1–2 (April–July 1974): 103–10.

[32]Even if men in predominantly female occupations earn less than men in predominantly male occupations, they may still earn more than *women* in predominantly female jobs. As we saw in Chapter 10, there is some evidence this is the case; this phenomenon has been termed a "glass escalator."

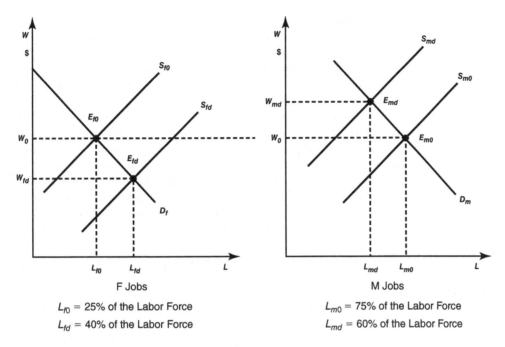

FIGURE 11-1 An Illustration of the Overcrowding Model

women who "crowd" into these jobs due to their preferences for the work or a lack of alternative opportunities.

This model is illustrated in Figure 11-1. F jobs and M jobs are considered. As in the previous models of discrimination, it is assumed that male and female workers are (potentially) equally productive. The hypothetical situation of no discrimination is represented by demand curves D_f and D_m and supply curves S_{f0} and S_{m0}. The non-discriminatory equilibrium points in the two markets (E_{f0} and E_{m0}) are determined so that the wage rate (W_0) is the same for both types of jobs.

To understand why, in the absence of discrimination, the wage rate will be the same for both types of jobs, recall that we assumed all workers are equally well qualified for F and M jobs and that employers are indifferent between hiring male and female workers. Suppose that, by chance, the equilibrium wage in F jobs is higher than the equilibrium wage in M jobs. Then workers attracted by the higher wage rates would transfer from M jobs to F jobs. This process would continue until wages in F jobs were bid down to the level of wages in M jobs. Similarly, if by chance wages in M jobs were set above those in F jobs, workers would move from F jobs to M jobs until the differential was eliminated. Thus, in the absence of discrimination, worker mobility ensures that the wages paid for both types of work are the same, at least after allowing time to make adjustments. This outcome, of course, assumes that no *nonpecuniary* differences exist in the relative attractiveness of the two jobs that would result in a compensating wage differential.

In the hypothetical example given in Figure 11-1, demand conditions are such that, in the nondiscriminatory equilibrium, L_{f0} workers (25 percent of the labor force) are employed in F jobs and L_{m0} workers (75 percent of the labor force) work in

M jobs. F and M jobs have no sex labels associated with them, and both women and men are randomly divided between the two sectors.

How does the situation differ when there is discrimination against women in "male" occupations or when, for a variety of reasons, women choose to concentrate in typically female jobs? The consequences of such segregation may be ascertained by comparing this situation to the hypothetical situation of no segregation. In our example, the restriction of M jobs to men results in an inward shift of the supply curve to M jobs from S_{m0} to S_{md}, causing wages to be bid up to W_{md}. At this higher wage, only L_{md} workers (60 percent of the labor force) are employed in M jobs. The exclusion of women from M jobs means that all the women must (or choose to) "crowd" into the F jobs. The expanded supply of labor in F jobs, represented by an outward shift of the supply curve from S_{f0} to S_{fd}, depresses wages there to W_{fd}. Now L_{fd} workers (40 percent of the labor force) are employed in F occupations.

The overcrowding model shows how gender segregation in employment may cause a wage differential between otherwise equally productive male and female workers. This differential will occur if the supply of women seeking employment is large relative to the demand for labor in the F jobs. This may well be what takes place in the labor market. Nevertheless, the analysis also shows that gender segregation in employment need not always result in a wage differential between men and women. If it so happens that the wage rate that equates supply and demand in the F sector is the same as the wage that equates supply and demand in the M sector, no wage differential will result (i.e., if the F sector is not overcrowded). However, this will happen only by chance. Labor market discrimination (or some other barrier) eliminates the free mobility of labor between the two sectors that would otherwise ensure wage equality between M and F jobs.

Returning to the more likely situation illustrated in Figure 11-1, in which segregation does lower women's pay, we may examine its impact on the *productivity* of women relative to men. Employers of women in F jobs accommodate a larger number of workers (L_{fd} rather than L_{f0}) by substituting labor for capital. The relatively low wages of the women, W_{fd}, make it profitable to use such labor-intensive production methods. On the other hand, the higher wage in the male sector, W_{md}, encourages employers to substitute capital for labor to economize on relatively high-priced labor. In the overcrowding model, women earn less than men, but both are paid in accordance with their productivity. Discrimination causes differences in both wages and productivity between *potentially* equally productive male and female labor—women are less productive than men because, due to segregation and crowding, they have less capital to work with.

The claim that the supply of labor to a particular occupation (or industry) helps to determine the wage rate is relatively noncontroversial. But the crowding hypothesis, in and of itself, does not explain why so many women are employed in typically female sectors. Controversy centers on the question of whether this segregation and crowding result because men and women have inherently different talents or preferences for different types of work; because, due to differences in socialization or in household responsibilities, women are willing to trade higher wages and steeper lifetime earnings profiles for more favorable working conditions and lower penalties for discontinuous labor force participation; or because employers, coworkers, or customers discriminate against women in some occupations but not in others.

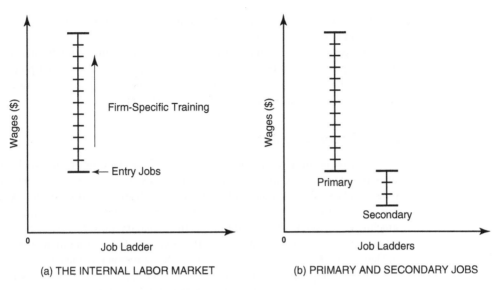

FIGURE 11-2 An Illustration of the Institutional Model

Institutional Models

The idea that the male–female pay gap is closely related to employment segregation is echoed in **institutional models of discrimination**.[33] Such explanations emphasize that labor markets may not be as flexible as the simple competitive model assumes. Rigidities are introduced both by the institutional arrangements found in many firms and by various barriers to competition introduced by the monopoly power of firms in the product market or of firms or unions in the labor market.

The Internal Labor Market

Institutionalists point out that the job structure of many large firms looks like the illustration in Figure 11-2a. Firms hire workers from the outside labor market for entry jobs. The remaining jobs are internally allocated by the firm as workers progress along well-defined promotion ladders by acquiring job-related skills, many of which are firm-specific in nature. When firm-specific skills are emphasized and a high proportion of jobs are filled from internal sources, the firm has an **internal labor market**. That is, it determines wages for each job category and the allocation of workers among categories and is insulated to some extent (although not entirely) from the impact of market forces.

To administer their personnel systems, larger firms often take the occupational category as the decision unit, establishing pay rates for each category (with some

---

[33]For important early work on this concept, see Peter B. Doeringer and Michael J. Piore, *Internal Labor Markets and Manpower Analysis* (Lexington, MA: D.C. Heath, 1971), and Michael J. Piore, "The Dual Labor Market: Theory and Implications," in *Problems in Political Economy: An Urban Perspective*, ed. David M. Gordon (Lexington, MA: D.C. Heath, 1971), 90–94. For an application to gender, see Francine D. Blau and Carol L. Jusenius, "Economists' Approaches to Sex Segregation in the Labor Market: An Appraisal," *Signs: Journal of Women in Culture and Society* 1, no. 3, pt. 2 (Spring 1976): 181–99.

allowance for seniority and merit considerations) and linking jobs together into promotion ladders. Thus, group treatment of individuals is the norm, and it will be to the employer's advantage to make sure that workers within each job category are as similar as possible. If it is believed that men and women differ in their productivity-related characteristics (like quit and absenteeism rates), statistical discrimination is likely to result in their being channeled into different jobs.

Primary and Secondary Jobs

The **dual labor market model** developed by Peter Doeringer and Michael Piore takes this analysis a step further and emphasizes the distinction between primary and secondary jobs.[34] Primary jobs emphasize high levels of firm-specific skills and, thus, pay high wages, offer good promotion opportunities, and encourage long-term attachment between workers and firms. In secondary jobs, firm-specific skills are not as important. Such jobs pay less, offer relatively fewer promotion opportunities, and have fairly high rates of labor turnover. This situation is depicted in Figure 11-2b. Applying the dual labor market model to gender discrimination leads us to expect that men would be more likely to be in primary jobs and women in secondary jobs.

The distinction between primary and secondary jobs may occur within the same firm—say, between the managerial and clerical categories. In addition, it is believed that primary jobs are more likely to be located in monopolistic industries that are generally higher-paying and have traditionally offered more stable employment[35] and that secondary jobs are more likely to be found in lower-paying, competitive industries with more labor turnover. This is an additional reason for expecting women to be more concentrated in the competitive sector.

Segmentation of male and female workers into primary and secondary jobs is likely to produce both pay and productivity differences between them due to unequal access to on-the-job training. Institutionalists also point out that feedback effects are likely to magnify any initial productivity differences as women respond to the lower incentives for employment stability in the secondary sector.

Institutional analyses also reinforce the point made earlier that labor market discrimination against women is not necessarily the outcome of conscious, overt acts by employers. Once men and women are channeled into different types of entry jobs, the normal, everyday operation of the firm—"business as usual"—will virtually ensure gender differences in productivity, promotion opportunities, and pay. This process is termed **institutional discrimination**.[36] Even gender differences in initial occupational assignment may be in part due to adherence to traditional practices that tend to work against women—for example, referrals from current male employees or an informal network of male colleagues at other firms, sexist recruitment materials

---

[34]Doeringer and Piore, *Internal Labor Markets*; and Piore, "The Dual Labor Market."

[35]The original formulation emphasized that these would likely also be union jobs as well, but as we saw in Chapter 7, there has been a steep decline in the extent of unionization in the United States. In addition, today, given the greater degree of international competition, even when there are a relatively small number of domestic manufacturers of a product, the firm may nonetheless face considerable competition and instability—witness the US auto industry.

[36]For business practices that may adversely affect women, see Barbara F. Reskin and Denise D. Bielby, "A Sociological Perspective on Gender and Career Outcomes," *Journal of Economic Perspectives* 19, no. 1 (Winter 2005): 71–86; Patricia A. Roos and Barbara F. Reskin, "Institutional Factors Contributing to Occupational Sex Segregation," in *Sex Segregation in the Workplace: Trends, Explanations, Remedies,* ed. Barbara Reskin (Washington, DC: National Academies Press, 1984), 235–60; and Reskin, "The Proximate Causes of Employment Discrimination."

picturing women in traditionally female jobs and men in traditionally male jobs, and lack of encouragement of female applicants to broaden their sights from traditional areas.

Feedback Effects

As noted several times already in this and earlier chapters, labor market discrimination or unequal treatment of women in the labor market may adversely affect women's own decisions and behavior.[37] These **feedback effects** are illustrated in Figure 11-3. Human capital theory and other supply-side explanations for gender differences in economic outcomes tend to emphasize the role of the gender division of labor in the family in causing differences between men and women in labor market outcomes and are indicated by the arrow pointing to the right in the figure.

This relationship undoubtedly exists; however, such explanations tend to neglect the impact of labor market discrimination in reinforcing the traditional division of labor (shown by the arrow pointing to the left). Even a relatively small amount of initial labor market discrimination can result in greatly magnified effects if it discourages women from making human capital investments, weakens their attachment to the labor force, and provides economic incentives for the family to place priority on the husband's career. Although labor market discrimination is not responsible for initially causing the traditional division of labor in the family, which clearly predates modern labor markets, it may well help to perpetuate it by inhibiting more rapid movement toward egalitarian sharing of household responsibilities today.

The net result is what might be viewed as a vicious circle. Discrimination against women in the labor market reinforces traditional gender roles in the family, while

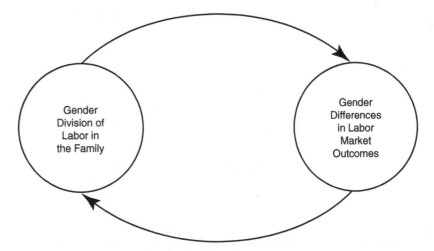

FIGURE 11-3 An Illustration of Feedback Effects

---

[37]A number of authors emphasize the importance of feedback effects in analyzing discrimination in pay and employment. See, for example, Arrow, "The Theory of Discrimination"; Shelly J. Lundberg and Richard Startz, "Private Discrimination and Social Intervention in Competitive Labor Markets," *American Economic Review* 73, no. 3 (June 1983): 340–47; and Yoram Weiss and Reuben Gronau, "Expected Interruptions in Labour Force Participation and Sex-Related Differences in Earnings Growth," *Review of Economic Studies* 48, no. 4 (October 1981): 607–19.

adherence to traditional roles by women in the family provides a rationale for labor market discrimination. However, this also means that effective policies to end labor market discrimination can be expected to have far-reaching effects, particularly when combined with simultaneous changes in social attitudes toward women's roles. A decrease in labor market discrimination will have feedback effects as the equalization of market incentives between men and women induces further changes in women's supply-side behavior. These changes in turn are likely to further encourage employers to reduce statistical discrimination against women. In addition, as more women enter previously male-dominated fields, the larger number of female role models for younger women is likely to induce still further increases in the availability of women for such jobs. Thus, demand-side policies can be expected to play an important role in sustaining a process of cumulative change in women's economic status.

Conclusion

In Chapter 10, we reviewed the evidence suggesting that labor market discrimination against women exists. In this chapter, we reviewed theories that focus on the following possible sources of discrimination:

- Employers, coworkers, or customers have tastes for discrimination against women.

- Discrimination may be unconscious and implicit, rather than conscious and overt, taking the form of subtle barriers that negatively affect women.

- Employers judge individual women in terms of the average characteristics of the group (statistical discrimination).

- Women's wages are depressed because they are "crowded" into predominantly female occupations.

- Women are concentrated in dead-end jobs with few opportunities for on-the-job training and promotion.

Each of the models of discrimination that we have considered contributes to our understanding of a complex reality, where the factors keeping women in segregated and poorly paid jobs, rather than being mutually exclusive, are likely to reinforce each other. By the same token, however, we pointed out that any improvements in women's labor market outcomes are likely to have positive feedback effects. By rewarding women more highly for their human capital, women are encouraged to accumulate more human capital on which they can gather rewards.

Questions for Review and Discussion

1. Summarize Becker's model of employer discrimination. Are its predictions consistent with some of the gender differences we observe in the labor market? Why do economists question whether gender differences due to employer discrimination can persist in the long run?

2. Male-only private social clubs are generally legal under federal antidiscrimination laws. Suggest arguments in support of and against such a policy.

3. "If employers pay women less due to employers' correct perception of average gender differences in productivity, this does not constitute discrimination as economists define it." Is this statement true or false? Explain your answer fully.

4. Use the crowding model to explain the relationship between occupational segregation of women and the gender wage gap. Can you think of a real-world example where overcrowding may play a role in explaining the gender wage gap? Explain your reasoning.

5. To the extent that it is true that women earn less because they spend less time in the labor market and that they spend less time in the labor market because they are paid less, how can this vicious circle be broken?

Suggested Readings

Akerlof, George A., and Rachel E. Kranton. *Identity Economics: How Our Identities Shape Our Work, Wages and Well-Being.* Princeton, NJ: Princeton University Press, 2010.

Becker, Gary S. "Prize Lecture: The Economic Way of Looking at Life." (1992). http://www.nobelprize.org/nobel_prizes/economics/laureates/1992/becker-lecture.html.

Becker, Gary S. *The Economics of Discrimination*, 2nd ed. Chicago: University of Chicago Press, 1971.

Bertrand, Marianne, Dolly Chugh, and Sendhil Mullainathan. "Implicit Discrimination." *American Economic Review* 95, no. 2 (May 2005): 94–98.

Blau, Francine D., Mary C. Brinton, and David B. Grusky, eds. *The Declining Significance of Gender?* New York: Russell Sage Foundation, 2006.

Blau, Francine D., and Lawrence M. Kahn. "The Gender Wage Gap: Extent, Trends, and Sources." NBER Working Paper 21913 (National Bureau of Economic Research, Cambridge, MA, January 2016) (*Journal of Economic Literature*, forthcoming).

Blau, Francine D., and Lawrence M. Kahn. "Women's Work and Wages." In *The New Palgrave Dictionary of Economics*, 2nd ed., edited by Steven N. Durlauf and Lawrence E. Blume, 762–72. London: Palgrave Macmillan, 2008.

Fiske, Susan T. "Stereotyping, Prejudice, and Discrimination." In *Handbook of Social Psychology*, edited by D. T. Gilbert, S. T. Fiske, and G. Lindzey, 357–411. New York: McGraw-Hill, 1998.

Goldin, Claudia. "A Pollution Theory of Discrimination: Male and Female Differences in Occupations and Earnings." In *Human Capital in History: The American Record*, edited by Leah Platt Boustan, Carola Frydman, and Robert A. Margo, 313–48. Chicago: University of Chicago Press, 2014.

Hersch, Joni. "Sex Discrimination in the Labor Market." *Foundations and Trends in Microeconomics* 2, no. 4 (2006): 281–361.

Key Terms

labor market discrimination (301)

marginal product (302)

tastes for discrimination (302)

nonpecuniary cost (303)

discrimination coefficient (303)

employer discrimination (303)

monopsony power (305)

implicit discrimination (307)

employee discrimination (307)

compensating wage differential (308)

identity model (310)

pollution theory of discrimination (310)

customer discrimination (310)

subtle barriers (310)

statistical discrimination (312)

overcrowding model (314)

institutional models of discrimination (317)

internal labor market (317)

dual labor market model (318)

institutional discrimination (318)

feedback effects (319)

Government Policies to Combat Employment Discrimination

12

CHAPTER HIGHLIGHTS

- ■ Rationales for Government Intervention
- ■ Equal Employment Opportunity Laws and Regulations
- ■ Effectiveness of the Government's Antidiscrimination Effort
- ■ Affirmative Action
- ■ Comparable Worth

In Chapters 10 and 11, we reviewed empirical evidence on the extent of labor market discrimination and economic models of labor market discrimination. We now turn to a consideration of government antidiscrimination policies. As we have noted previously, such policies are motivated by both equity and efficiency concerns. We explore these rationales in more detail in the first section. We then turn to a summary of the existing laws and regulations, including a consideration of the legal treatment of a number of issues that have received considerable attention in the news, including sex discrimination in the form of sexual harassment and discrimination on the basis of sexual orientation and gender identity. This is followed by an assessment of the effectiveness of the government's antidiscrimination policies. We close with an analysis of a policy that has been proposed for the United States and implemented in a number of other countries, comparable worth.

Rationales for Government Intervention

Government policies to combat labor market discrimination against women can potentially be justified on at least two grounds. One is equity or fairness—"a matter of simple justice."[1] Thus, government intervention may be rationalized as an effort to assure equal treatment for all participants in the labor market, regardless of gender (or race, ethnic origin, etc.).

In addition to being unfair, unequal treatment on the basis of gender may result in an inefficient allocation of resources. This inefficiency provides a second rationale for government intervention. Consider the case where equally productive men and women are hired for different jobs and women's jobs are lower-paid (as in the overcrowding model). Under these circumstances, prices do not serve as accurate indicators of social costs. In comparison with the nondiscriminatory situation, society produces "too little" of the outputs that use "overpriced" male labor, given that equally productive female labor is available at a lower price to expand production. Society produces "too much" of the outputs that use "underpriced" female labor, given that the contribution of equally productive labor is valued more highly in the male sector (as measured by its price).

Discrimination is also inefficient to the extent that it results in the underutilization of women's talents and abilities. This is the case when, for example, qualified women are not hired for or promoted into higher-level positions. The inefficiency caused by discrimination is even greater when we take into account feedback effects. If women are deterred from investing in their human capital because of discrimination, society loses a valuable resource. Thus, opening doors previously closed (or only slightly ajar) to women potentially benefits society as well as individual women by bringing their talents and abilities to bear in new areas.[2]

Weighed against these potential gains are the costs of the increased government intervention in society that may be necessary to produce this result. These costs loom large indeed to those who are skeptical of the evidence of labor market discrimination against women presented in Chapter 10. Some may also fear what they regard as the possible excesses of antidiscrimination policies in the form of reverse discrimination or preferential treatment for women and minorities, although, as we shall see, research to date provides no evidence that the increased employment of women and minorities encouraged by legislation and government regulation entailed such efficiency costs.[3]

---

[1]This phrase provided the title of the Report of the President's Task Force on Women's Rights and Responsibilities (Washington, DC: US Government Printing Office, April 1970).

[2]It has been estimated that reduction in the barriers to occupational choice facing women and blacks in the United States between 1960 and 2010 can explain about one-quarter of growth in productivity (output per person); see Chang-Tai Hsieh, Erik Hurst, Charles I. Jones, and Peter J. Klenow, "The Allocation of Talent and U.S. Economic Growth," unpublished working paper, Chicago Booth (August 2016), http://klenow.com/HHJK.pdf . See also Tiago Cavalcanti and José Tavares, "Gender Discrimination Lowers Output Per Capita (A Lot)," *VOX*, October 16, 2007, http://voxeu.org.

[3]Jonathan S. Leonard, "Antidiscrimination or Reverse Discrimination: The Impact of Changing Demographics, Title VII, and Affirmative Action on Productivity," *Journal of Human Resources* 19, no. 2 (Spring 1984): 145–74; Harry Holzer and David Neumark, "Are Affirmative Action Hires Less Qualified? Evidence from Employer–Employee Data on New Hires," *Journal of Labor Economics* 17, no. 3 (July 1999): 534–69; and Fred L. Pincus, *Reverse Discrimination: Dismantling the Myth* (Boulder, CO: Lynne Rienner, 2003). For a helpful review of the evidence on this question and other issues related to affirmative action, see Harry J. Holzer and David Neumark, "Affirmative Action: What Do We Know?" *Journal of Policy Analysis and Management* 25, no. 2 (Spring 2006): 463–90.

Equal Employment Opportunity Laws and Regulations[4]

There is a long history of government involvement in shaping conditions encountered by women in the labor market. During the period following the Civil War, in response to concern and agitation by workers and their sympathizers, a number of states passed protective labor laws limiting hours and regulating other terms of employment for all workers. At first, the Supreme Court struck down these laws as unconstitutional on the basis that they interfered with the freedom of workers to enter into contracts. Subsequently, in its 1908 decision in *Muller v. Oregon*,[5] the court upheld such laws when they were confined to women alone, arguing that individual rights may be abridged because the state has a legitimate interest in the possible social effects of women's work. Louis Brandeis, later to become a Supreme Court justice known for his support of individual human rights, wrote the following about the case:

> The two sexes differ in structure of body, in the functions performed by each, in the amount of physical strength, in the capacity for long-continued labor, particularly when done standing, the influence of vigorous health upon the future well-being of the race, the self-reliance which enables one to assert full rights, and in the capacity to maintain the struggle for subsistence. The difference justifies a difference in legislation, and upholds that which is designed to compensate for some of the burdens which rest upon her.

In time, however, the concern shifted from protection to equal opportunity. Indeed, protective laws eventually came to be viewed as undesirable impediments to the advancement of women. Supreme Court Justice Brennan expressed this view well in a 1973 case: "Traditionally, discrimination was rationalized by an attitude of romantic paternalism which in practical effect put women not on a pedestal but in a cage."[6]

The 1960s ushered in the legislation and regulations that are most pertinent to women today, including the Equal Pay Act, Title VII of the Civil Rights Act, and Executive Order 11246.

Equal Pay Act

As early as 1961, President Kennedy issued an executive order calling for a presidential commission on the status of women. Two years later, the **Equal Pay Act** of 1963 was passed, which requires employers to pay the same wages to men and women who do substantially equal work, involving equal skill, effort, and responsibility

---

[4]For summaries of the law and legal issues, see Mack A. Player, *Federal Law of Employment Discrimination in a Nutshell*, 7th ed. (St. Paul, MI: Thomson/West, 2013), and Lenora M. Lapidus, Emily J. Martin, and Namita Luthra, *The Rights of Women: The Basic ACLU Guide to a Woman's Rights*, 4th ed. (New York: NYU Press, 2009). For this chapter, we also draw on Susan Deller Ross, Isabelle Katz Pinzler, Deborah A. Ellis, and Kary L. Moss, *The Rights of Women: The Basic ACLU Guide to a Woman's Rights*, 3rd ed. (Carbondale: Southern Illinois University Press, 1993). For a useful description of the role of economists in employment litigation, see Joni Hersch and Blair Bruhan, "The Use and Misuse of Econometric Evidence in Employment Discrimination Cases," *Washington and Lee Law Review* 71, no. 4 (Fall 2014): 2365–2429.
[5]Muller v. Oregon, 208 U.S. 412 (1908).
[6]Frontiero v. Richardson, 411 U.S. 677 (1973).

and performed under similar conditions in the same establishment. This law, for instance, makes it illegal for a firm to have separate pay scales for women and men doing the same job. It applies only to wage discrimination for the same job in the same firm and does not address discrimination in hiring, promotion, training programs, and so on.

Title VII of the Civil Rights Act

More comprehensive legislation was enacted in 1964 when **Title VII of the Civil Rights Act** was passed.[7] This legislation was originally written to prohibit discrimination in employment on the basis of race, religion, and national origin but was amended at the last minute to include the word *sex*.[8] Title VII comprises the centerpiece of the federal government's antidiscrimination enforcement effort; it broadly prohibits sex discrimination in virtually all aspects of employment, including hiring and firing, training, promotions, wages, fringe benefits, or other terms and conditions of employment. As amended, it covers all businesses employing 15 or more workers, including federal, state, and local governments and educational institutions. It also prohibits discrimination by employment agencies and labor organizations. The **Equal Employment Opportunity Commission (EEOC)** is the federal agency charged with enforcing the Equal Pay Act and Title VII. Enforcement of Title VII may involve litigation over individual complaints but may also take the form of **class action lawsuits** in which one or more individuals sue on behalf of a larger group of affected individuals. Class action lawsuits are arguably more efficient in that a larger group will be affected by the judgment in the case, although a larger case is likely to be more costly to prosecute.

Executive Order 11246 and Affirmative Action

Executive Order 11246, issued in 1965 and amended in 1967 to include *sex*, bars discrimination in employment by all employers with federal contracts and subcontracts. It also requires that firms with federal contracts or subcontracts that have more than 50 employees and $50,000 in contracts take "affirmative action" for classes of workers disadvantaged by past discrimination. In general, **affirmative action** refers to a set of proactive policies established by the firm that seek to provide equal employment opportunities and "to erase differences between women and men, minorities and nonminorities, etc."[9] In the context of the executive order, contractors are required to analyze their employment patterns to determine where women and minorities are underrepresented.[10] Whenever such deficiencies are found, contractors are required to set up "goals and timetables" for the hiring of women and minorities

---

[7]For a useful review of the history, scope, and impact of the Civil Rights Act of 1964 50 years after its passage, see Joni Hersch and Jennifer Bennett Shinall, "Fifty Years Later: The Legacy of the Civil Rights Act of 1964," *Journal of Policy Analysis and Management*, 34, no. 2 (Spring 2015): 424–56.

[8]Because it was Howard Smith, a conservative congressman from Virginia, who proposed this amendment, it is widely believed that his purpose in doing so was to increase opposition to the bill and reduce the chances of its passage.

[9]Harry Holzer and David Neumark, "Assessing Affirmative Action," *Journal of Economic Literature* 38, no. 3 (September 2000): 483–568; quotation is from p. 484.

[10]In the case of the construction industry, it is the Office of Federal Contract Compliance that sets the targeted percent of female construction workers to be hired, not the firm itself. A goal of 6.9 percent was set as a target in 1980 and continues today; see US Department of Labor website, http://www.dol.gov/ofccp/regs/compliance/aa.htm, accessed January 11, 2013.

and to make good faith efforts to reach their goals in the specified period. The executive order is enforced by the Office of Federal Contract Compliance. Violators face possible loss of their government contracts, although this sanction is seldom invoked.

It should be noted that while government contractors are mandated by the executive order to have affirmative action plans, other firms have sometimes been required by the courts to implement affirmative action plans in connection with the resolution of employment discrimination cases or have voluntarily chosen to adopt such plans. We discuss these points later in the chapter in the section on "Affirmative Action."

Major Court Decisions and Legislation That Have Shaped the Equal Employment Laws and Regulations

In the years since their passage and implementation, the federal antidiscrimination laws and regulations have been interpreted and clarified by the courts, with the final arbiter being the US Supreme Court. This process is especially important in understanding the provisions of Title VII of the Civil Rights Act, the broadest law and the centerpiece of the federal government's antidiscrimination enforcement effort. In some cases, the court's interpretations of the law changed as the membership on the court shifted, which is likely to continue to be the case in the future. Bearing this likelihood in mind, in order to better understand what activities are currently prohibited under Title VII, we turn to a brief summary of some of the more important court decisions.

EXCEPTIONS TO TITLE VII DUE TO BONA FIDE OCCUPATIONAL QUALIFICATIONS Title VII permits exceptions to its ban on gender discrimination when sex is found to be a **bona fide occupational qualification (BFOQ)**. When the law was passed in the mid-1960s, it was not entirely clear what this exemption would mean as a practical matter, particularly as only gender could be a basis for a BFOQ in the legislation, not race, religion, or national origin. At that time, it was widely accepted that a considerable number of jobs were particularly suitable for women and a number of others especially appropriate for men. Indeed, newspapers routinely divided portions of their help-wanted sections into "help wanted male" and "help wanted female." The former might include openings for jobs such as manager or construction worker, while the latter might include what used to be referred to as a "girl Friday" (i.e., administrative assistant) or receptionist.[11] Thus, the interpretation of the BFOQ exemption by the courts was extremely important. If interpreted broadly, to match the social views of the day, considerable gender discrimination would have been permissible under Title VII in that sex might have been viewed as a valid qualification for a host of traditionally male and traditionally female jobs.

However, both the EEOC and the courts have taken the position that the BFOQ exception should be interpreted narrowly. That is, men and women are entitled to consideration on the basis of their individual capabilities, rather than on the basis of characteristics generally attributed to the group. The court, for example, has rejected the BFOQ exemption for predominantly male jobs in which heavy lifting is required as well as for the predominantly female position of flight attendant, where

---

[11]In 1968, the EEOC issued guidelines stating that help-wanted advertisements that used male and female headings violated Title VII; see, "Milestones in the History of the U.S. Equal Employment Opportunity Commission," accessed November 12, 2016, https://www.eeoc.gov/eeoc/history/50th/milestones.cfm.

it was argued by the employer that airline passengers preferred women in the job. Also, the court has ruled that it is discriminatory to bar all women of childbearing age from jobs where they would work with substances that might be hazardous to a developing fetus.[12] In the only major case to date in which gender was found to be a BFOQ, the 1977 *Dothard v. Rawlinson* case, the Supreme Court allowed the hiring of only males for the position of prison guard in Alabama's maximum-security male prisons. The court reasoned that due to the nature of the prison population, as well as the atmosphere of the prison, women would be particularly subject to sexual assault, which would interfere with their job performance. Regardless of whether or not one agrees with this reasoning, this case has not resulted in substantially greater acceptance by the courts of the BFOQ exception for other jobs, given its unusual circumstances.[13]

RULINGS REGARDING SEX PLUS ANOTHER CHARACTERISTIC   The court has also found in a number of cases that sex cannot be used in combination with some other factor as a legal basis for differentiating between women and men under Title VII. (This is termed "sex-plus discrimination.") The court has held, for example, that an employer cannot refuse to hire women with preschool-age children while men with preschool-age children are hired.[14] Furthermore, it is illegal to pay women lower monthly pension benefits than men.[15] In this case, the other factor would be longevity—the practice was justified on the basis that, on average, women live longer and, thus, it would be more costly to provide them with the same monthly benefit. The courts ruled that each woman is entitled to be treated as an individual, rather than as a group member.

DISPARATE TREATMENT AND DISPARATE IMPACT   **Disparate treatment** of women and minorities, that is, differential treatment of these groups with the intention to discriminate, is a clear violation of Title VII. A more complex issue addressed by the courts in interpreting Title VII concerns unintentional discrimination. This type of discrimination arises when apparently neutral practices or policies of a firm, say with regard to hiring or promotion, result in a **disparate impact** that is, have disproportionately adverse effects on women or minorities. An example of disparate impact as it relates to women might be a minimum height and weight requirement for the position of police officer that screens out a higher proportion of women than men. Based on a 1971 Supreme Court decision in *Griggs*, apparently neutral practices resulting in a disparate impact on women and minorities may be illegal even

---

[12]Major cases in which the court has rejected a BFOQ exemption include Weeks v. Southern Bell Telephone and Telegraph, 408 F. 2d 228 (5th Cir. 1969); Rosenfeld v. Southern Pacific Company, 444 F. 2d 1219 (9th Cir. 1971); Diaz v. Pan American World Airways, Inc., 442 F. 2d 385 (5th Cir. 1971); and United Auto Workers v. Johnson Controls, Inc., 499 U.S. 187 (1991). The Johnson controls case, which focused on workplace hazards, raised a particularly controversial issue. The court found the exclusion of women of childbearing age from such employments to be discriminatory because "fertile men, but not fertile women, are given a choice as to whether they wish to risk their reproductive health for a particular job." It clarified that the BFOQ exemption of Title VII "must relate to ability to perform the duties of the job" rather than to any danger or risk to the woman herself. The court also concluded that the risk of employer liability was slight given that "Title VII bans sex-specific fetal-protection policies, the employer fully informs the woman of the risk, and the employer has not acted negligently." See Bureau of National Affairs, *Daily Labor Report*, no. 55 (March 21, 1991), A1–A3, D1–D11.
[13]Dothard v. Rawlinson, 433 U.S. 321 (1977).
[14]Philips v. Martin Marietta Corp., 400 U.S. 542 (1971).
[15]City of Los Angeles, Dept. of Water v. Manhart, 435 U.S. 702 (1978).

if the discrimination is not intentional. Once the plaintiffs show that the practice creates a disparate impact, the burden of proof shifts to the employer to show that the practice is a matter of "business necessity" or that the requirement is job-related; otherwise, the practice is discriminatory.[16]

1991 CIVIL RIGHTS ACT   In 1991, the Civil Rights Act was reauthorized, and several provisions were added. The new law permits women to obtain compensatory and punitive damages for *intentional* discrimination, in addition to back pay, although the amounts are limited. Prior to this law, only racial minorities had such rights. In addition, the new law allows discrimination cases to be argued before juries as well as judges. As we shall see shortly, these changes made it much more likely that private law firms would be willing to take on sex discrimination cases, particularly class action cases.

SEXUAL HARASSMENT   A gender-related employment issue that has captured considerable public attention is sexual harassment[17] As we saw in Chapter 8, sexual harassment in education programs and activities is prohibited under Title IX. In this section, the focus is on sexual harassment in *employment*. **Sexual harassment** in the workplace potentially encompasses a broad range of objectionable behaviors, from the making of sexual demands where a refusal results in an adverse action (e.g., dismissal, the loss of a promotion, reduced benefits), generally called *quid pro quo* harassment, to various actions that are sufficiently offensive to result in a *hostile work environment*. Deciding whether sexual harassment is indeed covered under Title VII and demarcating the conditions under which the behavior is egregious enough to be illegal proved to be challenging for the courts. A major step forward was the Supreme Court's 1986 decision in *Meritor*, which held that sexual harassment is illegal under Title VII if it is unwelcome and "sufficiently severe or pervasive to alter the conditions of the victim's employment and create an abusive working environment."[18] Some controversy followed the court's ruling over what constituted evidence of a hostile environment, with some lower courts requiring evidence of severe psychological injury or diminished job performance.

---

[16]Griggs v. Duke Power Co., 401 U.S. 424 (1971). The *Griggs* case related to race, and the requirement at issue was a high school diploma for higher-paid jobs. A later 1989 Supreme Court decision (Wards Cove Packing Co. v. Atonio, 490 U.S. 642 [1989]) held that even after a disparate impact was demonstrated, the burden of proof remained with the plaintiffs to show that the employer had no business necessity justification for the practice. This decision was widely criticized by civil rights advocates, and the original interpretation of the law that places the burden of proof on the *employer* was reestablished by Congress with the passage of the 1991 Civil Rights Act.

[17]This issue first attracted particular attention during the 1991 confirmation hearings of Supreme Court Justice Clarence Thomas, when charges of sexual harassment were made against the nominee by Anita Hill, a law professor who had formerly worked as his assistant. Although Justice Thomas was confirmed, the airing of this issue in a national forum greatly heightened public awareness of the problem. Kaushik Basu discusses the extent and rationale for government intervention in this area in "The Economics and Law of Sexual Harassment in the Workplace," *Journal of Economic Perspectives* 17, no. 3 (Summer 2003): 141–57. See also Heather Antecol and Deborah A. Cobb-Clark, "The Changing Nature of Employment-Related Sexual Harassment: Evidence from the U.S. Federal Government (1978–1994)," *Industrial and Labor Relations Review* 57, no. 3 (April 2004): 443–61. For an excellent review of the evolution of the law in this area, see Joanna L. Grossman, "Moving Forward Looking Back: A Retrospective on Sexual Harassment Law," *Boston University Law Review* 95 (2015): 1029–48.

[18]Meritor Savings Bank v. Vinson, 477 U.S. 57 (1986); the quotation was cited in "Ending Sexual Harassment: Business Is Getting the Message," *Business Week*, March 18, 1991, 99.

In its 1993 *Harris*[19] case, the Supreme Court clarified this issue, overturning a lower court ruling that an employee who was subjected to the company president's repeated offensive and demeaning comments of a sexual nature was not entitled to redress under the law because she had not suffered sufficient psychological damage. The standard put forth by the court in its decision is essentially that a hostile environment is one that a *reasonable person* would perceive to be "hostile or abusive." Writing for the majority, Justice Sandra Day O'Connor said that the protection of federal law "comes into play before the harassing conduct leads to a nervous breakdown." The court has since ruled that Title VII prohibits sexual harassment between members of the same sex under the same legal standards as those used to evaluate claims of sexual harassment by a member of the opposite sex.[20]

Because sexual harassment generally results from interactions between employees, the question arises as to when employers are held liable for the actions of their employees. This issue is important because employers are regarded as having "deep pockets"; that is, they can potentially pay financial compensation to individuals who are the victims of harassment. The stakes involved may be considerable. In 1998, in the largest sexual harassment settlement negotiated up to that point, Mitsubishi Motor Corporation agreed to pay $34 million to end a government lawsuit charging that hundreds of female employees at its automobile assembly plant in Normal, Illinois, had been sexually harassed.[21] Prior to two 1998 Supreme Court decisions,[22] it was believed, based on a lower court ruling, that employers could only be held liable for sexual harassment if they knew or should have known that the harassment had taken place. In its 1998 decisions, however, the Supreme Court extended the employer's liability well beyond this situation, making it clear that employers bear the fundamental responsibility for preventing and eliminating sexual harassment from the workplace. The court ruled that when sexual harassment results in "a tangible employment action, such as discharge, demotion or undesirable assignment" (as in the quid pro quo type of case described earlier), the employer's liability is absolute. In cases of no tangible action (including hostile work environment cases), an employer could still be liable but can defend itself by establishing that it took "reasonable care to prevent and correct promptly any sexually harassing behavior" and that the employee "unreasonably failed to take advantage of any preventive or corrective opportunities" provided.

It is generally believed that a strong, well-publicized employer policy against harassment coupled with an effective grievance (complaint) procedure are the best tools available to employers to combat sexual harassment at the workplace and to safeguard themselves from legal liability. Such a policy cannot simply be "on the

---

[19]Harris v. Forklift Systems Inc., 510 U.S. 17 (1993). The summary of the case and quotation from the opinion are from Linda Greenhouse, "Court, 9–0, Makes Sex Harassment Easier to Prove," *New York Times*, November 10, 1993, A1–A14; see also Bureau of National Affairs, "Psychological Injury Not Needed to Prove Sex Harassment, Unanimous Supreme Court Rules," *Daily Labor Report*, no. 216, November 10, 1993, AA1–AA2.

[20]This ruling came in the 1998 case of Oncale v. Sundowner Offshore Services, Inc., 523 U.S. 75 (1998); see Charles J. Muhl, "The Law at Work: Sexual Harassment," *Monthly Labor Review* 121, no. 7 (July 1998): 61–62.

[21]Barnaby J. Feder, "$34 Million Settles Suit for Women at Auto Plant," *New York Times*, June 12, 1998, www.nytimes.com.

[22]The two cases, both decided in 1998, are Faragher v. City of Boca Raton, 524 U.S. 775, and Burlington Industries, Inc. v. Ellerth, 524 U.S. 742. The quotations are from Linda Greenhouse, "The Supreme Court: The Workplace; Court Spells Out Rules for Finding Sex Harassment," *New York Times*, June 27, 1998, www.nytimes.com. See also Muhl, "The Law at Work," and Steven Greenhouse, "Companies Set to Get Tougher on Harassment," *New York Times*, June 28, 1998, www.nytimes.com.

books." The employer must make sure that the policy is effectively communicated to employees; complaints are promptly investigated; and corrective action, where merited, is promptly taken.[23]

SEXUAL ORIENTATION AND GENDER IDENTITY   A final substantive issue is employment discrimination based on sexual orientation or gender identity.[24] While a 2015 Supreme Court ruling legalized same-sex marriage throughout the United States, as of 2016 no federal law *explicitly* prohibited employment discrimination based on sexual orientation or gender identity. As we have seen, Title VII does prohibit discrimination based on "sex," but historically the courts have not interpreted this to mean that the law bars discrimination based on sexual orientation or gender identity. This situation may be changing. One step in this direction was when a 1998 Supreme Court decision found that Title VII prohibits sexual harassment between members of the same sex on the same terms as between members of the opposite sex.[25] Another important development is that, since 2012, the EEOC, which is charged with enforcing Title VII, has held that the law's prohibition of discrimination based on sex extends to discrimination based on gender identity and, since 2015, that it extends to sexual orientation.[26] However, the reception of the federal courts to the EEOC position has been mixed.[27] Thus, the current legal situation at the federal level as it applies to private sector employment is ambiguous. A new law, the Employment Non-Discrimination Act (ENDA), has been proposed to address this situation; it would explicitly prohibit employment discrimination on the basis of sexual orientation or gender identity. However, as of 2016, ENDA had not been enacted into law.[28]

While the legal status of protections against discrimination based on sexual orientation and gender identity for workers in private sector employment remains unclear based on federal law, some states and localities have moved forward and passed laws explicitly banning such discrimination. As of 2016, 19 states and the District of Columbia prohibited discrimination based on sexual orientation or gender identity, while an additional three states prohibited discrimination based on sexual orientation only.[29]

---

[23]For additional information, see, for example, Mark I. Schickman, "Sexual Harassment: the Employer's Role in Prevention," American Bar Association, Solo, Small Firm and General Practice Division, accessed January 13, 2013, http://www.americanbar.org; and US Equal Employment Opportunity Commission, "Questions and Answers for Small Employers on Employer Liability for Harassment by Supervisors," accessed January 13, 2013, http://www.eeoc.gov/policy/docs/harassment-facts.html.

[24]In this section we draw in part on the summary provided in Katz, Marshall & Banks, LLP, "Sexual Orientation and Transgender Discrimination," accessed October 30, 2016, http://www.kmblegal.com/practice-areas/discrimination-retaliation/sexual-orientation-transgender-discrimination. See also Workplace Fairness, "Sexual Orientation Discrimination" and "Gender Identity Discrimination," accessed October 30, 2016, http://www.workplacefairness.org.

[25]*Oncale*, 523 U.S. 75; see Muhl, "The Law at Work."

[26]For the EEOC guidelines and rationale, see US Equal Employment Opportunity Commission, "What You Should Know about EEOC and the Enforcement Protections for LGBT Workers," accessed October 30, 2016, https://www.eeoc.gov/eeoc/newsroom/wysk/enforcement_protections_lgbt_workers.cfm.

[27]For an example of a case in which the EEOC interpretation was not upheld, see Kevin McGowan, "Title VII Doesn't Cover Sex Orientation, 7th Cir. Rules," August 1, 2016, accessed November 12, 2016, bna.com.

[28]See Ed O'Keefe, "The Fix: ENDA, Explained," *Washington Post*, November 4, 2013, Washingtonpost.com. For details of the bill, see https://www.congress.gov/bill/113th-congress/senate-bill/815 (accessed October 28, 2016).

[29]See "Non-Discrimination Laws: State by State Information—Map," accessed October 28, 2016, www.aclu.org; and Katz, Marshall & Banks, LLP, "Sexual Orientation and Transgender Discrimination."

In addition, in the public sector, federal government workers are protected against discrimination on the basis of sexual orientation and gender identity.[30] Moreover, under a 2014 executive order signed by then-president Barack Obama, employees of federal government contractors (firms that do work for the federal government) are also protected against discrimination based on sexual orientation or gender identity.[31]

THE LILLY LEDBETTER CASE   Judicial decisions on procedural as well as substantive matters can also have important consequences for the implementation of Title VII and thus its potential effects. A controversial 2007 decision by the Supreme Court in *Ledbetter v. Goodyear Tire & Rubber Co.*[32] was viewed by many as a setback in combating gender discrimination. Lilly Ledbetter, the plaintiff in the court case, worked as a supervisor at Goodyear Tire & Rubber for 19 years. When she began her job in 1979 she was paid the same as her male colleagues, but due to smaller raises, a disparity arose; by 1998 (when she brought suit), she was paid significantly (40 percent) less than her male counterparts. The court did not rule on the merits of the case but held that employees alleging discrimination in pay under Title VII may not bring suit unless they have filed a formal complaint with the EEOC within 180 days after the original discriminatory pay-setting decision (the statute of limitation established in the act). Surprisingly to many observers, this timeline was found to apply, "even if the effects of the initial discriminatory act were not immediately apparent to the worker and even if they continue to the present day." It was widely believed that adherence to this standard would bar many of the pay discrimination cases that had been brought under Title VII and were still pending. The decision rejected the view of the EEOC that each (lower) paycheck received reflected the initial discrimination and in effect reset the 180-day clock.

In a strongly worded dissent, Supreme Court Justice Ruth Bader Ginsburg argued that many employees lack information on the salaries of their coworkers and thus would not know within the 180-day limit that they had been underpaid. Moreover, if the initial disparity is small, an employee, particularly a woman or minority "trying to succeed in a nontraditional environment," might disregard it so as not to "make waves"; but small differences could cumulate to large ones over many pay periods (as they did in the Ledbetter case). In 2009, legislation was passed by Congress that restored the EEOC interpretation; that is, it defined the 180-day clock as restarting each time discriminatory compensation is received, rather than when the employer discriminates for the first time.[33]

---

[30]See Office of Personnel Management, "Addressing Sexual Orientation and Gender Identity Discrimination in Federal Civilian Employment: A Guide to Employment Rights, Protections, and Responsibilities," June 2015, accessed November 13, 2016, www.opm.gov; and US Equal Employment Opportunity Commission, "Facts about Discrimination in Federal Government Employment Based on Marital Status, Political Affiliation, Status as a Parent, Sexual Orientation, and Gender Identity," accessed November 13, 2016, www.eeoc.gov.

[31]Peter Baker, "President Calls for a Ban on Job Bias against Gays," *New York Times*, July 21, 2014, nytimes.com.

[32]Ledbetter v. Goodyear Tire & Rubber Co., 550 U.S. 618 (2007). For more on this case, see "Ledbetter v. Goodyear Tire & Rubber Co., United States Supreme Court," www.bna.com, and Linda Greenhouse, "Justices Limit Discrimination Suits over Pay," *New York Times*, May 29, 2007, www.nytimes.com. We draw heavily on Greenhouse's article, and the quotations in the text are from that.

[33]For more on the Lilly Ledbetter Fair Pay Act of 2009, see http://www.govtrack.us (accessed December 24, 2012).

THE FAILED WAL-MART CLASS ACTION SUIT   Another case, *Wal-Mart Stores Inc. v. Dukes,* with potentially far-reaching consequences, involved a class action suit against Wal-Mart (generally known to consumers as Walmart) on behalf of as many as 1.5 million current and former female Wal-Mart employees.[34] The plaintiffs claimed that a company-wide policy of giving individual store managers discretion to make their own decisions was vulnerable to gender stereotypes and had resulted in discrimination against women. The case was struck down by the majority of the Supreme Court because, in the words of Justice Antonin Scalia, the plaintiffs "have identified no 'specific employment practice'—much less one that ties all their 1.5 million claims together." The decision did not address whether or not Wal-Mart had discriminated against women but only determined that the case could not proceed as a class action suit.[35]

This is potentially an extremely important decision because class action cases are generally a more efficient way to challenge an employer's practices than proceeding with cases on behalf of one individual at a time. They allow individual plaintiffs to pool their resources in pursuing the suit and result in rulings or settlements that affect a much larger number of workers. The long-run implications of the Wal-Mart case for the viability of class action employment discrimination suits are not fully known at this point. However, many experts believe that, while the ruling does not foreclose future class action employment discrimination cases, it has probably raised the bar—adding a higher burden of proof for certifying a class. Early indications are that this assessment is correct. Evidence indicates that both the payouts from class action discrimination settlements and the number of new employment discrimination class action lawsuits have decreased since the *Dukes* decision.[36]

Effectiveness of the Government's Antidiscrimination Effort

Much remains to be learned about the functioning of these laws and regulations. Questions have been raised both about their effectiveness in improving opportunities for protected groups and about the possibility that they might result in reverse discrimination against groups not covered.

While there has been little research examining the impact of the Equal Pay Act, it is likely that its effect has been fairly minimal. Even today, due to gender segregation by occupation and, within occupation, by job level and firm, men and women often do not do exactly the same kind of work in the same firm—as would be required for gender pay differences to be covered by the law. Moreover, as discussed earlier, the law does not address discrimination more broadly in hiring, promotion, training programs, and so on. However, as occupational segregation has declined

---

[34]We draw on Adam Liptak, "Justices Take Up Crucial Issue in Wal-Mart Suit," *New York Times,* March 29, 2011, www.nytimes.com; Adam Liptak, "Justices Rule for Wal-Mart in Class-Action Bias Case," *New York Times,* June 20, 2011, www.nytimes.com; "Justices Hand Wal-Mart a Big Victory, Reversing Sex Bias Class Certification," *Daily Labor Report,* Bloomberg BNA, June 20, 2011; and Margaret Cronin Fisk and Greg Stohr, "Wal-Mart Ruling Hurts Bias Cases, May Spare Other Class Actions," Bloomberg, June 20, 2011, www.bloomberg.com. The quotation is from Fisk and Stohr, "Wal-Mart Ruling."

[35]The Wal-Mart case also highlights the use and impact of econometric (statistical) analysis in court cases alleging discrimination; see the write-up of the case in Joni Hersch and Blair Druhan Bullock, "The Use and Misuse of Econometric Evidence in Employment Discrimination Cases," *Washington and Lee Law Review* 71, no. 4 (Fall 2014): 2365–2429.

[36]Nina Martin, "The Impact and Echoes of the Wal-Mart Discrimination Case," ProPublica, September 27, 2013, accessed November 13, 2016, www.propublica.org.

and more women and men are working side by side, the protection offered by this law has likely grown and may be expected to continue to grow more important in the future if there are further reductions in segregation.

Although considerably more research has been devoted to studying the effects of Title VII and Executive Order 11246, the results are not entirely conclusive, in part because it is difficult to isolate the effect of legislation, regulations, and major court decisions from other changes that have occurred.

One reasonable starting point is to consider whether trends in the gender pay gap appear consistent with an impact of these antidiscrimination efforts. A review of the trends in the male–female pay gap was presented in Chapter 7. It gave no indication of a notable improvement in women's economic status in the immediate post-1964 period that might be attributable to the effects of the government's antidiscrimination effort; the gender pay ratio remained basically flat through 1980, after which it began to increase. In contrast, African Americans experienced considerable increases in their earnings relative to whites in the immediate post-1964 period that many scholars ascribe, at least in part, to the impact of the antidiscrimination laws.[37]

Despite the fact that we do not see a marked improvement in women's earnings immediately after the passage of Title VII and Executive Order 11246, some detailed studies do find positive effects of the government's policies on women's employment, earnings, and occupations.[38] Studies focusing specifically on the impact of affirmative action also suggest modest employment gains for women attributable to this program. Such programs also appear to boost the relative wages of women, both because establishments using affirmative action are higher-paying, even after controlling for the characteristics of workers employed in them, and because sex differences in wages are smaller in such establishments.[39]

It might also be argued that the improvement in women's wages that began around 1980 could be due at least in part to the opportunities created by the government's antidiscrimination laws and regulations, which perhaps took some time to have an effect. This influence could potentially include both the direct effect of improving the treatment of women in the labor market and, in response to that, the indirect effect of increasing the incentives for women to train for nontraditional jobs.

The government's enforcement of antidiscrimination laws and regulations and the number of cases filed have varied considerably over time. In the 1980s, during the Reagan era, the government scaled back its antidiscrimination enforcement efforts. During that time, enforcement of affirmative action in the contract sector declined,[40]

---

[37]See, for example, Donohue J. and James Heckman, "Continuous Versus Episodic Change: The Impact of Civil Rights Policy on the Economic Status of Blacks," *Journal of Economic Literature* 29, no. 4 (December 1991): 1603–43.

[38]See, for example, Andrea H. Beller, "The Impact of Equal Opportunity Policy on Differentials in Earnings and Occupations," *American Economic Review* 72, no. 2 (May 1982): 171–75; and William J. Carrington, Kristin McCue, and Brooks Pierce, "Using Establishment Size to Measure the Impact of Title VII and Affirmative Action," *Journal of Human Resources* 35, no. 3 (Summer 2000): 503–23.

[39]Holzer and Neumark, "Assessing Affirmative Action"; see also Holzer and Neumark, "Affirmative Action: What Do We Know?" and Holzer and Neumark, "What Does Affirmative Action Do?"; Fidan Ana Kurtulus, "The Impact of Affirmative Action on the Employment of Minorities and Women over Three Decades: 1973–2003," Upjohn Institute Working Paper 15-221 (W.E. Upjohn Institute for Employment Research, Kalamazoo, MI, 2015); Fidan Ana Kurtulus, "Affirmative Action and the Occupational Advancement of Minorities and Women During 1973–2003," *Industrial Relations* 51 no. 2 (April 2012): 213–46; and Jonathan S. Leonard, "Women and Affirmative Action," *Journal of Economic Perspectives* 3, no. 1 (Winter 1989): 61–75.

[40]Leonard, "Women and Affirmative Action."

and the number of class action cases brought by the EEOC under Title VII (alleging a pattern and practice of discrimination against women or minorities on the part of an employer) also fell.[41] As discussed earlier, the resolution of class action suits on behalf of the plaintiffs potentially results in a much larger labor market impact than the resolution of individual complaints. However, the passage of the 1991 federal antidiscrimination law mentioned earlier ushered in a new era. This is because the 1991 law makes it more lucrative for private law firms to represent employees alleging discrimination. Under the original antidiscrimination legislation, monetary redress was generally limited to back pay. Since 1991, in cases of intentional discrimination, it is possible to sue for distress, humiliation, and punitive damages. In addition, the 1991 law allows discrimination cases to be argued before juries, who tend to be more favorable to plaintiffs than judges, also increasing the incentives for private firms to take them on.[42] After the passage of the law, the number of class action and other employment discrimination suits increased substantially.[43] In 2007, charges filed by the EEOC (which enforces the Equal Pay Act and Title VII) also began to rise, reaching a record high in 2011 and continuing at a relatively high level through 2015 (the most recent year available).[44]

Affirmative Action

Just as there is disagreement on the effectiveness of the government's antidiscrimination effort, so is there controversy about the form it should take. Debate particularly centers on the desirability of affirmative action to remedy the underrepresentation of women and minorities. Recall that *affirmative action* refers to a set of *proactive* policies established by the firm that seek to provide equal employment opportunities and to eliminate differences between women and men and between minorities and nonminorities. Affirmative action contrasts with laws and regulations that simply require employers not to discriminate against these groups.[45] Thus, *affirmative action* refers to a broad array of possible activities ranging from efforts

---

[41]Erin Kelly and Frank Dobbin argue that employers' Equal Employment Opportunity/affirmative action (EEO/AA) programs survived the Reagan-era cutbacks because in the previous decade EEO/AA programs and practices had developed a constituency within the firm in the form of EEO/AA specialists. Increasingly, however, the rationale for these efforts was shifted from legal compliance to "diversity management." See "How Affirmative Action Became Diversity Management: Employer Response to Anti-Discrimination Law, 1961–1996," *American Behavioral Scientist* 41, no. 7 (April 1998): 960–84.

[42]Brooke A. Masters and Amy Joyce, "Costco Is the Latest Class-Action Target: Lawyers' Interest Increases in Potentially Lucrative Discrimination Suits," *Washington Post*, August 18, 2004, www.washingtonpost.com; see also Allen Myerson, "As U.S. Bias Cases Drop, Employees Take Up Fight," *New York Times*, January 12, 1997, www.nytimes.com.

[43]Detailed trends for the period 1992–2003 are provided in Donald L. Zink and Arthur Guttman, "Statistical Trends in Private Sector Employment Discrimination Suits," in *Employment Discrimination Litigation: Behavioral, Quantitative, and Legal Perspectives*, ed. Frank Landy (Hoboken, NJ: Wiley, 2005), 101–31.

[44]US Equal Employment Opportunity Commission, "Charge Statistics FY 1997 through FY 2015," accessed November 1, 2016, http://eeoc.gov/eeoc/statistics/enforcement/charges.cfm. The number of charges peaked at 99,947 in 2011; 89,385 charges were filed in 2015.

[45]Holzer and Neumark, "Assessing Affirmative Action," 484. This article as well as Holzer and Neumark, "Affirmative Action: What Do We Know?" and Barbara R. Bergmann, *In Defense of Affirmative Action* (New York: Basic Books, 1996), provide extremely useful treatments of the issues surrounding affirmative action and assessments of the empirical evidence.

to more vigorously recruit women and minorities for job openings to some sort of preferences for women and minorities and, very rarely, even quotas under certain circumstances.

Affirmative action plans are legally mandated in only two situations. First, as we have seen, Executive Order 11246 requires affirmative action by government contractors who are found to underutilize women or minorities. Such employers are required to set goals based on estimates of the availability of protected groups for similar types of positions and to set reasonable timetables for meeting those goals. Thus, the government contract compliance program under the executive order does not impose hiring quotas on employers but rather requires the establishment of employment goals and timetables for meeting them. Second, affirmative action may be imposed by the courts in cases where employers are found guilty of discrimination or settlements are reached in discrimination suits. Although quotas may sometimes be ordered in such instances, quotas remain extremely rare in the labor market. In addition to these legal requirements, some employers have voluntarily adopted affirmative action programs. They may be motivated by a sincere desire to expand their utilization of women and minorities, the hope of heading off potential lawsuits by women and minorities, the potential public relations benefits of such efforts, or some combination of all of these factors.

There is considerable disagreement about the desirability of affirmative action. First, some argue that there is no conclusive evidence that serious discrimination against women and minorities (still) exists and that, even if there were, removing it would be sufficient and affirmative action is not needed. Second, others accept the need for some form of affirmative action but oppose the use of goals and timetables for fear that they will be too rigidly enforced and become de facto quotas. A difference of opinion, even among strong proponents of affirmative action, focuses on whether it should take the form of sincere efforts to find and encourage fully qualified candidates from the protected groups or go so far as to hire them preferentially. Some believe that preferential treatment may at times be needed to overcome the effects of past discrimination, while others do not believe such steps are warranted.

Although affirmative action programs that include preferences for women or minorities in employment are controversial in the public debate, such programs have generally been found by the courts to be legitimate approaches to remedying past discrimination in the labor market. Moreover, the legal status of court-mandated affirmative action plans that include employment preferences is not in question. Similarly, those required by Executive Order 11246 have generally not been challenged.[46]

The Supreme Court has also found that voluntary programs incorporating employment preferences are legal under certain circumstances. Specifically, court rulings in 1979 and 1987 held that employers can give employment preferences to women and minorities as a temporary measure to remedy manifest imbalances in traditionally segregated job categories.[47] A subsequent court ruling, in 2003,

---

[46]The Supreme Court's ruling in the 1995 *Adarand* case placed significant limits on federal government programs that favor racial minorities (and presumably women); see Adarand Constructors, Inc. v. Peña, 515 U.S. 200 (1995). However, that case dealt with preferences for minority-owned firms in awarding contracts rather than with employment.

[47]Steelworkers v. Weber, 443 U.S. 193 (1979); and Johnson v. Santa Clara County Transportation Agency, 480 U.S. 616 (1987).

upheld affirmative action based on race in admission to the University of Michigan Law School. The ruling was interpreted by some experts as possibly providing (through extension) an additional rationale for affirmative action in the employment arena, namely, achieving diversity. Specifically, the court's majority opinion, written by Justice Sandra Day O'Connor, cited the views put forward by a number of major companies in "friend of the court" briefs in finding that the educational benefits of diversity are "not theoretical but real, as major American businesses have made clear that the skills needed in today's increasingly global marketplace can only be developed through exposure to widely diverse people, cultures, ideas, and viewpoints."[48] The Supreme Court echoed this reasoning in a 2016 case that upheld the use of affirmative action in student admissions to the University of Texas.[49]

At the same time, the court has stressed the need for affirmative action plans to be flexible, gradual, and limited in their adverse effect on men and whites; it has also tended to disapprove of strict numerical quotas except where necessary to remedy demonstrated cases of severe past discrimination. Furthermore, although the court has ruled that employers may give preference to women and minorities in hiring and promotion under certain circumstances, it has rejected the use of such preferences to protect women and minorities from layoffs.[50] This distinction may be due to a concern over the rights of third parties, that is, members of nonprotected groups who may be adversely affected by an affirmative action program. Being denied a potential benefit such as being hired for a particular job, gaining admittance to a training program, or securing a promotion may be viewed as a less serious cost than being laid off from a job, especially after accumulating considerable seniority.

It is important to recognize, however, that most affirmative action programs do not require that employers favor one group. Rather, far more often, employers respond by improving their human resource management systems, such as by implementing wider and more systematic search procedures and developing more objective criteria and procedures for hiring and promotion.[51] Not only are such changes likely to make human resource management systems more effective, but they should also help to create more objective evidence when considering women and minority candidates for promotions or other employment opportunities.

In studies comparing workers in firms that used affirmative action and in firms that did not, little evidence indicated that women or minorities hired under

---

[48]Cited in Lisa E. Chang, "*Grutter v. Bollinger*, et al.: Affirmative Action Lessons for the Private Employer," *Employee Relations Law Journal* 30, no. 1 (Summer 2004): 3–15. This article includes a useful appraisal of the impact of the *Grutter* decision on employers. See also Steven Greenhouse and Jonathan D. Glater, "Companies See Court Ruling as Support for Diversity," *New York Times*, June 24, 2003, www.nytimes.com. Note that the court struck down an affirmative action program used for *undergraduate* admissions at Michigan for giving too much weight to race, in contrast to the law school that considered race as one factor among many. This ruling was interpreted in the employment arena as reinforcing the court's negative stance on quotas.
[49]Adam Liptak, "Supreme Court Upholds Affirmative Action Program at University of Texas," *New York Times,* June 23, 2016, accessed November 13, 2016, www.nytimes.com.
[50]Lex K. Larson, "Layoffs, Seniority, and Affirmative Action," in *Larson on Discrimination* (Conklin, NY: Matthew Bender & Company, 2012), chap. 96, accessed January 14, 2013, See also Stuart Taylor, "Court's Change of Course," *New York Times*, March 27, 1987, 1; and Steven A. Holmes, "Quotas: Despised by Many, but Just What Are They?" *New York Times*, June 2, 1991, 20.
[51]Holzer and Neumark, "What Does Affirmative Action Do?"

affirmative action performed worse. Where affirmative action was used in *recruitment only* (rather than in hiring), the results indicated that women and minorities, if anything, performed better than white males. When affirmative action was used in the hiring process, it was found that new female hires possessed similar qualifications and job performance. Some evidence of lesser qualifications was found "on paper" for minorities, but once hired, most minority groups performed at a level equivalent to their white male peers.[52] These findings strongly suggest that rigid employment quotas and reverse discrimination are not the norm in the labor market.

As in the case of affirmative action, it has been found, with respect to the broader issue of antidiscrimination policy as a whole, that the increased employment of women has been achieved without substantial reverse discrimination. Specifically, no evidence at the industry level indicates that the productivity of women fell relative to that of men as their employment increased—as would be expected if there were substantial reverse discrimination. Direct tests at the company level of the effect of affirmative action pressure, Title VII litigation, and changing proportions of women and minorities on profits also fail to show any adverse effect.[53]

Given that there is little evidence that affirmative action has produced ill effects, one may wonder why affirmative action programs have sometimes provoked public controversy and opposition. One reason may be that it is unclear who the "victims" of affirmative action efforts are and, hence, it is easy to form exaggerated views of their numbers. For example, when a woman or minority gets a position, observers may leap to the conclusion that the individual is an "affirmative action hire," which may or may not be true in the first place. Then, since it is generally not known who would have otherwise been hired, all those who did not get the job may feel that it was "because" of affirmative action. Of course, in reality, no more than one of the rejected applicants would have been hired. A second possible reason for public concern about affirmative action is that, as we saw in Chapter 10, recent decades have been in some respects difficult and uncertain times for the less skilled, in particular. Affirmative action becomes a ready scapegoat for those who feel adversely affected by what are in truth broader economic trends that are unrelated to the government's antidiscrimination effort.

Exaggerated public perceptions of the negative effects of affirmative action and other government antidiscrimination programs constitute a serious concern because they may adversely affect attitudes toward women and minorities in the workplace. A related problem is that women and minorities may, as noted earlier, be branded as affirmative action hires and stigmatized as less competent. Such perceptions could sap their confidence and make it difficult for them to function effectively in their jobs. On the other hand, if the alternative to affirmative action is greater discrimination against women and minorities, the absence of good advancement opportunities could, through feedback effects, discourage these groups from investing in job skills.

---

[52]Holzer and Neumark, "Are Affirmative Action Hires Less Qualified?" and Holzer and Neumark, "What Does Affirmative Action Do?"
[53]Leonard, "Antidiscrimination or Reverse Discrimination"; see also Holzer and Neumark, "Are Affirmative Action Hires Less Qualified?"

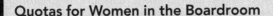

Quotas for Women in the Boardroom

While quotas in any aspect of employment are rare in the United States, a growing number of west European countries have sought to move women more rapidly into the top ranks of corporations by adopting corporate board quotas. **Corporate board quotas** require corporations to reserve a percentage of seats on corporate boards for women. Norway took the lead in 2003, setting aside 40 percent of seats for women. A number of other European countries have followed suit. The motivation for this policy is that women's representation on corporate boards is very low. (For instance, in the United States, in 2016, women held just 20 percent of board seats in S&P 500 firms.)* And, as we saw in Chapter 10, there is some evidence that a higher representation of women at the top has a positive effect on women's representation and pay at the lower ranks. While proponents argue that corporate board quotas are one way to swiftly increase women's representation at the highest ranks, opponents point to the fact that such policies, like comparable worth in the case of pay (which will be discussed shortly), interfere with the workings of the market. In evaluating the usefulness of corporate board quotas, there are at least two important dimensions to consider. One is whether this policy has the intended effect of improving gender equity within the firm. Another is what impact, if any, this policy has on corporate performance.

Does incorporating more women on corporate boards enhance gender equity within the firm? Unfortunately, there is not yet much evidence on this topic. One study looked at the effect of Norway's 2003 adoption of a 40 percent female quota. It reported mixed evidence. On the one hand, the study found that, despite the large increase in the fraction of women on corporate boards, there was no evidence of a "watering down" of female board members' qualifications. On the contrary, the study found that the new board seats due to the quotas were filled with women who were better qualified than their predecessors, "suggesting that previously untapped networks of top business women were activated by the policy." At least in part for this reason, the new

policy was associated with a decreased earnings gap between men and women on boards. The study also found evidence that there was an increase in the representation of women among top-level, senior executives in the affected firms. On the other hand, disappointingly, the study found no evidence of female gains beyond these very high levels—the gains at the top had not yet "trickled down" by 2010, the last year of data included in the study. This finding does not, however, rule out the possibility that broader-based gains could emerge in the future.**

What about the impact of corporate board quotas on firm performance? This was the focus of another study of the policy change in Norway. In this case, the authors compared outcomes for Norwegian firms covered by quotas to otherwise similar firms in other Scandinavian countries that did not have such quotas. The study found that firms covered by quotas undertook fewer workforce reductions and increased employment more than comparison firms. This increased their relative labor costs and reduced their short-term profits. The researchers suggest that fewer layoffs could reflect a more "stakeholder-oriented" attitude on the part of female directors; that is, female directors may consider worker preferences as well as the preferences of stockholders in making their decisions.*** While the decision to retain workers may not have maximized short-run profits, it is possible that such a strategy could contribute to long-run profitability by building a more loyal, better-trained, and more experienced workforce. Also, putting the findings of the two studies we just reviewed together, reductions in discrimination against women at the top (on the board and in the senior management ranks) could be expected to lead to productivity gains as women's capabilities are more fully utilized. And if the policy eventually results in broader female gains (beyond the top ranks), any such effects may be enhanced. Thus, the long-term effect on profits of increasing female directors could be positive.

Finally, evidence on stock market performance can also shed light on the effect on the firm's bottom line of increasing female representation on corporate boards. This evidence is mixed. One study from

continues

Australia finds that that the stock market valuation of a firm increased with the addition of female directors to the board. On the other hand, a study that compared firms' stock valuations before and after the introduction of the Norwegian corporate board quota policy found that firms' valuations dropped when female representation increased.****

Given that corporate board quotas are a relatively new policy, more evidence is needed before one can draw any definitive conclusions regarding the net benefits of adopting such policies. From the perspective of the United States, this policy is unlikely to be adopted any time in the near future given the very decentralized nature of the US labor market, especially compared to countries in western Europe which have adopted such a policy and the fact that, as we noted at the outset, employment quotas of any kind are quite rare in the US context.

*See David A. Matsa and Amalia R. Miller, "A Female Style in Corporate Leadership? Evidence from Quotas," American Economic Journal: Applied Economics 5, no. 3 (July 2013): 136–69; and Oliver Staley, "You Know Those Quotas for Female Board Members in Europe? They're Working," QUARTZ, accessed November 1, 2016, qz.com. The figure for the United States is from Catalyst, Pyramid: Women in S&P 500 Companies (New York, Catalyst, September 19, 2016), accessed November 13, 2016, www. catalyst.org.
**Marianne Bertrand, Sandra E. Black, Sissel Jensen, and Adriana Lleras-Muney, "Breaking the Glass Ceiling? The Effect of Board Quotas on Female Labor Market Outcomes in Norway," NBER Working Paper 20256 (National Bureau of Economic Research, Cambridge, MA, June 2014).
***Matsa and Miller, "A Female Style in Corporate Leadership?"
****The Australian study is Renée Adams, Stephen Gray, and John Nowland, "Does Gender Matter in the Boardroom? Evidence from the Market Reaction to Mandatory New Director Announcements," University of Queensland (November 2, 2011), accessed December 24, 2012, http:// papers.ssrn.com/sol3/papers.cfm?abstract_id=1953152; the Norwegian study is Kenneth R. Ahern and Amy K. Dittmar, "The Changing of the Boards: The Impact on Firm Valuation of Mandated Female Board Representation," Quarterly Journal of Economics 127, no. 1 (February 2012): 137–97.

Comparable Worth

In the latter half of the 1970s, impatience with the slow progress in closing the male–female earnings gap at that time, as well as some reluctance to accept the movement of women out of traditionally female occupations as a necessary component of the solution, led to considerable interest in a possible alternative approach to increasing women's wages. The idea that emerged, in simple terms, amounts to extending the notion of equal pay for equal work to the broader concept of equal pay for work of **comparable worth** within the firm.[54] Proponents argue that this is a reasonable interpretation of Title VII and a feasible way of achieving a more rapid reduction in the male–female pay gap. Opponents point to the difficulties involved in determining

[54]For an early article articulating the legal basis for this approach, see Ruth G. Blumrosen, "Wage Discrimination, Job Segregation, and Title VII of the Civil Rights Act of 1964," *University of Michigan Journal of Law Reform* 12, no. 3 (Spring 1979): 399–502. For examinations of the economic and social issues involved, see, for example, Barbara R. Bergmann, *The Economic Emergence of Women*, 2nd ed. (New York: Palgrave, St. Martin's Press, 2002); Paula England, "The Case for Comparable Worth," special issue, *Quarterly Review of Economics and Finance* 39, no. 3 (Fall 1999): 743–55; and Mark R. Killingsworth, "Comparable Worth and Pay Equity: Recent Developments in the United States," supplement, *Canadian Public Policy* 28, no. s1 (May 2002): S171–86.

exactly what comparable worth means in practical terms. They are also concerned about interfering with the working of the market and the possibility of bringing about a substantial imbalance in the supply of and demand for female workers.

Comparing the value to the firm of workers employed in different jobs is a difficult task that involves the establishment of equivalences for various levels of education, different types of skill, and varying work environments. Nonetheless, a procedure that provides a mechanism to do this is available in the form of job evaluation (explained in greater detail in the "Job Evaluation" box). Job evaluation is widely used to determine pay scales, not only by governments but also by many larger firms. This wide usage certainly shows that the approach is feasible. However, it should be noted that such a procedure is generally used in conjunction with information about market wage rates, rather than as a completely separate alternative to the market. Moreover, existing job evaluation schemes have themselves been criticized for undervaluing the skills and abilities that are emphasized in female jobs. Finally, when unions are involved in determining and implementing comparable worth or pay equity adjustments, alterations in pay rates across jobs may in part be determined through the negotiation process rather than solely through job evaluation.

Turning to the issue of setting wages at a level other than that determined by the market, the strongest opposition to such a policy comes primarily from those who believe that the existing labor market substantially resembles the neoclassical competitive model. In such a market, only the person's qualifications and tastes limit access to jobs, and all workers are rewarded according to their productivity. In this view, raising women's wages not only is unnecessary but would lead to excess supply and, hence, unemployment and a misallocation of resources.

On the other hand, many of those in favor of the comparable worth approach begin with a view of a segmented labor market, where workers' access to highly paid positions is often limited by discriminating employers, restrictive labor organizations, entrenched internal labor markets, and differences in the prelabor market socialization of men and women. Under such circumstances, the crowding of women into traditionally female occupations is believed to represent a misallocation of resources, which is permitted to continue by societal and labor market discrimination against women. Mandating higher wages would bring the earnings of those who remain in women's jobs closer to the level of comparably qualified men.

However, raising women's wages without changing the underlying conditions that produced them could still result in job loss. This may be illustrated with reference to Figure 11-1 in Chapter 11. Suppose we begin with the discriminatory situation. The relevant supply curves are S_{fd} and S_{md}, and wages are W_{fd} and W_{md}, in the female and male sectors, respectively. Suppose further that a comparable worth system sets wages in female jobs at W_0, the rate that would prevail in the absence of discrimination. At that wage, only L_{f0}, rather than L_{fd}, workers would be demanded by employers. The remainder, $L_{fd} - L_{f0}$, would be displaced from their jobs. Thus, the employment costs associated with this policy depend on how many workers are displaced and what happens to them.

It is also worth noting that the alternative approach of raising women's pay through the principles of equal pay for equal work and equal employment opportunity also offers the potential for increasing the wages even of women who remain in female jobs. This scenario may also be illustrated in Figure 11-1. Suppose that we again begin with the discriminatory situation. If the barriers to entry into male jobs are reduced, women will transfer from lower-paying F jobs to higher-paying M jobs. The supply curve in F jobs will shift inward toward S_{f0}, while the supply curve in M jobs shifts outward toward S_{m0}. Wages in the female sector are increased by the reduction of overcrowding there. A completely successful antidiscrimination policy would result in a wage of W_0 being established for both types of jobs. Proponents of comparable worth contend, however, that existing policies have not achieved adequate success as yet and that a new strategy is called for.

Thus far, we have emphasized the economic issues relevant to the subject of comparable worth—issues that are paramount in concluding whether, and for whom, such a policy would be beneficial. However, the courts have made decisions concerning the issue on purely legal grounds. Currently, the status of comparable worth as a legal doctrine under Title VII is unclear because the matter has not been definitively addressed by the Supreme Court.[55] Nor is there much evidence of the adoption of comparable worth in the private sector, although some state and local governments have implemented a version of comparable worth.[56] In addition, some unions, particularly those in the public sector, have pressed for pay equity as a collective bargaining demand.

Empirical evidence on the potential impact of comparable worth in the United States is based on analyses of its implementation for state and municipal government employees since the private sector has little experience with comparable worth. Such studies tend to find positive effects on women's relative wages. When employment effects are also examined, adverse effects on the growth of women's relative employment are usually found, although such effects are generally small.[57] Some additional light can be shed on these issues by examining what happened in Australia when wages in female occupations were abruptly raised by introducing a comparable worth policy. The experience of that country is described in Chapter 18, but overall it tends to be relatively positive in that a considerable narrowing of the gender pay gap was achieved with relatively modest negative employment effects.

However, it may be difficult to extrapolate the results of studies that focus on government employees to the impact of the adoption of a nationwide comparable worth policy that includes the private sector. Even studies of comparable worth as implemented in Australia may be less than fully instructive because the labor market in that country tends to be highly centralized with a large role for government tribunals and unions in setting wage rates (though the wage system has become somewhat more decentralized in recent years). This contrasts strongly with the highly decentralized US labor market, which relies much more heavily on the market and

---

[55]In County of Washington v. Gunther, 452 U.S. 161 (1981), the Supreme Court removed a major legal stumbling block to the comparable worth doctrine by ruling that it is not required that a man and woman do "equal work" in order to establish pay discrimination under Title VII. However, many other issues remain unresolved, and the court stopped short of endorsing the comparable worth approach. See Ross et al., *The Rights of Women*, 26–29.

[56]See Susan E. Gardner and Christopher Daniel, "Implementing Comparable Worth/Pay Equity: Experiences of Cutting-Edge States," *Public Personnel Management* 27, no. 4 (Winter 1998): 475–89, and Killingsworth, "Comparable Worth and Pay Equity."

[57]See, for example, Mark R. Killingsworth, *The Economics of Comparable Worth* (Kalamazoo, MI: W.E. Upjohn Institute for Employment Research, 1990); Peter F. Orazem and J. Peter Mattila, "The Implementation Process of Comparable Worth: Winners and Losers," *Journal of Political Economy* 98, no. 1 (February 1990): 134–52; and June O'Neill, Michael Brien, and James Cunningham, "Effects of Comparable Worth Policy: Evidence from Washington State," *American Economic Review* 79, no. 2 (May 1989): 305–09.

generally gives firms considerable autonomy in setting wages. In this respect, the consequences of a pay equity initiative that was implemented in one Canadian province, Ontario, beginning in the early 1990s, may be of particular interest because the Canadian labor market is more similar to that of the United States in being relatively decentralized. The results of a study of the Ontario experience suggest some caution in implementing comparable worth in such circumstances. Substantial lapses in compliance and implementation of the law were found. These lapses tended to center on small firms that lacked the resources to undertake the necessary job evaluation programs and often did not have a sufficient sample of male and female jobs to make meaningful comparisons. (See the "Job Evaluation" box for a detailed discussion of

Job Evaluation

The implementation of comparable worth requires an evaluation of the contribution of the many different jobs within an enterprise.* At present, formal **job evaluation** procedures are already used by the federal government, a number of state governments, and many large private firms as an aid in determining pay rates. Employers rely on such evaluations because, as explained in our discussion of internal labor markets in Chapter 11, many positions, particularly in large firms, are filled entirely from within the firm itself through promotion and upgrading of the existing workforce. Job evaluation may be useful in setting pay rates in such jobs, especially since some of them are unique to a particular enterprise. This means that the "going rate" in the local labor market is often not known for such internally filled jobs. Thus, employers may find it necessary to use some other mechanism to determine wages for such jobs since they cannot simply accept those determined by the market. However, it is important to bear in mind that, when wages are set in this way, it does not mean that market forces are ignored. In setting wages, most firms and governmental units that use job evaluation try to take into account whatever information is available to them on prevailing wages for different types of labor. However, the existence

of job evaluation and other procedures for setting wages tends to make wages less responsive to short-term shifts in market conditions than they would otherwise be.

The actual methods used differ in detail but share the same basic rationale and approach. The first step is always a description of all the jobs within the given organization. The next step is to rate each job according to all the various features that are believed to determine pay differences across jobs. Last, these ratings are combined to create a score for each job, which may then be used to help determine wages.

Among the factors used to construct job scores are characteristics such as level of education, skills, and responsibility needed for the job, as well as the environment in which the work is performed. Commonly, multiple regression is used to link these to the existing pay structure. At other times, weights are assigned according to the judgment of the experts constructing the scale. In theory, various jobs can be assigned values objectively, presumably not influenced by irrelevant factors such as the gender and race of the incumbents, and quite different jobs may be assigned equal values, if warranted.

*Job evaluation is discussed in Konrad Reiher, "Compensation and Benefits: Job Evaluation," Handbook of Human Resource Management, ed. Matthias Zeuch (Berlin: Springer-Verlag, 2015): 1–14; and Donald J. Treiman and Heidi I. Hartmann, eds., Women, Work and Wages: Equal Pay for Jobs of Equal Value (Washington, DC: National Academies Press, 1981),

71–74. Institutional models, discussed in Chapter 11, emphasize the importance of job evaluation and other administrative procedures for determining wages. See Peter B. Doeringer and Michael J. Piore, Internal Labor Markets and Manpower Analysis (Lexington, MA: D.C. Heath, 1971).

job evaluation programs.) Because such small firms employed the majority of both male and female workers in Ontario, little evidence was found of a positive impact of the pay equity policy on women's relative pay overall. Even among large firms, where compliance was fairly complete, estimated positive effects on women's pay in female jobs were modest and typically statistically insignificant.[58] It is also possible that the ineffectiveness of pay equity legislation in this case reflects additional factors specific to the situation in Ontario, such as the particular law implemented there or a change in the governing party that occurred a few years after the passage of the law.

Conclusion

In this chapter, we examined the government's equal employment opportunity policies, including the Equal Pay Act, Title VII of the Civil Rights Act, and Executive Order 11246 barring discrimination on the part of federal contractors. In recent decades, coverage of Title VII has broadened to include sexual harassment in the workplace. There is also growing recognition of the need to address employment discrimination on the basis of sexual orientation and gender identity. While there are now protections in some states and for federal workers, such discrimination in the private sector is not yet explicitly prohibited by federal law. We also considered the effectiveness of the government's antidiscrimination effort. Finally, we considered the pros and cons of a policy that has been proposed as an additional measure to combat the gender wage gap, comparable worth.

As we shall see in Chapter 18, the United States was a leader among the economically advanced countries in its adoption of antidiscrimination legislation. Our review of the effectiveness of these policies indicates that, while the consequences of the government's efforts are difficult to measure, the evidence suggests that they have improved labor market outcomes for women and minorities with little evidence of negative effects on worker productivity.

Looking forward, firms' adoption of "best practices" regarding diversity in the workplace, *alongside* the government's antidiscrimination policies described here, is critical in addressing discriminatory workplace behavior. Some evidence suggests that the most effective firm strategy for increasing the representation of women and minorities is for the organization to take specific measures that assign organizational responsibility for change, such as setting forth an affirmative action plan or establishing a committee or manager in charge of creating and maintaining a diverse workplace. Another useful strategy, though not found to be as effective, is to reduce the social isolation of women and minorities through mentoring and networking. Least effective appears to be efforts at reducing bias via diversity training and evaluating managers based on their diversity performance.[59] It is to be hoped that further research may shed additional light on best practices that can be adopted by firms to reduce discrimination and even bolster the firm's bottom line by doing so.

---

[58]Michael Baker and Nicole M. Fortin, "Comparable Worth Work in a Decentralized Labor Market: The Case of Ontario," *Canadian Journal of Economics* 37, no. 4 (November 2004): 850–78. See also Judith A. McDonald and Robert J. Thornton, "Coercive Cooperation? Ontario's Pay Equity Act and the Gender Pay Gap," *Contemporary Economic Policy* 33, no. 4 (2015): 606–18.

[59]Alexandra Kalev, Frank Dobbin, and Erin Kelly, "Best Practices or Best Guesses? Assessing the Efficacy of Corporate Affirmative Action and Diversity Policies," *American Sociological Review* 71, no. 4 (August 2006): 589–617.

Questions for Review and Discussion

1. Is the Equal Pay Act likely to be effective in reducing the gender pay gap? Why or why not? Explain your answer fully.

2. Antidiscrimination policy and affirmative action are both possible means of reducing the gender pay gap. Which is likely to be more effective? Why? Do you see them as substitutes or as complements, and why?

3. "Affirmative action policies have been shown to lead to reverse discrimination and the hiring of less-qualified women and minorities. Not only are such policies unfair, but they exact a high cost in reducing efficiency." Fully evaluate this statement based on this chapter's material. Explain your answer fully.

4. What is *comparable worth*, and how could it be applied in the labor market to reduce the gender pay gap? Discuss the arguments for and against applying such a policy nationwide. Illustrate your answer with a diagram.

5. Use economic theory to explain how antidiscrimination policies that successfully increase the access of women to predominantly *male* occupations could affect wages in predominantly *female* occupations. Illustrate your answer with a diagram.

6. "An employer policy that excludes women from occupations that require physical strength is justified because men tend to be stronger than women." Evaluate the legal validity of this argument.

Suggested Readings

Basu, Kaushik. "The Economics and Law of Sexual Harassment in the Workplace." *Journal of Economic Perspectives* 17, no. 3 (Summer 2003): 141–57.

Bergmann, Barbara R. *In Defense of Affirmative Action.* New York: Basic Books, 1996.

Grossman, Joanna L. "Moving Forward Looking Back: A Retrospective on Sexual Harassment Law." *Boston University Law Review* 95 (2015): 1029–48.

Hersch, Joni, and Blair Druhan Bullock. "The Use and Misuse of Econometric Evidence in Employment Discrimination Cases." *Washington and Lee Law Review* 71, no. 4 (Fall 2014): 2365–2429.

Hersch, Joni, and Jennifer Bennett Shinall. "Fifty Years Later: The Legacy of the Civil Rights Act of 1964." *Journal of Policy Analysis and Management*, 34, no. 2 (Spring 2015): 424–56.

Holzer, Harry J., and David Neumark. "Affirmative Action: What Do We Know?" *Journal of Policy Analysis and Management* 25, no. 2 (Spring 2006): 463–90.

Key Terms

Equal Pay Act (325)

Title VII of the Civil Rights Act (326)

Equal Employment Opportunity Commission (EEOC) (326)

class action lawsuit (326)

Executive Order 11246 (326)

affirmative action (326)

bona fide occupational qualification (BFOQ) (327)

disparate treatment (328)

disparate impact (328)

sexual harassment (329)

corporate board quotas (339)

comparable worth (340)

job evaluation (343)

PART IV

The Economics of the Family: Theory, Evidence, and Policy

Changing Work Roles and Family Formation

13

CHAPTER HIGHLIGHTS

- ■ Economic Explanations for Family Formation
- ■ Marriage
- ■ Divorce
- ■ Cohabitation: Opposite-Sex Couples
- ■ Cohabitation and Marriage: Same-Sex Couples
- ■ Fertility

This chapter examines the effect of economic factors on family formation and fertility. In doing so, we provide evidence and offer explanations for the dramatic changes that have taken place. These changes include delays in and the decline of marriage, the rise of opposite-sex cohabitation, the increase in mother's age at first birth, and the increase in the proportion of births to unmarried women. We also point to evidence on the growing divergence in these outcomes by educational attainment. This chapter also examines the effect of economic factors on the formation of same-sex couples and discusses the 2015 Supreme Court ruling that legalized same-sex marriage throughout the United States. In the next chapter, we follow up by looking at the relationship between changes in the American family and the economic well-being of family members.

Economic Explanations for Family Formation

What is the expected effect of economic factors, including women's increased labor force participation, on family formation? From the viewpoint of neoclassical economics, the determining factor in decisions concerning family issues such as marriage, divorce, and fertility is whether the benefits exceed the costs.[1] Thus, the question arises as to the effect of women's increasing labor force participation and other economic factors on the costs and benefits associated with these decisions—do more or fewer couples choose to marry, divorce, or cohabit? As we shall see, the answer to this question is not obvious from a theoretical point of view. That is, forces operate both to reduce and to increase the benefits and costs of these decisions, leaving the outcome uncertain from a theoretical perspective.

The Role of Gains to Specialization in Production

A useful starting point follows from our discussion of Gary Becker's model of specialization and exchange in Chapter 3. To summarize, we found that specialization according to comparative advantage and exchange between spouses (or partners) has the potential to increase the couple's productivity and economic well-being. Recall that comparative advantage in a particular activity, like producing home versus market goods, is determined by identifying which individual is able to do the activity at lower opportunity cost. In general, the larger the *difference* between two partners in their comparative advantage in producing home and market goods, the greater the economic gain to their partnership. Such a situation not only encourages specialization but results in it having a relatively high productivity payoff. The implication of this model for family formation is as follows: The larger the *difference* between partners in their comparative advantage in each activity, the greater the gains to marriage and, for those already married, the larger the deterrent to divorce.

However, as discussed in Chapter 3, there are other gains to marriage, and, even if comparative advantage in the household and market is identical for two partners, marriage still confers these other benefits. These benefits include gains from **shared consumption**.[2] That is, individuals likely derive greater utility from doing activities with those who have common interests. In addition, marriage allows for the enjoyment of **public goods** (goods that can be jointly consumed). It also provides **economies of scale** because two can live more inexpensively together than they can separately. In other words, the cost of housing and food is usually much lower on a per-person basis if shared. And marriage allows **risk-pooling** between spouses; if one of them loses a job or wants to make a career switch, he or she can rely on the earning power of his or her spouse. While these benefits can also be reaped, at least to some extent, by unmarried couples, roommates, or those living in extended families, a particular advantage of marriage is that it offers greater legal protections than these alternatives if the relationship were to end. As a result, marriage fosters investments in **marriage-specific capital**, that is, skills and knowledge developed by an individual that are worth more within the marriage than if the relationship were to

---

[1]Seminal work by neoclassical economists on the economics of the family was first done by Gary S. Becker and is summarized by him in *A Treatise on the Family* (Cambridge, MA: Harvard University Press, 1991). See also Shelly Lundberg and Robert A. Pollak, "The American Family and Family Economics," *Journal of Economic Perspectives* 21, no. 2 (Spring 2007): 3–26.

[2]Betsey Stevenson and Justin Wolfers, "Marriage and Divorce: Changes and Their Driving Forces," *Journal of Economic Perspectives* 21, no. 2 (Spring 2007): 27–52; Lundberg and Pollak, "The American Family." Early discussions of the benefits of shared consumption include Francine D. Blau and Marianne A. Ferber, *The Economics of Women, Men, and Work*, 1st ed. (Upper Saddle River, NJ: Prentice Hall, 1986), chaps. 3 and 5; and David Lam, "Marriage Markets and Assortative Mating with Household Public Goods," *Journal of Human Resources* 23, no. 4 (Fall 1988): 462–87.

end. Prime examples include specialization in nonmarket production and children. Just as they increase the benefits to marriage, these marriage-specific investments serve as a deterrent to divorce.

Declining Gains from Specialization in Production

In recent years, gains from specialization in production have declined for both women and men. Women have acquired more job-oriented education and training, which has led to higher potential market wages and rising rates of labor force participation. They have also encountered less discrimination in the labor market than in the past, further raising their market wages and spurring investments in their human capital. The availability of reliable contraceptive technology, particularly the birth control pill, which became available to married women in the early 1960s and to single women in the late 1960s and early 1970s, also permitted women to focus on their careers, without the risk of pregnancy.[3] Over the past decade, a further development is the considerable rise in the use of **long-acting reversible contraceptives (LARC)** such as the intrauterine device (IUD) and contraceptive implants, which would be expected to have the same effect.[4] One consequence of these developments for married couples, as discussed further in Chapter 14, is a rise in the share of dual-earner couples.

Gains from specialization have also fallen as a result of changes in how household goods are produced. The near ubiquity of household appliances such as the microwave oven along with the emergence of high-quality market substitutes for home-cooked meals have reduced the relative value of time spent on household production and hence the gains from specialization and exchange. A further factor reducing the gains from specialization is the liberalization of state divorce laws that started in the 1970s. As discussed further shortly in the "Divorce" section, these changes in divorce laws, which increased the bargaining power of the partner most interested in exiting the marriage, reduced incentives for investment in marriage-specific capital including home production.[5]

Changes in men's market productivity also affect the gains from specialization and exchange and, hence, marriage. Higher male earnings increase the gains to specialization and thereby raise the likelihood of marriage.[6] This also means that falling male earnings have the reverse effect. As discussed in earlier chapters, economic outcomes for less educated men, in particular, have deteriorated considerably since 1980. The decline in market productivity for this group, which has reduced the gains to specialization and exchange, is undoubtedly an important explanation behind recent decreases in marriage among those with less education.

---

[3]Claudia Goldin and Lawrence F. Katz, "Career and Marriage in the Age of the Pill," *American Economic Review* 90, no. 2 (May 2000): 461–65.

[4]See Sabrina Tavernise, "Use of Long-Acting Birth Control Method Surges among US Women," *New York Times*, November 10, 2015.

[5]Betsy Stevenson, "The Impact of Divorce Laws on Marriage-Specific Capital," *Journal of Labor Economics* 25, no. 1 (January 2007): 75–94.

[6]Further, as will be discussed in the "Marriage" section, the opportunities for specialization that marriage affords appear to increase men's market productivity and hence their earnings. Thus, for men, marriage and earnings likely have reinforcing effects. See Avner Ahituv and Robert I. Lerman, "How Do Marital Status, Work Effort, and Wage Rates Interact?" *Demography* 44, no. 3 (August 2007): 623–47.

Other Benefits from Marriage Remain and Some May Be Increasing

As discussed, a number of factors have substantially reduced the gains to marriage from specialization in production, and this development is expected to lead to a decrease in marriage and a rise in divorce, all other factors held constant. However, even as the gains to specialization have declined, not only do many of the other advantages to marriage remain, including economies of scale and the enjoyment of public goods, but still other benefits have likely increased. For instance, Betsey Stevenson and Justin Wolfers convincingly argue that the gains from shared consumption have risen as the proportion of two-earner couples has grown.[7] This is expected to be the case to the extent that two-earner couples have more similar tastes and experiences than couples who pursue a traditional division of labor. And, with two incomes, spouses are also able to spend more money on leisure activities that they can enjoy together, further enhancing joint consumption. Another benefit reaped by two earners that has likely become increasingly important given the uncertainties of our ever-changing global economy is that spouses are able to share risk and so are not entirely dependent on one income.

Finally, Robert Pollak and Shelly Lundberg argue that the rising returns to education and other types of human capital (see Chapters 8 and 9 for a discussion of these trends) may explain why marriage rates remain relatively strong among the highly educated—notably college graduates—while they have declined for those with less education. Those who are highly educated have the greatest incentive to marry and reap the benefits of marriage-specific investments. That is, they are best positioned, in terms of financial resources, to take advantage of the rising returns to human capital (in the form of greater future labor market success for their children) and intensively invest in their children within the marriage. As discussed earlier, because it is relatively costly to end, marriage encourages such investments.[8]

All told, without empirical evidence it is not possible to say whether the net impact of economic factors, including women's rising labor force participation, has served to decrease or increase marriage and divorce rates. In the next sections, we consider these and other factors that likely affect family formation decisions and look at evidence for the 1960s to the present. In doing so, we first discuss marriage, divorce, and cohabitation for opposite-sex couples. We next discuss factors affecting same-sex couples and the key legal change in their status, notably the legalization of same-sex marriage throughout the United States in 2015. We take this approach because, historically, for both cultural and legal reasons, women's and men's family decisions primarily focused on forming opposite-sex unions, principally marriage, though cohabitation is a growing alternative. In addition, there is considerably more research and data on opposite-sex couples, though this will undoubtedly change in the coming years. In fact, it is only since fall 2014 that the US Census Bureau began counting same-sex married couples among the set of all married couples.

---

[7]Stevenson and Wolfers, "Marriage and Divorce."
[8]Shelly Lundberg and Robert Pollak, "The Evolving Role of Marriage, 1956–2010," *The Future of Children* 25, no. 2 (fall 2015): 29–50.

Marriage

As discussed earlier, declining gains to specialization, in large part due to women's rising labor force participation, are expected to reduce marriage. On the other hand, other potential benefits of marriage remain unaffected, and the gains to shared consumption and benefits of risk sharing have arguably increased. In addition to these broad considerations, a number of other specific factors affect the decision to marry and thus the trends in marriage.[9] One of these is the availability of marriage partners. Demographic trends, for one, may lead to an insufficient supply of women or men in particular groups and, in turn, reduce marriage rates.[10] For example, consider the US baby boom, a period of relatively high birth rates that began after World War II. Birth rates rose through the mid-1950s and then began to fall, although they remained at historically high levels through the early 1960s. Women born during the early part of the baby boom encountered an imbalance in the marriage market because the men that they typically sought to marry, generally 2 or 3 years older than themselves, were from smaller birth cohorts. The shortage of men in these age groups created what has been called a "marriage squeeze," likely reducing or delaying marriage rates and changing the age gap between some spouses.[11]

William Julius Wilson has further observed that women's propensity to marry depends not only on the number of men in the marriage market but also on the availability of men with decent earnings prospects, who he has termed **marriageable men**.[12] Wilson's point is closely related to our earlier discussion of decreasing gains to specialization for the less educated due to declining labor market earnings of less educated men. Further, evidence suggests that, not only do men's absolute earnings matter, but their *relative* earnings do as well: men are perceived as more economically attractive if their earnings are higher than other men who live near them and share similar characteristics such as race, ethnicity, and education.[13] High incarceration rates of males have also been identified as a contributing factor to an insufficient

---

[9]For a review, see Stevenson and Wolfers, "Marriage and Divorce"; Andrew Cherlin, "Demographic Trends in the United States: A Review of the Research in the 2000s," *Journal of Marriage and the Family* 72, no. 3 (June 2010): 403–19; Steven Ruggles, "Patriarchy, Power, and Pay: The Transformation of American Families, 1800–2015," *Demography* 52 (2015): 1797–1823; and Ron Haskins and Isabel V. Sawhill, "The Decline of the American Family: Can Anything Be Done to Stop the Damage?' *Annals of the American Academy of Political and Social Science* 667, no l (September 2016): 8–34.

[10]Shoshana Grossbard-Shechtman, *On the Economics of Marriage* (Boulder, CO: Westview Press, 1993), chaps. 4 and 5; and Joshua Angrist, "How Do Sex Ratios Affect Marriage and Labor Markets? Evidence from America's Second Generation," *Quarterly Journal of Economics* 117, no. 3 (August 2002): 997–1038. Post–World War I France provides another useful example; see Ran Abramitzky, Adeline Delavande, and Luis Vasconcelos, "Marrying Up: The Role of Sex Ratio in Assortative Mating," *American Economic Journal: Applied Economics* 3, no. 3 (July 2011): 124–57.

[11]Paul Glick, "Fifty Years of Family Demography: A Record of Social Change," *Journal of Marriage and the Family* 50, no. 4 (November 1988): 861–73.

[12]This theory is presented in William J. Wilson and Kathryn Neckerman, "Poverty and Family Structure: The Widening Gap between Evidence and Public Policy Issues," in *Fighting Poverty: What Works and What Doesn't*, ed. Sheldon Danziger and Daniel Weinberg (Cambridge, MA: Harvard University Press, 1986), 232–59. For further discussion on the relationship between male economic success and marriage, see David Autor and Melanie Wasserman, *Wayward Sons and the Emerging Gender Gap in Labor Markets and Education*, (Washington, DC: Third Way, March 2013).

[13]Tara Watson and Sara McLanahan, "Marriage Meets the Joneses: Relative Income, Identity, and Marital Status, *Journal of Human Resources* 46, no. 3 (2011): 482–517. For a broader discussion of how relative income matters, see Ruggles, "Patriarchy, Power, and Pay."

supply of men and hence lower marriage rates among those with less education. To the extent that African American men have lower average educational attainment as well as higher incarceration rates compared to white men, these factors help to explain their lower rates of marriage.[14]

Government transfer programs and tax policies also have the potential to affect whether and when to marry. For instance, prior to the passage of the federal welfare reform legislation of 1996, there was concern that the existing welfare program, Aid to Families with Dependent Children (AFDC), which largely provided benefits to single mothers and their children, discouraged marriage. This was one of a number of reasons that changes in this program were advocated, leading to reform of the welfare system in 1996. However, despite all the public attention, considerable research indicates that AFDC could not have led to the large shift away from marriage that began in the 1970s.[15]

Another relevant factor is changes in social norms, principally the dramatic liberalization in attitudes toward divorce, cohabitation, and sex outside of marriage beginning in the 1960s and 1970s. These changes have undoubtedly affected the decision to marry, its timing, and whether childbearing occurs within marriage or outside of it.[16] In particular, by reducing the benefits to marriage (or the costs of remaining unmarried), these trends have likely contributed to a delay of marriage and a reduction in marriage rates. Finally, technological change via the rise of online dating sites and, more broadly, the diffusion of the Internet, play a potential role by reducing search costs associated with finding a partner. Some evidence indicates that the diffusion of the Internet worked to increase marriage rates (relative to what they would have otherwise been); it also contributed to a shift away from more traditional approaches to finding a partner, such as introductions from family and friends.[17]

Table 13-1 shows the trends in marriage rates from 1960 to 2014. These trends may be viewed as representing the net effect of the various factors we have discussed. From 1960 to 1970, marriage rates rose from 8.5 to 10.6 marriages per 1,000 population; they remained at about that level until 1980 and have declined steadily since then, standing at 6.9 marriages per 1,000 population in 2014. Based on the research evidence, it appears that the rapid entry of women into the labor market, which occurred as women's labor market opportunities expanded, is indeed an important factor that is responsible for at least part of the decline in marriage rates.[18] This finding suggests that the decline in the gains to specialization and exchange

---

[14]Kerwin Kofi Charles and Ming Ching Luoh, "Male Incarceration, the Marriage Market and Female Outcomes," *Review of Economics and Statistics* 92, no. 3 (August 2010): 614–27. For recent data regarding black men, see Justin Wolfers, David Leonhardt, and Kevin Quealy, "1.5 Million Missing Black Men," *New York Times*, April 20, 2015.

[15]Robert A. Moffitt, "The Temporary Assistance for Needy Families Program," in *Means-Tested Transfer Programs in the United States*, ed. Robert A. Moffitt (Chicago: University of Chicago Press, 2003), 291–363.

[16]Arland Thornton and Linda Young-DeMarco, "Four Decades of Trends in Attitudes toward Family Issues in the United States: The 1960s through the 1990s," *Journal of Marriage and the Family* 63 (November 2001): 1009–37. For more recent evidence, see Jill Daugherty and Casey Copen, "Trends in Attitudes about Marriage, Childbearing, and Sexual Behavior: United States, 2002, 2006–2010, and 2011–2013," *National Health Statistics Reports* 92 (March 17, 2016): table 1.

[17]Andriana Bellou, "The Impact of Internet Diffusion on Marriage Rates: Evidence from the Broadband Market," *Journal of Population Economics* 28, no. 2 (2015): 265–97.

[18]Evidence that better labor market opportunities for women are negatively related to marriage rates is provided by T. Paul Schultz, "Marital Status and Fertility in the United States," *Journal of Human Resources* 29, no. 2 (Spring 1994): 637–69; and Francine D. Blau, Lawrence M. Kahn, and Jane Waldfogel, "Understanding Young Women's Marriage Decisions: The Role of Labor Market and Marriage Market Conditions," *Industrial and Labor Relations Review* 53, no. 4 (July 2000): 624–47.

TABLE 13-1 TRENDS IN MARRIAGE AND DIVORCE RATES, 1960–2014

	1960	1970	1980	1990	2000	2010	2014
Marriage Rate per 1,000 Population	8.5	10.6	10.6	9.8	8.2	6.8	6.9
Divorce Rate per 1,000 Married Women	9.2	14.9	22.6	20.9	18.8	16.4	n.a.
Divorce Rate per 1,000 Population	2.2	3.5	5.2	4.7	4.0	3.6	3.2

Notes: n.a. = not available.

The divorce rate per 1,000 married women reported for 2010 is from 2009.

Sources: US Census Bureau, *Statistical Abstract of the United States: 2000*, table 144, and *2007*, table 76; ProQuest Statistical Abstract of the United States 2016 Online Edition, "Marriage and Divorce Rates by State: 1990 to 2014," table 143; University of Virginia, The National Marriage Project, *The State of Our Unions 2011*, figure 5; CDC/NCHS National Vital Statistics System: National Marriage and Divorce Rate Trends 2000–2014, accessed May 11, 2016, www.cdc.gov; and US Department of Health, Education, and Welfare, *Divorces and Divorce Rates: United States* 21, no. 29 (repr. 1980): table 1.

has been the dominant factor in determining marriage trends, offsetting the impact of any increase in the benefits of shared consumption that may have also occurred. Undoubtedly, the liberalization of social attitudes has also played a role. However, some of the decline in the overall incidence of marriage reflects a postponement of marriage by young men and women rather than their forgoing it completely.

This postponement may be seen in the rising median age at first marriage for both women and men shown in Table 13-2. As of 2015, the median age at first marriage was 27 for women and 29 for men, up from 21 for women and 23 for men in 1970. Table 13-2 also points to a dramatic increase in the fraction of young women and men who have never been married. In 1970, for example, only 36 percent of women ages 20 to 24 were never married compared with 84 percent in 2015.

Women's rising economic opportunities, which encouraged young women to stay in school longer and not only to enter the labor force but, in many cases, to pursue challenging careers, are likely a major factor behind this postponement. Claudia Goldin and Larry Katz point to the pivotal role of the birth control pill in fostering this delay, which, as we have noted, became widely available to *single* women starting in the late 1960s and early 1970s. It allowed young women to postpone marriage and pursue college and professional training without incurring the cost of abstinence or facing a substantial risk of an unwanted pregnancy that could derail their studies. Further, as more and more women delayed marriage, the risk of waiting to marry and then losing out on finding a good marriage partner also fell.[19]

As would be expected, based on this discussion, a long-standing pattern has been that highly educated women delay marriage.[20] A notable new development is that delayed marriage is now the predominant pattern for all women, regardless of educational attainment. Indeed, one study found that by 2010 the median age at first

---

[19]Goldin and Katz, "Career and Marriage in the Age of the Pill." See also Martha J. Bailey and Brad J. Hershbein, "U.S. Fertility Rates and Childbearing 1800 to 2010," in *Oxford Handbook of American Economic History* (New York and Oxford: Oxford University Press, forthcoming).

[20]For a discussion, see Adam Isen and Betsey Stevenson, "Women's Education and Family Behavior: Trends in Marriage, Divorce and Fertility," in *Demography and the Economy*, ed. John Shoven (Chicago: University of Chicago Press, 2010), 107–140; and Wendy D. Manning, Susan L. Brown, and Krista K. Payne, "Two Decades of Stability and Change in Age at First Union Formation," *Journal of Marriage and Family*, 76 (April 2014): 247–60.

TABLE 13-2   TIMING OF MARRIAGE AND PERCENTAGE MARRIED, 1970–2015

	1970	1980	1990	2000	2010	2015
Median Age at First Marriage						
Men	23.2	24.7	26.1	26.8	28.2	29.2
Women	20.8	22.0	23.9	25.1	26.1	27.1
% Never-Married Men						
Age 20–24	54.7	68.8	79.3	83.7	88.7	90.5
Age 40–44	6.3	7.1	10.5	15.7	20.4	20.3
% Never-Married Women						
Age 20–24	35.8	50.2	62.8	72.8	79.3	84.0
Age 40–44	4.9	4.8	8.0	11.8	13.8	15.5
% Married Adults, Ages 18+	71.7	65.5	61.9	59.5	56.6	55.1
White, Non-Hispanic	72.6	67.2	64.0	62.1	59.8	58.8
Black	64.1	51.4	45.8	42.1	38.8	38.3
Asian	n.a.	n.a.	n.a.	n.a.	64.3	62.7
Hispanic Origin	71.8	65.6	61.7	60.2	53.8	52.0

Notes: Beginning in 2000, data on whites are for white, non-Hispanics. Also, beginning in 2000, individuals were able to report more than one race. In this table, whites are defined as persons who selected this race group only, and blacks (Asians) are defined as persons who selected black (Asian) alone or in combination with other races. For all years, persons of Hispanic origin may be of any race.
2015 figures for percent married adults, ages 18+, are from 2014.
Percent married adults include married spouse present, married spouse absent, and separated.
n.a. = not available.
Source: US Census Bureau, detailed tables from www.census.gov: table MS-2, "Estimated Median Age at First Marriage, by Sex, 1890 to the Present" and table A1, "Marital Status of People 15 Years and Over by Age, Sex, Personal Earnings, Race, and Hispanic Origin;" US Census Bureau, *America's Families and Living Arrangements* (2000, 2010, and 2014); US Census Bureau, "Marital Status and Living Arrangements: March 1994," *Current Population Report* P20–484 (February 1996), tables A-1, A-2, and A-3; and US Census Bureau, *Statistical Abstract of the United States: 2008*, table 55.

marriage for those who completed high school or less was only slightly lower (1 year) than the age at first marriage for more highly educated women. One important remaining difference by educational attainment, however, is the *timing* of women's first union. More highly educated women delay both marriage and cohabitation, while the typical pattern is for less educated women to start their first union (cohabitation) several years prior. In other words, for less educated women, early cohabitation has increasingly replaced early marriage.[21]

Table 13-3 provides figures on cohabitation rates among all women aged 15 to 44 over the last few decades. The table shows a substantial rise in rates, from just 3 percent in 1982 to 15 percent in 2013. The table further shows that in 2013 fully 57 percent of women in this age range had cohabited at some point in their lives, if only briefly.

While most individuals nonetheless continue to marry, the share who do not is rising and may continue to increase in the future. Referring back to Table 13-2, we see that, by ages 40 to 44, in 1970, just 5 percent of women had never married. But, by 2015, 15.5 percent of women in this age group had never married (of

---

[21]Manning, Brown, and Payne, "Two Decades of Stability."

TABLE 13-3 COHABITATION OF WOMEN AGED 15–44 WITH A MALE PARTNER, SELECTED YEARS

	1982	1995	2002	2013
% Women Cohabiting	3.0	7.0	9.0	15.0
% Women Who Ever Cohabited	n.a.	41.2	50.0	57.3

Notes: Figure for 2013 is from 2011–2013. n.a. = not available.
Source: US Centers for Disease Control and Prevention, "Current Cohabitation Status," and "Ever Cohabited," *Key Statistics from the National Survey of Family Growth*, accessed February 22, 2016, http://www.cdc.gov/nchs/nsfg/key_statistics/c.htm.

course, some of this group may still marry). Looking forward, demographers have estimated that, if current trends continue, as many as one-fourth to one-third of those currently in their 20s will remain unmarried by age 50.[22] Another notable difference from past patterns is that due to postponement of marriage, as well as the increase in the share that is likely never to marry, more children are now being born to unmarried mothers.

Table 13-2 also provides figures on the fraction of adults who are currently married. These figures reflect trends in the rate and timing of first marriage as well as trends in divorce and remarriage.[23] As may be seen in the table, the fraction of currently married adults has declined for all racial and ethnic groups but has decreased most among blacks. This shift appears to reflect black women's rising economic opportunities combined with black men's often poor job prospects. In addition, especially in inner cities, high rates of homicide and incarceration have further contributed to the decline in marriage rates by reducing the number of "marriageable" young black men.[24]

Marriage Patterns by Educational Attainment

One development that has garnered increasing attention is the *reversal* in historical marriage patterns by educational attainment, as shown in Figure 13-1. In 1970, with the exception of those with less than 4 years of high school, education was *inversely* related to the share currently married. Differences across education groups were not, however, very large at that time. For example, high school graduates were only *slightly more* likely to be currently married than those with 4 or more years of college (85 vs. 81 percent). Between 1970 and 2015, marriage rates declined for all educational groups, but they declined *most dramatically* for those with less education. Further, while divorce rates declined for all educational groups, the decline was greater for the college-educated, as discussed in the next section. Thus, by 2015, the share currently married was *positively* related to education; and, in particular, those with 4 or more years of college were *substantially more* likely to be currently

[22]The one-third figure is from Steven Ruggles, "Patriarchy, Power, and Pay," and the one-fourth figure is from Wendy Wang and Kim Parker, "Record Share of Americans Have Never Married," Pew Research Center, September 24, 2014, www.pewresearch.org.
[23]Isen and Stevenson, "Women's Education and Family Behavior."
[24]Charles and Luoh, "Male Incarceration;" and Shannon Seitz, "Accounting for Racial Differences in Marriage and Employment," *Journal of Labor Economics* 27, no. 3 (July 2009): 385–437. For a detailed discussion by race, see R. Kelly Raley, Megan M. Sweeney, and Danielle Wondra, "The Growing Racial and Ethnic Divide in U.S. Marriage Patterns," *The Future of Children* 25, no. 2 (2015): 89–109. One puzzling finding raised by the authors is the substantial decline in marriage rates for highly educated black men.

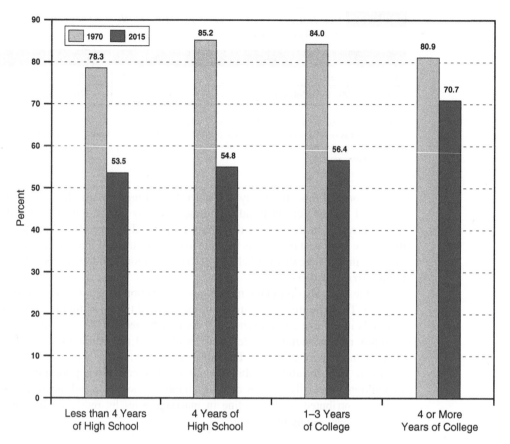

FIGURE 13-1 Share of Women Currently Married, Ages 30–50, 1970 and 2015

Source: Authors' Calculations from March Current Population Survey accessed from IPUMS.

married than women in the other educational categories. For example, the share currently married was 71 percent for college graduates versus 55 percent for high school graduates.

While most research has pointed to low earnings and employment difficulties of men as substantial obstacles to marriage among the less educated, other factors contribute to the educational marriage divide as well. It turns out that from the standpoint of economic resources, wealth is regarded by many couples as a "prerequisite" to marriage, whether measured as owning a car or a home or having savings in the bank.[25] Researchers point to noneconomic barriers as well. Among these, disadvantaged women may be avoiding marriage or remarriage because of concerns about future divorce. Such concerns are not unfounded given higher rates of divorce for this group. Another factor found to be important is women's concerns about whether they can fully rely on and trust male partners. These views are likely related, at least in part, to the fragile economic situation of many of these couples.[26] Taking these findings as a whole, sociologist Andrew Cherlin suggests that marriage continues to

---

[25]Daniel Schneider, "Wealth and the Marital Divide," *American Journal of Sociology* 117 (2011): 627–67.
[26]Kathryn Edin and Joanna M. Reed, "Why Don't They Just Get Married? Barriers to Marriage among the Disadvantaged," *The Future of Children* 15, no. 2 (2005): 117–37.

be important in the lives of many Americans but its nature has changed. For many, marriage is now viewed as a "capstone experience"—a goal to be strived for—rather than a necessary first step to building a family.[27]

Finally, another notable marriage trend, though not shown in Table 13-1, is a rise in intermarriage across racial and ethnic lines. Estimates vary somewhat, but one study estimates that about 15 percent of new marriages in 2010 were between spouses of different races or ethnicities, up from about 7 percent in 1980.[28] Intermarriage is increasingly common among more highly educated individuals. One explanation is that, although there is likely still some social cost associated with intermarriage, the gains to pairing up with those of similar (high) levels of education, regardless of race or ethnicity, increasingly exceed these costs.[29]

In conclusion, despite the decline in the overall marriage rate in the United States since 1980, marriage remains central to the lives of many Americans. This is reflected in the fact that the majority (55 percent) of adults are currently married. Also, it is instructive to note that the share of Americans who have remarried (defined as the percent who ever remarried among those who were previously married) is at about the same level as in 1960. Part of the explanation for the stability in this figure is that while the share of those who have remarried has fallen for those under 35, it has increased markedly for those ages 55 and over, in part due to increased life expectancy.[30] From a comparative perspective, the US marriage rate remains one of the highest among economically advanced nations.[31]

Divorce

A number of factors affect a couple's decision to divorce.[32] For traditional married couples, the interdependence of husband and wife due to specialization and exchange is probably the single most important economic deterrent to divorce. Both partners have invested in a very specific set of skills in their sphere, whether the home or market. Over the years, investments by the spouses, particularly the wife, in marriage-specific human capital further cement this interdependent relationship. With women's rising labor force participation, the gains from specialization and exchange are reduced and the propensity to divorce is likely to increase. On the other hand, as discussed in the case of marriage, the similar experiences of husbands and wives in dual-earner couples may enhance the quality of their married lives, thereby making their union more enduring.

---

[27]Andrew J. Cherlin, "In the Season of Marriage, a Question. Why Bother?" *New York Times*, April 27, 2013.

[28]Pew Research Center, "The Rise of Intermarriage: Rates, Characteristics Vary by Race and Gender," February 16, 2012, www.pewresearch.org. See also Sharon M. Lee and Barry Edmonston, "New Marriages, New Families: U.S. Racial and Hispanic Intermarriage," *Population Bulletin* 60, no. 2 (June 2005): 1–36.

[29]Roland G. Fryer Jr., "Guess Who's Been Coming to Dinner? Trends in Interracial Marriage over the 20th Century," *Journal of Economic Perspectives* 21, no. 2 (Spring 2007): 71–90.

[30]Gretchen Livingston, "Four-in-Ten Couples Are Saying 'I Do,' Again: Growing Number of Adults Have Remarried," Pew Research Center, November 14, 2014, www.pewresearch.org.

[31]For the most recent international comparisons, see the Organisation for Economic Co-operation and Development's OECD Family Database, www.OECD.org.

[32]See Gary S. Becker, Elisabeth M. Landes, and Robert T. Michael, "An Economic Analysis of Marital Instability," *Journal of Political Economy* 85, no. 6 (December 1977): 1141–87.

Another reason why women's increased labor force participation may be correlated with divorce is because it increases the financial viability of a woman exiting a marriage and being able to support herself and her children. For partners in an unhappy marriage, a divorce may be an improvement for all concerned. In such instances, we may observe a positive relationship between women's paid work and divorce, but it is not necessarily the case that paid employment *caused* the divorce but rather that women's market earnings provided the means to exit an unhappy situation. For instance, evidence indicates that the relationship between women's increased labor force participation and divorce depends on whether the spouses were happily married. The wife's labor force participation was found to have no effect on the likelihood of divorce for couples with a fulfilling marriage, but her participation was found to increase the likelihood of divorce among unhappy couples.[33]

Unanticipated events that occur in a marriage are another factor that may tip the decision toward divorce. One example is a sudden job loss for one of the partners.[34] Another example is the shift in long-accepted norms regarding gender roles, such as the increases in married women's labor force participation that occurred during the 1960s and 1970s. These changes, which were likely unanticipated by husbands and wives who married under very different circumstances and assumptions, probably altered their preferences and needs, thereby increasing their propensity to divorce.

Considerable interest continues to surround the impact of the liberalization of state divorce laws in the 1970s on the divorce rate. These changes included the adoption of **no-fault divorce**, where the spouse who is seeking a divorce does not have to show that the other partner did something wrong in order to obtain it, and **unilateral divorce**, where divorce can proceed if just one spouse seeks to terminate the marriage rather than requiring both spouses to agree to termination. These changes not only made it easier to divorce but effectively increased the bargaining power of the partner most interested in exiting the marriage. On the one hand, some have argued that these changes should not increase the divorce rate if spouses are able to make adequate adjustments within marriage, such as shifting resources toward the partner with the newly increased bargaining power. On the other hand, others have argued that divorce rates should rise either because bargaining within the marriage would be difficult or because the changes in the law reduced legal costs. Although the research evidence is mixed, one authoritative study finds that, while the liberalization of divorce laws increased the divorce rate temporarily, there was no long-term effect on the rate.[35] The changes in the rules governing divorce might also affect which couples marry in the first place. It has been argued that now that it is easier for either partner to dissolve a marriage, couples who choose to marry these days tend to be those who are better matched and thus have more to gain from marriage.[36] To the extent that this argument is valid, the propensity to divorce is expected to decline.

---

[33]For example, see Liana C. Sayer, Paula England, Paul D. Allison, and Nicole Kangas, "She Left, He Left: How Employment and Satisfaction Affect Women's and Men's Decisions to Leave Marriages," *American Journal of Sociology* 116, no. 6 (May 2011): 1982–2018.

[34]Interestingly, one study finds that the likelihood of divorce tends to increase after a layoff not so much due to the financial loss but rather due to the negative "signal" about the partner's employment prospects; see Kerwin Kofi Charles and Melvin Stephens Jr., "Job Displacement, Disability, and Divorce," *Journal of Labor Economics* 22, no. 2 (April 2004): 489–522.

[35]For this finding and a review of the literature, see Justin Wolfers, "Did Unilateral Divorce Raise Divorce Rates: Reconciliation and New Results," *American Economic Review* 96, no. 5 (December 2006): 1802–20.

[36]Imran Rasul, "Marriage Markets and Divorce Laws," *Journal of Law, Economics, and Organization* 22, no. 1 (Spring 2006): 30–69.

Given that many couples who divorce have children, changes in rules governing child support—income provided by noncustodial parents—and changes in rules regarding child custody may also affect spouses' decisions regarding divorce. One study argues that rising rates of joint custody of children and stricter child support enforcement shift bargaining power to the spouse who does *not* want to exit. Consistent with this argument, the study finds that both changes contributed to a decline in the divorce rate since 1980.[37]

As would be expected, divorce is also influenced by religious beliefs and broad social attitudes. The role of broad social attitudes is illustrated by the finding that divorce in the United States occurs less frequently in families with sons. This finding suggests some preference for male children even in the United States, although this preference is not nearly as strong as in some other countries, notably those in East Asia.[38]

For some time, the factors that served to increase divorce appeared to dominate those that encouraged the continuation of marriage. As shown in Table 13-1, the divorce rate stood at 9.2 divorces per 1,000 married women in 1960, rose to 14.9 in 1970, and then further increased to 22.6 in 1980.[39] This suggests that, for this period, the reduction in the gains to specialization and the reduced economic dependence of wives associated with women's rising labor force participation outweighed any larger gains to joint consumption of dual-earner couples.[40] It may also be that divorce rates during this period rose at least in part as a consequence of the unexpected change in gender roles associated with wives' rising labor force participation. Interestingly, after 1980, the divorce rate leveled off and then declined, decreasing from 22.6 divorces per 1,000 married women in 1980 to 16.4 in 2009 (the most recent year data are available for this measure)—a substantial decrease, returning the divorce rate to somewhat above its 1970 level.[41] These trends for all ages combined match the experiences of younger cohorts. However, there is recent evidence of a rise in divorce rates for older Americans, a shift that is discussed at greater length shortly.[42]

One explanation for the leveling off and subsequent decline of the overall divorce rate is that, for the later period, the factors we have noted reversed. That is, the impact of the more similar experiences of husbands and wives in dual-earner couples started to outweigh the reduction of the gains to specialization and exchange.

---

[37]Rafael González-Val and Miriam Marcén, "Unilateral Divorce versus Child Custody and Child Support in the U.S.," *Journal of Economic Behavior & Organization* 81 (2012): 613–43.

[38]For evidence on this point in the United States, see Gordon Dahl and Enrico Moretti, "The Demand for Sons," *Review of Economic Studies* 75, no. 4 (October 2008): 1085–120. The preference for sons in East Asia is discussed further in Chapter 17.

[39]The advantage of looking at divorces per 1,000 married women versus divorces per 1,000 population (for which data are also shown) is that marriages rates have been changing at the same time; the former figure tells us what has been happening to divorce among the married population.

[40]Evidence regarding the relationship between labor force participation and divorce has been mixed. For a review of the research findings, see Berkay Özcan and Richard Breen, "Marital Instability and Female Labor Supply," *Annual Review of Sociology* 38 (2012): 463–81.

[41]For those married from the 1950s through 1970s, around one-half of marriages ended in divorce within 25 years. The figure for more recent cohorts is likely to be slightly lower, given declines in the divorce rate. See Stevenson and Wolfers, "Marriage and Divorce."

[42]Susan L. Brown and I-Fen Lin identify a rise in divorce rates for older Americans, specifically for those aged 50 and over, in "The Gray Divorce Revolution: Rising Divorce among Middle-Aged and Older Adults, 1990–2010," *Journals of Gerontology, Series B: Psychological Sciences and Social Sciences* 67, no. 66 (2012): 731–41. In another study Sheela Kennedy and Steven Ruggles adjust the overall divorce rate per 1,000 married women by age and find that rates have been declining or stable for younger cohorts but since around 1990 they have been rising for those over age 35; see "Breaking Up Is Hard to Count: The Rise of Divorce in the United States, 1980–2010," *Demography,* 51 (2014): 587–98.

Indicative of this type of shift in the nature of marital partnerships are the results of one study that looked at patterns of marital stability for couples formed from the 1950s to 1980s relative to those formed from the 1990s to early 2000s. Among couples formed since the 1990s, those in which the spouses have the same level of education are now less likely to break up than those where the husband has the educational advantage, contrary to the pattern for earlier cohorts. And, for those in which the wife has the educational advantage, they are now no more likely to break up than other married couples, also a shift from the earlier pattern.[43] A related research study reaches a different conclusion. It finds that couples in which the wife outearns her husband are more susceptible to break up. The findings differ, perhaps, because the latter study includes couples formed in earlier periods or because of difference in the measures analyzed (relative earnings versus relative educational attainment).[44]

Other factors may have also contributed to the leveling off and decline of the divorce rate. As we have seen, the age at first marriage has been rising, and this has been found to contribute to the decline in the divorce rate.[45] It makes sense that the delay of marriage would promote marital stability since it has been found that people who get married in their late 20s are less likely to break up than those who marry at younger ages. Another explanation that has been offered is that rising cohabitation contributes to recent trends because the breakup of such unions is not counted in the divorce statistics. However, a study that examined this possibility found that rising cohabitation played only a minor role at most.[46] A final explanation is better matching of spouses. Better matching may be a consequence of the rising age at first marriage (partners' interests and preferences are more firmly established), the liberalization of divorce laws (so only those with the most to gain marry), and the rise of online social media (which expands the pool of potential partners with common interests and goals).[47]

In examining trends in divorce, there are important differences by educational attainment and age. First, while the overall divorce rate has declined since its peak in 1980, it has fallen considerably more for college-educated women than for their less educated counterparts.[48] Recall that we earlier mentioned that those with less education also had larger declines in marriage rates. At least part of the explanation for both trends likely lies with deteriorating labor market opportunities for less-skilled male workers.

Finally, another trend that has garnered considerable recent attention is the substantial rise in divorce rates of older individuals, what has been labeled "gray divorce." A recent study estimates that the divorce rate among those over age 50

---

[43]Christine R. Schwartz and Hongyun Han, "The Reversal of the Gender Gap in Education and Trends in Marital Dissolution," *American Sociological Review* 79, no 4. (2014): 605–29.

[44]Marianne Bertrand, Emir Kamenica, and Jessica Pan, "Gender Identity and Relative Income within Households," *Quarterly Journal of Economics* 130, no. 3 (2015): 571–614.

[45]Dana Rotz finds that the rise in women's age at first marriage can explain as much as 60 percent of the decline in the divorce rate for those marrying between 1980 and the mid-2000s; see "Why Have Divorce Rates Fallen? The Role of Women's Age at Marriage," *Journal of Human Resources* 51, no. 4 (fall 2016): 961–1002.

[46]Joshua R. Goldstein, "The Leveling of Divorce in the United States," *Demography* 36, no. 3 (August 1999): 409–14.

[47]Stevenson and Wolfers, "Marriage and Divorce."

[48]See Steven P. Martin, "Trends in Marital Dissolution by Women's Education in the United States," *Demographic Research* 15, no. 20 (December 2006): 537–60; and Isen and Stevenson, "Women's Education and Family Behavior."

doubled between 1990 and 2010.[49] Reasons for this increase remain to be sorted out, but it may be that, with child-raising years largely past and overall life expectancy increasing, older women and men may be reassessing how they want to spend their remaining years from a marital standpoint.

Cohabitation: Opposite-Sex Couples

Opposite-sex cohabitation represents an increasingly common living arrangement.[50] As may be seen in Table 13-3, not only is an increasing share of women cohabiting at a point in time (15 percent in 2013) but it is estimated that 57 percent of women aged 15 to 44 have cohabited at some point in their lives. In some instances, cohabitors may be individuals who never marry; in other instances, women and men may cohabit prior to their first marriage or after they have been divorced or widowed. Opposite-sex cohabitation is in some ways similar and in other ways different from marriage. Like marriage, cohabitation involves two individuals living together in a single household. Here again, the situation presents possibilities for specialization and economies of scale as well as the other gains derived from couples living together that were discussed earlier. Why then do some couples choose to cohabit while others marry? One factor may, of course, be the level of commitment of the partners, but beyond that a number of economic and social factors likely play a role.

The current financial and economic resources of the two partners, especially the male's, are an important consideration. Many couples believe that they should be financially secure before taking the "next step" to marriage. This may further mean that some couples do not move to this "next step" if the male's economic situation does not improve.[51]

Marriage also provides a set of legal protections that are not available to opposite-sex cohabitors. For instance, it establishes property rights for each individual regarding assets brought into or acquired after setting up a joint household.[52] As another example, even if cohabitors have been together for a long time, neither partner in such a relationship is legally entitled to a spousal benefit under Social Security. Such legal considerations may play a role in the decision to cohabit versus marry. For example, one would expect individuals who want to live together to be more likely to cohabit rather than marry if little or no legal protection of property is at issue. In addition, the desire for or presence of children may increase the importance of these property rights. Finally, the propensity to cohabit is influenced by prevailing social attitudes toward sex and childbearing outside of marriage,

---

[49]Brown and Lin, "The Gray Divorce Revolution."

[50]Although the term *mixed-sex* or *different-sex* is used by some researchers to distinguish men–women couples from gay and lesbian couples, we use the term *opposite-sex couple* here because it is used by the US Census Bureau and the general public.

[51]Some also wait until they have funds to cover the traditional wedding they envision; see Pamela Smock, Wendy Manning, and Meredith Porter, "'Everything's There Except Money': How Money Shapes Decisions to Marry among Cohabitors," *Journal of Marriage and Family* 67, no. 3 (August 2005): 680–96.

[52]For a discussion of the legal standing of opposite-sex cohabitors, see Cynthia Grant Bowman, *Unmarried Couples, Law, and Public Policy* (New York: Oxford University Press, 2010); and "When Unmarried Parents Split: Family Law Has Not Kept Up with the Changes in Families," *The Economist*, January 16, 2016.

which, except among the very religious, have grown more liberal.[53] Indeed, as cohabitation has become more common, attitudes have grown more tolerant, further encouraging couples to choose this arrangement.

Cohabitation is expected to be of shorter duration than marriage. This is due to some important differences in the circumstances of married couples and cohabitors. For one thing, cohabitors are less likely to become as economically interdependent. This is because an individual in a cohabiting relationship who specializes in homemaking and forgoes the opportunity to maintain and increase labor market skills does not receive the same legal protections as a married person would. Thus, cohabitors have less incentive than married couples to specialize. In addition, the fact that cohabitation creates few, if any, legal commitments makes it more likely that any personal problems or economic setbacks that arise will lead to breakups. Consistent with these expectations, data from the late 2000s indicate that for couples cohabiting for the first time (and who were never previously married), the median length of time in this arrangement is relatively short—just under 2 years, though up from around 1 year in 1995. These data also show that 3 years after first cohabiting, 40 percent of these couples went on to marry and 27 percent broke up.[54] Overall figures such as these mask important differences by age cohort, race, and economic status. Evidence indicates that younger cohorts who cohabit have lower intentions to ever marry than older cohorts.[55] And cohabitation is far less likely to be a prelude to marriage for those who are more economically disadvantaged and for minorities.[56]

One recent trend that is receiving particular attention is a rise in **serial cohabitation**, that is, living with one partner and then moving in with another. One study documents a 40 percent increase in serial cohabitation from 1995 to 2002 compared to just a 26 percent increase in cohabitation overall. As might be expected, since marriage tends to go hand in hand with economic stability, serial cohabitation tends to be more common among those who are young and those who are more economically disadvantaged.[57]

---

[53]Thornton and Young-DeMarco, "Four Decades of Trends in Attitudes."

[54]The figures on cohabitation are from Casey E. Copen, Kimberly Daniels, and William D. Mosher, "First Premarital Cohabitation in the United States: 2006–2010 National Survey of Family Growth," *National Health Statistics Reports* 64 (April 4, 2013). See also Sheela Kennedy and Larry Bumpass, "Cohabitation and Children's Living Arrangements: New Estimates from the United States," *Demographic Research* 19 (2008): 1663–92. Early research found that premarital cohabitation was associated with increased marital instability, perhaps because those who cohabit are less committed than those who marry immediately. However, as cohabitation has grown more common, research finds less of an association with marital instability and even some evidence that premarital cohabitation is associated with greater marital stability for those in second and subsequent marriages; see Steffen Reinhold, "Reassessing the Link between Premarital Cohabitation and Marital Instability," *Demography* 47, no. 3 (August 2010): 719–33.

[55]Jonathan Vespa, "Historical Trends in the Marital Intentions of One-Time and Serial Cohabitors," *Journal of Marriage and Family* 76, no. 1 (February 2014): 207–17.

[56]Daniel T. Lichter, Zenchao Qian, and Leanna M. Mellott, "Marriage or Dissolution? Union Transitions among Poor Cohabiting Women," *Demography* 43, no. 2 (2006): 223–40; and Richard Fry and D'Vera Cohn, "Living Together: The Economics of Cohabitation," Pew Research Center, June 27, 2011, www.pewresearch.org. While most research focuses on patterns of the most and least educated, Andrew J. Cherlin observes that more focus should be placed on those in the middle—the largest group—those with high school and possibly some college. When partnerships include marriage and cohabitation, he finds that white high school–educated women, age 35 to 40, had the greatest number of partnerships. See "Between Poor and Prosperous: Do the Family Patterns of Moderately Educated Americans Deserve a Closer Look?" in *Social Class and Changing Families in an Unequal America*, ed. Marcia Carlson and Paula England (Stanford, CA: Stanford University Press, 2011), 68–84.

[57]Daniel T. Lichter, Richard N. Turner, and Sharon Sassler, "National Estimates of the Rise in Serial Cohabitation," *Social Science Research* 39 (2010): 754–65.

With rising rates of cohabitation, increasing numbers of children are living in such arrangements. In some cases, children are born to cohabiting parents, while, in other cases, one or both partners may have children from a previous relationship.[58] For instance, in 2015, 40 percent of cohabiting couples included at least one child under age 18, nearly identical to the percent of married-couple families with children under age 18 present.[59] Moreover, it is projected that 40 percent of *all* children under age 12 will spend at least some of their childhood in a cohabiting family.[60]

These changes in family structure have potentially important implications for children's well-being. For one, as we have seen, cohabitors are considerably more likely to break up than married couples, putting children at greater risk of the often negative consequences of family disruption. In addition, cohabiting couples have considerably lower incomes than married couples, on average, and a much larger fraction live in poverty.[61] As will be discussed in Chapter 15, these economic difficulties would not be fully remedied by simply having these couples marry; even if they were to do so, they would still have lower earnings, on average, than married couples, mainly because they tend to have less education and work experience. Moreover, marriage, per se, would not likely reduce the breakup rate of couples who previously cohabited because cohabiting couples may be more susceptible to breakup in the first place.

Finally, it is useful to place opposite-sex cohabitation in the United States in an international context. Cohabitation rates are higher in a number of other economically advanced countries, including Sweden, where as many as 19 percent of persons age 20 and over are cohabiting at a given point in time compared to 7 percent in the United States.[62] (Note that the US figure here differs from that in Table 13-3 because of the difference in age ranges—20 and over here and 15–44 in the table.) Not only do countries differ in their incidence of cohabitation but some researchers have argued that there are several stages of cohabitation in a society, and countries are at different stages. In the first stage, cohabitation is rare; in the second stage, cohabitation serves as a prelude to marriage but does not involve childbearing; in the third stage, cohabitation is even more socially acceptable and includes childbearing; and in the fourth stage, cohabitation and marriage become "indistinguishable" in terms of duration and childbearing. According to this view, Sweden and other Nordic countries are in the fourth stage, while recent patterns for the United States suggest that, generally speaking, more highly educated couples are in the second stage and less educated couples are in the third stage.[63]

---

[58]Pamela J. Smock and Fiona Rose Greenland, "Diversity in Pathways to Parenthood: Patterns, Implications and Emerging Research Directions," *Journal of Marriage and Family* 72 (June 2010): 576–93.

[59]US Census Bureau, "America's Families and Living Arrangements: 2015," detailed tables FG3 and UC3, accessed May 2016, www.census.gov.

[60]Kennedy and Bumpass, "Cohabitation and Children's Living Arrangements."

[61]These and other findings on cohabitation and children are discussed in Wendy D. Manning, "Cohabitation and Child Well-Being," *The Future of Children* 25 no. 2 (Fall 2015): 51–66.

[62]These figures are from the OECD Family Database, table SF3.3.A, "Partnerships and Cohabitation: 2011," accessed August 19, 2016, www.oecd.org.

[63]Kathleen Kiernan set forth the stages of cohabitation, see "Unmarried Cohabitation and Parenthood: Here to Stay? European Perspectives," in *The Future of the Family*, ed. Daniel P. Moynihan, Timothy M. Smeeding, and Lee Rainwater (New York: Russell Sage Foundation, 2004), 66–95. For recent discussion, see Megan M. Sweeney, "The Reproductive Context of Cohabitation in the United States," *Journal of Marriage and Family* 72, no. 1 (October 2010): 1155–70.

Cohabitation and Marriage: Same-Sex Couples

Like traditional married couples and unmarried opposite-sex couples, **same-sex couples** also reap economic benefits, including the ability to share economic resources and enjoy joint consumption and to realize economies of scale. However, even though same-sex partners may also differ in terms of their comparative advantage in housework and market work, neither partner is likely to specialize in home production to the same extent as an average woman in an opposite-sex marriage.[64]

First, until recently, same-sex couples were not legally permitted to marry and thus had fewer legal protections than married couples, thereby making investment in homemaking skills particularly costly in the event that the couple broke up. However, efforts to legalize marriage, beginning with Massachusetts in 2004 and culminating in the Supreme Court ruling of *Obergefell v. Hodges* in 2015, changed this calculation. As discussed at length in the "State of Unions" box in Chapter 4, same-sex marriage is now legal throughout the United States, and spouses in such couples now have access to precisely the same benefits and protections as their opposite-sex married-couple counterparts.[65]

Second, to the extent that young women know they are not likely to enter an opposite-sex relationship, they have less incentive to specialize in homemaking skills. On the contrary, those expecting to have partnerships with other women are more likely, all else equal, to accumulate human capital useful for the labor market compared with those expecting to be members of a more traditional opposite-sex household. For the same reason, they are also likely to choose more career-oriented, male-dominated occupations.

Turning to men in same-sex partnerships, while they are also likely to acquire skills useful for the labor market, they are unlikely to be as specialized in market-oriented activities as their heterosexual male counterparts since they are not expecting to fulfill the traditional breadwinner role. Thus, both women and men in same-sex couples are likely to be less specialized in traditional gender roles than their opposite-sex counterparts.

While figures vary depending on the survey used,[66] it has been estimated that same-sex couples comprised around 1 percent of all married and unmarried couples in 2013. And, for that same year, around 21 percent of same-sex couples were married. By October 2015, 4 months after the decision that legalized same-sex marriage in all states, this figure stood at more than double, 45 percent.[67] These figures are likely to increase further as public support for same-sex relationships and same-sex marriage continues to rise and as more unmarried same-sex couples legalize their relationship through marriage.

---

[64]Dan A. Black, Seth G. Sanders, and Lowell J. Taylor, "The Economics of Lesbian and Gay Families," *Journal of Economic Perspectives* 21, no. 2 (Spring 2007): 53–70.

[65]The box in Chapter 4 also discusses *United States v. Windsor*, a 2013 Supreme Court decision which overturned the 1996 Defense of Marriage Act.

[66]Concerns have been raised about the accuracy of the counts obtained; see D'Vera Cohn, "How Accurate Are Counts of Same-Sex Couples?" Pew Research Center, August 25, 2011, www.pewresearch .org. Moreover, it was only in fall 2014 that the US Census Bureau began including married same-sex couples among the set of all married couples; see D'Vera Cohn, "Census Says It Will Count Same-Sex Marriages, but with Caveats," Pew Research Center, May 28, 2014, www.pewresearch.org.

[67]Figures in this paragraph are drawn from Gary Gates, "Marriage and Family: LGBT Individuals and Same-Sex Couples," *The Future of Children* 25, no. 2 (Fall 2015): 67–87; and Gary Gates and Taylor N. T. Brown, *Marriage and Same-Sex Couples after Obergefell* (Los Angeles: Williams Institute, November 2015).

A considerable number of children are raised in same-sex families, most often born into one of the adult's prior opposite-sex unions. For the year 2013, it has been estimated that 27 percent of married same-sex couples and 15 percent of unmarried same-sex couples were raising children under the age of 18. As a point of comparison, figures for opposite-sex married and unmarried couples were 44 and 43 percent, respectively. With the legalization of marriage, it is expected that in the years to come an increasing number of children will be born to or adopted at birth by same-sex couples compared to the current situation.[68]

Fertility

Neoclassical economic theory sheds considerable light on the determinants of **fertility**: people's decisions about whether to have children and how many to have. According to the economic approach, parents' **demand for children** (how many they would like to have)[69] depends not only on the benefits (or utility) they expect to derive from having children but also on the costs of raising them, including the **opportunity cost of time** (income foregone during time spent in caring for children), and the family income available.[70]

Estimates are available for some of these costs. For 2013, the US Department of Agriculture estimated that the expenditures on clothing, housing, and education required for an average married couple to raise a child through age 17 amounted to $245,340.[71] This is a substantial sum and does not take into account expenditures on post–secondary education. Also omitted from this estimate is the opportunity cost of the time parents devote to child-rearing, which is a large part of their contribution to raising children. Even when a great deal of childcare is purchased, parents, most often mothers, still spend a good deal of time finding suitable caregivers, taking care of emergencies, and helping with schoolwork, as well as providing recreation and other enrichment. The time and energy parents devote to these purposes could otherwise be used to obtain more education or training for themselves, to advance their own careers, to earn more income by working longer hours, or to enjoy more leisure.[72]

---

[68]Figures and discussion are from Gates, "Marriage and Family."

[69]Gary S. Becker, *A Treatise on the Family*, defines demand for children in terms of child services. We use a simplified definition here.

[70]Richard A. Easterlin offers a different explanation for changes in fertility and female labor force participation. In his model, the driving force behind changes in these outcomes is that young people aspire to achieve at least the same income their parents had when they were growing up. If members of a particular birth cohort are worse off than their parents were, female labor force participation will rise to compensate, and fertility will decline. If, on the other hand, their income is higher than what their parents achieved, the effect on fertility will be positive. See Richard A. Easterlin, "On the Relation of Economic Factors to Recent and Projected Fertility Changes," *Demography* 3 (August 1966): 131–53. For a review of Easterlin's work and influence, see Diane J. Macunovich, "Fertility and the Easterlin Hypothesis: An Assessment of the Literature," *Journal of Population Economics* 11, no. 4 (1998): 53–111. For a discussion of other ways to broaden the economic model of fertility, see Robert Pollak and Susan Cotts Watkins, "Cultural and Economic Approaches to Fertility: Proper Marriage or Mesalliance?" *Population and Development Review* 19, no. 3 (September 1993): 467–96.

[71]Figure is from US Department of Agriculture, "Parents Projected to Spend $245,340 to Raise a Child Born in 2013, According to USDA Report," news release 0179.14, August 18, 2014. See also Sabino Kornrich and Frank Furstenberg, "Investing in Children: Changes in Parental Spending on Children, 1972–2007," *Demography* 50, no. 1 (February 2013): 1–23.

[72]See Nancy Folbre, *Valuing Children: Rethinking the Economics of the Family* (Cambridge, MA: Harvard University Press, 2008); and Carl Bialik, "Kids Can Be Costly after They Turn 18," *Wall Street Journal*, June 22, 2012.

Higher income is expected to increase a couple's demand for all "commodities" from which they derive utility or satisfaction, including children. Moreover, higher income enables a family to more easily meet the money costs of raising more children. Thus, one might expect to see a positive relationship between income and fertility. In fact, however, fertility tends to decline with income. One reason is that higher income is believed to increase parents' demand for **child quality** (investment per child) rather than for **child quantity** (the number of children).[73] Child quality includes investments parents make in the education and health of each of their children. Child quality may be enhanced by education- or skill-related expenditures like piano lessons, a spot at soccer camp, or advanced classes in science, as well as tuition for private school and college and perhaps graduate school later on. Because education and skills are particularly valued in today's labor market, these kinds of expenditures provide children with considerable advantages. Another dimension of child quality, children's health, also requires expenditures, through either paying insurance premiums or out-of-pocket costs. Parents with strong preferences for child quality are likely to have fewer children because higher expenditures on child quality increase the costs of child quantity. For instance, parents who are committed to providing a college education for each of their children will find an additional child more costly than those committed to just getting their children through high school.

Changing economic opportunities of women and men are also expected to affect the fertility decision. As women's wages rise, the opportunity cost of the time they spend with children increases, leading to a negative substitution effect on their demand for children. In other words, as children become more expensive (in opportunity cost terms), the individual is likely to substitute away from children toward the consumption of other goods or services that provide utility. Even though a higher wage is expected to also have a positive income effect encouraging fertility (but see our discussion of child quality earlier), the substitution effect of the wage increase is likely to dominate for women because they generally continue to be the primary caregivers. Similarly, because women's wages are a key determinant of their labor force participation, we would expect to observe a negative relationship between fertility and women's labor market activity.

Over the long term, the relationship between women's wages (or labor force participation) and fertility depends on the relative strength of competing factors. On the one hand, as women become better educated and more career-oriented, the opportunity cost of child-rearing is increased, thereby reducing the demand for children.[74] On the other hand, the availability of affordable high-quality childcare, as well as the increasing acceptance of using it, probably reduces the opportunity cost of child-rearing to some extent. Certainly, access to childcare makes it easier for women to combine employment with having a family.

---

[73]Becker, *A Treatise on the Family*; Gary Becker and Nigel Tomes, "Child Endowments and the Quantity and Quality of Children," *Journal of Political Economy* 84, no. 4, pt. 2 (August 1976): S143–62. Matthias Doepke provides a useful review and shows how subsequent research work built on it, see "Gary Becker on the Quantity and Quality of Children," *Journal of Demographic Economics* 81 (2015): 59–66.

[74]For instance, McKinley L. Blackburn, David E. Bloom, and David Neumark found that late childbearers tend to invest more heavily in their human capital than early childbearers in "Fertility Timing, Wages and Human Capital," *Journal of Population Economics* 6, no. 1 (1993): 1–30. Late childbearing would also be expected to reduce the number of children per woman, all else equal. See also Steven P. Martin, "Women's Education and Family Timing: Outcomes and Trends Associated with Age at Marriage and First Birth" in *Social Inequality*, ed. Kathryn Neckerman (New York: Russell Sage Foundation, 2004), 79–118.

For men, the income effect of a wage increase is likely to dominate the substitution effect because they generally do not give up as much of their time to providing childcare. Therefore, as men's wages increase, we would expect to see a rise in fertility, all else equal.[75] However, as already discussed, families are also likely to use some of the added income to increase spending per child by investing in child quality.

In addition to women's and men's wages and family income, changes in contraceptive technology such as the birth control pill and LARCs, along with changes in reproductive technology, such as those that permit women to have children at older ages, have enhanced women's ability to control their own fertility, whether in terms of the timing or the number of children born.[76] Government policies, including the diffusion of family planning services in the 1960s and legal decisions such as the legalization of abortion in 1973, also have the potential to affect fertility rates and timing. Indeed, evidence indicates that both of these developments served to delay childbearing and reduce fertility.[77] Government tax policies and transfer programs may also affect fertility. For instance, in the federal individual income tax, the personal exemption increases with the number of children, as do several tax credits including the Child Tax Credit and the Earned Income Tax Credit. These tax features subsidize childbearing and thus provide positive incentives for fertility.[78]

Trends in Fertility Rates: World War II to Present

Table 13-4 and Figure 13-2 present data on the **total fertility rate** since the 1940s. The total fertility rate is an estimate of the number of births that a cohort of 1,000 women would have if they experienced the age-specific birth rates occurring in the indicated year throughout their childbearing years. When this figure is divided by 1,000, as is commonly done for ease of interpretation, it provides an estimate of the average number of children a woman would have over her lifetime.

As the data make clear, the total fertility rate has fluctuated considerably over time. The period that lasted from the end of World War II until the early 1960s is known as the **baby boom** (and those born during this period are known as **Baby Boomers**). As shown in the figure, fertility rates for this period were considerably higher than those in the prior and subsequent periods; rates reached a peak of 3.7

---

[75]For instance, using evidence on the coal boom in Appalachia during the 1970s, one study found that men's wages and fertility rose in areas that benefited from the boom (thus, a positive income effect) compared to areas that did not experience the boom. See Dan A. Black, Natalia Kolesnikova, Seth G. Sanders, and Lowell J. Taylor, "Are Children 'Normal'?" *Review of Economics and Statistics* 95, no. 1 (March 2013): 21–33.

[76]For evidence on the role of the pill, see Goldin and Katz, "Career and Marriage in the Age of the Pill"; and Bailey and Hershbein, "U.S. Fertility Rates and Childbearing." Regarding LARCs, see Ron Haskins, Isabel Sawhill, and Sara McLanahan, "The Promise of Birth Control," *The Future of Children Policy Brief* (Fall 2015).

[77]See, for instance, Elizabeth Oltmans Ananat, Jonathan Gruber, and Phillip B. Levine, "Abortion Legalization and Life Cycle Fertility," *Journal of Human Resources* 42, no. 2 (Spring 2007): 375–97; and Bailey and Hershbein, "U.S. Fertility Rates and Childbearing." Recent research by Kaitlyn Myers ascribes a greater role to abortion policy than the birth control pill in affecting family formation; see "The Power of Abortion Policy: Re-examining the Effects of Young Women's Access to Reproductive Control," *Journal of Political Economy* (forthcoming).

[78]In the case of the Earned Income Tax Credit, the credit does not increase further for four or more children. Regarding incentive effects of tax policies, see Stacey Dickert-Conlin and Reaghan Baughman, "The Earned Income Tax Credit and Fertility," *Journal of Population Economics* 22, no. 3 (2009): 537–63; regarding the effects of welfare programs, see Moffitt, "Temporary Assistance for Needy Families Program."

TABLE 13-4 TOTAL FERTILITY RATES, 1940–2015

YEARS	TOTAL FERTILITY RATE
1940–1949	2,754
1950–1959	3,514
1960–1964	3,449
1965–1969	2,622
1970–1974	2,094
1975–1979	1,774
1980–1984	1,817
1985–1989	1,900
1990–1994	2,042
1995–1999	1,986
2000–2004	2,041
2005–2009	2,072
2010–2014	1,885
2015	1,843

Note: The total fertility rate is the number of births that a cohort of 1,000 women would have if they experienced the age-specific birth rates occurring in the current year throughout their childbearing years. Dividing by 1,000 provides a measure of births per woman.

Sources: US Census Bureau, *Statistical Abstract of the United States*, 1984; US Department of Health and Human Services, "Births: Final Data for 2014," *National Vital Statistics Reports* 64, no. 12 (December 23, 2015); and "Births: Preliminary Data for 2015," *National Vital Statistics Reports* 65, no. 3 (June 2, 2016), www.cdc.gov/nchs.

FIGURE 13-2 Total Fertility Rates, 1940–2015

Sources: US Census Bureau, *Statistical Abstract of the United States*, 1984; US Department of Health and Human Services, "Births: Final Data for 2014," *National Vital Statistics Report* 64, No. 12 (December 2015); and US Department of Health and Human Services, "Births: Preliminary Data for 2015," *National Vital Statistics Report* 65, no. 3 (June 2016); and *Vital Statistics of the United States* (1964 and 1969).

children per woman (3,690 children per 1,000 women) between 1955 and 1959, extremely high by recent historical standards and far above the replacement rate of 2.1 children per woman.

By the mid 1970s, however, during the "baby bust," the rate declined to as low as 1.7, well below the replacement rate. The cohort that was born after the baby boom and includes the baby bust period is referred to in the media as **Generation X**. After a number of years of relatively low fertility, the fertility rate began to rise modestly in the mid-1980s; it reached approximately the replacement rate by 1990 and remained at roughly that level into the 2000s. Starting in 2008, the rate again fell below replacement level and declined modestly thereafter.

In addition to the fertility rate, the total number of births is related to the number of women in their childbearing years. The prime example is the recent cohort known early on as the *echo* of the baby boom, Generation Y, and now almost universally referred to as **Millennials**, who are the offspring of the baby boom cohort. Millennials are generally defined as those born between 1980 and the early 2000s. Millennials are the largest cohort ever, not because the baby boom cohort had high birth rates—on the contrary, birth rates were relatively low for this group—but rather because so many women were of childbearing age at that time. Among the characteristics that differentiate Millennials, they are the first cohort to have been exposed to the Internet, cell phones, and other similar technologies during childhood.[79]

The fluctuations in the total fertility rate shown in Figure 13-2 occurred, in substantial part, as a result of variations in the strength of the factors discussed earlier. The baby boom took place during a time of prosperity and rising real wages of men and women. Because relatively few married women of childbearing age were employed in those days, the main effect of rising real wages was an increase in fertility due to the income effect of husbands' rising wages.[80] Research also points to the role of falling prices of labor-saving appliances, such as the vacuum cleaner, washing machine, and clothes dryer, in spurring the adoption of these conveniences, thereby reducing the burden of larger families.[81] In addition, the magnitude of the baby boom probably cannot be fully explained without taking into account the postponement of births that occurred during the Great Depression of the 1930s and World War II, as well as a variety of social and cultural factors.

The subsequent sharp drop in fertility beginning in the early 1960s coincided with both rapid increases in the labor force participation rate of young women and advances in contraceptive technology. As labor market opportunities opened up for women and as women became increasingly career-oriented, their opportunity cost of dropping out of the labor force to bear and raise children was increased. The modest rise in the total fertility rate from the mid-1980s to the early 1990s may reflect a "catching-up" phenomenon as women who did not have children earlier chose to have them at a later time.[82] It may also, in part, reflect the decision of some

---

[79]Council of Economic Advisers, *15 Economic Facts about Millennials* (October 2014) accessed February 24, 2017, https://obamawhitehouse.archives.gov.

[80]William P. Butz and Michael P. Ward, "The Emergence of Countercyclical U.S. Fertility," *American Economic Review* 69, no. 3 (June 1979): 318–28.

[81]"Jeremy Greenwood, Ananth Seshadri, and Guillaume Vandenbroucke, "The Baby Boom and Baby Bust," *American Economic Review* 95, no. 1 (March 2005): 183–207. Another study has challenged these findings, noting, for instance, that fertility increased for the Amish during the same period, although they did not use the new technology; see Martha J. Bailey and William J. Collins, "Did Improvements in Household Technology Cause the Baby Boom? Evidence from Electrification, Appliance Diffusion, and the Amish," *American Economic Journal: Macroeconomics* 3, no. 2 (April 2011): 189–217.

[82]Julie DaVanzo and M. Omar Rahman, "American Families: Trends and Correlates," *Population Index* 59, no. 3 (Fall 1993): 350–86. Blackburn, Bloom, and Neumark, "Fertility Timing," suggest that this postponement was associated with women's greater investment in their human capital.

couples to start their families earlier in light of publicity about the difficulties that some older women face in becoming pregnant. As noted, from the early 1990s into the 2000s, the level fluctuated modestly at about 2.1 children per woman. Starting in 2008, around the start of the Great Recession, the fertility rate declined, as would be expected in a situation of higher unemployment.[83] What is more surprising is that, as shown in Figure 3-2, fertility rates continued to decline, albeit at a very slow pace, well beyond the period of the Great Recession and its aftermath. In 2015, the rate stood at 1.8 children per woman.

Future trends in fertility are difficult to predict. It is still possible that rates may rebound, reflecting fertility "catch up" now that the Great Recession is in the past, though there has been no such rebound thus far. Looking longer term, even if the overall fertility rate again rises to reach replacement level, it is unlikely that it will rise much further than that, especially in light of the continued increase in women's educational attainment and their continued commitment to market work discussed in earlier chapters. One might even speculate that the US fertility rate might decline somewhat more given the generally lower rates in most other economically advanced countries, as discussed in Chapter 18.[84] However, the level in the United States is not likely to fall too far below the replacement rate because of above-average fertility of some immigrant groups; fertility rates for Hispanic immigrant women average just over three births per woman.[85]

Apart from fluctuations in overall fertility rates, there are other important aspects of women's fertility patterns to consider, many of which have changed in notable ways. For one, there has been a steady rise in women's mean age at first birth. Table 13-5, which provides data on trends from 1970 to 2014, shows that their mean age at first birth rose from 21.4 in 1970 to 26.3 in 2014. This increase reflects a compositional change in first births: a declining share of such births are to teens and a rising share are to older women.[86] Other noteworthy trends that are discussed in the remaining sections of this chapter include a growing divergence in the timing of first births by educational attainment as well as a considerable rise in the share of births to unmarried women.

Timing of Fertility by Educational Attainment

Recent evidence points to an increasing divergence in women's timing of childbearing by educational attainment. There has been a long-standing pattern of college-educated women delaying childbearing somewhat more than less educated women, not only because college takes at least 4 years but also because they tend to be more

---

[83]For further discussion, see Daniel Schneider and Orestes P. Hastings, "Socioeconomic Variation in the Effect of Economic Conditions on Marriage and Nonmarital Fertility in the United States: Evidence from the Great Recession," *Demography* 52, no. 6 (December 2015): 1893–1915.

[84]The substantial fertility decline that has occurred in some of these countries may, however, reflect greater challenges to combining work and family than in the United States; see James Feyrer, Bruce Sacerdote, and Ariel Dora Stern, "Will the Stork Return to Europe? Understanding Fertility within Developed Nations," *Journal of Economic Perspectives* 2, no. 3 (Summer 2008): 3–22.

[85]For second-generation Hispanic women (those born in the United States with at least one parent who is foreign-born), fertility rates are just slightly below replacement, though still higher than rates of their non-Hispanic white counterparts. See Pew Research Center, "Modern Immigration Wave Brings 59 Million to U.S., Driving Population Growth and Change through 2065," Pew Research Center, September 26, 2015, table A2, www.pewresearch.org.

[86]Gretchen Livingston and D'Vera Cohn, "The New Demography of American Motherhood," Pew Research Center, May 6, 2010, www.pewresearch.org.

TABLE 13-5 SELECTED BIRTH RATES, 1970–2014

	1970	1980	1990	2000	2010	2014
Women's Mean Age at First Birth	21.4	22.7	24.2	24.9	25.4	26.3
Birth Rates (Births per 1,000 Women in Specified Group)[a]						
Overall Birth Rate, Ages 15–44	87.9	68.4	70.9	65.9	64.1	62.9
Teen Birth Rate, Ages 15–19	68.3	53.0	59.9	47.7	34.2	24.2
Older Mother Birth Rate						
Ages 35–39	31.7	19.8	31.7	39.7	45.9	51.0
Ages 40–44	8.1	3.9	5.5	8.0	10.2	10.6
Unmarried Birth Rates (Births per 1,000 Unmarried Women in Specified Group)[b]						
Unmarried Birth Rate, Ages 15–44	26.4	29.4	43.8	44.1	47.6	43.9
White, Non-Hispanic	13.9	18.1	24.4	28.0	32.9	31.8
Black	95.5	81.1	90.5	70.5	65.3	61.5
Unmarried Teen Birth Rate, Ages 15–19	22.4	27.6	42.5	39.0	31.1	22.0
White, Non-Hispanic	10.9	16.5	25.0	24.7	20.3	15.0
Black	96.9	87.9	106.0	75.0	50.8	34.4
Unmarried Older Mother Birth Rate						
Ages 35–39	13.6	9.7	17.3	19.7	29.6	33.4
Ages 40–44	3.5	2.6	3.6	5.0	8.0	8.5
Types of Births (%)						
Unmarried Births as % of All Births	10.7	18.4	28.0	33.2	40.8	40.2
White, Non-Hispanic	5.7	9.5	16.9	22.1	29.0	29.2
Black	37.6	55.5	66.5	68.5	72.1	70.4
Unmarried Teen Births as % of All Unmarried Births	50.1	40.8	31.0	27.4	19.8	13.7

[a]For instance, birth rate for ages 15–44 refers to births to women ages 15–44 per 1,000 women in that age group.
[b]For instance, unmarried birth rate for ages 15–44 refers to births to unmarrried women ages 15–44 per 1,000 unmarried women in that age group.
Notes: For data stratified by race, race refers to child's race for 1970; data refers to mother' race for other years. Beginning in 1990, data on whites are for white, Non-Hispanic.
Sources: US Department of Health and Human Services, "Births: Final Data for 2010," *National Vital Statistics Reports* 61, no. 1 (August 28, 2012); and "Births: Final Data for 2014," *National Vital Statistics Reports* 64, no. 12 (December 23, 2015), www.cdc.gov/nchs; US Department of Health and Human Services, "Nonmarital Childbearing, by Detailed Race and Hispanic Origin of Mother, and Maternal Age: United States, Selected Years 1970–2014, table 4, *Health 2015*,www.cdc.gov; US Department of Health and Human Services, "Mean Age of Mother, 1970–2000," *National Vital Statistics Reports* 51, no. 1 (December 11, 2002); and T. J. Mathews and Brady E. Hamilton, "Mean Age of Mothers is on the Rise: United States, 2000–2014," NCHS *Data Brief* no. 232 (January 2016), www.cdc.gov.

career-oriented and the opportunity cost of having children early in their careers is more substantial for them.[87] Thus, it is not surprising that, while the age at first birth rose for all women (as we saw in Table 13-5), it increased substantially more for college-educated women than for those with less education.[88] The net result, as

---

[87]See Amalia R. Miller, "The Effects of Motherhood Timing on Career Path," *Journal of Population Economics* 24, no. 3 (2011): 1071–1100.
[88]See Martin, "Women's Education and Family Timing"; and Isen and Stevenson, "Women's Education and Family Behavior."

TABLE 13-6   PERCENT OF WOMEN WHO HAVE GIVEN BIRTH TO AT LEAST ONE CHILD, BY AGE, MARITAL STATUS, AND SELECTED EDUCATION, 2014

	TOTAL	LESS THAN HIGH SCHOOL	HIGH SCHOOL	BACHELOR'S ONLY	MORE THAN BACHELOR'S
Age 20–29	37.4	66.8	51.9	20.6	23.2
Ever-Married	66.0	88.7	76.4	49.5	40.6
Never-Married	24.6	52.2	40.0	7.6	10.2
Age 30–39	76.1	91.7	83.4	68.9	60.6
Ever-Married	85.5	96.5	90.4	82.0	75.1
Never-Married	49.8	80.1	65.8	25.8	10.3
Age 40–50	83.9	90.1	85.0	81.8	77.5
Ever-Married	89.3	94.0	89.4	88.4	85.9
Never-Married	50.4	74.3	59.8	30.9	21.9

Source: US Census Bureau, *Fertility of American Women: 2014*, table 3, "Children Ever Born per 1,000 Women and Percent Childless," accessed May 11, 2016, www.census.gov.

shown in Table 13-6, is that, in 2014, among women aged 20 to 29, a much lower share of college-educated women had given birth than had those with a high school education or less. Nonetheless, by ages 40 to 50, there is considerable "fertility catch-up" by college-educated women in terms of having at least one child; for example, 85 percent of high school–educated women had given birth to a child by those ages compared to 82 percent of women with a bachelor's degree and 78 percent of women with more than a bachelor's degree.

Births to Unmarried Mothers

Another notable trend has been the marked increase in the share of births to unmarried mothers starting in the 1970s. As shown in Table 13-5, the share of births to unmarried mothers rose sharply from 11 percent of all births in 1970 to a high of nearly 41 percent in 2010. It remained at around that level in 2014. In thinking about unmarried births, there are two key points to keep in mind. First, for the past few decades, the majority of all unmarried births have been to women over age 20, not teens. In fact, in 2014, this figure was just over 86 percent (so just 14 percent of all such births were to teen mothers), and a rising share were to mothers 35 and over. Second, children born to cohabiting parents are included in this statistic. It is estimated that 50 percent of these children are born to unmarried cohabiting parents and so have two parents in their lives at birth.[89]

As in the case of marriage and divorce, there is again a substantial educational divide when it comes to which women have unmarried births. In 2011, just 9 percent of all unmarried births to women aged 15 to 50 were to women who completed a bachelor's degree or more.[90] This pattern is also suggested by the figures in

---

[89]Gladys Martinez, Kimberly Daniels, and Anjani Chandra, "Fertility of Men and Women Aged 15–44 Years in the United States: National Survey of Family Growth, 2006–2010," *National Health Statistics Report* 51 (April 12, 2012).

[90]Rachel M. Shattuck and Rose M. Kreider, "Social and Economic Characteristics of Currently Unmarried Women with a Recent Birth: 2011," *American Community Survey Reports* ACS-21 (Washington, DC: US Census Bureau, May 2013).

Table 13-6, which show a much higher share of never-married women who have given birth among those with high school or less than among the college-educated.

The share of all births that are to unmarried women depends on both the number of unmarried women (and hence the marriage rate) and the probability of married and unmarried women giving birth. Changes in either component affect the trend in the overall share. The birth rate of unmarried women increased substantially, particularly between 1980 and 2010, when it rose from 29.4 to 47.6 births per 1,000 unmarried women (see Table 13-5). Nonetheless, the largest source of the increase in the share of births to unmarried women was actually the substantial increase in the *number* of unmarried women of childbearing age, rather than the rise in the birth rate of unmarried women.[91]

Table 13-5 also points to a new development in the birth rate of unmarried women: after decades of continuous increase, it declined, from 47.6 births per 1,000 unmarried women in 2010 to 43.9 in 2014. This decline, albeit modest, explains why the share of unmarried births has stabilized at around 40 percent. Also quite notable is that, while the birth rate of unmarried women remains higher for blacks than for whites, the rate for blacks has declined considerably since 1990. As a consequence, the race difference in the unmarried birth rate is considerably lower than several decades ago.

Births to unmarried women are related to many of the same factors that affect incentives to marry. Women's increased labor market opportunities have made it easier for them to financially support a family on their own, while at the same time men's ability to make a substantial economic contribution to their family has declined among the less educated.[92] In addition, premarital sex and unmarried childbearing have become much more widely accepted than in the past, and unmarried mothers are now far less likely to get married before the baby's birth.[93] One useful qualification to bear in mind, as mentioned earlier, is that for around 50 percent of unmarried births, the father is around at the time of birth. Government policies also have the potential to influence nonmarital fertility. For instance, stricter child support enforcement in recent years, which increased the costs of fatherhood, appears to have discouraged unmarried births at least to some extent.[94]

Delays and declines in marriage have led to another development that is receiving increasing attention, called **multipartner fertility**.[95] Multipartner fertility

[91]JoAnna Gray, Jean Stockard, and Joe Stone, "The Rising Share of Nonmarital Births: Fertility Choice or Marriage Behavior?" *Demography* 43, no. 2 (May 2006): 241–53. See also Elizabeth Wildsmith, Nicole R. Steward-Streng, and Jennifer Manlove, "Childbearing Outside of Marriage: Estimates and Trends in the United States," *Child Trends research brief*, Publication 2011-29 (Washington, DC: Child Trends, 2011).

[92]Timothy M. Smeeding, Irwin Garfinkel, and Ronald Mincy, "Young Disadvantaged Men: Fathers, Families, Poverty, and Policy," *Annals of the American Academy of Political and Social Science* 635 (May 2011): 6–21.

[93]George A. Akerlof, Janet L. Yellen, and Michael L. Katz argue that the availability of the birth control pill and legal abortion reduced the cost of premarital sex as well as unmarried women's ability to "bargain" for marriage in the event of pregnancy. These changes, in turn, led to a reduction in the number of marriages following pregnancy and a rise in nonmarital fertility; see "An Analysis of Out-of-Wedlock Childbearing in the United States," *Quarterly Journal of Economics* 111, no. 2 (May 1996): 277–317.

[94]Robert D. Plotnick, Irwin Garfinkel, Sara S. McLanahan, and Inhoe Ku, "The Impact of Child Support Enforcement Policy on Nonmarital Childbearing," *Journal of Policy Analysis and Management* 26, no. 1 (Winter 2007): 79–98; and Anna Aizer and Sara McLanahan, "The Impact of Child Support Enforcement on Fertility, Parental Investments, and Child Well-Being," *Journal of Human Resources* 41, no. 1 (Winter 2006): 28–45.

[95]Karen Benjamin Guzzo, "New Partners, More Kids: Multiple-Partner Fertility in the United States," *Annals of the American Academy of Political Science* 654, no. 1 (July 2014): 61–86. For a theoretical perspective, see Robert J. Willis, "A Theory of Out-of-Wedlock Childbearing," *Journal of Political Economy* 107, no. S6 (December 1999): S33–64.

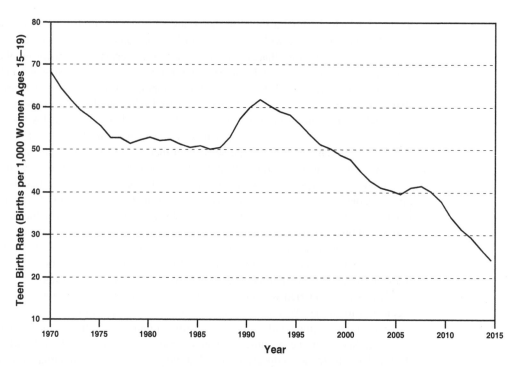

FIGURE 13-3 Teen Birth Rate (Births per 1,000 Women Ages 15–19), 1970–2014

Sources: National Center for Health Statistiics, "National and State Patterns of Teen Births in the United States 1940–2013," *National Vital Statistics Reports 63, no. 4* (August 20, 2014) and "Births: Final Data for 2014," *National Vital Statistics Reports* 64, no. 12 (December 23, 2015).

occurs when a man or a woman has children with more than one partner. While multipartner fertility may occur through the process of marriage, divorce, and remarriage, it is most common among women and men who have a first child born outside of marriage. As discussed in the next chapter, not only does this trend increase the complexity of family structure—for example, blended (step-parent) families and siblings living in different households—it also has practical implications, such as making the collection of child support from noncustodial parents more complicated.

Teen Births

The figure that continues to receive perhaps the greatest attention is the rate of teen births in the United States, which is considerably higher than in other economically advanced countries.[96] Figure 13-3 provides trends for 1970 through 2014. Although the US teen birth rate remains quite high, it has declined substantially since the early 1990s, from a high of 61.8 births per 1,000 teens to a historic low of 24.2 births per 1,000 teens in 2014. Despite this encouraging trend, the level of teen births remains a particular concern because these young women, the majority of whom are unmarried, have not yet had an opportunity to fully build their human capital, so their incomes are often low and likely to remain so.

Teen pregnancy and births to unmarried teens are, in part, related to economic factors, including poor labor market prospects, which lower the opportunity cost of

---

[96]Melissa S. Kearney and Phillip B. Levine, "Why Is the Teen Birth Rate in the United States So High and Why Does It Matter?" *Journal of Economic Perspectives* 26, no. 2 (Spring 2012): 141–66.

pregnancy for some young women.[97] It has also been suggested that a host of public policies may affect rates of teenage childbearing. Policies often cited that might reduce teen births include abstinence education, mandatory sex education, stricter abortion rules, family planning benefits through Medicaid, and less generous welfare benefits. Notably, one study, which sought to explain the decline in the US teen birth rate from 1991 to 2008, found that only two of these policies—reduced welfare generosity and expanded family planning access—played a role, and together they could account only for 12 percent of the total decline. For the more recent period from 2008 to 2012, these same authors further found that the Great Recession, which increased unemployment rates, as well as the US television program titled *16 and Pregnant*, which expanded teens' awareness about the challenges of being very young parents, had a dampening effect on fertility. These specific factors, however, cannot explain the concurrent decline in teen births that occurred outside of the United States. They also point to broader (non-US-specific) explanations including the increased use of LARCs and women's rising educational attainment, which are both expected to decrease fertility.[98]

Births to Older Mothers

A final interesting trend revealed by Table 13-5 is the substantial rise in birth rates among women age 35 and older since 1980. Birth rates of older women are now higher than they were in 1970, substantially so for both women aged 35 to 39 and those aged 40 to 44. In fact, the *share* of births to women over age 35 now exceeds the share of births to teens.[99] While the table indicates birth rates for women over age 35 were also fairly high in 1970, there are important differences. In earlier years, older mothers tended to be women with large families who started their childbearing in their 20s and continued to have children into their 30s and even into their early 40s. As discussed earlier, especially with the delay in fertility associated with increased educational attainment, women are now much more likely to begin their childbearing at later ages. Another major difference is that a rising share of these births are to unmarried mothers. Since 1980, there has been a threefold increase in the unmarried birth rate for women aged 35 to 39 and aged 40 to 44.[100] Many of these births are to very highly educated women, including those with M.D.s and Ph.D.s.[101]

---

[97]Kearney and Levine, "Why Is the Teen Birth Rate?" For earlier work, see Barbara Wolfe, Kathryn Wilson, and Robert Haveman, "The Role of Economic Incentives in Teenage Nonmarital Childbearing Choices," *Journal of Public Economics* 81, no. 3 (September 2001): 473–511.

[98]See Melissa S. Kearney and Phillip B. Levine, "Teen Births Are Falling: What's Going On?" *Policy Brief* (Washington, DC: Brookings Institution, March 2014). For evidence on the effect of LARCs during the latter period, see Nicholas Bakar, "Unplanned Pregnancies Hit Lowest Level in 30 Years," *New York Times*, March 7, 2016.

[99]Livingston and Cohn, "The New Demography of American Motherhood."

[100]Reproductive technology such as in vitro fertilization (IVF), which especially enhances older women's chances of bearing children, is very costly; such births are more common in states that require private insurance companies to cover such costs. See Lucie Schmidt and Marianne P. Bitler, "Utilization of Infertility Treatments: The Effects of Insurance Mandates," *Demography* 49, no. 1 (February 2012): 124–49.

[101]Gretchen Livingston, "Childlessness Falls, Family Size Grows among Highly Educated Women," Pew Research Center, May 7, 2015, www.pewresearch.org; "Having It All, and Then Some: Why the Best-Educated Women Are Opting for More Children," *The Economist*, May 23, 2015; and Qingyan Shang and Bruce A. Weinberg, "Opting for Families: Recent Trends in the Fertility of Highly Educated Women," *Journal of Population Economics* 26, no. 1 (January 2013): 5–32.

Conclusion

This chapter examined economic explanations for the changing American family. We have seen that in the past a major economic motivation for individuals to marry was to reap gains from specialization in production. Today, as a result of rising women's wages and the growing availability of household appliances and market substitutes for household production, the gains to specialization have been greatly eroded. The decline in the gains to specialization reduces the economic benefits to marriage. As we saw in this chapter, although marriage remains central to the lives of most Americans, many individuals are delaying marriage, and marriage rates are falling. Moreover, it is likely that marriage, when it does occur, is increasingly based on the shared gains in consumption, rather than specialization. The move away from marriage is also reflected in a rise in opposite-sex cohabitation as well as a rise in single parenthood. While single parenthood may arise after divorce or widowhood, the major source of the increase has been a rise in nonmarital fertility. One striking recent development is that, after a long period of substantial increase, the nonmarital birth rate has modestly declined since 2010. As a result, the often-cited figure of unmarried births as a share of all births has levelled off at around 40 percent. The broad trends reviewed here, as well as the increase in same-sex couples (who are now permitted to marry throughout the United States) have contributed to an increase in the diversity of living arrangements. In the next chapter, we look at the implications of recent changes in family structure on the well-being of children and families.

Questions for Review and Discussion

1. Describe the main changes in the typical family in the United States over the past 30–40 years and explain their causes.

2. Women's rising labor force participation might either increase or reduce marriage rates. Explain why the effect could go either way.

3. A negative relationship is observed between women's labor force participation and fertility. Is higher labor force participation the cause of the lower birth rate or vice versa? Discuss.

4. Increasing numbers of children are being raised in families in which mothers are cohabiting, either with the child's father or with a boyfriend. Consider the pros and cons for children of these arrangements versus living with a single parent.

5. In what ways are marriage and cohabitation similar, and in what ways do they differ?

6. What are the advantages and disadvantages of the rising age at first marriage?

7. Women who become mothers when they are teenagers are less likely to obtain a college degree than those who delay their childbearing until at least their mid-20s. Discuss why this outcome is generally the case and what the consequences for these women and their families are likely to be. [*Hint*: Refer back to the human capital model in Chapter 8.]

Internet-Based Data Exercise

The major source of US data on marriage, divorce, cohabitation, and fertility is the National Center for Health Statistics (NCHS), which is part of the Centers for Disease Control (CDC).

Visit the National Center for Health Statistics at http://www.cdc.gov/nchs/.

1. On this website, go to "FastStats." FastStats provides the latest key demographic findings. Update the figures for the marriage rate per 1,000 population and the divorce rate per 1,000 population in Table 13-1. How do the new figures compare?

2. On this website, find the "Marriage and Divorce" page. Find the most recent statistics on marriage rates per 1,000 population and the divorce rate per 1,000 population by *state*. What state has the highest and lowest rates for each? What about the state in which you are presently located? Discuss these statistics and the general pattern you see across states.

Suggested Readings

Amato, Paul R., Alan Booth, Susan M. McHale, and Jennifer Van Hook, eds. *Families in an Era of Increasing Inequality: Diverging Destinies*. New York: Springer, 2015.

Bailey, Martha J., and Thomas A. DiPrete, "Five Decades of Remarkable Change in U.S. Women's Economic and Social Status." *Russell Sage Foundation Journal of the Social Sciences* 2, no. 4 (2016): 1–32.

Black, Dan A., Seth G. Sanders, and Lowell J. Taylor. "The Economics of Lesbian and Gay Families." *Journal of Economic Perspectives* 21, no. 2 (Spring 2007): 53–70.

Carlson, Marcia, and Paula England, eds. *Social Class and Changing Families in an Unequal America*. Stanford, CA: Stanford University Press, 2011.

Cherlin, Andrew. *The Marriage Go-Round*. New York: Knopf, 2009.

Ellwood, David T., and Christopher Jencks. "The Spread of Single-Parent Families in the United States since 1960." In *The Future of the Family*, edited by Daniel P. Moynihan, Timothy M. Smeeding, and Lee Rainwater, 25–65. New York: Russell Sage Foundation, 2004.

England, Paula, and Kathryn Edin, eds. *Unmarried Couples with Children*. New York: Russell Sage Foundation, 2007.

Furstenberg, Frank F. "Fifty Years of Family Change: From Consensus to Complexity." *Annals of the American Academy of Political and Social Science* 654 (July 2014): 12–30.

Grossbard, Shoshana. *The Marriage Motive: A Price Theory of Marriage. How Marriage Markets Affect Employment, Consumption, and Savings*. New York: Springer, 2015.

Lundberg, Shelly, Robert A. Pollak, and Jenna E. Stearns. "Family Inequality: Diverging Patterns in Marriage, Cohabitation, and Childbearing." *Journal of Economic Perspectives* 30, no. 2 (April 2016): 79–101.

Ruggles, Steven. "Patriarchy, Power, and Pay: The Transformation of American Families, 1800–2015." *Demography* 52, no. 6 (December 2015): 1797–1823.

Sawhill, Isabel. *Generation Unbound: Drifting into Sex and Parenthood without Marriage.* Washington, DC: Brookings Institution Press, 2014.

Stevenson, Betsey, and Justin Wolfers. "Marriage and Divorce: Changes and Their Driving Forces." *Journal of Economic Perspectives* 21, no. 2 (Spring 2007): 27–52.

Key Terms

shared consumption (350)

public goods (350)

economies of scale (350)

risk-pooling (350)

marriage-specific capital (350)

long-acting reversible contraceptive (LARC) (351)

marriageable men (353)

no-fault divorce (360)

unilateral divorce (360)

opposite-sex cohabitation (363)

serial cohabitation (364)

same-sex couples (366)

fertility (367)

demand for children (367)

opportunity cost of time (367)

child quality (368)

child quantity (368)

total fertility rate (369)

baby boom (369)

Baby Boomers (369)

Generation X (371)

Millennials (371)

multipartner fertility (375)

The Changing American Family and Implications for Family Well-Being

14

CHAPTER HIGHLIGHTS

- Changing Family Structure
- Poverty: Incidence and Measurement
- Implications for Children's Well-Being

In this chapter, we look at the relationship between the changes that have occurred in the American family and the economic well-being of family members. As we shall see, family structure has substantial implications for the well-being of individuals and their families, in terms of both economic status and consequences for children's development. Thus, after reviewing changes in family structure, we provide an in-depth consideration of the incidence and measurement of poverty, highlighting the particular challenges faced by female-headed families. We conclude by reviewing the literature on the effect of maternal employment on children's development and the effects of income and family structure on measures of children's future success. The policy issues raised by changing family structure are discussed in the next chapter.

Changing Family Structure

The US labor force was once composed almost entirely of workers with few, if any, responsibilities for homemaking. The majority were married men with wives who were full-time homemakers, while most of the others were single. Today the labor force includes a growing proportion of workers from **dual-earner married-couple families**, in which both husbands and wives participate in the paid labor force, and from **single-parent families**, generally mothers and their children.

Dual-Earner Married-Couple Families

Among married couples, dual-earner couples have replaced the breadwinner husband–homemaker wife as the dominant paradigm, as shown in Figure 14-1, which provides employment trends for husbands and wives in married couples with children. The share of dual-earner families rose from 54 percent in 1976 (the first year for which data are available) to nearly 70 percent in 1990, and then it effectively plateaued, increasing slightly to 70.6 percent by 2000. The share subsequently declined to 64 percent in 2010 (not shown in the figure) and remained at that level through 2014. This trend (especially the rise and subsequent plateau in the 1990s) closely mirrors the trend in married women's labor force participation that we reviewed in Chapters 5 and 6.

Figure 14-1 also shows that the decline in dual-earner couples between 2000 and 2014 was offset by rising shares of husband-only employed, wife-only employed, and neither spouse employed families. Husband-only employed families (often viewed as synonymous with stay-at-home mother families) rose from 24 percent to nearly 28 percent, wife-only employed families (often viewed as synonymous with stay-at-home father families) rose from 3.2 to 4.5 percent, and couples in which neither spouse was employed rose from 2.1 to 3.4 percent.[1]

The aforementioned trends are of interest, but the bottom line remains that, in 2014, dual-earner families comprised the majority of married couples with children. Additional

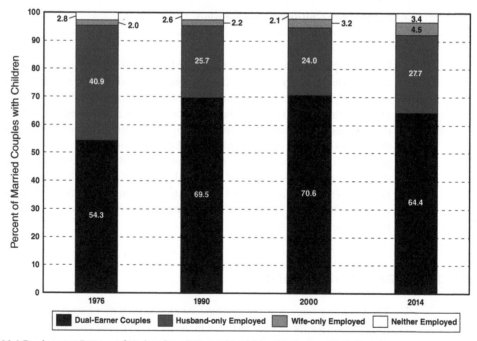

FIGURE 14-1 Employment Patterns of Husbands and Wives with Children Under Age 18, Selected Years, 1976 to 2014, in percent

Note: Employed is defined as having positive earnings.
Sources: US Census Bureau, Table FINC-04, "Presence of Related Children Under 18 Years Old—Married Couple Families, by Total Money Income and Work Experience, Race and Hispanic Origin of Reference Person" (2000 and 2014); and US Census Bureau, "Work Experience of Husband and Wife—Married Couple Families, "Tables F-14, F-15, and F-17 (1976 and 1990); accessed May 11, 2016, www.census.gov.

---

[1]For discussions, see D'Vera Cohn, Gretchen Livingston, and Wendy Wang, "After Decades of Decline, a Rise in Stay-at-Home Mothers," Pew Research Center, April 18, 2014; and Gretchen Livingston, "Growing Number of Dads Home with the Kids: Biggest Increase among Those Caring for Family," Pew Research Center, June 5, 2014, www.pewresearch.org.

data indicate that the labor force commitment of wives in such families is often quite substantial, as is their contribution to family income. For example, in 2014, both spouses worked full-time, full-year in nearly half of dual-earner families. And married women's earnings are an important source of family income today. All told, the incomes of dual-earner married couples are, on average, 50 percent higher than those with just an employed husband.[2] Over time, women's financial contribution to married-couple families has expanded as a result of the factors that we have discussed in earlier chapters—women's rising labor force attachment, improved qualifications, and increasing labor market opportunities.

Another consequence of labor market advancements for women, in conjunction with declines in the real earnings of less educated men, is that the percentage of wives with higher annual earnings than their husbands also increased, from just 16 percent in 1981 to 28 percent by 2014.[3] Researchers have taken a closer look at this trend and its implications. One dimension investigated is whether, in families in which wives earn more than their husbands, wives outearn their husbands year after year or whether the pattern is more transitory. Looking at a 3-year period, one study finds that, for a vast majority of couples (60 percent) the pattern persists for all 3 years.[4] One would expect women's bargaining power in the family—which depends in part on earnings—to be greater in couples where this pattern is more permanent.

Perhaps not surprisingly there is some evidence that a wife who outearns her husband conflicts with enduring norms about women's gender-appropriate roles and that this role conflict may influence wives' behavior. For example, one study finds that a wife whose earnings are predicted to be greater than her husband's is less likely to participate in the labor force, all else equal, and that, if she does work, she earns less than predicted, in part due to lower work hours. Possibly, she may reduce her hours worked to hold down her earnings. Moreover, the wife spends more time in household tasks, perhaps to make the situation more acceptable to her husband.[5] This last finding is particularly surprising given that the theory of comparative advantage, which we explored in Chapter 3, would lead us to expect the opposite—as the wife's relative earnings increased she would spend less time on household tasks. The study also reports that couples in which the wife earns more than her husband tend to be less happy and more likely to divorce.

The findings described above are certainly concerning; however, it is possible that the strength of this gender norm may be diminishing. First, as we have seen, the share of married-couple families in which the wife outearns her husband has been growing and, in such couples, the female earnings advantage tends to be permanent. Second, a related study, which we discussed in Chapter 13, finds that married couples formed since the early 1990s in which the wife holds the educational advantage are less prone to divorce then earlier cohorts and are now no longer more likely to divorce than couples in which the husband has the educational advantage. This suggests a shifting pattern regarding divorce, at least in terms of educational

---

[2]These figures are from US Census Bureau, "Presence of Related Children under 18 Years Old—Married Couple Families, by Total Money Income in 2014, Work Experience in 2014, Race and Hispanic Origin of Reference Person," table FINC-04 (accessed February 12, 2016), www.census.gov.

[3]Figure is from US Census Bureau, "Married-Couple Families with Wives' Earning Greater than Husbands' Earnings: 1981 to 2014 (Selected Years)" table F-22 (accessed February 12, 2016), www.census.gov. For discussion, see Sara B. Raley, Marybeth J. Mattingly, and Suzanne M. Bianchi, "How Dual Are Dual-Income Couples? Documenting Change from 1970 to 2001," *Journal of Marriage and Family* 68 (February 2006): 11–28.

[4]Anne E. Winkler, Timothy D. McBride, and Courtney Andrews, "Wives Who Outearn Their Husbands: A Transitory or Persistent Phenomenon for Couples?" *Demography* 42, no. 3 (August 2005): 523–35.

[5]Marianne Bertrand, Emir Kamenica, and Jessica Pan, "Gender Identity and Relative Income within Households," *Quarterly Journal of Economics* 130, no. 3 (2015): 571–614. For a useful summary, see Marianne Bertrand, Emir Kamenica, and Jessica Pan, "Economic Consequences of Gender Identity," VOX CEPR's Policy Portal, April 13, 2015, voxeu.org.

differences between spouses.[6] Third, and consistent with this, attitudes seem to be becoming more permissive along this dimension. A 2013 attitude survey found that only 28 percent of adults agreed that "It's generally better for a marriage if the husband earns more than his wife" compared to 40 percent in 1997. College graduates had especially permissive views, with only 18 percent supporting this statement.[7]

With the increase in women's labor force participation and the rise in dual-earner families, there is the question of how children and employment of a spouse affect women's and men's wages. As reviewed in Chapter 9, some evidence suggests that employed women with children earn less than their childless counterparts, even after accounting for differences in work experience, while married men appear to receive an earnings boost from being married and fatherhood. There is also evidence that wives' wages, especially, may suffer to the extent that typically husbands' careers are given precedence, thereby limiting wives' job opportunities.

Another important issue is what effect, if any, women's increasing labor force participation and the rise in dual-earner families has had on trends in earnings inequality among families. Evidence indicates that family earnings inequality has increased substantially since the 1980s. The primary factor producing this increase has been the pronounced rise in male earnings inequality we discussed in Chapter 10. It is possible that women's rising labor force participation has served to restrain this rise, or, alternatively, it may have further contributed to it. On the one hand, the larger proportion of wives in the labor force works to reduce income inequality because now there are fewer couples in which the wife has no earnings. On the other hand, the positive association between the earnings of husbands and wives, which has always existed, has grown stronger. The phenomenon that men and women with higher earnings potential tend to be married to one another is called **positive assortative mating**.[8] A number of studies have found that, on net, the rising employment and earnings of wives have led family income inequality to rise less than might have been the case otherwise, though one recent study challenges this conclusion.[9]

Single-Parent Families

Single-parent families are increasingly common in the United States, especially families maintained by mothers.[10] Table 14-1 indicates that, among families with

---

[6]Christine R. Schwartz and Hongyun Han, "The Reversal of the Gender Gap in Education and Trends in Marital Dissolution," *American Sociological Review* 79, no 4. (2014): 605–29. As indicated in the text, this study differed not only in looking at a more recent cohort but also by examining a different measure (educational advantage versus earnings advantage).

[7]Wendy Wang, Kim Parker, and Paul Taylor, "Breadwinner Moms: Mothers Are the Sole or Primary Provider in Four-in-Ten Households with Children; Public Conflicted about the Growing Trend," Pew Research Center, 2013, www.pewresearch.org.

[8]For data and discussion on assortative mating by educational attainment, see Esther Lamidi, Susan L. Brown, and Wendy D. Manning, "Assortative Mating: Educational Homogamy in U.S. Marriages, 1964–2014," FP-15-14, National Center for Family & Marriage Research (2014), http://www.bgsu.edu/ncfmr.html; and Christine R. Schwartz and Robert D. Mare, "Trends in Educational Assortative Marriage from 1940 to 2003," *Demography* 42, no. 4 (November 2005): 621–46.

[9]For recent evidence that women's labor force participation has stemmed rising family inequality, see Dmytro Hryshko, Chinhui Juhn, and Kristin McCue, "Trends in Earnings Inequality and Earnings Instability among U.S. Couples: How Important Is Assortative Matching?" IZA Discussion Paper 8729 (IZA, Bonn, Germany, December 2014). Earlier work that reaches this same conclusion includes Maria Cancian and Deborah Reed, "The Impact of Wives' Earnings on Income Inequality: Issues and Estimates," *Demography* 36, no. 2 (May 1999): 173–84. For recent evidence on the other side, see Jeremy Greenwood, Nezih Guner, Georgi Kocharkov, and Cezar Santos, "Marry Your Like: Assortative Mating and Income Inequality," *American Economic Review* 104, no. 5 (2014): 348–53.

[10]For an excellent discussion, see David T. Ellwood, and Christopher Jencks, "The Spread of Single-Parent Families in the United States Since 1960" in *The Future of the Family*, edited by Daniel P. Moynihan, Timothy M. Smeeding, and Lee Rainwater (New York: Russell Sage Foundation, 2004).

TABLE 14-1 TRENDS IN FAMILIES WITH OWN CHILDREN UNDER AGE 18, 1970–2015

	AS A % OF ALL FAMILIES					
	1970	1980	1990	2000	2010	2015
Mother-Only Families						
All Races	11.5	19.4	24.2	25.8	25.6	25.6
White, Non-Hispanic	8.9	15.1	18.8	19.2	18.9	18.9
Black	33.0	48.7	56.2	55.3	53.6	54.3
Hispanic Origin	n.a.	24.0	29.3	28.4	29.7	28.9
Father-Only Families						
All Races	1.3	2.1	3.9	5.5	4.5	4.9
White, Non-Hispanic	1.2	2.0	3.8	5.4	4.5	5.2
Black	2.6	3.2	4.3	6.1	5.5	5.3
Hispanic Origin	n.a.	1.9	4.0	5.7	4.3	4.3
Married-Couple Families						
All Races	87.1	78.5	71.9	68.7	65.3	64.3
White, Non-Hispanic	89.9	82.9	77.4	75.5	72.8	71.7
Black	64.3	48.1	39.4	38.6	35.4	34.6
Hispanic Origin	n.a.	74.1	66.8	65.9	59.1	59.1
Unmarried-Couple Families						
All Races	n.a.	n.a.	n.a.	n.a.	4.6	5.2
White, Non-Hispanic	n.a.	n.a.	n.a.	n.a.	3.8	4.2
Black	n.a.	n.a.	n.a.	n.a.	5.6	5.8
Hispanic Origin	n.a.	n.a.	n.a.	n.a.	6.9	7.7

Notes: Families include those heading their own households and those living in the households of others (subfamilies). Prior to 2011 unmarried (cohabiting) couples with at least one child under age 18 in common were not separately identified.
Beginning in 2000, data on whites are for white, non-Hispanics. Also, starting in 2000, individuals were able to report more than one race. In this table, whites are defined as persons who selected this race group only, and blacks are defined as persons who selected black alone. For all years, persons of Hispanic origin may be of any race.
n.a. = not available.
Sources: US Census Bureau, detailed tables from www.census.gov: table FM-2, "All Parent/Child Situations by Type, Race, and Hispanic Origin of Householder or Reference Person: 1970 to Present;" table FG10, "Family Groups," (2010 and 2015); table FG5, "One-Parent Family Groups with Own Children Under 18, March 2000;" and table FG7, "Family Groups by Family Type, Sex, and Race and Hispanic Origin, March 2000," www.census.gov.

children, the percentage of mother-only families increased from slightly less than 12 percent in 1970 to 26 percent in 2015, though most of the rise had occurred by 1990. In addition, in 2015 nearly 5 percent of families were father-only families, a figure that has quintupled since 1970. Prior to 2000, cohabiting couples with children were included in the count of mother-only or father-only families. However, given the rise in cohabitation discussed in Chapter 13, starting in 2010 data for this group are now shown separately. Table 14-1 shows that cohabiting couples comprised just over 5 percent of families with children in 2015.

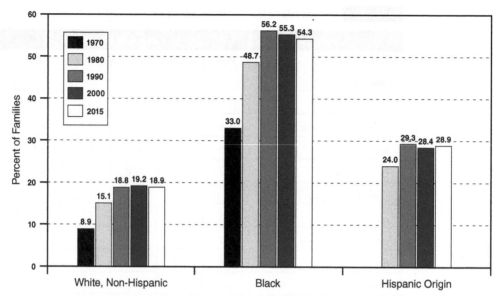

FIGURE 14-2 Mother-Only Families by Race and Ethnicity, 1970–2015 (%)

Note: Source and notes are provided in Table 14-1.

Historically, mother-only families have been more common among blacks, and this pattern remained true in 2015. For blacks, mother-only families represented 54 percent of families with children compared to 19 percent of white, non-Hispanic and 29 percent of Hispanic families. However, there have been important shifts in the trends, as shown in Figure 14-2 and Table 14-1. Since 1990, the share of mother-only families among blacks has slightly declined, while rates have effectively stabilized for non-Hispanic whites and Hispanics.

Single-parent families raise concerns about children's well-being. These families tend to have lower incomes, and, even after accounting for income, children growing up with a single parent may not do as well as children raised by two biological parents in a number of dimensions. These topics are covered further in the next sections.

Poverty: Incidence and Measurement

Table 14-2 shows the income and poverty status of families with children in 2014. Most strikingly, the median income of female-headed families was only one-third that of married couples. Nearly 40 percent of female-headed families were poor compared to around 8 percent of married couples. Poverty rates were particularly high for black and Hispanic female-headed families, with 46 percent of both groups living in poverty. Even among white, non-Hispanic female-headed families, the poverty rate was 32 percent. The rates for 2014 remain higher than prior to the Great Recession. As a point of comparison, in 2006, the poverty rate for female-headed families was 36.5 percent and the rate for married-couple families was 6.4 percent.[11]

---

[11]US Census Bureau, Historical Poverty Tables, table POV04, "Families by Age of Household, Number of Children, and Family Structure: 2006," accessed April 22, 2016, www.census.gov.

TABLE 14-2 INCOME AND POVERTY RATES FOR FAMILIES WITH CHILDREN, 2014[a]	PERCENT IN POVERTY 2014	MEDIAN INCOME ($) 2014
All Families	17.6	63,767
White, Non-Hispanic	10.8	80,271
Black	31.4	36,790
Asian	11.1	89,988
Hispanic Origin	27.8	41,363
Type of Family		
Married-Couple Families	8.2	87,420
Male Householder, No Wife Present	22.0	41,436
Female Householder, No Husband Present	39.8	26,374
White, Non-Hispanic	32.0	30,418
Black	45.6	23,559
Asian	27.8	36,017
Hispanic Origin	46.3	22,991

[a]Figures are for families heading their own households, with related children under age 18.
Notes: White, non-Hispanic refers to those who reported their race as white alone and reported Hispanic origin. Black (Asian) includes those who reported this race alone or in combination with one or more other race groups. Persons of Hispanic origin may be of any race.
Source: US Census Bureau, table 4, "Poverty Status of Families, by Type of Family, Presence of Related Children, Race, and Hispanic Origin: 1959 to 2014;" and FINC-03, "Presence of Related Children under 18 Years Old—All Families by Total Money Income in 2014, Type of Family, Experience in 2014, Race and Hispanic Origin of Reference Person," www.census.gov.

Inevitably, the high rates of poverty among single-parent families are a major factor behind the high rates of poverty for children overall. In 2014, 20.7 percent of all children—nearly 12 percent of white, non-Hispanic, 31 percent of Hispanic, and 36 percent of black children—lived in poverty.[12]

When interpreting poverty statistics, it is important to understand the way the **official poverty rate** is calculated. A family is defined as poor if their income falls below a specified threshold. In the official poverty measure, established in the 1960s, *income* refers to cash income. The threshold is based on consumption patterns in the 1950s, when food was one-third of total consumption expenditures, and is updated annually to account for inflation. In 1995, a major national report documented the inadequacies of this measure.[13] On the one hand, the income measure used to determine poverty status does not include such items as food stamps and the Earned Income Tax Credit (EITC), so it understates the total resources available to the

---

[12]US Census Bureau, Historical Poverty Tables, table 3, "Poverty Status of People by Age, Race, and Hispanic Origin: 1959 to 2014," accessed April 22, 2016, www.census.gov. For a discussion, see Bruce Western, Deirdre Bloome, Benjamin Sosnaud, and Laura M. Tach, "Trends in Income Insecurity among U.S. Children, 1984–2010," *Demography* 53, no. 2 (April 2016): 419–48.
[13]For more on poverty measurement, see Robert Haveman, Rebecca Blank, Robert Moffitt, Timothy Smeeding, and Geoffrey Wallace, "The War on Poverty: Measurement, Trends, and Policy," *Journal of Policy Analysis and Management* 34, no. 3 (Summer 2015): 593–638.

low-income families that receive these benefits. On the other hand, although the poverty threshold is updated to account for inflation, it ignores the fact that the pattern of consumer expenditures has changed considerably since the 1950s; for instance, today food is only about one-seventh of expenditures, on average.

In 2010, after much study, the federal government introduced the **Supplemental Poverty Measure (SPM)**, which addresses these criticisms. In the SPM, the threshold is calculated using information on expenditures on food, clothing, shelter, and utilities for those at the 33rd percentile of the income distribution, with additional allowance for discretionary expenditures. The figure is adjusted for regional differences in housing costs as well as for whether the family owns or rents. The SPM modifies the calculation of income by including the value of food stamps and the EITC and by deducting work-related expenses such as the cost of childcare and out-of-pocket medical expenses. Finally, another notable difference in calculating family poverty is that, unlike the official poverty measure, the SPM assumes that cohabiting couples are a single unit (akin to a married couple) and therefore that the cohabitors' incomes are pooled. The SPM is now tracked alongside the official poverty rate, though the official poverty rate continues to be the major indicator of the economic status of those at the bottom of the income distribution. As just one point of comparison, the poverty rate for all persons in 2014 was calculated to be 15.3 percent using the SPM and 14.9 percent using the official measure.[14] While this difference does not appear all that large at a point in time, *trends* in poverty rates differ considerably, depending on the measure used. Using this alternative measure, which is arguably superior at measuring resources and needs, poverty rates have declined since the mid-1960s, rather than appearing relatively unchanged, as shown by trends in the official poverty measure. This finding is important because it suggests that the increased generosity of government transfer programs has been effective at reducing poverty.[15]

Returning to the patterns shown in Table 14-2, it is not difficult to understand why the incomes of single-parent families are so much lower than those of married-couple families. First, they have a lower ratio of adults to children and, thus, fewer potential earners. This also means that they have fewer caregivers per dependent, making it far more difficult for the adult to do justice to both work and family and, thus, potentially lowering the adult's earnings. Second, as implied by our discussion of marriage and fertility patterns in Chapter 13, the incidence of female-headed families is higher among the less educated, which further contributes to the lower income of such families.[16] Third, women tend to earn considerably less than men with comparable qualifications, and mothers tend to accumulate less labor force experience than other workers.

Single mothers may live independently or in extended households, with their parents (their children's grandparents), other relatives, or an unmarried male partner (cohabit). Doubling up with parents does involve some loss of privacy but also

---

[14]These figures are from US Census Bureau, "The Supplemental Poverty Measure: 2014," table 2, *Current Population Report* P60-264 (September 2014).

[15]See Liana Fox, Irwin Garfinkel, Neeraj Kaushal, Jane Waldfogel, and Christopher Wimer, "Waging War on Poverty: Historical Trends in Poverty Using the Supplemental Poverty Measure," *Journal of Policy Analysis and Management* 34, no. 1 (Summer 2015): 567–92.

[16]For recent evidence, see Sara McLanahan and Christopher Jencks, "Was Moynihan Right? What Happens to Children of Unmarried Mothers?" *Education Next* (Spring 2015): 14–20; and Wendy Wang, Kim Parker, and Paul Taylor, "Breadwinner Moms," Pew Research Center, May 29, 2013, www.pewresearch.org. The seminal paper that first pointed to the divergence in this and other outcomes by educational attainment is Sara McLanahan, "Diverging Destinies: How Children Are Faring under the Second Demographic Transition," *Demography* 4, no. 1 (2004): 607–27.

reduces costs because of economies of scale. In addition, other household members often provide financial assistance and emotional support as well as in-house child-care.[17] In the case of unmarried couples with children, one would suspect that there is a good deal of income sharing. The official poverty rate assumes that no such sharing occurs, but as noted earlier, income sharing is assumed in the computation of the newly developed poverty measure, the SPM. Studies have found that the poverty rate for children in cohabiting families would decline if cohabitors' incomes were taken into account, but nonetheless many of these families would remain poor, principally because the male partners often have low income themselves.[18]

The economic circumstances of families maintained by women also vary considerably depending on the woman's age and marital status. Never-married mothers tend to have particularly low incomes, in part because they tend to be younger and have less education, and also because they are less likely than divorced mothers to receive child support from absent fathers. Women who become parents as teenagers, most of whom are not married, tend to remain at a pronounced economic and social disadvantage throughout their lives. Many have little education and, if employed, generally earn low wages. At first, researchers assumed that it was early childbearing itself that led to these negative outcomes. Subsequently, however, studies suggested that many of these women would not have done particularly well even if they had delayed childbearing until their 20s because many are, themselves, from economically and socially disadvantaged backgrounds. While the research evidence to date is mixed, it does appear that early childbearing, per se, does have some detrimental effect on the economic status of these young women.[19]

Divorced mothers tend to fare somewhat better than never-married mothers because they are more likely to receive child support from nonresident fathers. Nonetheless, as of 2013, only 58 percent of divorced mothers were awarded child support (compared to just 42 percent of never-married mothers) and only 57 percent received full payment (compared to just 34 percent for never-married mothers).[20] One study

[17]For a broader discussion on doubling up, see Natasha V. Pilkauskas, Irving Garfinkel, and Sara S. McLanahan, "The Prevalence and Economic Value of Doubling Up," *Demography* 51, no. 5 (2014): 1667–76. For a discussion on financial transfers between parents and their adult children and how these patterns have changed over time, see Joan R. Kahn, Frances Goldscheider, and Javier García-Manglano, "Growing Parental Economic Power in Parent–Adult Child Households: Coresidence and Financial Dependency in the United States, 1960–2010," *Demography* 50 (2013): 1449–75.

[18]See Susan L. Brown, Wendy D. Manning, and Krista K. Payne, "Family Structure and Children's Economic Well-Being: Incorporating Same-Sex Cohabiting Mother Families," *Population Research and Policy Review* 35, no. 1 (February 2016): 1–21. The text refers to figures from table 1 on poverty rates for children in opposite-sex cohabiting families. The study also provides estimates for children in cohabiting same-sex mother families. Regarding income sharing, see also Steven J. Haider and Kathleen McGarry, "Recent Trends in Resource Sharing among the Poor," in *Working and Poor: How Economic and Policy Changes Are Affecting Low-Wage Workers*, ed. Rebecca M. Blank, Sheldon H. Danziger, and Robert F. Schoeni (New York: Russell Sage Foundation, 2006), 205–32.

[19]For a very readable exposition of alternative research methods and why they might reach different conclusions, see Christina J. Diaz and Jeremey E. Fiel, "The Effects of Teen Pregnancy: Reconciling Theory, Methods, and Findings," *Demography* 53, no. 1 (February 2016): 85–116. See also Saul D. Hoffman and Rebecca A. Maynard, eds., *Kids Having Kids: Economic Costs & Social Consequences of Teen Pregnancy*, 2nd ed. (Washington, DC: Urban Institute, 2009). Less studied is the effect of teen fatherhood, though one study identifies negative consequences on own educational attainment; see Barbara Wolfe and Jason Fletcher, "The Effects of Teen Fatherhood on Young Adult Outcomes," *Economic Inquiry* 50, no. 1 (January 2012): 182–201.

[20]Timothy Grall, US Census Bureau, "Custodial Mothers and Fathers and Their Child Support, 2013," *Current Population Report* P-60-255 (January 2016), table 2. Regarding the effect of child support on income, see Maria Cancian and Daniel R. Meyer, "Child Support and the Economy," in Blank, Danziger, and Schoeni, eds., *Working and Poor*, 338–65.

found that after the first year of divorce, children's family income was 40 percent lower, on average, than if their parents had stayed together. After 6 years, their economic situation was somewhat better, and their postdivorce family income was only 20 percent lower on average, though the latter figure varies considerably depending on whether the mother remarries.[21]

Implications for Children's Well-Being

In this section we look at the implications of the changing American family on the well-being of children. First, we focus on the relationship between mother's employment and children's well-being. Next, we look at the consequences of economic disadvantage for children. As we have seen, a much higher fraction of children in single-parent families live in poverty compared to those who live with both parents. Low income not only translates into fewer household resources, which in the most dire situation may lead to a lack of food or homelessness, but may also affect children's achievement and behavioral outcomes. Finally, we look at how family structure affects children's outcomes, after accounting for differences in income.

Maternal Employment, Childcare, and Children's Outcomes

The increased labor force participation of married women with infants and small children, along with the rise in single-mother families, has prompted considerable and continuing research on the effect of maternal employment on children's development. This question became all the more important with the passage of the 1996 federal welfare legislation, which requires single (and married) parents to seek employment as a condition for receiving welfare benefits. In principle, the question should be asked about parental rather than just maternal employment, but it is still commonly accepted that the father will be working for pay full-time, as is still generally the case. Even so, some limited attention is now being paid to the influence of fathers' employment as well.[22]

As would be expected, research clearly shows that children's development is determined by a great many factors in addition to mother's employment. These factors include the sex and other innate characteristics of each child; the number of children in the family; the family's level of resources; parents' characteristics, such as their level of educational attainment and their sensitivity and responsiveness to the children's needs; the role of their father, of other family members, and of close friends in the children's lives; the quality of their alternative care; and last, but by no

---

[21]Marianne E. Page and Ann Huff Stevens, "The Economic Consequences of Absent Parents," *Journal of Human Resources* 39, no. 1 (Winter 2004): 80–107. See also Laura M. Tach and Alicia Eads, "Trends in the Economic Consequences of Marital and Cohabitation Dissolution in the United States," *Demography* 52, no. 2 (April 2015): 401–32.

[22]See, for instance, Susan L. Averett, Lisa A. Gennetian, and H. Elizabeth Peters, "Paternal Child Care and Children's Development," *Journal of Population Economics* 18, no. 3 (September 2005): 391–414; Christopher J. Ruhm, "Parental Employment and Child Cognitive Development," *Journal of Human Resources* 39, no. 1 (Winter 2004): 155–92; Joseph H. Pleck, "Why Could Father Involvement Benefit Children? Theoretical Perspectives," *Applied Development Science* 11, no. 4 (December 2007): 196–202; and Maureen R. Waller, "Family Man in the Other America: New Opportunities, Motivations, and Supports for Paternal Caregiving," *Annals of the American Academy of Political and Social Science* 624 (July 2009): 156–76.

means least, the nature of the community where they live. In addition, many aspects of children's development merit consideration other than merely test scores, educational attainment, and whether a girl becomes pregnant in her teens, the criteria most frequently employed by economists to gauge child outcomes. Social and emotional development is obviously important as well, as are such long-term outcomes as the stability of their marriages and their success in raising their own children. Again, the evidence shows that many different factors influence these various outcomes.[23]

It is also important to remember, as discussed in Chapter 4, that while employed mothers spend less time directly engaged with their children than those who are not employed, the difference tends to be fairly modest. Among the reasons, many mothers work only part-time or take time from their own leisure activities to spend time with their children. In addition, increasing numbers of children attend preschool and hence are not at home, even if their mother is not employed. Another point to be kept in mind is that, as discussed in Chapter 4, parental time spent with children has been rising since the mid-1980s; this is true for all mothers, both married and single, employed and nonemployed. Fathers in two-parent families are spending more time with their children as well.[24]

The general consensus among researchers is that children between the ages of 2 and 4 tend to do better both cognitively and socially when they are cared for in childcare centers than children cared for entirely at home.[25] For those in the first year of life, however, the evidence has been more mixed, with some studies, in particular, finding negative effects on children's later cognitive development when their mother is employed.[26] An important qualification is that studies that reach this conclusion are often not able to fully account for the quality of nonmaternal care, which might attenuate any negative effects. Also, maternal employment provides additional economic resources to the families, which tend to benefit children and might help to offset any negative effects of such employment. Finally, researchers in this field and those interpreting their findings face the challenge that factors affecting children's outcomes are highly interrelated, making it extremely difficult to isolate the influence of a single factor.[27]

---

[23]For a review of the issues, see Jack P. Shonkoff and Deborah A. Phillips, eds., *From Neurons to Neighborhoods: The Science of Early Child Development* (Washington, DC: National Research Council, 2000), esp. chaps. 10 and 11; and Christopher J. Ruhm, "Maternal Employment and Child Development," in *Handbook of Family and Work*, ed. D. Russell Crane and E. Jeffrey Hill (Lanham, MD: University Press of America, 2009), 331–54.

[24]This discussion is drawn from Suzanne M. Bianchi, "Maternal Employment and Time with Children: Dramatic Change or Surprising Continuity?" *Demography* 37, no. 4 (November 2000): 401–14. Chapter 4 discusses recent trends.

[25]For reviews of findings, see Jane Waldfogel, *What Children Need* (Cambridge, MA: Harvard University Press, 2006); and Rachel G. Lucas-Thompson, Wendy A. Goldberg, and JoAnn Prause, "Maternal Work Early in the Lives of Children and Its Distal Associations with Achievement and Behavior Problems: A Meta-Analysis," *Psychological Bulletin* 36, no. 6 (2010): 915–42.

[26]For an overview of the findings, see Waldfogel, *What Children Need*, chaps. 2 and 3; and Jeanne Brooks-Gunn, Wen-Jui Han, and Jane Waldfogel, "First-Year Maternal Employment and Child Development in the First Seven Years," *Monographs of the Society for Research in Child Development* 75, no. 2 (2010): 1–148.

[27]See, for instance, Tamar Lewin, "A Child Study Is a Peek. It's Not the Whole Picture," *New York Times*, July 21, 2002, 4; and Shonkoff and Phillips, *From Neurons to Neighborhoods*, chap. 11. Causation between mothers' employment and children's outcomes may go either way. For instance, mothers of children with developmental delays may be slower to return to employment or remain out completely; see Paul Frijters, David W. Johnston, Manisha Shah, and Michael A. Shields, "To Work or Not to Work? Child Development and Maternal Labor Supply," *American Economic Journal: Applied Economics* 1, no. 3 (July 2009): 97–100.

One study which used particularly rich data, including information on key factors mentioned earlier—mother's sensitivity to her child, mother's earnings, and the type and quality of childcare—found that, on net, relative to the alternative of non-employment, part-time maternal employment during the child's first year had no negative effect on measures of children's social, emotional, and cognitive development at ages 1 to 7. Results for women employed full-time were somewhat less favorable than those for women employed part-time. Even this detailed study is not the "last word," however, because the main results obtained were for white non-Hispanic women, and these findings may not be fully generalizable.[28]

As already mentioned, a critical issue is the extent to which the *quality* of non-maternal childcare affects children's development. Studies of specific childcare programs provide evidence on this point. Quality is measured either in terms of institutional features of childcare settings, such as teacher training, group size, and child–teacher ratios, or in terms of children's experiences in childcare, such as how much verbal interaction occurs between children and teachers or whether "developmentally appropriate" activities are provided. As might be expected, programs that tend to be of high quality in one dimension tend to also be of high quality in others. Although findings vary somewhat, evidence indicates that quality of care does matter. For instance, research has found that the amount of verbal interaction between childcare providers and children positively influences children's outcomes, though factors related to the child's own family environment are consistently stronger determinants of their development than attributes of day care.[29]

The conclusion that the quality of childcare matters is also supported by positive results from early intervention programs. Probably the best-known early childhood program aimed at disadvantaged children is Head Start. Numerous studies have evaluated its success. The general consensus is that Head Start has positive effects on children's development while enrolled, but some research has found that achievement test score gains fade out after children leave the program. Investigating these effects is an area of intense research inquiry, especially in light of proposals to dramatically reshape the program.[30] Apart from quality of childcare is the issue of access. Children in low-income families are arguably in the greatest need of quality childcare, but regrettably, they are also the least able to get it because privately purchased quality care is expensive and government-funded programs like Head Start have a limited number of slots.[31]

Turning to adolescents, mothers' employment can have both positive and negative effects on their development. On the one hand, employed mothers provide positive role models, and they bring more income into the household. On the other hand,

---

[28]Brooks-Gunn, Han, and Waldfogel, "First-Year Maternal Employment."

[29]See Shonkoff and Phillips, *From Neurons to Neighborhoods*, chaps, 10 and 11; Chantelle J. Dowsett, Aletha C. Huston, Amy E. Imes, and Lisa Gennetian, "Structural and Process Features in Three Types of Child Care for Children from High and Low Income Families," *Early Childhood Research Quarterly* 2 (2008): 69–93; David Blau and Janet Currie, "Preschool, Day Care, and Afterschool Care: Who's Minding the Kids," in *Handbook of the Economics of Education,* vol. 2, ed. Eric Hanushek and Finis Welch (Amsterdam: North Holland, 2006), chap. 20; and Council of Economic Advisers, *The Economics of Early Childhood Investments* (Washington, DC: Council of Economic Advisers, 2014).

[30]For a review of findings, see Chloe Gibbs, Jens Ludwig, and Doug Miller, "Head Start Origins to Impacts," in *Legacies of the War on Poverty,* ed. Martha Bailey and Sheldon Danziger (New York: Russell Sage Foundation Press, 2013), 39–65.

[31]Jens Ludwig and Deobrah Phillips, "Leave No (Young) Child Behind: Prioritizing Access in Early Childhood Education," in *Investing in Young Children: New Directions in Federal Preschool and Early Childhood Policy*, ed. Ron Haskins and W. Steven Barnett (Washington, DC: Brookings Institution, 2010), 49–58.

adolescents of employed mothers may have more home responsibilities, reducing time for homework, as well as less supervision, possibly leading to more risky behaviors. Evidence regarding the net effect of mothers' employment on adolescent development is mixed, with some studies finding a negative effect and other research finding no effect overall.[32]

Finally, research has looked at the relationship between maternal employment during children's early years and their adult children's employment and time spent in home production. A recent study of individuals in 24 countries for the years 2002 and 2012 finds that adult daughters of employed mothers (compared to those with nonemployed mothers) are more likely to be employed and earn higher wages, among other favorable labor market outcomes, and they spend less time on housework. Adult sons of employed mothers (again compared to those of nonemployed mothers) tend to spend more home time with children.[33] These findings suggest that maternal employment has effects on children that extend beyond the child-raising years and, in fact, has the potential to shift gender roles in the next generation.

Family Economic Disadvantage and Children's Outcomes

An important dimension of economic disadvantage is income. As we have seen, economic disadvantage is also associated with single parenthood and lower levels of education. Considerable research has focused on the relationship between measures of economic disadvantage and children's outcomes. Children raised in lower-income families tend to do worse, on average, on a range of outcomes: achievement test scores, years of school completed, health status, criminal behavior, and teen pregnancy. Part of the impacts may come through family structure (as discussed in the next section), as well as through the negative characteristics of the neighborhoods in which they can afford to live and the poorer quality of the schools that they attend. Children raised in low-income families also tend to experience more stress, whether related to worrying about the next meal or dealing with crowded or poor housing conditions.[34] While a fairly new area of research inquiry, some research also finds a positive relationship between family income and children's non-cognitive (socio-emotional) skills. As we saw in Chapter 9, such skills are highly valued in the labor market, and so children who lack adequate development of these skills are likely to have more difficulties in the future for this reason as well.[35] Finally, as would be expected, the negative effects

---

[32]For discussion and evidence, see Waldfogel, *What Children Need*, chap. 5; Christopher J. Ruhm, "Maternal Employment and Adolescent Development," *Labour Economics* 15 (2008): 958–83; and Robert Crosnoe and Shannon E. Cavanagh, "Families with Children and Adolescents: A Review, Critique, and Future Agenda," *Journal of Marriage and Family* 72 (June 2010): 594–611.

[33]Kathleen L. McGinn, Elizabeth Long Lingo, and Mayra Ruiz Castro, "Mums the Word! Cross-National Relationship between Maternal Employment and Gender Inequalities at Work and at Home," Harvard Business School Working Paper 15-094 (Harvard Business School, Boston, MA, June 2015). See also Claire Cain Miller, "Mounting Evidence of Advantages for Children of Working Mothers," *New York Times*, May 15, 2015.

[34]See Greg J. Duncan, Kathleen M. Ziol-Guest, and Ariel Kalil, "Early Childhood Poverty and Adult Attainment, Behavior, and Health," *Child Development* 81 (2010): 306–25; and Timothy Smeeding, "Multiple Barriers to Economic Opportunity for the 'Truly' Disadvantaged and Vulnerable," *Russell Sage Foundation, Journal of the Social Sciences* 2, no. 2 (May 2016): 98–122; Thomas B. Edsall, "Separated at Birth," *New York Times*, June 9, 2016; and Jane Waldfogel, "Presidential Address: The Next War on Poverty," *Journal of Policy Analysis and Management*, 35, no. 2 (2016): 267–78.

[35]Jason Fletcher and Barbara L. Wolfe, "The Importance of Family Income in the Formation and Evolution of Non-Cognitive Skills in Childhood," NBER Working Paper 22168 (National Bureau of Economic Research, Cambridge, MA, April 2016).

of poverty on a child's outcomes are magnified if he or she experienced poverty year after year versus a short time in this situation.[36]

The previous discussion suggests that "income matters" in the lives of children. Indeed, some evidence indicates that income transfers, such as those provided through the EITC (discussed further in Chapter 15), improve children's reading and math test scores, with larger benefits going to children from more disadvantaged backgrounds. Moreover, researchers find that income transfers have the largest payoff for children's development when they are made earlier in children's lives.[37]

Of particular import, given the focus of this text, is the extent to which the impact of economic disadvantage differs by children's gender. Evidence points to more detrimental effects for boys. One detailed study, which compared outcomes for boys and girls raised in the same economically disadvantaged family, found that boys tend to have both relatively lower levels of academic achievement as measured by test scores and high school graduation, and relatively more behavioral issues, as measured by school absences and suspensions. Moreover, evidence indicates that these differences emerge as early as kindergarten.[38] This latter finding again points to the potential payoffs from early interventions and investments in children.

Family Structure and Children's Outcomes

As evident from the statistics we have seen, an increasing number of children are being born to single or cohabiting parents. Other children, while born to married parents, are in families in which that marriage has ended in divorce. Indeed, as discussed in Chapter 4, in 2014 just 58.4 percent of children lived with both biological parents in a married-couple family. A large fraction of children (28 percent) lived with a single parent, most often with a single mother, and the remainder lived with cohabiting parents (4 percent), in a married-couple family with at least one step-parent (5 percent), or with a nonparent adult (4 percent).[39] Also quite telling are findings from a study which focused exclusively on the family structure of firstborn children of unmarried mothers. It found that by age 10 as many as 60 percent of these children had at least one half-sibling, from a subsequent relationship by the mother, the father, or both.[40] These figures, among others, point to children's varied living arrangements as well as the fact that many children, especially those born to unmarried and cohabiting parents, experience family transitions (family instability) as their parents form new households as a result of subsequent cohabitation or (re)marriage.[41]

---

[36]Carolyn Ratcliffe, *Child Poverty and Adult Success* (Washington, DC: Urban Institute), 2015.

[37]Gordon B. Dahl and Lance Lochner, "The Impact of Family Income on Child Achievement: Evidence from the Earned Income Tax Credit," *American Economic Review* 102, no. 5 (2012): 1927–56. For further discussion, see Greg J. Duncan, Katherine Magnuson, and Elizabeth Votruba-Drzal, "Boosting Family Income to Promote Child Development," *The Future of Children* 24, no. 1 (Spring 2014): 99–120. Importantly, not all researchers find that more income benefits children; see Susan E. Mayer, "Revisiting an Old Question: How Much Does Parental Income Affect Child Outcomes? *Focus* 27, no. 2 (Winter 2010): 21–26.

[38]David Autor, David Figlio, Krzysztof Karbownik, Jeffrey Roth, and Melanie Wasserman, "Family Disadvantage and the Gender Gap in Behavioral and Educational Outcomes," NBER Working Paper 22267 (National Bureau of Economic Research, Cambridge, MA, May 2016).

[39]Another 1.1 percent of children had one or more adoptive parents. They are not included with biological married parents here (which is often done) because the data source did not indicate whether they were in married-couple or cohabiting families.

[40]This finding is from Maria Cancian, Daniel R. Meyer, and Steven Cook, "The Evolution of Family Complexity from the Perspective of Children," *Demography* 48, no. 3 (2011): 957–82.

[41]See David M. Blau and Wilbert van der Klaauw, "A Demographic Analysis of the Family Structure Experiences of Children in the United States," *Review of Economics of the Household* 6 (2008): 193–221; and Susan L. Brown, J. Bart Stykes, and Wendy D. Manning, "Trends in Children's Family Instability, 1995–2010," *Journal of Marriage and Family* 78, no 5 (October 2016): 1173–83.

An obvious next question is whether and to what extent family structure affects children's well-being, typically measured in research studies by their educational attainment, labor force participation, or a teen pregnancy or birth. Early research, beginning with a landmark 1994 study by Sara McLanahan and Gary Sandefur, examined outcomes for children raised in single-mother families and step-father families compared to those raised with both biological parents present. They found that children raised by single mothers have a higher high school dropout rate and a higher rate of teen births than those raised by two biological parents, even after taking account of differences in parents' educational levels, race, and incomes.[42] Some of their evidence also indicated that a number of outcomes are not as favorable for children in step-father families as for those living with both biological parents.

Since the landmark 1994 study, research has moved forward in several directions. First, the study generated considerable interest and debate about whether, and to what extent, growing up in a single-parent family is the real *cause* of children performing poorly in school, among other negative outcomes. Some argue that there might be other factors that are the underlying cause of both children's poor school performance and parents' divorce, such as a parent's substance abuse problem or a high degree of family conflict. In these cases, the child might well perform poorly in school even if the parents did not separate. As a result, subsequent research has made concerted efforts to disentangle causation from correlation. Some of this research tends to confirm McLanahan and Sandefur's findings that living in arrangements other than an intact biological two-parent family, such as a single-parent or step-parent family, results in unfavorable effects on educational outcomes, but others find no such effect.[43]

Second, a growing body of research is looking at the extent to which growing up with a single mother (and other measures of family disadvantage, including income) differentially affects boys' and girls' outcomes. One notable study that focused on children's behavior finds that boys raised by single mothers are more likely to be suspended from school compared to boys who are raised with both biological parents present.[44] The authors find that it is not so much that parental inputs (e.g., amount of time spent reading to children or doing other activities with them) vary by gender but rather that single-parent families provide lower levels of these inputs and boys respond more negatively than girls.

Third, there is greater recognition that studies that focus on the impact of family structure on children's outcomes at a point in time (e.g., when the child is age 5 or age 16) fail to capture the impact of family structure transitions and associated residential change on children's outcomes. In other words, family stability (or lack thereof) may also play a role. As discussed earlier, increasing numbers of children are born to cohabiting and unmarried parents who are likely to form new households

---

[42]Sara McLanahan and Gary Sandefur, *Growing Up with a Single Parent: What Hurts, What Helps?* (Cambridge, MA: Harvard University Press, 1994). In this study, adopted children are included with biological children. They focus on single-mother and step-father families because they are the most prevalent types of single-parent and step-parent families.

[43]For a discussion of the methodological challenges and a review of evidence on both sides, see Sara McLanahan, Laura Tach, and Daniel Schneider, "The Causal Effects of Father Absence," *Annual Review of Sociology* 39 (2013): 399–427. Some research has also focused on the effect of an incarcerated parent on children's outcomes; see, for instance, Amanda Geller, Carey E. Cooper, Irwin Garfinkel, Ofira Schwartz-Soicher, and Ronald B. Mincy, "Beyond Absenteeism: Father Incarceration and Child Development," *Demography* 49 (February 2012): 49–76.

[44]Marianne Bertrand and Jessica Pan, "The Trouble with Boys: Social Influences and the Gender Gap in Disruptive Behavior," *American Economic Journal: Applied Economics* 5, no. 1 (2013): 32–64.

at a future point. And while married-couple families tend to be more stable, children in these families may similarly experience family instability if their parents decide to divorce.[45] Research focused on the impact of family instability finds that it has detrimental effects for children, particularly in terms of their behavioral and socioemotional development.[46] Suggestive of the benefits of stability, a related line of research finds that outcomes for children raised by both biological parents in long-term cohabiting unions are quite similar to those raised by their married-couple counterparts.[47]

In interpreting the research findings we have reviewed, it is important to keep in mind that even if growing up in a single-parent family or with a step-parent has negative effects, this only means that the risk of less desirable outcomes is increased, *not* that it is assured or nonexistent for children living in families with both biological parents.

Conclusion

Changes in family structure have important implications for family well-being. We began by looking at economic well-being and found that dual-earner families earn considerably more, on average, than single-earner families. Married women's increased earnings most likely improve their bargaining power in the family. We also saw that single-mother families face particularly difficult challenges, especially as a consequence of their much higher poverty rates. Next, we looked at the implications of maternal employment for children's well-being. Some evidence suggests that maternal employment during a child's first year of life may negatively affect the child's later cognitive development. In evaluating this finding, it is important to keep in mind that maternal employment is only one of many interrelated factors that affect children's well-being and achievement. Out-of-home care for preschoolers, on the other hand, is generally found to be beneficial. With respect to family structure, some evidence indicates that children growing up in a family without both biological parents present do not, on average, fare as well as those raised in married-couple families with both biological parents present, though again this is an area of active research. In the next two chapters, we look at policies to support low-income families as well as policies to help all family types better balance the dual demands of paid work and family.

---

[45]In his review of the benefits of marriage for child well-being, David Ribar points to the greater stability of married-couple families, among other benefits; see "Why Marriage Matters for Child Wellbeing," *The Future of Children* 25, no.2 (Fall 2015): 11–27.

[46]Regarding the impact, see Paula Formby and Andrew J. Cherlin, "Family Instability and Child Well-Being," *American Sociological Review* 72, no. 2 (April 2007): 181–201; and Dohoon Lee and Sara McLanahan, "Family Structure Transitions and Child Development: Instability, Selection, and Population Heterogeneity," *American Sociological Review* 80, no. 4 (2015): 738–63.

[47]See Wendy D. Manning, "Cohabitation and Child Wellbeing," *The Future of Children* 25, no. 2 (Fall 2015): 51–66. Family stability has also been identified as a key factor that must be taken into account in comparing outcomes for children raised in same-sex couples with those raised with two biological parents. As discussed in Chapter 13, the majority of children raised by same-sex parents are born to opposite-sex parents from a prior union and so tend to experience family instability as the parent(s) forms a new household. As more children are born into married same-sex families, stability should increase. See Gary Gates, "Marriage and Family: LGBT Individuals and Same-Sex Couples," *The Future of Children* 25, no. 2 (Fall 2015): 67–87.

Questions for Review and Discussion

1. Children raised in mother-only families are generally at an economic and social disadvantage compared to those raised in two-parent families. Explain the major reasons why.

2. What are the major differences between the official poverty measure and the newer Supplemental Poverty Measure (SPM)? Provide a rationale for each of the changes made.

3. Explain why the distinction between causation and correlation is so important in understanding the relationship between family structure and children's well-being. Suggest another factor that may affect both children's outcomes and family structure.

Internet-Based Data Exercise

Note: In doing this exercise, students should be aware that the precise names of documents and their location within a website may change over time.

The US Census Bureau is the primary source of government data on many topics included in this text including income, education, health insurance, and poverty.

Visit the home page of the US Census Bureau at http://www.census.gov.

1. Click on "Poverty." On the poverty data page, look for the most recent document titled "Income and Poverty" (or a similar title). (This is the same publication used in the data exercise for Chapter 7). Find Table 3, which provides information on *people* in poverty by selected characteristics. (Table 14-2 of this chapter focused on *families*.)

   Using these data, look at differences in (official) poverty rates for individuals by age, race, nativity, and work experience. What might explain these differences given discussions in this chapter and earlier ones?

2. The Census Bureau website also provides "Historical Tables" on poverty and other topics. On the poverty data page, look for Historical Table 2: "Poverty Status of People by Family Relationship, Race, and Hispanic Origin."

   Using these data, compare the overall poverty rate for individuals (people) for the most recent year with rates from the early 2000s. Discuss these trends in light of changes in economic conditions in the overall US economy during this period.

Suggested Readings

Bartik, Timothy J. *From Preschool to Prosperity: The Economic Payoff to Early Childhood Education.* Kalamazoo, MI: W. E. Upjohn Institute for Employment Research, 2014.

Bertrand, Marianne, Emir Kamenica, and Jessica Pan. "Economic Consequences of Gender Identity." VOX CEPR's Policy Portal, April 13, 2015, voxeu.org.

Bradbury, Bruce, Miles Corak, Jane Waldfogel, and Elizabeth Washbrook. *Too Many Children Left Behind: The U.S. Achievement Gap in Comparative Perspective.* New York: Russell Sage Foundation, 2015.

Carlson, Marcia, and Paula England, eds. *Social Class and Changing Families in an Unequal America*. Stanford, CA: Stanford University Press, 2011.

Currie, Janet M. *The Invisible Safety Net: Protecting the Nation's Poor Children and Families*. Princeton, NJ: Princeton University Press, 2008.

Duncan, Greg J., and Richard J. Murnane, eds. *Whither Opportunity? Rising Inequality, Schools, and Children's Life Chances*. New York: Russell Sage Foundation, 2011.

Ellwood, David T., and Christopher Jencks. "The Spread of Single-Parent Families in the United States since 1960." In *The Future of the Family*, edited by Daniel P. Moynihan, Timothy M. Smeeding, and Lee Rainwater. New York: Russell Sage Foundation, 2004, 25-65.

Haskins, Ron, Irv Garfinkel, and Sara McLanahan, eds. *The Future of Children: Two Generation Programs*. Princeton, NJ: Princeton University Press, 2014.

Haveman, Robert, Rebecca Blank, Robert Moffitt, Timothy Smeeding, and Geoffrey Wallace. "The War on Poverty: Measurement, Trends, and Policy." *Journal of Policy Analysis and Management* 34, no. 3 (Summer 2015): 593–638.

Hoffman, Saul D., and Rebecca A. Maynard, eds. *Kids Having Kids: Economic Costs and Social Consequences of Teen Pregnancy*, 2nd ed. Washington, DC: Urban Institute, 2009.

McLanahan, Sara. "Diverging Destinies: How Children Are Faring under the Second Demographic Transition." *Demography* 41, no. 4 (November 2004): 607–28.

Shonkoff, Jack P., and Deborah A. Phillips, eds. *From Neurons to Neighborhoods: The Science of Early Child Development*. Washington, DC: National Research Council, 2000.

Waldfogel, Jane. *What Children Need*. Cambridge, MA: Harvard University Press, 2006.

Key Terms

dual-earner families (381)	positive assortative mating (384)	Supplemental Poverty Measure (SPM) (388)
single-parent families (381)	official poverty rate (387)	

Government Policies Affecting Family Well-Being

15

CHAPTER HIGHLIGHTS

- Policies to Alleviate Poverty
- Aid to Families with Dependent Children: The Former US Welfare Program
- Temporary Assistance to Needy Families: The Current US Welfare Program
- The Earned Income Tax Credit
- Employment Strategies
- Child Support Enforcement
- Taxes, Specialization, and Marriage
- Federal Income Tax
- Social Security

A host of programs and policies have emerged and evolved over time that influence the well-being of individuals and families. This chapter begins where Chapter 14 left off, by discussing government policies to alleviate poverty, especially those that affect mother-only families, because these families often face the greatest difficulties. Next, we review some major features of the US federal income tax and Social Security systems and point to some of their potential effects on dual- versus single-earner couples and on family formation decisions.

Policies to Alleviate Poverty

Federal welfare reform was a major policy change in the mid-1990s and remains the focus of much ongoing policy discussion. For this reason, we begin by briefly describing the prior federal welfare program, Aid to Families with Dependent Children

(AFDC), which was replaced by Temporary Assistance to Needy Families (TANF) in 1996.[1] Next, we examine the Earned Income Tax Credit (EITC), government employment programs, and policies designed to increase child support paid by noncustodial parents. We also review marriage promotion initiatives intended to improve the economic well-being of families.

Aid to Families with Dependent Children: The Former US Welfare Program

Aid to Families with Dependent Children (AFDC), initiated in 1935 as part of the Social Security Act, was a federal entitlement program that provided all eligible families, principally those headed by single mothers, with cash assistance. Over the years, the government also established a number of in-kind benefit programs for which AFDC recipients typically qualified. **In-kind benefits** are noncash benefits targeted at specific goods. One such benefit program, **Food Stamps**, was initiated in 1964 to provide food assistance for lower-income households. This program, which has evolved over time, was renamed the **Supplemental Nutrition Assistance Program (SNAP)** in 2008. Eligibility is household-based, and in recent years benefits are delivered through an electronic benefit transfer card.[2] Another in-kind benefit program, **Medicaid**, was established in 1965 to provide health insurance for low-income parents and children and persons with disabilities. A few years later it expanded to cover the low-income elderly, and in the mid-1980s it further expanded to include low-income pregnant women. Most recently, under the Affordable Health Care for America Act ("Obamacare"), states have the option of expanding Medicaid eligibility to include all individuals with less than 133 percent of the poverty line. As of June 2016, nearly two-thirds of states had done so.[3]

Despite the fact that AFDC made up only about 1 percent of the federal budget, it came to be one of the most hotly debated government transfer programs. There were four major reasons for this. One often-cited concern was that because AFDC mainly provided benefits to single mothers, it might create an incentive for couples not to get married or to break up, in order for the mother and her children to be eligible for welfare.[4] Public concern was heightened when it became

---

[1]For overviews of programs and policies designed to reduce poverty and assist families, see John Karl Scholz, Robert Moffitt, and Benjamin Cowan, "Trends in Income Support," in *Changing Poverty, Changing Policies*, ed. Maria Cancian and Sheldon Danziger (New York: Russell Sage Foundation, 2009), 203–41. For overviews of the AFDC and TANF programs, see James P. Ziliak, "The Temporary Assistance for Needy Families Program," in *The Economics of Means-Tested Transfer Programs in the United States*, vol. 1, ed. Robert A. Moffitt (Chicago: University of Chicago Press, 2016), pp. 303–94; and Thomas Gabe, *Welfare, Work, and Poverty Status of Female-Headed Families with Children: 1987–2013* (Washington, DC: Congressional Research Service, November 2014).

[2]In the AFDC period, Food Stamps were distributed as paper coupons—hence the name of the program. For the evolution of this program, see Jacob A. Klerman and Caroline Danielson, "The Transformation of the Supplemental Nutrition Assistance Program," *Journal of Policy Analysis and Management* 30, no. 4 (Fall 2011): 863–88.

[3]In 1997 the federal government also initiated the Children's Health Insurance Program (CHIP). For the history of Medicaid, CHIP, as well as discussion of the major provisions of the Affordable Health Care for America Act, see Barbara Wolfe, "The Legacy of the War on Poverty's Health Programs for Non-Elderly Adults and Children," in *Legacy of the War on Poverty*, ed. Martha J. Bailey and Sheldon Danziger (New York: Russell Sage Foundation, 2013), 237–67. The most recent information on Medicaid eligibility can be found at www.healthcare.gov.

[4]Policy changes in 1961 and 1988 expanded benefits to two-parent families with an unemployed spouse, but single mothers remained the overwhelming majority of welfare recipients.

clear that the program, originally intended to help families of poor widows, in fact mainly served divorced women and, over the years, increasing numbers of never-married mothers. For instance, from 1970 to 1993 (when caseloads were at their peak level), the percentage of families on AFDC headed by never-married mothers increased from 28 to 53 percent.[5] It was, therefore, argued that this program discouraged marriage and encouraged unmarried women to have children. Evidence suggests, however, that even though AFDC appears to have affected these decisions, it cannot explain the dramatic rise in female headship or in births to unmarried women since the 1970s.[6]

A second concern was that AFDC created potential disincentives for paid work because it provided the maximum benefit, termed the **AFDC guarantee**, for recipients who were not employed. As we saw in Chapter 6, the availability of nonlabor income increases the reservation wage, thereby reducing the probability of labor force participation. Another important parameter of the AFDC program was the **AFDC tax rate**, the amount by which the AFDC guarantee was reduced for each dollar earned in the labor market. In the later years of the program, if a recipient entered the labor market, benefits were reduced by a dollar for each dollar earned on the job—this is equivalent to a 100 percent tax rate on earnings. Needless to say, for any individual, on welfare or not, this would provide a considerable disincentive to work. Evidence indicates that the AFDC guarantee did reduce labor supply, but again the effects were found to be relatively small. Further, altering the tax rate was not found to have much impact on recipients' propensity to work.[7] AFDC was also believed to discourage paid work because, by keeping their hours low, recipients could remain on the AFDC program and thus retain access to Medicaid.[8] However, during the late 1980s, this disincentive was reduced as a result of a number of benefit expansions in the Medicaid program to low-income individuals who were not on welfare.

A third concern was that AFDC promoted welfare dependency because benefits were not time-limited. Evidence indicates, however, that most recipients did not rely on AFDC for long periods of time.[9]

Finally, AFDC and other transfer programs were also subject to much criticism because they produced only modest success in alleviating poverty.[10] Part of the reason these programs were not more successful was that the amount of money available from AFDC became increasingly inadequate. The value of the AFDC

[5]US Department of Health and Human Services, *Indicators of Welfare Dependence*, Annual Report to Congress (Washington, DC, 2007 ed.), table TANF7, accessed March 3, 2016, http://aspe.hhs.gov.

[6]See Robert A. Moffitt, "The Temporary Assistance for Needy Families Program," in *Means-Tested Transfer Programs in the United States*, ed. Robert A. Moffitt (Chicago: University of Chicago Press, 2003), 291–363. For evidence that AFDC may also have encouraged cohabitation, see Robert A. Moffitt, Robert Reville, and Anne E. Winkler, "Beyond Single Mothers: Cohabitation and Marriage in the U.S. Welfare System," *Demography* 35, no. 3 (August 1998): 359–78.

[7]Moffitt, "The Temporary Assistance for Needy Families Program."

[8]Regarding work disincentives in Medicaid, see, for instance, Anne E. Winkler, "The Incentive Effects of Medicaid on Women's Labor Supply," *Journal of Human Resources* 26, no. 2 (Spring 1991): 308–37; and Erin Strumpf, "Medicaid's Effect on Single Women's Labor Supply: Evidence from the Introduction of Medicaid," *Journal of Health Economics* 30, no. 3 (May 2011): 531–48.

[9]See, for instance, Moffitt, "The Temporary Assistance for Needy Families Program."

[10]For extended discussions, see Sheldon H. Danziger, Gary D. Sandefur, and Daniel H. Weinberg, eds., *Confronting Poverty: Prescriptions for Change* (Cambridge, MA: Harvard University Press and New York: Russell Sage Foundation, 1994); and Sheldon H. Danziger and Robert H. Haveman, eds, *Understanding Poverty* (Cambridge, MA: Harvard University Press and New York: Russell Sage Foundation, 2002).

TABLE 15-1 STATISTICS ON FAMILIES RECEIVING SELECTED TRANSFER PROGRAM BENEFITS, 1975–2014

	PERIOD OF AFDC PROGRAM/EARLY EITC		PERIOD OF TANF/LATER EITC			
	1975	1993	2000	2008	2010	2014
AFDC/TANF[a]						
AFDC/TANF Families (in Thousands)	3,481	5,011	2,303	1,700	1,918	1,650
As % of All Families	6.2%	7.4%	3.2%	2.2%	2.4%	2.0%
AFDC/TANF Recipients (in Thousands)	11,318	14,205	6,143	4,001	4,594	3,957
As % of Population	5.2%	5.5%	2.2%	1.3%	1.5%	1.2%
AFDC/TANF Cash Benefits (in Millions of $2014)[b]	$37,015	$36,511	$15,370	$9,510	$11,615	$8,443
Food Stamps (SNAP) Program						
SNAP Recipients (in Thousands)	17,064	26,987	17,194	28,223	40,302	46,664
As % of Population	7.9%	10.5%	6.1%	9.3%	13.0%	14.7%
SNAP Benefits (in Millions of $2014)	$19,298	$36,053	$20,599	$38,054	$70,244	$69,999
Earned Income Tax Credit (EITC)						
EITC Recipient Families (in Thousands)	6,215	15,117	19,277	24,757	27,368	27,500
As % of All Families	11.2%	22.2%	26.8%	31.8%	34.7%	33.8%
EITC Benefits (in Millions of $2014)	$5,500	$25,454	$44,400	$55,714	$64,663	$66,700

[a]AFDC/TANF recipient figures are for the calendar year. TANF figures also include State Separate Program (SSP) and Maintenance of Expenditure (MOE) funds.

[b]Figures reported are for federal and state funds (SSP and MOE) used for cash assistance only. Total TANF spending also includes expenditures on childcare and work-related activities. AFDC = Aid to Families with Dependent Children; TANF = Temporary Assistance for Needy Families

Sources: Department of Health and Human Services: "TANF Caseload Data—Number of Families and Recipients," various years; "TANF Financial Data," various years, www.acf.hhs.gov. and Welfare Indicators and Risk Factors: Thirteenth Report to Congress, table TANF 4: "Total AFDC/ TANF Expenditures on Cash Benefits and Administration: 1970 - 2011 (March 1, 2014); US Department of Agriculture, Food and Nutrition Service, "Supplemental Nutrition Assistance Program Participation and Costs," accessed February 2, 2016, www.fns.usda.gov; Tax Policy Center, "Earned Income Tax Credit: Number of Recipients and Amount of Credit, 1975–2013," www.taxpolicycenter.org; Internal Revenue *Service, EITC and Other Refundable Tax Credits*, "Statistics for Tax Returns with EITC," accessed February 2, 2016, https://www.eitc.irs.gov/EITC-Central/eitcstats; and US Census Bureau, table FM-1, "Families, by Presence of Own Children Under 18: 1950 to Present," www.census.gov.

guarantee (averaged across the states) fell by well over 50 percent between 1970 and 1993 in inflation-adjusted terms. The impact of this decline was cushioned somewhat by an increase in in-kind benefits, most notably by Food Stamps (SNAP). As seen in Table 15-1, as real spending on AFDC decreased, real spending on Food Stamps (SNAP) increased. Nonetheless, as of 1993, the combined value of the two benefits for a family of three still provided only two-thirds of the amount needed to reach the poverty threshold.[11] The decline in real wages for less educated individuals, which we have discussed in earlier chapters, further compounded the difficulty of raising low-income households out of poverty. While the concern that AFDC had only limited success in reducing poverty remains valid, we note that a more recent analysis of trends in poverty rates undertaken using the new Supplemental Poverty

---

[11]The calculations reported in this paragraph are based on data provided in US Department of Health and Human Services, *Indicators of Welfare Dependence* (Washington, DC, 2005).

Measure (SPM) indicates that government transfer programs as a whole were more effective at reducing poverty rates than previously thought.[12]

Pressure to restructure welfare grew, beginning in the 1980s. Probably best known is President Clinton's promise during the 1992 presidential campaign to "end welfare as we know it." To this end, early in his presidency, President Clinton encouraged states to experiment with different aspects of their policies. In response, some states placed time limits on benefits, while others capped AFDC benefits for those who had additional children.[13]

Temporary Assistance to Needy Families: The Current US Welfare Program

In 1996 AFDC was replaced with a new program called **Temporary Assistance to Needy Families (TANF)**, which altered the federal provision of welfare transfers in a number of important ways. For one, it changed the way welfare is funded. AFDC was a federal entitlement program, meaning that the federal government provided assistance to families deemed needy by federal rules. Instead, under TANF, states are given fixed block grants and have greater discretion regarding program rules, eligibility, and how funds are used. This shift was based on the view that states would be better able to tailor aid to their population because of their greater knowledge of the residents' needs. Second, TANF required that a large fraction of recipients work. As of 2016, 50 percent of single parents receiving welfare were required to be employed in some capacity for a minimum of 30 hours.[14] One argument for the work requirement is that today most married women, including those with small children, are employed, so it is not unreasonable to require single women maintaining families to also be employed. To put "teeth" into these rules, the legislation gave states greater authority to sanction recipients who do not follow program rules. Third, to reduce welfare dependency, TANF mandated a 5-year cumulative time limit on receiving federally funded welfare, albeit with exemptions possible for up to 20 percent of families. TANF also set forth a number of other new rules: it restricted eligibility for teen parents so that only those who stay in school and live with their parents can receive benefits; stepped up enforcement of child support by noncustodial parents, most often fathers; and limited eligibility for Food Stamps for some adults.[15] The legislation also sought to discourage nonmarital fertility and promote two-parent families. The "Beyond Traditional Income and Work Support Policies" box discusses specific efforts to promote marriage.

---

[12]As discussed in Chapter 14, the SPM includes the value of Food Stamps and the Earned Income Tax Credit, in addition to other adjustments. See Liana Fox, Irwin Garfinkel, Neeraj Kaushal, Jane Waldfogel, and Christopher Wimer, "Waging War on Poverty: Historical Trends in Poverty Using the Supplemental Poverty Measure," *Journal of Policy Analysis and Management* 34, no. 1 (Summer 2015): 567–92.

[13]For further discussion of state experimentation with alternative policies during the "waiver period," see Ziliak, "Temporary Assistance for Needy Families Program."

[14]In the case of two-parent families, 90 percent of such families were required to have an employed adult, and minimum work hours were set higher than for single-parent families. These requirements are reduced for those states that are successful at reducing the number of individuals receiving benefits. See Center on Budget and Policy Priorities, *Policy Basics: An Introduction to TANF* (Washington, DC: Center on Budget and Policy Priorities, June 15, 2015), www.cbpp.org .

[15]US House of Representatives, *2004 Green Book* (Washington, DC: US Government Publishing Office, 2004).

As might be expected, the states (and the District of Columbia) have taken advantage of the greater latitude given to them by the federal government under TANF and are now essentially running 51 different welfare experiments. For instance, in calculating welfare benefits, states now differ greatly as to the tax rate applied to a welfare recipient's earnings, with some states choosing very low tax rates in an effort to increase work incentives.[16] States have also made different choices regarding eligibility for two-parent families and whether benefits are increased if recipients have additional children. Because the state-level policies generally include both "carrots" and "sticks" in an effort to encourage or discourage certain behaviors, it is virtually impossible to classify individual states as more harsh or generous across the board. Also, program evaluation is challenging because it is difficult to isolate the influence of these individual policies. Complicating things even further, the EITC, which encourages labor force participation, was expanded (as discussed further later in the "Earned Income Tax Credit" section) at around the same time that TANF was introduced.

Given that 20 years have passed, it is now possible to draw some conclusions about the success of the 1996 welfare reform. In reviewing the evidence, it is useful to divide the discussion into two periods, the period from 1996 to 2007, when the economy was generally strong, and post-2007, with the advent of the Great Recession and its aftermath. The Great Recession began in December 2007 and, while it officially ended in June 2009, its after-effects continued for quite some time, with the national unemployment rate still hovering at just under 8 percent in early 2013. The rate finally returned to its pre-recession level of just under 5 percent in 2015.

The overall consensus regarding the impact of welfare reform for the period prior to the Great Recession is quite positive. The national welfare caseload fell by 50 percent from 1993, when the size of the welfare (AFDC) caseload was at or near its most recent peak, to 2000, a few years after TANF's inception. This decrease was unprecedented in the history of the program and far larger than policy makers anticipated. As shown in Table 15-1, in 2000, just 2.2 percent of the US population was receiving welfare benefits compared with 5.5 percent in 1993. However, caution must be exercised in attributing the full decline in welfare caseloads to the introduction of TANF; considerable evidence indicates that the expansion of the EITC and the booming US economy of the late 1990s also played critical roles.[17] Together, these three factors (the booming economy, expansion of the EITC, and welfare reform) contributed to a considerable reduction in the rate of families entering welfare, as well as an increase in the rate of families exiting the program.[18]

Prior to the onset of the Great Recession, TANF, coupled with the expansion of the EITC, also had considerable success in moving individuals from welfare to work, particularly in the buoyant 1990s. As we saw in Figure 6-4 (see Chapter 6), starting in the mid-1990s, the labor force participation rate of single mothers (both never-married and ever-married) increased considerably more rapidly than for married mothers. Even during the recession of 2001, which was relatively mild, the labor force participation rate for single mothers only declined briefly before attaining its

---

[16]Jordan Matsudaira and Rebecca M. Blank, "The Impact of Earnings Disregards on the Behavior of Low Income Families," *Journal of Policy Analysis and Management* 33, no. 1 (2014): 7–35.

[17]Numerous studies have sought to untangle the role of each factor. For reviews, see, for instance, Ziliak, "The Temporary Assistance for Needy Families Program"; and Jeffrey Grogger and Lynn A. Karoly, *Welfare Reform: Effects of a Decade of Change* (Cambridge, MA: Harvard University Press, 2005).

[18]Jeffrey Grogger, Steven J. Haider, and Jacob Klerman, "Why Did the Welfare Rolls Fall during the 1990s? The Importance of Entry," *American Economic Review* 93, no. 2 (May 2003): 288–92.

all-time peak level in 2002.[19] It appears that these changes in welfare and the EITC also led to increases in family earnings and reductions in poverty. However, some evidence suggests that the economic well-being of women on the very lowest rungs of the economic ladder may have worsened during this time period.[20]

The impact of welfare reform on economic well-being is far less favorable when we examine the period during and after the Great Recession. In marked contrast to its role in prior recessions, welfare—now TANF—no longer served as a meaningful safety net despite the sharply rising unemployment rates associated with the Great Recession: in two-thirds of states, caseloads rose only modestly, and in the other one-third of states, caseloads actually fell.[21] Consistent with this, as shown in Table 15-1, from 2008 (just after the start of the recession) through 2010, the national TANF caseload barely increased as a percent of the population. Rather, it was the Food Stamp (SNAP) program that provided the most critical assistance to those in need. Table 15-1 shows that the percentage of the population receiving SNAP rose from 9.3 percent in 2008 to 13 percent in 2010 and, in fact, further increased through 2014.[22]

One explanation for why TANF provided a much weaker safety net than its predecessor, AFDC, is that it is a fixed block grant, not a federal entitlement program, so states have limited funds. Another is that the 1996 welfare reform required states to meet high work participation targets, and as a consequence many states shifted their allocation of TANF funds away from cash assistance that provides a true safety net to other forms of assistance that focus on moving the most job-ready recipients into employment. For instance, spending on TANF cash assistance (the figures reported in Table 15-1) declined as a portion of total TANF spending from just over 70 percent in 1997 to just 30 percent by the late 2000s.[23] A federal TANF contingency fund, which was created to deal with economic crises, proved inadequate to address the depth of the Great Recession, although some additional emergency TANF funds were made available through the 2009 federal stimulus enacted under President Obama.[24]

---

[19]Participation rates for married mothers also declined slightly, suggesting that the slight decline for single mothers reflected a broader weakness in the labor market.

[20]For a review of findings see Ziliak, "Temporary Assistance to Needy Families Program," and Grogger and Karoly, *Welfare Reform.*

[21]Sheila Zedlewski and Paula Loprest, *What Role Is Welfare Playing in this Period of High Unemployment?* Urban Institute Fact Sheet 3 (Washington, DC: Urban Institute, August 2011), www.urban.org.

[22]Along with SNAP, the Unemployment Insurance program also provided important support. For an overview and analysis of the effectiveness of multiple safety net programs during the Great Recession, see Marianne Bitler and Hilary Hoynes, "The More Things Change, the More They Stay the Same? The Safety Net and Poverty in the Great Recession," *Journal of Labor Economics* 34, no. 1, pt. 2 (2016): S403–44. What remains puzzling is the high rate of SNAP receipt well after the end of the Great Recession. Explanations offered include continued lack of employment opportunities and program policy changes; see Chad Stone, Arloc Sherman, and Brynne Keith-Jennings, *No Mystery Why SNAP Enrollment Remains High: It's Still the Economy* (Washington, DC: Center on Budget and Policy Priorities, March 18, 2015), www.cbpp.org; and Peter Ganong and Jeffrey B. Liebman, "The Decline, Rebound, and Further Rise in SNAP Enrollment: Disentangling Business Cycle Fluctuations and Policy Changes," National Bureau of Economic Research Working Paper 19363 (National Bureau of Economic Research, Cambridge, MA, 2013).

[23]Figures for 1997 and 2013 are from, respectively, US Department of Health and Human Services, *Indicators of Welfare Dependence* (2007) and (2009–2013), table TANF5. The figure remained at 30 percent in 2013; see US Department of Health and Human Services, *Welfare Indicators and Risk Factors* (2013), table TANF5.

[24]This discussion is drawn from Zedlewski and Loprest, *What Role Is Welfare Playing?*; Bitler and Hoynes, "The More Things Change"; and Danilo Trisi and LaDonna Pavetti, *TANF Weakening as a Safety Net for Poor Families* (Washington, DC: Center on Budget and Policy Priorities, March 13, 2012), www.cbpp.org. For an overall assessment of the success of welfare reform from multiple viewpoints, see Richard V. Burkhauser, ed., "Welfare Reform: A 20-Year Retrospective," *Journal of Policy Analysis and Management*, 35, no. 1 (Winter 2016): 223–24.

One consequence of the changes in welfare, undoubtedly exacerbated by the Great Recession, is growth in what have been termed "disconnected mothers." **Disconnected mothers** are those who receive little to no welfare support and have little, if any, earnings.[25] This development raises concern for the well-being not only of these women but also of their dependent children. Robert Moffitt argues that the rise in this group is part of a more general shift in the US transfer system; it has shifted resources from single mothers toward persons with disabilities and the elderly and from the poorest of the poor (including the nonemployed) to those employed or not quite as disadvantaged.[26]

Beyond Traditional Income and Work Support Policies: Marriage Promotion

Efforts to alleviate poverty among families and improve children's well-being have long relied on welfare programs including AFDC and, more recently, TANF. As discussed further in the "Earned Income Tax Credit" section, these efforts were buttressed by expansions in the federal EITC, a tax credit that supplements the income of families with low earnings, as well as by policies to strengthen child support enforcement. Considerable attention has also focused on another strategy—promoting and supporting healthy marriages. As discussed in the "State of Unions" box in Chapter 4, the 1996 welfare legislation explicitly mentioned supporting two-parent families as a goal and, in response, a substantial number of states began **marriage promotion** policies. Marriage promotion policies have ranged from providing bonuses to married recipients in state welfare programs to funding local marriage education programs. The federal government first funded the Healthy Marriage Initiative in 2002, which was subsequently expanded into the Healthy Marriage and Responsible Fatherhood Program.*

Proponents point to a range of benefits of marriage including the fact that married-couple families are, on average, on considerably better financial footing than single-parent families, as shown in Table 14-2. Married couples also have considerably higher incomes than cohabiters. In addition, Chapter 14 pointed to evidence that suggests that children tend to do better in married families with both biological parents present than when raised by a single parent. However, when comparing the economic well-being of married and unmarried couples or of single mothers and their potential mates, it is important to bear in mind that these couples have very different characteristics, on average. This is most readily illustrated by comparing married couples and cohabiters. For instance, adults in married-couple families tend to be older and more highly educated. Thus, it is not reasonable to assume that if all cohabiting couples were to marry they would achieve the same economic well-being as married couples. One study does find that when marriage is "simulated" among cohabiting couples, the poverty rate of children in these families falls from over three to two times the rate for children in married-couple families. Nonetheless, this improvement would still leave a considerable fraction of children in poverty.**

continues

---

[25]Rebecca M. Blank and Brian K. Kovak, "The Growing Problem of Disconnected Mothers," in *Making the Work-Based Safety Net Work Better*, ed. Carolyn J. Heinrich and John Karl Scholz (New York: Russell Sage Foundation, 2009), 227–58. For a discussion of how these mothers make ends meet, see Kristin S. Seefeldt and H. Sandstrom, "When There Is No Welfare: The Income Packaging Strategies of Disconnected Mothers following an Economic Downturn," *Russell Sage Foundation Journal of Social Sciences* 1 (2015): 139–58.

[26]Robert A. Moffitt, "The Deserving Poor, the Family, and the U.S. Welfare System," *Demography* 52, no. 3 (2015): 729–49.

While marriage promotion has enjoyed considerable support, concerns have been raised about such an emphasis in government programs.*** For instance, given scarce government resources, marriage promotion efforts might divert government funds from traditional assistance programs for lower-income families. And even if marriage promotion efforts are found to encourage marriage, such policies might have the unintended consequence of prolonging or increasing domestic violence in unhealthy marriages. Further, as discussed in Chapter 14, some research finds negative effects associated with growing up with a step-parent, suggesting that all marriages may not be equally beneficial for children.

A number of evaluations of marriage promotion programs have now been completed. They find no effect or only a small positive effect on couples' relationship quality and no evidence that these programs encourage marriage or keep married couples together.**** In light of these findings as well as the continued weakening of the link between marriage and childbearing (as discussed in Chapters 4 and 13), support for these policies appears to be waning. Indeed, Isabel Sawhill, a longtime advocate of efforts to support marriage, has come to the view that government funds would be put to better use by promoting "responsible parenthood," including efforts to encourage young women to defer pregnancy.*****

*Information on the federal government's Healthy Marriage and Responsible Fatherhood Initiatives can be found at US Administration for Families and Services, Office of Family Assistance, http://www.acf.hhs.gov. For discussion of the arguments made for and against marriage promotion, see Susan L. Brown, "Marriage and Child Well-Being: Research and Policy Perspectives," Journal of Marriage and Family 72 (October 2010): 1059–77; and Melanie Heath, One Marriage Under God: The Campaign to Promote Marriage in America (New York: New York University Press, 2012).
**Gregory Acs, "Can We Promote Child Well-Being by Promoting Marriage?" Journal of Marriage and the Family 69 (2007): 1326–44; and Daniel Lichter and Deborah Roempke Graefe, "Men and Marriage Promotion: Who Marries Unwed Mothers?" Social Service Review 81, no. 3 (September 2007): 397–421.
***See Robert G. Wood, Quinn Moore, Andrew Clarkwest, Alexandra Killewald, and Shannon Monahan, The Long-Term Effects of Building Strong Families: A Relationship

Skills Education Program for Unmarried Parents (Princeton, NJ: Mathematica, November 2012); and Erika Lundquist, JoAnn Hsueh, Amy E. Lowenstein, Kristen Faucetta, and Daniel Gubits, A Family-Strengthening Program for Low-Income Families: Final Impacts from the Supporting Healthy Marriage Evaluation, OPRE Report 2014-09A (Washington, DC: US Department of Health and Human Services, Office of Planning, Research and Evaluation, January 2014).
****See, for instance, Theodora Ooms, "Marriage and Government: Strange Bedfellows?" Policy Brief 1 (Washington, DC: Center for Law and Social Policy, August 2002); and Daniel T. Lichter, Marriage as Public Policy (Washington, DC: Progressive Policy Institute, September 2001).
*****Isabel Sawhill, Generation Unbound: Drifting into Sex and Parenthood without Marriage (Washington, DC: Brookings Institution Press, 2014). See also Brigid Schulte, "A Longtime Proponent of Marriage Wants to Reassess the Institution's Future," Washington Post, January 3, 2015.

The Earned Income Tax Credit

The **Earned Income Tax Credit (EITC)** is a refundable tax credit based on household earnings that both raises income and encourages individuals with low potential wages to seek employment. In contrast to many tax credits, which benefit only households with an income high enough to pay taxes, the refundable feature of the tax credit means that the government provides a refund if the amount of the credit exceeds taxes owed. Thus, unlike these other tax policies, the EITC transfers income to low-income households. Further, unlike the minimum wage, it targets only low-wage workers living in poor and near-poor households.[27] The EITC also avoids the possible negative employment effects that economic theory leads us to expect from the imposition of a minimum wage, although empirical evidence on such an effect has been mixed.[28]

The EITC was initially a small program established in 1975 to offset the Social Security payroll tax for low-earner households with children. It was then expanded considerably in the early 1990s by President Clinton to "make work pay." As shown in Table 15-1, it has become the single largest cash transfer program for low-income families in the United States, dwarfing TANF.

The amount of the EITC credit varies according to the presence of children as well as the level of family earnings.[29] The credit has three earnings ranges: in the *phase-in* range, the amount of the credit increases with earnings; in the *stationary* range, the maximum credit is provided; and in the *phase-out* range, the EITC payments are phased out, and the value of the credit declines with earnings. A payment structure like this is needed since the EITC is targeted on low-income families and, thus, the amount received from the program must eventually decline as family income increases. As an example, consider a single-parent family with two children in 2016. For families with earnings between $0 and $13,931 (the phase-in range), earnings were subsidized at a rate of 40 percent. Families with earnings of $13,931 through $18,190 (the stationary range) received the maximum credit of $5,572. Finally, for families with earnings between $18,190 and $44,648 (the phase-out range), the credit fell by 21 cents for every additional dollar earned, reaching $0 at earnings of $44,648.[30]

The impact of the EITC on raising families out of poverty is substantial.[31] For instance, as shown in Table 15-2, in 2016, the EITC increased the income of an employed single parent with two children who worked full-time, full-year at the federal minimum wage from $14,500 to $20,072, a figure just around the relevant poverty threshold.[32] As discussed in the "Minimum Wage: What Is It?" box in Chapter 10, as of 2016, over one-half of states had set their minimum wages to be higher than the federal level. In these states (or if Congress were to increase the federal minimum wage), the poverty-reducing impact of the EITC, which serves as an earnings subsidy, is amplified. This simple example makes a second point that has received increased attention by policymakers. While the EITC and the minimum wage might

---

[27]For an excellent review, see Austin Nichols and Jesse Rothstein, "The Earned Income Tax Credit (EITC)," in Moffitt, ed., *Economics of Means-Tested Transfer Programs*, vol. 1.

[28]For reviews of the research, see David Neumark, "The Effects of Minimum Wages on Employment," *FRBSB Economic Letter* (San Francisco: Federal Reserve Bank, December 2015), and *Keeping Up with a Changing Economy: Indexing the Minimum Wage, Hearing Before the US Senate Committee on Health, Education, Labor, and Pensions*, 113th Cong. (2013) (statement of Andrajit Dube); for influential early work, see David C. Card and Alan B. Krueger, *Myth and Measurement: The New Economics of the Minimum Wage* (Princeton, NJ: Princeton University Press, 1995).

[29]Since 1994, low-income households without children have also been eligible, though only for a small credit. Since 2009, there has been a somewhat higher credit for families with three or more children.

[30]Figures are from Tax Policy Center (Washington, DC: Urban Institute, January 5, 2016), accessed November 7, 2016, www.taxpolicycenter.org.

[31]For a review of the evidence see Nichols and Rothstein, "The Earned Income Tax Credit."

[32]Notably, David T. Ellwood finds that financial resources remain at about the level of "earnings plus EITC" reported in Table 15-2 even if a fuller analysis is done, which takes account of other income support programs like Food Stamps (which increase financial resources) as well as payroll taxes and work expenses (which reduce resource to about an equal extent); see "The Impact of the Earned Income Tax Credit and Social Policy Reforms on Work, Marriage, and Living Arrangements," *National Tax Journal* 53 no. 4, part 2 (December 2000): 1063–1106.

TABLE 15-2 MAKING ENDS MEET FOR A LOW-EARNER SINGLE-PARENT FAMILY WITH TWO CHILDREN, 2016

Earnings (Assume Employed at Minimum Wage Job Full-Time, Full-Year)[a]	$14,500
EITC (Maximum Credit)	$5,572
Earnings plus EITC	$20,072
Poverty Threshold[b]	$19,337
Ratio of Earnings Plus EITC to Official Poverty Threshold	1.0

[a]Earnings are computed as $7.25 per hour (federal minimum wage) multiplied by 40 hours per week multiplied by 50 weeks per year.
[b]This figure, calculated by the US Census Bureau, is the poverty threshold for 2016 for a family of 3 with two related children under age 18; see "Poverty Thresholds for 2016 by Size of Family and Number of Children Under 18 Years," accessed March 5, 2017, www.census.gov. EITC = Earned Income Tax Credit.

be considered *substitutes* in that they are alternative policy approaches—albeit very different—to raising low incomes, they function in some respect as complementary policies in that a higher minimum wage increases the income boost associated with the EITC.[33]

In contrast to AFDC, which provided maximum payments to those who were not employed and imposed a high marginal tax rate on earnings for program participants, the EITC encourages individuals to seek employment by subsidizing earnings of recipients. For individuals in the phase-in range, the amount of the EITC increases with additional hours worked, providing an incentive for those initially out of the labor force to enter. As discussed in Chapter 6, this positive participation effect is a result of the substitution effect of the wage change, which increases the opportunity cost of not working.[34]

At the same time, however, the EITC may cause some workers to reduce the number of hours worked. The provision of a fixed credit over the stationary range, for instance, provides these workers with a pure increase in income. As discussed in Chapter 6, with higher nonlabor income, individuals tend to work fewer hours. The work disincentive is even greater for individuals in the phase-out range of the EITC. For them, the credit and thus the net wage are reduced as earnings increase. Individuals with earnings in this range are expected to substitute toward nonmarket time and away from paid work because of the decrease in the opportunity cost of nonmarket time. At the same time, total income is still higher than it would otherwise be without the EITC program, also providing an incentive for individuals to work less. Hence, in this range, both the substitution and income effects operate to reduce hours worked.

The effect of the EITC program thus varies depending on the family's earnings. Overwhelming evidence indicates that the EITC provides a strong incentive for single mothers to enter the paid labor force. In fact, one study found that nearly

---

[33]Nichols and Rothstein, "The Earned Income Tax Credit," among others, have also recognized that the EITC potentially increases the supply of labor to the low-wage market, thereby reducing the wage received by workers. A higher minimum wage serves to offset this effect.
[34]For those already in the labor force but working very low hours, the EITC also has an income effect, which works in the opposite direction. However, the strength of the substitution effect is expected to dominate in the phase-in range.

60 percent of the substantial increase in single mother's employment from 1984 to 1996 was due to the expansion of the EITC.[35] On the other hand, as discussed in Chapter 6, the design of the EITC also may cause some secondary earners in married-couple families, typically wives, to leave the labor force.[36] This is the case because wives' additional earnings may place the family in the high-income range of the credit or even above it, thereby leading to receipt of a lower EITC or none at all.[37]

The EITC not only results in a "second-earner" penalty for some married-couple families but also alters incentives for couples to marry or stay married because eligibility is largely based on family income. For instance, a single mother with children who is employed full-time, full-year at the minimum wage and her employed male partner may be better off cohabiting because then only her income is counted in the EITC calculation. If instead they were to marry, both incomes would be counted.[38] Interestingly, the EITC might also encourage marriage for other couples. For instance, if a nonemployed mother with children who is ineligible for the EITC marries a low-earner male, the family will gain eligibility.

Employment Strategies

The employment outlook for welfare recipients tends to be especially bleak because, as a rule, they have little education and few job skills. Many also face other barriers to employment, including discrimination and often physical or mental health problems.[39] In addition they may encounter problems getting to work due to a lack of transportation. The government could, of course, assist people in finding jobs, which tends to be quite inexpensive to do; but jobs alone are not likely to help many welfare recipients to escape poverty. The alternative is to provide education and skills that raise the earnings of both welfare recipients and those who are poor but not on welfare. However, this approach involves considerable costs in the short run compared with merely maintaining welfare payments, and it takes some time for such expenditures to pay off.

The federal government has been active to some extent in providing training and employment programs for at least some disadvantaged and unemployed workers since the 1960s. The most recent program, which received bipartisan approval by Congress in 2014, is called the **Workforce Innovation and Opportunity Act (WIOA)**. This program, like its predecessors, provides funds for job training and job support services at the state and local levels. Because it is new, it is far

---

[35]Bruce D. Meyer and Dan T. Rosenbaum, "Welfare, the Earned Income Tax Credit, and the Labor Supply of Single Mothers," *Quarterly Journal of Economics* 116, no. 3 (August 2001): 1063–1114; and for a review of this and other studies, Nichols and Rothstein, "The Earned Income Tax Credit."

[36]Nada Eissa and Hilary W. Hoynes, "Behavioral Responses to Taxes: Lessons from the EITC and Labor Supply," in *Tax Policy and the Economy*, vol. 20, ed. James M. Poterba (Cambridge, MA: MIT Press, 2006), 73–110.

[37]Starting in 2001, the George W. Bush administration eased the EITC's secondary earner penalty slightly by expanding the phase-out range for married couples (though not for singles), and additional efforts in this regard were made in subsequent years. However, these changes have, by no means, eliminated the penalty.

[38]For an illustrative example, see Melissa S. Kearney and Leslie J. Turner, "Giving Secondary Earners a Tax Break: A Proposal to Help Low- and Middle-Income Families," Hamilton Project Discussion Paper 2013-07 (Washington, DC: Brookings Institution, December 2013).

[39]Rebecca M. Blank, "Improving the Safety Net for Single Mothers Who Face Serious Barriers to Work," *The Future of Children* 17, no. 2 (2007): 183–97.

too early to evaluate its effectiveness. However, the prior program, the **Workforce Investment Act (WIA)** was the subject of considerable criticism. By its end, funding was so low that it has been argued that the combination of Pell Grants and community colleges (to provide training) played a larger role in workforce development than the WIA.[40]

Also, beginning in the 1980s, states and subsequently the federal government initiated some education and training programs explicitly designed to move AFDC recipients from welfare to work. Analyses of a number of these welfare-to-work programs indicate that, in some cases, such programs increased earnings but generally not enough to lift individuals out of poverty.[41] The 1996 welfare legislation that followed largely shifted the emphasis of the employment strategy for helping welfare recipients away from job training and education and toward a focus on employment per se. Many states now pursue a "work first" strategy, which emphasizes job search and tries to get welfare recipients into paid employment as quickly as possible. If this effort is unsuccessful, states may place welfare recipients in unpaid work or subsidized employment or offer them limited opportunities for education and training. The success of a work first approach depends most notably on a sustained healthy economy that creates sufficient jobs for lower-skilled workers. Also, this approach must be sufficiently flexible to assist individuals who lack adequate qualifications or face any of the other types of employment barriers mentioned earlier. The EITC, which raises earnings in the low-paying jobs that such workers usually obtain, is another crucial ingredient needed for success.

Child Support Enforcement

Child support enforcement is another strategy for aiding single-parent families. Over the last several decades, child support enforcement in the United States has changed considerably, shifting from a "complaint-driven, court-enforced system" subject to considerable discretion by judges to a system guided by state and federal laws and regulations.[42] The first major child support legislation, enacted in 1975, was aimed at enforcing payments by noncustodial parents. Additional legislation in 1984 and 1988 considerably strengthened this law by requiring states to adopt numerical guidelines in setting child support awards and allowing them to collect income withheld by employers (garnish wages) and retain income tax refunds from noncustodial parents who do not make the required payments. The 1996 welfare legislation went further and instituted rules that make the establishment of paternity faster and easier, added a national registry system that makes tracking down delinquent parents across

---

[40]Regarding the WIA and related programs, see Harry J. Holzer, "Workforce Development Programs," in *Legacies of the War on Poverty*, ed. Martha J. Bailey and Sheldon Danziger (New York: Russell Sage Foundation, 2013), 121–51. See also Paul T. Decker and Jilliam A. Berk, "Ten Years of the Workforce Investment Act (WIA): Interpreting the Research on WIA and Related Programs," *Journal of Policy Analysis and Management* 30, no. 4 (Fall 2011): 906–26; and Timothy Williams, "Seeking New Start, Finding Steep Cost Workforce Investment Act Leaves Many Jobless and in Debt," *New York Times*, August 17, 2014.

[41]The most cited example of success is the Riverside California GAIN program. See Ziliak, "Temporary Assistance for Needy Families Program."

[42]This characterization is from Elaine Sorensen and Ariel Halpern, "Child Support Reforms: Who Has Benefited?" *Focus* 21, no. 1 (Spring 2000): 38–41. For a concise review of the major changes in the relevant federal laws, see "Child Support Enforcement Policy and Low-Income Families," *Focus* 21, no. 1 (Spring 2000): 1–4.

state lines possible, and set forth tough new penalties for nonpayment, including re-voking professional licenses and seizing assets. Subsequently, a law passed in 1998 made the sanctions even tougher, including penalties of up to 2 years in prison, for "deadbeat" parents.

Mothers who receive welfare are required to pursue child support as one of the conditions for receiving cash benefits. Since 2008, the federal government has per-mitted a portion of the child support monies received to "pass through" to children. This income source is also disregarded in calculating eligibility for TANF. These policies provide at least a modest incentive for noncustodial parents to make formal child support payments because they can assume that their children would get some benefit from their payments.[43]

Recent evidence indicates that the government policies outlined here do lead to higher rates of child support receipt by families, especially by those on welfare. Not surprisingly, these effects are even stronger when combined with greater state expenditures on enforcement.[44] Nonetheless, rates for both child support awards es-tablished and full payment received remain disappointingly low. Even as of 2013, only 58 percent of divorced and just 42 percent of never-married custodial parents, largely women, had a child support agreement in place. Of those due child support, 57 per-cent of all divorced custodial parents received full payment, up quite a bit from just 43 percent in 2009. For never-married parents, this same figure was 34 percent in 2013, little changed from 2009.[45]

Although recent policies have had the intended effect of increasing child sup-port awards at least to some extent, these positive gains have been accompanied by concerns that the current system is not sufficiently flexible to deal with the diverse economic circumstances of noncustodial parents, typically fathers. The current guidelines are designed for those with stable employment and adequate incomes, while many noncustodial fathers face a different economic reality of little education, unstable employment, and consequently low earnings. The rise in multipartner fer-tility has further complicated the situation as an increasing number of fathers have child support obligations for children living in more than one household. Fathers with employment difficulties, sometimes labeled *dead-broke dads* (to contrast with the term *deadbeat dads,* which has been used to negatively characterize fathers who flout their child support obligations), may simply not be able to financially support their children and so, for them, existing child support policies may be counterpro-ductive. Child support enforcement efforts may lead such men to shift from legal em-ployment to "under-the-table" work, with all its attendant disadvantages, or they may give up employment altogether. Some fathers may also have limited social contact

---

[43]Jennifer Roff, "Welfare, Child Support, and Strategic Behavior: Do High Orders and Low Disregards Discourage Child Support Awards?" *Journal of Human Resources* 45, no. 1 (Winter 2010): 59–86. Evi-dence indicates that informal payments are made (that is, payments outside of the official child support system) when policies are set to limit the "pass through" of child support monies to children; see Samara Potter Gunter, "Effects of Child Support Pass-Through and Disregard Policies on In-Kind Child Sup-port," *Review of Economics of the Household* 11 (2013): 193–209.

[44]For evidence, see Maria Cancian and Daniel Meyer, "Child Support and the Economy," in *Work-ing and Poor: How Economic and Policy Changes Are Affecting Low-Wage Workers,* ed. Rebecca M. Blank, Sheldon H. Danziger, and Robert F. Schoeni (New York: Russell Sage Foundation, 2006), 338–65; and Roff, "Welfare, Child Support, and Strategic Behavior."

[45]Timothy Grall, US Census Bureau, "Custodial Mothers and Fathers and Their Child Support, 2013," *Current Population Report* P-60-255 (January 2016), table 2; figures for 2009 are from US Census Bureau, "Custodial Mothers and Fathers and Their Child Support: 2009," *Current Population Reports* P60-240 (December 2011), table 2.

with their children because they are unable to pay support. One policy solution is to improve the labor market opportunities of disadvantaged fathers. Indeed, the federal government has funded a variety of initiatives with this intent.[46]

One alternative to the patchwork of child support policies in the United States would be to establish a **child support assurance system** similar to the one that exists in Sweden, where both parents and government are responsible for the support of children.[47] Under such a system, awards from nonresident parents could be set as a percentage of their income and withheld from their earnings, just as taxes are. If, for whatever reason, the amount paid by the parent is less than the minimum benefit assured by the government, then the government fills the financial gap so that the child receives at least the minimum benefit. While such a program might better ensure that children have adequate financial resources, it faces little chance of being adopted in the United States in the near future given the reluctance of many to see the role of the federal government expanded.

Taxes, Specialization, and Marriage

Up to this point, we have largely ignored the role of the federal income tax system, but it is in fact quite important in this context. Income taxes help to finance the federal programs discussed here, along with many others. At the same time, when income is taxed, this means that individuals do not retain all their labor market earnings, in other words they have lower take-home pay. Given the structure of the federal income tax this also means that the after-tax wage received by the individual is affected. Consequently decisions regarding whether and how much to work as well as decisions regarding family formation may be influenced. For similar reasons, payroll taxes and the Social Security payments they fund also affect these decisions.[48] Both the federal income tax and Social Security evolved when the one-earner family was the norm and, as currently structured, subsidize married women who stay home. Thus, both programs have been criticized for favoring the traditional, one-earner family. In this section, we examine the ways in which their design may discourage married women's employment. In addition, concerns have been raised about the equity or fairness of these programs. One of the primary rules proposed by economists for fair taxation is **horizontal equity**, which means that those in similar circumstances should be treated similarly.[49] Thus, we also specifically consider

---

[46]For an excellent discussion of these issues and policy solutions, see Maria Cancian, Daniel R. Meyer, and Eunhee Han, "Child Support: Responsible Fatherhood and the Quid Pro Quo," *Annals of the American Academy of Political and Social Science* 635 (2011): 140–62; and Virginia Knox, Philip A. Cowan, Carolyn Pape Cowan, and Elana Bildner, "Policies that Strengthen Fatherhood and Family Relationships: What Do We Know and What Do We Need to Know?" *Annals of the American Academy of Political and Social Science* 635, no. 1 (May 2011): 216–39.

[47]For a discussion of child support systems elsewhere, see Irwin Garfinkel and Lenna Nepomnyaschy, "Assuring Child Support: A Re-Assessment in Honor of Alfred Kahn" in *From Child Welfare to Child Well-Being: An International Perspective on Knowledge in the Service of Making Policy*, ed. Sheila B. Kamerman, S. Phipps, and A. Ben-Arieh (New York: Springer, 2010), 231–53.

[48]Here, we focus on two major federal programs only; but most states also have their own income tax, and an array of other taxes are imposed at the federal, state, and local levels.

[49]The view that "there is a generally accepted standard of equity or fairness with respect to public finance measures: equal treatment of those equally circumstanced" was first expressed by Carl S. Shoup, *Public Finance* (Chicago: Aldine, 1969), 23, and has been widely shared ever since.

whether the current income tax and Social Security systems violate this rule in their treatment of one-earner and two-earner families.[50]

Federal Income Tax

First and foremost, the present federal income tax system may be considered inequitable because the value of goods and services produced in the home is not taxed, whereas money income is subject to taxation. As a result, two couples with different levels of economic well-being may have the same taxable incomes. Suppose, for instance, that Ellen and Ed earn $25,000 each and produce $10,000 worth of goods and services in the household. Suppose too that Jim earns $50,000 and Jane, a full-time homemaker, produces $30,000 worth of goods and services in the home. Although Jim and Jane produce a total income of $80,000, including the value of home production, while Ellen and Ed only produce an income of $60,000, taxable income is $50,000 for both couples. Thus, because home production is not taxed, the tax system violates horizontal equity and favors the traditional one-earner family such as Jim and Jane.

The federal income tax structure further provides a disincentive for married women to participate in the labor force because of two specific features. First, the family is the unit of taxation, which means that there are separate schedules depending on a taxpayer's family status. For the typical married couple, the spouses sum their incomes and taxes are determined using the "married filing jointly" schedule. There are separate schedules for single individuals and single heads of household (such as heads of single-parent families).[51] Second, the United States has a **progressive income tax** structure, meaning that higher levels of income are taxed at a higher rate than lower levels. As shown in panel (a) of Table 15-3, this means, for example, that if a married couple earns $50,000, part of this amount is subject to a 10 percent tax rate and the remainder is subject to a 15 percent rate. In general, progressive tax rates are considered to be desirable because they result in wealthier families paying a proportionately larger share of their incomes in taxes.

The degree of progressivity in the tax system has varied considerably since the mid-1980s. The Tax Reform Act of 1986, which was enacted during the Reagan administration, reduced the number of tax brackets from 15, with a top rate of 50 percent, to only 2, with stated rates of 15 and 28 percent. Under President Clinton, the top tax rate was increased to 39.6 percent. In 2001, under President George W. Bush, a 10 percent bracket was introduced, and all other rates were lowered, including the top rate, from 39.6 to 35 percent. In 2013, under President Obama, the top rate was restored to 39.6 percent, as shown in Table 15-3.

---

[50]These topics have been discussed by economists for some time, dating at least from Nancy R. Gordon, "Institutional Responses: The Federal Income Tax System" and "Institutional Responses: The Social Security System," in *The Subtle Revolution*, ed. Ralph E. Smith (Washington, DC: Urban Institute, 1979), 201–21, 223–55. For a more recent consideration, see Edward J. McCaffery, "Where's the Sex in Fiscal Sociology? Taxation and Gender in Comparative Perspective," in *Taxation in Perspective: Comparative and Historical Approaches to Fiscal Sociology*, ed. Isaac Martin, Ajay K. Mehrota, and Monica Prasad (Cambridge: Cambridge University Press, 2009), 216–36.

[51]There is also a schedule that permits married couples to file separately. (This is distinct from the "single" schedule—using the single schedule is not an option for married couples.) However, the vast majority of couples file jointly because the taxes owed using this schedule are generally lower. The married filing jointly schedule is the one discussed in the text and shown in Table 15-3.

TABLE 15-3 FEDERAL INDIVIDUAL INCOME TAX RATES AND CALCULATION OF MARRIAGE PENALTY/BONUS

(a) 2016 FEDERAL INDIVIDUAL INCOME TAX RATE SCHEDULES[a]

SINGLE SCHEDULE		MARRIED FILING JOINTLY SCHEDULE	
Taxable Income	Tax Rate	Taxable Income	Tax Rate
$0–$9,275	10%	$0–$18,550	10%
$9,275–$37,650	15%	$18,550–$75,300	15%
$37,650–$91,150	25%	$75,300–$151,900	25%
$91,150–$190,150	28%	$151,900–$231,450	28%
$190,150–$413,350	33%	$231,450–$413,350	33%
$413,350–$415,050	35%	$413,350–$466,950	35%
$415,050+	39.6%	$466,950+	39.6%

(b) CALCULATION OF MARRIAGE PENALTY/BONUS USING 2016 TAX RATE SCHEDULE[b]

COUPLE	VALUE OF HOME PRODUCTION (NOT TAXABLE)	HUSBAND'S INCOME (TAXABLE)	WIFE'S INCOME (TAXABLE)	COMBINED INCOME (TAXABLE)	TAX LIABILITY IF:		MARRIAGE PENALTY OR BONUS
					Married Couple	Both Single	
Ellen and Ed	$10,000	$25,000	$25,000	$50,000	$6,573	$6,573	$0 Penalty
Jane and Jim	$30,000	$50,000	$0	$50,000	$6,573	$8,271	$1,699 Bonus
Gina and Greg	$10,000	$80,000	$80,000	$160,000	$31,786	$31,543	$244 Penalty
Debra and Dave	$30,000	$160,000	$0	$160,000	$31,786	$37,837	$6,051 Bonus

[a]There are two other schedules not shown here, the head of household schedule for single individuals with a dependent child and a married filing separately schedule for couples who are separated.
[b]This table makes several simplifying assumptions. It assumes that there are no children and that taxable income equals gross income. In actual practice, taxable income is calculated as gross income less personal exemptions and less the standard deduction.

The current tax structure means that a married woman, still generally considered to be the secondary earner by most families, will often face a high marginal tax rate on her potential income, should she decide to enter the labor market. This is because the first dollar of her earnings is taxed at her husband's top marginal tax rate. In this situation the wife bears what is known as a **secondary earner penalty**; the labor market return to working is lowered, thereby reducing her incentive to enter the labor market.[52] In the case of Jane and Jim, for example, if Jane decides to work for pay, the first dollar she receives is taxed at a 15 percent rate, rather than at the lowest rate of 10 percent. This is because her income will be added on to Jim's and their tax liability will be determined using the married filing jointly tax schedule. This disincentive increases considerably with couples' income. For instance, consider a couple in which the husband, Dave, has $160,000 in earnings and his wife, Debra, is presently a full-time homemaker. If Debra were to enter the labor market, her first dollar of pay would be taxed at a 28 percent rate, not at the bottom tax rate of 10 percent. Further, as noted earlier, the EITC, which is part of the federal tax code, discourages participation by a secondary earner in low-earning families because the value of the EITC eventually declines as family earnings rise.

The "marriage penalty" is another disincentive created by the current structure of the US tax system. A **marriage penalty** refers to the additional taxes a couple owes if they are married compared to the taxes they would pay if they remained single. Couples could also possibly receive a **marriage bonus**, which refers to tax savings due to marriage compared to remaining single. Under our current tax system, two-earner couples may incur a marriage penalty, while single-earner couples receive a marriage bonus. Because single-earner couples receive a marriage bonus, the tax system provides incentives for such couples to marry. On the other hand, the marriage penalty that arises for some dual-earner couples may discourage such couples from marrying.[53]

The marriage penalty occurs when the income brackets for married couples are less than twice as wide as the brackets for singles. The marriage penalty came about as the result of a policy change initiated in 1969 to reduce taxes paid by single taxpayers relative to married couples. This change inevitably increased the relative tax liability for some married couples compared to single taxpayers. In 2001 President George W. Bush introduced tax changes to partly deal with this situation. The Bush changes made the new 10 percent bracket for married couples twice as wide as for singles and instituted the same change for the existing 15 percent bracket. The value of the standard deduction for married couples was also increased so that it is now twice the value for singles. Importantly, although these changes eliminated the marriage penalty for some two-earner married couples and reduced it for others, they also had the effect of considerably *increasing* the marriage bonus for traditional, one-earner couples.

To get a better idea of how marriage bonuses and penalties arise, let us look at panel (b) of Table 15-3, which illustrates the size of the bonus or penalty for different types of married couples using 2016 tax rates. For instance, consider again Jim

[52]Among its provisions, the Tax Reform Act of 1986 eliminated many deductions, including one designed to reduce this very penalty. A recent proposal suggests bringing a variant of it back; see Kearney and Turner, "Giving Secondary Earners a Tax Break."
[53]Regarding the impact of taxes and subsidies on fertility, marriage, and divorce decisions, see Adam Carasso and C. Eugene Steurle, "The Hefty Penalty on Marriage Facing Many Households with Children," *The Future of Children* 15, no. 2 (Autumn 2005): 157–75.

and Jane and Ellen and Ed, but now suppose that they are unmarried. If Jim earns $50,000 and marries Jane, who has no earnings, their combined tax liability declines by $1,699, providing a marriage bonus of this amount. Conversely, if Ellen and Ed each earn $25,000 and marry, they receive no bonus. Because their top tax bracket is 15 percent, they also do not face a marriage penalty as a result of the Bush tax changes described earlier.

Marriage penalties remain, however, for couples whose income is taxed in brackets higher than 15 percent. For instance, Gina and Greg, who each earn $80,000, face a marriage penalty of $244. In contrast, consider the situation of Debra and Dave, who have the same combined family income of $160,000 but Dave brings in all the earnings. They receive a *bonus* of $6,051. What explains the very different tax consequences for Debra and Dave versus Gina and Greg (or, for that matter, Jane and Jim vs. Ellen and Ed)? The simplest answer points to the two features of our tax structure reviewed earlier: progressive taxation combined with separate schedules for married-couple and single taxpayers. Debra and Dave receive such a large bonus because, as a married couple, a larger portion of their income is taxed at a lower rate in the married-couple tax schedule than in the single schedule. These examples illustrate the general pattern we noted earlier: single-earner couples generally receive a marriage bonus, while two-earner couples receive no marriage bonus and may bear a penalty. Indeed, as we have seen, marriage penalties persist for those in higher tax brackets; they also tend to be larger when the spouses' incomes are fairly equal.[54] Finally, as discussed earlier in this chapter, the marriage penalty is also quite large (as a percentage of income) for low-earning couples with children who qualify for the EITC.[55]

It is also instructive to compare the examples in Table 15-3 to a system that taxes each person as an individual, as is the case in most other economically advanced countries and as was the case in the United States prior to 1948.[56] This alternative eliminates the secondary earner penalty because each individual's first dollar is taxed at the same rate he or she would pay if single. It also eliminates marriage penalties (and bonuses) because there is one tax schedule regardless of family structure. Such a change would clearly be to the advantage of two-earner couples such as Gina and Greg, who face a penalty under the current system. On the other hand, single-earner couples (Jane and Jim and Debra and Dave) would no longer receive large marriage bonuses.[57] Which system is viewed as more equitable in its treatment of money income (in the sense of horizontal equity) depends on whether the individual or the family is viewed as the appropriate tax unit.[58] The fact that single-earner families would be made worse off under individual taxation than under the current arrangement points to the considerable political challenges involved in changing from

---

[54]Couples cannot get around this "penalty" by filing separate returns because the tax rates for married filing separately are higher than those for single individuals.

[55]For a discussion of penalties and bonuses in the EITC, see Carasso and Steurle, "Hefty Penalty on Marriage."

[56]Jonathan Gruber, *Public Finance and Public Policy*, 3rd ed. (New York: Worth, 2010), 551–52.

[57]Another option would be to make the household, not the family, the unit of taxation. This option would place cohabiting couples and married couples on equal footing but would not address the issue of secondary earner bias associated with joint filing. For a fuller consideration of this and alternative proposals, see Anne L. Alstott, "Updating the Welfare State: Marriage, the Income Tax, and Social Security in the Age of the New Individualism," 66 *Tax Law Review* 695 (2013).

[58]For instance, some argue that the family should be the unit of taxation because it is a basic economic unit in society and because husbands and wives pool income. See Edward J. McCaffery, *Taxing Women* (Chicago: University of Chicago, 1997), chap. 1.

one regime to another even if it were viewed as desirable to do so. Another option that would also meet the goal of horizontal equity and surfaces periodically is a "flat tax," which imposes the same rate on all incomes and provides a personal exemption. Still, even with a large personal exemption such a tax would be much less progressive than the current system.

Social Security

Social Security, the federal social insurance program instituted in 1935, which provides retirement and survivor benefits as well as disability coverage for workers and their dependents, also poses problems of equity between one-earner married couples, on the one hand, and two-earner married couples, unmarried couples, and single people, on the other hand.[59] The problem arises because payroll taxes paid by workers are based on each individual's employment history, while the Social Security benefits they receive are family-based.

As of 2016, individuals in jobs covered by Social Security (and Medicare) faced a 15.3 percent tax rate on earnings up to a specified maximum level, half to be paid by the employer and half by the worker. To receive benefits, individuals must work in jobs covered by Social Security for at least 40 calendar quarters. Benefits received reflect contributions paid, so low-wage workers and those with long periods out of the labor force receive correspondingly lower benefits. However, the Social Security system has special rules for married couples: spouses of covered workers are entitled to receive Social Security benefits equal to 50 percent of the amount received by the covered worker and survivor benefits of 100 percent if the covered worker dies, even if they have never paid payroll taxes.[60] Alternatively, the spouse may opt to receive benefits based on his or her own earnings record if that amount is greater.

One consequence of these various rules is that married couples fare very differently under Social Security in terms of taxes paid in (contributions) and benefits received, depending on how much each spouse earns. To illustrate this point, we look at three situations ranging from more to less traditional: (1) the husband is the sole earner; (2) both spouses are employed, but the wife works intermittently or at low wages; and (3) both spouses are employed, and both have considerable earnings records.[61]

In the case of a married couple where the husband is the sole earner, only the husband pays payroll taxes, while the family (husband and wife) receives 150 percent of his individual Social Security benefit. In this situation, the difference between payroll taxes paid in and benefits received is the greatest, and hence, this family structure is most favored by the Social Security system.

Next, consider a couple where the wife is employed, but she earns substantially lower wages or has a shorter work life than her husband. Such a family is likely to

---

[59]Useful overviews of these issues are provided in Melissa M. Favreault and C. Eugene Steurle, "Measuring Social Security Proposals by More than Solvency: Impacts on Poverty, Progressivity, Horizontal Equity, and Work Incentives," Working Paper 2012-15 (Center for Retirement Research at Boston College, Chestnut Hill, MA, 2012); and McCaffery, *Taxing Women.*

[60]Since 1977, spouses divorced after at least 10 years of marriage are entitled to the same benefit as current spouses. For more discussion on program changes over the years, see Patricia P. Martin and David A. Weaver, "Social Security: A Program and Policy History," *Social Security Bulletin* 66, no. 1 (2005): 1–15.

[61]The rules are gender-neutral and would apply equally if the wife were the sole wage earner.

maximize benefits by claiming the spouse benefit. In this case, although the wife pays payroll taxes into the system too, the family still receives 150 percent of the husband's Social Security benefit, precisely the same amount as they would have if she had not been employed and had paid no payroll taxes. Nevertheless, the husband and wife together receive more benefits than they would if they were each single.

Finally, consider the case of the wife who earns enough to receive larger benefits in her own right than she would receive as a spouse.[62] The benefits received by this family (calculated as the wife's individual benefit plus the husband's individual benefit) are somewhat larger than the amount received by the married couples in the prior two cases. However, unlike the couples discussed previously, the couple in this case does not benefit from being married. She and her husband receive exactly the same amount in benefits as if they were both single.

The results in the preceding descriptions violate the rule of horizontal equity, namely that equal contributions should secure equal returns. Each employed wife pays in as much as she would if she were single, but only the one who earns considerably less than her husband receives additional benefits as a spouse. Moreover, a wife who is not employed receives benefits as a spouse without making any tax payments. Clearly, this system provides secondary earners, typically wives, with yet another disincentive to work for pay.[63]

One way to bring about equity among couples under the Social Security system would be through *earnings sharing*.[64] This approach assigns an equal share of total household earnings to each spouse and eliminates dependent benefits. Earnings sharing recognizes that the division of labor in the home represents a joint decision and that both spouses contribute to family welfare through their market and/or non-market work. Unlike the present system, earnings sharing would not penalize dual-earner couples. In addition, the Social Security system would move in the direction of greater horizontal equity, in that equal contributions to Social Security by each family member would yield equal benefits.[65] No couple would have an advantage compared to any other type of couple or compared to an unmarried individual. Such a change would, however, create problems for traditional couples who presumably made their labor supply decisions under the existing rules. This difficulty could, however, be overcome by giving couples who married before the new policy was adopted the option of remaining under the current system. A change to earnings sharing also raises concerns about the adequacy of benefit levels for single-earner families. Although such issues remain to be addressed, continued growth of the two-earner

---

[62]As a result of demographic changes including declining rates of marriage combined with past increases in women's labor force participation, increasing numbers of women have benefits based entirely on their own earnings records. For discussion, see Barbara A. Butrica and Karen E. Smith, "The Impact of Changes in Couples' Earnings on Married Women's Social Security Benefits," *Social Security Bulletin*, 72, no. 1 (2012): 1–9; and for projections, see Social Security Administration, Current Law Projections, "Women & Dual Entitlement, 2025–2090," accessed March 10, 2016, www.socialsecurity.gov.

[63]For a more in-depth analysis of the incentives inherent in the system, see Andrew G. Biggs, Gayle L. Reznik, and Nada O. Eissa, "The Treatment of Married Women by the Social Security Retirement Program," Working Paper 2010-18 (Center for Retirement Research at Boston College, Chestnut Hill, MA, November 2010).

[64]For details on this alternative, see Marianne Ferber, Vanessa Rouillon, and Patricia Simpson, "The Aging Population and Social Security: Women as the Problem and the Solution," *Challenge* 49, no. 3 (May/June 2006): 105–19; and Howard M. Iams, Gayle Reznik, and Christopher R. Tamborini, "Earnings Sharing in the U.S. Social Security System: A Microsimulation Analysis of Future Female Retirees," *The Gerontologist* 50, no. 4 (2010): 495–508.

[65]No Social Security taxes are paid on the value of what is produced in the household, but neither does the family accumulate benefits.

family is likely to increase support for policies that eliminate the advantages that single-earner families realize under the current structure of Social Security.

Another concern that has long been raised about the current system is the adequacy of Social Security benefits for women, especially for those who are never-married, divorced, and widowed, because these groups have the highest poverty rates among the elderly. In recent years, this concern has been amplified in light of declines in marriage, as discussed in Chapter 13, which are expected to increase the ranks of those who cannot claim a spousal benefit. Moreover, to the extent that declines in marriage are most pronounced among those with the least income and education, these individuals will be at even greater risk of poverty in future years.[66]

Women's higher poverty rates are in part due to the fact that, on average, they earn lower wages and work fewer hours per week than men and are much more likely to have spent time out of the labor market to raise children or to take care of other family members.[67] For this reason, they are also much less likely to have pensions from employers and much more likely to have to rely on Social Security as their major source of income in their old age.[68] Widows, for instance, typically receive just half to two-thirds of the combined benefit of a married couple, which results in a considerable drop in their standard of living because the cost of maintaining a one-person household is considerably more than half of the cost of maintaining a household of two.[69] Never-married women and divorced women who were married fewer than 10 years receive benefits based on their own earnings record only. Elderly women at greatest risk of poverty are those who spent a good deal of time on welfare in earlier years. Their shorter work lives and most often low earnings lead to extremely low Social Security benefits. Even though they are likely to be eligible for **Supplemental Security Income (SSI)**, which provides cash benefits for the low-income elderly, the combined benefits of the two programs are generally insufficient to lift them out of poverty.[70] One way to address these problems would be to increase the value of the minimum Social Security benefit. Others advocate increasing the size of the spousal and survivor benefit or perhaps giving women "credit" for time spent out of the labor force to raise children, but these changes would further increase the advantage of

---

[66]US General Accountability Office, *Trends in Marriage and Work Patterns May Increase Economic Vulnerability for Some Retirees*, GAO-14-33 (Washington, DC: General Accountability Office, January 15, 2014).

[67]For evidence on the difficulties facing women and policy options to strengthen Social Security for women, see Carroll L. Estes, Terry O'Neil, and Heidi Hartmann, "Breaking the Social Security Glass Ceiling: A Proposal to Modernize Women's Benefits" (Washington, DC: Institute for Women's Policy Research, May 2012).

[68]US General Accounting Office, "Retirement Security: Women Still Face Challenges," July 2012; and Women's Bureau, US Department of Labor, "Older Women Workers and Economic Security" (Washington, DC: February 2015).

[69]These figures are calculated as follows. As discussed in the text, a one-earner couple receives a couple benefit equal to 150 percent of the husband's individual benefit. If the wife becomes widowed, she receives 66 2/3 percent of the couple benefit (equivalent to 100 percent of his sole benefit). For couples in which the spouses have similar earnings, the couple receives a couple benefit equal to 200 percent of his or her individual benefit. If he or she becomes widowed, he or she receives 50 percent of what the couple previously received (precisely equal to his or her own 100 percent benefit). See David A. Weaver, "Widows and Social Security," *Social Security Bulletin* 70, no. 3 (2010).

[70]Sheila R. Zedlewski and Rumki Saha, "Social Security and Single Mothers," in *Social Security and the Family: Addressing Unmet Needs in an Underfunded System*, ed. Melissa M. Favreault, Frank J. Sammartino, and C. Eugene Steurle (Washington, DC: Urban Institute, 2002), 89–121. For more on the SSI program, see Mark Duggan, Melissa S. Kearney, and Stephanie Rennane, "The Supplemental Security Income (SSI) Program," in Moffitt, ed., *Economics of Means-Tested Transfer Programs*, vol. 2.

one-earner over two-earner families and increase incentives for women to stay out of the labor force.[71]

As the baby boom cohort enters retirement age, policy discussion has focused on reforming Social Security to ensure that the program will be on sound financial footing in years to come. Among the policy options, payroll taxes could be raised, the cap on the maximum amount of earnings subject to Social Security taxes could be increased or even removed, benefits could be reduced, the eligibility age for receiving benefits could be further increased, or some combination of these reforms could be instituted.[72] In addition to such reforms, a number of proposals have circulated including a "two-tier" system, comprised of a Social Security program much like the present one coupled with a second tier of private investments.[73] The merits of this specific reform remain the subject of considerable debate, particularly because it is such a radical departure from the existing system. Part of the discussion has focused on the implications of such a change for women.[74] One concern is that women who spend time out of the labor market to rear children, especially those who were never employed, would be disadvantaged because they would have accumulated little in the investment component of the program. Even employed women would likely accrue smaller amounts than men because of their lower earnings levels. However, if the two-tier system were combined with earnings sharing (discussed earlier), these concerns would be mitigated. A second concern highlighted by the financial crisis of 2008 is that private investments are risky and can be subject to considerable market fluctuations.

Conclusion

This chapter began by reviewing the major changes that occurred in the US welfare program in the mid-1990s. TANF replaced AFDC. TANF was implemented at a time of unprecedented economic prosperity. It resulted in a considerable decline in welfare caseloads, a rise in the employment of single mothers, and increased earnings and reduced poverty for many, though not all, single-mother families. However, in contrast to its predecessor AFDC, TANF did not serve as an adequate safety net during the Great Recession, as evidenced by the fact that the national caseload increased only slightly during the recession. Rather, the most important transfer program to buffer families during the economic crisis was SNAP, which experienced a tremendous

---

[71]For a discussion of alternatives, see US General Accountability Office, *Trends in Marriage and Work Patterns*, appendix II; and Estes, O'Neil, and Hartmann, "Breaking the Social Security Glass Ceiling." On caregiver credits, specifically, see John Jankowski, "Caregiver Credits in France, Germany, and Sweden: Lessons for the United States," *Social Security Bulletin*, 71, no. 4 (November 2011).

[72]Carole Green points out that a seemingly neutral policy such as raising the eligibility age for Social Security may have a disparate impact by race and ethnicity given differences in health status, financial need, and occupation; see "Race, Ethnicity, and Social Security Retirement Age in the US," *Feminist Economics* 11, no. 2 (July 2005): 117–43.

[73]For details on one proposal, see John F. Cogan and Olivia S. Mitchell, "Perspectives from the President's Commission on Social Security Reform," *Journal of Economic Perspectives* 17, no. 2 (Spring 2003): 149–72. For a critique of this and other similar proposals, see Ferber, Rouillon, and Simpson, "Aging Population and Social Security."

[74]US General Accounting Office, *Social Security Reform: Implications for Women*, Report T-HEHS-99–52 (Washington, DC: General Accounting Office, February 1999). Although many concerns have been raised, a simulation by Rudolph G. Penner and Elizabeth Cove suggests that women might actually benefit from such a change. See "Women and Individual Accounts," in Favreault, Sammartino, and Steurle, eds., *Social Security and the Family*, 229–70.

increase in its caseload size and expenditures. As a consequence of these developments, there is considerable concern about the growing number of disconnected single mothers who have little government income support or earnings to rely on.

This chapter has also looked at the role of two other federal programs designed to address the problems of low-income, particularly female-headed, families: the EITC and child support. The EITC has played a critical role in reducing poverty. It is now the single largest cash transfer program to working families with low earnings, and as we have seen, it raises the incomes of the working poor to just about the official poverty line. In addition, child support awards increased for many single-parent families, particularly never-married mothers, as a direct result of changes in federal child support rules. Still, some concern surrounds these policies. For instance, the size of the marriage penalty associated with the EITC may discourage some unmarried couples from marrying and may encourage some married couples to get divorced. And, while stepping up child support enforcement transfers more resources to children, an ongoing concern is that many noncustodial parents, generally fathers, have very low incomes themselves, limiting the amount they can potentially pay.

Finally, in this chapter, we have identified a number of important ways that federal income taxes and Social Security affect the work and family decisions of individuals. Both these policies favor families with full-time homemakers compared to those with two earners, although two-earner couples are now the norm. We also noted that it is critical for policymakers to consider the effects of such policies on incentives for secondary earners to work for pay, especially when evaluating proposals to revamp the income tax system or restructure Social Security.

Questions for Review and Discussion

1. In what fundamental ways does the TANF program differ from the former AFDC program?

2. The EITC receives bipartisan support, while AFDC was far less widely accepted. What are the key differences in these programs that led one to be popular and the other (now defunct and replaced by TANF) to have received so much less support?

3. In recent decades, child support enforcement was stepped up considerably. Explain the pros and cons of this policy change.

4. Consider a married couple where the husband and the wife each has $85,000 in taxable earnings. Assume they have no children and all income is from earnings. Using the information in Table 15-3,

   a. Compute their tax liability as a married couple.

   b. Compute their tax liability if they live together but are not married.

   c. Assuming they are married, compute their marriage bonus or penalty. Is this outcome what you would have expected based on the discussion in the chapter? Explain.

   d. Answer the prior questions again, but this time assume that the husband has $170,000 in taxable earnings and the wife has no earnings. Do your findings differ? If so, explain why.

e. Suppose the wife in part d is deciding whether to enter the labor force. What income tax rate affects this decision? Explain your answer.

5. Discuss the pros and cons of taxing each spouse as an individual without regard to marital status.

Suggested Readings

AEI/Brookings Working Group on Poverty and Opportunity. *Opportunity, Responsibility, and Security: A Consensus Plan for Reducing Poverty and Restoring the American Dream.* Washington, DC: AEI/Brookings, 2015.

Bailey, Martha J., and Sheldon Danziger, eds. *Legacies of the War on Poverty.* New York: Russell Sage Foundation, 2013.

Bartfield, Judith, Craig Gundersen, Timothy M. Smeding, and James P. Ziliak. *SNAP Matters. How Food Stamps Affect Health and Well-Being.* Palo Alto, CA: Stanford University Press, 2015.

Beller, Andrea H., and John W. Graham. "The Economics of Child Support." In *Marriage and the Economy*, edited by Shoshana Grossbard-Shechtman, 153–76. Cambridge: Cambridge University Press, 2003.

Currie, Janet M. *The Invisible Safety Net: Protecting the Nation's Poor Children and Families.* Princeton, NJ: Princeton University Press, 2008.

Edin, Kathryn J., and H. L. Shaefer. *$2.00 a Day: Living on Almost Nothing in America.* Boston: Houghton Mifflin Harcourt, 2015.

Grogger, Jeffrey, and Lynn A. Karoly. *Welfare Reform: Effects of a Decade of Change.* Cambridge, MA: Harvard University Press, 2005.

Heinrich, Carolyn J., and John Karl Scholz, eds. *Making the Work-Based Safety Net Work Better: Forward-Looking Policies to Help Low-Income Families.* New York: Russell Sage Foundation, 2009.

Luce, Stephanie, Jennifer Luff, Joseph Anthony McCartin, and Ruth Milkman. *What Works for Workers? Public Policies and Innovative Strategies for Low-Wage Workers.* New York: Russell Sage Foundation, 2014.

McCaffery, Edward J. "Where's the Sex in Fiscal Sociology? Taxation and Gender in Comparative Perspective." In *Taxation in Perspective: Comparative and Historical Approaches to Fiscal Sociology*, edited by Isaac Martin, Ajay K. Mehrota, and Monica Prasad, 216–36. Cambridge: Cambridge University Press, 2009.

Moffitt, Robert, ed. *Economics of Means-Tested Transfer Programs.* Chicago: University of Chicago, 2016.

Moffitt, Robert A. "The Deserving Poor, the Family, and the U.S. Welfare System," *Demography* 52 (2015): 729–49.

Newman, Katherine S., and Hella Winston. *Reskilling America: Learning to Labor in the Twenty-First Century.* New York: Metropolitan Books, 2016.

Smeeding, Timothy M., and Marcia J. Carlson. "Family Change, Public Response: Social Policy in an Era of Complex Families." In *Social Class and Changing Families in an Unequal America*, edited by Marcia J. Carlson and Paula England, 161–95. Stanford, CA: Stanford University Press, 2011.

Ziliak, James P., ed. *Welfare Reform and Its Long-Term Consequences for America's Poor.* New York: Cambridge University Press, 2009.

Key Terms

Aid to Families with Dependent Children (AFDC) (400)

in-kind benefits (400)

Food Stamps (400)

Supplemental Nutrition Assistance Program (SNAP) (400)

Medicaid (400)

AFDC guarantee (401)

AFDC tax rate (401)

Temporary Assistance to Needy Families (TANF) (403)

disconnected mothers (406)

marriage promotion (406)

Earned Income Tax Credit (EITC) (407)

Workforce Innovation and Opportunities Act (WIOA) (410)

Workforce Investment Act (WIA) (411)

child support enforcement (411)

child support assurance system (413)

horizontal equity (413)

progressive income tax (414)

secondary earner penalty (416)

marriage penalty (416)

marriage bonus (416)

Social Security (418)

Supplemental Security Income (SSI) (420)

Balancing the Competing Demands of Work and Family

16

CHAPTER HIGHLIGHTS

- The Competing Demands of Work and Family
- Rationales for Government and Employer Policies to Assist Workers
- Family Leave
- Childcare
- Other Family-Friendly Policies

This chapter starts with a discussion of the competing demands of paid work and family that an increasing number of individuals are confronting as single-parent and dual-earner families replace the traditional family of a breadwinner husband and homemaker wife. Next, we discuss the potential role for government and employers in alleviating these conflicts and review family-friendly policies, including family and medical leave, childcare, and alternative work schedules offered by firms.

The Competing Demands of Work and Family

A growing share of the workforce has family responsibilities. There are greater numbers of two-earner families, including those with small children; more single-parent families; and more people with elderly parents. In the United States, the burden of balancing the competing demands of work and family is still largely borne by individuals. Nonetheless, government and employers offer some policies to assist workers as discussed in this chapter.

Many individuals inevitably confront a trade-off between doing full justice to their job and fully meeting family responsibilities. Balancing these demands is generally most difficult for employed women with families. Before they start their workday and after it ends, they typically do most of the housework, as well as childcare, essentially working a "second shift."[1] As seen in Chapter 4, although the gender gap in housework has narrowed, employed wives still spend one and one-half as much time in housework as their husbands. Further, as discussed in Chapter 9, this appears to reduce their wages, perhaps by limiting the energy and time they are able to expend on market work. In addition, the need for elder care, mainly provided by women, is placing increasing demands on women's time. The Census Bureau projects that the size of the US population aged 65 and over will more than double from 2015 to 2060. Moreover, as a result of improved health care and nutrition, the size of the "old old" population, typically defined as those aged 85 and over, will more than triple over the same period; this group is even more likely to require care.[2] Demands are especially great on women responsible for the care of both their parents and their children at the same time, typically those who delayed childbearing until their 30s or 40s.[3]

Workplace culture and expectations can pose a serious obstacle to successfully combining paid work and family.[4] The specific challenges differ considerably, depending on whether the position is professional (e.g., a lawyer) or nonprofessional (e.g., a retail sales job), and by gender. Especially for those in professional positions, the maintained assumption by employers is that work should take precedence over family matters. As a result, workers may be deemed unprofessional if they admit that they are delayed due to childcare problems or if they want to attend a child's soccer game. Rising weekly work hours for professionals and other highly skilled workers, discussed in Chapter 5, have further intensified work–family conflicts.[5] To avoid stigma or career repercussions (e.g., fewer opportunities for advancement, lower raises), workers may offer a nonfamily reason such as car repair when arriving late to work or leaving earlier than usual. Setting up meetings outside of the office is another example of a strategy that provides "cover" to leave the physical workplace to attend to family matters. Even when supportive policies are available, workers may feel reluctant to take advantage of them, as evidenced by low rates of utilization.

---

[1]The pioneering book on this subject is Arlie Hochschild, *The Second Shift* (New York: Viking Press, 1989). For an excellent review of the issues and policies discussed in this chapter, see Heather Boushey, *Finding Time: The Economics of Work–Family Conflict* (Cambridge, MA: Harvard University Press, 2016). See also, Shelley J. Correll, Erin L. Kelly, Lindsey Trimble O'Connor, and Joan C. Williams, "Redesigning, Redefining Work," introductory essay for special issue, *Work and Occupations* 41, no. 1 (February 2014): 3–17.

[2]US Census Bureau, National Population Projections, "Projections of the Population by Sex and Selected Age Groups for the United States: 2015 to 2060," table 3, accessed June 14, 2016, www.census.gov. For evidence on the extent and impact of elder care responsibilities, see, for example, Richard W. Johnson and Anthony T. Lo Sasso, "The Employment and Time Costs of Caring for Elderly Parents," *Inquiry* 43, no. 3 (Fall 2006): 195–210; and Ann Bookman and Delia Kimbrel, "Families and Elder Care in the Twenty-First Century," *The Future of Children* 21, no. 2 (Fall 2011): 117–40.

[3]See, for example, Kim Parker and Eileen Patten, "The Sandwich Generation: Rising Financial Burdens for Middle-Age Americans," Pew Research Center, January 30, 2013, www.pewresearch.org. For recent data, see US Bureau of Labor Statistics, "Unpaid Eldercare in the United States—2013–14 Summary," *News Release* USDL-15-1851, September 23, 2015.

[4]Considerable recent media attention has focused on this issue. See Tara Siegel Bernard, "The Unspoken Stigma of Workplace Flexibility," *New York Times*, June 13, 2013; Anne Weisberg, "The Workplace Culture that Flying Nannies Won't Fix," *New York Times*, August 24, 2015; Erin Reid, "Why Some Men Pretend to Work 80 Hour Weeks," *Harvard Business Review*, April 28, 2015; and Noam Scheiber, "Attitudes Shift on Paid Leave: Dads Sue, Too," *New York Times*, September 15, 2015.

[5]Jerry A. Jacobs and Kathleen Gerson, *The Time Divide: Work, Family, and Gender Inequality* (Cambridge, MA: Harvard University Press, 2005; Peter Kuhn and Fernando Lozano, "The Expanding Workweek? Understanding Trends in Long Work Hours among U.S. Men, 1979–2006," *Journal of Labor Economics* 26, no. 2 (April 2008): 311–43; and Heather Boushey and Bridget Ansel, *Overworked America: The Economic Causes and Consequences of Long Work Hours* (Washington, DC: Washington Center for Equitable Growth, May 16, 2016), equitablegrowth.org.

The reasons why professional women and men may suffer career-wise when making overt decisions to focus on family differ. For men, it is argued that they are penalized because they are engaging in "gender nonconforming behavior" since the idealized male worker focuses on his career to the exclusion of family. For women, they are penalized for engaging in gender-conforming behavior since they are validating that the workplace is not their main focus.[6] While progress remains slow, a number of prominent firms are taking steps to change workplace culture.[7]

Workers in nonprofessional jobs face a different set of workplace flexibility issues. For instance, retail sales workers may be expected to be available at a moment's notice (termed "open availability" or "just in time" scheduling) so that the firm can avoid overstaffing and the attendant costs. However, workers with small children may not have a caregiver ready to take over without sufficient advanced notice.[8] Another practice that leads to irregular shifts and unpredictable earnings is when employers send workers home earlier than expected due to slow demand. Further, when low-wage workers request more flexible hours, they are often instead offered fewer hours, which is not equivalent from an earnings standpoint. This lack of employment flexibility contributes to greater tardiness and absenteeism, as well as more quits.[9]

Some women respond to the competing demands of paid work and family, if they can do so financially, by taking part-time rather than full-time jobs; and for women in demanding careers, this often means putting opportunities for career advancement on hold.[10] Nonetheless, Table 16-1 shows that in 2015 nearly 50 percent of all employed married mothers with children under 18 years of age were employed full-time. The corresponding figure for married mothers with a child under age 3 was 43 percent. Those who do work full-time are more securely attached to the labor force and earn higher incomes, but many undoubtedly face a time squeeze. In the remainder of this section we look at the specific difficulties of two groups: low-wage workers with families and highly educated women seeking to combine paid work and family.

Work–Family Challenges Faced by Low-Wage Workers with Families

It is arguably low-wage workers with families, especially low-income single mothers, who face the greatest challenges when it comes to combining paid work and family. For instance, as discussed in Chapter 15, welfare programs such as Temporary

[6]See Joan C. Williams, Mary Blair-Loy, and Jennifer L. Berdahl, "Cultural Schemas, Social Class, and the Flexibility Stigma," *Journal of Social Issues* 69, no. 2 (2013): 209–34; see also David S. Pedulla and Sarah Thébaud, "Can We Finish the Revolution? Gender, Work–Family Ideals, and Institutional Constraint," *American Sociological Review* 80, no. 1 (February 2015): 116–39. For a historical perspective, see Andrea Rees Davies and Brenda D. Frink, "The Origins of the Ideal Worker: The Separation of Work and Home in the United States from the Market Revolution to 1950," *Work and Occupations* 41, no. 1 (February 2014): 18–39.
[7]Claire Cain Miller and David Streitfeld, "Big Leaps for Parental Leave, if Workers Actually Take It," *New York Times*, September 1, 2015.
[8]In fact, this practice by Starbucks and others received considerable media attention in 2014, and Starbucks swiftly adjusted its specific policy. See Jodi Kantor, "Working Anything but 9 to 5," *New York Times*, August 13, 2014; and Jodi Kantor, "Starbucks to Revise Work Scheduling Policies," *New York Times*, August 15, 2014. See also Steven Greenhouse, "A Push to Give Steadier Shifts to Part-Timers," *New York Times*, July 15, 2014.
[9]Williams, Blair-Loy, and Berdahl, "Cultural Schemas, Social Class."
[10]For further discussion, see Suzanne M. Bianchi, "Changing Families, Changing Workplaces," *The Future of Children* 21, no. 2 (Fall 2011): 15–36.

TABLE 16-1   WORK EXPERIENCE OF MOTHERS, BY AGE OF YOUNGEST CHILD, 2015

	ALL MOTHERS	MARRIED MOTHERS
With Child under Age 18		
% Employed	66.2	65.3
% Employed Full-Time[a]	50.4	49.4
With Child under Age 3		
% Employed	57.3	57.2
% Employed Full-Time[a]	41.7	42.5
With Child under Age 1		
% Employed	54.2	55.8
% Employed Full-Time[a]	39.3	41.3

[a]Full-time refers to a person who usually works 35 hours or more per week at all jobs.
Source: Bureau of Labor Statistics, *Employment Characteristics of Families—2015*, USDL-16-0795 (April 22, 2016), tables 5 and 6.

Assistance for Needy Families (TANF) have work requirements, but government-provided childcare to support this employment is often inadequate. Even those single mothers who are employed full-time, full-year, with their earnings supplemented by the Earned Income Tax Credit (EITC), still find themselves with incomes at just above the poverty line.

They also confront a lack of affordable *high-quality* child care. Lower-wage jobs also tend to lack adequate flexibility, as described earlier, making it difficult, if not impossible, to both work enough hours to pay the bills and take time out to fully meet the needs of their children.[11] Finally, lower-wage workers typically have less access to **fringe benefits**—additional benefits of employment beyond pay—such as paid leave and health insurance. Regarding the latter benefit, while the 2010 Affordable Health Care Act expanded access to health insurance for the lowest-income individuals, gaps remain for the working poor if their employer does not provide access to health insurance or they live in a state that did not expand Medicaid to the working poor. Inequalities in fringe benefits further magnify the extent of **earnings inequality**—the gap between higher- and lower-wage workers—discussed in earlier chapters.[12]

Work–Family Challenges for Highly Educated Professional Women

In a 2003 *New York Times Magazine* piece, Lisa Belkin famously raised attention to the idea of an "opt out" revolution. Following the long and dramatic rise in women's labor force participation rate and subsequent plateau (as discussed in Chapter 6),

[11]For discussions, see Randy Albeda, "Time Binds: US Antipoverty Policies, Poverty, and the Well-Being of Single Mothers," *Feminist Economics* 17, no. 4 (October 2011): 189–214. See also Jane Waldfogel, "The Role of Family Policies in Antipoverty Policy," in *Changing Poverty, Changing Policies*, ed. Maria Cancian and Sheldon Danziger (New York: Russell Sage Foundation, 2009), 242–65.
[12]For details on access to Medicaid and to health insurance, more generally, through the Affordable Care Act, see https://healthcare.gov. For broader discussion of gaps in workplace policies by income and educational attainment, see Council of Economic Advisers, "The Economics of Family-Friendly Workplace Policies," *The Economic Report of the President* (Washington, DC: GPO, 2015), chap. 4.

there was a decline in the labor force participation rate of college-educated women with infants from the late 1990s to early 2000s. Noting this decrease, Belkin posed the possibility that these mothers were "opting out" of the labor market. A closer look at evidence for that time period suggests that labor force participation rates declined for other groups as well, so the decline could not be fully ascribed to a sweeping change by highly educated women to give up employment for family.[13] Nonetheless, attention to this issue remains strong—including the extent to which lack of adequate workplace policies may play a role—in light of the fact that women continue to be underrepresented in the top echelons of government, management, and unions, as discussed in earlier chapters.

Census Bureau data for 2013 confirm the strong labor force commitment among highly educated women. Only 56 percent of mothers of infants who completed high school were in the labor force compared with 74 percent who completed 4 years of college or more. Historical evidence on stay-at-home mothers provides similar evidence. While it is the case that stay-at-home mothers have risen in recent years (this trend is reflected in the rise in husband-only employed married couples with children in Figure 14-1), it is less educated, not college-educated, mothers who comprise a steadily growing share of stay-at-home mothers.[14]

Claudia Goldin has further investigated the extent to which recent college graduates are "opting out" of the labor market using a unique data set that follows the career and family patterns of female graduates of selective colleges from around 1980 (when they graduated) until 15 years later. These data provide information about the length of time they spent out of the labor force, something that cannot be discerned from Census Bureau data. She found considerable evidence of strong labor force attachment for this group. For instance, on average, women with children spent just 2 of the 15 years out of the labor market, and half of women with children had not been out of the labor market (or an educational institution) for more than 6 months.[15]

Nonetheless, of course, some highly educated women do opt out. The reasons why they do so, to the extent that they do, are varied. In part, this decision may reflect a strong valuation of nonmarket activities, most notably time investments in small children.[16] However, there is also considerable evidence, as discussed in the "In the Media" box and throughout this chapter, that workplaces continue to lack

---

[13]Lisa Belkin, "The Opt-Out Revolution," *New York Times Magazine*, October 26, 2003. For subsequent evidence, see, for instance, Sharon R. Cohany and Emy Sok, "Trends in Labor Force Participation of Married Mothers with Infants," *Monthly Labor Review* 130, no. 2 (February 2007): 9–16.

[14]Data on participation rates for mothers with infants are from US Census Bureau, "Births in the Past Year and Labor Force Participation by Education: 2006–2013," Fertility of American Women, Historical Table 5, accessed June 15, 2016, www.census.gov. Trends in stay-at-home mothers are from Rose M. Kreider and Diana B. Elliott, *Historical Changes in Stay-at-Home Mothers: 1969 to 2009* (Washington, DC: US Census Bureau, 2010); and Gretchen Livingston, "Opting Out? About 10% of Highly-Educated Moms are Staying at Home," Pew Research Center, May 7, 2014.

[15]Claudia Goldin, "The Quiet Revolution that Transformed Women's Employment, Education, and Family," *American Economic Review* 96, no. 2 (May 2006): 1–20. For further discussion, see Heather Antecol, "The Opt-Out Revolution: Recent Trends in Female Labor Supply," *Research in Labor Economics* 33 (2011): 45–83.

[16]For evidence, see Joni Hersch, "Opting Out among Women with Elite Education," *Review of Economics of the Household* 11 (2013): 469–506. She compared labor force participation rates for highly educated women who attended selective and nonselective educational institutions. After accounting for a host of personal factors, she found lower labor force participation rates for women from elite schools, especially those who earned MBAs. She argues that this difference cannot be fully explained by inflexibility of the workplace. One possibility she suggests is that women from elite schools may place a higher value on investing time in children, all else equal.

In the Media: Prominent Women Debate Whether Highly Educated Women Can "Have It All"

A 2012 article in *The Atlantic* titled "Why Women Still Can't Have It All," by Anne-Marie Slaughter, the first woman to be head of Policy Planning at the US State Department, reignited a long-simmering debate about the ability of women to balance high-powered careers and "be there" for their families. Her piece, which answers the question with a "qualified, no" stands in stark contrast to the views expressed by another high-powered woman, Sheryl Sandberg, chief operating officer of Facebook, who advocated for women with children to push as hard as they can to get to the top in her 2013 book *Lean In*.*

In 2009 Slaughter accepted a 2-year post at the US State Department in Washington, DC. Prior to this position, she served as dean of Princeton's Woodrow Wilson School of Public and International Affairs in New Jersey and lived nearby with her husband and two sons. Her new high-powered position in Washington, DC, entailed long hours and considerable face time, leaving no opportunity to spend time with her family (who remained in Princeton) except on weekends, when she returned by train. Even with a very supportive husband taking care of things at home, after 18 months she confessed to a colleague that she found it incredibly hard to do justice to both her career and her family, especially with a teenage son who was having difficulties. The key difference between her DC and Princeton jobs was *flexibility*; in the DC position, she had no ability to set her own schedule, and technology (e.g., conference calls from home) was not a substitute for being physically present. The high-profile articles and books on the career decisions of highly educated women by Slaughter, Sandberg, and others point to the critical role that family policies and supportive family members play.

Slaughter's initial account of her personal experience in the 2012 *Atlantic* article acknowledged but did not delve into the even more immense challenges faced by single parents and those who work low-paid jobs to make ends meet. (College-educated women are just one group, albeit a significant one, in the labor force.) In her subsequent 2015 book, she broadened the scope of her argument and policy solutions to address these workers. Also, more recently, following the sudden death of her husband in 2015, Sandberg modified her earlier thinking. In Sandberg's book, she had effectively assumed the presence of a supportive spouse who would help with household tasks and children. She writes, "Before, I did not quite get it."** In doing so, she acknowledges that a key difference between her new situation and that of so many other single mothers is that she is financially secure.

What should give? One key we have already discussed is the opportunity for greater flexibility in terms of working hours. Further, in the *Atlantic* piece, Slaughter suggests that "women should think about the climb to leadership not in terms of a straight upward slope, but as irregular stair steps, with periodic plateaus (and even dips)" to accommodate the demands of family when they are greatest. These are interesting ideas, but given the current setup of the labor market, women would likely bear significant penalties for this type of career path. In one of a number of follow-up pieces, Ross Douthat, a conservative columnist for the *New York Times*, offers additional thought-provoking commentary. He makes the observation that this is not a "left" or "right" issue; he agrees that both greater flexibility and a nonlinear career path make sense. Where he disagrees is the idea that accommodations would make it possible for women (and men) to "have it all." His point is that time is limited to 24/7, and the current set of work–life balance policies and practices can no doubt be improved; but ultimately trade-offs have to be made.*** There is little question that he is right about trade-offs, but much progress remains to minimize the sacrifices that might still need to be made.

Pursuing the most demanding career involves serious trade-offs, as documented firsthand by Slaughter and discussed by many others. However, it is important to remember that many women, including Slaughter herself, have reached high-level positions (dean of Princeton's Woodrow Wilson School) and had a family. There is also no doubt that the cost of a full exit from the labor force for women (as well as

continues

for men who withdraw to raise children full-time), particularly for those who are more highly educated, is substantial, including the loss of work experience and firm-specific human capital. In other words, there may be perceived short-term benefits to staying home, but the opportunity cost can be quite significant from a longer-term perspective. For this reason, it makes sense to promote policies that support women's ability to both remain attached to the labor force and raise a family, if they so choose.

*See Anne-Marie Slaughter, "Why Women Still Can't Have It All," The Atlantic. July/August 2012, www.atlantic.com; and Sheryl Sandberg, Lean In: Women, Work, and the Will to Lead (New York: Knopf Doubleday, 2013). Slaughter's views are contrasted with Sandberg's in Jodi Kantor, "Elite Women Put a New Spin on an Old Debate," New York Times, June 21, 2012.
**See Anne-Marie Slaughter, Unfinished Business: Women, Men, Work, Family (New York: Random House, 2015); and Sheryl Sandberg, "Sheryl Sandberg Reflects on Single Motherhood, Says Lean In Critics 'Were Right,'" Fortune, May 7, 2016, fortune.com.
***Ross Douthat, "Having It All," New York Times, June 22, 2012. For further discussion, see Claire Cain Miller, "More Than Their Mothers, Young Women Plan Career Pauses," New York Times, July 22, 2015; and Sylvia Ann Hewlett and Carolyn Buck Luce, "Off-Ramps and On-Ramps: Keeping Talented Women on the Road to Success," Harvard Business Review 83, no. 3 (March 2005).

adequate policies to help professional women (and professional men with significant caregiver responsibilities) combine their careers with family. Further, many professions, notably those requiring an MBA and law, have been found to impose considerable wage penalties for workers who want to work a part-time schedule and for those who want to work full-time but prefer more flexible, shorter, or more predictable hours. Claudia Goldin broadly refers to flexibility in the timing and number of hours of work as **temporal flexibility**. As discussed in Chapters 9 and 10, she has identified pharmacy as a prime example of an occupation that allows women (and men) to adjust their time without a wage penalty. For instance, if pharmacists increase their hours from 23 to 24 hours per week or 38 to 39, the additional earnings are exactly the same.[17]

Particular Challenges for Women in Balancing Work and Family

In the absence of adequate provisions for maternity leave, women in the labor force who bear children also face a number of unique challenges. For instance, as a general rule, pregnant women must be careful to avoid heavy lifting and excessive physical exertion. If employers do not accommodate the needs of pregnant women in jobs where this is required by assigning them to alternative duties, these women may not be able to keep their jobs. In fact, even when requesting minor accommodations such as additional restroom breaks, some pregnant women may confront employer resistance.[18] Also, breastfeeding, a practice strongly encouraged by the American

[17]See Claudia Goldin, "A Grand Gender Convergence: Its Last Chapter," American Economic Review 104, no. 4 (2014): 1091–1119; and Claudia Goldin and Lawrence F. Katz, "A Most Egalitarian Profession: Pharmacy and the Evolution of a Family Friendly Occupation," Journal of Labor Economics 34, no. 3 (July 2016): 705–46.
[18]Dina Bakst, "Pregnant, and Pushed Out of a Job," New York Times, January 30, 2012; and Brigid Schulte, "States Move to Ensure Pregnant Workers Get Fair Chance to Stay on Job," Washington Post, September 8, 2014.

Academy of Pediatrics, especially during the first months of children's lives, is often impossible or at least difficult for employed mothers.[19]

Given women's primary role as caregivers, they would be the main beneficiaries of more family-friendly policies. Adoption of such policies would make it easier for them to remain attached to the labor force and to succeed on the job, while also continuing to take care of their families. Such policies would, in turn, increase the incentives for women and their employers to invest in women's human capital. In addition, men who already shoulder sizable housework and childcare responsibilities would benefit as well, and others would find it easier to take on a larger share. Thus, family-friendly policies would also be expected to promote a more equal division of labor in the household.

Rationales for Government and Employer Policies to Assist Workers

As we have seen, many workers face difficulties doing full justice to the demands of paid work and family. The question arises as to whether the government or employers have a role in easing such conflicts. In the following sections, we examine the rationales that might justify a role for each.

Rationales for Government Policies

In all economically advanced countries, government plays some role in childcare through such policies as mandated or government-provided parental leave, providing for or financing day care, and so on. However, there is considerable variation across countries, and, in contrast to most other economically advanced countries, the government's role in the United States remains quite limited. Even unpaid family leave was not mandated until passage of the Family and Medical Leave Act (FMLA) in 1993, while all other economically advanced nations provide *paid* leave and most had been doing so prior to the passage of the FMLA in the United States. Also, the US government does not provide day care, although it does subsidize childcare for poor families and offers tax deductions to others. Consequently, families must make their own arrangements or take advantage of benefits offered by some firms such as on-site childcare or help in finding childcare. In comparison, France, Sweden, and Denmark, among others, provide free or heavily subsidized day care through the government sector.

The question of how the costs of raising children should be shared among parents, the government, and employers is controversial.[20] Economic theory provides both efficiency and equity rationales for government playing a role.

---

[19]See Phyllis L. F. Rippeyoung and Mary C. Noonan, "Is Breastfeeding Truly Cost Free? Income Consequences of Breastfeeding for Women," *American Sociological Review* 20, no. 10 (March 2012): 1–24. In addition to lack of adequate breaks and access to a private room, this study points to large earnings losses for mothers who breastfeed for 6 months or longer. Effective 2010, the Affordable Care Act requires that large employers (those with 50 or more workers) provide breaks and a private room for workers to pump milk until their child is age 1.

[20]For excellent discussions of these issues, see Arleen Leibowitz, "Child Care: Private Cost or Public Responsibility?" in *Individual and Social Responsibility: Child Care, Education, Medical Care, and Long-Term Care in America*, ed. Victor R. Fuchs (Chicago: University of Chicago Press, 1996), 33–57; Nancy Folbre, "Children as Public Goods," *American Economic Review* 84, no. 2 (May 1994): 86–90; Nancy Folbre, *Valuing Children: Rethinking the Economics of the Family* (Cambridge, MA: Harvard University Press, 2008); and Douglas A. Wolf, Ronald D. Lee, Timothy Miller, Gretchen Donehower, and Alexandre Genest, "Fiscal Externalities of Becoming a Parent," *Population and Development Review* 37, no. 2 (June 2011): 241–66.

One efficiency argument for government involvement is that there are externalities associated with bearing and raising children. **Externalities** are benefits or costs that accrue to a third party when an economic decision is made. So, for example, when a consumer purchases a product such as a smoke alarm, neighbors also benefit. Similarly, it is argued that when partners decide to have a child, there are broader social benefits. Not only do the parents receive a direct benefit from their own children in terms of enjoyment and other consumption benefits, but the rest of society also benefits because the children of today are the potential taxpayers and workers of tomorrow. The rewards to the rest of society are expected to be even larger to the extent that children are healthier, better-educated, and better-trained. Thus, while parents should bear part of the costs of raising children since they receive direct benefits, government should help finance the costs as well since society as a whole also benefits.[21]

A second efficiency-related reason for government intervention is that private markets may not be able to efficiently provide benefits such as family leave and health insurance. This is due to a phenomenon called adverse selection. **Adverse selection** refers to the tendency for those workers who need family leave or health insurance the most (because they have private information about their own family situation or health) to seek out firms that offer these benefits; that is, workers will be adversely selected from the perspective of the firm's costs. To understand the problem adverse selection poses, consider the following example. Suppose no federal family leave policy exists and instead only one firm offers it, basing its estimate of costs on the percentage of the total workforce that might use it. It would then provide the benefit and offer its workers a somewhat lower wage that would cover its costs. Given the scarcity of this benefit, however, this firm would likely attract workers with a higher probability of using family leave than the workforce at large. Hence, it would face higher costs than anticipated and might well try to reduce wages even more. This would further aggravate the adverse selection problem because those willing to work for these lower wages would increasingly consist of those who are most likely to take advantage of leave. In the end, the firm might well stop offering this benefit because it is too costly. More generally, adverse selection is likely to result in too few firms offering family leave relative to the optimal number, given workers' preferences. A government mandate requiring all firms to provide such a policy would, however, eliminate this problem and thus be desirable on these grounds.[22]

Issues of **equity** or fairness provide another rationale for government to play a role. Government support for young children through such policies as subsidies for day care, parental leave, and infant nutrition serve to ensure that all children have a more equal chance at life, regardless of the economic status of the family into which they are born. Currently, various levels of government in the United States subsidize primary, secondary, and, to some extent, higher education. Arguably, it makes little sense to help educate children from age 5 or 6 on but not to help ensure that they will be ready to benefit from that education. Parental leave, when taken by fathers as well

---

[21]Nobel Laureate James J. Heckman has produced a voluminous amount of research drawn from economics and the child development literature pointing to the efficiency benefits of investing in young disadvantaged children. He further observes that such investments also increase equity. See, for instance, James J. Heckman and Dimitry V. Masterov, "The Productivity Argument for Investing in Young Children," *Review of Agricultural Economics* 29, no. 3 (2007): 446–93.

[22]This example is drawn from Christopher J. Ruhm and Jacqueline L. Teague, "Parental Leave Policies in Europe and North America," in *Gender and Family Issues in the Workplace*, ed. Francine D. Blau and Ronald G. Ehrenberg (New York: Russell Sage Foundation, 1997), 133–56. For a discussion of the adverse selection problem in general, see Harvey Rosen and Ted Gayer, *Public Finance*, 10th ed. (New York: McGraw Hill, 2014).

as mothers, and subsidized day care also enhance equity because they place female and male workers on a more equal footing.

The preceding discussion provides both efficiency and equity reasons as to why the government should play a role in raising children. However, in fully assessing the issue, potential costs should be considered as well. For one, government financing of any program requires tax collection. Some research suggests that taxes cause individuals to work and save less than they would otherwise, thus reducing output.[23] For this and other reasons, employer-mandated leave, be it paid or unpaid, may be more efficient than leave paid for by the government, especially if the group that benefits from the mandate bears the cost of the leave in the form of lower wages.[24] At least one study provides some evidence that wages do adjust and, thus, the policy is efficient.[25] Mandates would also boost economic efficiency to the extent that they encourage women to stay in the labor force, thereby raising the firm-specific human capital of the labor force.[26] On the other hand, mandates for employer-provided leave, financed through wage reductions of the affected groups, effectively eliminate any subsidy for parents. Recall that there is a case for such subsidies because of the benefits that society as a whole derives from children, who become the next generation of productive citizens and workers. Moreover, wage reductions are likely to fall on women to a much greater extent than men because, even when leave is available to both mothers and fathers, it is disproportionately taken by mothers. In addition, lower wages would reduce the incentive for mothers to stay in the labor force and thus might diminish the positive effects such policies would otherwise have in encouraging women's labor force attachment. The wage reductions would likely affect all women of childbearing age; the impact would be felt not just by mothers who took the fully allowed length of leave but even mothers who took a short leave as well as those who did not go on to have children. Finally, such wage reductions are particularly burdensome for low-income workers, whose wages would be reduced further.

This discussion shows that the issues regarding family leave and subsidized day care are complex. It is therefore not surprising that the extent of government's involvement differs considerably across countries, as do the manner in which policies are instituted and the generosity of these policies.

Rationales for Employer Policies

Employers may institute family-friendly policies in lieu of wage increases and other benefits or because they expect the gains of the policies to outweigh the costs. There

---

[23]For evidence of the negative effect of taxes on labor supply, see, for instance, Michael P. Keane, "Labor Supply and Taxes: A Survey," *Journal of Economic Literature* 49, no. 4 (December 2011): 961–1075. A recent paper which focused on expansions of paid leave in Norway from 13 to 35 weeks identifies considerable increased costs to taxpayers of doing so without corresponding benefits in terms of children's educational attainment or women's increased labor force participation; see Gordon B. Dahl, Katrine V. Løken, Magne Mogstad, and Kari Vea Salvanes, "What Is the Case for Paid Maternity Leave?" *Review of Economics and Statistics,* 98, no. 4 (October 2016): 655–70.

[24]As we shall see with federal leave policy in the United States, even if leave is unpaid, employers still bear health insurance costs and, in some cases, costs associated with training a replacement worker or the costs of lost productivity as tasks are shifted around.

[25]Jonathan Gruber, "Incidence of Mandated Maternity Benefits," *American Economic Review* 84, no. 3 (June 1994): 622–41.

[26]Christopher J. Ruhm, "The Economic Consequences of Parental Leave Mandates: Lessons from Europe," *Quarterly Journal of Economics* 113, no. 1 (February 1998): 285–318.

are a number of potential benefits. One is that family-friendly benefits may serve as a means of attracting and retaining workers. For example, in the tech sector, a number of leading companies—Microsoft, Accenture, Netflix, to name just a few—are ramping up the length of paid parental leave and other such policies that especially appeal to younger workers as they compete against each other for top talent.[27] The improvement in worker retention is likely to be beneficial to the firm because it is often much less costly to provide workers with family-friendly benefits than to train new employees. Other potential benefits to firms include greater productivity and reductions in tardiness and absenteeism. It is also becoming increasingly clear that family-friendly policies lead to many positive results for employees. Such policies can dramatically increase workers' satisfaction with the firm, and they may also reduce work–family conflict by lowering stress.[28]

On the other hand, firms will also incur costs associated with these policies. For one, there are the costs of finding replacements for workers who are on leave. This is likely to be less of a problem for large firms because they are not as dependent on one or a few highly trained and specialized individuals and, given their larger staffs, may be able to shift current workers around. There are also the costs of setting up the programs themselves. Such costs are likely lower for large firms (in this case, on a per-worker basis) because they are able to reap the advantages of economies of scale conferred by having a larger number of workers who can potentially take advantage of the programs put into place. A very detailed study finds that, on net, family-friendly policies may not necessarily enhance the bottom line, but they also do not reduce it.[29]

While large firms have been at the forefront of change, largely for the aforementioned reasons, adoption of family-friendly policies has nonetheless occurred at a rather slow pace in the United States.[30] One likely reason is that their adoption requires a change in workplace "culture." As discussed earlier, family issues continue to be seen as separate from the work sphere. Second, in many firms, workers are evaluated on the basis of "face time" (i.e., the number of hours spent at the office or plant) rather than on output. Finally, there is also concern that with more flexible policies, including home-based work and flextime, it may be harder to monitor employees.

In the sections that follow we examine major family-friendly policies offered in the United States by the government and employers: family leave, childcare assistance, as well as other policies that might help families better juggle paid work and family including alternative work schedules and flexible benefit plans.

---

[27]Miller and Streitfeld, "Big Leaps for Parental Leave"; and Nick Wingfield, "Following Netflix, Microsoft Sweetens Parental Leave Benefits," *New York Times*, August 5, 2015.

[28]For discussion and evidence of benefits for both workers and firms, see Council of Economic Advisers, "Economics of Family-Friendly Workplace Policies"; and Erin L. Kelly, Ellen Ernst Kossek, Leslie B. Hammer, Mary Durham, Jeremy Bray, Kelly Chermack, Lauren A. Murphy, and Dan Kaskubar, "Getting There from Here: Research on the Effects of Work–Family Initiatives on Work–Family Conflict and Business Outcomes," *Academy of Management Annals* 2, no. 1 (2008): 305–49.

[29]Nick Bloom, Tobias Kretschmer, and John Van Reenen, "Are Family-Friendly Workplace Practices a Valuable Firm Resource?" *Strategic Management Journal* 32 (2011): 343–67.

[30]See Stephen Sweet, Marcie Pitt-Catsouphes, Elyssa Besen, and Lonnie Golden, "Explaining Organizational Variation in Flexible Work Arrangements: Why the Pattern and Scale of Availability Matter," *Community, Work and Family* 17, no. 2 (2014): 115–41; and Correll et al., "Redesigning, Redefining Work."

Family Leave

Family leave allows workers to take time off from their job for such reasons as pregnancy, childbirth, infant care, and tending to ill family members. Without such a policy, workers may have to deal with these complications by giving up their jobs, with loss not only of earnings but of accrued benefits and seniority as well. The availability of family leave, even a relatively short and unpaid one, with provisions for job security and some other entitlements, is often helpful in enabling workers, particularly women workers, to avoid these high costs. It also increases incentives for women to invest in firm-specific training and for employers to provide them with opportunities to do so.

Government Leave Policies at the Federal Level

The US government has promulgated two specific policies regarding leave. The first, the **Pregnancy Discrimination Act** of 1978 (an amendment to Title VII of the Civil Rights Act of 1964), prohibits employers from discriminating against workers on the basis of pregnancy. An employer may not, for example, terminate or deny a job to a woman because she is pregnant. Employers who have a short-term disability program must provide paid disability leave for pregnancy and childbirth on the same basis as for other medical disabilities.[31] While the 1978 act prohibits discrimination, there is mounting attention to the fact that it does not address the issue that pregnant women may need temporary accommodations during their pregnancy, whether additional short breaks or exemptions from heavy lifting or climbing ladders. In response, an increasing number of states are passing laws to require these types of accommodations.[32]

The second is the **Family and Medical Leave Act (FMLA)** of 1993, which allows eligible workers to take up to 12 weeks of unpaid leave for birth or adoption; acquiring a foster child; illness of a child, spouse, or parent; or their own illness.[33] Workers may also take shorter leaves intermittently, pending the firm's approval. During the leave, the firm must continue health insurance coverage; and afterward, the employee must be given the same or an equivalent position, with the same benefits, pay, and other conditions of employment. The FMLA applies to public and private sector workers who have been with the same employer for at least 1 year and

---

[31]Employers who do not have a short-term disability program, however, are not required to provide paid disability for pregnancy and childbirth. For extended discussion on pregnancy discrimination and the effectiveness of the act, see Deborah L. Brake and Joanna L. Grossman, "Unprotected Sex: The Pregnancy Discrimination Act at 35," *Duke Journal of Gender Law and Policy* 21 (2014): 67–123.

[32]In a recent high-profile case, a pregnant female UPS worker requested that she be reassigned to light duties but was instead put on unpaid leave. She sued under the Pregnancy Discrimination Act. After losing at the lower court level, the Supreme Court ultimately decided in the pregnant worker's favor, ruling that if employers offered an accommodation to other workers, then pregnant workers should be granted the same accommodation; see Liz Morris, Cynthia Thomas Calvert, and Joan C. Williams, "What Young vs. UPS Means for Pregnant Women and Their Bosses," *Harvard Business Review*, March 26, 2015. For further discussion of these issues and recent state efforts, see Schulte, "States Move to Ensure Pregnant Workers."

[33]For details on the FMLA, see Gerald Mayer, *The Family and Medical Leave Act (FMLA): An Overview*, 7-5700 (Washington, DC: Congressional Research Service, September 28, 2012). From the late 1980s until the time the legislation passed, approximately one-half of states adopted their own legislation. See Jacob Klerman and Arleen Leibowitz, "Labor Supply Effects of State Maternity Leave Legislation," in *Gender and Family Issues in the Workplace*, ed. Francine D. Blau and Ronald G. Ehrenberg (New York: Russell Sage Foundation, 1997), 65–85.

worked at least 1,250 hours. However, the act applies only to private sector establishments with at least 50 workers. (It covers all public sector workers, regardless of the number of workers at a given site). To the extent that some states mandate more generous benefits, they supersede the federal law. Initially, the FMLA was hotly debated. Opponents of the measure were particularly concerned about the costs imposed on employers, who must continue to pay for health insurance for workers on leave and bear the costs of training replacement workers. (Pay for replacement workers, however, is not an added cost because workers on leave do not draw a paycheck.) The net costs of implementing the policy are reduced, however, to the extent that family leave reduces the costs of turnover; such costs can be quite substantial when hiring and training expenses are considered. Also, this policy may enhance workers' commitment to the firm and hence their productivity. The 1995 bipartisan Commission on Leave, as well as a study commissioned by the Department of Labor in 2000, found that providing short, unpaid leaves was not been unduly onerous for business in terms of profitability or growth.[34] The most recent survey, conducted in 2012, reached a similar conclusion. This study found that the majority of employers reported few negative effects of the FMLA in terms of compliance or productivity.[35]

The overall effect of family leave on women's labor force attachment and wages is ambiguous a priori. On the one hand, availability of leave is likely to increase labor force attachment by enabling workers to return to the same employer following an absence, and thus to maintain job continuity. This would be expected to result in a positive effect on wages by encouraging longer job tenure and associated investments in firm-specific training, the maintenance of a good "job match," and the opportunity to continue climbing the firm's career ladder. On the other hand, to the extent that leave encourages women to stay out of the labor market longer than they would without such a policy, leave or the extension of leave time might have a negative effect due to the depreciation of human capital. This is probably more of a concern in other countries where leaves may be as long as 12 months or more but is less likely to be an issue in the United States where the mandated length of leave is quite short. As noted earlier, however, there is concern that even short leaves might reduce women's relative wages to finance the benefit, although any negative effect on the gender pay gap would be mitigated if men were to avail themselves of leave as well. Finally, it is possible that employers might respond to increased costs by cutting back on employment.

Empirical evidence thus far indicates that the effect of the FMLA has been modest; it has been found to have a small positive effect on employment and no effect on wages.[36] These findings reflect the situation in the United States, where leaves

---

[34]Commission on Leave, *A Workable Balance: Report to Congress on Family and Medical Leave Policies* (Washington, DC: US Department of Labor, 1996); and David Cantor, Jane Waldfogel, Jeffrey Kerwin, Mareena McKinley Wright, Kerry Levin, John Rauch, Tracey Haggerty, and Martha Stapleton Wright, *Balancing the Needs of Families and Employers: The Family and Medical Leave Surveys: 2000 Update* (Rockville, MD: Westat, 2001), www.dol.gov.

[35]Jacob Alex Klerman, Kelly Daley, and Alyssa Pozniak, *Family and Medical Leave in 2012: Technical Report* (Cambridge, MA: Abt Associates, September 7, 2012; revised April 18, 2014). See also Laura D'Andrea Tyson, "The Family and Medical Leave Act, 20 Years Later," *New York Times*, February 8, 2013.

[36]See, for example, Charles L. Baum II, "The Effects of State Maternity Leave Legislation and the 1993 Family and Medical Leave Act on Employment and Wages," *Labour Economics* 10, no. 5 (October 2003): 573–96; and Jane Waldfogel, "The Impact of the Family and Medical Leave Act," *Journal of Policy Analysis and Management* 18, no. 2 (Spring 1999): 281–302. For a review of these and other studies, see Christopher Ruhm, "Policies to Assist Parents with Young Children," *The Future of Children* 21, no. 2 (2011): 38–68.

are generally unpaid and of short duration. Analyses of international differences in leave mandates have also found that leave of short duration has few, if any, negative effects; but where leave is paid and of medium or long duration, some evidence indicates negative effects on earnings.[37]

Turning next to the effect of leave on children, it has also been argued that children may be the beneficiaries of a generous family leave policy. With such a policy, parents are able to take time out prior to the birth if there are pregnancy complications and, postbirth, they have an opportunity to spend more time with their children, when bonding is likely to be most important. Moreover, longer leave encourages breastfeeding, which has been found to have beneficial effects for children.[38]

The effect of the FMLA on time away from employment after having a child is, however, not clear a priori. Since the FMLA offers the advantage of allowing parents to return to their previous job after taking a leave of 12 weeks, some workers may take more time out than without this policy, when they might have felt pressured to return sooner. Alternatively, others may return to work more quickly after a birth. For example, prior to the leave policy, workers who felt unable to return to work immediately postbirth might have quit their jobs and, once their tie to the firm was severed, ended up staying out of the labor force for an extended period of time. With a leave policy in place that provides for a feasible period of leave, they may instead feel able to remain with their employer and return to work sooner. For a third group, the FMLA may have no effect on the amount of leave taken because they may not be interested in staying out for longer than they would have prior to the policy, or they may be unable to afford to take time off without pay. Evidence suggests that, on balance, family leave increases the length of time away from work, especially for college-educated parents and for women in higher-income families, perhaps because they have greater financial means to support themselves temporarily without a paycheck coming in.[39]

Family leave, if taken by men as well as women, tends to promote greater gender equality by encouraging fathers to share in caring for infants and meeting family emergencies. Nevertheless, while both men and women are eligible to take advantage of the FMLA, female workers are more likely to seek time off under this policy than their male counterparts, though the gender gap narrowed between 1995 and 2012. Specifically, over this period, the percentage of men reporting they took an FMLA leave (for any reason) in the prior 18 months increased from 12.7 to 16 percent, while the percent of women rose from just 20 to 21 percent. A gender gap also persists in the number of days of leave taken in the last 12 months for birth, adoption, or child's illness: mothers took an average of 58 days compared to 22 days for fathers.[40]

---

[37]Ruhm and Teague, "Parental Leave Policies"; and Ruhm, "Economic Consequences of Parental Leave Mandates."

[38]For evidence on breastfeeding, see Michael Baker and Kevin Milligan, "Maternal Employment, Breastfeeding and Health: Evidence from Maternity Leave Mandates," *Journal of Heath Economics* 27, no. 4 (2008): 871–87. Maya Rossin-Slater finds that leave provides health benefits for children, especially for those of college-educated parents (who are most able to utilize such leave); see "The Effect of Maternity Leave on Children's Birth and Infant Health Outcomes in the United States," *Journal of Health Economics* 30, no. 2 (2011): 221–39.

[39]For recent evidence, see Sari Pekkala Kerr, "Parental Leave Legislation and Women's Work: A Story of Unequal Opportunities," *Journal of Policy Analysis and Management* 35, no. 1 (Winter 2016): 117–44; and Wen-Jui Han, Christopher Ruhm, and Jane Waldfogel, "Parental Leave Policies and Parents' Employment and Leave-Taking," *Journal of Policy Analysis and Management* 28, no. 1 (Winter 2009): 29–54.

[40]These figures are from Klerman, Daley, and Pozniak, *Family and Medical Leave in 2012*, exhibits 7.2.5 and 7.2.8.

From the point of view of workers, a major problem with the FMLA is that it provides limited coverage. As noted earlier, it does not cover workers in private sector establishments with fewer than 50 employees. Furthermore, it does not cover workers who work fewer than 1,250 hours per year nor those employed for less than a year. Hence, it is estimated that the FMLA covers just under 60 percent of private sector workers.[41] For the remainder, coverage depends on state- and firm-specific parental leave policies. Leaves, whether paid or unpaid, are less frequently available in smaller firms and for those working part-time.[42]

As already noted, another problem with the FMLA is that it provides for only unpaid leave, which limits the ability of many covered workers, particularly those with low incomes, to take advantage of its provisions.[43] It is estimated that just 13 percent of all private sector firms provide paid family leave, though in the case of pregnancy and childbirth, some workers have access through their employers' short-term disability plan.[44] Others must use paid vacation time or paid sick leave, if they have the benefits available.

While paid leave at the federal level in the United States does not appear likely in the near term, the Obama administration expanded policies for federal workers and those working for federal contractors. For instance, in 2015, federal workers, both women and men, were granted access to up to 6 weeks of paid leave through their paid sick leave policy in the case of the birth or adoption of a child or for other health situations covered by sick leave.[45]

Paid Leave: Action on Leave Policies at the State Level

Momentum for paid leave is growing at the state and local levels. A handful of states including California, New Jersey, Rhode Island, and New York have long provided paid leave for pregnancy under their state's temporary disability insurance program.[46] In 2004, building on the structure of this program, California became the first state to expand the availability of this leave to include new fathers as well as those who must care for an ill family member, including a spouse, parent, or domestic partner. The California paid family leave program replaces 55 percent of earnings, up to a specified maximum, and leave can be taken for up to 6 weeks per year.[47] The paid leave is financed by workers through a payroll deduction.

---

[41]Klerman, Daley, and Pozniak, *Family and Medical Leave in 2012*.

[42]US Bureau of Labor Statistics, *National Compensation Survey: Employee Benefits in the United States, March 2016*, Bulletin 2785 (Washington, DC: Bureau of Labor Statistics, September 2016), table 32.

[43]Moreover, Kerr finds that the FMLA had no effect on reducing the gap in leaving-taking or length of leave by family income; see "Parental Leave Legislation and Women's Work."

[44]US Bureau of Labor Statistics, *National Compensation Survey*, table 32.

[45]White House, "Presidential Memorandum—Modernizing Federal Leave Policies for Childbirth, Adoption and Foster Care to Recruit and Retain Talent and Improve Productivity" (January 15, 2015), https://obamawhitehouse.archives.gov. These benefits are available as an "advance" on paid sick leave; they are not a new formal paid leave policy. President Obama also issued an executive order mandating paid sick leave for employees of federal contractors; see Peter Baker, "Obama Orders Federal Contractors to Provide Workers Paid Sick Leave," *New York Times*, September 7, 2015.

[46]Hawaii and the territory of Puerto Rico also had such a program as of 2016.

[47]For details see Eileen Appelbaum and Ruth Milkman, *Leaves that Pay: Employer and Worker Experiences with Paid Leave in California* (Washington, DC: Center for Economic and Policy Research, January 2011). In 2016, San Francisco became the first city to pass an ordinance that provides 100 percent wage replacement for new parents who bear or adopt a child. Effectively, the city placed 45 percent of the burden on employers, with the other 55 percent financed by workers through the state's temporary disability program, as described in the text; see Thomas Fuller, "San Francisco Approves Fully Paid Parental Leave," *New York Times*, April 5, 2016.

Following California's lead, New Jersey and Rhode Island have since adopted similar policies, and New York will offer state-wide paid leave beginning in 2018.

Here we focus on California's paid leave program since it has been in existence for the longest period of time and has received the most research attention. Research finds that the program increased the length of leave taken by mothers, especially for those who would not be in a financial position to take such a long leave otherwise. These results confirm that part of the reason for the low utilization rate of the FMLA by those eligible is due to the fact that it is unpaid.[48] Another study looked at the effect of California's paid leave program on the leave-taking decision of parents in families in which both are employed. The share of fathers taking leave prior to the program was estimated to have been exceptionally low, around 2 percent, and the policy expanded this share by 1 percentage point (a 50 percent increase) to 3 percent. The authors attribute about half of the identified increase to fathers who took the leave at the same time as mothers (so both were home together bonding with their newborn), while they attribute the other one-half of the increase to fathers who took leave while the child's mother worked.[49] While father's leave-taking remains very low, this evidence points to the potential benefits for infants in terms of more time with fathers and for more shared caregiving among dual-employed parents going forward. As with the FMLA, this policy also raised attendant concerns about costs and administrative burdens on employers. Other research has looked at the implications of this leave on firms' bottom line. One study found that, despite initial concerns from business, over 90 percent of employers reported either no effect or a favorable effect on their firm's productivity and profitability.[50] One caveat to keep in mind, however, is that many workers surveyed did not know about the program, so cost implications might rise with greater take-up of the program.

Finally, another notable recent development is that a number of states and localities, following the lead of Connecticut in 2012, have mandated that employers offer paid sick leave. As in Connecticut, this leave typically not only covers workers themselves but also their family members, including spouses and children. For instance, with such leave, a parent can take his or her children to a doctor's appointment or stay home with them if they are sick. Laws vary somewhat, but Connecticut provides a good example. In Connecticut, eligible workers are those who earn an hourly wage (including those who work part-time) in service occupations and are employed in large firms (those with 50 or more workers). While this law is relatively new, it has been found to disproportionately benefit part-time workers. This finding reflects the fact that prior to the new law this subgroup was generally not eligible for paid sick leave under their employers' policies.[51]

---

[48]Maya Rossin-Slater, Christopher J. Ruhm, and Jane Waldfogel, "The Effects of California's Paid Family Leave Program on Mothers' Leave-Taking and Subsequent Labor Market Outcomes," *Journal of Policy Analysis and Management* 32, no. 2 (2015): 224–45.

[49]Ann Bartel, Maya Rossin-Slater, Christopher Ruhm, Jennifer Stearns, and Jane Waldfogel, "Paid Family Leave, Fathers' Leave-Taking, and Leave-Sharing in Dual-Earner Households," NBER Working Paper 21747 (National Bureau of Economic Research, Cambridge, MA, December 2015).

[50]Appelbaum and Milkman, *Leaves that Pay.*

[51]Eileen Appelbaum, Ruth Milkman, Luke Elliot, and Teresa Kroeger, *Good for Business? Connecticut's New Paid Sick Leave Law* (Washington, DC: Center for Economic and Policy Research, March 2014).

Childcare

Finding affordable, quality **childcare** is a critical concern for most single parents and dual-earner couples with children.[52] In fact, a substantial fraction of such families face this problem shortly after their child's birth, given that 58 percent of all women with infants (children less than 1 year old)—and, of course, the great majority of fathers—were in the labor force as of 2015.[53] In making their decision about whether to stay in the labor force or leave to spend time raising children, parents must decide how much they value their time spent in the labor market compared to the value of time at home. That is, as we discussed in Chapter 6, they compare the value of market time (w) to the value of home time (w^*). The value of market work includes not only earnings but also nonwage compensation, the nonpecuniary benefits of work, and the impact of current employment on future career prospects. The value of home time includes not only the value of time with children but also the leisure they would enjoy and the goods and services they would produce if they remain at home. In Chapter 6, we looked at the effect of childcare costs on women's labor force participation. We saw that this factor effectively reduces the net wage, thereby reducing the likelihood of labor force participation, while childcare subsidies for employed parents work in the opposite direction and encourage it.

In the United States, most of the costs of caring for young children are borne by parents, though the federal government does provide some subsidies to assist parents. In this section, we review the major government programs and policies that subsidize childcare. As discussed earlier, there are both efficiency and equity motives for the government to play such a role. Nevertheless, there is some opposition to subsidies, particularly to subsidies that directly benefit employed parents who purchase childcare. One common argument against such subsidies is that they benefit two-earner families at the expense of those with stay-at-home mothers. In evaluating this argument, it is useful to recall from our earlier discussion on taxes that, without such subsidies, the federal tax system heavily favors traditional families because home production is untaxed and because the tax schedules favor one-earner couples. Thus, childcare subsidies may be seen as a way to offset this imbalance. Furthermore, even though these subsidies may encourage some mothers to work outside the home who might not otherwise do so, many are already employed and will remain employed in any case. In the case of single mothers on welfare, the 1996 welfare reform requires that recipients take a job, as discussed earlier in Chapter 15, and some government childcare subsidies are specifically designed to make this more feasible.

There is also some concern that, by reducing parents' costs of caring for children, subsidies will encourage fertility. However, as mentioned, providing subsidized

---

[52]A thorough discussion of these issues is found in Myra H. Strober, "Formal Extrafamily Child Care—Some Economic Observations," in *Sex, Discrimination and the Division of Labor*, ed. Cynthia B. Lloyd (New York: Columbia University Press, 1975); Council of Economic Advisers, "The Economics of Early Childhood Investments" (Washington, DC: Council of Economic Advisers, December 2014), https://obamawhitehouse.archives.gov; and David M. Blau, "Child Care Subsidy Programs," in *Means-Tested Transfer Programs in the United States*, vol. 1, ed. Robert A. Moffitt (Chicago: University of Chicago Press, 2003), 443–516.

[53]Figure is from US Bureau of Labor Statistics, *Employment Characteristics of Families*, USDL-15-0689 (Washington, DC: Bureau of Labor Statistics, April 23, 2015), table 6. As shown in Table 16-1, the percent of all *employed* women with infants was slightly lower, at 54.2 percent.

day care also encourages mothers to enter the labor market. To the extent that women acquire more—and more market-oriented—education in anticipation of this and accumulate more work experience as a consequence, they will have higher earnings. Hence, the opportunity cost of additional children will also increase. Further, it may be that employed women develop stronger preferences for market goods and perhaps for having their own income, which gives them a greater feeling of independence. Therefore, it is not possible to determine a priori which set of forces is likely to be stronger.[54]

Another concern frequently voiced by opponents of publicly subsidized day care involves children's well-being. As discussed in Chapter 14, even though some studies have found a negative effect of maternal employment on child outcomes, particularly nonparental care in the first year of life, these studies are generally not able to control fully for childcare quality, which would be expected to attenuate or even negate any such effects. And children between the ages of 2 and 4 tend to do better in center-based childcare both cognitively and socially than children cared for entirely at home. Moreover, as noted earlier, children's development is affected by a host of other factors, most importantly family characteristics.

We review the major ways that government reduces the costs of caring for children in the United States. As we shall see, it is a largely a patchwork system, with differing amounts and types of subsidies depending on income level and the number of children. We shall also see that almost all of these policies are expected to unambiguously encourage mothers' labor force participation.

For low-income families, the majority of support comes through the **Child Care and Development Block Grant**, which provides states with funds to expand day-care services for low-income families, including those on welfare, as well as to improve the overall quality and supply of day care. For instance, states might provide part of these funds to childcare providers, who can then allow families to pay for care on a sliding-scale basis, depending on their income. Alternatively, states might give vouchers directly to low-income families who would then use them to buy childcare from an eligible provider or even from a friend or relative living outside their home. A smaller but important amount of federal support goes to **Head Start**, a program which is explicitly designed to provide early childhood education for low-income preschoolers.[55] One recent development which also merits mention is the growing number of states and a number of localities that are investing their own tax dollars in *universal* preschool programs. *Universal* refers to the fact that all children, regardless of income, are eligible, in contrast to the federal Head Start program. Oklahoma and Georgia were the first two states to do so. Major cities with universal preschool programs include Washington, DC, Los Angeles, and most recently New York City.[56]

Other childcare subsidies, which operate through the federal tax system, are targeted toward middle- and higher-income families. Parents who purchase childcare can receive a subsidy through the federal **Dependent Care Tax Credit**. This credit

---

[54]For evidence that subsidies have a pronatalist effect, see Kevin Milligan, "Subsidizing the Stork: New Evidence on Tax Incentives and Fertility," *Review of Economics and Statistics* 87, no. 3 (March 2006): 539–55.

[55]For more on federal childcare subsidies for low-income families, see Ruhm, "Policies to Assist Parents."

[56]Regarding states' role in administering federal policies, see Karen Schulman and Helen Blank, *Turning the Corner: State Child Care Assistance Policies* (Washington, DC: National Women's Law Center, 2014). Regarding state and local prekindergarten efforts, see National Institute for Early Education Research, *State of Preschool 2015* (Washington, DC: NIEER, 2015).

operates on a sliding scale so that benefits decline as earnings increase. However, since the credit is nonrefundable, low-earner families who do not pay federal taxes do not benefit.[57] Another way in which the federal tax code provides some subsidy for childcare expenses is through **flexible spending accounts** provided by some employers. In firms that provide this option, employees may have money deducted from their paychecks for dependent care expenses on a pretax basis. Since they do not owe taxes on the money set aside for this purpose, the costs of such care are thereby reduced.

All of the aforementioned types of government childcare subsidies—subsidized day care, subsidized preschool, tax credits, and favorable tax treatment for paid childcare—are theoretically expected to encourage women's labor force participation, by reducing the cost of doing so. And, as discussed in Chapter 6, evidence indicates that such programs and policies generally have this expected effect.[58]

The federal government also provides other forms of income support which are not specifically earmarked to subsidize childcare but might be used for this purpose. One such subsidy is the **Child Tax Credit**, a tax credit which provides up to $1,000 for each child under age 17 in the family, though it phases out for higher-income families. It is also partly refundable, which means that, unlike the Dependent Care Tax Credit, it provides some benefit to families with lower earnings who do not pay federal taxes.[59] The impact of this tax credit on mothers' labor force participation is ambiguous. On the one hand, as we saw in Chapter 6, economic theory suggests that such an increase in nonlabor income is expected to discourage labor force participation, all else equal. On the other hand, it is possible that, as a practical matter, the funds might be used to defray childcare costs, thereby encouraging participation. Finally, some families may use funds from the **Earned Income Tax Credit (EITC)** to pay for childcare. Recall that this program provides a fully refundable tax credit, which is related to the number of children present; as of 2016, it provided a maximum of $5,572 to a low-income working single-parent family with two children. For those mothers who are initially out of the labor force, the EITC functions as a wage subsidy and is expected to encourage labor force participation due to the substitution effect. However, its overall impact on labor supply is ambiguous, both points discussed at length in Chapter 15. The EITC has been shown to have a strong positive effect on the labor force participation of single mothers.

To varying degrees, employers also play a role in assisting workers with their childcare needs. In 2015, 11 percent of private employers paid for the partial or full

[57]For discussion and a suggested policy modification, see James P. Ziliak, "Proposal 10: Supporting Low-Income Workers through Refundable Child Care Credits" in *Policies to Address Poverty in America*, ed. Melissa S. Kearney and Benjamin H. Harris (Washington, DC: Brookings Institution, 2014), 109–17.
[58]See, for instance, David Blau and Erdal Tekin, "The Determinants and Consequences of Child Care Subsidies for Single Mothers in the USA," *Journal of Population Economics* 20, no. 4 (October 2007): 719–41; Pierre Lefebvre and Philip Merigan, "Child-Care Policy and the Labor Supply of Mothers with Young Children: A Natural Experiment from Canada," *Journal of Labor Economics* 2008 26, no. 3 (2008): 519–48; and Michael Baker, Jonathan Gruber, and Kevin Milligan, "Universal Child Care, Maternal Labor Supply, and Family Well-Being," *Journal of Political Economy* 116, no. 4 (August 2008): 709–45. For one study that finds no effect, see Maria Donavan Fitzpatrick, "Preschoolers Enrolled and Mothers at Work? The Effects of Universal Prekindergarten," *Journal of Labor Economics* 28, no. 1 (2010): 51–85.
[59]For details on how it works, see "Taxation and the Family: What is the Child Tax Credit?" *The Tax Policy Briefing Book* (Washington, DC: Tax Policy Center, 2016). C. Eugene Steuerle points out that it may make sense to have both the dependent care credit and the child credit. The child credit adjusts for differences in family size, while the dependent care credit adjusts for the costs of purchased childcare; see "Systematic Thinking about Subsidies for Child Care, Part Three: Application of Principles" (Washington, DC: Urban Institute, February 1998). For another useful discussion, see Barbara R. Bergmann, "Subsidizing Child Care by Mothers at Home," *Feminist Economics* 6, no. 1 (March 2000): 77–88.

cost of their workers' day-care expenses, whether on-site or off-site. These benefits are more often provided by larger establishments and to managerial and professional workers.[60] The fact that some of these programs are on-site raises the issue of how desirable such an arrangement is. Such care has both advantages and drawbacks for employees. On the one hand, parents do not have to make a separate trip to take children elsewhere, they are nearby in case of emergencies, and the children receive care during whatever hours the parent works.[61] On the other hand, children often are taken out of their own neighborhood, perhaps travel long distances, and must change caregivers when parents change jobs.

Table 16-2 shows the diversity of childcare arrangements used by employed mothers of preschool children. In 2011, 25 percent of these mothers had their children in organized childcare facilities. While this figure has increased only slightly since 1997, it nevertheless reflects a considerable increase from the late 1970s, when just 13 percent of employed mothers used this arrangement.[62] This increase is no doubt related to the aforementioned federal subsidies as well as the expansion of on-site care provided by employers.[63] Still, as shown in Table 16-2, the largest percentage of families, 46 percent, continue to use childcare provided by the child's father or other relatives, either in their own home or in a relative's home. An additional 13 percent used the services of a nonrelative, either in their own home or at the home of the day-care provider. The remainder of mothers (nearly 16 percent) cared for their children at work or did not have a regular childcare arrangement.

In choosing a childcare arrangement, cost is, no doubt, a major consideration. Data for the period 1985 to 2011 indicate a nearly 70 percent rise in the inflation-adjusted weekly cost of childcare for families with employed mothers who pay for care.[64] Due at least in part to high costs of care, poor families are much less likely to use center care and more likely to have their children cared for by relatives at no cost. Among poor families that pay for childcare, they pay less in total because of the type of care they use, whether it is provided at low cost by relatives or through subsidized programs targeted at the low-income population like Head Start. Nonetheless, because their incomes are so low, poor families with employed mothers who purchase care spend a much greater share of their income on childcare than nonpoor families; in 2011 the difference was 30 percent versus 8 percent of weekly income.[65]

Another factor that affects the type of childcare chosen is the child's age. A much smaller percentage of infants are in organized group day care compared to preschool-age

[60]US Bureau of Labor Statistics, *National Compensation Survey*, table 40.

[61]Many such day-care centers are at hospitals, where large numbers of women of childbearing age who have to work nonstandard hours are employed. For more on this arrangement, see Rachel Connelly, Deborah S. DeGraff, and Rachel A. Willis, *Kids at Work: The Value of Employee-Sponsored On-Site Child Care Centers* (Kalamazoo, MI: Upjohn Institute, 2004).

[62]US Census Bureau, Historical Time Series, Table A, "Primary Child Care Arrangements Used for Preschoolers by Families with Employed Mothers: Selected Years, 1977 to 1994," accessed December 2008, www.census.gov.

[63]William Goodman, "Boom in Day Care Industry the Result of Many Social Changes," *Monthly Labor Review* 118, no. 8 (August 1995): 3–12.

[64]Figures in this paragraph are from Lynda Laughlin, *Who's Minding the Kids? Child Care Arrangements: Spring 2011*, Current Population Report P70-135 (Washington, DC: US Census Bureau, April 2013), www.census.gov. Chris M. Herbst attributes part of the rising real costs of childcare to a greater use of formal (nonrelative) care and a rise in the number of hours women are employed; see "The Rising Cost of Child Care in the United States: A Reassessment of the Evidence" Discussion Paper 9072 (IZA, Bonn, German, May 2015).

[65]Laughlin, *Who's Minding the Kids?* 17.

TABLE 16-2 CHILDCARE ARRANGEMENTS USED BY EMPLOYED MOTHERS OF PRESCHOOLERS, 1997 AND 2011 (PERCENT DISTRIBUTION)

	1997	2011
Organized Childcare Facilities	20.4	25.2
Parents	20.8	22.0
Mother Cares for Child at Work	3.2	2.4
Father	17.7	19.6
Other Relatives	24.9	26.6
Grandparent	17.5	21.1
Sibling and Other Relative	7.4	5.5
Nonrelative Care	20.2	12.9
In Child's Home	3.8	3.1
In Provider's Home	16.3	9.8
Other Arrangement[a]	13.7	13.2
Total	100.0	100.0

[a]This category includes no regular arrangement and a very small percentage of childen who are in kindergarten/grade school.

Note: Columns may not sum to 100 due to rounding.

Source: Lynda Laughlin, "Who's Minding the Kids? Child Care Arrangements: Spring 2011," *Current Population Reports* P70-135 (Washington, DC: US Census Bureau, April 2013), table 3, www.census.gov.

children. Parents of infants who can afford to do so may hire a nanny or find some other way to have their children cared for in their own home because at home the children generally receive more one-on-one attention and their exposure to infectious diseases is limited. For preschoolers, on the other hand, group care provides the advantages of contact with other children and teaches them to share and cooperate.[66] For school-age children, the question of after-school care arises. A 2011 survey indicated that 4.6 percent of children aged 5 to 11 (elementary school age) and 27 percent of children aged 12 to 14 (middle school age) were regularly left unsupervised.[67] Even though "self-care" can build self-esteem and independence for older children, it is generally viewed as a poor and even a dangerous alternative for younger children. Alternatives include not only after-school programs that offer supervised educational or recreational activities but also greater workplace flexibility on the part of employers, which would allow for more parental supervision as well as permit parents to attend parent–teacher conferences.[68]

Not all childcare is equivalent from the standpoint of children's development. As discussed earlier in Chapter 14, a key factor is the quality of childcare.[69] Quality of care varies considerably across different settings—center-based care, family day care

---

[66]Jane Waldfogel provides a comprehensive discussion of the benefits of various childcare arrangements by child's age in *What Children Need* (Cambridge, MA: Harvard University Press, 2006).

[67]Laughlin, *Who's Minding the Kids?* table 5.

[68]For evidence on the effects of unsupervised care, see Anna Aizer, "Home Alone: Supervision after School and Child Behavior," *Journal of Public Economics* 88, no. 9–10 (August 2004): 1835–48. For more on the benefits of greater workplace flexibility, see Kathleen Christiansen, Barbara Schneider, and Donnell Butler, "Families with School Children," *The Future of Children* 21, no. 2 (Fall 2011): 69–90.

[69]See, for instance, Waldfogel, *What Children Need*, and Council of Economic Advisers, "Economics of Early Childhood Investments."

(care provided in the home of a nonrelative), and relative care. Quality is typically measured in terms of both the structural characteristics of the childcare arrangement and children's experiences in that setting. Structural characteristics include the level of teachers' education and training, group size, and the child–teacher ratio. Criteria for evaluating children's experiences in childcare include the way caregivers relate to children, such as how much they talk to them, and the continuity of care with the same caregiver.[70]

In recent decades, access to childcare—and better childcare—has been at the forefront of policy attention as a consequence of several developments: the rise in the fraction of women who are employed full-time, full-year; government policies that moved more low-income women from welfare to work; and the shift in economic activity to 24 hours a day, 7 days a week ("24/7"). The latter development means that there is increasing need for care very early in the morning, in the evenings, and on weekends. These changes, taken together, have raised concerns about the extent to which government childcare policies are adequately addressing these changing needs.[71] Just on the most basic level of funding, the answer seems to be no. Evidence shows that federal childcare funds are insufficient to cover all eligible children. And even when subsidies are available, such as those made available through the Child Care and Development Block Grant, they focus solely on supporting parents' paid work, not on providing early childhood education like Head Start.[72] These concerns have not gone unnoticed by policymakers, and at least some efforts are being made to address them.[73]

A range of other policies have been suggested, from sweeping to more modest, to address concerns raised about the affordability, accessibility, and quality of childcare. The most ambitious proposal, which is unlikely to be adopted in the United States anytime soon, is universal government-provided childcare.[74] A more modest proposal that has been suggested is to restructure the Child Dependent Care Credit so that it is available to low-income families and, furthermore, incentivizes the

---

[70]Nancy L. Marshall, "The Quality of Early Child Care and Children's Development," *Current Directions in Psychological Science* 13, no. 4 (2004): 165–68.

[71]Heather Hahn, Gina Adams, Shayne Spaulding, and Caroline Heller, *Supporting the Child Care and Workforce Development Needs of TANF Families*, Research Report (Washington, DC: Urban Institute, April 2016).

[72]For evidence that federal childcare subsidies are associated with low-quality care, see Anna D. Johnson, Rebecca M. Ryan, and Jeanne Brooks-Gunn, "Child Care Subsidies: Do They Impact the Quality of Care Children Experience?" *Child Development* 83, no. 4 (2012): 1444–61. Herbst and Tekin further find that children who received care financed by the federal childcare subsidy had lower math and reading scores at kindergarten entry and during kindergarten than children who did not receive the subsidy, perhaps due to the low quality of childcare obtained with the subsidy; see "Child Care Subsidies and Child Development," *Economics of Education Review* 29, no. 4 (2010): 618-38.

[73]For instance, the 2014 reauthorization of the Child Care and Development Block Grant included a host of provisions aimed at improving both childcare quality and access to it; see Hannah Matthews, Karen Schulman, Julie Vogtman, Christine Johnson-Staub, and Helen Blank, *Implementing the Child Care and Development Block Grant Reauthorization: A Guide for States* (Washington, DC: National Women's Law Center and CLASP, 2015).

[74]The province of Quebec offers universal childcare from infancy through age 4. Of concern, some research has identified negative impacts of the program on children's development, but a recent study which examines subgroups of children, rather than average effects, finds benefits for economically disadvantaged children; see Michael J. Kottelenberg and Steven F. Lehrer, "Targeted or Universal Coverage? Assessing Heterogeneity in the Effects of Universal Childcare," NBER Working Paper 22126 (National Bureau of Economic Research, Cambridge, MA, March 2016). For an influential earlier study, see Baker, Gruber, and Milligan, "Universal Child Care."

purchase of high-quality childcare.[75] For children ages 3 to 5, recent efforts by states and localities to expand public preschool also appear promising.[76] If high-quality, these programs yield a double-dividend of improving children's developmental outcomes and making it easier for parents to combine work and family during school hours. However, these programs do not address the lack of affordable, quality care for nonschool hours or for children ages 0 to 3.

Other Family-Friendly Policies

Previously, we discussed family leave and childcare policies where both government and employers play a role. We now turn to other family-friendly policies, in this case focusing on a number of policies provided by employers. These include policies that, to varying extents, permit greater temporal flexibility—flexibility in the number of hours and timing of work, a concept discussed earlier, as well as flexibility as to where work is performed (at a conventional workplace or at home). Such policies fall under the umbrella term of *alternative* work schedules and include flextime, nonstandard work schedules, part-time employment, "right to request" time off, job sharing, and home-based work. Some firms also offer the option of flexible benefits as well as policies specifically crafted to assist couples. As discussed earlier, the number and types of policies offered vary considerably across firms, with larger firms often having greater ability to extend such benefits.[77]

Alternative Work Schedules

Alternative work schedules provide greater flexibility for workers to take care of family responsibilities and to arrange their personal lives more conveniently. A policy known as **flextime** permits some variation in work schedules at the discretion of the employee, ranging from modest changes in starting and quitting times to varying the number of hours worked per day, week, or pay period. For instance, in 2014, just over 80 percent of large firms (those with over 50 workers) offered at least some workers an opportunity to periodically adjust their hours, and 43 percent of such firms permitted at least some workers the option to work more hours over fewer days.[78] Such flexibility can be advantageous, especially for workers with young children or other family members who depend on their care. Also, workers on flextime can avoid driving in rush hour, thereby reducing their commuting time. In fact, as more workers take advantage of flextime, even workers who do not have a flexible schedule benefit from less rush-hour traffic. The degree of flexibility offered depends on the nature of the enterprise and the type of work. Some employers may be reluctant to offer

[75]For discussion of federal universal preschool and more modest alternatives, see Suzanne Helburn and Barbara Bergmann, *America's Child Care Problem: The Way Out* (New York: Palgrave, St. Martin's Press, 2002). The more modest proposal is from Ziliak, "Proposal 10: Supporting Low Income Workers."

[76]Elizabeth U. Cascio and Diane Whitmore Schanzenbach, "The Impacts of Expanding Access to High-Quality Preschool Education," *Brookings Papers on Economic Activity* (Fall 2013): 127–92.

[77]For an excellent review of the literature, see Council of Economic Advisers, "Economics of Family-Friendly Policies."

[78]Figures are from Council of Economic Advisers, "Economics of Family-Friendly Policies," figure 4-12. See also Lonnie Golden, "Flexible Daily Work Schedules in U.S. Jobs: Formal Introductions Needed?" *Industrial Relations* 48, no. 1 (January 2009): 27–54.

this benefit because they need key employees to be present during standard business hours, perhaps to be available to handle customers or to meet workflow demands. Others may be concerned about the potential for abuse.

Other workers have **nonstandard work schedules**, where they are employed on alternating shifts, nights, or weekends. (The term *nonstandard* as used here refers to work schedules, rather than to the type of worker or employment, as in Chapter 7.) These schedules have expanded considerably as economic activity has moved to virtually 24/7.[79] The availability and widespread adoption of technologies such as laptop computers and smaller electronic devices (e.g., smart phones, tablets, and the like) explain part of this change. Another factor is the rise in the number of dual-earner and single-parent families, who must do their shopping on weekends and evenings. It is estimated that, in 2011, about 20 percent of all employed Americans worked a nonstandard schedule, defined as 50 percent of employed time spent during the evenings, nights, or weekends. This figure stood at 28 percent for workers in low-earner families.[80] Nonstandard schedules appear to be something of a US phenomenon. A recent study that compared work schedules in five countries finds that the percentage of individuals working evenings and weekends in the United States is considerably higher than in France, Germany, The Netherlands, and, to a somewhat lesser degree, the United Kingdom.[81] Like flextime, nonstandard work schedules potentially provide some flexibility for workers juggling childcare, or perhaps schooling, and a job. However, unlike flextime, these schedules are typically set by employers rather than at the discretion of employees. As discussed earlier, recent attention has focused on the difficulties faced by workers when employers require that they be "available" for work in the case of high demand or find themselves released early if business is slow. To the extent that workers are not able to choose their schedules, those with young children may face considerable difficulties finding childcare to match their needs, especially on weekends and at night. Moreover, when a family member has this type of schedule, there are often adverse effects for the worker and her or his family. Many people have biological difficulties adjusting to night work. In addition, family members have less time together, leading to potentially negative consequences for marriages and children's behavior.[82]

Another alternative is **part-time employment**. This arrangement is especially common among women (as well as young people going to school and older workers retired from their full-time jobs) and does offer some flexibility compared to a regular full-time job. In 2015, 25.2 percent of employed women and 12.4 percent of employed men worked less than full-time (defined as at least 35 hours per week).[83]

---

[79]See Janet C. Gornick, Harriet B. Presser, and Caroline Batzdorf, "Outside the 9-to-5," *The American Prospect* (2005): 21–25; and Harriet B. Presser, *Working in a 24/7 Economy* (New York: Russell Sage Foundation, 2003).

[80]María E. Enchautegui, "Nonstandard Work Schedules and the Well-Being of Low-Income Families," Low-Income Work Families Paper 26 (Washington, DC: Urban Institute, July 2013).

[81]Daniel S. Hamermesh and Elena Stancanelli, "Long Workweeks and Strange Hours," *ILR Review* 68 no. 5 (October 2015): 1007–18.

[82]For instance, recent studies find that nonstandard parental work schedules, specifically night shifts, are associated with more risky behaviors by teens and more aggressive and anxious behavior by very young children; see Wen-Jui Han, Daniel P. Miller, and Jane Waldfogel, "Parental Work Schedules and Adolescent Risk Behaviors," *Developmental Psychology* 46, no. 5 (September 2010): 1245–67; and Rachel Dunifon, Ariel Kalil, Danielle Crosby, and Jessica Houston Su, "The Cost of the Night Shift: Mothers' Night Work and Children's Behavior Problems," *Developmental Psychology* 49 (2013): 1874–85.

[83]US Bureau of Labor Statistics, "Household Data Annual Averages, 2015," table 8, accessed June 28, 2016, www.bls.gov. For more on the attributes of those working part-time, including a distinction between those who are primary and secondary workers in the family, see H. Luke Schaefer, "Part-Time Workers: Some Key Differences between Primary and Secondary Earners," *Monthly Labor Review* (October 2009): 3–15.

While part-time work offers a solution to the difficulties of combining work and family responsibilities, one concern is that it offers few fringe benefits (such as health care and pensions), frequently poor compensation, and few opportunities for promotion.[84]

A new policy that has been adopted in other countries including the United Kingdom and New Zealand and is gaining traction in the United States is called "right to request." A **right to request policy** is one where the worker can ask a supervisor for flexibility in terms of number of days, hours per day, or where work is performed, without fear of retaliation for doing so. The supervisor has the ultimate authority as to whether or not to grant the request.[85] In 2014 Vermont became the first state and San Francisco the first city to implement such a policy.

Some firms may offer the possibility of **job sharing**, where two individuals share one position. For people seeking less than full-time work, this arrangement can be a good way to obtain a more attractive part-time position, while employers may find that this option helps them retain valuable employees. A disadvantage is that people who share jobs, like all part-time workers, may receive only partial benefits or none at all.

Finally, an increasing number of workers are choosing **home-based employment**. Estimates of the extent of home-based work vary depending on the definition used. For instance, for 2010, it is estimated that 9.5 percent of employed persons worked at least 1 full day at home per week, while a somewhat smaller figure, 6.6 percent of workers, worked entirely from home. As would be expected, using either definition, home-based workers are more likely to be self-employed and more likely to be highly educated.[86]

The increase in prevalence of home-based employment is due to several factors working together. For one, increases in women's labor force participation have increased the desirability of home-based versus "office-based" work to better balance the demands of earning a living and raising a family. Second, the major advancements that have occurred in information technology (noted previously) have made it increasingly possible for work to be conducted off-site. One recent study concludes that it was the second factor, advancements in information technology, which was primarily responsible for the growth in home-based employment during the period from 1980 to 2000.[87]

Home-based work has typically been associated with lower pay to the extent that workers are willing to trade wages at a place-bound job for the flexibility of home-based work. Importantly, the aforementioned study also found that the wage penalty associated with home-based work declined considerably for both women and men over the 1980 to 2000 period. One explanation for the reduction in the wage penalty is that computer advancements (and presumably declining prices of this technology) reduced employer costs associated with this type of employment.[88]

---

[84]Claire Cain Miller, "How a Part-Time Pay Penalty Hits Working Mothers, *New York Times*, August 21, 2014.

[85]Council of Economic Advisers, "Economics of Family-Friendly Policies"; and Steven Greenhouse, "A Push to Give Steadier Shifts to Part-Timers," *New York Times*, July 15, 2014.

[86]Figures are from Peter J. Mateyka, Melanie A. Rapino, and Liana Christin Landivar, "Home-Based Workers in the United States: 2010," *Current Population Reports* (Washington, DC: US Census Bureau, 2012), 70–132. See also Gerald S. Oettinger, "The Incidence and Wage Consequences of Home-Based Work in the United States, 1980–2000," *Journal of Human Resources* 46, no. 2 (Spring 2011): 237–60.

[87]Oettinger, "Incidence and Wage Consequences." See also Linda N. Edwards and Elizabeth Field-Hendry, "Home-Based Work and Women's Labor Force Decisions," *Journal of Labor Economics* 20, no. 1 (January 2002): 170–200.

[88]Oettinger, "Incidence and Wage Consequences."

It is important to be realistic about the drawbacks as well as the benefits of home-based work. For instance, home-based work blurs the distinction between paid work and home responsibilities and may thus come at a professional cost for women. This is because the home has been women's traditional sphere, so a woman working at home may be perceived as not having a "real" job.[89] There is also the question of how well home-based work solves the problem of balancing paid work and family. For one, there is the issue of how much work can be accomplished when children or an infirm parent are present and require attention. For another, one recent study finds that those who telecommute tend to work more hours than would otherwise be the case.[90] Finally, another possible drawback of home-based work is the isolation the individual may experience without having coworkers in close physical proximity.

Flexible Benefits

As the workforce has become more diverse, with some workers who are members of traditional families, some who have employed spouses, some who are single, and others who live with partners they are not married to, **flexible benefit plans** (also known as *cafeteria plans*) have become increasingly important as an alternative to standard or fixed benefit packages. These plans allow employees to select from an assortment of benefits worth up to a specified amount predetermined by the employer. They increase the value of fringe benefits to workers because workers can choose the benefits that best meet their needs. Thus, such benefits may provide a further inducement to individuals to enter or to remain attached to the labor market in general and to the firm in particular.[91] For example, two-earner couples derive no benefit from the double health insurance coverage they receive when one or both are covered under their own employer's health insurance program and under their spouse's. With a flexible benefit plan, one of the spouses could instead choose to receive childcare benefits, contributions into a pension fund, or any one of the other benefits available.

Policies to Assist Couples

Dual-earner couples, married or unmarried, whether same sex or opposite sex, face particular problems in the workplace. Such couples, especially those with two professionals, must deal with the often daunting task of finding two jobs commensurate with their respective skills in the same location, or having a "commuting relationship," if both are to successfully pursue their careers. As discussed in Chapter 9, many opposite-sex married couples still give priority to the husband's career, often at the expense of the wife's, although husbands are increasingly making sacrifices too.

Employers can reduce the negative consequences for the "trailing partner" in a number of ways. For example, firms, acting alone or with others, can help partners find employment. Assistance might take the form of sending out a spouse's résumé to employers or making use of personal contacts. Many universities as well as some

---

[89]For an interesting discussion, see Debra Osnowitz, "Managing Time in Domestic Space: Home-Based Contractors and Household Work," *Gender and Society* 19, no. 1 (February 2005): 83–103.

[90]Mary C. Noonan and Jennifer L. Glass, "The Hard Truth about Telecommuting," *Monthly Labor Review* (June 2012): 38–45.

[91]Moreover, employer-provided benefits such as health insurance are not subject to federal or state taxation, thereby increasing the financial gain from access to these benefits; see Jonathan Gruber, "The Tax Exclusion for Employer-Sponsored Health Insurance," *National Tax Journal*, 64 (June 2011): 511–30.

other establishments have set up programs for hiring couples or offer jobs to partners of employees, whenever suitable positions can be found.[92] Businesses can also reduce difficulties for such couples by not penalizing employees who decline a promotion because they have family responsibilities or decline a transfer to a branch in a different location because their partner might find it difficult to locate a satisfactory job there.

Antinepotism rules, once widely used to restrict the hiring or retention of relatives of employees but most particularly spouses of employees, have virtually disappeared in academia and are less common elsewhere as well. These rules not only prevented both members of the couple from being hired but if two employees married, one—usually the wife—would have to go. Restrictions that still exist today are less severe. Some employers restrict spouses, unmarried partners, and, in some cases, even couples with romantic attachments from working in the same department or at least avoid having one partner directly supervising the other. In these cases, the concern is that a partner who has influence may use it to have the other hired or promoted or that the couple would form a working alliance that may be resented by their coworkers. Such abuses undoubtedly take place, but there is no evidence that they are more common than among close friends. In fact, couples might be somewhat more circumspect because favoritism would be so obvious. In any case, the risk that such problems may occur must be weighed against the disadvantage of not being able to hire and retain the best-qualified people regardless of their relationships. One problem with even the remnants of antinepotism rules is that as long as husbands are most often senior to their wives and in higher positions, it is the woman who will be viewed as more expendable. Further, employment of the partner by a competitor may even create its own problems. For instance, the partners may inadvertently share confidential business information such as trade secrets, putting the firm at risk.

While policies that are helpful to married couples, with and without children, may have benefits, they raise questions about fairness to those who do not have families.[93] For instance, singles are at a disadvantage if employers pay lower wages to all employees as a result of providing benefits such as family leave, on-site day care, or subsidized spousal health care and pensions. Also, singles may be far less interested in flexible schedules and may regret the reduction in face time with coworkers. In addition, some single individuals observe that they are often called upon to shoulder extra responsibilities at work when a coworker's child becomes sick and at times are expected to work weekends, nights, or holidays so that others can spend time with their families. Regarding inequities in benefits, one solution is for firms to offer flexible benefit plans so that workers can choose the benefits they want. Another solution, recently adopted by some larger firms, is to extend benefits to a broader set of household members, including workers' grown children, elderly parents, or unmarried partners, so as to increase the share of their workforce that benefits from the policies.[94] Few would likely benefit from the more radical alternative of scaling back all such benefits because people's situations change—singles marry, childless

---

[92]See, for instance, Londa Schiebinger, Andrea Davies Henderson, and Shannon K. Gilmartin, *Dual-Career Academic Couples: What Universities Need to Know* (Stanford, CA: Stanford University, Michelle R. Clayman Institute for Gender Research, 2008).

[93]Wendy J. Casper, Dennis J. Marquardt, Katherine J. Roberto, and Carla Buss, "The Hidden Family Lives of Single Adults without Dependent Children," in *The Oxford Handbook of Work and Family*, ed. Tammy D. Allen and Lillian T. Eby (New York: Oxford University Press, 2016), chap. 14; and Susan J. Wells, "Are You Too Family Friendly?" *HR Magazine* 52, no. 10 (2007).

[94]Wells, "Are You Too Family Friendly?"

adults have children or adopt, married people get divorced or become widowed, and parents become ill—so that most workers are likely to benefit from even the existing set of policies at some point in their lives.

Also, unmarried couples, whether opposite sex or same sex, still tend to be at a disadvantage relative to married couples because they are generally not eligible for the substantial fringe benefits that are usually available to spouses including dental, health, and life insurance. However, starting in the early 1980s, a growing number of employers began extending such benefits to unmarried partners as a result of the domestic partnership movement.[95] With the 2015 Supreme Court ruling that legalized same-sex marriage, same-sex couples in all states now have the option to marry and have access to the same benefits and rights as opposite-sex married couples. This change, while benefitting many, may have had the unintended consequence of reducing benefit access to those who choose to remain unmarried. Prior to this decision, some employers provided benefits such as health insurance to the unmarried partners in same-sex couples on the grounds that they otherwise would not have access to them. With the legalization of same-sex marriage, some of these same employers have rescinded benefits to such individuals since they can now gain access through marriage. And an employer survey conducted after the decision suggests that some firms are now also limiting (or considering limiting) access to employer-provided benefits for unmarried opposite-sex partners.[96]

How to Handle a Job Interview

How much should you tell a potential employer about your current and expected family responsibilities during a job interview?* This question is not easy to answer. On the one hand, mentioning that you plan to marry or have children, currently have young children, or perhaps have other family members who need care or that you have a spouse who would also need to relocate may reduce your chances of being offered a position for which you are fully qualified. On the other hand, in order for you to be sure that you and the firm will be a "good match," you may need to learn about the employer's willingness to accommodate your family concerns. You might like to know whether the employer would make it easier for you to handle possible family emergencies or whether your progress would be impeded if you were reluctant to move. The question might even arise as to whether you would want to work for an organization that looks askance at anyone who has a life outside the workplace.

At the same time, it is likely that because of the high costs of hiring and training workers, employers who interview you are also interested in making a good long-term match and therefore want to learn as much as possible about you. They too, however, face challenges and constraints. On the one hand,

continues

---

[95]For the rationale for these policies, see *Domestic Partner Benefits: Facts and Background* (Washington, DC: Employee Benefit Research Institute, February 2009). Importantly, access does not necessarily mean equal treatment. For instance, even though some employers may offer access to health insurance to unmarried partners (same or opposite sex), this benefit is taxed as income, while the benefit is tax-exempt (and thus more favorably treated) for married spouses.

[96]Tara Siegel Bernard, "Fate of Domestic Partner Benefits in Question after Marriage Ruling," *New York Times*, June 28, 2015. Stephen Miller, "Poll: Many Will Now Drop Domestic Partner Benefits," Society for Human Resource Management website (July 13, 2015), accessed September 15, 2016, https://www.shrm.org/resourcesandtools/hr-topics/benefits/pages/domestic-partner-benefits-poll.aspx.

employers would like to learn about your commitment to the job. On the other hand, they are not allowed under our antidiscrimination laws to ask directly about your family situation, including current or intended pregnancies, whether any family members have disabilities, or even your marital status.** One problem is that some employers may nevertheless ask questions that are illegal, fall into a gray area, or are at least "unwise," depending on how they are asked. Their questions confront you with the difficult decision of how to handle the situation.

Although it is impossible to offer suggestions on precisely what to say and do under all circumstances that may arise, it has generally been recommended that you avoid an explicit discussion about your current or expected family responsibilities. For instance, one approach is to ask your potential employer to describe a "typical day" or a "typical week" for a person who holds this type of job. The answer would give you a sense of whether you would be expected to work late hours during the week or on weekends, without your asking the question directly and thus perhaps giving the appearance that you are not willing to work hard. Also, at a later stage in the interview process, you could ask for materials regarding conditions of employment, which may include information about options for flextime and various fringe benefits, such as on-site childcare. In addition, discrete conversations with potential coworkers may serve to answer questions you would be reluctant to raise with the employer directly.

While the general rule has been to convey as little information about family demands as possible, one study finds that applicants may actually benefit from explicitly sharing information about children, at least as far as explaining "gaps" on a résumé due to time out of the labor force to raise children. (Recall, as discussed earlier, that an employer cannot initiate this discussion.) Using an online survey, the researchers asked currently employed individuals to read short "vignettes" about female applicants with a 10-year gap in their work history. The vignettes varied, with some describing the real reason for the gap—staying home to raise children—while other vignettes omitted this information. The researchers found that, *among those with gaps*, the survey respondents strongly preferred the candidates who explicitly mentioned child-rearing. Their reasoning for this perhaps somewhat surprising finding is that "more information is better"; that is, employers prefer greater certainty about job candidates.*** While heartening, this does not preclude the possibility that employers nonetheless prefer applicants who do not have such gaps to those who do. Moreover, at the next stage of the interview process, they may still look askance at job applicants who inquire directly about workplace flexibility, thereby signaling a current need to balance paid work and family.

Concerns about family responsibilities remain especially problematic for women because they continue to bear the primary responsibility for the family and household. Under these circumstances, employers may be tempted to hire men who tend to have fewer family commitments that will interfere with their devotion to their jobs, although, of course, explicitly discriminating in favor of men would be illegal. This suggests that public policies emphasizing equal opportunity are only part, though a very crucial part, of the effort to promote gender equity in the workplace. Work–family policies are also crucial, as is, more fundamentally, a greater sharing of family responsibilities by women and men themselves.

---

*This discussion is drawn from Sue Shellenbarger, "What You Should Say about Family Duties in a Job Interview," Wall Street Journal, April 10, 1996, B1; "Advice to Help You Get Ahead from the Experts: Business Newsletters, Magazines and Books; Job Seekers Should Beware," Atlanta Journal and Constitution, June 20, 1999; Kirsten Downey Grimsley, "Awkward Queries in Interviews," San Francisco Chronicle, February 25, 2000, B3; Eileen P. Gunn, "How to Ask about Flexible Hours without Derailing Your Candidacy," Wall Street Journal, February 8, 2007; and Alissa Quart,

"Why Women Hide Their Pregnancies," New York Times, October 6, 2012.
**"Five Illegal Interview Questions and How to Dodge Them," Forbes, April 20, 2012.
***Joni Hersch and Jennifer Bennett Shinall, "Something to Talk About: Information Exchange under Employment Law," University of Pennsylvania Law Review 165 (2016): 49–90; and Patricia Cohen, "A Child Care Gap in the Résumé: Whether to Explain or Not," New York Times, May 19, 2016.

Conclusion

This chapter looked at how and the extent to which government and employers have implemented policies to help people meet the dual demands of paid work and family. These policies have received increasing attention as women have joined the paid labor force in record numbers and men have taken on more household responsibilities, including childcare and elder care. Nevertheless, concerns remain. First, we pointed to the continued lack of mandated paid federal leave. Even with the existing federal leave policy—the Family and Medical Leave Act (FMLA), which mandates unpaid leave—large fraction of workers are not eligible, including those who are employed in small firms or work part-time. Moreover, for those who are eligible, the fact that the FMLA is unpaid means that many workers may not be able to take advantage of the policy. We noted a promising new development, which is a growing trend among states to offer paid family leave. It is important that men utilize the various leave policies in order to reduce any negative repercussions that women might otherwise experience from taking leave.

Second, we pointed to the continued lack of flexibility in the workplace. While part-time work is an option used by many women to gain flexibility, such employment tends to offer few, if any, opportunities for career advancement and often pays less on an hourly basis. Policies that offer full-time workers greater temporal flexibility, including a "right to request" policy, have the potential to help them better balance work and family. Again, for the reasons mentioned earlier, it is important that men as well as women utilize these policies. A third ongoing concern is the lack of affordable, quality childcare, not just for infants but also for school-age children and disadvantaged children of all ages. These problems have increased as a greater fraction of businesses operate 24/7, resulting in a growing number of individuals working nights, weekends, and irregular hours. It is in the interest of firms that want a focused, committed workforce now and in the future as well as society at large to find solutions to these problems. Greater temporal flexibility for workers as well as increased funding for before- and after-school programs and additional childcare subsidies would be important steps in that direction.

Questions for Review and Discussion

1. When the FMLA was passed in the United States in 1993, it was attacked as overly generous by some and as inadequate by others. Discuss the arguments behind each of these views.

2. Suppose you work for a "singles" lobby group. Point to the various policies that "work against singles." What sort of policies would be useful to families but would be more neutral with respect to family structure?

3. Make the best case you can for the following:

   a. Parents being entirely responsible for the care of their children

   b. Employer-financed day care

   c. Government-financed day care

4. Discuss the pros and cons of mandating that employers provide relatively long paid parental leaves of, say, 1 year.

5. Based on the discussion in this chapter, what do you think are the key factors that a supervisor likely takes into account when deciding whether or not to approve a request under a "right to request" policy? Such policies typically include language that bars retaliation by employers when employees request flexibility. Explain the importance of such language.

Suggested Readings

Blau, David M. *The Child Care Problem: An Economic Analysis*. New York: Russell Sage Foundation, 2001.

Boushey, Heather. *Finding Time: The Economics of Work–Life Conflict*. Cambridge, MA: Harvard University Press, 2016.

Clawson, Dan, and Naomi Gerstel. *Unequal Time: Gender, Class, and Family in Employment Schedules*. New York: Russell Sage Foundation, 2014.

Council of Economic Advisers. "Family Friendly Policies." In *Economic Report of the President*, chap. 4. Washington, DC: GPO, 2015.

Folbre, Nancy. *Valuing Children: Rethinking the Economics of the Family*. Cambridge, MA: Harvard University Press, 2008.

Jacobs, Jerry A., and Kathleen Gerson. *The Time Divide: Balancing Work and Family in Contemporary Society*. Cambridge, MA: Harvard University Press, 2004.

Milkman, Ruth, and Eileen Appelbaum. *Unfinished Business: Paid Family Leave in California and the Future of U.S. Work–Family Policy*. Ithaca, NY: ILR Press and Cornell University Press, 2013.

Moynihan, Daniel P., Timothy M. Smeeding, and Lee Rainwater, eds. *The Future of the Family*. New York: Russell Sage Foundation, 2004.

Presser, Harriet B. *Working in a 24/7 Economy*. New York: Russell Sage Foundation, 2003.

US Department of Labor. *The Cost of Doing Nothing. The Price We All Pay without Paid Leave Policies to Support America's 21st Century Working Families*. Washington, DC: US Department of Labor, 2015.

Waldfogel, Jane. *What Children Need*. Cambridge, MA: Harvard University Press, 2006.

Key Terms

fringe benefits (428)	temporal flexibility (431)	adverse selection (433)
earnings inequality (428)	externalities (433)	equity (433)

Pregnancy Discrimination Act (436)

Family and Medical Leave Act (FMLA) (436)

childcare (441)

Child Care and Development Block Grant (442)

Head Start (442)

Dependent Care Tax Credit (442)

flexible spending accounts (443)

Child Tax Credit (443)

Earned Income Tax Credit (EITC) (443)

flextime (447)

nonstandard work schedules (448)

part-time employment (448)

right to request policy (449)

job sharing (449)

home-based employment (449)

flexible benefit plans (450)

PART V

The Economic Status of the World's Women

Gender Differences around the World

17

CHAPTER HIGHLIGHTS

- ◼ **Indicators of Women's Economic Status**
- ◼ **Labor Force Participation**
- ◼ **Time Spent in Unpaid Work**
- ◼ **Educational Attainment**
- ◼ **Cross-National Trends in Fertility Rates**
- ◼ **Variations in Sex Ratios at Birth**
- ◼ **Women's Political and Legal Empowerment**
- ◼ **Multidimensional Measures of Women's Status**
- ◼ **Economic Development, Globalization, and Women's Status**

Up to this point, we have focused almost entirely on the situation in the United States. Throughout, we have emphasized the influence of economic factors in determining the status of women. This is not, however, to suggest that nothing else matters but rather that, everything being the same, economic considerations play an important role. Of course, in the real world, everything else is generally not the same. Societies differ in their political systems, economic and social policies, cultures, and religions. In this chapter, we turn to a consideration of women in other countries, both to shed light on the causes of the substantial diversity in their status and to see what we can learn about institutions and policies elsewhere that have retarded or enhanced improvements in the position of women. We begin with a broad description of the economic status of women compared to men throughout the world, with special attention to women's labor market activity and the forces that influence it. In the subsequent chapter, we examine the United States in the context of other economically advanced countries.

459

Indicators of Women's Economic Status

A number of measures are, by general agreement, regarded as useful indicators of women's economic status: women's labor force participation, the degree of occupational segregation by sex, the female–male earnings ratio, women's educational attainment compared to men's, the fertility rate, the allocation of housework, and women's political and legal empowerment. These indicators are of interest both because they are themselves direct indicators of women's economic status and because they are causally intertwined with one another. Their importance is underscored by the influential Millennium Development Goals set forth by the United Nations in 2000, which sought to achieve gender equality in primary education and promote gender equality and women's empowerment through increases in their paid labor market activity and share of political representation. In 2016 the United Nations established the Sustainable Development Goals to continue these efforts.[1]

The International Context

As we shall see, there is considerable variation in women's situation across regions and even within countries located within the same region. For ease of discussion, we categorize countries by region and, within region, using income-based definitions from the World Bank. In doing so, it should be kept in mind that income is only one dimension of a country's level of economic development.[2] Most high-income countries are located in western and northern Europe and North America, but there are a number of notable exceptions, as shown in Table 17-1. For instance, high-income countries also include major oil-exporting countries in the Middle East such as Kuwait and Saudi Arabia and the countries of Australia, Japan, and South Korea in East Asia and the Pacific. Following the World Bank, we refer to low- and middle-income countries as **developing countries**. There are large income differences among the countries in this group. Some can only euphemistically be called *developing*, while others are soon likely to be reclassified as *economically advanced*. They also differ considerably with respect to religion, customs, geographic location, and economic resource bases, among other factors. Progress within countries may also be very uneven, as is well illustrated by developments in China and India. Both of these countries have experienced considerable growth in per capita income along with the creation of modern cities, while their rural populations have been left behind to a great extent.[3]

Women in developing countries face particular challenges and difficulties, as a result of the extremely low income levels of these countries.[4] A telling statistic is that the poorest

[1]For details on these efforts, see United Nations, *The Millennium Development Goals Report 2015* (New York: United Nations, 2015); and United Nations, "Sustainable Development Goals," accessed July 6, 2016, www.un.org.
[2]See World Bank, "Country Classifications," Data and Statistics, www.worldbank.org.
[3]Shubham Chaudhuri and Martin Ravallion, "Partially Awakened Giants: Uneven Growth in China and India," in *Dancing with Giants: China, India, and the Global Economy*, ed. L. Alan Winters and Shahid Yusuf (Washington, DC: World Bank, 2006), 157–88.
[4]A number of useful books and many interesting articles on women in developing countries have been published since Ester Boserup's landmark 1970 volume, *Women's Role in Economic Development*, including, for example, Ester Boserup, *Economic and Demographic Relationships in Development* (Baltimore: Johns Hopkins University Press, 1990); Ester Boserup, "Obstacles to Advancement of Women," in *Investments in Women's Human Capital*, ed. T. Paul Schultz (Chicago: University of Chicago Press, 1995), 51–60; and World Bank, *Gender at Work: A Companion to the World Development Report on Jobs* (Washington, DC: World Bank, 2014).

50 percent of the world's population receives only 8 percent of the income, while the wealthiest 16 percent receives 64 percent.[5] Not surprisingly, then, developing countries are generally characterized by an extremely low standard of living, high rates of infant mortality, short life expectancy, and high rates of illiteracy. In many instances, their high rates of fertility tend to exacerbate some of the other problems. Thus, most people in developing countries live in extremely difficult circumstances. In addition, women most often bear a disproportionate share of the burdens of economic and social deprivation.[6]

Labor Force Participation

Labor force participation is arguably the most important indicator of women's economic status. Although it is true that women perform a great deal of work in all economies, the total amount of time spent on household and paid work and how it is allocated between these activities differs substantially across countries. Paid work is deemed to be particularly important because it provides women with status in their own right, gives them greater power and influence in decision-making within the family, and raises the family's standard of living overall.[7]

Table 17-1 provides figures on women's labor force participation rates in 1990 and 2014 for those aged 15 and over by world region and level of income and for selected countries in these regions.[8] International differences in female labor force participation rates reflect differences across countries in women's participation in paid work but are also influenced by a number of measurement issues. Differences across countries in the age range of the population that is included may influence the comparison.[9] And, even when the age range being compared is the same, international differences may be affected by a number of other factors, including the age distribution of the population and the typical school-leaving and retirement ages.

Table 17-1 indicates considerable variation in labor force participation rates across regions and selected countries. For example, the data for 2014 show that women's labor force participation rates given by the regional averages for developing countries vary widely, from 63 percent in East Asia and 64 percent in sub-Saharan Africa to 20 percent in the Middle East and North Africa. Considerable variation

[5] Calculated from World Bank, *World Development Indicators,* accessed August 2, 2016, www.worldbank.org.

[6] Allen Tuovi, "Economic Development and the Feminization of Poverty," in *Women's Work in the World Economy,* ed. Nancy Folbre, Barbara Bergmann, Bina Agarwal, and Maria Floro (New York: New York University Press, 1992), 107–19. For an updated discussion of these issues, see Lourdes Benería, Günseli Berik, and Maria S. Floro, *Gender, Development, and Globalization,* 2nd ed. (New York and London: Routledge, 2016).

[7] The pioneering work on this subject is Ester Boserup, *Women's Role in Economic Development* (New York: St. Martin's Press, 1970). For further discussion, see Esther Duflo, "Women Empowerment and Economic Development," *Journal of Economic Literature* 50, no. 4 (December 2012): 1051–79; Shelly Lundberg, "The Sexual Division of Labour" in *The Shape of the Division of Labour: Nations, Industries and Households,* ed. Robert M. Solow and Jean-Philippe Touffut (Cheltenham, UK, and Northampton, MA: Edward Elgar 2010), 122–48; World Bank, *World Development Report 2012: Gender Equality and Development* (September 19, 2011); and International Labour Organization, *Women at Work Trends 2016* (Geneva: International Labour Organization, March 2016).

[8] For purposes of brevity, we focus on women's labor force participation here. Other indicators of women's economic activity include the share of women in the labor force and the ratio of women's to men's labor force participation rates.

[9] In our more detailed comparison of the economically advanced countries in Chapter 18 (Table 18-1) we examine labor force participation rates of those 25 to 54, thereby excluding those who are most likely to be going to college (under age 25) or retired (over age 54).

TABLE 17-1   INDICATORS OF WOMEN'S ECONOMIC STATUS, BY WORLD REGIONS AND SELECTED COUNTRIES

	GROSS NATIONAL INCOME PER CAPITA (IN $) 2014	GENDER INEQUALITY INDEX[a] 2014	FEMALE LABOR FORCE PARTICIPATION RATE (%) (AGE 15 AND OLDER)	
			1990	2014
I. WORLD				
Low and Middle Income (Average)	4,602	n.a.	53	50
High Income (Average)	42,705	n.a.	50	53
II. BY WORLD REGION AND INCOME				
Sub-Saharan Africa Region				
Low and Middle Income (Regional Average)	1,727	0.58	59	64
Ethiopia	550	0.56	72	78
Kenya	1,300	0.55	70	62
Niger	420	0.71	25	40
Nigeria	2,970	n.a.	39	48
South Africa	6,790	0.41	39	45
East Asia and Pacific Region				
Low and Middle Income (Regional Average)	6,157	0.33	69	63
China	7,400	0.19	73	64
Indonesia	3,630	0.49	50	51
Thailand	5,780	0.38	76	64
Vietnam	1,900	0.31	74	73
High Income				
Australia	64,620	0.11	52	59
Japan	41,900	0.13	50	49
Singapore	55,330	0.09	51	59
South Korea	26,970	0.12	47	50
South Asia				
Low and Middle Income (Regional Average)	1,496	0.54	36	31
Bangladesh	1,080	0.50	62	58
India	1,560	0.56	35	27
Pakistan	1,400	0.54	13	25
Central and Eastern Europe and Central Asia				
Low and Middle Income (Regional Average)	9,607	0.30	50	46
Moldova	2,560	0.25	61	38
Romania	9,590	0.33	52	49
Uzbekistan	2,070	n.a.	46	48
High Income				
Russia	14,330	0.28	60	57
Czech Republic	18,690	0.09	52	51
Poland	13,690	0.14	55	49
Slovenia	23,560	0.02	48	52

ADULT ILLITERACY RATE (%)				TOTAL FERTILITY RATE[c]	
FEMALE		MALE			
1980	2005–2013	1980	2005–2013	1970	2013
48	24	29	14	5.5	2.6
b	b	b	b	2.5	1.7
72	48	51	31	6.7	5.0
89	71	72	51	7.0	4.5
57	33	30	22	8.1	4.4
97	91	87	77	7.4	7.6
78	59	55	39	6.5	5.7
25	7	22	5	5.6	2.4
43	8	20	3	5.7	1.8
48	7	22	3	5.7	1.6
40	10	21	4	5.5	2.5
17	4	8	4	5.6	1.5
19	9	7	4	6.5	2.0
b	b	b	b	2.9	1.9
b	b	b	b	2.1	1.4
26	5	9	b	3.1	1.2
11	b	3	b	4.5	1.2
75	43	48	24	5.8	2.6
83	44	59	37	6.9	2.2
74	41	45	21	5.6	2.5
86	57	59	30	6.6	3.7
8	3	3	b	2.8	1.9
8	b	b	b	2.6	1.3
7	b	b	b	2.9	1.4
33	b	17	b	6.5	2.3
b	b	b	b	2.0	1.7
b	b	b	b	1.9	1.5
b	b	b	b	2.2	1.3
b	b	b	b	2.2	1.6

continues

TABLE 17-1 INDICATORS OF WOMEN'S ECONOMIC STATUS, BY WORLD REGIONS AND SELECTED COUNTRIES

	GROSS NATIONAL INCOME PER CAPITA (IN $) 2014	GENDER INEQUALITY INDEX[a] 2014	FEMALE LABOR FORCE PARTICIPATION RATE (%) (AGE 15 AND OLDER)	
			1990	2014
Middle East and North Africa Region				
Low and Middle Income (Regional Average)	4,598	0.54	17	20
Algeria	5,490	0.41	10	15
Egypt	3,210	0.57	26	24
Iran	6,550	0.51	10	17
Jordan	4,590	0.47	9	16
Morocco	3,080	0.52	26	27
High Income				
Israel	35,340	0.10	41	58
Kuwait	49,300	0.39	35	44
Saudi Arabia	25,500	0.28	14	20
Latin America and Caribbean Region				
Low and Middle Income (Regional Average)	9,503	0.42	41	55
Brazil	11,790	0.46	45	59
Honduras	2,270	0.48	33	43
Mexico	10,080	0.37	34	45
High Income				
Trinidad and Tobago	18,830	0.37	39	53
Argentina	12,330	0.38	41	48
Uruguay	16,210	0.31	45	56
North America and Western Europe				
High Income				
Canada	51,770	0.13	58	61
Germany	47,500	0.04	43	54
Italy	34,540	0.07	35	40
Spain	29,380	0.10	34	53
Sweden	60,590	0.05	62	60
United Kingdom	43,350	0.18	53	56
United States	54,400	0.28	56	56

ADULT ILLITERACY RATE (%)				TOTAL FERTILITY RATE[c]	
FEMALE		MALE			
1980	2005–2013	1980	2005–2013	1970	2013
72	30	44	15	6.7	2.9
76	36	46	19	7.6	2.9
75	33	47	17	5.9	3.3
61	22	38	11	6.4	1.7
46	3	18	b	7.9	3.5
85	42	58	24	6.7	2.5
13	b	5	b	3.8	3.0
39	6	26	4	7.3	2.2
67	9	33	3	7.3	2.8
23	9	18	8	5.4	2.2
27	8	23	9	5.0	1.8
40	15	37	14	7.3	2.4
22	7	14	5	6.8	2.3
16	b	7	b	3.6	1.8
6	2	6	2	3.1	2.3
b	b	b	2	2.9	2.0
b	b	b	b	2.3	1.6
b	b	b	b	2.0	1.4
5	b	3	b	2.4	1.4
8	3	3	b	2.8	1.3
b	b	b	b	1.9	1.9
b	b	b	b	2.4	1.8
b	b	b	b	2.5	1.9

Notes: Figures are for closest year available. n.a. = not available

Gross national income (GNI) per capita in low- and middle-income countries was below $12,735 in 2014, while GNI per capita exceeded this figure in high-income countries. Figures are for closest year available.

[a]The Gender Inequality Index ranges between 0 (least inequality) and 1 (greatest inequality), with an average across the world of .45; regional averages provided if available.

[b] Figure is less than 2% or not available.

[c] The total fertility rate is defined as the number of births that a cohort of 1,000 women would have if they experienced the age-specific birth rates occurring in the current year throughout their childbearing years (see Table 13-4). Here it is divided by 1,000 to measure births per woman.

Sources: World Bank, World Development Indicators (various years), published and online database (accessed July 8, 2016 and November 15, 2016); the 1980 illiteracy data are from the published version of World Development Indicators, 2000; and United Nations, *Human Development Report* (2015), "Gender Inequality Index and Related Indicators," table 5.

is also found within some of these regions. For instance, in East Asia, the female labor force participation rate for Vietnam was 73 percent compared to 51 percent for Indonesia. And in sub-Saharan Africa, the female labor force participation rate was 78 percent in Ethiopia but just 40 percent in Niger.

There is also considerable variation in women's participation rates across high-income countries. In these countries, labor force participation rates for 2014 ranged from just 20 percent in Saudi Arabia to around 40 percent in Italy and Kuwait to closer to 60 percent for a number of the high-income countries in North America and western Europe. Chapter 18 provides a more in-depth look at labor force participation rates in economically advanced countries.[10]

The region of central and eastern Europe and central Asia comprises the countries of the former Soviet bloc as well as the countries that were previously part of Yugoslavia. For four decades, from the end of World War II until the late 1980s or so, these countries were dominated to a great extent by a communist ideology. Countries in this region traditionally had relatively high female labor force participation rates, but female (and male) participation rates declined to varying extents following the breakup of the Soviet bloc and the transition to market economies. For instance, the data reported in Table 17-1 show a modest decline in women's participation rates in Russia from 60 percent in 1990 to 57 percent in 2014.[11]

How do we explain the considerable diversity in labor force activity by gender across countries and, more generally, across regions? Part of the explanation is that countries or regions are in various stages of economic development, ranging from agricultural to industrial and postindustrial. As discussed in Chapter 2, one hypothesis that receives some support from the evidence is that the relationship between economic development and women's labor force participation rates tends to be U-shaped. Referring back to Figure 2-1, female labor force participation is high in the stage of subsistence agriculture, when women tend to be heavily involved as family workers, but then declines during the early stages of economic development as the nature of agricultural work changes and the locus of much production moves out of the household and into factories and offices. This stage is effectively the "bottom" of the U. One argument for the much lower female labor force participation at this stage is that societal norms often work against women, particularly married women, performing manual, factory-type work. Then, as countries become more developed and women's education and opportunities for white-collar employment rise, women's labor force participation once again increases.[12] Consistent with this pattern, we see in Table 17-1

---

[10]As shown in Table 18-1, when rates are computed for those aged 25–54, the Nordic countries have noticeably higher rates than the United States.

[11]One caution in looking at trends in transition countries is that survey methods may have changed. See UNIFEM, *The Story behind the Numbers: Women and Employment in Central and Eastern Europe and the Western Commonwealth of Independent States* (New York: UNIFEM, March 2006).

[12]Claudia Goldin, "The U-Shaped Female Labor Force Function in Economic Development and Economic History," in *Investment in Women's Human Capital*, ed. T. Paul Schultz (Chicago: University of Chicago Press, 1995), 61–90. For additional evidence, see Kristin Mammen and Christina Paxson, "Women's Work and Economic Development," *Journal of Economic Perspectives* 14, no. 4 (Fall 2000): 141–64. While there is quite a bit of cross-sectional evidence in support of a U shape, a study by Isis Gaddis and Stephan Klasen finds weaker evidence of the declining portion of the U for those countries currently defined as "developing"; see "Economic Development, Structural Change, and Women's Labor Force Participation: A Reexamination of the Feminization U Hypothesis," *Journal of Population Economics* 27 (2014): 639–81. On this point, see also Claudia Olivetti, "The Female Labor Force and Long-Run Development: The American Experience in Comparative Perspective," in *Human Capital in History: The American Record*, ed. L. Platt Boustan, C. Frydman, and R. A. Margo (Chicago: University of Chicago Press, 2014), 161–204.

relatively high rates of participation in countries with economies that are predominantly agricultural, such as those in sub-Saharan Africa, but lower rates at the next stage of development, as is true of countries in Latin America. Higher rates are found once again in many of the more economically advanced countries.

As we saw in Chapter 6, the key to women's labor force participation decision is the value of market earnings (w) compared to the value of time spent in household production (w^*). Differences in women's labor market activity from place to place and over time may also be influenced by demand factors (affecting w) and supply factors (affecting w^*). So, for example, the demand for women workers is influenced by such factors as the industrial mix of the economy and the relative size of the market and nonmarket sectors, which help to determine the nature of the jobs available in the labor market. In addition, a larger service sector provides substitutes for household production and encourages female labor force participation.[13] The preferences of employers for male versus female workers, perhaps reflecting deep-seated cultural ideas regarding the appropriate role of women, may also play a role. Taken together these factors influence the wages that women can earn in the labor market and the quality of the labor market opportunities available to them.

On the supply side, the value of home time is strongly influenced by fertility rates, the availability of goods and services for purchase in the market, general attitudes toward the appropriate roles for women and men, and tastes for market goods compared to commodities mainly produced at home. Social forces such as religion, ideology, and culture also influence women's labor market activity.[14] For instance, women's labor force participation tends to be lower in countries dominated by religious faiths that particularly emphasize women's traditional roles as wives and mothers, such as in Latin America, with its predominantly Catholic population, and in the Middle East and North Africa, which is largely Muslim. Marxist ideology, which strongly advocates women's entry into the workforce, surely helps to explain why women's participation came to be extremely high in many of the former Soviet bloc countries as well as in China. Similarly, concern for gender equality in the Nordic countries was one of the reasons for the introduction of policies that encouraged female labor force participation such as a tax structure favorable to two-earner couples, family leave, and subsidized day care. Indeed, Chapter 18, which focuses on economically advanced countries, points to the potential impact of these and other government and employer policies on women's labor force participation decisions. Apart from their direct effect, such policies in turn likely influence attitudes about women's role in the economy.

Time Spent in Unpaid Work

As discussed at some length in earlier chapters, the roles of women and men in the labor market are interrelated with their roles in the household. In our review of the situation in the United States in Chapter 4, we found a considerable gender difference in time spent in household production remains despite women's increasing

---

[13]For instance, Richard B. Freeman and Ronald Schettkat point out that in the countries of the European Union more household services are produced in the home rather than purchased in the market than is the case in the United States, thus reducing their female labor supply relative to that of the United States; see "Marketization of Household Production and the EU–US Gap in Work," *Economic Policy* (January 2005): 5–50.

[14]See, for instance, World Bank, "Removing Social Barriers and Building Social Institutions," *World Development Report 2000/2001: Attacking Poverty* (Washington, DC: World Bank, 2000).

attachment to the labor force, though there is some evidence that married fathers are spending more time on childcare. The continued unequal division of household responsibilities between men and women potentially influences both the amount of leisure time available to women and their achievements on the job. For instance, data from around 2010 indicate that the ratio of women's to men's time in unpaid work was around 1.3 in Sweden, 1.6 in the United States, and considerably higher, at around 5, in South Korea and Japan.[15] In the latter two countries, a long-standing custom has been that wives of eldest sons are responsible for their in-laws, a duty which adds considerably to women's caregiving responsibilities.

Women's burden is undoubtedly greatest for those in developing countries, especially those living in rural areas; in addition to the usual housework, they often do a large amount of unpaid work needed for their families' subsistence, including carrying water and firewood as well as growing agricultural products.[16]

Educational Attainment

Women's educational attainment is also important as an indicator of their economic status, in part because it influences their occupations and earnings, which are themselves indicators of women's status. Also, it allows women to make better-informed decisions about affairs in their own household, their community, and their nation. Gender differences in educational attainment are fairly small among economically advanced countries but vary considerably across all countries, as a result of, and related to, differences in levels of affluence as well as differences in fertility, social customs, and government policies.

In developing countries, women's educational attainment has historically been lower than men's for several reasons. From a purely economic standpoint, to the extent that girls do more housework than boys, including caring for siblings, the opportunity cost of sending daughters rather than sons to school is greater. (However, at older ages boys may face a higher opportunity cost due to the higher wages they can earn in the labor market.) Moreover, as discussed in Chapter 8, to the extent that girls receive a smaller return on their educational investments than boys due to a shorter expected work life or gender discrimination in pay, it may be that they or their families opt to invest less in it. Tradition may also play a role. For instance, in many cultures boys are expected to support their parents in their old age, while girls marry into another family, thereby giving parents a greater economic motive to invest in sons. As another example, in some societies, education, beyond a minimal level, may reduce a woman's chance of marrying, given social norms.[17]

---

[15]Figures are calculated from Organisation for Economic Co-operation and Development (OECD), "Time Spent in Paid and Unpaid Work," OECD.Stat, accessed March 2, 2016, www.oecd.org. See also Clair Cain Miller, "How Society Pays When Women's Work Is Unpaid," *New York Times*, February 22, 2016. For an interesting discussion, see Michael Burda, Daniel S. Hamermesh, and Philippe Weil, "Total Work Hours and Gender," *Journal of Population Economics* 26 (2013): 239–61.

[16]Miranda Veerle, "Cooking, Caring and Volunteering: Unpaid Work around the World," OECD Social, Employment and Migration Working Paper 116 (OECD, Paris, France, 2010); and Benería, Berik, and Floro, *Gender, Development, and Globalization*, chap. 5.

[17]For discussion, see M. Anne Hill and Elisabeth M. King, "Women's Education and Economic Well-Being," *Feminist Economics* 1, no. 2 (Summer 1995): 21–46; and World Bank, *World Development Report 2012*.

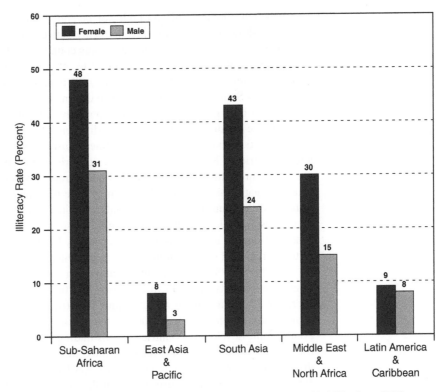

FIGURE 17-1 Illiteracy Rates, Low & Middle-Income Economies, World Regions, 2013

Note: See Table 17-1 for notes and sources.

Illiteracy rates provide one useful measure of educational attainment, especially in the developing world. As shown in Table 17-1 and Figure 17-1, female illiteracy rates in 2013 stood at 43 percent in South Asia, 48 percent in sub-Saharan Africa, and 30 percent in the developing countries of the Middle East and North Africa.[18] The rates for men were also high but considerably lower than those of women in each region, with male illiteracy rates of 24 percent in South Asia, 31 percent in sub-Saharan Africa, and 15 percent in the developing countries of the Middle East and North Africa.[19] An important factor that contributes to low levels of educational attainment for both men and women in the poorest countries is that large numbers of children do not even attend school because many of them, especially girls, are helping out at home, while others are employed as child laborers.[20]

---

[18]The data in Table 17-1 and Figure 17-1 are based on World Bank data for the period 2005–2013. For brevity, the text refers to 2013.

[19]For data on average years of schooling for women relative to men by broad region for 1950–2010, see Robert J. Barro and Jong-Wha Lee, "A New Data Set of Educational Attainment in the World, 1950–2010," *Journal of Development Economics* 104 (2013): 184–98, table 4. The authors maintain a website with these data at http://www.barrolee.com (accessed July 6, 2016).

[20]For more on child labor, see Eric V. Edmonds and Nina Pavcnik, "Child Labor in the Global Economy," *Journal of Economic Perspectives* 19, no. 1 (Winter 2005): 199–220; and Kathleen Beegle, Rajeev Dehejia, and Roberta Gatti, "Why Should We Care about Child Labor?" *Journal of Human Resources* 44, no. 4 (Fall 2009): 871–89. Girls are a disproportionate share of domestic workers (those who work in someone else's household). They tend to be "hidden" and, as a consequence, particularly vulnerable to abuse; see International Labour Organization, *Ending Child Labour in Domestic Work and Protecting Young Workers from Abusive Working Conditions* (Geneva: International Labour Organization, June 2013).

Although illiteracy rates for both women and men remain high in some regions, Table 17-1 shows that they declined markedly between 1980 and 2013 across all regions and selected countries. In the developing countries of the Middle East and North Africa, female illiteracy rates fell from 72 to 30 percent and from over 70 percent in sub-Saharan Africa and South Asia to 48 percent in sub-Saharan Africa and 43 percent in South Asia. Men's rates also declined, so there has been a reduction in illiteracy for both groups. Improvement in relative educational attainment is also reflected in the **gender education gap**, the difference between men's and women's average education levels. This gap has declined considerably and even reversed in quite a few countries.[21] Rising enrollment rates of girls in primary and secondary school are the main factors behind falling illiteracy rates and the decline in the gender education gap. The observed changes may have been hastened by the 2000 United Nations Millennium Development Goals, mentioned earlier, which placed pressure on nations around the world to achieve universal primary education and eliminate gender inequality at the primary and secondary levels by 2015. Even with these efforts, the region of sub-Saharan Africa, in particular, still lags considerably behind.[22]

Another notable development is that women comprise a large and rising fraction of college students not only in countries like the United States and its economic peers but also in a number of developing countries. In fact, women now constitute a larger proportion of college students than men in all economically advanced and even in some developing countries.[23] This finding for economically advanced countries is consistent with trends for the United States that we reviewed in Chapter 9; there we saw that women have comprised over half of US college students since the 1980s. It is perhaps more surprising that this pattern also holds in a number of developing countries, given that girls' enrollments continue to lag at the primary and secondary levels in a number of these countries. An explanation for this seemingly contradictory finding is that when girls do have the opportunity to go to school they are less likely to drop out than boys.[24] One cautionary note, however, discussed in the "Middle East and North Africa" box, is that despite women's considerable gains in educational attainment, their labor force participation rates do not always increase commensurately.

The Benefits of Educating Girls

One reason for the emphasis on reducing or eliminating gender differences in education by the United Nations and other institutions is that investing in women's education not only benefits the individual receiving the education but contributes to broader

---

[21]Barro and Lee, "A New Data Set of Educational Attainment"; and Ina Ganguli, Richard Hausmann, and Martina Viarengo, "Closing the Gender Gap in Education: Does It Foretell the Closing of the Employment, Marriage, and Motherhood Gaps?" *International Labour Review* 153, no. 2 (June 2014): 173–207.

[22]United Nations, *Millennium Development Goals Report 2015.* Stephan Klasen and Simon Lange observe that the Millennium Development Goals were unrealistic because they imposed the same goal on all countries, regardless of their initial starting point. An alternative way to evaluate success is to compare a country's performance at moving toward the goal compared to past progress. Even under this more modest goal, most sub-Saharan countries still lag behind; see Klasen and Lange, "Getting Progress Right: Measuring Progress Towards the MDGs against Historical Trends," Discussion Paper 87 (Courant Research Centre, Göttingen, Germany, February 2012).

[23]See World Bank, *World Development Report 2012,* chap. 3; and Francisco Parro, "International Evidence on the Gender Gap in Education over the Past Six Decades: A Puzzle and an Answer to It," *Journal of Human Capital* 6, no. 2 (2012): 150–85.

[24]Monica J. Grant and Jere R. Behrman, "Gender Gaps in Educational Attainment in Less Developed Countries," *Population and Development Review* 36, no. 1 (March 2010): 71–89.

social gains as well. The gains to the individual are clear. As discussed in earlier chapters, acquiring education leads to greater opportunities for employment and better earnings and working conditions. Beyond these gains to the individual receiving the education, investments of scarce government resources targeted at girls' and women's education can be justified from a broader societal standpoint on the grounds of equity and efficiency. On the basis of equity (fairness) alone, it can be argued that girls deserve to be treated the same as boys. Thus, policies targeted at girls and women reduce the often substantial disadvantage that many girls and women in developing countries face. Such investments would be expected to reduce gender differences in labor market outcomes and increase women's bargaining power in the family.

Less obvious, but no less important, is that investments in girls' and women's education may also improve efficiency to the extent that such investments produce positive externalities, that is, spillover benefits to family members and society at large.[25] The positive externalities associated with investments in female education that have been most often cited include reductions in fertility, improvements in children's health including declines in child mortality, increases in children's schooling, and greater economic growth of the country overall. Here we briefly discuss each in turn.

As discussed in earlier chapters, greater education gives women the incentive to have fewer children because it increases the opportunity cost of raising children (due to the increased value of women's market time). And indeed, the evidence does show that increased education reduces fertility in developing countries.[26] Smaller families in turn allow parents to devote more of their limited resources to each child, improving outcomes for them.

Increasing mother's education may also improve children's health in a number of ways. For instance, with greater education women are better able to read labels and instructions and can better understand and evaluate information about nutrition, proper hygiene, and medical procedures. In line with this reasoning, research finds that mothers' numeracy and literacy skills improve their children's health outcomes in developing countries.[27] Mother's education has also been found to reduce child mortality, though some research has questioned whether mother's education is *relatively* more important than father's.[28]

It has also been argued that mothers play a critical role in determining their children's schooling, largely because they have primary responsibility for child-rearing.[29]

[25]T. Paul Schultz, "Why Governments Should Invest More to Educate Girls," *World Development* 30, no. 2 (2002): 207–25; and Hill and King, "Women's Education and Economic Well-Being."

[26]Rachel Heath and Seema Jayachandran, "The Causes and Consequences of Increased Female Education and Labor Force Participation in Developing Countries," NBER Working Paper 22766 (National Bureau of Economic Research, Cambridge, MA, October 2016); and Hill and King, "Women's Education and Economic Well-Being."

[27]Paul Glewwe, "Why Does Mother's Schooling Raise Child Health in Developing Countries?" *Journal of Human Resources* 34, no. 1 (Winter 1999): 124–59; and Pinar Mine Güneş, "The Role of Maternal Education in Child Health: Evidence from a Compulsory Schooling Law," *Economics of Education Review* 47 (August 2015): 1–16. See also Duncan Thomas, John Strauss, and Maria-Helena Henriques, "How Does Mother's Education Affect Child Height?" *Journal of Human Resources* 26, no. 2 (Spring 1991): 183–211. For a broader discussion of this and other benefits, see Heath and Jayachandran, "Causes and Consequences."

[28]See World Bank, *World Development Report 2012*; Hill and King, "Women's Education and Economic Well-Being"; and Schultz, "Why Governments Should Invest More." The critique is raised by Esther Duflo; see "Women Empowerment and Economic Development," *Journal of Economic Literature* 50, no. 4 (December 2012): 1051–79.

[29]For evidence that women's education matters more, see Hill and King, "Women's Education and Economic Well-Being"; and World Bank, *World Development Report 2012*, chap. 3.

Middle East and North Africa: Low Female Labor Force Participation Rates Despite Rising Educational Attainment

In this box, we examine the region of the Middle East and North Africa, with particular attention paid to two indicators of women's economics status: educational attainment and labor force participation rates. In doing so, it is important to recognize that the countries in this region vary considerably as a consequence of their diverse history and experiences as well as due to differences in their natural resources, culture, government, and religion.* Thus, it is to be expected that the status of women and economic opportunities for both women and men within this region differ as well.

Some of the countries in the region have colonial legacies, while others do not. For instance, Syria and Lebanon were previously under French control and Iraq, Jordan, and Egypt have a British legacy. Turkey, on other hand, remained independent. Some have a history of hereditary rulers, such as the Saudi royal family, while others, notably Iran, have experienced a variety of political regimes, including monarchy and, in more recent decades, an Islamic republic.

Similarly, resources vary considerably among these countries. Many, though not all, of the nations in this region have considerable reserves of oil and gas as well as other natural resources. Oil has made some of them among the richest nations in the world, such as Saudi Arabia and the Gulf states, including the United Arab Emirates, Oman, and Kuwait. However, the economic growth of these countries has, for the most part, been unbalanced, with a primary focus on extractive industries. Other countries, among the most populous in the region, such as Egypt, Jordan, Morocco, and Tunisia, lack such natural resources. Israel, a Jewish state also located in this region, is a high-income country with a highly-diversified economy. It is fairly similar to economically advanced countries in other regions of the world. Thus, here we focus on the other countries in the Middle East and North Africa.

The countries in the Middle East and North Africa are predominantly Islamic (with the obvious exception of Israel), although religion in the region is not entirely monolithic, not even among people who classify themselves as Arabs. Some Islamic countries are predominantly Shia, while others are Sunni; and in Lebanon about 40 percent of the population is Christian. One common feature of virtually all of the countries in the region is the growth in political Islam since the 1970s. This development is generally attributed to their history as colonies of Western countries and more recently to their high rates of unemployment and a lack of economic opportunities, as well as to "growing hostility to the West and to Israel."** Earlier we pointed to the case of Iran, which became an Islamic republic in 1979. As a second example, since 2006 Gaza has been governed by the Islamic group Hamas.

While, again, there are considerable differences among countries in this region, a notable development is the considerable general rise in women's educational attainment. For instance, as shown in Figure 17-1, in the developing countries of the Middle East and North Africa region the female illiteracy rate declined from 72 to 30 percent between 1980 and 2013. Female illiteracy rates in the region tend to be quite a bit lower in higher-income countries such as Kuwait and Saudi Arabia, though a notable exception is Jordan, where the rate stands at just 3 percent. In addition, in quite a number of countries, women outnumber men at the college level.***

What remains most striking, however, is that women's labor force participation rates have not kept pace with the considerable progress in women's educational attainment. As shown in Table 17-1, women's labor force participation rate averaged only 20 percent for the developing countries in the Middle East and North Africa and 44 and 20 percent, respectively, in the oil-rich nations of Kuwait and Saudi Arabia. The religion of Islam and the generally patriarchal nature of the society in many of these countries are among the reasons typically cited. Women's mobility is more restricted than in other parts of the world, with, perhaps, the best-known example being prohibitions in Saudi Arabia against women driving cars. However, these factors are not the sole causes.**** For one, there are other countries with large Islamic populations, such as Indonesia, with substantially

continues

higher rates of female labor force participation than in most Muslim countries in the Middle East and North Africa. For example, as also shown in Table 17-1, in 2014 women's labor force participation rate stood at 51 percent in Indonesia, considerably higher than in the Middle East and North Africa. Another explanation that has been proffered is the often unbalanced nature of the economic growth occurring in the region. Extractive industries, such as oil, minerals, and gas, which dominate many of the economies of the Middle East, tend to offer women fewer employment opportunities than are provided by countries with a more balanced economic structure. Also, men's higher incomes in the oil-rich countries reduce the economic incentive for women's employment.*****

Even for those women who are in the labor force, employment in sectors other than agriculture remains quite low compared to that in other regions. Moreover, those women who find employment outside of agriculture tend to be in jobs in the public sector. Thus, gender segregation by industry and occupation remains substantial. Women, especially those with higher education, must also confront unemployment rates that considerably exceed those of men. This lack of progress in female employment represents a lost economic opportunity because this valuable resource is not being put to its best use.******

*The Middle East is typically defined to include Algeria, Bahrain, Egypt, Jordan, Iran, Iraq, Israel, Kuwait, Lebanon, Libya, Morocco, Oman, Qatar, Saudi Arabia, Syria, Tunisia, Turkey, United Arab Emirates, West Bank and Gaza, and Yemen. See, for instance, World Bank, "World Development Indicators," accessed August 1, 2016, www.worldbank.org. The background in this section draws on Nikki R. Keddie, Women in the Middle East: Past and Present (Princeton, NJ, and Oxford: Princeton University Press, 2007); Farzaneh Roudi-Fahimi and Mary Mederios Kent, "Challenges and Opportunities—The Population of the Middle East and North Africa," Population Bulletin 62, no. 2 (June 2007): 2–19; Karen Pfeifer and Marsha P. Posusney, "Arab Economies and Globalization: An Overview," in Women and Globalization in the Arab Middle East, ed. Eleanor A. Doumato and Marsha P. Posusney (Boulder, CO, and London: Lynne Rienner, 2003), 25–54; Ebru Kongar, Jennifer C. Olmsted, and Elora Shehabuddin, "Gender and Economics in Muslim Communities: A Critical Feminist and Postcolonial Analysis," Feminist Economics 20, no. 4 (2014): 1–32; Tarik M. Yousef, "Development, Growth and Policy Reform in the Middle East and North Africa," Journal of Economic Perspectives 18, no. 3 (Summer 2004): 91–116; and James E. Rauch and Scott Kostyshak, "Three Arab Worlds," Journal of Economic Perspectives 23, no. 3 (Summer 2009): 165–88.

**See Keddie, Women in the Middle East, 160–65; quotation is from p. 160.

***World Bank, Opening Doors: Gender Equality and Development in the Middle East and North Africa (Washington, DC: World Bank, 2013); and Rana F. Sweis, "In Jordan, Educated Women Face Shortage of Jobs," New York Times, May 4, 2014.

****See Olmsted, "Gender, Aging, and the Evolving Arab Patriarchal Contract"; Rauch and Kostyshak, "Three Arab Worlds"; Ghazal Bayanpourtehrani and Kevin Sylwester, "Female Labor Force Participation and Religion: A Cross Country Analysis," Bulletin of Economic Research 65, no. 2 (2012): 1–27; Seema Jayachandran, "The Roots of Gender Inequality in Developing Countries," Annual Review of Economics 7 (August 2015): 63–88; World Bank, Opening Doors; and Michael Ross, The Oil Curse: How Petroleum Wealth Shapes the Development of Nations (Princeton, NJ: Princeton University Press, 2012).

***** Olmsted, "Gender, Aging and the Evolving Arab Patriarchal Contract;" and Michael Ross, The Oil Curse: How Petroleum Wealth Shapes the Development of Nations (Princeton, NJ: Princeton University Press, 2012).

****** World Bank, Opening Doors.

Indeed, research has found a strong positive association between mothers' and children's education levels. However, what is more difficult to ascertain is the extent to which mothers' greater education, in fact, *causes* their children's educational attainment to be higher.[30]

Finally, to the extent that a gender gap in educational attainment persists, this means that some women do not have the opportunity to fully develop and utilize

[30]For further discussion, see Jere R. Behrman and Mark R. Rosenzweig, "Does Increasing Women's Schooling Raise the Schooling of the Next Generation?" *American Economic Review* 92, no. 1 (March 2002): 323–34.

their talents, thereby diminishing their contribution to the market economy. Consistent with this line of reasoning, there is some evidence that countries with smaller gender gaps in education experience higher rates of economic growth.[31] Thus, increases in girls' education have the potential to improve the well-being of society as whole by contributing to economic development.

This brief review points to the efficiency gains associated with investing in girls: society at large benefits from reduced fertility, improvements in child health, decreases in child mortality, increased education of future generations, as well as higher economic growth rates. Moreover, as mentioned at the outset, it is important to keep in mind that even if there were no efficiency gains associated with girls' education, such investments increase equity and place girls and boys and men and women on a more level playing field, both at home (in terms of bargaining power) and in the workplace.

Cross-National Trends in Fertility Rates

There is a strong relationship between fertility, educational attainment, and labor market activity. Fertility rates are an important indicator of women's economic status because with fewer children, women have greater opportunities to acquire education and engage in paid employment. Conversely, when birth rates are high, women have more difficulty staying in school and more incentive to remain full-time homemakers. As noted in earlier chapters, however, causation runs in the other direction as well. As women invest more in education and increase their participation in market work, particularly when it is away from the household, the opportunity cost of children rises, thereby providing an incentive to have fewer children. In addition, fertility is at times related to explicit government policies, as well as to religion and ideology. For instance, some governments have implemented policies explicitly designed to increase fertility or that might be expected to have such an effect. Such policies include relatively generous child allowances, paid parental leaves, and subsidized childcare. Some have also introduced laws prohibiting various types of family planning, often justifying them on the grounds of religious strictures. Other countries, however, have sought to control population growth; many have done so by making birth control information available, while China went so far as to impose severe economic penalties for having more than one child, which came to be known as the **one-child policy**. The "China's One-Child Policy" box takes a closer look at this policy and its consequences.[32]

Given the various factors that influence fertility, it is not surprising that fertility rates differ dramatically across regions. As shown in Table 17-1 and Figure 17-2, in 2013 fertility rates were as high as 5 births per woman in sub-Saharan Africa, followed by the developing countries of the Middle East and North Africa as well

---

[31] Stephan Klasen and Francesca Lamanna, "The Impact of Gender Inequality in Education and Employment on Economic Growth: New Evidence for a Panel of Countries," *Feminist Economics* 15, no. 3 (2009): 91–132; and Aniruddha Mitra, James T. Bang, and Arnab Biswas, "Gender Equality and Economic Growth: Is It Equality of Opportunity or Equality of Outcomes?" *Feminist Economics* 21, no. 1 (2015): 110–35.

[32] The policies adopted by India have been less coercive, but at times the government's tactics have not been far from compulsion. See Amartya Sen, "Fertility and Coercion," *University of Chicago Law Review* 63 no. 3 (Summer 1996): 1035–61.

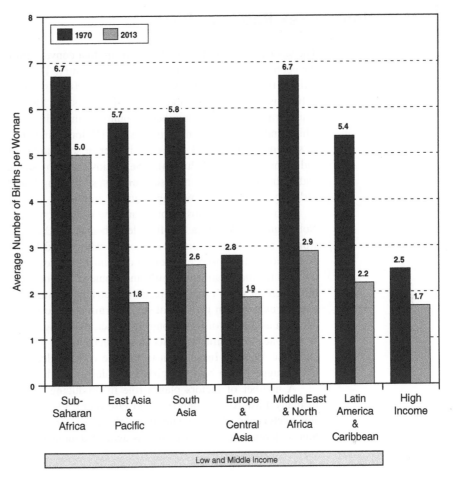

FIGURE 17-2 Total Fertility Rates, World Regions, 1970 and 2013

Note: See Table 17-1 for notes and sources.

as South Asia, with rates of just under 3 births per woman. In sharp contrast, the US rate was 1.9, just below the replacement level, and the average rate among all high-income economies was even lower at 1.7.[33] Table 17-1 and Figure 17-2 further show that fertility rates in all regions have fallen considerably from levels in past decades. Indeed, in light of these trends, Ronald Lee observed, "The question about their fertility transition is no longer 'whether,' but rather 'how far' and 'how fast.'"[34] Sub-Saharan Africa remains the one region where fertility declines are thus far quite modest.

---

[33]The US fertility rate fell to 1.9 in the aftermath of the Great Recession.
[34]Ronald Lee, "The Demographic Transition: Three Centuries of Fundamental Change," *Journal of Economic Perspectives* 17, no. 4 (Fall 2003): 167–90; quote is from p. 175. See also David Lam, "How the World Survived the Population Bomb: Lessons from 50 Years of Extraordinary Demographic History," *Demography* 48, no. 4 (2011): 1231–62; and Nicholas Eberstadt, "The Global Flight from the Family," *Wall Street Journal*, February 21, 2015.

Variations in Sex Ratios at Birth

The **sex ratio at birth** is another measure that conveys important information about the economic status of women in a given country. This figure is constructed as the ratio of the number of boys born for every 100 girls. At normal rates, the sex ratio at birth is expected to be about 105 to 106 boys per 100 girls; however, this figure is considerably higher in a number of countries, including the most populous nations of China and India.[35] Recent estimates are 116 for China and 111 for India as a whole, as shown in Figure 17-3, and even higher in some areas of China and in the north Indian provinces (e.g., Punjab).[36] Sex ratios are also especially distorted in second- and higher-order births in these countries, suggesting that if a couple already have a girl, they are much less willing to accept another.

Lop-sided sex ratios at birth are one dimension of a larger phenomenon that Nobel laureate Amartya Sen first described in 1990 as "missing women." **Missing women** refers to the number of women who would be expected to be part of the population in the absence of gender discrimination resulting from sex-selective abortion and the maltreatment of girls and women.[37] In the past, imbalanced sex ratios at birth were in some cases the result of outright infanticide. In more recent decades, a major explanation is prenatal sex-determination tests and the use of sex-selective abortion as a form of birth control. In fact, these high sex ratios prevail despite the fact that sex-determination tests have been officially banned in both China and India since the 1990s.[38] In addition to the use of sex-selective abortion, evidence from China suggests that births of girls are underreported.[39]

A number of factors play a role in producing the lop-sided sex ratios found in many East Asian countries and elsewhere. One factor of great importance is **son preference**, the long-standing cultural preference for sons in these societies. Son preference has resulted in bias against daughters and women in general. One

---

[35]World Bank, *Toward Gender Equality in East Asia and the Pacific: A Companion to the World Development Report* (Washington, DC: World Bank, 2012). Skewed sex ratios are not unique to East Asia; see Susan Brink, "Selecting Boys over Girls Is a Trend in More and More Countries," *NPR* (August 26, 2015), www.npr.org. Even in the United States, some slight preference for sons is evident, as demonstrated by the sex ratios for third-born children in US families of Chinese, Korean, and Indian descent; see Douglas Almond and Lena Edlund, "Son-Biased Sex Ratios in the 2000 United States Census," *Proceedings of the National Academy of Sciences* 105, no. 15 (April 15, 2008): 5681–82.

[36]"The Worldwide War on Baby Girls," *The Economist*, March 4, 2010.

[37]Amartya Sen, "More than 100 Million Women Are Missing," *New York Review of Books* 37, no. 20 (December 1990): 61–66; and Amartya Sen, "Missing Women—Revisited," *British Medical Journal* 327 (6 December 2003): 1297–98. Research that looks at sex ratios by age finds that most of the "missing women" in China occur around the time of birth, but, in contrast, for India the sex ratio is most skewed at *older* ages; see Siwan Anderson and Debraj Ray, "Missing Women: Age and Disease," *Review of Economic Studies* 77, no. 4 (October 2010): 1262–1300.

[38]For discussions on the sex ratio at birth in China, see, for instance, Yuyu Chen, Hongbin Li, and Lingsheng Meng, "Prenatal Sex Selection and Missing Girls in China: Evidence from the Diffusion of Diagnostic Ultrasound," *Journal of Human Resources* 48, no. 1 (2013): 36–70; and Judith Banister, "Shortage of Girls in China Today," *Journal of Population Research* 21, no. 1 (May 2004): 19–45. On India, see, for instance, Prabhat Jha, Maya A. Kesler, Rajesh Kumar, Faujdar Ram, Usha Ram, Lukasz Aleksandrowicz, Diego G. Bassani, Shailaja Chandra, and Jayant K. Banthia, "Trends in Selective Abortions of Girls in India: Analysis of Nationally Representative Birth Histories from 1990 to 2005 and Census Data from 1991 to 2011," *Lancet* 377 (June 4, 2011): 1921–28; and V. Bhaskar and Bishnupriya Gupta, "India's Missing Girls: Biology, Customs, and Economic Development," *Oxford Review of Economic Policy* 23, no. 2 (Summer 2007): 221–38.

[39]Daniel Goodkind, "Child Underreporting, Fertility and Sex Ratio Imbalance in China," *Demography* 48, no. 1 (February 2011): 291–316.

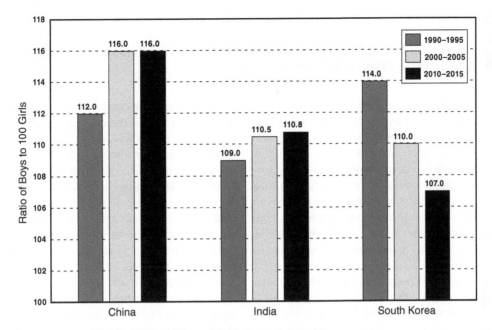

FIGURE 17-3 Sex Ratios at Birth for China, India, and South Korea, Selected Years

Note: At normal rates, the sex ratio is expected to be about 105-106; the ratio for the United States is 105.
Source: United Nations, *World Population Prospects: The 2015 Revision* (New York: UN 2015), available from www.un.org, accessed November 14, 2016.

explanation for son preference is that many of these societies are patrilineal, meaning that inheritance tends to pass through the male line. (Such societies also tend to be patrilocal, meaning that the wife goes to live with her husband and his family.) Moreover, it has long been viewed as the obligation of sons, but not daughters, to support their parents in old age, thereby making boys more economically valuable to their parents.[40]

Another factor affecting girls' value is the nature of the financial arrangement expected to be made at the time of their marriage. Girls' status appears to be improved in cultures where they are seen as a source of a **bride price** (a payment received by the bride's family from the groom's family upon marriage) rather than as a financial drain on the family, as in the case where the bride's family may pay a **dowry** (a payment to the groom's family from the bride's family upon marriage).[41]

---

[40]For discussions of son preference and its role in driving skewed ratios, see Monica Das Gupta, Jiang Zhenghua, Li Bohua, Xie Zhenming, Woojin Chung, and Bae Hwa-Okm, "Why Is Son Preference so Persistent in East and South Asia? A Cross-Country Study of China, India, and the Republic of Korea," *Journal of Development Studies* 40, no. 2 (2003): 153–87; and Charis Loh and Elizabeth J. Remick, "China's Skewed Sex Ratio and the One-Child Policy," *China Quarterly* 222 (June 2015): 293–319. In India, *firstborn* sons are especially favored; see Seema Jayachandran and Rohini Pande, "Why Are Indian Children so Short?" NBER Working Paper 21036 (National Bureau of Economic Research, Cambridge, MA, March 2015). It has also been conjectured that parents' preference for sons, along with a preference for children who eventually marry, may lead to a society in which upper-class families have boys because they have a good chance in life and a good chance to marry, while lower-income parents tend to choose daughters, who would have a good chance to marry men who are as well or better off than they are; see Lena Edlund, "Son Preference, Sex Ratios, and Marriage Patterns," *Journal of Political Economy* 107, no. 6, pt. 1 (December 1999): 1275–304.

[41]Siwan Anderson, "The Economics of Dowry and Brideprice," *Journal of Economic Perspectives* 21, no. 4 (Fall 2007): 151–74.

China's One-Child Policy: A Case Study of the Unintended Consequences of a Seemingly Neutral Fertility Policy*

China's one-child policy is an example of how a policy intended to control population size exacerbated discrimination against girls. This policy was instituted in a society in which boys are highly valued. Given this context, the one-child policy contributed to high sex ratios at birth as parents took measures to ensure the birth of at least one boy.** In addition, this policy has led to unintended consequences for the country as a whole. We describe the broad outlines of China's one-child policy and its current situation.

With roughly 20 percent of the world's population, China has the distinction of being the most populous country in the world. In 1979, it instituted a particularly rigid one-child policy for urban residents unless the first child was incapacitated or died. In rural areas, couples who had a girl for their first child were allowed to have a second child, what has been termed the "1.5-child policy." The one-child policy was pursued through political and social pressure, as well as by creating powerful economic incentives. Couples with a single child were entitled to such perks as cash bonuses, longer maternity leaves, better childcare, and preferential housing. However, couples who had more than the number allowed, particularly in the city, could face steep fines or the loss of their jobs or other benefits.

This policy was rigorously administered until 1983, when it became clear that it was not accepted by the public and was thus eased somewhat. Greater emphasis was placed on other ways of reducing fertility such as later marriage and education about contraception. Also, more control was given to autonomous regions and provinces in setting their own policies, including exemptions for minority groups. Starting in the late 1990s, the one-child policy was eased further. For instance, married men and women living in large urban areas who were both "only" children were permitted to have two children. And,

in some instances, wealthier couples were able to pay the required fines and have a larger family. China's easing of its policy was likely prompted not only by social pressures but also by rising incomes and economic growth and the fact that the fertility rate in China had fallen to just under the replacement level. In fall 2015, the Chinese government announced the official end of the one-child policy. Married couples are now permitted to have two children.***

On its face, the one-child policy appears to be a seemingly gender-neutral fertility policy. However, when coupled with long-standing son preference, it had the unintended consequence of contributing to the skewed sex ratios seen in Figure 17-3 as many families tried to ensure that their only child was a boy. Among the long-term consequences, fewer baby girls translate into a shortage of marriageable women. The phrase "bare branches" has come to describe the large number of sons who do not marry.**** There appear to be other significant social consequences of the one-child policy. For example it appears that skewed sex ratios can explain at least a portion of the rise in crime in China as unattached young men are more prone to commit crimes. Further, it has been suggested that the gender imbalance may contribute to the kidnapping and trafficking of women and perhaps even foment social unrest.*****

Ironically, the declining supply of women, which resulted from a bias against women, may end up benefiting women in a variety of ways. Perhaps most important is that girls who are the only children in their families may benefit from greater parental investments than would have been the case if they grew up with brothers. While some of these highly educated women are choosing not to marry, others who do seek marriage find their value in the "marriage market" increasing as they become scarcer. Indicative of these changes, some evidence suggests

continues

that parents of boys may be saving more than in the past to increase the financial resources available to their son if he were to marry, thereby increasing his marriage market potential.******

The one-child policy was a national policy, but implementation long varied at the local level, with less rigid rules in rural areas; see Gu Baochang, Wang Feng, Guo Zhigang, and Zhang Erli, "China's Local and National Fertility Policies at the End of the Twentieth Century," Population and Development Review 33, no. 1 (Mar 2007): 129–47. For additional description, see Judith Banister, "Shortage of Girls in China Today," Journal of Population Research 21, no. 1 (May 2004): 19–45; and Judith Bannister, China's Changing Population (Stanford, CA: Stanford University Press, 1987).
** See, for instance, Abraham Ebenstein, "The Missing Girls of China and the Unintended Consequences of the One Child Policy," Journal of Human Resources 45, no. 1 (2010): 87–11.*
***"China Ends One Child Policy Allowing Two Children," New York Times, October 30, 2015; and Amartya Sen, "Women's Progress Outdid China's One Child Policy," New York Times, November 11, 2015.*
****See Christophe Z. Guilmoto, "Skewed Sex Ratios at Birth and Future Marriage Squeeze in China and India, 2005–2100," Demography 49 (2012): 77–100; "Bare Branches, Redundancy of*

Males," The Economist, April 18, 2015; and Valerie M. Hudson and Andrea M. den Boer, Bare Branches: Security Implications of Asia's Surplus Male Population (Cambridge, MA: MIT Press, 2004).
*****On crime, see Lena Edlund, Hongbin Li, Junjian Yi, and Junsen Zhang, "Sex Ratios and Crime: Evidence from China," Review of Economics and Statistics, December 95, no. 5 (2013): 1520–34. For broader discussions of consequences, see Lisa Cameron and Xin Meng, "China's One Child Policy," in The New Palgrave Dictionary of Economics, ed. Steven N. Durlauf and Lawrence E. Blume (London: Palgrave MacMillan, 2014); and Hudson and den Boer, Bare Branches.*
******For evidence, see Vanessa L. Fong, "China's One-Child Policy and the Empowerment of Urban Daughters," American Anthropologist 104, no. 4 (2002): 1098–1109; Amie Tsang and Zhang Tiantian, "Marriage Falls in China, Transforming Finances and Families," New York Times, September 11, 2016; and Shang-Jin Wei and Xiabo Zhang, "The Competitive Saving Motive: Evidence from Rising Sex Ratios and Savings Rates in China," Journal of Political Economy 119, no. 3 (2011): 511–64.*

There is also an important relationship between women's role in production and basic survival rates. As discussed in Chapter 2 and later in this chapter, evidence indicates that in regions where women are more economically valuable, there is a higher ratio of women to men in the population (in other words, fewer missing women).[42] This pattern suggests that girls are more highly valued and better-treated—as reflected by higher survival rates—when girls and women make a substantial economic contribution outside the household. However, a high participation rate for women does not always correspond to less skewed sex ratios. China is an example of a country that, despite having a high overall female participation rate, also has a very high male–female sex ratio at birth. The situation in China points to the high societal value placed on sons and the wide-ranging impact of this preference, despite the role that women's productive activity plays. As discussed in the next section, China's one-child policy likely further contributed to its skewed sex ratio at birth.

While sex ratios remain skewed in China and India, a very promising development in East Asia is the considerable decline in the sex ratio in South Korea, which historically had both a strong son preference and a high sex ratio. As shown in Figure 17-3, the sex ratio at birth in South Korea stood at around 114 in 1990, but in more recent years the figure is very close to what would be expected based on normal rates. Rising urbanization and education are believed to lie behind this decrease in the sex ratio. One study further points to a considerable reduction in

---

[42]Jean Dreze and Amartya Sen, Hunger and Public Action (Oxford: Clarendon Press, 1989), chap. 4; and Stephan Klasen and Claudia Wink, "'Missing Women': Revisiting the Debate," Feminist Economics 9, no. 2–3 (2003): 263–99.

son preference as measured by wives' reports regarding whether they "must" have a son. In fact, evidence indicates that social norms are changing across the population at large, not just among those who are highly educated.[43]

Women's Political and Legal Empowerment

Women's political and legal empowerment has considerable impact on their status. Greater representation of women among public officials is expected to increase the extent to which women's issues receive attention from the government, and greater equality before the law affects, among other things, women's right to inherit and own property, as well as their rights within the family and in case of divorce. Although women today have the right to vote in virtually all countries with representative institutions, they continue to be substantially underrepresented in public positions, especially at high levels. For instance, in 2016, there were just 12 female presidents and 7 female prime ministers out of nearly 200 countries around the world.[44] Also, as of 2016, although women occupied slightly more than 40 percent of all parliamentary seats in the Nordic countries, they held just 19 percent in Asia, 23 percent in sub-Saharan Africa, and 18 percent in North Africa and the Middle East.[45] Women remain underrepresented in high-level government positions in the United States as well. In 2016, only 19 percent of representatives and 20 percent of senators were women (the same percentage as in 2012). Women also continue to be underrepresented in US cabinet and cabinet-level appointments, though recent administrations have generally included more women than in the past.[46]

To hasten women's advancement in the political arena, a diverse group of countries, including Norway, Egypt, South Africa, Sudan, and Mexico, have implemented a policy of some type to achieve this objective. Notably, the United States is not among the countries that have taken any steps in this direction. Efforts range from instituting voluntary quotas, where political parties must include a certain percentage or number of female candidates on a slate for a specific office, to reserving a specific number of seats in parliament for women.[47]

Next, turning to women's progress toward equality before the law, it has been slow and uneven. In the United States, it was not until 1974 that Congress passed the

---

[43]Woojin Chung and Monica Das Gupta, "Why Is Son Preference Declining in South Korea? The Role of Development and Public Policy," *Population and Development Review* 33, no. 4 (December 2007): 757–83. See also Christophe Z. Guilmoto, "The Sex Ratio Transition in Asia," *Population and Development Review* 35, no. 3 (September 2009): 519–49.

[44]"Worldwide Guide to Women in Leadership," accessed on July 8, 2016, www.guide2womenleaders. com. For a comprehensive discussion of the situation, Farida Jalalzai, *Shattered, Cracked, or Firmly Intact: Women and the Executive Glass Ceiling Worldwide* (Oxford: Oxford University Press, 2013).

[45]Inter-Parliamentary Union, "Women in National Parliaments, Situation as of 1 June 2016," accessed July 8, 2016, http://www.ipu.org. For discussions regarding why women's political participation may matter, see Marianne A. Ferber and Michael Brun, "Does Your Legislator's Sex Matter?" *Policy Matters* 4 (Autumn 2006): 11–15; Raghabendra Chattopadhyay, "Women as Policy Makers: Evidence from a Randomized Policy Experiment in India," *Econometrica* 72, no. 5 (September 2005): 1409–43; and Lori Beaman, Raghabendra Chattopadhyay, Esther Duflo, Rohini Pande, and Petia Topalova, "Powerful Women: Does Exposure Reduce Bias?" *Quarterly Journal of Economics* 124, no. 4 (2009): 1497–1540.

[46]For more details, go to the Center for American Women and Politics, Eagleton Institute of Politics, Rutgers University, www.cawp.rutgers.edu.

[47]See World Bank, *Women Business and the Law: Getting to Equal* (Washington, DC: World Bank, 2016).

Equal Credit Opportunity Act, which allowed women to apply for credit on their own (without a male to cosign). In some countries, women are still not able to own land or other property or receive bank loans.[48] On the other hand, as of 2016, 189 countries (over 90 percent of member nations of the United Nations) had ratified an "international bill of rights for women" known as the **Convention for the Elimination of All Forms of Discrimination against Women (CEDAW)**, though the United States remains one notable exception.[49] At the same time, "even when legal discrimination is removed, it can take generations for practice to catch up with the revised law."[50]

In recent decades, despite wide cultural differences, women from around the world have joined together in international efforts to reduce gender inequality and improve women's status. For instance, in 1995, women from nearly 190 countries attended the United Nations Fourth World Conference on Women in Beijing and put together a "Plan for Action" that focused on education as a key to women's progress, at which US Democratic presidential nominee Hillary Clinton famously proclaimed that "women's rights are human rights." In addition, the conference addressed a broad range of other issues, from violence against women to economic development. At follow-up conferences, including the most recent called "Beijing + 20" in 2015, women representatives again came together to take stock of the progress made since 1995, as well as to press for additional rights and to reaffirm each government's commitment to change.[51] Other significant international efforts include the UN's Millennium Development Goals and Sustainable Development Goals mentioned previously.

Multidimensional Measures of Women's Status

Thus far we have looked at specific indicators of women's status such as labor force participation, fertility, educational attainment, and political empowerment, but it is increasingly accepted in the discipline of economics that status is multidimensional. Today there are not only indexes that rank countries based on a number of dimensions of economic development, such as the Human Development Index of the United Nations or Amartya Sen's Capability Index, but also indexes that rank countries based on gender equity.[52] Such indexes are a useful way to summarize the situation, but it is important to keep in mind that they require decisions about what factors should be accounted for and the weighting scheme to be attached to each factor. For these reasons, one country may rank higher in one index but lower in another.

---

[48]For evidence and discussion see World Bank, *Women Business and the Law*; and Matthias Doepke, Michele Tertilt, and Alessandra Voena, "The Economics and Politics of Women's Rights," *Annual Review of Economics* 4 (2012): 339–72.

[49]United Nations Treaty Collection, treaties.un.org.

[50]United Nations, *Human Development Report 1995* (New York: United Nations, 1995) 42–43. In addition, as Diane Elson points out, legal equality often means little for poor rural women as long as they are concentrated in the informal sector or in female ghettoes of the formal sector, and intrahousehold distribution is not necessarily affected by these changes. See her "Introduction" in *Male Bias in the Development Process* (Manchester, UK: Manchester University Press, 1991), 1–28.

[51]For details on the 1995 through 2015 conferences, see UN Commission on the Status of Women, accessed November 14, 2016, http://www.unwomen.org/en/csw/csw59-2015.

[52]Work by Nobel laureate Amartya Sen, who developed the "capability" approach for thinking about poverty, inequality and human development, has pushed the discipline of economics in this direction; see Amartya Sen, *Development as Freedom* (Oxford: Oxford University Press, 1999). For further discussion, on these indexes see Benería, Berik, and Floro. *Gender, Development, and Globalization*, chap. 1.

One index of gender inequality that has been widely referenced is the **Gender Inequality Index (GII)** calculated by the United Nations and reported in Table 17-1. For each country, this index takes account of information on women's reproductive health (e.g., maternal mortality and teen fertility), empowerment (gender differences in secondary school completion and representation in parliamentary seats), and gender differences in labor force participation. The GII ranges from 0 (no inequality) to 1 (greatest inequality), with an average of 0.45 across the world. As shown in Table 17-1, the index is less than 0.1 in the Nordic countries such as Sweden compared to 0.5 or more for countries in the Middle East and North Africa, South Asia, and sub-Saharan Africa. The index for the United States stands at 0.3, quite a bit higher than for most other economically advanced countries. The reason for the relatively high index in the United States is that it has substantially higher rates of maternal mortality and teen fertility and a lower share of women in Congress.

Economic Development, Globalization, and Women's Status

In recent years, the relationship between economic development and gender equality has received increasing attention by policymakers. As observed by Esther Duflo, the direction of causation may go both ways.[53] First, consider the effect of economic development on gender equality. The impact of economic development on women's status is generally positive. With reductions in the most extreme levels of poverty, families that previously faced daunting decisions about the allocation of scarce resources to their sons and daughters are able to adequately provide for both, thereby reducing any discrimination against girls that might exist. In addition, economic development expands women's economic opportunities and their economic value to their families. One piece of evidence is provided by a study conducted by Nancy Qian which examined the effect of a set of economic reforms in rural China that included the production of cash crops such as tea. Qian found that girls' survival rates increased in tea-growing regions, where women's labor was more economically valuable (due to the fact that women tend to be shorter and their fingers are more deft at harvesting tea leaves), relative to regions where men had a comparative advantage in production.[54] As we saw in Chapter 2, economic development also creates incentives for men to extend property rights to women because, in their role as husbands and fathers, they themselves will benefit from the resulting greater economic contributions of women.

Still, economic development is not a panacea for producing gender equality.[55] As already mentioned, technology has made sex-selective abortion possible, contributing to discrimination against girls at birth. And even in the most economically advanced countries, women still face a glass ceiling in the workplace, as discussed in Chapter 11 for the United States and in Chapter 18 for other economically advanced countries including Sweden.

---

[53]See, for instance, Duflo, "Women Empowerment and Economic Development"; and World Bank, *World Development Report 2012*, chap. 12.

[54]Nancy Qian, "Missing Women and the Price of Tea in China: The Effect of Sex-Specific Earnings on Sex Imbalance," *Quarterly Journal of Economics* 123, no. 3 (August 2008): 1251–85.

[55]Duflo, "Women Empowerment and Economic Development"; and Seema Jayachandran, "Does Economic Development Mean Less Discrimination against Women?" *Milken Institute Review* (First Quarter 2015): 36–47.

As mentioned, it is also possible that causation runs the other way—increases in gender equality may spur economic development.[56] We have already seen that not only women themselves but also their families and most especially their children benefit from enhanced labor market and educational opportunities for women. In fact, mounting evidence indicates that mothers tend to spend a larger share of resources on children, whether boys or girls, than do fathers.[57] Such investments should lead their children to be healthier and presumably more productive, as well as reduce the considerable imbalance in the allocation of resources between girls and boys in countries that have traditionally favored boys. And, as noted earlier, there is also evidence that countries with smaller gender gaps in education and employment experience higher rates of economic growth.[58] In addition to wage employment, women's access to microcredit loans, which permits them to start or expand a small business, is another way of improving their economic status and possibly even spurring economic growth (see the "Microcredit for Women" box).

Another increasingly important dimension to consider in evaluating the effect of economic development on women's status is the impact of globalization.[59] Economic activity is increasingly global in nature, with goods produced and services (such as call centers to help with information technology [IT] difficulties) provided both at home and abroad. With these changes, the status of women is affected not just by economic and cultural factors within their own countries but also by the larger world economy. For example, the spread of cable and satellite television in developing nations has exposed the population to new information about the world and other ways of life. One study identified a number of highly beneficial effects resulting from the introduction of cable television in rural India, including decreases in the reported acceptability of domestic violence toward women, reduced son preference, lower fertility, and increases in women's autonomy.[60]

Globalization also provides potential benefits in the form of enhanced job opportunities and pay. Evidence indicates that foreign-owned firms operating in developing countries generally have higher productivity and pay higher wages on average than domestically owned firms.[61] Similarly, export industries—a result of the dramatic expansion in international trade—typically offer a wage premium.[62] Globalization has also led to the rapid development of the relatively high-paying IT services industry. One study that used experimental methods points to the direct

---

[56]As an example of the prominence of this view, see Ian Talley, "Gender Equality an 'Economic No-Brainer,' Says IMF Chief," *Wall Street Journal*, September 6, 2015.

[57]For example, see Duncan Thomas, "Intra-Household Resource Allocation: An Inferential Approach," *Journal of Human Resources* 25, no. 4 (Fall 1990): 635–64; Shelly J. Lundberg, Robert A. Pollak, and Terence J. Wales, "Do Husbands and Wives Pool Their Resources? Evidence from the U.K. Child Benefit," *Journal of Human Resources* 32, no. 3 (Summer 1997): 463–80. Grandmothers behave similarly to mothers; see Esther Duflo, "Grandmothers and Granddaughters: Old Age Pensions and Intra-Household Allocations in South Africa," *World Bank Economic Review* 17, no. 1 (2003): 1–25.

[58]Klasen and Lamanna, "Impact of Gender Inequality."

[59]For an excellent overview of the issues, see World Bank, *World Development Report 2012*, chap. 12; and Benería, Berik, and Floro. *Gender, Development, and Globalization*, chaps. 3 and 4.

[60]Robert Jensen and Emily Oster, "The Power of TV: Cable Television and Women's Status in India," *Quarterly Journal of Economics* 124, no. 3 (August 2009): 1057–94.

[61]See Robert E. Lipsey, "Home- and Host-Country Effects of Foreign Direct Investment," in *Challenges to Globalization: Analyzing the Economics*, ed. Robert E. Baldwin and L. Alan Winters (Chicago: University of Chicago Press, 2004), 333–82.

[62]For evidence on wage premiums for workers in export industries, see, for example, Irene Brambilla, Nicolas D. Chauvin, and Guido Porto, "Examining the Export Wage Premium in Developing Countries," *Review of International Economics* (forthcoming).

benefits to women from such job opportunities. In the experiment, young women in randomly selected villages in India were provided with 3 years of recruiting services (e.g., information about job openings, assistance with interview skills) to help them get jobs in various "back office" positions in the IT services sector. The study found that women who received the recruiting services were less likely to marry and have children during this period and instead obtained more schooling or entered the labor market.[63] Also, to the extent that globalization leads firms to acquire new technology that is "complementary" with female labor, it has the potential to increase their share of employment and their wages.[64]

Nonetheless, these findings do not mean that such job opportunities are without their own set of concerns. Workers in traditional industries may be displaced by more productive foreign-owned firms or by competition from imports and, thus, may have to learn new skills. And even if employment by foreign-owned firms and export industries generally pays more than other domestic opportunities, there may still be questions about pay in specific instances, as well as adherence to **labor standards**, generally defined to include the right of labor to organize, prohibitions against forced labor and the worst forms of child labor, as well as provisions to address humanitarian concerns regarding working conditions.[65] As just one example of the latter, critics point to the often unsafe and unhealthy work conditions associated with low-skilled, export-based manufacturing jobs in the maquiladoras in Mexico and parts of Asia.[66]

Another aspect of globalization is that an economic downturn in one part of the world, such as the Great Recession in the United States (which officially began in December 2007 and ended in June 2009) can have repercussions on the economies and economic well-being of individuals around the globe. One study that looked at the impact of the Great Recession found that it had a disproportionately negative impact on women in developing countries because women in these countries are relatively disadvantaged to begin with and such countries typically lack safety nets for the most vulnerable.[67]

On net, it is difficult to assess whether women's status is improved or not by economic globalization given the considerable variation in the nature of this employment and the alternatives otherwise available. Also, within a given country, globalization may improve women's situation in some respects but not necessarily in others. What is clear, however, is that globalization is here to stay.

---

[63]Robert Jensen, "Do Labor Market Opportunities Affect Young Women's Work and Family Decisions? Experimental Evidence from India," *Quarterly Journal of Economics* 127, no. 2 (May 2012): 753–92.

[64]See, for instance, Chinhui Juhn, Gergely Ujhelyi, and Carolina Villegas-Sanchez, "Men, Women, and Machines: How Trade Impacts Gender Inequality," *Journal of Development Economics* 106 (January 2014): 179–93.

[65]For more on labor standards, see Drusilla K. Brown, "Labor Standards: Where Do They Belong on the International Trade Agenda?" *Journal of Economic Perspectives* 15, no. 3 (Summer 2001): 89–112. Regarding child labor and international efforts to reduce the worst forms, see International Labour Organization, *Tackling Child Labor: From Commitment to Action* (Geneva: International Labour Organization, 2012).

[66]Edme Dominguez, Rosalba Icaca, Cirila Quintero, Silvioa Lopez, and Asa Stenman, "Women Workers in the Maquiladoras and the Debate on Global Labor Standards," *Feminist Economics* 16, no. 4 (2010): 185–209; and World Bank, *World Development Report 2012*.

[67]Naoko Otobe, "Global Economic Crisis, Gender and Employment: The Impact and Policy Response," ILO Employment Sector Working Paper 74 (International Labour Organization, Geneva, 2011).

Microcredit for Women: Lifeline or Mirage?

Starting a small business is one way for individuals to support themselves and their families. In developing countries, the amounts needed are often rather small but nonetheless beyond the reach of millions of poor people, particularly poor women, who tend to lack contacts with potential lenders, have no collateral, and are generally regarded as poor credit risks. **Microcredit**—very small loans—fills this gap. In this box we discuss microcredit and research findings regarding its impact on women and, more generally, on the lives of the poor.

In 1976, Muhammad Yunus founded Grameen Bank, which was the first institution to extend microcredit. Subsequently, similar institutions were founded in numerous other developing countries.* One of the distinctive features of microcredit institutions is that they mainly extend credit to women. It is estimated that women receive 70 percent of all such loans, and among the poor, women comprise an even higher share.** In 2006, Muhammad Yunus, along with the bank itself, received the Nobel Peace Prize in recognition of their efforts to "create social and economic development from below."***

Microcredit works as follows. Local groups of borrowers guarantee one another's loans, and no one receives a second loan until all the first loans are repaid. This arrangement has led to high repayment rates, which have enabled microcredit institutions not only to continue but to expand.

Microcredit provides loans for activities such as the production and sale of food, agricultural products, and handicrafts, as well as funding for other entrepreneurial activities. In more recent years, microcredit has come to be part of a broader concept called "microfinance." **Microfinance** further includes broader financial assistance such as access to savings accounts and various kinds of insurance. Also, some lending has moved beyond group liability lending, which we just described, to individual loans.

Other useful services include providing technical information and offering workshops on what kind of business to start and how to run it, as well as information on broader topics related to improving literacy and health. Participants in such programs have an opportunity to share information and learn from one another.****

A large number of studies have examined the impact of microcredit and identified positive effects, but a serious challenge to evaluating the effects of microcredit is properly disentangling correlation from causation. It could simply be that those who borrow have characteristics that are likely to be associated with better outcomes, such as greater decision-making ability in the family or better health, rather than microcredit directly causing favorable outcomes for them.***** To address this concern, subsequent studies have conducted field experiments using a method called random assignment in which microcredit is extended to some individuals but not to others. They then examine how these otherwise identical groups respond. The emerging consensus, based on this more rigorous research method, is that microcredit has modest effects at most. As expected, it does permit businesses to expand and others to start up. It also provides the ability for families to smooth out consumption during difficult times, which would not otherwise be possible without such credit access. However, contrary to earlier findings, studies using an experimental approach do not find that microcredit improves education, health, or women's bargaining power. This evidence suggests that microcredit and the broader umbrella of microfinance benefit the poor but that the effects are modest, a much more tempered conclusion than reached by early studies. However, these same experiments have provided valuable information about how microcredit might be more effective in the future. For instance, they point to

continues

the importance of flexibility in the timing of repayment and the value of social relationships, not just through shared liability in lending but also through group meetings.******

*For an excellent discussion of microcredit and the broader field of microfinance, see Beatriz Armendariz de Aghion and Jonathan Morduch, The Economics of Microfinance, 2nd ed. (Cambridge, MA: MIT Press, 2010).
**Armendariz de Aghion and Morduch, Economics of Microfinance, chap. 7.
***www.nobelprize.org (accessed November 11, 2016).
****See, for instance, Signe-Mary McKernan, "The Impact of Microcredit Programs on Self-Employment Profits: Do Noncredit Program Aspects Matter?" Review of Economics and Statistics 84, no. 1 (February 2002): 93–115.
*****For just two examples of early studies, see Rosintan D. M. Panjaitan-Drioadisuryo and Kathleen Cloud, "Gender, Self-Employment, and Microcredit Programs: An Indonesian Case Study," special issue, Quarterly Review of Economics and Finance 39, no. 5 (1999): 769–79; and Mark Pitt and Shahidur

R. Khandker, "The Impact of Group-Based Credit Programs on Poor Households in Bangladesh: Does the Gender of Participants Matter?" Journal of Political Economy 106, no. 5 (1998): 958–96. For more recent evidence based on experimental methods and a synthesis of research to date, see Erica Field, Abraham Holland, and Rohini Pande, "Microfinance: Points of Promise" in Contemporary and Emerging Issues, ed. Jean Kimmel (Kalamazoo, MI: W. E. Upjohn Institute for Employment Research, forthcoming); Armendariz de Aghion and Morduch, Economics of Microfinance; and Abhijit Vinayak Banerjee, "Microcredit under the Microscope: What Have We Learned in the Past Two Decades, and What Do We Need to Know?" Annual Review of Economics 5 (2013): 487–519.
******See, for instance, Field, Holland, and Pande, "Microfinance: Points of Promise," and Banerjee, "Microcredit under the Microscope."

Conclusion

In this overview of the status of the world's women, we found that considerable differences remain between women's and men's outcomes. Nonetheless, while women's status remains precarious in many parts of the world, especially in developing countries and the region of the Middle East and North Africa, progress is being made to varying degrees. One very promising development is the rising educational attainment of girls and the narrowing of the gender education gap. Of concern, however, is that this development has not necessarily led to increased labor force participation of women, most notably in the Middle East and North Africa. As we discussed, women's labor force participation is important because it not only leads to higher living standards but also affects women's status in the family and the resources available to their children. Another positive development is the considerable decline in women's fertility in much of the developing world, though a notable exception is the region of sub-Saharan Africa, where rates remain high, albeit lower than in past decades. Also of concern for women's status is the persistence of skewed sex ratios at birth in a number of countries, including the two most populous, China and India. One encouraging development on the policy front is the official end of China's one-child policy, which exacerbated discrimination against girls and has led to broader negative societal consequences.

In the next chapter, we focus on women in other economically advanced countries to learn more about women's status in those countries, to see the ways in which the United States is similar or different, and to identify lessons that might be learned to improve women's status in the United States and in other countries across the globe.

Questions for Review and Discussion

1. Explain why economists pay so much attention to the role of paid work within a given country in determining women's status.

2. Explain the ways in which a reduction in fertility can improve women's status.

3. What are some specific policies that might improve women's well-being in the poorest countries? What are the difficulties and challenges entailed in undertaking them?

4. It has been argued that government investments in women's education in developing countries result in societal as well as private benefits. Discuss each.

5. Apart from religion, what other factors affect women's experiences and opportunities in the Middle East and North Africa?

6. If you were creating an index of gender inequality, identify four key factors you would include. Which factor(s) would you weight the most in your index, and why?

Suggested Readings

Armendariz de Aghion, Beatriz, and Jonathan Morduch. *The Economics of Microfinance,* 2nd ed. Cambridge, MA: MIT Press, 2010.

Banerjee, Abhijit V., and Esther Duflo. "The Economic Lives of the Poor." *Journal of Economic Perspectives* 21, no. 1 (Winter 2007): 141–67.

Benería, Lourdes, Günseli Berik, and Maria S. Floro. *Gender, Development, and Globalization*, 2nd ed. New York and London: Routledge, 2016.

Charles, Maria. "A World of Difference: International Trends in Women's Status." *Annual Review of Sociology* 37 (2011): 355–71.

Duflo, Esther. "Women Empowerment and Economic Development." *Journal of Economic Literature* 50, no. 4 (December 2012): 1051–79.

Gregory, Mary. "Gender and Economic Inequality." In *Oxford Handbook of Economic Inequality*, edited by Wiemer Salverda, Brian Nolan, and Timothy M. Smeeding, 284–314. Oxford: Oxford University Press, 2009.

Heath, Rachel, and Seema Jayachandran. "The Causes and Consequences of Increased Female Education and Labor Force Participation in Developing Countries." NBER Working Paper 22766, National Bureau of Economic Research, Cambridge, MA, October 2016.

International Labour Organization. *Women at Work Trends 2016*. Geneva: International Labour Organization, 2016.

Jacquette, Jane S., and Gale Summerfield, eds. *Women and Gender Equity: Development Theory and Practice*. Durham, NC, and London: Duke University Press, 2006.

Jalalzai, Farida. *Shattered, Cracked, or Firmly Intact: Women and the Executive Glass Ceiling Worldwide.* Oxford: Oxford University Press, 2013.

Jayachandran, Seema. "The Roots of Gender Inequality in Developing Countries." *Annual Review of Economics* 7 (August 2015): 63–88.

Lundberg, Shelly. "The Sexual Division of Labour." In *The Shape of the Division of Labour: Nations, Industries and Households*, edited by Robert M. Solow and Jean-Philippe Touffut, 122–48. Cheltenham, UK, and Northampton, MA: Edward Elgar, 2010.

Veerle, Miranda. "Cooking, Caring and Volunteering: Unpaid Work around the World." OECD Social, Employment and Migration Working Paper 116, Organisation for Economic Co-operation and Development, Paris, 2010.

World Bank, *Gender at Work: A Companion to the World Development Report on Jobs.* Washington, DC: World Bank, 2014.

World Bank, *Opening Doors: Gender Equality and Development in the Middle East and North Africa.* Washington, DC: World Bank, 2013.

World Bank. *Toward Gender Equality in East Asia and the Pacific: A Companion to the World Development Report.* Washington, DC: World Bank, 2012.

World Bank, *Women Business and the Law: Getting to Equal.* Washington, DC: World Bank, 2016.

World Economic Forum. *The Global Gender Gap Report.* Geneva: World Economic Forum, 2015.

Key Terms

developing countries (460)

gender education gap (470)

one-child policy (474)

sex ratio at birth (476)

missing women (476)

son preference (476)

bride price (477)

dowry (477)

Convention for the Elimination of All Forms of Discrimination against Women (CEDAW) (481)

Gender Inequality Index (GII) (482)

labor standards (484)

microcredit (485)

microfinance (485)

A Comparison of the United States to Other Economically Advanced Countries

18

CHAPTER HIGHLIGHTS

- International Differences in Policies and Institutions
- US Women's Labor Force Participation in an International Context
- The US Gender Wage Ratio in an International Context
- Understanding Low Fertility in Economically Advanced Countries

This chapter places the experience of the United States in an international context. Many of the major labor market and social trends that have occurred in the United States since the 1970s—increases in female labor force participation rates, increases in the gender earnings ratio, and significant demographic shifts—have also occurred in other economically advanced countries, although to varying degrees. Explanations for these trends are similar to those offered for the United States in earlier chapters. However, other factors, including differences in government employment policies (e.g., antidiscrimination legislation), government tax policies, wage-setting institutions (e.g., whether the labor market is more or less decentralized), and family-friendly policies (e.g., family leave and childcare subsidies), are particularly important in explaining cross-country differences in outcomes.[1] In addition, international differences in religion, culture, and ideology play a role. This chapter reviews differences among economically advanced countries and explores the ways in which these

---

[1]For overviews, see Organisation for Economic Co-operation and Development (OECD), "Female Labour Force Participation: Past Trends and Main Determinants in OECD Countries," *Economic Policy Reforms: Going for Growth* (Paris: OECD, 2005), chap. 6; Francine D. Blau and Lawrence M. Kahn, "Women's Work and Wages," in *The New Palgrave Dictionary of Economics*, 2nd ed., ed. Steven N. Durlauf and Lawrence E. Blume (London: Palgrave Macmillan, 2008), 762–72; European Commission, *Report on Equality between Women and Men—2010* (Luxembourg: European Commission, 2010); and "Women and Work: Closing the Gap," *The Economist*, November 26, 2011.

factors are related to labor market and demographic outcomes. This review also provides a roadmap of possible policies the United States might undertake based on the experiences of other countries.

International Differences in Policies and Institutions

In this section our goal is to highlight the variation in policies and in the timing of adoption of policies that may affect labor market outcomes. In our focus on economically advanced countries, we pay particular attention to the experiences of Sweden and Japan. Sweden, like other Nordic countries, has made notable progress toward greater equality between men and women in the home as well as in the labor market, while Japan has experienced slower change. Beginning in the 1960s, Sweden instituted a comprehensive set of policies to achieve the goal of equal treatment of women and men.[2] For instance, efforts were made to discourage gender-based stereotypes at all levels of the educational system. All gender differences in public aid were removed. Legislation was introduced to make marriage an equal partnership. Full participation of women and men in the labor market became the established goal. To this end, Sweden adopted a broad set of family-friendly policies. However, a distinction between the United States and Sweden is that Sweden passed antidiscrimination legislation considerably later than the United States. In contrast to the broad-based Swedish efforts, Japan's efforts toward gender equality have generally lagged behind those of the United States and many other countries, though one notable difference from the United States is that it offers more generous family leave. Also, it is instructive to note that in 2013 the Japanese government announced concerted efforts to increase gender equality in an effort to spur economic growth. These policy reforms, termed "womenomics," seek to increase women's and, more specifically, mothers' labor force participation rates, as well as move greater fractions of women into leadership positions.[3]

Labor Market Policies to Combat Gender Discrimination

Explicit labor market policies to address gender discrimination include antidiscrimination legislation, comparable worth pay policies, and employment (corporate board) quotas. As discussed in Chapter 12, the United States was an early leader in adopting antidiscrimination legislation. Starting in the early 1960s, the United States promulgated the Equal Pay Act, Title VII of the Civil Rights Act, and, through an executive order, the policy of affirmative action. Starting a bit later, in the 1970s, other economically advanced countries began to enact similar measures aimed at ensuring women's rights to equal opportunity in employment. Both Sweden and Japan were

---

[2]See, for instance, Asa Lundqvist and Christine Roman, "Construction of Swedish Family Policy, 1930–2000," *Journal of Family History* 33, no. 2 (2008): 216–36.

[3]For an excellent comparison of the policies and situation in the United States, Japan, Sweden, and Spain, see Margarita Estévez-Abe, "An International Comparison of Gender Equality: Why Is the Japanese Gender Gap so Persistent?" *Japan Labor Review* 10, no. 2 (Spring 2013): 82–100. See also Helina Melkas and Richard Anker, *Towards Gender Equity in Japanese and Nordic Labour Markets: A Tale of Two Paths* (Geneva: International Labour Organization, 2003). For more on "womenomics," see "Holding Back Half the Nation," *The Economist*, March 29, 2014; and Emma Chanlett-Avery and Rebecca M. Nelson, *"Womenomics" in Japan: In Brief* (Washington, DC: Congressional Research Service, August 2014).

relative latecomers. Sweden did not pass antidiscrimination laws in employment until 1980 and 1992.[4] Nonetheless, Sweden's 1992 Equal Opportunity Act goes further than legislation in many other countries, requiring that employers try to obtain a well-balanced sex distribution in various jobs and make it easier for workers to combine work and family. Japan did not enact any antidiscrimination legislation until 1985, and that initial legislation only required that employers voluntarily comply. Subsequent legislation passed in 1997 and 2006 considerably strengthened the earlier legislation by explicitly prohibiting discrimination in hiring, training, and promotion; imposing stricter rules regarding sexual harassment in the workplace; and providing greater protections for women against pregnancy-related discrimination.[5]

Australia is notable because it was a leader in adopting a country-wide policy of **comparable worth**. In 1972 a federal tribunal moved toward a policy of comparable worth by deciding that the "equal pay for equal work" concept that was previously adopted in 1969 should be expanded to "equal pay for work of equal value" in order to cover employees in predominantly female jobs. The "Comparable Worth in Australia" box discusses the effects of this policy change.

More recently, to help women break though the corporate glass ceiling and move more quickly into top decision-making roles, a growing number of western European countries and Japan (as of 2015) have established corporate board quotas.[6] **Corporate board quotas** require public and state-run corporations to set aside a fixed percentage of seats on corporate boards for women. This policy approach is very different from that pursued in the United States; as discussed in Chapter 12, employment quotas rarely exist, if at all, in the United States. Norway took the lead in 2003, setting aside 40 percent of board seats for women. Such policies might have positive spillovers such as the increased hiring of women into the upper ranks of management as well as on the employment status of women more generally. While no firm conclusion can yet be drawn, one study that looked at the impact of Norway's 2003 quota found that, apart from directly increasing the share of women on the board and the ranks of the most senior executives, it did not have these hoped for spillover effects.[7] It has also been suggested that women leaders may differ in their management "style," including the decisions that they make, with possible effects on the corporate bottom line. One study that looked at this question identified a gender

[4]See Helina Melkas and Richard Anker, *Gender Equality and Occupational Segregation in Nordic Labour Markets* (Geneva: International Labour Organization, 1998), chap. 4.

[5]The details of the legislation are described in Hiroya Nakakubo, "'Phase III' of the Japanese Equal Employment Opportunity Act," *Japanese Labor Review* 4, no. 3 (Summer 2007): 9–19; and Yukiko Abe, "The Equal Employment Opportunity Law and Labor Force Behavior of Women in Japan," *Journal of the Japanese and International Economies* 25 (2011): 39–55. Linda N. Edwards, Takuya Hasebe, and Tadashi Sakai find that while this legislation encouraged women's college completion, it may have had the unintended consequence of discouraging marriage; see "Education and Marriage Decisions of Japanese Women and the Role of the Equal Employment Opportunity Act," (working paper, City University of New York, New York, September 2015).

[6]See International Labour Organization, *Women in Business and Management—Gaining Momentum* (Geneva: International Labour Organization, 2015); Eleanor Warnock, "A Step Forward for 'Womenomics' in Japan," *Wall Street Journal*, August 28, 2015; and Rohini Pande and Deanna Ford, "Gender Quotas and Female Leadership, Background Paper for World Bank," *World Development Report 2012* (Washington, DC: World Bank, 2011).

[7]Alina Dizik, "Do Quotas for Corporate Boards Help Women Advance?" *Chicago Booth Review*, June 15, 2015; and for specific evidence, see Marianne Bertrand, Sandra E. Black, Sissel Jensen, and Adriana Lleras-Muney, "Breaking the Glass Ceiling? The Effect of Board Quotas on Female Labor Market Outcomes in Norway," NBER Working Paper 20256 (National Bureau of Economic Research, Cambridge, MA, June 2014).

difference in decision-making; it found that corporate boards with a larger share of women were more likely to avoid layoffs, a decision that protected workers but reduced short-run profits.[8]

Wage-Setting Institutions

Wage-setting institutions also differ considerably across countries. These differences affect wage structures and, hence, wage inequality and the gender earnings ratio. As discussed in Chapter 10 in our consideration of trends in the gender wage gap, *wage structure* refers to the relative wages paid for various labor market qualifications, such as the proficiency of an experienced worker compared to a new hire or a college graduate compared to someone who finished only high school. It also includes wage premiums associated with higher-paying occupations or industries. International differences in wage-setting institutions and wage inequality are considerable, especially between the United States and other economically advanced nations.

In many of the economically advanced countries, wages are determined in a highly centralized way, with a strong role for unions and government in wage setting. Wages in the union sector are determined by collective bargaining, and, where unions are strong, collective bargaining agreements are often extended to nonunion workers or may cause nonunion firms to voluntarily imitate union pay structures.[9] Unions tend to raise the wages of less-skilled (low-wage) workers and lead to a more compressed wage structure. As a relatively low-wage group in all countries, women disproportionately benefit from wage policies that "bring up the bottom" of the wage distribution. In contrast, in the United States, the wage-setting process is quite decentralized, with only a small proportion of the labor force in labor unions and wages largely determined by employers. For example, in 2013, only 11 percent of workers in the United States were union members compared with rates of 26 to 27 percent in Canada and the United Kingdom and rates as high as 52 to 86 percent in the Nordic countries. Thus, in the United States, with its more dispersed wage distribution, less-skilled (low-wage) workers tend to receive lower relative pay than in most other economically advanced countries.[10] This difference in wage-setting institutions between the United States and other economically advanced countries tends to increase the gender wage gap in the United States relative to these other countries.[11]

Family-Friendly Policies

When it comes to family policy, the United States continues to lag behind other economically advanced countries. As discussed in Chapter 16, only in 1993 did the United States mandate that firms provide workers with *unpaid* **family leave** of

---

[8]David A. Matsa and Amalia R. Miller, "A Female Style in Corporate Leadership? Evidence from Quotas" *American Economic Journal: Applied Economics* 5, no. 3 (July 2013): 136–69.

[9]See, for instance, Francine D. Blau and Lawrence M. Kahn, "International Differences in Male Wage Inequality: Institutions versus Market Forces," *Journal of Political Economy* 104, no. 4 (August 1996): 791–837.

[10]Figures are from "Trade Union Density" in the OECD database, OECD.stat, accessed October 7, 2016, www.oecd.org. For a discussion, see Francine D. Blau and Lawrence M. Kahn, *At Home and Abroad: U.S. Labor Market Performance in International Perspective* (New York: Russell Sage Foundation, 2002); and Blau and Kahn, "International Differences in Male Wage Inequality."

[11]See Lawrence M. Kahn, "Wage Compression and the Gender Pay Gap," *IZA World of Labor* (April 2015), http://wol.iza.org. The role of wage structure is discussed at length later in this chapter.

12 weeks.[12] All other economically advanced countries preceded the United States in providing or mandating leave, generally paid leave, for mothers or for both parents. Indeed, Sweden began offering paid maternity leave to all mothers in the mid-1950s and was the first to extend such leave to fathers, in 1974.[13] Its policy is extremely generous compared to that of the United States: it provides 12 months of paid leave that may be taken by either parent at 80 percent replacement pay plus an additional 3 months with a flat-rate payment. Workers are guaranteed their jobs back when they return to work and must be offered the option of working part-time (6 hours per day) until their youngest child is age 8. Turning to the case of Japan, its leave policy is also more generous than that of the United States. Mothers are entitled to 14 weeks leave at 60 percent replacement pay, and either parent may take unpaid leave for up to a year.[14]

Even when parental leave is available to both parents, it tends to be disproportionately taken by mothers rather than fathers. In light of this, an increasing number of countries are offering an innovative policy called a **father's quota** or "daddy leave." This policy provides a period of paid leave that is available exclusively to the father after the birth of a child on a "use it or lose it" basis.[15] The fact that the father cannot transfer the benefit to the mother incentivizes paternal leave-taking if the family wishes to fully avail itself of leave allotments. Further, by especially singling out the father for this leave, it may reduce the stigma of paternal leave-taking and thereby encourage fathers to take leave. Norway was the first to adopt such a policy, in 1993, and Sweden followed shortly thereafter. In 2015, the length of these policies was 10 weeks in both countries. A number of other countries as well as the Canadian province of Quebec have similarly adopted this policy.[16]

Many economically advanced countries provide family-friendly policies that extend well beyond parental leave, and the prevalence of such policies has increased considerably in recent years. One such policy is **part-time work**. Perhaps the most striking case is The Netherlands, where just over 60 percent of women and 19 percent of men are employed part-time.[17] Another family-friendly policy is the option of switching to a part-time or flexible schedule after the birth of a child, to care for aged relatives, or to accommodate training and education. For instance, the United Kingdom, New Zealand, and Australia provide a **"right to request policy"** whereby parents of preschool-age children may ask their employer for flexible or

---

[12]Given the lack of progress at the federal level, as discussed in Chapter 16, a few US states have taken measures to offer at least a short amount of paid leave.

[13]The evolution of this policy is described in Britta Hoem and Jan M. Hoem, "Sweden's Family Policies and Roller-Coaster Fertility," *Journal of Population Problems* 52, no. 3–4 (November 1996): 1–22.

[14]For a discussion and comparison of policies, see Willem Adema, Chris Clarke, and Valérie Frey, "Paid Parental Leave: Lessons from OECD Countries and Selected U.S. States," OECD Social, Employment and Migration Working Paper 172 (Paris, OECD, 2015); and OECD Family Database, www.oecd.org.

[15]For more on the father's quota, see Linda Haas and Tine Rostgaard, "Fathers' Rights to Paid Parental Leave in the Nordic Countries: Consequences for the Gendered Division of Leave," *Community, Work & Family* 14, no. 2 (May 2011): 177–95; Christina Boll, Julian Leppin, and Nora Reich, "Paternal Childcare and Parental Leave Policies: Evidence from Industrialized Countries," *Review of Economics of the Household* 12, no. 1 (March 2014): 129–58; and Ankita Patnaik, "Reserving Time for Daddy: The Short and Long-Run Consequences of Fathers' Quotas," (January 18, 2016), www.ssrn.org.

[16]OECD, "Parental Leave: Where Are the Fathers?" OECD Policy Brief (Paris: OECD, March 2016), www.oecd.org.

[17]The figures are from the OECD database, OECD.Stat, accessed July 16, 2016, www.oecd.org. Part-time work is defined as 30 weeks or fewer in this source; for the United States, the standard definition is fewer than 35 weeks. For discussion, see Alison L. Booth and Jan C. van Ours, "Part-Time Jobs: What Women Want?" *Journal of Population Economics* 26, no. 1 (January 2013): 263–83.

reduced hours, without fear of negative repercussions. Parents do not have to offer a specific justification such as a child's illness, and employers have the right to say no if the change is not feasible on business grounds.[18] Turning to the United States, a few states had mandated a "right to request" policy by 2016.

Countries also differ when it comes to government support for childcare. Sweden and France are examples of two countries that have committed a large amount of resources for this purpose. For instance, in Sweden, publicly provided day care is available for nearly half of children ages 0 to 2 and more than 90 percent of children ages 3 to 5. France subsidizes childcare even more generously. There, all children ages 3 to 5 are eligible for free preschool, and virtually all of them do attend even if their mother is not employed. In addition, 50 percent of children ages 0 to 2 are in day care.[19] As discussed in Chapter 16, in the United States, government involvement in childcare differs considerably. For low-income children, there is some subsidized preschool available through the federal Head Start program as well as some childcare subsidies provided through federal grants. However, access to childcare, especially affordable high-quality childcare, remains limited. Higher-income parents receive some subsidies for childcare via the federal tax system, but again there is the issue of availability of quality care. One notable development in the United States is that a handful of states and most recently the city of New York offer universal prekindergarten.

A related, albeit different, policy that is available in most economically advanced countries is a **child allowance** or child benefit. The motivation for government to provide an allowance is to help families defray the costs of raising children (regardless of whether or not they use childcare). The amount is based on the number of children and typically does not depend on parents' employment or income.[20] The United States does not provide such an allowance. The most closely related US policy is the Child Tax Credit. As discussed in Chapter 16, given the design of the credit, it is not available for high-income families and provides limited benefits for the poorest families. Finally, unlike the United States, most of the other economically advanced countries offer either national health insurance or a national health care system. Such programs reduce the cost of rearing children and potentially improve the health and, thus, the productivity of present as well as future workers.

What lessons might the United States learn from family-friendly policies implemented elsewhere? In Chapter 16 we made the point that family-friendly policies such as paid leave and part-time and flexible schedules can be quite important to women in maintaining their attachment to the labor force and to their current firm. As discussed in an upcoming section, the fact that the United States lags behind in offering family-friendly policies is a primary reason why a growing number of countries now have labor force participation rates that exceed the US rate.[21] However, such policies may also reinforce traditional gender roles in the family and thus

---

[18]See Ariane Hegewisch and Janet C. Gornick, *Statutory Routes to Workplace Flexibility in Cross-National Perspective* (Washington, DC: Institute for Women's Policy Research, 2008).

[19]For information on a large number of countries, see OECD, Family Database, table PF3.2.A, "Childcare and Pre-School Services for 0-2 Year Olds, 2006 and 2013"; and table PF.3.2.C, "Participation Rates for 3-5 Year Olds in Pre-Primary Education or Primary School, 2002 and 2012" (September 22, 2015), accessed July 14, 2016, www.oecd.org.

[20]See OECD, Family Database, table PF1.3A, "Family Cash Benefits, 2010," accessed November 1, 2016, www.oecd.org. For more discussion, see Nancy Folbre, *Valuing Children: Rethinking the Economics of the Family* (Cambridge, MA: Harvard University Press, 2007), 159.

[21]Francine D. Blau and Lawrence M. Kahn, "Female Labor Supply: Why Is the US Falling Behind?" *American Economic Review* 103, no. 3 (May 2013): 251–56.

help to perpetuate differences in labor market outcomes between men and women. On the demand side, firms may engage in statistical discrimination, by not hiring or offering women training or promotion opportunities in anticipation that they will utilize available family policies. And, on the supply side, women who make use of these policies may choose sectors and positions that are most accommodating, or, particularly when parental leave is quite long, they may stay out of the labor force longer following a birth.[22] The evidence indicates that while relatively short leaves have been found to increase women's labor force attachment and wages, the situation appears more ambiguous for longer leaves. Such leaves (more than 3 months in one study) have been found to have a negative effect on women's wages.[23] And, to the extent that women disproportionately take leaves compared to men, this reduces the effectiveness of leave policies at mitigating gender differences in the workplace.[24] In addition, as discussed in earlier chapters, part-time work frequently provides less opportunity for upward mobility than full-time employment.

Turning specifically to the Nordic countries including Sweden, it has been further suggested that while their extensive family policies have raised women's labor force participation and increased their attachment to the labor force, they have not opened up new career paths for women and may have had the unintended consequence of segmenting women into "female" jobs, thereby contributing to a "glass ceiling" for women workers. Women in these countries continue to be disproportionately employed in traditionally female clerical and white-collar jobs, most notably in the government sector and in health care, education, and childcare.[25] Indeed, despite women's high labor force participation rates in these countries (as we will see shortly, in Table 18-1), Sweden and other Nordic countries continue to have the highest levels of occupational sex segregation (as measured by various indexes) among economically advanced countries.[26]

Childcare subsidies, in contrast, are an example of a policy that unambiguously supports women's labor force entry and attachment as well as their career advancement. In Chapter 6, we reviewed findings from the United States that showed this positive relationship. As an additional piece of evidence, a study conducted in

---

[22]For a nice overview, see Janet C. Gornick and Ariane Hegewisch, "Gender, Employment, and Parenthood: The Consequences of Work Family Policies," in *Lessons from Europe? What Americans Can Learn from European Policie*s, ed. R. Daniel Kelemen (Thousand Oaks, CA: CQ Press, 2015), 17–42.

[23]Christopher J. Ruhm, "The Economic Consequences of Parental Leave Mandates: Lessons from Europe," *Quarterly Journal of Economics* 113, no. 1 (1998): 285–317; and Joya Misra, Michelle Budig, and Irene Boeckmann, "Work–Family Policies and the Effects of Children on Women's Employment Hours and Wages," *Community, Work & Family* 14, no. 2 (May 2011): 139–57.

[24]For instance, in the Nordic countries, while most fathers tend to take the "father quota," they are much less likely to take advantage of the shared parental leave available; see Linda Haas and Tine Rostgaard, "Fathers' Rights to Paid Parental Leave."

[25]Nabanita Datta Gupta, Nina Smith, and Mette Verner, "The Impact of Nordic Countries' Family Friendly Policies on Employment, Wages, and Children," *Review of Economics of the Household* 6, no. 1 (March 2008): 65–89; and Ariane Hegesisch and Janet C. Gornick, "The Impact of Work–Family Policies on Women's Employment: A Review of Research from OECD Countries," *Community, Work & Family* 14, no. 2 (May 2011): 119–38.

[26]For recent evidence, see Jennifer Jarman, Robert M. Blackburn, and Girts Racko, "The Dimensions of Occupational Gender Segregation in Industrial Countries," *Sociology* 46, no. 6 (December 2012): 1003–19, table 1. This has long been the pattern; see Richard Anker, *Gender and Jobs: Sex Segregation of Occupations in the World* (Geneva: International Labour Organization, 1998). These policies may also widen the gender earnings gap; see Hadas Mandel and Moshe Semyonov, "Family Policies, Wage Structures, and Gender Gaps: Sources of Earnings Inequality in 20 Countries," *American Sociological Review* 70, no. 6 (December 2005): 949–67; and James Albrecht, Peter S. Thoursie, and Susan Vroman, "Parental Leave and the Glass Ceiling in Sweden," *Research in Labor Economics* 41 (2015): 89–114.

Norway, which looked at the combined effect of a rise in subsidized childcare and an increase in the length of the father's quota (these policy changes occurred at around the same time), found that these policies speeded up women's reentry into the labor force, at least partly reducing the negative effect of long leave-taking on women's labor supply.[27] This finding also suggests that it is important to consider how policies operate together, in addition to thinking about their separate effects on women's work, occupations, and earnings.

Tax Policies

Another factor that contributes to international differences in labor market outcomes is tax policy. In a number of countries, the structure of the income tax creates a **secondary earner penalty**, whereby the labor market return for the wife (typically regarded as the secondary earner) is lowered, thereby discouraging labor force participation. As discussed in Chapter 6 and in greater detail in Chapter 15, one way this penalty may arise is if the family is the unit of taxation. A progressive tax code combined with this tax structure creates a secondary earner penalty because the wife's first dollar of earnings is taxed at the top rate of her husband's last dollar. In contrast, if the individual is the unit of taxation, then each spouse's first dollar is taxed at the same rate. Indeed, in the early 1970s as part of its effort to achieve equal participation of women and men in the labor force, Sweden eliminated the joint income tax for spouses (except for nonwage income) and replaced it with a system of individual taxation. These days the United States and Germany are two of only a handful of economically advanced countries in which the family remains the unit of taxation.

What is less recognized is that even if the individual is the unit of taxation, an income tax structure can still impose a secondary earner penalty if there is a dependent credit or allowance that is reduced or eliminated when a spouse enters the labor force or increases hours worked. Japan's tax structure is one such example. Since World War II, Japan has had a system of individual taxation, but starting in 1961, and with a subsequent adjustment in 1987, the tax system permits a deduction (called an "allowance") for the primary earner if the employed spouse's earnings are below a certain threshold. This deduction provides an incentive for married women to keep their hours, and thus their earnings, low.[28]

US Women's Labor Force Participation in an International Context

Table 18-1 provides figures on the labor force participation rates of prime-age (ages 25–54) women and men for a large set of economically advanced countries for 1984 and 2015. (These figures are not completely comparable with those in Table 17-1 because the age ranges differ.) It shows that the trends in women's and men's labor

---

[27]Marit Rønsen and Ragni Hege Kitterød, "Gender-Equalizing Family Policies and Mothers' Entry into Paid Work: Recent Evidence from Norway," *Feminist Economics*, 21, no. 1 (2015): 59–89.
[28]OECD, "Special Feature. Measuring the Tax on Second Earners," *Taxing Wages* (Paris, France: OECD, May 2016); and Hideo Akabayashi, "Labor Supply of Married Women and Spousal Tax Deduction in Japan—A Structural Estimation," *Review of Economics of the Household* 4, no.4 (2006): 349–78. As we saw for the United States in Chapter 15, retirement systems may also create secondary earner penalties.

| TABLE 18-1 | TRENDS IN LABOR FORCE PARTICIPATION RATES FOR WOMEN AND MEN, AGES 25–54, SELECTED ECONOMICALLY ADVANCED COUNTRIES, 1984 AND 2015 |

	PERCENT OF WOMEN IN THE LABOR FORCE		PERCENT OF MEN IN THE LABOR FORCE	
	1984	2015	1984	2015
Australia	57.3	76.6	93.4	90.3
Belgium	57.1	80.2	94.0	89.9
Canada	68.6	82.0	93.4	90.9
Denmark	84.5	83.4	93.5	90.8
Finland	86.9	83.5	93.5	89.6
France	68.4	82.7	96.0	92.4
Germany	59.2	82.5	93.5	92.5
Greece	47.8	77.7	94.8	93.1
Ireland	37.1	73.4	92.5	89.8
Italy	47.9	65.9	95.0	87.7
Japan	60.3	75.2	96.7	95.5
Netherlands	44.4	82.1	91.7	92.1
Norway	75.8	83.9	95.8	89.1
Portugal	61.6	86.0	93.8	91.7
South Korea	48.4	65.4	93.5	91.1
Spain	35.1	82.0	94.5	92.6
Sweden	89.0	88.3	95.2	93.3
United Kingdom	67.7	80.0	95.4	91.7
United States	69.6	73.7	93.9	88.3

Source: The Organisation for Economic Co-operation and Development (OECD), Online Database, stats.oecd.org, accessed July 13, 2016.

force participation rates that we reviewed in Chapter 5—rising rates for women and declining rates for men—were experienced by a broad set of economically advanced countries during this period.[29] The table also points to substantial cross-country differences in participation levels in 1984 as well as a substantial convergence in these rates over the next 30 years.[30] Nonetheless, variation remains. For instance, as of 2015, the female labor force participation rate was 88 percent in Sweden (the highest of the countries included) compared to 74 and 75 percent for the United States and

---

[29]As in the United States, female participation rates also tend to be higher among the more highly educated; see Paula England, Janet Gornick, and Emily Fitzgibbons Shafer, "Women's Employment, Education, and the Gender Gap in 17 Countries," *Monthly Labor Review* (April 2012): 3–12.

[30]Steven J. Haider, Helena Skyt Nielsen, and Elizabeth U. Cascio point to this convergence in "The Effectiveness of Policies that Promote Labor Force Participation of Women with Children: A Collection of National Studies," *Labour Economics* 36 (October 2015): 64–71. For the United States in comparative perspective since 1850, see Claudia Olivetti, "Gender Gaps in Developed Economies, *NBER Reporter* 2 (2016).

Japan, respectively. Rates in Italy and South Korea were approximately 66 percent, the lowest of the included countries.[31]

An advantage of looking at the United States in an international context is that other economically advanced countries provide a benchmark with which the US experience can be compared. Indeed, the figures in Table 18-1 indicate that although female participation rates increased in the United States over this period, the relative position of US women fell compared to other countries. In 1984, the United States ranked 5th out of the 19 countries shown in the table; by 2015, the United States ranked 16th. One study found that, over the 1990–2010 period, a substantial portion (nearly 30 percent) of the decrease in US women's labor force participation rates relative to other economically advanced nations was due to the greater expansion in these other countries of family-friendly policies, including the provision of parental leave and rights to part-time work. However, consistent with our earlier discussion, this study also presented evidence suggesting that these policies appear to encourage women's employment in part-time work and lower-level occupations.[32] Thus, the participation gains may come at a cost in terms of advancing women's status in the labor market.

The US Gender Wage Ratio in an International Context

Table 18-2 shows the ratio of women's to men's median earnings for full-time workers for the period from 1975 to 2013 in a number of economically advanced countries. As shown in the table, in all the selected countries women continue to be paid less than men, although the ratio of women's to men's earnings has risen since at least 1975 (or the earliest year for which data are provided) in all cases. Interestingly, however, the most rapid increases did not occur at the same time, nor did the ratios reach the same level in each of these countries. Instead, there have been a variety of patterns, including intermittent increases, interrupted by periods of stagnation, and even temporary reversals.

As we saw in Chapter 7, the gender ratio of median earnings of full-time workers in the United States increased substantially over the 1980s, rising from .63 in 1980 to .72 in 1990. Progress was less dramatic and more uneven subsequently, but the ratio continued to increase, rising to .77 in 2000 and .82 by 2013. In the case of Sweden, on the other hand, most of the gains in the ratio had occurred by the early 1980s, and the ratio has remained virtually unchanged since then, albeit at a relatively high level, with a ratio of .87. Of the included countries, Denmark, New Zealand, and Norway had the highest ratios at .93 in 2013. Turning to Japan, its earnings ratio was among the lowest in 1975 and remained at that level for some time, finally rising in the 1990s. Nonetheless, Japan's ratio continues to lag behind the ratios in all other countries, standing at just .73 in 2013. A final case of interest is Australia, which introduced a policy of comparable worth in 1969, as discussed in greater detail in the "Comparable Worth in Australia" box. The adoption of this policy explains its relatively high level of .78 as early as 1975.

[31]Interestingly, Sweden was hardly a leader in this respect in earlier days; married women there were not even granted the legal right to enter into work contracts or to control their own earnings until 1920, as discussed in Christina Jonung and Inga Persson, "Combining Market Work and Family," in *Population, Economy and Welfare in Sweden*, ed. Tommy Bengtsson (New York: Springer-Verlag, 1994), 37–64.
[32]Blau and Kahn, "Female Labor Supply." Data are for women aged 25–54 in 22 countries. In this sample the US ranking fell from 6th in 1990 to 17th in 2010.

TABLE 18-2 RATIO OF WOMEN'S TO MEN'S MEDIAN EARNINGS FOR FULL-TIME WORKERS, SELECTED YEARS, 1975–2013

	1975	1980	1990	2000	2010	2013
Australia	0.78	0.81	0.82	0.83	0.86	0.82
Canada	n.a.	n.a.	0.75	0.76	0.81	0.81
Denmark	n.a.	n.a.	n.a.	n.a.	0.91	0.93
Finland	0.72	0.73	0.77	0.80	0.81	0.80
France	n.a.	n.a.	0.85	0.85	0.86	0.86
Germany	n.a.	n.a.	0.73	0.79	0.83	0.86
Japan	0.58	0.58	0.59	0.66	0.71	0.73
Netherlands	n.a.	n.a.	n.a.	0.85	0.81	n.a.
New Zealand	n.a.	0.79	0.83	0.93	0.93	0.93
Norway	n.a.	n.a.	0.90	0.90	0.92	0.93
Sweden	0.82	0.87	0.81	0.85	0.86	0.87
Switzerland	n.a.	n.a.	0.75	0.76	0.80	0.83
United Kingdom	0.60	0.63	0.67	0.74	0.81	0.83
United States	0.62	0.63	0.72	0.77	0.81	0.82

Notes: OECD provides data on the unadjusted gender wage gap, which is defined as the percentage gap between the median earnings of men and women. This table reports the gender wage ratio, which is calculated as 100 − the gender wage gap; it is reported in decimal form.
Data are provided for the closest year available; n.a. = not available.
Source: The Organisation for Economic Co-operation and Development (OECD) Online Database, stats.oecd.org, accessed November 14, 2016.

In sum, there is evidence for the countries examined that women's wages have been rising relative to those of men. It is difficult to sort out the reasons for the trends in these series, and they need not be the same for all countries. It is, however, likely that changing wage structures within countries, the degree of enforcement of antidiscrimination laws,[33] and changes in the relative qualifications of women workers play a greater or lesser role. Another factor may be industrial composition, with women faring better in countries with larger service sectors where demand for female labor is higher.[34]

Another issue that deserves attention is the relationship between the female–male earnings ratio and occupational segregation by sex. If one looks at the supply side (the human capital explanation) and at the demand side (discrimination), one might expect a negative relationship: the higher the degree of segregation, the lower the female–male earnings ratio. However, if earnings for women are relatively high in predominantly female fields, women will have less incentive to enter predominantly

---

[33]An interesting finding in this regard is that the ratification by countries of two International Labour Organization conventions supporting equal treatment of men and women has been found to have a strong and significant effect on reducing the "unexplained" gender wage gap; see Doris Weichselbaumer and Rudolf Winter-Ebmer, "The Effects of Competition and Equal Treatment Laws on Gender Wage Differentials," *Economic Policy* 22, no. 50 (April 2007): 235–87. For evidence of a glass ceiling in 10 European Union countries, see Wiji Arulampalam, Alison L. Booth, and Mark L. Bryan, "Is There a Glass Ceiling over Europe? Exploring the Gender Pay Gap across the Wages Distribution," *Industrial and Labor Relations Review* 60, no. 2 (November 2006): 163–86.
[34]Claudia Olivetti and Claudia and Barbara Petrongolo, "The Evolution of the Gender Gap in Industrialized Countries," *Annual Review of Economics* 8 (2016): 405–34.

male occupations so that one could observe both a high degree of segregation and a relatively high earnings ratio. This might occur in countries with strong union policies that serve to compress the overall wage structure, as is the case in Sweden, or where comparable worth policies have been adopted, as is the case in Australia.

It is also worthy of note that the earnings ratio in the United States currently falls in the middle of the selected countries and, in earlier years, lagged considerably behind most of the countries.[35] One might have expected the United States to have ranked close to the top throughout this period because it was among the first to promulgate antidiscrimination laws and US women have tended to have similar, if not higher, levels of human capital relative to men, as well as relatively low levels of occupational segregation, as compared to women in these other countries. The answer to this puzzle lies in the fact that the size of the gender gap is determined not only by differences across countries in women's qualifications and in the extent of discrimination against them but also, as previously mentioned, by international differences in wage structure.[36]

A comparison with Sweden is particularly instructive. As we have seen, the female–male wage ratio is much higher in Sweden than in the United States. One study suggests this is due to differences between the two countries in wage structure, with Sweden's reward structure being considerably more compressed than that in the United States, largely due to the significant role of unions.[37] This study suggests that the United States would have as high a gender wage ratio as Sweden if it had the same compressed wage structure. In fact, the high level of US wage inequality raises the gender wage gap in the United States compared to many other economically advanced countries. In contrast, the even larger gender wage gap in Japan (which was not included in this study) likely reflects factors specifically related to gender, including the high degree of segregation of women within broad occupational categories there.

Another factor influencing differences in the gender wage gap across countries is the self-selection of women into employment, a topic we considered earlier in Chapter 10. The impact of this factor can be seen in a comparison of female labor force participation rates and gender earnings ratios in European countries. A number of southern European countries have tended to have both lower gender wage gaps and lower labor force participation rates than other European countries. One study suggests that the reason for the relatively low gender wage gaps in these southern European countries is "probably not . . . more equal pay treatment for women" but rather that in these countries, where market work among women is less common, it is concentrated among women who can earn especially high wages when they enter the labor market. This lowers the measured gender wage gap. In countries with higher participation rates, on the other hand, more low-wage women are included in the labor force and the measured gender wage gap is larger.[38]

[35]See Francine D. Blau and Lawrence M. Kahn, "Gender Differences in Pay," *Journal of Economic Perspectives* 14, no. 4 (Fall 2000): 75–99.
[36]For a more detailed discussion and evidence, see Blau and Kahn, "Gender Differences in Pay"; Francine D. Blau and Lawrence M. Kahn, "Wage Structure and Gender Earnings Differentials: An International Comparison," supplement, *Economica* 63 (1996): 29–62; Francine D. Blau and Lawrence M. Kahn, "Understanding International Differences in the Gender Pay Gap," *Journal of Labor Economics* 21, no. 1 (January 2003): 106–44; Mandel and Semyonov, "Family Policies, Wage Structures, and Gender Gaps"; and Anne Daly, Xin Meng, Akira Kawaguchi, and Karen Mumford, "The Gender Wage Gap in Four Countries," *Economic Record* 82, no. 257 (June 2006): 165–76.
[37]Blau and Kahn, "Wage Structure and Gender Earnings Differentials."
[38]Claudia Olivetti and Barbara Petrongolo, "Unequal Pay or Unequal Employment? A Cross-Country Analysis of Gender Gaps," *Journal of Labor Economics* 26, no. 4 (October 2008): 621–54; quotation is from p. 625.

Comparable Worth in Australia

Along with the Nordic countries, Australia has the distinction of long having one of the highest gender earnings ratios among economically advanced countries. As described here, the implementation of equal pay and, particularly, of comparable worth in Australia in the 1970s played a major role in raising the relative earnings of women.*

Australia's wage determination system is markedly different from that in the United States. In Australia, minimum wage rates for occupations are determined by government wage tribunals, and unions play a large role, though the wage system has become somewhat more decentralized in recent years, as discussed shortly.

Up to 1969, the Australian pay structure explicitly discriminated against women. Until 1950, female award rates were set at 54 percent of male rates; that year they were raised to 75 percent. In 1969, the concept of equal pay for equal work was implemented, and the award rate was raised to 100 percent. In 1972, the federal tribunal moved toward a policy of comparable worth by deciding that the "equal pay for equal work" concept should be expanded to "equal pay for work of equal value" in order to cover employees in predominantly female jobs.

The result of the implementation of these policies, particularly of comparable worth, was a 30 percent rise in the gender pay ratio from 1970 to 1975 (a few years after implementation of comparable worth).** One might expect that if such policies increased the gender earnings ratio, they might have resulted in lower female employment. Research suggests that female employment did indeed grow more slowly than would have been expected if women's wages had not risen but that the negative employment effect was fairly small. One explanation for the small employment effect is that women and men held very different jobs, so the high degree of occupational segregation may have constituted a substantial barrier to women being replaced by men even as their relative wages increased.

Since 1996, Australia's wage determination system has grown more decentralized; individual firms can now negotiate wage agreements, unions possess less bargaining power, and government wage tribunals play a much more modest role in determining wages. These changes prompted a new set of concerns about possible negative effects on women's employment and earnings. One study examined the impact of these changes and found that women's labor force participation increased since the 1996 reform, a positive development, but much of the increase was in part-time rather than full-time work. Regarding pay, the same study found a slight decline in the gender wage ratio in the private sector in the post-1996 reform period.*** Nonetheless, as seen in Table 18-2, Australia's gender pay ratio remains on a par with other economically advanced countries, fluctuating between .82 and .86 over the past several decades.

*This account of comparable worth is based on Robert G. Gregory, Roslyn Anstie, Anne Daly, and Vivian Ho, "Women's Pay in Australia, Great Britain, and the United States: The Role of Laws, Regulations and Human Capital," in Pay Equity Empirical Inquiries, ed. Robert T. Michael, Heidi I. Hartmann, and Brigid O'Farrell (Washington, DC: National Academies Press, 1989), 222–42; Mark Killingsworth, The Economics of Comparable Worth (Kalamazoo, MI: Upjohn Institute for Employment Research, 1990); and Angela Barns and Alison Preston, "Is Australia Really a World Leader in Closing the Gender Gap?" Feminist Economics 16 (October 2010): 81–103.

**See Francine D. Blau, Marianne A. Ferber, and Anne E. Winkler, The Economics of Women, Men, and Work, 4th ed. (Upper Saddle River, NJ: Pearson, 2001), table 11.4; based on data from Francine D. Blau and Lawrence M. Kahn, "The Gender Earnings Gap: Some International Evidence," in Differences and Changes in Wage Structures, ed. Richard B. Freeman and Lawrence F. Katz (Chicago: University of Chicago Press, 1995).
***Barns and Preston, "Is Australia Really a World Leader?" Efforts at increasing pay equity are ongoing; see Sara Charlesworth and Fiona McDonald, "Australia's Gender Pay Equity Legislation: How New, How Different, What Prospects?" Cambridge Journal of Economics 39, no. 2 (2015): 421–40.

Understanding Low Fertility in Economically Advanced Countries

Figure 18-1 provides data on trends in fertility rates for selected economically advanced countries for 1980 through 2013. As would be expected in line with the increasing labor force participation rate of women in all these countries, the graph shows that fertility rates generally declined after 1980. Many countries reached unprecedented lows in the late 1990s, though rates have rebounded a bit in most of the included countries.[39] Nonetheless, fertility rates in a number of these countries (Germany, Italy, Japan, and Spain) remain quite low at 1.4 or fewer births per woman, well below the replacement rate of 2.1 births per woman. The US fertility rate, which had been at or near the replacement level for many years, declined to 1.9 in the aftermath of the Great Recession and remained at that level through 2013.

A second pattern that has been noted by researchers considering a larger set of economically advanced countries than shown in Figure 18-1 is that countries with the highest female labor force participation rates also tend to have the highest fertility rates and vice versa. This *positive* relationship is surprising given that, as we saw in Chapter 6, economic theory leads us to expect a *negative* or inverse relationship between fertility and female labor force participation when we consider these decisions at the individual level, and the empirical evidence is consistent with that. Researchers have pointed to a number of factors behind the positive relationship between female labor force participation and fertility at the country level for economically advanced countries: the degree to which family-friendly policies are available; the flexibility of the labor market, including the availability of part-time work; the extent to which childcare time is distributed more equally between parents; and the rate of nonmarital fertility in the face of declining marriage rates.[40]

In the Nordic countries, for instance, both fertility rates and female labor force participation are boosted by strong family-friendly policies combined with the fact that fathers share substantially in childcare. The United States has traditionally had relatively high levels of both fertility and female labor force participation, although, as we have seen, the US female labor force participation rate has fallen relative to other countries in recent decades. While there are a number of factors working to boost both female labor force participation rates and fertility in the United States, including the general availability of out-of-home childcare (at least for children over age 2) and part-time work, as well as fathers playing an important and growing role in childcare, the lack of family-friendly policies appears to have depressed female labor force participation in the United States relative to other countries. Nonetheless, the relatively high fertility rate in the United States (compared to other economically

---

[39]There is debate among demographers, however, over the extent to which this increase was simply due to changes in the timing of fertility; see John Bongaarts and Tomas Sobotka, "A Demographic Explanation for the Recent Rise in European Fertility," *Population and Development Review* 38, no. 1 (March 2012): 83–120.

[40]For evidence of a positive relationship between fertility and women's labor force participation and a discussion of possible explanations, see Ronald Rindfuss and Minja Kim Choe, "Diverse Paths to Low and Lower Fertility: An Overview," in *Low and Lower Fertility Variations across Developed Countries*, ed. Ronald Rindfuss and Minja Kim Choe (Cham, Switzerland: Springer, 2015), chap. 1; and James Feyrer, Bruce Sacerdote, and Ariel Dora Stern, "Will the Stork Return to Europe and Japan? Understanding Fertility within Developed Nations," *Journal of Economic Perspectives* 22, no. 3 (Summer 2008): 3–22.

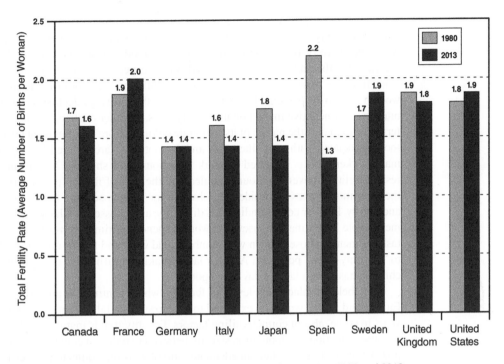

FIGURE 18-1 Total Fertility Rates, Selected Economically Advanced Countries, 1980 and 2013

Note: The total fertility rate is defined as the number of births that a cohort of 1,000 women would have if they experienced the age-specific birth rates occuring in the current year throughout their childbearing years (see Table 13-4). Here it is divided by 1,000 to measure average number of births per woman.
Source: Fertility rates are from World Bank, World Development Indicators, Online Database, accessed November 15, 2016, www.worldbank.org.

advanced countries) coupled with still substantial female labor force participation is notable. One factor contributing to the relatively high US fertility rate (though it has declined slightly since the Great Recession) is that, as discussed in Chapter 13, the United States has experienced sustained immigration, and fertility rates of immigrant women have tended to be higher, on average, than those of native-born women.

In contrast, countries in southern Europe (e.g., Greece, Italy, and Spain) have been noted to have both low fertility and low female labor force participation, though this pattern appears to be changing. As shown in Table 18-1, Spain's female participation rate is now quite high and Greece's rate is not all that far behind. Explanations as to why women have not combined employment and motherhood to the extent that they have elsewhere include high unemployment rates for younger people, which raise the cost of children (thereby reducing fertility) by making reentry difficult for employed women who leave the labor force to bear children. The lack of adequate part-time work and adequate out-of-home childcare, along with a more traditional division of labor in the home, are additional factors that have been cited.[41]

Japan has been observed to have a very low fertility rate coupled with a relatively lower female labor force participation rate (though the rate has increased in recent years). The explanations are again varied, but one distinctive factor is a declining

[41]See, for instance, Alicia Adsera, "Where Are the Babies? Labor Market Conditions and Fertility in Europe," *European Journal of Population* 27, no. 1 (February 2011): 1–32; and Daniela Del Boca, Silvia Pasqua, and Chiara Pronzato, "Fertility and Employment in Italy, France, and the UK," special issue, *Labour* 19 (2005): 51–77.

marriage rate coupled with very low rates of nonmarital fertility.[42] Its marriage rate fell considerably from 1970 to 2012, from 10 to 5.3 marriages per 1,000 persons, while the share of births to unmarried women stood at just 2 percent in 2014.[43] In contrast, for the same years, the United States experienced a decline in marriage from 10 to 6.8 marriages per 1,000 persons, while the share of births to unmarried women rose to 40 percent. The net result is that the marriage decline in Japan had a much greater negative impact on its fertility rates. Another contributing factor to low fertility in Japan is the nature of its corporate culture. "Core" employment positions—those associated with wage increases and promotions—are tailored for a traditional male worker who is expected to work long hours and shoulder few, if any, home responsibilities. Given the hours entailed and the lack of flexibility, the structure of these positions poses a considerable obstacle for women seeking to combine career and family. Further compounding this difficulty, as discussed in Chapter 17, Japanese men devote little time to housework; women spend four times as much time on these tasks as men.[44] Those women who combine paid work and family are often relegated to "mommy-track" positions. Another factor making it difficult to combine work and children has been a lack of day-care spots.[45]

The below-replacement levels of fertility, which continue to prevail in much of Europe and Japan, would be expected to lead to substantial declines in population in years to come, absent countervailing factors. Fertility trends matter to policymakers because reductions in population size are believed to reduce a country's international power and prestige. Further, an adequate ratio of working adults to retirees is necessary to finance social security programs. Immigration moderates the effects of such declines, and, indeed, the European countries experienced a considerable increase in immigration even prior to the refugee crisis of 2015, when over 1 million people left their homes for refuge in Europe.[46] Japan, in contrast, has not experienced any such influx. Another approach, and one that is, of course, not mutually exclusive, would be to adopt policies that better enable women to combine employment and child-rearing.[47]

---

[42]For excellent discussion, see Rindfuss and Choe, "Diverse Paths to Low and Lower Fertility"; and Sawako Shirahase, "Women's Economic Status and Fertility: Japan in Cross-National Perspective," in *The Political Economy of Low Fertility: Japan in Comparative Perspective*, ed. Frances McCall Rosenbluth (Stanford, CA: Stanford University Press, 2007), chap. 2. The situation in South Korea is very similar to that of Japan.

[43]Marriage figures are from table SF3.1.A, "Crude Marriage Rate for 1970, 1995, and 2012," and unmarried birth share is from table SF2.4A, "Share of Births Outside of Marriage, 2014," both available from OECD Family Database, www.oecd.org (accessed October 3, 2016).

[44]Noriko O. Tsuya, Larry L. Bumpass, Minja Kim Choe, and Ronald R. Rindfuss also find that marriage considerably increases women's housework time, with little change for men; "Employment and Household Tasks of Japanese Couples, 1994–2009," *Demographic Research* 27 (November 2012) 27: 705–18.

[45]The "womenomics" reforms discussed earlier seek to improve day-care access to remedy this problem; see Nathalie Stucky, "Womenomics: Success or Failure?" *Japan Today*, December 1, 2015.

[46]For evidence on the rise in immigration patterns prior to the 2015 crisis, see Francine D. Blau and Lawrence M. Kahn, "Immigration and the Distribution of Incomes," *Handbook of the Economics of International Migration*, vol. 1B, ed. Barry R. Chiswick and Paul Miller (Amsterdam: Elsevier, 2015), chap. 15, table 3. For details on the refugee crisis, see BBC, "Migrant Crisis: Migration to Europe Explained in Seven Charts," March 4, 2016, accessed November 2, 2016, bbc.com.

[47]Ronald Lee, "The Demographic Transition"; contributions in Alan Booth and Ann C. Crouter, eds., *The New Population Problem: Why Families in Developing Countries Are Shrinking and What It Means* (Mahwah, NJ: Lawrence Erlbaum, 2005); and Frances McCall Rosenbluth, ed., *The Political Economy of Japan's Low Fertility* (Stanford, CA: Stanford University Press, 2007), chap. 9. Immigration as a solution is emphasized in David E. Bloom, David Canning, Guenther Fink, and Jocelyn E. Finlay, "The Cost of Low Fertility in Europe," *European Journal of Population* 26, no. 2 (2010): 141–58.

Conclusion

In this chapter, we found that a number of economically advanced countries, especially the Nordic countries, have adopted a variety of policies to encourage women's labor force participation while also making it possible for them to take care of their families. Even there, the situation is still far from perfect, however, mainly because occupational segregation remains high. Nonetheless, innovative policies including the father's quota are being adopted and expanded to help level the playing field for women seeking to pursue careers. We also saw that low fertility is creating substantial difficulties for a number of countries. Again, family policies, if carefully crafted, may better help women combine careers and family and raise these rates. Finally, from the standpoint of the United States, our review points to several policy options that the United States might consider adopting to increase women's overall labor force participation rate, which has not seen any measurable increase since the early 1990s.

Questions for Review and Discussion

1. As seen in Table 18-1, women's labor force participation rates in economically advanced countries vary considerably. What economic and noneconomic factors might explain this disparity?

2. Evidence indicates that fathers are more likely to take family leave when it is offered as a "father's quota" rather than when it is available as part of a more standard leave policy where the leave allowance can be shared by the father and mother. Based on course material, why do you think this is the case?

3. Occupational segregation by sex in Sweden is very high, yet it has the smallest gender earnings gap of any economically advanced country in the world. "This proves that occupational segregation does not reduce women's earnings relative to the earnings of men." Evaluate the validity of this statement.

4. A number of countries have policies intended to encourage people to have larger families, while others offer inducements to reduce family size. Would you favor either policy for the United States? Why or why not?

5. Based on the discussion in Chapter 18, what policies would you recommend to increase women's labor force participation in the United States, over and above those policies already in place, as described in Chapter 16? Justify your recommendations.

6. Governments in some countries are concerned that fertility rates are too low, while in other countries, there is concern that fertility rates are too high. Based on material in Chapters 17 and 18, explain the concerns raised in both situations and what measures the respective governments might take to address them.

Suggested Readings

Blau, Francine D., and Lawrence M. Kahn. "Gender Differences in Pay." *Journal of Economic Perspectives* 14, no. 4 (Fall 2000): 75–100.

Charles, Maria. "A World of Difference: International Trends in Women's Status." *Annual Review of Sociology* 37 (2011): 355–71.

Gornick, Janet C., and Ariane Hegewisch. in "Gender, Employment, and Parenthood: The Consequences of Work Family Policies." In *Lessons from Europe? What Americans Can Learn from European Public Policies*, edited by R. Daniel Kelemen, 17–42. Thousand Oaks, CA: CQ Press, 2015.

International Labour Organization. *Women in Business and Management—Gaining Momentum*. Geneva: International Labour Organization, 2015.

Jalalzai, Farida. *Shattered, Cracked, or Firmly Intact? Women and the Executive Glass Ceiling Worldwide*. Oxford: Oxford University Press, 2013.

Melkas, Helina, and Richard Anker. *Towards Gender Equity in Japanese and Nordic Labour Markets: A Tale of Two Paths*. Geneva: International Labour Organization, 2003.

Olivetti, Claudia, and Barbara Petrongolo. "The Evolution of the Gender Gap in Industrialized Countries." *Annual Review of Economics* 8 (2016): 405–34.

Rindfuss, Ronald R., and Minja Kim Choe. *Low and Lower Fertility: Variations across Developed Countries*. Cham, Switzerland: Springer, 2015.

Rosenbluth, Frances McCall, ed. *The Political Economy of Japan's Low Fertility*. Stanford, CA: Stanford University Press, 2007.

Strober, Myra H., and Agnes Miling Kaneko Chan. *The Road Winds Uphill All the Way: Gender, Work, and Family in the United States and Japan*. Cambridge, MA: MIT Press, 1999.

World Bank. *World Development Report 2012: Gender Equality and Development* (Washington, DC: World Bank, September 19, 2011).

Key Terms

comparable worth (491)

corporate board quotas (491)

wage-setting institutions (492)

family leave (492)

father's quota (493)

part-time work (493)

"right to request policy" (493)

child allowance (494)

secondary earner penalty (496)

Author Index

Subject Index

Note: Page references followed by a "*t*" indicate table; "*f*" indicate figure.

Printed in the USA/Agawam, MA
July 15, 2020

758191.006